PAUL GIFFORD

anity

Its Public Role

D1334268

HURST & COMPANY, LONDON

First published in the United Kingdom by
C. Hurst & Co. (Publishers) Ltd.,
38 King Street, London WC2E 8JZ
© Paul Gifford, 1998
All rights reserved.
2nd impression, corrected, 2001
Printed in Malaysia

ISBNs
1-85065-340-2 *casebound*
1-85065-335-6 *paperback*

PREFACE

From 1973 to 1976 the Leverhulme Trust funded a research programme entitled 'Christianity in Independent Africa', directed by Richard Gray, Professor of African History at the School of Oriental and African Studies (SOAS) of the University of London, with Adrian Hastings as Leverhulme Fellow. That project resulted in the publication of three books which have been central to African Christianity as a field of academic study ever since.[1] In 1992 the Leverhulme Trust agreed to fund another three-year project, to be directed by J.D.Y. Peel, Professor of Anthropology and Sociology at SOAS, and Adrian Hastings, Professor of Theology and Religious Studies at the University of Leeds. I was appointed Leverhulme Fellow. This new project was not to be simply a replay of the 1970s project, a review of how things stood twenty years on. The main focus of the earlier study was on how Christianity, in its various forms, had adjusted to the epochal change and challenge posed by African independence (South Africa fell almost entirely outside its scope). This second study is concerned not only with how the churches are responding to political developments, but just as much with how they are helping to shape them.

The first part of this 1992-5 project was to convene a conference to examine the role of the churches in the democratising of individual African countries. The proceedings of this conference were published as Paul Gifford (ed.), *The Christian Churches and the Democratisation of Africa* (Leiden: E.J. Brill, 1995). The second part largely entailed researching and elaborating the case studies which form the core of this book. For this I made extended visits to each of the countries selected. On these visits I travelled widely, making a conscious effort to go beyond the most important cities and towns. I conducted interviews, both structured and unstructured, with local churchmen and churchwomen of many denominations, with politicians and academics – indeed, with a wide range of people whose only qualification was their readiness to talk to me. I attended services, Bible studies, crusades, conferences and workshops. I also collected as much relevant literature as I could, ranging from books through magazines, newspapers and newsletters to the merest ephemera. I also established contacts with people prepared to forward more material to me in London.

---

[1]   E. Fashole-Luke, R. Gray, A. Hastings and G. Tasie (eds), *Christianity in Independent Africa*, London: Rex Collings, 1978; Adrian Hastings, *African Christianity*, London: Geoffrey Chapman, 1979; Adrian Hastings, *A History of African Christianity, 1950-1975*, Cambridge University Press, 1979.

I owe considerable gratitude to numerous people: to the trustees of the Leverhulme Foundation who made the project possible; to Professor Haddon Willmer and colleagues of the Department of Theology and Religious Studies of the University of Leeds, who generously appointed me a research fellow of the department for the year 1995-6, to allow me to finish the research; to the numerous individuals prepared to share ideas with me on my visits to their countries; and above all to Richard Gray, Adrian Hastings and John Peel, for whose encouragement over many years I am extremely grateful. None of them, however, is responsible for the views expressed here.

September 1997   P. G.

CONTENTS

MAPS

ABBREVIATIONS

AACC	All Africa Conference of Churches
ACIB	Assemblée du clergé indigène du diocèse de Bafoussam
AEA	Association of Evangelicals of Africa
AFM	Apostolic Faith Mission
AFRC	Armed Forces Revolutionary Council
AIC	African Independent (Instituted) Church
AME	African Methodist Episcopal
AMECEA	Association of Member Episcopal Conferences of East Africa
APS	All Africa Press Service
CAFM	Christian Action Faith International
CBC	Cameroon Baptist Convention
CCC	Calvary Charismatic Centre
CCG	Christian Council of Ghana
CCJP	Catholic Commission for Justice and Peace
CCZ	Christian Council of Zambia
CDC	Cameroon Development Corporation
CENC	National Episcopal Conference of Cameroon
CFA	Communauté Financière Africaine (Franc)
CIA	Central Intelligence Agency
CoP	Church of Pentecost
COU	Church of Uganda
CSMC	Conference of Major Superiors of Cameroon
EBC/NBC	Eglise Baptiste Camerounaise/Native Baptist Church
ECZ	Episcopal Conference of Zambia
EEC	Eglise Evangélique Camerounaise
EFZ	Evangelical Fellowship of Zambia
ELCC	Evangelical Lutheran Church in Cameroon
EPC	Eglise Presbytérienne Camerounaise
EU	European Union
FEMEC	Fédération des Eglises et des Missions Evangéliques du Cameroun
FGBMFI	Full Gospel Businessmen's Fellowship International
FODEP	Foundation for the Democratic Process
GATT	General Agreement on Tariffs and Trade
GDP	Gross Domestic Product
GEC	Ghana Evangelism Committee
ICGC	International Central Gospel Church
ICT	Institute for Contextual Theology
IFI	International Financial Institution
IMF	International Monetary Fund
JMAS	*Journal of Modern African Studies*
JRA	*Journal of Religion in Africa*
JW	Jehovah's Witness

KPC	Kampala Pentecostal Church
LCC	Lutheran Church in Cameroon
MMD	Movement for Multi-Party Democracy
MRND	Mouvement Révolutionnaire National pour la Démocratie
MSRDP	Multi-Sectoral Rural Development Programme
NCCK	National Council of Churches of Kenya
NCNC	National Council of Nigeria and the Cameroons
NDC	National Democratic Congress
NGO	Non-Governmental Organisation
NRA	National Resistance Army
NRM	National Resistance Movement
OAU	Organisation of African Unity
PACLA	Pan-African Christian Leadership Conference
PAOG	Pentecostal Assemblies of God
PCC	Presbyterian Church of Cameroon
PCUSA	Presbyterian Church (USA)
PDC	People's Defence Committee
PNDC	Provisional National Defence Council
RC	Resistance Council
RDPC	Rassemblement Démocratique du Peuple Camerounais
RoAPE	*Review of African Political Economy*
RPF	Rwanda Patriotic Front
SAP	Structural Adjustment Programme
SCC	Small Christian Community
SDA	Seventh Day Adventist
SDF	Social Democratic Front
SECAM	Symposium of Episcopal Conferences of Africa and Madagascar
SOAS	School of Oriental and African Studies
UAOG	Uganda Assemblies of God
UBC	Uganda Broadcasting Commission
UCAC	Université Catholique d'Afrique Centrale
UCZ	United Church of Zambia
UEBC	Union des Eglises Baptistes Camerounaises
UJCC	Uganda Joint Christian Council
UNIP	United National Independence Party
UNISA	University of South Africa
UNLA	Uganda National Liberation Army
UPC	Uganda People's Congress
VAT	Value Added Tax
WCC	World Council of Churches
WDC	Workers' Defence Committee
ZCCM	Zambia Consolidated Copper Mines
ZEC	Zambian Episcopal Conference
ZEMEC	Zambia Elections Monitoring Coordinating Committee

1

THE CONTEXT: AFRICA NOW

This book has two aims. First, it seeks to situate Africa's churches in their wider context, to see what light can be shed on recent developments in African Christianity by using concepts taken from political and social analysis. Second, it seeks to examine the public role that the churches are playing in Africa. Let me sketch these two aims in slightly more detail.

I will briefly outline the history of sub-Saharan Africa over the last thirty years. I will relate the dynamics within African state and society to the dynamics of African Christianity. I will be asking to what extent the forces operative in Africa's social, political and economic sphere are operative in or reflected by African Christianity. Observers analyse African developments by means of concepts like neo-patrimonialism, reciprocal assimilation and co-optation of élites, personalism, extraversion and civil society. We will enquire whether these analytical tools shed any light on the dynamics within African churches.

The second aim works in the other direction. It attempts to shed light on what the churches are contributing or might contribute in Africa's current social changes. Many observers of Africa refer to the significance of Christianity in African society. A popular overview of the continent remarks simply: 'Today...the Christian church is probably the most powerful institution in sub-Saharan Africa.' The author does not, however, explain what this power consists of or how it is exercised.[1] Others refer to the influence of the churches, either in general or in particular countries, but then leave the issue unexamined. An important volume on civil society in Africa admits that religious groupings are the most significant on the continent, but deliberately does not consider them.[2] This book attempts to make up for this lack.

Even if Africa's plight in the mid-1990s is plain for all to see, there is no agreement about the reasons for it or about the remedy. Received wisdom about Africa has also changed quite considerably since the 1960s. At the risk of oversimplifying, we can note three major shifts in per-

---

[1]   David Lamb, *The Africans*, London: Methuen, rev. edn 1985, 141.
[2]   Larry Diamond, Juan J. Linz and Seymour Martin Lipset, *Democracy in Developing Countries: Africa*, Boulder, CO: Lynne Rienner, 1988, xxii.

ception. In the 1960s, around the time of independence, modernisation theory held sway, presuming that Third World countries would swiftly be transformed into participative, pluralist and democratic regimes. The state and the ruling élites would be the primary agents of political and economic development, and the principal bearers of modernisation. Development was conceived as a centre-outwards and top-downwards process. By the 1970s it was becoming clear that this theory was not working. Modernisation theory was superseded (at least on the left) by dependency theory, already well established in Latin America in the 1950s. The *dependencistas* reversed many of the assumptions of modernisation theory: they saw metropolitan influence as pernicious, not beneficent; foreign investment as masking even greater financial outflow; modernising élites as essentially parasitic, serving their own and foreign interests, not that of their people; and world trade as perpetuating structures of underdevelopment, not removing them. Dependency theory was even more evanescent than modernisation theory: by the early 1980s it was being superseded by the 'new realism', which held that at independence power had been given to the wrong people. Africa's corrupt élites and their self-seeking policies bore overwhelming responsibility for the disaster in Africa. The new realists were equally sure about the required remedy – structural adjustment. This is the dominant view in the mid-1990s, promoted by the International Financial Institutions (IFIs, essentially the World Bank and the International Monetary Fund) and American policy-oriented academics, even if it is fiercely opposed by a vigorous minority, and the proposed remedy of structural adjustment can show little evidence of success.[3]

It is not necessary here to trace all the twists of this debate. Here I want merely to sketch Africa's socio-political context today, to provide a backdrop against which we can view the functioning of Africa's churches. (In sketching this context, it will become clear that I think there is some truth in all three theories accounting for Africa's decline.)

The legacy of colonialism

Britain had been exploiting Africa without great opposition and without bothering to govern it for some decades before the scramble; it had exclusive rights to most of Africa in an informal or invisible empire, but

---

[3]   The best survey of these trends is Colin Leys, *The Rise and Fall of Development Theory*, London: James Currey, 1995. For sharply conflicting views see David E. Apter and Carl G. Rosberg, 'Changing African Perspectives' in David E. Apter and Carl G. Rosberg (eds), *Political Development and the New Realism in Sub-Saharan Africa*, Charlottesville, VA: University Press of Virginia, 1994, 1-57; Joel D. Barkan, 'Resurrecting Modernisation Theory and the Emergence of Civil Society in Kenya and Nigeria' in Apter and Rosberg, *Political Development*, 87-116; Jeff Haynes, *Religion in Third World Politics*, Buckingham: Open University Press, 1993, 20-7.

by 1881 France and Belgium were mounting a challenge that precipitated the scramble itself.[4] This scramble for Africa lasted about three decades, being complete by 1912. Colonialism had considerable effects, creating capital cities, railway networks, administrative structures and Western schools, and introducing European languages. But it affected different areas in different ways, according to which Western power exerted control, whether minerals or other resources could easily be extracted, and above all whether Europeans settled there.[5] And although colonialism could be brutal if challenged (for example, the German suppression of the Herero revolt in 1904 exterminated about 70% of the Herero, and almost the same percentage of the neighboring Nama), in many areas the impact was much milder, and quite soon was channelled into essentially progressive directions laid down by African society itself.[6] The greatest single effect was the totally artificial boundaries which united at least two but usually many more recognisably distinct 'peoples', and conversely divided homogeneous groups between two or more different countries.[7] Besides the heterogeneity of citizens, the colonial state left other negative legacies. Colonial administrations were both centralised and authoritarian. Just as important, the rulers manifested a sense of superiority over those they ruled, and power was experienced as coming from above rather than flowing from below. Thus the ruled developed a sense of the state as an alien institution, to be feared but also to be deceived and exploited, since it existed on a plane above the people whom it governed, beyond any chance of control.

Colonialism in Africa not only had a very short life – in many places it lasted only a single generation – but the end, when it came, was remarkably swift. The scramble out of Africa (1957-68) was pursued at the same headlong pace as the scramble into it.[8] Britain had learned from experience in India that independence there was inevitable; once the principle was admitted, withdrawal from Africa could not be long delayed. The Belgians left the Congo precipitately in 1960, leaving chaos behind them. The French were more determined to hold on to their world empire, but the resistance in Vietnam (1946-54) and especially Algeria (1954-62) brought de Gaulle back to power and, with him, a reversal of policy. Only the Portuguese continued to resist decolonisation, in the view of

4   Thomas Pakenham, *The Scramble for Africa*, London: Abacus, 1992, 111.

5   For the difference between British and French colonialism, see Christopher Clapham, *Third World Politics: an Introduction*, London: Routledge, 1985, 20-4; much of the following is dependent on Clapham.

6   Adrian Hastings, *The Church in Africa 1450-1950*, Oxford University Press, 1995, pp. 400-1.

7   Clapham, 'The African State' in Douglas Rimmer (ed.), *Africa 30 Years On*, London: James Currey, 1991, 96, warns against placing too much emphasis on this artificiality.

8   Pakenham, *Scramble*, 671.

many because their backward and politically isolated metropolitan economy could not afford neo-colonialism.[9] It took the 1974 'carnation revolution' in Portugal – intimately connected with the conscript army's reluctance to continue suppressing its colonial subjects – to bring about independence for the country's overseas territories.

Most African countries became independent in the 1960s, the local élite taking over the instruments of rule from the colonial powers. Independence coincided with a most important global phenomenon, a period of unparalleled economic growth (1945-75) which achieved 'the most dramatic, rapid and profound revolution in human affairs of which history has record.[10] Africa shared in both the economic boom and the resultant social transformation. Thus Africa came to independence on a surge of optimism, even euphoria. The new governments set about modernising their societies, making up for lost time. For this modernising process there was no effective model other than Western economic and techno-scientific development, either in its capitalist or socialist variant.[11] The euphoric and often highminded determination to modernise could even take the form of such ambitious social engineering as Nyerere's Ujamaa villages in Tanzania.

Before long, however, the euphoria of the early 1960s turned sour. It will pay us to consider in some detail the political systems that came to take root in Africa. As adumbrated above, colonial states had been above all about control: they were essentially about securing the obedience of an alien people. They were hierarchical, with their primary aim being the maintenance of order. Moreover, as the colonial states had to pay for themselves, they were geared to extracting resources from the domestic economy, or from the trade flowing from the economy's incorporation into the global trading system. Only after that was the state concerned with the provision of services. So the African state from birth was essentially an agency for control and extraction. There was never any merging of state and society as common expressions of shared values. Thus there has been little in the way of legitimacy, or popular commitment to public institutions.[12]

9   Eric Hobsbawm, *Age of Extremes: the Short Twentieth Century, 1914-1991*, London: Abacus, 1995, 221.

10 Hobsbawm, *Age*, 286; Hobsbawm also claims that 'the extraordinary economic explosion' of those years, 'with its consequent social and cultural changes [caused] the most profound revolution in society since the stone age' (16).

11 *Ibid.*, 200-4.

12 See the chapter 'Colonial Roots of the Contemporary Crisis' in Richard Sandbrook, *The Politics of Africa's Economic Stagnation*, Cambridge University Press, 1985, 42-62.

Neo-patrimonialism

This complete lack of shared values makes African states very different from developed Western societies. Western societies (albeit of a strictly ideal type) rest on what Weber described as 'rational-legal authority'; power has come to be exercised through legally defined structures, for a publicly acknowledged aim. Operating these structures are officials who in exercising the powers of office treat other individuals impersonally, according to criteria which the structures demand. If an official moves to a new post, he will immediately act according to the rules of this new post, and his successor in his previous position will act as he had done. This rational-legal ideal (admittedly nowhere achieved in its fulness) has proved to be the most efficient and legitimate way of running a complex modern state.

African states have failed even to approximate to this rational-legal mode of operation. They can best be described through another of Weber's authority types, that of patrimonialism. This, as the name implies, is based on the kind of authority a father has over his children. Here, those lower in the hierarchy are not subordinate officials with defined powers and functions of their own, but retainers whose position depends on a leader to whom they owe allegiance. The system is held together by loyalty or kinship ties rather than by a hierarchy of administrative grades and functions.

Africa's modern patrimonial systems have two particular manifestations: corruption and clientelism.[13] Corruption is the use of public office to achieve private goals. In the classic patrimonial system, the idea of corruption makes no sense because there is no distinction between the public and the private, the very distinction that underpins Weber's rational-legal ideal type. In a 'neo-patrimonial' system, however, the system is formally constituted on the principle of rational-legality. African states function with the apparatus of a modern nation state, but officials tend to exercise their powers as a form not of public service but of private property. In Africa the distinction between public and private has been hardly recognised, and public office has been accepted as the route to personal wealth and power. This attitude is expressed in proverbs like 'The goat eats where it is tethered', and the whole phenomenon has been analysed in terms of the phrase that Bayart has popularised: '*La politique du ventre*',

[13] For essentially the same phenomenon analysed as 'prebendalism', see Richard J. Joseph, *Democracy and Prebendal Politics in Nigeria: the Rise and Fall of the Second Republic*, New York: Cambridge University Press, 1987; Crawford Young, 'Democratisation in Africa: the Contradictions of a Political Imperative' in Jennifer A. Widner (ed.), *Economic Change and Political Liberalisation in Sub-Saharan Africa*, Baltimore, MD: Johns Hopkins University Press, 1994, 230-50; Nicolas van de Walle, 'Neopatrimonialism and Democracy in Africa, with an Illustration from Cameroon' in Winder, Economic Change, 129-57.

or 'The politics of the belly'.[14] Of course, some aspects of this system can be seen as rooted in traditional society. Distinguishing between the personal and the official self is not normal in tribal societies where loyalty to one's kin group is the primary social and moral value. Also, gift-giving constitutes a normal recognition of a superior's authority in a tributary system. Admittedly, some corruption may lead to the redistribution and exchange of benefits within a community, but most leads to the siphoning of resources from it. The resources plundered may be considerable, for in Africa the enormous powers of office are normally unchecked by countervailing powers such as those developed by business and property in the evolution of Western liberal states. Hence the labels often applied to the African state: the 'personally-appropriated state', 'vampire state', 'extraction state', 'opportunity state' or 'predatory state'.

In a neo-patrimonial state, support is ensured by clientelism, a relationship of exchange in which a superior provides security for an inferior, who as a client then provides political support for his patron. Control of the state carries with it the ability to provide (and, of course, to withhold) security, and to allocate benefits in the form of jobs, development projects and so on. Where the government is under no obligation to allocate benefits according to recognised criteria such as justice or efficiency or need, it may do so at its own discretion to encourage political support. Often this clientelism works through local power brokers, in which case the central authority looks around for a local leader with a following in his own area. The central figure delivers benefits to the local grandee, who in turn delivers the support of his area to the supremo. The local leader thus becomes a broker between his own community and central government, passing benefits in both directions, and probably taking his share in the process. Most often in Africa, given the totally artificial colonial boundaries which have left few states corresponding to ethnic identities, clientelism functions to mobilise ethnic support. The leadership obliges itself to look after the interests of its constituent tribe or group, and in return acquires a kind of legitimacy as the authentic representative of that group, regardless of the enormous gulf between the leader and his followers. In this way clientelism both maintains ruling class interests and at the same time effectively prevents the rise of class as a political factor.[15] Clientelism has thus militated against the rise of revolutionary movements in Africa.[16]

---

[14]   J.-F. Bayart, *The State in Africa: the Politics of the Belly,* London: Longman, 1993.
[15]   'In most African countries precapitalist relations of production [mean that] most people tend to see policies favouring notables from their own ethnic group more as favouring their ethnic group than as discriminating against small farmers' (Leys, *Rise and Fall,* 92).
[16]   'There is in Africa little revolutionary potential': J.-F. Bayart, 'Civil Society in Africa' in

To the extent that there is a dominant class, it has arisen from what Bayart calls 'hegemonic alliance' or 'the reciprocal assimilation of élites'. There exists between the administration, party, bureaucracy, army, intellectuals – sometimes even traditional chiefs – a privileged zone of interpenetration and mutual reinforcement, to produce a relatively homogeneous social group, an élite with Western education and well-paid public sector jobs, and often the former colonial residences. All the educated have tended to coalesce in this privileged group through processes described as 'straddling' or 'concatenation'. Even in single-party states the tendency has been to incorporate rather than to eliminate. Links are maintained through churches, lodges and social functions; in this web of personal relations, the private order is not separate from that of the state. The system involves co-optation, which extends to civil servants; to academics seeking preferment or appointment to commissions and diplomatic posts; to journalists who need access to information; to businessmen requiring contracts; to clergymen wanting tax-exempt status – in fact to all branches of the élite.[17]

In this way the state's tentacles stretch everywhere, from ethnic dependents in rural villages to all sectors of the élite. It is this aspect which Bayart has captured in his metaphor of 'the rhizome state', in which all sorts of 'little men' are linked through numerous capillaries of patronage and influence to some 'big man' through whom they can get a share of the good things of life.[18] Where there is no effective electoral process that offers real choice to clients, such a system admittedly brings some benefits, but its defects are obvious, not least that it does nothing to develop the efficiency, accountabilty and legitimacy necessary in the modern state.

What we have said of African states is as true of military as of civilian regimes. Military coups have been a feature of African rule – there were seven in 1966 alone – but even when the reason for the military's intervention was reform, this has proved beyond its capacities. The military's 'power to change the society was slight, whereas the society's power to subvert it was profound'.[19] To a large extent, a clear civilian-military dichotomy is difficult to use in categorising African states. Many regimes have the army behind them. In other cases, a military leader simply discards his uniform for a three-piece suit and goes on to 'win' an election, but the difference this makes is often not very clear.[20]

Similarly, the distinction between 'capitalist' and 'socialist' has not

Patrick Chabal (ed.), *Political Domination in Africa: Reflections on the Limits of Power*, Cambridge University Press, 1986, 113

[17] Bayart, *State*, esp. 150-79.

[18] *Ibid.*, 218-27.

[19] Clapham, 'African State', 94.

[20] Sandbrook, *Politics*, 85. For coups, see Hobsbawm, *Age*, 348-50.

proved particularly significant. Much of this labelling was for rhetorical effect during the Cold War. Some of the most statist and centralised regimes, like Mobutu's Zaïre, chose to style themselves pro-Western and anti-communist – but this was a ploy to receive aid. In the peculiar circumstances of the Cold War, it was often sufficient to achieve that aim.[21] Again, there has been little significant difference between the economic performance of socialist and capitalist regimes. The credit often given to the Ivory Coast and sometimes to Kenya for their relative economic success owes less to any 'capitalist' orientation than to Houphouet-Boigny's and to a lesser extent Moi's caution in Africanising, leaving many key economic positions to skilled expatriates.[22]

Externality

One factor, now obvious, is that many of Africa's states were completely unviable as autonomous entities. An important distinction here is that between empirical and juridical statehood (or between positive and negative statehood, exercised by substantive and quasi-states respectively). Western liberal states came into existence because they had developed the machinery of statehood: they controlled all the territory they claimed, could enforce laws, collect taxes, offer protection to their citizens, and repel invaders. As a result, they could demand recognition of their statehood from other states. There was often a considerable element of force in this process of establishing statehood: thus Bismarck forced all the German statelets into unity with Prussia, and after the withdrawal of French troops in 1869, the Papal States were powerless to withstand the forces of the *Risorgimento* intent on forging a united Italy under the House of Savoy. In Europe, there still exist some quaint reminders like Andorra, San Marino and Monaco of an era that has passed. However, since the Second World War, statehood has been granted to all sorts of entities that had never established any empirical statehood. Africa cannot claim all of these, but does have a fair share of them – it has about thirteen microstates, and all its offshore island countries except Madagascar are clearly of this kind.[23] Thus for many African states professed statehood

---

21 A former Acting British High Commissioner to Zimbabwe, writing of the 'four fundamental differences' between British and American policy towards Africa, gives as his fourth difference that for British policy 'marginal significance is attached to the label "Marxist" '– Roger Martin, 'How British Policy Toward Africa is Shaped and Executed', Centre for Strategic and International Studies, *CSIS Notes*, 87 (27 July 1988), 1.

22 Sandbrook, *Politics*, 117-21; Clapham, 'African State', 102.

23 See Robert H. Jackson and Carl G. Rosberg, 'Why Africa's Weak States Persist: the Empirical and the Juridical in Statehood', *World Politics*, 34 (1982), 1-24; Robert H. Jackson and Carl G. Rosberg, 'Sovereignty and Underdevelopment: Juridical Statehood in the African Crisis', *JMAS*, 24 (1986), 1-31; Robert H. Jackson, *Quasi-states: Sovereignty, International Relations and the Third World*, Cambridge University Press, 1990.

does not derive from any ability actually to do the things that are expected of a state – to impose taxation, build roads, provide education and health services, enforce the law and protect its citizens; many of them have no capacity to accomplish such things. They are states because the international community chooses to regard them as such, and the rules of the international game prevent fragmentation and interference on the part of others, or the recognition of other claimants who might perhaps be able or at least willing to provide such services. The Organisation of African Unity (OAU) was erected on just this principle of respecting existing sovereignties, and even censured Tanzania for attempting to depose Uganda's tyrant Amin in 1979. Such countries are said to have juridical statehood, but not empirical statehood (or negative but not positive statehood). This distinction serves to remind us that not a few countries in Africa are countries in a cartological sense only; they are presented in a distinctive colour on a map, so an unwary observer might think that they are countries of the same nature as Australia or Sweden. They are not: though they are recognised legal entities, they are not, in a functional sense, states.[24]

The notion of quasi-states shows how important are Africa's relations to the outside world. In many cases they are almost constitutive.[25] Many African countries have been independent for three decades, but in reality their dependence has enormously increased. They have become increasingly dependent on Western powers which are 'decreasingly willing to pay even lip-service to the mythology of state sovereignty'.[26] This does not mean that African states and societies are simple playthings of international systems, dancing to the tunes they play. On the contrary, African states have a life of their own, and opportunities to manipulate the external world and adapt it to their own needs. It is, however, the external element that created these states in the first place – the essential quality of the Third World is peripherality – and much of the freedom of action that African states possess lies in their ability to choose different ways of reacting to it.[27]

In the 1990s, with Africa's marginalisation, these links changed their character, through a process Clapham has called the privatisation or

---

[24] For an interesting example of a micro-state's powerlessness in the face of interference from foreign secret services, political parties and organised crime, see Stephen Ellis, 'Africa and International Corruption: the Strange Case of South Africa and Seychelles', *African Affairs*, 95(1996), 165-96.

[25] Bayart, *State*, esp. 20-32; the theme of 'externality' permeates Clapham's *Third World Politics*.

[26] Clapham, 'African State', 102.

[27] Clapham writes of the possible reactions of 'compliance, subversion, or defiance' to structural adjustment and political conditionality (*Africa and the International System: the Politics of State Survival*, Cambridge University Press, 1996, 176-81; 201-7).

de-stating of Africa's international relations.[28] After the Cold War, Western nations rapidly wound down their involvement with Africa. When,
for example, Eritrea became independent in 1993, the United States and
Italy (as the former colonial power) were the only states from outside
the immediate security zone to open embassies in Aṣmara. As the
possessor of a long coastline on the Red Sea immediately opposite Saudi
Arabia, if for no other reason, Eritrea might have expected far greater
interest. Western nations came to entrust their decreasing interests to
multinational bodies like the EU, the IFIs, the bodies overseeing the Lomé
conventions, or various United Nations organisations such as the UNDP,
UNHCR, UNICEF, WFP and WHO, much of whose work is in Africa.
More significantly for us, many of Africa's links with the West are now
through NGOs, whether as providers of famine relief, development aid
or residual social services. These Western NGOs often have greater
resources at their disposal than the recipient state itself. Their role in
Africa's current situation will be important for us throughout this study.

This notion of quasi-statehood explains why so few African governments can properly be described as totalitarian. Many, perhaps most, have
been authoritarian, some repressive and even brutal, but few have the
techniques and ability for total control which is the prerequisite for a
totalitarian regime. They simply have not had the capacity to be totalitarian.[29]
The incapacity of the state has preserved some private living space for
African peoples, and the depredations of the state have led many to retreat into this free space. Some scholars have come to concentrate on the
creativity of popular actors in this free space. A recent volume on African
Popular Culture finds, for example, in Mozambican anti-government songs
'a powerful sense of people naming the inequality they suffer from, and
recognising, often with humour and bitter irony, their own struggle and
endurance'. Peasants 'name their suffering because it is important to keep
its memory, which is itself empowering'.[30] It is necessary to preserve
this memory, and the study just cited analyses this phenomenon well,
but it is also necessary to keep a sense of proportion. Their resourcefulness has enabled Mozambican peasants to survive; but it would be
misleading to celebrate the empowerment of Mozambican peasants in
the last twenty years. Leys is right in calling for realism in the tragedy
affecting Africa. It is true that a 'black economy' (*magendo* in Uganda,
kalabule in Ghana) caters for between one- and two-thirds of economic

---

[28] *Ibid.*, 256-66.
[29] Samuel P. Huntington, *The Third Wave: Democratisation in the Late Twentieth Century*,
      Norman, OK: University of Oklahoma Press, 1991, 12.
[30] Karin Barber, 'Introduction' in Karin Barber (ed.), *Readings in African Popular Cul-
      ture*, London: James Currey, 1997, 5.

activity in many African economies. It is right that this be studied, but as
Leys remarks, 'this is part of the pathology of Africa's collapse, not a
seed-bed of renewal'; anyone who argues otherwise 'is not to be taken
seriously.'[31] The determination to prove that the masses in Africa are not
passive victims of external forces but make their own history is taken to
extreme lengths in Bayart's portrayal of refugees as heroes demonstrat-
ing the limitations of the state powerholders by exercising their 'exit option'.[32] Popular resourcefulness must be celebrated, but in any discussion of reshaping social and political structures its efficacy must be kept
in perspective.

Africa received its independence at the height of the Cold War. Initially, the impact was relatively slight. Some African countries were attracted to the USSR as a model for overcoming backwardness by means
of planned industrialisation.[33] In other cases nationalists like Neto in
Angola were forced to turn to the USSR after the West had refused help.
However, Africa was of little importance to the superpowers, especially
in comparison with the Middle East or South-east Asia. Thus African
states benefited from the paradox of impotence: since they did not matter
very much, it was not necessary for the superpowers to control them.
African rulers then used the Cold War as a resource and played the superpowers off one against the other. To some degree this changed in what
has been called the 'Second Cold War', from about 1975 to 1985. Between 1974 and 1979 a series of revolutions took place around the world;
these coincided with the American defeat in Vietnam, and the optimism
of Brezhnev's USSR. The United States became convinced that the Soviet Union was bent on expansion. Now Africa became embroiled in the
Great Power tussle, notably in the Angolan civil war of 1975-6, the Ogaden
war of 1977-8, and even the invasions of Zaïre in 1977 and 1978.
This was also the period of the emergence of a few African states (notably Angola, Ethiopia and Mozambique) which appeared to have opted
for Marxist-Leninist economic development. There was an enormous influx of arms into the continent, which provided African regimes with a
means of trying to control their own peoples, and encouraged these
same regimes to believe that external military backing would provide an
effective substitute for domestic political support. Thus the Cold War

---

[31] Colin Leys, 'Confronting the African Tragedy', *New Left Review,* 204 (1994), 35-6.

[32] *Ibid.*, 42-3; for examples highlighting peasant power, see J.F. Bayart, A. Mbembe, C.
     Toulabor, *Le politique par le bas en Afrique noire. Contributions à une problematique
     de la democratie*, Paris: Karthala, 1992. In the 'revenge of African societies' argument,
     claims Fatton, 'popular classes are presented as free to exit the public domain, victors
     over the macroeconomic programs of a state that now stands impotent, paralysed and
     powerless.' He argues that this view is deeply flawed (Robert Fatton, *Predatory Rule:
     State and Civil Society in Africa*, Boulder, CO: Lynne Rienner, 1992, 86).

[33] Hobsbawm, *Age*, 203.

from the mid 1970s played a role in reinforcing the levels of mis-government of African regimes, and the level of domestic insurgency against them.[34]

Although African countries gained independence during an economic boom, their economic base was very weak. Most adopted an economic strategy that centred on industrialisation through import substitution, protectionism, fixed exchange rates (invariably overvalued), the rationing of foreign exchange, the use of state-owned enterprises for development, and procurement and marketing through state agencies (normally called parastatals).[35] Much of this emphasis on industrialisation rather than agriculture was urged by foreign advisors, not least the World Bank itself. However, by the early 1980s it was obvious that these policies were not promoting development. There followed two important reactions. First, economic performance came to be seen as a function of politics. The World Bank's *From Crisis to Sustainable Growth* (1989) concluded that Africa's economic adversities could be largely attributed to a root political cause within Africa, namely bad governance (in World Bank terms, good governance comprised accountability, transparency, predictability, openness, and the rule of law).[36] Second, the emphasis on the state as an agent of development was considered discredited; now it was to be the markets that led to development. Previous policies had been obviously statist; they were all to be abandoned. The process of dismantling Africa's import-substituting industrial systems and the restrictive trade practices put in place to support them is normally called structural adjustment.[37] The shift in just a few decades from a perception of the state as the mechanism for the pursuit of public benefit to that of the state as an instrument of exploitation, managed purely in the interest of those who held power, was almost complete.[38]

Many of the most eloquent critics of the African state fail to take account of the international trade systems so stacked against Third World countries. They also ignore the undeniable fact that African states have lacked the base levels of national unity, the entrepreneurial classes, the organisational capacities and social controls on which Japan and Korea,

---

[34] Christopher Clapham, 'International Relations in Africa after the End of the Cold War', paper delivered at conference on 'The End of the Cold War: Effects and Prospects for Asia and Africa', SOAS, 21-2 Oct. 1994; Hobsbawm, *Age*, 245-6; 436; 452.

[35] These are all discussed in Michael F. Lofchie, 'The New Political Economy of Africa' in Apter and Rosberg, *Political Development*, 146-50.

[36] Robert H. Jackson and Carl G. Rosberg, 'The Political Economy of African Personal Rule' in Apter and Rosberg, *Political Development,* 314.

[37] Lofchie, 'New Political Economy', 170-1.

[38] Clapham, 'African State', 91-3.

or even Germany and France in an earlier era, could build.[39] So the degree to which Africa's plight can be attributed to mismanagement is disputed. However, it is undeniable that the neo-patrimonial systems of Africa have militated against development. It is often assumed that since economic underdevelopment is the principal problem (and indeed defining characteristic) of Third World countries, so development must be the overriding goal of their governments. But it is obvious from the internal dynamics of the neo-patrimonial state that this need not be so at all. Staying in power is the main objective. The army must be kept happy, urban masses must be fed, conflicting interests of political coalitions must be balanced. To this end every aspect of the economy becomes an instrument of patronage. Quotas, tariffs, subsidies, import licences, the overvalued currency and so on become channels of enrichment, through rent-seeking activity.[40] The privileges of the élite depend on the monopoly of power within a society, and not on the productivity of society as a whole, much less on any feelgood factor permeating the population at large. In the short term at least, a successful programme of economic development conflicts with that. The political and economic exigencies of personal rule follow their own logic. Mismanagement actually has a rationale within the neo-patrimonial political system.[41] This has been clearly expressed by one businessman explaining the chaos of Mobutu's Zaïre: 'Mobutu likes it this way. With hyperinflation it's easy for foreigners to make money, and it's the cut from foreigners that fills his pockets. With no roads, the army can never topple him. With no communications, the opposition can never organise. With total corruption, it's every man for himself, and people can be picked off one by one,'[42] Zaïre, admittedly an extreme case, illustrated the logic of underdevelopment.

Moves for reform

Pressure for reform, both internal and external, built up inexorably in the late 1980s. Internal pressure came from former politicians then in eclipse, and from the ranks of local community-based hierarchies: lawyers, community activists and church leaders. The latter groups had the advantage of

[39] *Ibid.*, 102.
[40] See Mark Gallagher, *Rent-Seeking and Economic Growth in Africa*, Boulder, CO: Westview, 1991.
[41] Clapham, *Third World Politics*, 91-2; Sandbrook, *Politics*, 153; Jackson and Rosberg, 'Political Economy', 302-3: Ernest Gellner, *Conditions of Liberty: Civil Society and its Rivals*, London: Hamish Hamilton, 1994, 175. See William Reno, *Corruption and State Politics in Sierra Leone*, Cambridge University Press, 1995.
[42] Cited in Christopher Hitchens, 'African Gothic', *Vanity Fair*, Nov. 1994, 53. See also Hobsbawm, *Age*, 23; Clapham, 'African State', 91; Jackson and Rosberg, 'Political Economy', 303-4.

professional associations, and often international links.[43] Although it was not as significant as internal pressure, international pressure helped. External pressure had been building up, but circumstances radically altered in 1989 with the end of the Cold War. Now leaders who before could rely on support from one or the other superpower were left to their own devices so that internal legitimacy and local support became far more important. The combination of both internal and external forces led about 1989 to pressure that could no longer be resisted. There occurred a series of national conferences in francophone countries, many one-party states were forced to permit opposition parties, elections were held, and some even achieved a change of regime. This led to a euphoria like that of the early 1960s; indeed, the phrase 'second liberation struggle' gained common currency for a time.

The impetus for political reform produced varying results. In as much as there is one explanation for the different outcomes, it seems to lie in the nature of the neo-patrimonial state. These systems need resources flowing through the system to remain functional. But economic collapse greatly reduced the leaders' ability to retain their clients' support. Leaders were unable to reward dependants because they no longer had the resources. They were unable to placate two groups in particular: urban élites, especially government employees, were no longer paid, and rulers did not have the wherewithal to provide the usual disproportionate rewards to the military and security forces, on whom they counted to suppress popular unrest. As a result, when an opposition formed, many regimes collapsed like a house of cards. It was the amount of resources available to leaders that determined whether they could preserve the patronage networks which sustained them. Thus Nigeria, Zimbabwe and Kenya could ride out the storm; Benin, Togo and Mali proved to be hollow shells as soon as pressure was applied.[44]

After a short time, the situation changed again. External pressure, exerted particularly through aid conditionality, diminished as Western powers became far more concerned about long-term stability in Africa and control of the drugs trade than political reform.[45] By mid-1993 when Babangida cynically aborted the return to civilian rule in Nigeria, that narrow window of opportunity had closed again.

By the mid-1990s, Africa was beyond a crisis; it was a tragedy. The economic collapse was evident to all. In Nigeria – and one out of every six Africans is a Nigerian – when Babangida left office in mid-1993 the

---

[43]   Robert H. Bates, 'The Impulse to Reform in Africa' in Widner, *Economic Change*, 21-2.

[44]   Jeffrey Herbst, 'The Dilemmas of Explaining Political Upheaval: Ghana in Comparative Perspective' in Widner, *Economic Change*, 194-6; van de Walle, 'Neopatrimonialism'; Michael Bratton, 'Economic Crisis and Political Realignment in Zambia' in Widner, *Economic Change*, 101-28.

[45]   Michael Bratton, 'International versus Domestic Pressures for "Democratisation" in Africa', paper delivered as part of conference referred to above, n. 34.

real income per head was one-tenth of what it was when he came to power eight years earlier.[46] In Cameroon income per head fell by half between 1985 and 1993.[47] According to the head of the United Nations Economic Commission for Africa, commenting on the failure of the UN Programme of Action for Africa's Economic Recovery and Development (1986-90), Africans were generally 40% worse off in 1991 than in 1980.[48] Per capita consumption in sub-Saharan Africa fell by one-fifth in the 1980s. Spending on health care declined by 50%, and on education by 25%. In the mid-1990s as many as 10,000 African children were dying each day from the effects of malnutrition and lack of rudimentary health care. It is estimated that Africa's share of global infant death will rise to 40% by the end of the decade. Between 1961 and 1995 Africa's food production per person decreased by 11.6% (by comparison, Latin America's increased by 31.4% and Asia's by 70.6%). The World Bank predicts that a third of all food requirements will have to be imported by the year 2000. Africa's share of world trade has all but disappeared – in 1950 it was 5.2%, in 1980 4.7% and in 1990 only 1.9%. Returns on investment in Africa dropped from 30.7% in the 1960s to 2.5% in the 1980s. Not surprisingly, then, there has been considerable disinvestment, and external private commercial investment in the continent totalled only $504m. in 1992, or 1.6% of the total private investment in Africa, Asia and Central and South America as a whole. The GDP of the whole of sub-Saharan Africa in 1992, at $270bn, was less than that of the Netherlands.[49] There has been a general collapse in infrastructure. By any standards of reckoning – statistics for life expectancy, child mortality, health, education, GDP – Africa has fallen well behind other developing areas of the world. The continent is slipping out of the Third World into its own bleak category of the nth world.[50] A recent World Bank statement has admitted that even if Africa were to implement all the required

---

[46] *Economist*, 21 Aug. 1993, 14 (survey).

[47] *Economist*, 22-26 Jan. 1994, 53.

[48] *24 Hours*, BBC World Service, 8 Sept. 1991. Of the numerous World Bank publications on Africa the most significant, portraying the changing situation, are *Accelerated Development in Sub-Saharan Africa: an Agenda for Action* (1981); *Towards Sustained Development in Sub-Saharan Africa* (1984); *Sub-Saharan Africa: from Crisis to Sustainable Growth: a Long Term Perspective Study* (1989); *The Social Dimensions of Adjustment Africa: a Political Agenda* (1990); *A Continent in Transition: Sub-Saharan Africa in the Mid-1990s* (1995); all published by the World Bank, Washington, DC.

[49] Clapham, *International System*, 164.

[50] Blaine Harden, *Africa: Dispatches from a Fragile Continent*, London: Harper Collins, 1991, 15. Harden balances this with a necessary positive note: 'Africa's problems, as pervasive and ghastly as they seem, are not the final scorecard on a doomed continent. They are the preliminary readings from the world's messiest experiment in cultural and political change' (*ibid.*, 16).

reforms correctly, the situation there would still deteriorate.[51]

And Africa's tragedy is not a narrowly political or economic one. It is also social and cultural. In Liberia and Rwanda it is obvious that whole populations have been brutalised. In other places too the situation is forcing people to kill, steal, beg and resort to drugs, prostitution and alcohol. Economic hardship has profound effects on family life, as young men unable to raise marriage payments leave young women to raise children without husbands. Kenyan human rights groups say the level of violence in society is spiralling: deaths in mob violence tripled within two years, far outstripping deaths due to ethnic clashes and banditry, and this communal violence is fast coming to be accepted.[52] Assuming that fertility rates fall in the coming years as they have in South Asia (a somewhat optimistic assumption) the World Bank expects that the population of sub-Saharan Africa will none the less double from about 500 million in 1990 to 1 billion in 2010, and reach 1.7 billion by 2050.[53] What this suggests in the way of pressure on already scarce fertile land and already crumbling urban infrastructures can only be dimly imagined. One observer notes that if the 1980s were the 'lost decade' for Africa, then the 1990s may well become the decade when 'Africa [is] rendered irrelevant to global development, so marginal[ised] that its people's only real resource is to call upon the pity of the world by threatening to die in mass starvation on television.'[54]

As Liberia, Sierra Leone, Somalia and Rwanda continued to unravel, some started to use the term 'Afropessimism'.[55] Others were talking about trusteeship, re-colonialism and similar concepts. Africans themselves feared that the biggest problem for Africa was not neo-colonialism but indifference on the part of the West. Determined to build democracy and capitalism in the former Eastern Bloc, the West might simply abandon Africa.[56] Of those proposing solutions, those on the left who argue for debt relief or that the subordination of African society to the market must be reversed are not listened to; the most dominant school, the neo-liberals of the IFIs and the policy-oriented American political scientists, have had few successes with structural adjustment, something admitted even by the World Bank itself.

---

[51] Leys, *Rise and Fall*, 190.

[52] *Guardian*, 2 May 1996, 11.

[53] World Bank, *Sub-Saharan Africa*, 33.

[54] Charles Bright and Michael Geyer, cited in John Mihevc, *The Market tells them so: the World Bank and Economic Fundamentalism in Africa*, London: Zed Books, 1995, 11.

[55] For a celebrated and influential example, see Robert D. Kaplan,'The Coming Anarchy', *Atlantic Monthly*, February 1994, 44-76; further elaborated as Robert D. Kaplan, *The Ends of the Earth: a Journey at the Dawn of the 21st Century*, New York: Random House, 1996.

[56] Clapham, 'African State', 102.

Civil society

One issue has become central in the discussion of Africa's plight: civil society. Since this will influence our focus in what follows, it is essential to outline the debate here.[57]

Civil society is defined as the 'set of diverse non-governmental institutions which is strong enough to counterbalance the state and, while not preventing the state from fulfilling its role as keeper of the peace and arbitrator between major interests, can nevertheless prevent it from dominating and atomising the rest of society.'[58] In Africa, as we have seen, there is little to counterbalance the state, and the state effectively means those who own it. As observers came to despair of the African state, they turned their focus to enhancing civil society as the way forward.

The notion of civil society is best explained by tracing its rise in the West. In eighteenth-century Europe a new kind of society began to take shape. This new society was relatively secularised. Faith had retreated more to the private area, at least to the extent that it had ceased to sacralise the social order. The social order was coming to be characterised by functional pragmatic compromise. No reality was treated as given. There was nothing that could not be questioned. At the same time, the division of labour was growing more refined and extensive. Economic and social activities began to be distinguished from centralised order-maintaining ones. Some were engaging in business, and simply leaving the protective or security arrangements to others. The new society was marked by individualism. People no longer identified with their position in village or lineage; they belonged to a much more mobile society. There arose a whole cluster of institutions and associations, and they could be entered and left freely; belonging to any one was not imposed by birth or sustained by ritual. 'Modular man' had been born.[59]

The novelty of this new society was particularly evident in the matter of authority. Many areas began to have real autonomy, not subject to central autocratic control. In many areas, it was no longer quite clear exactly who was boss. Other institutions could check the state; they were not supine before it. Power was reduced to an instrument, to be judged by its effectiveness and service, and was no longer a master. This taming

---

[57] Particularly, Gellner, *Conditions*; John A. Hall (ed.), *Civil Society: Theory, History, Comparison*, Cambridge: Polity Press, 1995; John W. Harbeson, Donald Rothchild, Naomi Chazan (eds), *Civil Society and the State in Africa*, Boulder, CO: Lynne Rienner, 1994; Dwayne Woods, 'Civil Society in Europe and Africa: Limiting State Power through a Public Sphere', *African Studies Review* 35 2 (1992), 77-100; Michael Bratton, 'Beyond the State: Civil Society and Associational Life in Africa', *World Politics* 41 (1989), 407-30; J. N. Moyo, 'Civil Society in Zimbabwe', *Zambezia* 20 (1993), 1-13.

[58] Gellner, *Conditions*, 5; my perspective here is from Gellner.

[59] Ernest Gellner, 'The Importance of Being Modular' in Hall, *Civil Society,* 32-55.

of power was, in Gellner's phrase, 'perhaps mankind's greatest triumph'.[60] Previously, since the state provided a source of power and wealth entirely disproportionate to that available from any other organised force within society, political power had been fought for with some ferocity. But now leaders were no longer paid out of all proportion to all others; on the contrary, their rewards became relatively feeble and nothing much out of the ordinary. Positions of power came to be rotated like all others. Those who amassed wealth did not use it for the acquisition of power, and thus they broke through the vicious circle which in the past obliged power-holders to suppress successful accumulators of wealth as an imminent political menace; the emerging bourgeoisie could be tolerated, as they themselves no longer sought power, at least as individuals. Indeed, these developments should be seen as the emerging middle class seeking a form of *collective* power in the name of the whole, increasingly understood as the modern nation state. Henceforth, in these commercial and industrial societies, using power as the way to personal wealth was not altogether unknown, but this route has been incomparably less important; in Gellner's phrase, in these societies 'the best way to make money is to make money'.[61]

The roots of this new order lay in the Reformation, and its development was intimately linked to the industrial revolution. This new order depended on economic expansion. Expectation of improvement replaced coercion as the ultimate basis of the social order. Only in conditions of overall growth can a majority have an interest in conforming, even without intimidation. Increasing wealth functioned effectively as a 'social bribery fund'; the new order could buy its way out of any external or internal threat.[62] Economic growth for its part required cognitive growth. It was the unending innovation of the scientific revolution that brought about an apparently unending exponential increase in productive power, until human skills rather than raw materials became the key element in wealth production. If such growth was to be maintained, ideological monopoly was impossible, and reason came to be applied not just to raw materials and productive processes but to society itself. Rational procedures were demanded by an informed public opinion; the rising bourgeoisie could not tolerate arbitrariness on the part of rulers. 'One of the most significant developments in Europe was the progress in bringing political arbitrariness to heel.'[63] In this way productive values came to

---

[60]   Gellner, *Conditions*, 206.

[61]   *Ibid.*, 74.

[62]   *Ibid.*, 73.

[63]   T. Callaghy, 'The State and the Development of Capitalism in Africa: Theoretical, Historical and Comparative Reflections' in D. Rothchild and N. Chazan (eds), *The Precarious Balance: State and Society in Africa*, Boulder, CO: Westview, 1988, 75.

triumph over all others. This new social order is almost defined by its strong civil society, the myriad groups which force the state to cater for their interests. It is precisely this associational life which is so weak in Africa, and which now is the focus of so much attention.

This emphasis on civil society as the solution for Africa has met with criticism. First, it is evident from the above just how Western the concept is, how rooted in a specific conjunture of circumstances in European history, and how inextricably linked with the pluralist, secularised, modular, scientific and capitalist societies of the West. For this reason, many claim that it is of limited application in Africa where a bourgeoisie, industrialisation and capitalism are in fact not in play (at least in the sense implied by the civil society debate). Also, to mark out Africa's future in terms of civil society is to present the West as some kind of model to which others must conform. Yet the notion of the West as a model is hard to maintain in the face of the unresolved problems of Western democratic institutions at the end of the twentieth century. This humility is reinforced now that Western supremacy is perhaps being overtaken. Asian countries are allegedly surpassing the industrial efficiency and the scientific and technological innovation of the West, yet without the individualism, modularity, and political freedoms regarded as crucial by civil society theorists.[64]

But the most serious criticism is not so much that the concept is unhelpful, as that it is ideological. 'Civil society' is allegedly part of the neo-liberal ideological project, something to be fostered as the alternative to the state. By strengthening African civil society, this criticism runs, the neo-liberals aim to undermine further the African state, and thus to leave Africa even more open to domination by Western forces. For such critics, the promotion of civil society is the obverse side of the 'vilification' of the African state. I regard this debate as somewhat misconceived, for surely there is no necessary opposition between the two. A strong civil society needs a strong state, that is, a state capable of exercising effectively certain functions such as repelling aggressors, maintaining order, guaranteeing health and education services and a certain infrastructure for transport and communication. Even the World Bank was admitting this by 1990.[66]

I have outlined the notion of civil society because religious groups

---

[64] See the review of Gellner's *Conditions* by John Gray, 'Our Way', *London Review of Books*, 22 Sept 1994, 8-9.

[65] For an example, see Bjorn Beckman, 'The Liberation of Civil Society: Neo-Liberal Ideology and Political Theory', *RoAPE* 58 (1993), 20-33; Tom Young, "A Project to be Realised": Global Liberalism and Contemporary Africa', *Millennium* 24 (1995), 527-46; Sandbrook, *Politics*, 154; Also: 'The most convenient world for multinational giants is one populated by dwarf states or no states at all' (Hobsbawm, *Age*, 281).

[66] Clapham, *International System*, 174-5; Diamond, Linz and Lipset, *Politics in Developing*

are widely admitted to be the strongest form of associational life in contemporary Africa. Much of our aim in what follows will be to shed light
on the internal functioning of Africa's churches as key elements of Africa's
'civil society'. This is a significant undertaking because, as Bratton admits, the precise workings of African associations are largely unknown.[67]
The attempt points up a certain paradox. In the West Christianity, while
arguably a key source of modernity, has declined in its public significance as modern society has taken shape. In Africa it may be that Christianity is assuming an increasing significance in the creation of a modern, pluralisitc African society.

Countries: Comparing Experiences with Democracy, 2nd edn, Boulder, CO: Lynne
Rienner, 1995, 30. 'The problem in Africa, to repeat, is not the state but the weakness
of the social formations on which the state rests' (Leys, 'Confronting', 46).

[67] Bratton, 'Beyond the State', 430. Bratton provides an example revealing the dynamics
of an element of African civil society in a study of farmers' unions in Zimbabwe, showing how they basically mirror the neo-patrimonial and authoritarian state of Zimbabwe
rather than foster worker participation; Michael Bratton, 'Micro-Democracy? The Merger
of Farmer Unions in Zimbabwe', *African Studies Review* 37 (1994), 9-37.

2

AFRICAN CHURCHES: THEIR
GLOBAL CONTEXT

The explicit involvement of Africa's churches in the public sphere was
drawn to the world's attention in the late 1980s, when francophone
countries began national conferences and Catholic bishops were appointed
to chair them. In Benin, Mgr Isidore de Sousa, Archbishop of Cotonou,
presided over the national conference, and then as president of the Haut
Conseil de la République overseeing the transition process, was the highest
authority in the land for the thirteen months leading up to elections. In
Gabon it was Mgr Basile Mve Engone, Bishop of Oyem. In Togo, Mgr
Sanouko Kpodzro, Bishop of Atakpame, presided over the process. In
the Congo, Mgr Ernest Kombo, Bishop of Owando, presided over the three-
month-long national conference and then the entire transitional process.
In Zaïre, Mgr Laurent Monsengwo Pasinya, Archbishop of Kisangani,
was elected in 1991 to preside over the national conference attempting
to halt that country's decline into anarchy.[1]

In many other countries, the churches' involvement was equally salient.
In Kenya the most articulate criticism of President Moi came from individual Anglican bishops, and later from the National Council of Churches
of Kenya. In Malawi the process of terminating President Banda's rule
was begun by the 1992 lenten pastoral of the Catholic bishops. In
Madagascar the Council of Churches was the core of the *Forces Vives*
that led to the ousting of President Ratsiraka in 1992. And in Zambia the
churches were among the most prominent local bodies involved in the
1991 transfer of power – at particular times of crisis playing a decisive
role in preventing deadlock.

That the churches played such a role is remarkable, since their involvement in Africa's liberation from colonialism was very minor. At
independence it was commonly thought that Christianity in Africa would
become ever less significant, because it was associated so closely with
colonialism, and depended so strongly on its school systems, which would
be taken over by the new African governments. This prediction has proved

---

[1] On these national conferences, see Fabien Eboussi Boulaga, *Les conférences
nationales en Afrique noire: une affaire à suivre*, Paris: Karthala, 1993; and *Jeune
Afrique*, 26, June-July 1991, 16-25. For the bishops as president, see Metena M'Nteba,
'Les Conférences Nationales Africaines et la figure politique de l'évêque-president',
Zaïre-Afrique, 276, June-Aug. 1993, 361-72.

completely false. Although precise figures are hard to verify (not least because of different definitions of 'Christian'), there is no doubting the enormous increase in Christianity south of the Sahara.[2] It has reached the stage that, as Adrian Hastings has written, 'Black Africa today is totally inconceivable apart from the presence of Christianity, a presence which a couple of generations ago could still be not unreasonably dismissed as fundamentally marginal and a mere subsidiary aspect of colonialism.'[3] This public prominence has been assessed in different ways.

In his much-quoted *The Third Wave* the political theorist Samuel Huntington has studied the movement to democracy of about thirty countries between 1974 and 1990 (the first two waves of democratisation he lists as 1828-1926 and 1943-62). He finds five factors responsible for these Third Wave transitions to democracy: the declining legitimacy of authoritarian regimes; global economic growth; changes in the policies of external actors like the United States; the 'snowball' or demonstration effect of successful transitions; and, directly relevant for our purposes, the 'changes in the doctrine and activities of the Catholic Church'. A strong correlation had long been noted between Protestantism and democracy, stemming from Protestantism's emphasis on the individual, its democratic rather than hierarchical church structures, and its encouragement of economic enterprise. But between the 1960s and the 1980s the Catholic Church changed, both at the global level of pronouncements of the Popes and the Vatican Council, and at the level of popular involvement, giving rise to 'a new church that almost invariably came into opposition to authoritarian governments'.[4] In Latin America, Eastern Europe, the Philippines and Korea churches lent their resources to the struggle against authoritarianism – buildings, radio stations, newspapers and international influence. At crucial times church leaders directly intervened. 'In country after country the choice between democracy and authoritarianism became personified in the conflict between the cardinal and the dictator.' Cardinal Sin in the Philippines may have exerted a larger role in changing political leadership 'than any Catholic prelate since the seventeenth century'. Huntington concludes: 'Catholicism was second only to economic development as a pervasive force making for democratisation in the 1970s and 1980s.'[5] Huntington

---

2   The figure commonly bandied about is an increase of 16,400 Africans each day; see Bob Coote, 'The Numbers Game in World Evangelisation', *Evangelical Missions Quarterly* 27, 2 (1991), 118-27.

3   Adrian Hastings, 'Christianity in Africa' in Ursula King (ed.), *Turning Points in Religious Studies*, Edinburgh: T. and T. Clark, 1990, 208.

4   Huntington, *Third Wave*, 79.

5   *Ibid.*, 85; he immediately continues: 'The logo of the third wave could well be a crucifix superimposed on a dollar sign.'

speculates whether democratisation will continue through the 1990s. He notes the spread of Christianity in Africa, and concludes: 'As the numbers of Christians multiply, presumably the activity of church leaders in support of democracy will not decline and their political power will increase.'[6] We will examine to what extent Huntington's optimism is warranted.

Huntington's study has little specific analysis of Africa. Other studies deal with Africa in the course of global presentations. The South African theologian John de Gruchy has studied the question of the relationship between Christianity and democracy across the world.[7] He distinguishes between the democratic *system*, or the principles and procedures, symbols and convictions that have developed over the centuries, and the democratic *vision*, or hope for a just and responsible society in which all people are equal and free. He argues that the democratic vision has its origins not so much in ancient Athens, the symbolic birthplace of the democratic system, as in the message of the Old Testament prophets. Above all – and this is his main interest – he outlines Christian theological concepts or ideals which should lead Christians to promote democracy. His richest contribution is his analysis of the themes, symbols and images preserved in various Christian traditions.[8] He is aware of how democratic rhetoric can be used to entrench power. He is also aware that much Northern concern is to promote a 'low-intensity democracy' whereby 'the United States in particular, and the North in general, seek to control the democratic process in the South in such a way that they retain their privileges.'[9] Some Christian involvement is of this sort: 'Much right-wing Christianity today equates its cause with the defence of Western interests under the ideological rubric of liberal democratic capitalism.'[10] But a large part of the book consists of case studies of the United States, Nicaragua, East Germany, South Africa (where 'there can be little doubt that the church played a key role in the ending of apartheid'[11]) and, of interest to us, sub-Saharan Africa. He is generally very positive in his assessment of the church's contribution to Africa's political transition.

---

6   *Ibid.,* 281.

7   John W. de Gruchy, *Christianity and Democracy*, Cambridge University Press, 1995. His African section depends heavily on a conference in Leeds in September 1993, published as Paul Gifford (ed.), *The Christian Churches and the Democratisation of Africa*, Leiden: E.J.Brill, 1995.

8   An accessible statement of this part is found in John de Gruchy, 'Theological Reflections on the Task of the Church in the Democratisation of Africa' in Gifford, *Christian Churches,* 47-60.

9   De Gruchy, *Christianity,* 162; see also 143, 247.

10   *Ibid.,* 127.

11   *Ibid.,* 211.

He elaborates different kinds of contribution: providing leaders of integrity and honesty; mediating between warring factions; facilitating national reconciliation and reconstruction; providing social cohesion; gathering international support; and linking élites with the people.[12] His argument is that the churches generally have been 'midwives of democratic transition and reconstruction'.[13]

A similarly positive assessment of the role of Christianity in global democratisation is offered by the Project on Christianity and Democracy of the Law and Religion programme of Emory University, Atlanta. Richard Joseph contributes the section on sub-Saharan Africa. He begins: 'At the center of most of [Africa's democratic] transformations and upheavals are religious leaders from a variety of Christian denominations.'[14] He makes his case from extended treatments of the churches in Cameroon and Zaïre, and briefer case studies of the churches in Benin, Togo, Kenya, Madagascar and Zambia. He traces a shift from churches as 'zones of liberty' to 'active agencies of political liberalisation',[15] and makes it clear that he is not referring merely to leaders: 'In most African countries, Christian groups have tended to provide general support for the contemporary democratic movement.'[16]

An even more positive assessment is found in John Mihevc's *The Market Tells Them So*, a wide-ranging analysis of the present state of Africa. He laments that academic studies do not pay sufficient attention to the contribution of the churches. For Mihevc 'Churches have been at the heart of the political upheavals sweeping through Africa.'[17] He writes of 'a rising number of church-supported and -inspired democratisation movements currently sweeping Africa.'[18] He states that the churches have 'in effect served to unleash the momentous political upheavals occurring in many African countries.'[19] They continue to have 'significant political impact.'[20]

However, if these surveys are, with qualifications, definitely positive about Christianity's current role, Jeff Haynes gives a different picture altogether. Haynes has written extensively on the role of religion, both

---

[12]   *Ibid.*, 181-7.

[13]   *Ibid.*, 193.

[14]   Richard Joseph, 'The Christian Churches and Democracy in Contemporary Africa', in John Witte Jr (ed.), *Christianity and Democracy in Global Context*, Boulder, CO: Westview Press, 1993, 231.

[15]   Joseph, 'Christian Churches', 234.

[16]   *Ibid.*, 237.

[17]   Mihevc, *Market*, 225.

[18]   *Ibid.*, 229.

[19]   *Ibid.*, 235.

[20]   *Ibid.*, 242.

Christianity and Islam, in sub-Saharan African politics. As regards Christianity, he distinguishes two kinds, mainline and popular. These are respectively 'an ideology of attempted hegemonic control' and a 'vehicle for mobilising community organisation, often to help fend off that control'.[21] In assessing the role of the leaders of the mainline churches, Haynes is extremely negative. Using Gramsci's concept of hegemony, he argues that mainstream religious leaders and the state interact 'to seek to achieve a hegemonic ideology that stresses the desirability of stability rather than progressive change... Senior religious figures usually seek to defuse, reduce and, when necessary, strive to help eliminate serious political challenges to the status quo.'[22] Where church leaders (notably the Catholic bishops in the much-trumpeted national conferences) did feature in democratic changes, such instances are 'best understood as examples of successful "passive revolutions" – another Gramscian term to describe the way that a dominant socio-political group may have to change its way of wielding power if it wants to maintain it.[23] On the other hand, popular religion caters for the real needs of the people, since it arises from 'a realisation that the best way to achieve individual and collective benefits [is] by practising methods of self-help.'[24] Popular Christianity is a creative response on the part of ordinary people to the destabilising effects of modernisation. Haynes distinguishes different kinds of popular Christianity: 'New Religious Movements' (like AICs, which, he claims, tend equally to preserve the *status quo*, and another sub-group consisting of rural movements like Lenshina's in Zambia or the Mozambican Nparamas), and the new Pentecostal or charismatic churches which he calls 'fundamentalist Christianity' and considers the counterpart of Islamic fundamentalism. He is much more approving of these fundamentalist groups, and sees them as popular movements catering for popular needs.[25]

By the end of this study, after consideration of the complexity and

21   Jeff Haynes, *Religion and Politics in Africa*, London: Zed Books, 1996, 123. See also his earlier book and articles: *Religion in Third World Politics,* Buckingham: Open University Press, 1993; 'Popular Religion and Politics in Sub-Saharan Africa', *Third World Quarterly* 16, 1 (1995), 89-108; 'The Revenge of Society? Religious Responses to Political Disequilibrium in Africa', *Third World Quarterly* 16, 4 (1995), 728-37.

22   Haynes, *Religion and Politics,* 104.

23   *Ibid.,* 105. For an extended criticism of the role of the Catholic Church, see 114-22. Also 'Roman Catholic leaders tended to be ambivalent about the concept of fundamental political reform because they feared emphatic change every bit as much as did the entrenched political élites. Although on occasion they headed conferences, it was not at all clear that they wished actually to personally endorse the demands for change until the groundswell of public opinion was such that not to do so would emphatically link them with the secular political elites at a time when demands for change [threatened the political élites]' (*ibid.,* 132).

24   *Ibid.,* 133.

25   *Ibid.,* 138-47, 169-87.

variety of the churches' involvement, we will be in a position to evaluate such diverse assessments of the role of Christianity in Africa's recent changes.

Theology

Although analysing essentially the same reality as the preceding authors, we will highlight one aspect that they largely leave aside, that of theology (de Gruchy's interest in the subject is prescriptive, rather than descriptive of the theology actually promoted by the churches). So many social science studies of African religion almost ignore this aspect. Thus Haynes, in explaining his Gramscian approach through hegemony, says that it is the social and class positions of the leaders that are crucial: 'What such leaders believe their religious message to comprise in a spiritual sense is of interest, but primarily the concern of theologians; what they seek to gain from their personal position or for their religious institution in competition with others is, however, relevant to a study of African politics and religion.'[26] However, a church's teachings cannot be entirely left aside in any adequate treatment, as though churches were groups like a women's institute or farmers' union or agricultural cooperative. An adequate treatment must allow space for those ideas, symbols, images, motifs, myths and metaphors which we can glorify with the title 'theology' or 'belief', although these terms usually indicate something more cerebral or conscious than I intend here.

A religion provides definitions, principles of judgement and criteria of perception. It offers a reading of the world, of history, of society, of time, of space, of power, of authority, of justice and of ultimate truth. Religion limits or increases the conceptual tools available, restricts or enlarges emotional responses, or channels them, and withdraws certain issues from inquiry. It inculcates a particular way of perceiving, experiencing and responding to reality. Religion can legitimise new aspirations, new forms of organisation, new relations and a new social order. Every religion involves struggles to conquer, monopolise or transform the symbolic structures which order reality. All these are issues for political analysis, and issues that are missed if questions of the political role of religion are asked purely in terms of church versus state.

Theology usually connotes reflective paradigmatic thought, elaborated by leisured professionals. Of all religions, it is Christianity, and indeed Western Christianity, that has elevated philosophical reflection to such prominence. We cannot presume that it is so central to African religion, even Africa's mainline Christianity. Some of the churches we will be studying place nearly all their emphasis on experience, on ecstatic

[26] *Ibid.*, 233.

worship, visions, healing, dreams and joyous bodily movement; their members would perhaps not claim to have any 'theology'. Most will not have any written theology. It is through their songs and prayers, sermons and testimonies that we will get to their symbolic cosmos; it is these we will draw on to establish their 'belief' or 'theology'.[27] I will not presume that every 'Christian' in an African church consciously holds the same beliefs, or to the same degree, or holds them in the way that church leaders (especially missionaries) might hope, and much less that he/she acts in accordance with them. This area is even more complicated because 'Christianity' does not constitute just one symbolic universe. There are very different forms of Christianity. I will constantly be looking for the different ways in which different forms of Christianity name, structure and reveal the true, the possible, the proper and the real, and create a symbolic order which is as social and political as it is theological.[28] I will refer to different theologies, not to evaluate them or judge between them theologically (e.g. between Catholic devotion to the saints and the Pentecostal gifts of the spirit, or between a sacramental system and justification by faith, or between the episcopal and the presbyterian polity) but to try to establish the symbolic cosmos of churches under discussion, on the grounds that it can play a considerable social role, even leading to side-effects which may not be adverted to. This is tricky terrain, difficult to negotiate, but it is necessary to attempt the task.

The approach is, moreover, of impeccable pedigree. After all, this was what Weber was doing in his *Protestant Ethic and the Spirit of Capitalism.*[29] He was tracing the socio-political effects of a belief or a religious idea. He argued that religious ideas had consequences, often independent of the motivation of those who held them. The early Puritans were interested merely in saving souls, but their particular form of belief had far-reaching socio-economic effects.[30] Moreover, Weber distinguished between the logical consequences of ideas and the psychological consequences.[31] He spent a great part of his work, and great erudition and subtlety, distinguishing between the religious ideas of Calvinists,

---

[27] Harvey Cox, *Fire from Heaven: the Rise of Pentecostal Spirituality and the Reshaping of Religion in the Twenty-First Century*, London: Cassell, 1996, 201; Michael Carrithers, *Why Humans have Cultures: Explaining Anthropology and Social Diversity*, Oxford University Press, 1992, 111-14; G. Lienhardt, *Divinity and Experience: the Religion of the Dinka* , Oxford University Press, 1961, 29-34.

[28] Achille Mbembe, *Afriques indociles. Christianisme, pouvoir et état en société postcoloniale*, Paris: Karthala, 1988. See especially 19-29.

[29] Max Weber, *The Protestant Ethic and the Spirit of Capitalism*, London: Routledge, 1992 (German original 1904-5, rev. edn 1920-1).

[30] For his understanding of the elective affinity between economic development and religious ideas, see *Protestant Ethic*, 277, n. 84.

[31] *Ibid.*, 128.

Lutherans, Pietists, Methodists and Baptists; because their beliefs differed, they played different roles in the rise of capitalism. With considerable sensitivity he argued that Pietism developing along Reformed lines could lead to an even greater religious stress on the ethic of the 'calling', and thus out-puritan the Calvinists; on the other hand, Pietism developing from a Lutheran basis led away from the all-important doctrine of predestination.[32] Of course Weber was not totally successful. He has been criticised, for example, in his understanding of Lutheranism as inevitably leading to fatalism.[33] But he shows how belief must be factored in, even if it is not quantifiable in any strictly scientific way. It is Weber's approach we will be following here. We will give great play to the religious ideas and attitudes and emphases characteristic of various churches, and our emphasis will be on the natural consequences of the beliefs, irrespective of the motivation of the holders. We will not be focusing on 'calling', the notion which was central for Weber, but on religious ideas like miraculous as opposed to natural agency, rationality in its relation to faith, human as opposed to divine responsibility, even human dignity and divine wrath. At times we will also note how consequences can be psychological rather than those necessitated by strict logic. Like Weber, we will distinguish between the teachings of different strains of Christianity – in our case, not so much denominations, but strands like mainline, independent or charismatic.[34]

Another celebrated example of the same approach is provided by E.P. Thompson's *Making of the English Working Class.* Thompson focuses on the Methodist revival, which Weber dealt with only tangentially. In a robust denunciation of the role of Methodism in the industrialisation of England, Thompson also devoted considerable attention to the role of theology. Wesley's doctrine of the universality of grace was incompatible with the Calvinist notion of 'election', and for him Christ's ransom was only provisional. It became Methodist doctrine that forgiveness of sin lasted only so long as the penitent went and sinned no more; the saved were in a state of conditional, provisional election. How then to keep grace? There were three obvious means: first through service to the church; second, through the cultivation of one's own soul; and third, through a methodical discipline in every aspect of life – above all, in labour. God's curse over Adam, when expelled from the Garden of Eden, provided

---

[32]   *Ibid.*, 132-3.

[33]   More basically, he has been criticised for a certain circularity; there is always the danger of interpreting theological belief in the light of what its adherents actually do. See Ernest Gellner, 'Concepts and Society' in Bryan R. Wilson (ed.), *Rationality*, Oxford: Blackwell, 1974, 19.

[34]   Like Weber (*Protestant Ethic*, 152), we will lay more stress on the consequences of a denomination's beliefs than on the consequences of its form of organisation (such as hierarchical or 'democratic').

irrefutable doctrinal support to the blessedness of hard labour, poverty and sorrow 'all the days of thy life'.[35] Thompson also analysed the imagery of Methodist hymns where, since joy was associated with sin and guilt, and pain with goodness and love, it became natural to suppose (Thompson is strong on psychological consequences too) that man or child found grace in God's eyes only when performing painful, laborious or self-denying tasks. Thus, Thompson argued, Wesley's theology became the ideological underpinning of the working class's acceptance of their suffering in providing the labour for Britain's industrial revolution.[36] Thompson has been criticised as much as Weber – and indeed his almost blanket condemnation of Methodism seems a caricature of a complex reality – but we too will make a similar attempt to assess the public consequences of Africa's current theologies.

Weber and Thompson were drawing out the essentially unintended socio-political and economic consequences of particular theologies. But since the 1960s there has developed a theology which explicitly addresses the public sphere. This developed primarily in Germany, where it is associated with the names of Johann Baptist Metz and Jürgen Moltmann. It has come to be most often associated with Latin America, where it was first given full expression in Gutiérrez's *A Theology of Liberation*. Its basic focus is the relation of Christianity to the socio-economic structures and systems in which Christians find themselves. Simultaneously, there developed a similar kind of theology in South Africa, which attracted the attention of the world as the apartheid era crumbled. South Africa's liberation theology finds a succinct expression in the *Kairos Document* produced under the aegis of Johannesburg's Institute for Contextual Theology. According to this, Christianity's task under apartheid was not to support the state or to focus on intra-ecclesiastical issues like bringing in more souls to people heaven, but to confront and destroy the satanic structures of apartheid.[37]

The existence of such an explicitly political theology in Africa north of the Limpopo will concern us too. There is a debate whether such an

---

[35] E.P. Thompson, *The Making of the English Working Class*, London: Penguin, 1980 (orig. 1963), 398-401. Also: 'Since salvation was never assured, and temptations lurked on every side, there was a constant inner goading to "sober and industrious" behaviour – the visible sign of grace – every hour of the day and every day of the year. Not only "the sack" but also the flames of hell might be the consequence of indiscipline at work' (*ibid.*, 406).

[36] For Thompson, Wesley 'dispensed with the best and selected unhesitatingly the worst elements of Puritanism' (*ibid.*, 398).

[37] *Kairos Document: Challenge to the Church: a Theological Comment on the Political Crisis in South Africa*, Braamfontein: the Kairos Theologians [1985]. See also Peter Walshe, 'South Africa: Prophetic Christianity and the Liberation Movement', *JMAS* 29, 1 (1991), 27-60; Peter Walshe, 'Christianity and Democratisation in South Africa: the Prophetic Voice within Phlegmatic Churches' in Gifford, *Christian Churches*, 74-94.

animal exists. De Gruchy, for instance, argues that 'theologians outside of southern Africa have not generally developed a critical political theology able to help the churches resist tyranny, overcome ethnic tension, and establish a just democratic order.'[38] However, a study of African theology by the British academic John Parratt denies this: 'It is clearly not accurate to characterise Christian theology outside South Africa as concerned only with the relationship of the Bible and Christian dogma to African traditions, any more than it is correct to describe theology within the Republic [of South Africa] as concerned only with politics.'[39] We will see in the course of this study that only to a limited extent could Christianity in large parts of Africa be said to espouse an explicitly political theology.

The churches' attitude to cultures will be another area of focus. As just mentioned, enhancement of culture is often said (by, for example, de Gruchy, in the section just cited) to be the major preoccupation of theology in Black Africa. Even if Parratt refuses to separate this too sharply from and elevate it over political interests, much of his book is given to expounding the concern of African theologians to re-value African traditions, in reaction to their supposed denigration by missionary Christianity.[40] The positive appraisal of African culture was stressed very early after independence. The proceedings of a 1965 consultation of African theologians, in a key statement, proclaimed:

We believe that God, the Father of our Lord Jesus Christ, Creator of Heaven and Earth, Lord of History, has been dealing with mankind at all times and in all parts of the world. It is with this conviction that we study the rich heritage of our African peoples, and we have evidence that they know him and worship him. We recognise the radical quality of God's self-revelation in Jesus Christ; and yet it is because of this revelation we can discern what is truly of God in our pre-Christian heritage; this knowledge of God is not totally discontinuous with our previous knowledge of him.[41]

This establishing of similarities or building bridges between the Bible and African traditional religions has considerable socio-political effects, too, since one's attitude to a culture determines how one assesses the

---

38 De Gruchy, *Christianity*, 191. He continues: 'The situation has been the reverse in South Africa where contemporary theologies have been honed in the struggle against apartheid and where, until more recently, theologians, wary of the abuse of ethnicity and culture by apartheid ideologists, have not engaged in the cultural task now incumbent on them'.

39 Parratt perceives 'an underlying unity in Christian theology throughout Africa'; John Parratt, *Reinventing Christianity: African Theology Today*, Grand Rapids, MI Eerdmans, 1995, 27.

40 For a more nuanced position on missionaries and African cultures, see Hastings, *Church*, 567.

41 Kwesi Dickson and Paul Ellingworth (eds), *Biblical Revelation and African Beliefs* Maryknoll: Orbis, 1969, 16.

actions determined or sanctioned by it. Pride in one's own culture can increase determination to preserve it and resist encroachment by another. Thus the attitude of the various strands of Christianity towards traditional African religion and culture will be another of our major interests.

Another theological emphasis that has political implications is a con-centration on the joys of the next life as a compensation for misery in this one. Third World theologians meeting in Dar es Salaam in 1976 sharply criticised Western missionaries for their 'services to Western imperialism by legitimising it and accustoming their new adherents to accept compensatory expectations of an eternal reward for terrestrial misfortunes, including colonial exploitation.'[42] These theologians were protesting that Western Christianity was used to reconcile Africans to hardship in this life rather than to struggle against it. Whether or not this was so earlier, it will be another of our tasks to assess to what degree African Christianity today can be said to play such a role.

Finally, even worship can be considered to have socio-political effects. For Thompson the emotionalism of early Methodism was essentially a diversion from rational assessment of the changes occurring, and a deterrent to opposing them: 'Social energies denied outlet in public life ... were released in sanctified emotional onanism', and 'Energies were not so much inhibited as displaced from expression in personal and in social life, and confiscated for the service of the church.'[43] In considering the charismatic emotionalism in African Christianity today, we will try to establish whether it too could be considered as diverting attention from active social involvement.

A new Pentecostal wave

Much of what can be called Christianity's explicit public involvement (issuing political pastoral letters, highlighting social ills, chairing national conferences) applies almost exclusively to the mainline churches, but this is not the only kind of involvement possible. There are other forms of involvement often associated with other branches of Christianity. In his magisterial survey of literature on this topic up to 1986,[44] Terence Ranger argued that the powerless have often found in religion a means of altering their situation and even reversing their status in both symbolic

---

42 Sergio Torres and Virginia Fabella (eds), *The Emergent Gospel: Theology from the Developing World*, London: Geoffrey Chapman, 1978, 266.

43 Thompson, *Making*, 44 and 404 respectively. Also: 'These sabbath orgasms of feeling made more possible the single-minded weekday direction of these energies to the consummation of productive labour'(406) and 'Methodism [was] in these years a ritualised form of psychic masturbation' (405).

44 Terence O. Ranger, 'Religious Movements and Politics in Sub-Saharan Africa', *African Studies Review*, 29, 2 (1986), 1-69.

and social terms. Religions can therefore become ideological and symbolic aspects of resistance to power. He cites the Watchtower in Zambia and Zionism in South Africa as illustrations. Such rural resistance, cultural and therefore political, can be resistance even though it is not armed conflict. Here Ranger highlights a crucial distinction, that between the articulated theological religion of the educated élites, and the less articulated religion of the rural members of the same denomination. Since the urban élites dominate the institutional structures and produce literary deposits that are easy to handle, there is always the tendency for observers to focus on these, and thus to slew the picture of the organisation by privileging the urban élite. But Ranger's distinction should not be made into a separation, for the larger African denominations are made up of both. In these cases the two parts can be understood only in relation to one another. Catholic or Anglican archbishops, for example, may live in the cities, but they are sometimes thought to be able to mobilise vast numbers in the countryside – which indeed was exactly what happened with the 1992 pastoral letter of the Catholic bishops of Malawi. The popular-élite dichotomy is still valid, and there must be proper under-standing of the creative cultural response of the marginalised; their imaginative resistance should be saved from the neglect or condescension of a radicalism focused on the urban proletariat.[45] But even here a sense of proportion must be maintained. We can talk of political resistance in a hard or an immediate sense, and this is the resistance commonly associated with the urban proletariat. They, for instance, were powerful enough to force Zambia's President Kaunda to abandon IMF structural adjustment. The responses of rural societies, creative and imaginative though they may be, are often not of that kind. Many African rulers have been forced to be actively concerned with dissent in cities, but they could not have cared less about dissatisfaction among the rural poor. In this study we will try to attend to both rural and urban Christianity; but we will not hide the fact that the unrest of an urban élite usually counts for a great deal more than any amount of rural discontent.

We will build upon many of the insights Ranger offers. He argues that religious movements may have such power, because they 'could draw on all the ambiguous power of myth and symbol and ritual; because they could mean many things at once and contain many potentialities.'[46] He insists that the symbolic, cultural, religious and creative elements, although not political in an immediate sense, cannot be too rigidly separated from the political. Ranger's clear distinction between the explicitly or narrowly political and the more generally cultural will be crucial in this study.

[45]   *Ibid.*, 22
[46]   *Ibid.*, 51

Ranger was writing in the mid-1980s before the second liberation struggle in the political sphere, and before, in the properly religious domain, a new wave of Pentecostalism had reached its peak. Pentecostalism is undoubtedly the salient sector of African Christianity today. Yet despite its salience, it is not particularly well understood. Thompson remarked of British Methodism: 'Too much writing on Methodism commences with the assumption that we all know what Methodism was, and gets on with discussing its growth-rates or its organisational structures.'[47] The same is true of Pentecostalism in contemporary Africa. Pentecostalism has been in Africa for most of this century – a good many of the classical AICs can rightly be called Pentecostal. But since the 1970s there has appeared a new variety of Pentecostalism which often sharply distinguishes itself from the earlier wave, and which is sometimes labelled 'charismatic' to distinguish it from earlier Pentecostal manifestations. These distinctions are sometimes not fully taken into account.

For example, in his perceptive study of the world-wide phenomenon, Cox tends to misrepresent Africa. He writes: 'The African Independent Churches constitute the African expression of the worldwide Pentecostal movement.'[48] He then gives as examples classical Independent churches like Zimbabwe's Apostolic Church of John Maranke, founded in 1932, and Bishop Samuel Mutendi's Zion Christian Church; Zambia's Lumpa Church, founded by Alice Lenshina in the 1950s; and the Church of the Lord Jesus Christ on Earth of the Prophet Simon Kimbangu, a movement originating in Zaïre about 1920. Cox writes of their use of drums and African instruments in worship; their rebellion against European expressions of the faith; and their incorporation of African elements like ancestor veneration.[49] While not disputing the application of the word 'Pentecostal' to these churches, we will see that by the 1990s African Pentecostalism was mushrooming in a different form and in a development which is incomprehensible if these older AICs are taken as paradigmatic. For example, the qualities cited above from Cox (use of African instruments, ancestor veneration, opposition to European expression) cannot today be presumed to be characteristic at all, as we shall see. The same misrepresentation is given by another book covering the same global phenomenon, even if it uses the word 'charismatic' in place of Pentecostal: *Charismatic Christianity as a Global Culture*. Its only sub-Saharan case study is of the Legio Maria Church in Kenya, which is likewise no longer typical of Africa's charismatic explosion.[50]

---

47   Thompson, *Making*, 918.
48   Cox, *Fire*, 246.
49   *Ibid.*, 146; see also 206, 247.
50   Karla Poewe (ed.), *Charismatic Christianity as a Global Culture*, Columbia, SC: University of South Carolina Press, 1994. This contains many good things but is not quite

The public role of African Pentecostalism and its socio-political effects, are key concerns in this study. That this 'born-again' Christianity has political ramifications is undeniable. Striking confirmation of this came in March 1996 when Mathieu (or from 1980, Ahmed) Kérékou, the Marxist military strongman and archetypal kleptocrat who had bankrupted Benin in his seventeen years of brutal repression (1972-90) and been the first African dictator to fall in the second liberation struggle, was re-elected to power – this time not as a Marxist but as a born-again Christian. In 1996 there was no political mileage in Marxism, but a great deal in Pentecostalism. Even if in Africa these churches are relatively under-researched, there have been two influential general studies of this phenomenon in Latin America. These are David Martin's *Tongues of Fire: the Explosion of Pentecostalism in Latin America,* and David Stoll's *Is Latin America turning Protestant? The Politics of Evangelical Growth.*[51] Both of these can help focus our enquiry.

First, the general religious context. For Martin particularly the recent religious transformation of Latin America forms part of a long process of global religious history, or part of a global theory of secularisation.[52] He traces this process from its beginnings in Britain to its logical conclusion in the United States, and eventually in the late 1980s to its impact on Latin America. His theory covers other countries as well – Europe, the white Commonwealth countries of Australia, Canada and New Zealand, and even the Caribbean. But Africa is hardly part of this global process.[53] Africa's colonisation was too recent and too different from Latin America's, and so few African countries were settled by colonists. Martin expounds his theory in terms of liberalism, socialism, secularism, communism, nationalism and anticlericalism, always relating religion to the rise of industrialisation and the bourgeoisie. All these 'isms' that have played such a role in the religious and secular history of Britain, Europe, the United States and Latin America have minimal importance in Africa. Most significantly, the role of Catholicism was simply different. Europe's history since the sixteenth century is tied up with movements

---

so relevant for us. The article on Legio Maria is Nancy Schwartz, 'Christianity and the Construction of Global History: the Example of Legio Maria', 134-75. Also, the book is not focused on the public role of churches, or even their internal structuring (although W.J. Hollenweger, 'The Pentecostal Elites and the Pentecostal Poor', 200-16, is suggestive here).

[51]   David Martin, *Tongues of Fire; the Explosion of Protestantism in Latin America,* Oxford: Blackwell, 1990; David Stoll, *Is Latin America Turning Protestant? The Politics of Evangelical Growth,* Berkeley, CA: University of California Press, 1990.

[52]   Martin, *Tongues,* 43. This book can be seen as a sequel to his *A General Theory of Secularisation,* Oxford: Blackwell, 1978.

[53]   South Africa might have been, had it not been distorted by apartheid (Martin, *Tongues,* 157-60).

reacting to Catholicism. Their struggles have determined the societies of Europe and its dependencies, and equally the forces operative in them. In Africa, however, Catholicism was generally just one among many competing denominations, entering the continent about the same time and on roughly the same footing. In British colonies Catholicism was given a perhaps surprisingly free rein, but to the extent that one can talk of an establishment, it was Anglicanism. France, though even today often called 'Catholic', has been marked by great tension between the church and state since the Revolution, and they have been officially separated since 1905. France's African colonies were run by often anti-clerical metropolitan governments, in no way disposed to give Catholicism any preference.[54] The lesser colonising powers of Belgium and Portugal were different, and privileged the Catholic Church. But Zaïre, where the colonial Catholic Church was certainly privileged, was hardly independent when Mobutu set out to tame it, and the Portuguese did so little to develop their colonies that the church-state question hardly arose in any Latin American sense. So in Black Africa Catholicism simply was not what it was in Latin America, and could not play the same role. Generally, in Africa, Catholicism has been an example of voluntarism, in exactly the same way as the Baptist, Lutheran and Pentecostal churches.

Stoll, likewise, relates the rise of Pentecostalism to Catholicism, though in a different way. He relates it to the rise of Liberation Theology, which he calls Pentecostalism's 'great rival',[55] and which he understands as a function of the breakup of the Catholic 'sacred canopy'. He shows that Pentecostalism and Liberation Theology react to and influence each other; for instance, he argues that the latter has forced Pentecostals to confront social issues. He also shows that where Liberation Theology is an attempt to conscientise and mobilise to change structures in the face of authorities, Pentecostalism has a more magical worldview.[56] The extent to which the rise of African Pentecostalism is related to or is influenced by a more politicised form of Christianity is another question to be considered here.

Both Martin and Stoll serve to highlight an important difference between African and Latin American society. Stoll in particular describes the violence and oppression in these national security states. In Africa, by contrast – again leaving aside South Africa – the undeniable violence and oppression have not been perpetrated for geopolitical or ideological reasons of national security, with Christianity part of the rationale. Although the violence can be very real, it has normally been ethnic, even sometimes mindless (as in Uganda), or has stemmed from anarchy and

---

54 For Catholicism in France's African colonies, see Hastings, *Church*, 430-1.
55 *Is Latin America?*, xix, 308.
56 *Ibid.*, 111-14.

warlordism. Nor is it structural, as for example part of a struggle against
landowners who have traditionally had the support of Christianity; in
many places in Africa there is still the option to move or revert to the
land. The undeniable and increasing hardship stems from poverty,
economic collapse, corruption, chaos and deteriorating services and
infrastructure.

Secondly, both Martin and Stoll distinguish clearly the political from
the cultural. Martin's whole argument turns on this distinction. He argues
that Pentecostal churches have an inherent cultural logic: we are dealing
with 'a voluntary, lay, participatory and enthusiastic faith... The cultural
logic of its forms [is] active, participatory, fissile, egalitarian and enthusiastic. In short, it represent[s] an autonomous mobilisation of mass-
consciousness, transforming and energising individual persons, and
bringing about myriads of competitive voluntary networks for sharing
and for mutual support.'[57] In these new churches, people can reinvent
themselves in an atmosphere of fraternal support. Qualities are
experienced and learned in churches; from there, when the time is ripe,
they may be transferred to the wider society. Martin highlights 'the latent
capacity of cultural changes held in religious storage to emerge over time
when circumstances are propitious', and 'the new potentials in the form
of models and images and concepts of the person and of organisation
stored in the religious capsule, and (maybe) later released into the
mainstream of society.'[58] Again we meet this distinction between culture
generally and politics proper which will be crucial to our discussion.

Of course, a debate turning on this distinction is not new in reference
to Christianity in Africa. It recalls a similar debate about the public role
of African Independent Churches (AICs). Some have emphasised the
radical potential of the AICs. One author claims: 'Black pastors of the
AIC were the ones who came forward in South Africa to advocate a broad
African nationalism and used their church organisations as the first functional
bases.'[59] This seems grossly overdrawn. Sundkler tells of Job Chiliza, the
founder of the African Gospel Church, who having caught sight of the
architect of apartheid in the corridor of a Pretoria government building could
say: 'I shall die satisfied to have seen the face of Dr Verwoerd.'[60] And Edward
Lekganyane, successor to his father as leader of South Africa's huge Zion
Christian Church, on Good Friday 1965 fêted the Minister of Bantu

---

[57]   Martin, *Tongues*, 274.

[58]   *Ibid*, 44 and 286.

[59]   T.A. Mofokeng, 'The Evolution of the Black Struggle and the Role of Black Theology'
      in Itumeleng Mosala and Buti Tlhagale (eds), *The Unquestionable Right to be Free*,
      Maryknoll: Orbis, 1986, 115.

[60]   B.G.M. Sundkler, *Zulu Zion and some Swazi Zionists*, London: Oxford University Press,
      1976, 89.

Affairs, hailing him as the new Moses who had led the African people and the Zion Christian Church out of bondage and into a land of freedom.[61] During the most repressive stage of apartheid, over 3 million members of the ZCC welcomed President P.W. Botha to their 1985 Easter gathering. These examples suggest far more accurately the directly political role of the AICs. But the AICs had a much more complex role, conveyed accurately by Thetele:

The AICs in South Africa in many ways are both pre-revolutionary and actively revolutionary at the same time. They are pre-revolutionary in the sense that they do not operate according to a set plan or strategy in trying to move society towards a definite gaol. But they are revolutionary in their impact on the fabric of the society, creating a change that provides the dispossessed people with a sense of hope and a vision for the future. They offer a place in society where people can begin to sense their role as creators of their own histories, rejecting a passive acceptance of the status quo and beginning to work out alternatives to dehumanisation.[62]

Frostin suggests that this role 'defies to be subordinated to European categories.'[63] I would prefer to say that it is explicable in European categories, provided one distinguishes the properly political and the more generally cultural, and admits that one church can be doing different things in the two different spheres.[64]

It must immediately be said, however, that although both Martin and Stoll argue for the long-term radical influence of the Pentecostal churches at the cultural level, they are extremely tentative about it. Martin adds a subtle 'maybe' at crucial steps of his argument. Stoll is perhaps even more hesitant in his conclusions; he would like to think that Pentecostalism will be a force for social change, but regrets that it probably will not.[65] It

---

[61]   Adrian Hastings, *A History of African Christianity 1950-1975* , Cambridge University Press, 1979, 183.

[62]   C. B. Thetele, 'Women in South Africa: the WAAIC' in Kofi Appiah-Kubi and Sergio Torres (eds), *African Theology en Route* , Maryknoll: Orbis, 1979, 151. Hastings makes the same point of the ZCC: 'It was able to provide very poor people with some lasting sense of status, of belonging to a successful institution which they could publicly identify with and be proud of by the standards of this world' (*History*, 183).

[63]   Per Frostin, *Liberation Theology in Tanzania and South Africa: a First World Interpretation* , Lund University Press, 1988, 228.

[64]   A similar debate has centred on black churches in the USA. Martin writes: 'It is perfectly possible ... to view the movement for black civil rights in the mid-twentieth century as an extrapolation from what had already been achieved symbolically in the "free space" created by the black churches' (*Tongues*, 44). Others dispute this; see Paul Gifford, *Christianity and Politics in Does Liberia,* Cambridge University Press, 1993, 49; and for another position, see de Gruchy, *Christianity,* 135.

[65]   Stoll, *Is Latin America?*, 315. Also xvi, 10. Note the 'maybe' at critical stages of Martin's argument, *Tongues,* 134, 224, 232, 267-8, 274, 286, 287, 288. Martin's more recent writing may be even more tentative: 'They run their churches as entrepreneurs seeking

will be one of our tasks to assess the probability in Africa.

Thirdly, both are aware of the links with North American Pente-costalism – Stoll particularly. Dealing with Nicaragua and Guatemala especially, in the 1980s, he is very sensitive to American political interest in the region; this was the height of Reaganism. He is no conspiracy theorist, and thinks the local dynamics of Pentecostalism are far more important, but realises that Latin American Pentecostalism cannot be analysed without reference to North American missionaries or partners, and particularly the Religious Right, who were at least one strand among many. He shows real discernment here; the Religious Right cannot be ignored, but must not be allowed to dominate the picture.[66] The nature of external connections must be considered in Africa too. In this regard, Stoll indirectly serves to emphasise how different the context is in Africa. Only South Africa, and to a lesser extent her neighbours sucked into her orbit, was ever considered an essential part of some divine geopolitical dispensation. The rest of Africa, even in Cold War days, was never essential. Even Liberia, with its military airfield and port, its Omega tracking station and the miles of radio masts at the CIA's African commu-nications system, was surprisingly dispensable. In 1990, at the very beginning of Liberia's unrest when even a small force might have been thought adequate to preserve order, the Americans were not prepared to intervene, and just walked away from all their plant, seemingly with few qualms.

Stoll too is very strong on the variations within Pentecostalism, their diverse social and political significance, and their shifting importance over time.[67] The 1980s were a time of important shifts; Pat Robertson, at that time a standard premillennialist, predicted the end of the world in 1982; by 1988 he was an exponent of Kingdom Theology and running for President to shape America for generations to come. Stoll detects

---

a market. In so doing they gain skills and capacities capable of redeployment in secular avocations, and they inculcate a discipline and priorities of consumption that could lead to modest advancement, at least in circumstances where inflation is under control.[...] Their combination of hard work and mutual aid probably gives them an edge in the search for survival. They are located at the social margin, where respectability and self-control and frugality assist survival and where aspirations can lead to small business ventures – or modest educational improvement. They could also be creating a new per-sonality, with a novel sense of self and of responsibility, capable of being converted into initiative. All this, one has to say, is latent and implied rather than realised and docu-mented' (David Martin, 'Evangelical and Charismatic Christianity in Latin America' in Poewe, *Charismatic Christianity*, 84-5). Cox ends his treatment of Pentecostalism in Latin America on a very negative note: 'The hopes that many people once held out that Pentecostalism would become a seed-bed of democracy in Latin America may prove to be a sad disappointment' (*Fire*, 183).

[66] Stoll, *Is Latin America?*, 102, 156-7.
[67] *Ibid.*, esp. 42-67.

equivalent differences within Pentecostalism in Latin America. We will attempt to be as alert to similar variations within African Pentecostalism.

The Faith Gospel

One factor neither Stoll nor Martin gives great attention to is the Faith Gospel, which characterises so many charismatic churches. Because it is so widespread in Africa, we will give a brief outline of it here. According to the Faith Gospel, God has met all the needs of human beings in the suffering and death of Christ, and every Christian should now share the victory of Christ over sin, sickness and poverty. A believer has a right to the blessings of health and wealth won by Christ, and he or she can obtain these blessings merely by a positive confession of faith. In its present form, several well-known names have helped create it: most notably, E.W. Kenyon, A.A. Allen, Oral Roberts, T.L. Osborn, Kenneth Hagin, Kenneth Copeland and John Avanzini. Each of these has made his own contribution. It was Allen, for example, who first made it an aid towards fundraising; he was the first to teach that God is a rich God, and that those who want to share in his prosperity must obey and support God's servant – the speaker himself. Roberts added the idea of seed faith, that you prosper by planting a seed in faith, the return on which will meet all your needs. The texts that are invariably utilised include Mk. 11: 23-24; Dt. 28-30; 3 Jn. 2; Mal. 3: 8-11; Mk. 10: 29-30; Phil. 4: 19; and for health in particular Ps. 91; Is. 53: 4-5 (=1 Pet. 2,24), Mt. 9: 27-31. This Faith Gospel has proved very functional among the religious entrepreneurs who constitute the media evangelists, for its 'seed faith' idea has brought in the enormous resources needed to sustain these extremely expensive ministries. Indeed, it developed in those circles precisely because it was so functional in this regard. Kenneth Copeland has admitted that only after committing himself to a TV series with no apparent capital did he come to understand the doctrine of 'biblical prosperity' properly.[68] Its widespread diffusion owes much to its pervasiveness in Christian broadcasting. However, it is not only its functionality but its general socio-

---

[68]   Kenneth Copeland, *The Laws of Prosperity*, Fort Worth, TX: Kenneth Copeland Ministries,1974, 74-6. Hagin claims he properly understood prosperity in January 1950 (Kenneth E. Hagin, *How God Taught Me about Prosperity*, Tulsa, OK: Kenneth Hagin Ministries, 1985, 15). The Copelands admit being influenced by Hagin, and started to think in terms of prosperity in 1967-8. See Gloria Copeland, *God's Will is Prosperity,* Fort Worth, TX: Kenneth Copeland Ministries, 1978, 32-3, and Kenneth Copeland, *The Laws of Prosperity*, 9. For the Faith Gospel, see Gifford, *Christianity and Politics*, 146-89. For an account of one of its main avenues into Africa, namely Bonnke's 1986 'Fire Conference' in Harare, see Paul Gifford, 'Prosperity: A New and Foreign Element in African Christianity', *Religion*, 20 (1990), 373-88. The best account of its origins and specifics is J.N. Horn, *From Rags to Riches: an Analysis of the Faith Movement and its Relation to the Classical Pentecostal Movement*, Pretoria: UNISA, 1989.

economic context that is significant. It appeared in the boom years of the 1960s and 1970s in the United States. These were the days when living standards were visibly increasing, opportunity was everywhere, and 'success through a positive mental attitude' was the rule. Indeed, the Faith Gospel's affinities to New Age thinking are obvious. We will meet this Faith Gospel, in varying degrees, across Africa. T.L.Osborn is well remembered for his crusades, and the literature of Hagin particularly was widely available throughout the 1980s. We will be interested specifically in the Faith Gospel's role in Africa's current socio-economic context.

Without some idea of the Faith Gospel, it is possible to misunderstand global developments within Christianity. Thus a recent article on Korean charismatic Christianity claims that 'Korean Christianity has become almost completely shamanised.' The author proves the 'shamanistic orientation' of the theology of Paul Yonggi Cho by expounding Cho's exegesis of 3 John 2 (not John 3: 2 as stated). Yet everything Cho understands by prospering has been taught in exactly that form by the Faith Gospel for years, and 3 John 2 has been one of its key texts. The emphasis on this-worldly blessing is too exclusively attributed to shamanism, with no reference to what is taught in a whole swathe of Christianity in America.[69] Cho and the Faith Gospel promoters generally cannot be understood in isolation from their American roots. Their symbols, hymns, denominational organisation, networks, rituals, technology, order of service, use of the Bible, instrumental music, literature and tapes on sale and theology – all of these characteristics and many more betray their origins.

A more satisfactory approach to global developments, and one which attends to both external and local factors, is found in Coleman's writings on *Livets Ord* (Word of Life), a faith church in Sweden: 'The Word of Life is a cultural product that cannot be understood merely in terms of its local or even national context. It must also be seen as formed from and reacting to international influences, and specifically as a product of North American religious culture.' However, Coleman immediately adds the equally important corollary: 'Its doctrines and forms of worship take on new symbolic resonances as they are transferred almost wholesale from one country to another.'[70] The reinterpretation exemplified by *Livets*

---

[69] Mark R. Mullins, 'The Empire Strikes Back: Korean Pentecostal Missions to Japan' in Poewe, *Charismatic Christianity*, 92-3. The author also oversimplifies the complex origins of the Korean theology of illness, much of which is also standard Faith Gospel. It is more complicated than is suggested by his statement that 'Paul Yonggi Cho's theology might best be viewed as a synthesis of Korean shamanism, Robert Schuller's "Positive Thinking", and the pragmatism of the church-growth school of missiology associated with Fuller Theological Seminary's School of World Mission' (*ibid.*).

[70] Simon Coleman, ' "Faith which Conquers the World'': Swedish Fundamentalism and the Globalisation of Culture', *Ethnos* 56, 1 (1991), 7; also Simon Coleman, 'Conserva-

Ord turns especially on Christian Zionism. (There is no intrinsic reason why the Faith Gospel should be linked with Christian Zionism; the combination of the two is itself largely due to purely contingent factors of recent American history.) Christian Zionism, embodying support for Israel and opposition to Russia, often fosters a keen antipathy towards the European Union (EU), for the Antichrist of the last days is supposed to arise from a reconstituted Roman Empire, which in this thinking is understood to be the EU created by the 1958 Treaty of Rome. In the 1990s Sweden was seriously split on the issue of joining the EU, and its Christian Zionism enabled the Word of Life Church to adopt a very high profile in this debate, in the vanguard of the anti-EU forces. Thus in Sweden Christian Zionism has proved very functional. Another aspect of Christian Zionism (the belief that the Jews of the diaspora must return home to Israel to usher in the return of Christ) has proved invaluable to the church itself. Word of Life had laboured for some years in East Asia, with virtually no success at all. Its evangelistic outreach was in danger of collapse, but at just the right time for it, the Soviet Union disintegrated, enabling Word of Life to switch its missionary thrust to a much more responsive area. Its phenomenal success in opening churches and Bible colleges and running crusades in former Soviet lands has not only revitalised the church but enabled it to focus on 'repatriating' Russian Jews to Israel. This task has almost come to define the church; Word of Life has bought and refitted an oceangoing ship solely for the purpose of transporting Jews to Israel – a Christian 'duty' that anyone who does not share its Christian Zionism could hardly credit. Of course this, too, sharpens the local church's identity. Sweden generally has been consistently pro-Palestinian in foreign policy; this Zionist orientation is one more way of standing out in Sweden. Thus in Sweden an element of a total religious package, which itself is hardly comprehensible outside its American roots, has, because of its functionality both in the nation generally and within the church itself, helped to establish the church's particular identity.[71] In studying Africa's faith churches, we will, like Coleman in Sweden, look for both continuity and adaptation.

Before leaving the Pentecostal churches, we must consider one more aspect: the church growth movement. In itself this is not exclusively Pentecostal; indeed it is most closely associated with Fuller Theological

---

tive Protestantism and the World Order: the Faith Movement in the United States and Sweden', *Sociology of Religion* 54 (1993), 353-73. Also: 'In all movements of religious conversion and change there is a dialectic of external influence and local adaptation' (Martin, *Tongues*, 282).

[71] For Word of Life's prosperity gospel, see Ulf Ekman, *Financial Freedom*, Uppsala: Word of Life, 2nd edn 1993; for its Zionism, see Ulf Ekman, *The Jews: People of the Future*, Uppsala: Word of Life, 1993, and especially the church's magazine, *Word of Life, passim*. Coleman perhaps underestimates the Zionism underlying the church's theology.

Seminary and the US Centre for World Mission, both of California, and with names like Donald McGavran and Ralph D. Winter.[72] As a distinct theory involving unreached people groups (*ethne*) it was first formulated by mission leaders of Billy Graham's Lausanne Congress on World Evangelisation in 1982. It is encountered most often in Africa in the form of the 'AD 2000 and Beyond' Movement, which was born out of the Lausanne Congress and has come to coordinate the efforts of many churches, denominations, mission agencies, parachurch bodies and Christian service groups. Its international chairman is Chinese and its director from Brazil, but behind AD 2000 are bodies like Campus Crusade, Concerts of Prayer, Discipling a Whole Nation (DAWN), Every Home for Christ, Generals of Intercession, Lausanne Global Prayer Strategy, March for Jesus, Mission Frontiers, Operation Mobilisation, Youth With A Mission (YWAM), Women's Aglow and others. AD 2000 has as its aim 'A Church for Every People and the Gospel for Every Person by the year 2000', and has a special focus on what it calls the '10/40 Window', that area from West Africa to East Asia between 10 and 40 degrees of latitude. The movement aims to have 200,000 new missionaries operating by the year 2000. It works through consultations, and 100 were held in preparation for its 1995 Global Consultation on World Evangelisation (GCOWE '95) in Seoul, Korea, which gathered 4,000 leaders from 186 nations in what some publicity called 'the most important global meeting in history'. The next such consultation will be in South Africa in 1997, followed by consultations in Hungary, India and (in AD 2000) Israel. The movement puts great stress on research and statistics. Its coordinating activity is increasingly evident in Africa, linked primarily to the Evangelical churches, but increasingly to all kinds of new churches, including Pentecostal mega-churches, and even mainline denominations.[73]

Two further issues require comment here; fundamentalism and sectarianism. In its classical Christian sense of denoting some belief in the Bible as inerrant,[74] almost all African Christianity is fundamentalist, for nearly all African Christians approach the Bible rather uncritically. In general, they love to quote it, refer to it and support any position by alluding to it. This is true also of Christians of the mainline churches, and is doubly true of the AICs. This was well expressed in a report on the history and theology of a group of Independent Churches, written by those churches themselves. After writing of how seriously they take the

---

72   A good introduction to church growth thinking is C. Peter Wagner, Win Arn and Elmer Towns, *Church Growth: State of the Art*, Wheaton, IL: Tyndale, 1989, esp. Wagner's article, 'The Church Growth Movement after Thirty Years', 21-39.

73   Information about AD 2000 and Beyond Movement is available from 2860 S Circle Dr., Suite 2112, Colorado Springs, CO 80906.

74   James Barr, *Explorations in Theology: the Scope and Authority of the Bible*, London: SCM, 1980, 65.

Bible, they continue: 'Some people will say that we are therefore "fundamentalists". We do not know whether that word applies to us or not.[...] We do not have the same problems about the Bible as White people have with their Western scientific mentality.'[75] But in recent years the word 'fundamentalist' has extended its meaning considerably, to cover all religions, and generally that sector of those religions with political involvement. Now the word carries considerable baggage, notably some element of political reaction, rejection of the modern world, return to the past.[76] A sizeable bloc of Christians described as fundamentalists in this sense are politically powerful in the United States. During the 1980s and '90s they have made missionary advances in Africa as great as those Stoll described in Latin America. They have established countless ministries, fellowships and churches of their own kind, and (through their workshops, literature and media involvement) have profoundly influenced already existing churches. So Africa now has a rapidly growing sector of Christianity which is closely related to US fundamentalism. However, when these US-influenced groups operate in Africa, they find themselves functioning in a context considerably different from that in the United States. In America there are particular issues that focus their energy and around which fundamentalists mobilise – issues like abortion, homosexuality, the equal rights amendment, 'welfare', the teaching of evolution in schools, New Age movements, and the alleged humanism of the supreme court, the media and the educational system. In Africa few of these are significant. In almost all African states, governments are strongly opposed to abortion, 'gay rights' are not an issue,[77] women are subordinate, welfare systems are inadequate, and the courts are usually subservient to the executive. Also, most of the electronic technology (cable TV, free-phone networks, computerised mailing) which has been an inseparable part of the emergence of the US fundamentalist coalition,

---

[75] African Independent Churches, *Speaking for Ourselves: Members of African Independent Churches report on their Pilot Study of the History and Theology of their Churches,* Braamfontein: ICT, 1985, 26.

[76] Martin E. Marty, 'Fundamentals of Fundamentalism' in Lawrence Kaplan (ed.), *Fundamentalism in Comparative Perspective,* Amherst, MA: University of Massachusetts Press, 1992, 18-22. For the wide-ranging Fundamentalism Project of the University of Chicago (which covered every possible 'fundamentalism' except Christianity in Black Africa) see Martin E. Marty and R. Scott Appleby, *Fundamentalisms Observed,* University of Chicago Press, 1991; subsequent volumes from the same editors and publishers include *Fundamentalisms and Society: Reclaiming the Sciences, the Family and Education* (1993) and *Fundamentalisms and the State: Remaking Polities, Economies and Militance* (1993). See also David Westerlund (ed.), *Questioning the Secular State: the Worldwide Resurgence of Religion in Politics,* London: Hurst, 1996.

[77] President Mugabe's anti-gay crusade in Zimbabwe 1995-7 was largely a political ploy to discredit human rights activists' criticisms of his government.

simply does not exist in Africa. Just as significant, the freedom of speech that enables US fundamentalists to denounce their government for all sorts of alleged inadequacies has not been widely honoured in Africa. Consequently, it is not clear what application the description 'fundamentalist' has in sub-Saharan Africa, or what debate is advanced by employing the term. The entire context is different. For this reason the term will be avoided here as much as possible.[78]

The second issue is that of sectarianism. 'Sect' is a label frequently used in Africa to describe the mushrooming new churches; in francophone countries '*les sectes*' is if anything more widely used. Mostly this is loosely used in something like Troeltsch's sense, as applying to groups distinct from the historic mainline churches.[79] There is a considerable body of literature on the religious sociology of 'sects'; for example, in the typology of Bryan Wilson a sect is described as manifesting qualities like exclusiveness or rejection.[80] I do not want to presume such qualities in the many African bodies to which the label is so readily applied; at the end of this study we will understand better how justifiable that presumption is.

Ecclesiastical externality

We have noted the importance given to external links in the analysis of sub-Saharan Africa. In the last decade Western governments wound down official links with Africa. To take their place there occurred one of the most remarkable developments of the 1980s, the NGO explosion. During the 1980s in Africa, as African governments collapsed and retreated from all kinds of areas, NGOs flooded in to take their place – in extreme cases such as Mozambique, to exert more power than the government.[81] Over the same period, in a similar way, missionaries have flooded into Africa, often with an effect on the Christian landscape just as substantial as that of the NGOs on the socio-political terrain. This missionary involvement is linked with the Pentecostal explosion, because so many of these new missionaries are part of the new Pentecostal wave. Already by the mid-1960s the mainline Protestant missionaries had been surpassed in numbers by those from non-ecumenical evangelical and 'unaffiliated' agencies. This trend has proceeded apace.[82]

---

[78]   Parratt is correct when he claims that Byang Kato, the first General Secretary of the Association of Evangelicals of Africa (AEA), by introducing the American debate, brought something quite foreign into African theology (*Reinventing*, 63).

[79]   Ernst Troeltsch, *The Social Teaching of the Christian Churches*, New York: Macmillan, 1931.

[80]   Bryan Wilson, *Religion in Sociological Perspective* , Oxford University Press, 1982, 89-120; Bryan Wilson, *Magic and the Millennium* , London: Heinemann, 1973, 11-30.

[81]   See, e.g., J. Hanlon, *Mozambique: Who Calls the Shots?* London: James Currey, 1991.

[82]   The two indispensable source books for mission statistics are John A Siewert and John

These missionaries are predominantly North American. It is not easy to plot trends in this matter. For one thing, statistics are not always collected on exactly the same basis.[83] It seems, however, that this American influence is, if anything, increasing. It is true that of all the Protestant missionaries around the world 65% in 1989 were North American, but by 1992 this percentage had fallen to 57%.[84] However, against this must be set other considerations. First, mission agencies have consciously adopted a new strategy of supporting locals rather than sending North Americans. Locals are both 'less expensive and less culturally intrusive'. In 1992 there were 24,213 locals fully supported and 17,737 partially supported by US agencies.[85] So the 'Americanness' of the modern missionary movement may not be in conflict with an apparently contradictory claim that by the year 2000 there will be a dominance of Third World missionaries around the world.[86]

Moreover, the missionary movement today includes various kinds of auxiliary forces. Many Evangelical Christian colleges in the United States now provide opportunities for students to spend at least some period of their summer vacation in mission fields; one estimate put the number of Americans in such short-term missions in 1989 at 120,000.[87] It must be said that much of this short-term work, even when it involves non-Americans, is on behalf of American multinational mission agencies like Youth With A Mission. Another important and novel feature of the contemporary missionary scene is the number of genuine 'independents': sent from independent charismatic churches in North America, they are not counted in statistics compiled according to mission agencies.

Comparing a representative number of African countries between 1989 and 1993, one finds that in general full-time American Protestant missionaries have increased: Ghana, for instance, had 158 American

---

A. Kenyon (eds), *Mission Handbook: USA/Canada Christian Ministries Overseas*, Monrovia, CA: Marc, 15th edn 1993 (13th edn 1986, 14th edn 1989); and Patrick Johnstone, *Operation World*, Carlisle: OM Publishing, 3rd edn 1978, 4th edn 1986 and 5th edn 1993.

83   For example, the 14th and 15th editions of *Mission Handbook* change the basic category from 'career' or 'life' missionary to missionary for 'more than four years'.

84   *Mission Handbook*, 14th edn, 576, and 15th edn, 76. Comparing the biggest agencies across these two categories between 1989 and 1993, the Southern Baptist Convention decreased from 3,839 to 3,660, the Wycliffe Bible Translators increased from 2,269 to 2,338, the New Tribes Mission increased from 1,807 to 1,837, the Christian Churches/ Churches of Christ decreased from 1,717 to 1,118, and the Assembles of God decreased from 1,530 to 1,485.

85   *Mission Handbook*, 15th edn, 59.

86   *Pulse*, 7 Feb 1992, 5.

87   *Mission Handbook*, 15th edn, 57. See Mark Robinson (ed.), *Summer Missions Handbook 1990*, La Mirada, CA: Biola University, 1989; of the ninety-nine mission agencies listed here, twenty-seven have summer activities in Africa.

Protestant missionaries in 1989 and 184 in 1993; in Kenya they increased from 1,225 to 1,337; in Malawi from 155 to 199; in Nigeria from 486 to 487; and in Zimbabwe from 239 to 309. However, over the same four-year period the US missionaries decreased in Cameroon (from 247 to 213) and in Zaïre (from 899 to 715, although this decline can easily be explained by the general flight of expatriates from the chaos engulfing the country since 1989). There were also in 1993 another 359 Protestant missionaries accredited to 'Africa' generally.[88] According to the successive editions of *Operation World*, the number of all expatriate Protestant missionaries (that is, not just American missionaries) in all these countries (except Nigeria) has steadily increased. For example, the figures for Ghana are 280 full-time Protestant missionaries in 1978, 380 in 1986 and 400 in 1993; for Kenya the corresponding figures are 1,150, 1,850 and 2,321; for Malawi 200, 220, and 366; for Zimbabwe 250, 600, 630; and for Zaïre 1,000, 1,300, 1406. Nigeria shows a decline: 1,300 in 1978, 950 in 1986, and 768 in 1993; the Nigerian authorities, in the light of increasing religious conflict, are reluctant to grant visas to missionaries. In this as in so many things Nigeria has a dynamic of its own.[89]

Within Protestantism, then, missionaries seem to be increasing in numbers, with the increase specially marked among non-mainline churches. Catholicism has its own dynamic. Even in the 1970s it was acknowledged that the changing balance between Africa's mainline Protestants and Catholics – decidedly to the advantage of the latter – 'depended to a very considerable extent upon a foreign force of priests and nuns.'[90] Twenty years on, Catholic missionaries still easily outnumber Protestant missionaries. In 1993 in Cameroon there were 1,640 Catholic missionaries to 689 Protestant; in Ghana 540 Catholic to 400 Protestant; in Kenya 3,210 to 2,321; in Malawi 578 to 366; in Nigeria 923 to 768; in Zimbabwe 905 to 630; and in Zaire 4,366 to 1,406.[91] Numbers of Catholic missionaries have fallen over the last fifteen years, although if those from the traditional sending countries have declined considerably, missionaries are increasing from places like India and Latin America. Only 7% of Catholic missionaries were North Americans in 1989.[92] American Catholic missionaries abroad[93] peaked at 9,655 in 1968 (in Africa at 1,184 in 1966);

---

88   *Mission Handbook*, 15th edn, *ad loc.* and 73.

89   Johnstone, *Operation World, ad loc.*

90   Hastings, *History*, 242; see all 239-42.

91   See Johnstone, *Operation World, ad loc.*

92   *Mission Handbook*, 14th edn, 576.

93   These missionaries are ageing and being replaced by lay missionaries; 90% of those under thirty are lay missionaries. See US Catholic Mission Association, *Annual Report on US Catholic Overseas Mission 1992-93*, Washington, DC: Catholic Mission Association, 1993.

in 1992 there were 5,467, a drop of 42 % since 1968, with 949 in Africa.

In our case studies, we will continually be alert to missionary influence – not only their numbers, but their resources, expertise and power. Africa's Christianity is both localised and part of a world religion. How this tension is resolved needs careful clarification and continual reassessment. In Africa, given the widespread and increasing dependence in so many fields, it is natural to ask whether the balance between the local and the external within Christianity is different from that in other less dependent parts of the world.

Method

Diverse claims are made about African Christianity, as we have already seen, and on all sorts of evidence and arguments. De Gruchy's *Christianity and Democracy* contains a selection of case studies. Obviously de Gruchy considers these case studies to support conclusions of a fairly hard kind. He writes that they 'broadly represent the global context, the varieties of Christian denomination, and the different ways in which churches have participated in the democratic process. They are also paradigmatic in illustrating the issues which are fundamental to the relationship between Christianity and democracy at the end of our century, and cumulative in their impact and significance.'[94] But a consideration of his chapter on sub-Saharan Africa shows how questionable this is. De Gruchy is concerned to show the 'role of the churches as midwives of democratic transition and reconstruction',[95] which leads him to choose his illustrations with that in mind. This leads him, for example, to write most positively of the Malawian Catholic bishops' 'opposition to one-party rule' which 'reached a climax in March 1992' with their pastoral letter which initiated Malawi's return to democracy.[96] But significant as this pastoral letter unquestionably was, it cannot be denied that the Catholic bishops' silent complicity for the previous twenty-seven years needs just as much explanation as the sudden decision to end it. De Gruchy is well aware that in Africa the churches' contribution has not been uniformly positive, and frequently alludes to their failure, silence, co-optation and excessive circumspection.[97] But he gives us no way of weighting the positive

94   De Gruchy, *Christianity*, 131.

95   *Ibid.*, 193.

96   *Ibid.*, 184.

97   See *ibid.*, 182, 183, 186. Similar qualifiers are expressed for Germany (196), South Africa (211), and American Black churches (135). Also, there is little differentiation within Christianity, with no references to evangelicals and very few to the Pentecostals and the new charismatics. Relatively, too much importance is placed on the AICs and their political significance, while the influence of Catholic bishops' pastoral letters and mainline Protestant symposia is taken for granted.

examples against the negative ones, or establishing a general pattern, or reaching an overall balance. We are left wondering whether de Gruchy is justified in his overall very positive assessment.

It is similar with Haynes, although he is arguing the opposite case. He analyses the mainline churches (or at least their leadership) through the concept of hegemony, arguing that their interests tend to coalesce with those of the ruling élite, and thus he views mainline churches as preserving élite privileges. This approach sheds considerable light in many instances. There are certainly countless examples of such hegemonic alliances. A clear example is Liberia. At the time of Doe's coup in 1980, the President, Tolbert, was also chairman of the Baptist Convention; Warner, his Vice-President, was the presiding Bishop of the Methodist Church; and Reginald Townsend, the National Chairman of the True Whig Party, in power since 1870, was the Moderator of the Presbyterian Church. So these three pillars of the political establishment were also the heads of Liberia's three oldest churches – an example of total fusion of church and political leadership. But even in Liberia it was not simple, for the Lutherans and Catholics had never been part of that system. The Lutherans had always worked among the tribal people inland, never with the Americo-Liberian élite. And anti-Catholicism was one of the principles on which Liberia had been established; it was only at its fourth attempt that Catholicism was even allowed into the country. Thus these two churches had some independence. The Catholic Archbishop of Monrovia spoke out courageously against corruption and abuses, and in favour of human rights; he could not be viewed as one of the local élite. The concept of hegemony fails to explain his role in the country.[98] Thus Haynes raises again the problem of procedure. One senses that he has adopted a position, and selected a number of examples to verify it. But in a continent as heterogeneous as Africa, examples are to hand to illustrate many different views. How many examples do you need to confirm an argument? Are there countervailing examples? How do you weight conflicting examples? Haynes's method is not as unproblematic as it may appear.[99]

To build up our picture we present below detailed case studies of the Christian churches in four African countries: Ghana, Uganda, Zambia and Cameroon. The selected countries are geographically spread and of roughly similar population and importance. All four are functioning countries – in a way that Zaïre, Liberia or Rwanda are not – and all have been prominently caught up in Africa's struggle to create new and more

---

[98]   Gifford, *Christianity and Politics*, esp. 71-87.

[99]   Cox's selection of material is also tendentious in places, e.g., his emphasis on ecology as a concern of African churches (*Fire*, 245, 258); above all his admittedly fascinating examples hardly prove Europe is undergoing a 'resurgence of primal spirituality' (*ibid.*, 211).

democratic societies. In addition to their similarities, they offer several important differences. Ghana and Uganda each enclose a great pre-colonial kingdom, respectively Ashanti and Buganda; Zambia and Cameroon have dominant ethnic blocs, but no equivalent of these kingdoms. Each one of four countries had a different experience of colonialism: the greater part of Cameroon was a German colony before becoming a French Mandated and then Trust Territory; Uganda was a British Protectorate; modern Ghana comprises three former British Protectorates; Zambia was a settler colony. Zambia and Cameroon have been remarkably stable since independence, Ghana has been plagued by coups and changes of regime, though with relatively little bloodshed, whereas Uganda suffered two regimes so savage that the country almost dissolved in the resulting welter of brutality (Amin 1971–9; Obote 1979–85). Zambia is extremely urbanised; the other countries are still predominantly rural. Zambia and Cameroon had a period of economic boom after independence, but in the mid-1990s both were on a sharp downward spiral; Uganda and Ghana both reached rock-bottom in the early 1980s, but at the time of writing, at least in the World Bank's view, they are perhaps the two glimmers of hope in Africa. A comparison of the four countries, with all their similarities and differences, will provide a better explanatory purchase on the phenomena, will buttress judgements with greater probability, and be more richly suggestive of general patterns and trends.

In comparing these countries, I have attempted to guard against slanting the material unduly, or against letting one case study determine what is looked for – and then probably found – in another. I have attempted to do justice to each country's particular dynamic. Thus there has been no presumption that what is important in one country is important in all or any of the others. The Catholic Church is treated in each country, because it is the biggest single church – by far – in all four, and therefore could not be omitted. Likewise, the new charismatic sector is of necessity covered in all four case studies. But the Anglican Church, though treated at length in Uganda, where it has traditionally formed a duopoly with the Catholic Church, scarcely deserves its single footnote in the discussion of the churches in Cameroon. Similarly, the Jehovah's Witnesses are very significant in Zambia, where their membership is proportionally greater (barring a few microstates) than in any other country in the world, but Witnesses have not warranted a mention in the other countries. From our case studies, then, some sort of direct comparison is possible across the four countries for the Catholic Church and the charismatics, but not for other churches. Obviously, deciding what constitutes the most significant features of the Christian dynamic in any country is to some degree subjective. However, many features select themselves. Statistics suggest a starting point. Other indications of relative importance are frequency of mention on news broadcasts, the number of column inches in newspapers, and even the scale and frequency of denunciation by irate government officials. Other observers might have balanced things differently, but the selection here is not entirely arbitrary.

Our case studies are fairly detailed, since a fruitful comparison requires sufficient contextual background. One may select something that is no doubt perfectly true, but in its full context it may signify something far more nuanced than appears at first sight.[100] We have already mentioned the Catholic bishops in Malawi, and it is perfectly true that their 1992 pastoral letter began the whole transition from one-party rule. This was undoubtedly a very positive contribution but, situating it in a wider context, it seems that rather than the Catholic Church, or even the Catholic bishops, it was one individual who was primarily responsible for the letter – and he an expatriate. And when the government rounded on the Catholic bishops, the other bishops were quite content for the expatriate to be deported. Likewise, any account of the socio-political role of the churches in Africa since the mid-1970s would have to mention Zimbabwe's Catholic Commission for Justice and Peace. But, directed predominantly by whites, it functions independently of the hierarchy, which enables the hierarchy effectively to disown the Commission whenever it suits them. The Commission is well known on the continent for its public involvement in issues of justice; what it reveals about Christianity – or even Catholicism – in Zimbabwe is less clear.[101]

In a work such as this a crucial task is that of discriminating between kinds of Christianity. Too many studies talk of the Christian church (or the Christian churches) as though Christianity was a single recognisable entity, playing exactly the same role wherever it appears. To some degree, if we are to talk about Christianity at all in the space available, we must generalise, and to order our material we must use broad categories. This study, however, does not presume that Christianity is one in all its manifestations, and even within broad categories like Protestant or Pentecostal it tries not to force churches artificially into a uniformity they do not possess. For example, we will see that the charismatic churches manifest considerable diversity. The presumption of uniformity flaws many important studies. In a significant article comparing the democratisation process in Zambia and Kenya, Bratton compares what he calls the 'lead institutions' in the two countries, respectively the trade unions and the churches. In the course of his description of Kenya, he

---

[100] An historical example of some relevance is the celebrated fellowship of the early Methodists, where they allegedly learnt democratic virtues. Thompson complains: 'The picture of the fellowship of the Methodists which is commonly presented is too euphoric; it has been emphasised to the point where all other characteristics of the church have been forgotten' (*Making*, 416).

[101] Diana Auret, *Reaching for Justice: the Catholic Commission for Justice and Peace 1972-1992*, Gweru: Mambo Press, 1992.

writes: 'The Protestant faiths are joined, along with the numerous independent African churches, in a countrywide umbrella body known as the National Council of Churches of Kenya (NCCK)', and proceeds to portray 'the church in Kenya [as] an informal, extraparliamentary opposition' to the Moi regime.[102] This is too simple. In Kenya, Protestant churches can be divided into many strands. First and most obviously there are the mainline Protestants, loosely grouped into the NCCK. Then there are the evangelicals, most prominently the Africa Inland Church, to which Moi belongs, which actually left the NCCK because of its perceived anti-Moi bias. Then there are the established Pentecostal churches, like the Gospel Redeemed Church, which has supported Moi at every turn. Then there are the Independents, which generally do not belong to the NCCK, and which could be said to be solidly behind Moi. In fact Archbishop Ondiek of the Legio Maria, one of the most significant Kenyan AICs, was till 1992 Moi's Minister of Employment – probably put there precisely to ensure the support of such a big independent church and those like it. Then there are the new charismatic US-type ministries, which were also solidly behind Moi. (One of them, World Intercessory Ministries, went on national TV the morning after the 1992 elections when the results were still being disputed, to counter the NCCK and urge opposition politicians to accept the results.) Thus to imply that the churches, as such, were 'lead institutions' in challenging the state is much too simple.

Nor do I presume here that any church or denomination is static. I am concerned with religion, an element within culture. Cultures are never static, for people pick and choose from their cultural pool, as they respond to new circumstances. I have stressed this incessant mutability and temporality, putting change and not permanence at the centre of vision. I try to view African Christianity less as an object, and more as an event or a series of events.[103] I seek to show that even a church like the Presbyterian can be in a process of considerable change, and in different countries can be changing in different ways. I readily admit that in Africa events are moving quickly, so some elements in the picture presented here may already be out of focus. I also try to be sensitive to different sectors within a church; urban or rural, élite or popular, official or less official. Throughout this study, even in dealing with the Catholic Church, often regarded as monolithic, I am open to finding change and differences. It is impossible to allow for every subtle distinction, but my presumption

---

102   Michael Bratton, 'Civil Society and Political Transitions in Africa' in John W. Harbeson, Donald Rothchild and Naomi Chazan, *Civil Society and the State in Africa* , Boulder, CO: Lynne Rienner, 1994, 66-7. Joseph generalises in exactly the same way about 'the Kenyan churches'; see 'Christian Churches', 242 and 245.

103   For this perspective, see Carrithers, *Why Humans?*

throughout will be to favour diversity rather than uniformity.

This book, then, is both ambitious and modest. It is ambitious in that it attempts to shed light on factors operative across all sub-Saharan Africa. Also, it tries to cover all sections of Christianity – Catholic, mainline Protestant, Evangelical, Pentecostal, Independent, new Charismatic, even Orthodox (in Uganda) – always given the proviso just mentioned, namely reference to some scale of public importance. At the same time, the aims are relatively modest. This study attempts to shed light on what is happening to African Christianity by using a range of concepts not normally used in the study of Christianity; and conversely to shed light, through selected examples, on the role Christianity is currently playing in African politics and society. It is not claimed that the countries treated are paradigmatic in a hard sense, that the discussion of them will produce some ironplated model revealing the dynamics within every African country. There are no paradigmatic African countries in that sense, just as there are no paradigmatic European countries. It would be as well to mention immediately two important elements of African Christianity that have only slight significance in our particular case studies. The first of these is Christian-Muslim tension. This is alluded to in various places below, but it will be obvious that this element would have featured far more prominently if, say, the Sudan, Nigeria or Tanzania had been one of the countries selected; unfortunately, Christian-Muslim conflict is increasingly important in many countries in both East and West Africa. The other factor that does not feature here but which will be important in determining the future character of African Christianity is the success or failure of South Africa's transition. The role of the various Christian churches in the creation and then dismantling of apartheid was considerable. In the newly emerging South Africa some churchmen like Archbishop Desmond Tutu are playing a significant role in the process of reconciliation. Should the churches advance reconciliation and reconstruction successfully, it is to be expected, given South Africa's regional dominance in so many areas, that the Christianity of neighbouring countries will be profoundly influenced.

One other reason for modesty is the level of analysis. Bratton has admitted that it is still too early to address the grand picture, or to say whether African civil society contributes to democratisation; before we can know the public function of civil society in Africa we must look closely at micro-level questions.[104] Much of this study is concerned with the churches as social organisations. I look, in connection with the running of the churches, at governance and legitimacy, at accountability, transparency, predictability, openness, observance of the law. I focus on the churches as creating a culture characterised by democratic virtues

[104]   Bratton, 'Beyond the State', 430.

like tolerance, respect, moderation and compromise. All the following questions need to be asked: Does the church have clear procedures? Does it have strict management standards? Is it marked by membership participation? How does it manage intra-organisational harmony, like that threatened by class and tribe? Are the churches democratic or authoritarian? How accountable are those in charge of the finances? How do they function at the periphery, as opposed to the urban centres? These are admittedly micro- or meso-level questions, but even to shed light in these areas would contribute greatly to our understanding of the wider social role of Africa's churches.

Situating this study

Aware of the link between social sciences and colonialism, and the attitudes of cultural superiority underlying much previous research, some scholars of Africa eschew any judgement of the phenomena they study. They take each culture as an entity to itself, not to be judged from outside. That approach is rejected here. Here we attempt not just to describe current expressions of Christianity, but also to judge their adequacy. Bourdillon has written of the 'obligation to make judgements about the political effects of certain types of religious knowledge.[...] While we must try to understand how and why people think the way they do, we cannot totally absolve ourselves from the question of whether they are right or wrong, no matter how complex this question may be in certain situations.'[105] Here we will try to address this complexity.

Two recent events constitute something of a watershed in the study of African Christianity, and have made this approach inevitable.These events were the implosion of Liberia and the genocide in Rwanda.

Liberia claimed to be built on Christianity. It prided itself on its Christian roots; indeed, its early Presidents gave one of their main reasons for the freed slaves returning to Africa as 'to convert the heathen', a motif repeated right up to the 1950s. Political rhetoric was saturated with Christian references and allusions. Political leaders were prominent in their churches – indeed, only with such Christian affiliation could they become political leaders. Evangelical and Pentecostal churches claimed to be apolitical, but were not: the omnipresent Faith Gospel and the almost exclusive stress on evangelisation not only left the regime totally unchallenged, but also offered nothing but support for any regime which promoted evangelisation. In 1990 came the civil war and Liberia's spiral to destruction. With hindsight it is plain to what degree Christianity had been part of the structures of oppression and was used to mask the

---

[105] M.F.C. Bourdillon, 'On the Theology of Anthropology', *Studies in World Christianity* 2, 1 (1996), 49-50. See also M.F.C. Bourdillon, 'Anthropological Approaches to the Study of African Religions', *Numen* 40 (1993), 217-39, esp. 229-37.

injustices that contributed so powerfully to the destruction of the country. Thus it is no longer adequate in a treatment of Liberia's Christianity to write: 'The civil war has unfortunately showed how little the spirit of the social gospel has penetrated the country.'[106] That misses the most crucial element of the dynamic.

Rwanda has proved even more destructive of any comfortable view of Christianity's public role in Africa. Statistically it was the most Christian country in Africa – overwhelmingly Catholic where Liberia was mainly Protestant. Here Christianity was an integral part of the 'genocidal culture' which collapsed under the weight of its own shortcomings in April 1994. Catholic missionaries had played an enormous role in creating the country under the Germans and then the Belgians; they had come with images of Constantine and Charlemagne, determined to replicate the Christian society of Europe's high Middle Ages. They had singled out the Tutsi as 'natural overlords', and had solidified the till then rather fluid categories of Tutsi and Hutu. Priest-anthropologists had played their part in providing the mythical understanding of the Tutsi as invaders, foreigners, Ethiopians – even Semites – which had buttressed Tutsi overlordship till the 1950s, and then after the rebellions in 1959 and through the period of independence had fuelled the Hutu repression of the Tutsi. In Rwanda everyone was 'wading in mythology', and the church was crucial in both creating the myths and preserving them. It was mythology which ensured that 'noble little Christian Rwanda' became the darling of the Christian Democrat International. 'Everything rested on a carefully controlled machinery of hypocrisy, with the church playing the role of Chief Engineer.'[107] Church leaders used Christian rhetoric to obfuscate and mystify, rather than to lay bare the structure of society. In the years of the Habyarimana regime (1973-94) the church turned a blind eye to the injustice of the system, in return for the prestige and influence that went with unchallenged control of education, health and development generally. Pastoral letters deliberately remained vague and non-specific, falling far short of denouncing those responsible for evils, even when they were widely known. Injustice was present even within the church – the Catholic bishops were predominantly Hutu, dominating a mainly Tutsi clergy. Church leaders were also personally linked to the regime; the Catholic Archbishop of Kigali was a member of the ruling party's central committee for fifteen years, and confessor to the President's wife. While Habyarimana delayed implementing reforms demanded by the international community, church leaders persisted in their evasions right till the end. Even when the genocide began, the bishops could claim that

---

[106] John Baur, *2000 Years of Christianity in Africa: an African History, 62-1992*, Nairobi: Paulines, 1994, 378.

[107] Gérard Prunier, *The Rwanda Crisis*, London: Hurst, 1995, 82.

what was happening was 'an invasion from Uganda' rather than something planned from within. A group of twenty-nine priests in the camps in Zaïre could even write to the Pope claiming that what had happened was slaughter by the invading Rwandan Patriotic Front, rather than genocide. In the genocide itself there is evidence that individual churchmen and women took part. Other mainline churches were also compromised in the structures of oppression.[108]

Both these cases have raised in a new way the question of the public role of Christianity in Africa. In the last twenty years, the stress has been (to use Ranger's words) on understanding the sense behind African religious responses. His survey showed that Africa's religious movements were eminently political, each making sense 'as a combined cultural-ideological-social-political response to its situation'.[109] Yet he continues: 'No one would say that such movements – or other manifestations of rural consciousness – made total sense, or enough sense, or the kind of sense that may be needed to transform [African society].'[110] And he adds a sentence that we will take up in this study: 'Maybe there has not been enough consideration of religious movements which have failed to make a creative response and which have constituted dangerous dead ends.'[111] When the Xhosa killed their cattle in 1857 at the urging of the prophetess, it made sense – in a way. But in the light of subsequent events, how adequate did that response prove to be? The belief of the followers of Patrice Lumumba or Alice Lakwena, or of the Nparamas of Mozambique, that their magic rendered them bulletproof made a kind of sense. But someone confronted with their bullet-ridden bodies is able to make a judgement of the validity of that belief.[112] Gellner has criticised anthropology 'which makes good sense of everything'. He has rejected the attitude *'tout comprendre c'est tout pardonner'*. 'In the social sciences at any rate, if we forgive too much we understand nothing.' Universal conceptual charity 'cannot deal with social change.[...] It precludes us from making sense of those social changes which arise at least in part

---

108 Ian Linden, *Chuch and Revolution in Rwanda*, Manchester University Press, 1977; Hugh McCullum, *The Angels have left Us: the Rwanda Tragedy and the Churches* Geneva: WCC Publications [1995], esp. 63-94; Saskia Van Hoyweghen, 'The Disintegration of the Catholic Church of Rwanda', *African Affairs* 95 (1996), 379-401; Timothy Longman, 'Christianity and Democratisation in Rwanda: Assessing Church Responses to Political Crisis in the 1990s' in Gifford, *Christian Churches*, 188-204. Priests and nuns allegedly participated in the atrocities; see African Rights, *Witness to Genocide*, Oct 1995.

109 Ranger, 'Religious Movements', 51.

110 *Ibid.*

111 *Ibid.*, 32.

112 M. Auge, *The Anthropological Circle*, Cambridge University Press, 1982, 4, quoted by Ranger, 'Religious Movements', 29.

from the fact that people sometimes notice the incoherences of doctrines and concepts and proceed to reform the institutions justified by them.[113] The inadequacy of the all-charitable understanding has been highlighted by the events in Rwanda and Liberia. Christianity in both countries did make a certain sense, and even if it did not make total sense, or the only sense, that particular Christianity was understandable. But Rwandan and Liberian Christians themselves no longer deny the inadequacy of their responses. We cannot avoid a similar question: how adequate has been the churches' contribution in Africa's current crisis? In the 1990s the possibility of a negative answer has to be faced in a way it need not have been in the 1980s. It is only now, after Rwanda and Liberia, that scholars, African and non-African alike, have been forced to re-examine the adequacy or appropriateness of many of Africa's Christian responses. This study is written as a contribution to this reappraisal.

[113]   Ernest Gellner, 'Concepts and Society', 46-8.

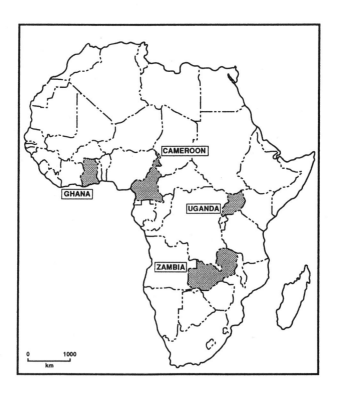

3

GHANA

Modern Ghana is made up of about seventy-five tribes, of which the most numerous are the Akan, the Mossi, the Ewe and the Ga. Although the numerous slaving forts along the shore testify to hundreds of years of European presence, European contact was initially restricted to the coast. The littoral known as the Gold Coast became a British crown colony in 1874, and over the next thirty years two more protectorates were established, one over the northern territories, and one over the Ashanti region in the centre – the latter effected by the British only with considerable difficulty. The Ashanti, members of the Twi-speaking branch of the Akan peoples, developed a powerful empire which reached its peak in the eighteenth and nineteenth centuries. The British finally occupied Ashanti in 1896.

Important in the creation of Ghana were the Protestant missions – the Basel Mission arrived in 1828, the Methodists in 1835 – and Ghana's history cannot be understood apart from the élite they created. Mission graduates were prominent along the coast in the mid-nineteenth century. Already in the 1870s there were Africans in the Legislative Council, and in the late nineteenth century Ghanaians with considerable Western education were becoming increasingly prominent. Even before the turn of the century, members of this élite had formed organisations like the Gold Coast Aborigines Rights Protection Society (ARPS) to advance their interests. Not the least important of the organs through which they articulated their criticism of British administration were those provided by Christian institutions like the *Gold Coast Methodist Times*. Another important factor in the development of Ghana's élite was the burgeoning cocoa industry – unlike manufacturing and mining, essentially an African enterprise – which saw Ghana become the world's biggest exporter of cocoa by 1911.

In 1947 nationalists, prominent among whom was Joseph Boakye Danquah, a sympathiser with traditional rulers, formed the United Gold Coast Convention. The UGCC appointed as their general secretary Kwame Nkrumah, who had been educated in the United States and was the organiser of the Pan African Conference in Manchester in 1945, but this eventually led to a split in the UGCC, as Nkrumah broke with the esssentially conservative lawyers, businessmen and traditional rulers to found his own Convention People's Party (CPP), advocating positive action in pursuit of 'self-government now', and supported by farmers, market women, small businessmen and half-qualified school-leavers – hence the label 'Verandah Boys'. In 1951, while Ghana was still a British colony, the CPP won the elections to the Legislative Council, with Nkrumah first 'Leader of Government Business' and then in 1952 Prime Minister. In further elections in 1954 the CPP repeated this success, this time defeating Kofi Busia's Ghana Congress Party. In the 1956 elections, Nkrumah's CPP was again victorious, although in this election the CCP failed to win the Ashanti region. Here we see the other important and abiding split in Ghanaian politics, besides that between the élite and the populists; that between the Ashanti and other groups. Thus Ghana came to independence – the first colonised African country to do so – in March 1957 with Nkrumah as Prime Minister.

Such has been the impact of the Protestant missions in setting the tone of Ghanaian society that the CPP had a distinctly Protestant revivalist flavour to it, so much so that it was quite natural for Nkrumah to express his pan-Africanism and socialism in Christian metaphors ('Lead kindly light...', 'Seek ye first the political kingdom...'). Athough a charismatic leader, and accorded great attention throughout Africa, in the communist world and in the West, hardship, corruption, repression, strong-arm tactics on the part of his Young Pioneers, along with a personality cult, came increasingly to characterise his regime. In February 1966, while on his way to China in an attempt to end the Vietnam war, he was overthrown in a military coup, which may have been externally supported but took place with apparently genuine popular approval.[1]

The ensuing National Liberation Council (1966-9) provided a breathing space before retiring to barracks in favour of Busia's Second Republic, run by the professional and merchant élite, in league with the Ashanti. This too descended into corruption and inefficiency, and was replaced in 1972 by a succession of military rulers. General I. Acheampong, the first of these, treated the state as his own personal property; he was replaced by General Fred Akuffo in 1978. The military were about to hand back to civilian government, when Flt Lt Jerry Rawlings attempted a coup in May 1979. His ensuing trial proved an occasion for frustration to overflow, and the lower ranks freed him from gaol on 4 June 1979 and took power as the Armed Forces Revolutionary Council (AFRC). Bowing to

---

[1]   For much of the details that follow, see Jeffrey Herbst, *The Politics of Reform in Ghana 1982-91*, Berkeley, CA: University of California, 1993; E. Gyimah-Boadi, *Ghana under PNDC Rule*, Dakar: Codesria, 1993; Douglas Rimmer, *Staying Poor: Ghana's Political Economy 1950-90*, Oxford: Pergamon Press, 1992; Donald Rothchild (ed.), *Ghana: the Political Economy of Recovery*, Boulder, CO: Lynne Rienner, 1991; a rather uncritical assessment of Rawlings is found in Kevin Shillington, *Ghana and the Rawlings Factor*, London: Macmillan, 1992.

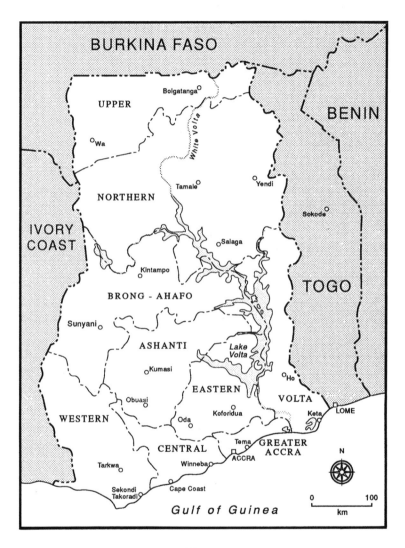

Ghana

popular rage at the ruling élite, they executed General Acheampong, and some weeks later General Akuffo and five others prominent in the previous regimes. After these few months of revolutionary and cathartic bloodletting, Rawlings made way for the Third Republic (1979-81), headed by Hilla Limann, a government of the élite, this time linked with the Ga and the north. This administration proved inept, and was somewhat intimidated by Rawlings watching from the wings. On 31 December 1981 Rawlings staged his second coup, and began the era of the Provisional National Defence Council (PNDC). This was revolutionary and contemptuous of the élite. People's Defence Committees (Military Defence Committees in the army, Workers' Defence Committees at the workplace) were established, which in December 1984 became Committees for the Defence of the Revolution (CDRs). Public Tribunals replaced courts, and even examined bank accounts to root out corruption among the élite. Throughout 1982 assaults and killings increased, unchecked by the PNDC, and reached their peak with the murder of three judges, one of them pregnant, and a retired army officer, who had been brave enough to resist some activity of the AFRC in 1979. This stirred such revulsion that the PNDC were forced to curtail excesses (and even execute a former PNDC member whom an enquiry had implicated in the murders). In 1983 famine and the expulsion from Nigeria of a million Ghanaians who had fled there from the chaos at home brought the country to its knees. Real income had fallen by 80% between 1970 and 1982.

At this juncture the PNDC changed direction entirely, submitting to a regime of structural adjustment prescribed by the IMF, and Rawlings, the socialist admirer of Libya and Cuba, returned to the fold. The roads, ports and railways were rehabilitated. The civil service was cut back. Agriculture was promoted. The forests were sold – indeed everything that could be was sold. User fees were introduced for education and health. Despite enormous suffering at the grassroots, Ghana came to be hailed as the World Bank's success story. (It had to be; the World Bank had poured in so much money, and had had such a free hand, that if Ghana was not a success the Bank had no authority to inflict its remedy elsewhere.[2])

With World Bank money flowing in, Rawlings rehabilitated the state, and was able to control the transition to civilian rule.[3] A Constitutional Assembly, weighted towards the PNDC (and introducing at the last minute an amnesty for all PNDC activity) drew up a new constitution, which was accepted by referendum in April 1992. Rawlings lifted the ban on political parties, declared himself (at the last moment) a candidate for

---

[2] Mihevc, *Market*, 155-65.

[3] E. Gyimah-Boadi, 'Associational Life, Civil Society, and Democratisation in Ghana' in Harbeson, Rothchild and Chazan, *Civil Society*, 140-1.

the presidency, and won 58% of the vote on election day, 3 November 1992, against 32% for his rival, the distinguished academic Adu Boahen. There was no doubting that Rawlings had manipulated the media, and used state resources to curry favour, but probably the election itself was relatively free and fair. The opposition parties cried foul, and refused to take part in the parliamentary elections a few weeks later.[4]

Thus Flt Lt Rawlings became President Rawlings of Ghana's Fourth Republic. Changes ensued – the press became much freer, and the opposition and Ghana's chattering classes can now vent their spleen on Rawlings in print – but this was hardly a transition to democracy. Rawlings is simply not the type of person to encourage participation or value consensus; his autocratic streak could even lead him to beat up his Vice-President in a cabinet meeting. Nor, for all the World Bank's stress on private enterprise, does Rawlings find it easy to encourage local businessmen; he would often harass them for supporting the opposition. And for all the much-trumpeted economic success in fields like mining, hardship at the grassroots has not eased. Protest marches took place in major cities in 1995 – with at least four killed in the Accra march. Ethnic tension has flared up, most seriously with the Konkomba demanding a paramount chieftainship from their traditional overlords, the Dagomba; over 1,000 were killed in early 1994, and the killing continued well into 1995.[5] At the beginning of 1995, the minimum wage was 780 cedis (about 80 cents) a day, when Ghana's Trades Union Congress claimed that 3,000 cedis a day were needed to feed a family of four. Education has become a privilege, with 57% of school age children ekeing out a living on the street.[6]

Rawlings had to submit himself to the electorate again towards the end of 1996. This time parts of the opposition formed a coalition (the Great Alliance), built from sectors of both the Danquah-Busia and the Nkrumahist traditions, with its candidate J.A. Kufuor; a third candidate was E.N. Mahama of the People's National Convention (PNC). Campaigning was relatively peaceful, although twenty were killed in clashes one weekend in early November. On election day, 7 December, after a mas-

---

4   I find broadly convincing the argument in Richard Jeffries and Clare Thomas, 'The Ghanaian Elections of 1992', *African Affairs* 92 (1993), 331-66, where they argue that Ghana's élite simply could not comprehend that Rawlings could receive a majority of votes in a free election. Yet for the majority, new roads and electricity perhaps mean more than the infringement of the rights so valued by the élite.

5   This antagonism has many longstanding causes, but not the least in the present eruption of violence is Rawlings' personal style. He evidently promised the Konkomba a paramountcy if they supported him in the elections; they did, but Rawlings in the new republic is not able to act as arbitrarily as before and deliver what he promised (*Statesman*, 27 Feb 1994, 5).

6   *APS Bulletin*, 21 Aug 1995.

sive 78% turn-out (compared with 50.2% in 1992), Rawlings was cred-
ited with 57.4% of the vote, Kufuor with 39.6%, and Mahama with 3%.
In the parliamentary elections held the same day, Rawlings' NDC won
134, or two-thirds, of the 200 seats. The opposition accepted the results,
and one of the features of Rawlings' subsequent swearing-in was the
handshakes from the defeated candidates. Although the voting was generally agreed to be free and fair, it was equally obvious that in campaigning the opposition was at a distinct disadvantage. Rawlings made
full use of state funds, a fleet of government vehicles, even helicopters,
state media – 'the advantages of incumbency were just too vast to contemplate'.[7] Internal feuding damaged the opposition's performance also.
Rawlings seemed again to have captured the vote of rural peasantry who
could see the drinking water, electricity and roads his rule had brought
('project politics', in the view of the opposition). However, the 'newspaper reading' classes voted for the opposition.

Facts and figures

Of the 19 million population, over 60% claim to be Christian, with about
16% Muslims and 20% adherents of traditional religions. In 1960 the
corresponding figures were 43%, 12% and 45%, so Christianisation has
been relatively recent. But beyond the statistics, Christianity in Ghana
has an obtrusiveness as great as in any African country. About 50% of
vehicles have Christian slogans painted across the front: 'God is King';
'Abide with Me'; 'God Never Gives to Curse'; some are a little more
cryptic: 'Don't Blame Judas'; 'Exodus 14,14'; or 'Talitha Kum'. Buses,
cars and taxis are bedecked with bumper stickers which are usually of a
Christian kind: 'God is greater than any problem I have'; 'Don't Give
Up – Your miracle is on the way'; 'I will make it in Jesus' Name'. Even
firms are frequently given Christian names: 'Jesus Way Upholstery'; 'King
of Kings Electrical'; 'Bethel Chop Bar'; 'Jehovah Jirah Motorbody Re-
pairs'; 'The Lord is my Light Car Wash'; 'Wonderful Jesus Hardware
Stores'; 'Saloon de Jesus the Lord'; and in Accra's Kaneshie market 'Jesus Saves Enterprises' almost next to 'Allah Alakbar Enterprises', but
these Muslim equivalents are rare. Even the distinctive Ghanaian *kente*
cloth on sale outside the national museum in Accra may have 'Jesus loves
you' or 'Jesus saves' printed on it. On Ghana's one TV channel, in the
public announcements slot every evening, up to one-third of the notices
can be of Christian events. On the cheapest form of public transport,
preachers will sermonise while the bus or van is filling up. In the lonely
hearts column in the tabloid *People and Places* about a third of all adver-

---

[7]   Joseph R.A. Ayee, 'The December 1996 General Elections in Ghana: a Post-Mortem',
paper delivered at SOAS, 6 Mar 1997, mimeo.

tisements are seeking a 'Christian' partner. And newspapers freely utilise Christian images and metaphors. For example, on the front page of
the opposition *Chronicle* for 15-17 May 1995, produced just after anti-
Rawlings demonstrations in which five lost their lives, the headlines were
'The Blood of Martyrs' and 'The Mark of the Beast', and across the
bottom were written the words: 'In the place that dogs licked up the
blood of Naboth shall dogs lick your own blood (1 Kings 21:19).'[8] It is
common to describe Rawlings' 1981 coup as his 'Second Coming'. Likewise everyone understands the frequent interpretation of J.J. Rawlings'
initials as 'Junior Jesus' (or, for the opposition, 'Junior Judas'), and everyone understands the allusion in the label 'Obaapa Jezebel' applied to his
wife. Public functions often give prominence to Christian ritual or
prayers – not exclusively (they can be combined with Muslim ritual, and
even the traditional pouring of libations – the state is fairly pragmatic),
but Christianity is given pride of place.

The Ghana Evangelism Committee conducted a survey of the entire
country, even remote rural areas, in 1986-7. The advantage of the survey
was that it counted those attending services on a Sunday; it did not rely
on numbers of alleged members or adherents given by denominations
themselves, which in Africa are notoriously unreliable. The survey was
repeated five years later. A comparison of the two surveys is revealing.
The traditional AICs are losing members, the larger ones substantially:
attendance at the Musama Disco Christo Church fell to 30,382, a decline
of 17% over the five years; the Church of the Twelve Apostles declined
to 34,808, a decrease of 22%; the African Faith Tabernacle declined to
29,051, a decrease of 23%. The mainline Protestant churches, those attached to the Christian Council of Ghana, overall held their own: the
Anglican Church fell to 29,354, a decrease of 2%; the Evangelical Presbyterian Church fell to 68,966, a decrease of 14%; the Methodist Church
grew to 188,725, an increase of 2%; the Presbyterian Church allegedly
grew to 178,870, an increase of 17% – it is thanks to the last that the
mainline churches overall can be said to have held steady, though their
small overall percentage growth of 7% in these five years is well below
the 17% increase of the whole population over the same period. The
Catholic Church, though still the largest single denomination, decreased
to 343,957, a decline of 2%.

The growth in Ghanaian Christianity occurred elsewhere, and in two
areas. The first was in those churches belonging to the Pentecostal Council, where the big winners were the Assemblies of God (up to 60,298, an
increase of 87%), the Church of Pentecost (up to 259,920, an increase of

8   The headline for 29-31 May 1995, in reference to the same demonstrations, was 'The
     Day the Walls of Jericho Came Down', and below was written: 'He who digs a pit will
     fall into it, and a stone will come back upon him who starts its rolling (Proverbs 26: 27).'

31%), the Apostolic Church (to 51,100, an increase of 27%), and Christ Apostolic (to 36,270, an increase of 36%). The second area was a group of churches that the survey categorises as 'mission-related', where the most successful were the Churches of Christ (up to 20,170, an increase of 36%) and, above all, the New Apostolic Church (up to 20,508, an increase of 369%). Another church (in a category of its own) which showed considerable increase was the Seventh Day Adventist (up to 79,491, an increase of 15%). These changes, monitored over a five-year period, would support the impression given in so many countries in Africa: the AICs are in serious difficulty; the mainline churches are static if not decreasing; and substantial growth lies with new Pentecostal and 'mission-related' churches.[9]

These 'mission-related' churches are not all the same, but they indicate that Ghana is experiencing something more complex than a 'Pentecostal explosion'. The most remarkable church here is the New Apostolic Church, with its headquarters now in Zürich (formerly Dortmund). It shows enormous growth. In the span of one year, between 1 January and 31 December 1993 (and thus after the period covered by the surveys discussed above), their Cape Coast District increased from 10,272 to 15,152 members (an increase of forty-two congregations), and their Accra membership from 7,631 to 11,065 (an increase of thirty-three congregations).

Before leaving the question of Christian statistics, it is worthwhile to refer to the Afrikania Movement, the attempt to re-establish African traditional religion as a world religion, begun in December 1982 by former Catholic priest Vincent Kwabena Damuah, who for a time served on Rawlings' PNDC. This movement is frequently referred to, and the Ghanaian theologian Kwame Bediako even attributes great significance to 'the Afrikania Challenge'. However, in the 1990s its numbers are almost non-existent, and the organisation is all but dead. This kind of thing seems not to meet Africans' needs. African traditional religion persists not as a separate 'African religion', but as enduring perceptions and habits within Christianity and Islam. As a self-conscious alternative to Christianity and Islam, Afrikania constitutes little challenge at all.[10]

---

9   Ghana Evangelism Committee, *National Church Survey, Update 1993: Facing the Unfinished Task of the Church in Ghana*, Accra: Ghana Evangelism Committee, 1993. For my purposes here I have ignored all churches with an attendance of less than 20,000. The report notes: 'The older orthodox churches and "spiritual" churches are failing to maintain their relative positions' (*ibid.*, 95). It notes under the heading of 'African Independent' churches, that 'sundry spiritual' (i.e. AICs) are decreasing by 3%; 'sundry charismatic' (i.e. new Pentecostal) are increasing by 99% (*ibid.*, 17). That such different churches as Otabil's ICGC (see below) and the Musama Disco Christo Church are lumped together under the category of 'African Independent' is a major defect of the survey.

10   Kwame Bediako, *Christianity in Africa: the Renewal of a Non-Western Religion*, Edinburgh University Press, 1995, esp. 17-38; Samuel Gyanfosu, 'The Development of Christian-related Independent Religious Movements in Ghana, with special reference to

The Catholic Church

The Catholic Church is now Ghana's largest denomination, and even by the 1970s it was challenging, in terms of significance, Ghana's Protestant ascendancy.[11] The Ghanaian bishops (all are local; there are no missionary bishops) possess considerable moral authority. In May 1995 their number increased from ten to fifteen, a 50% increase in one day. Of the five new bishops, one has a doctorate in church history from the University of Münster, another has a doctorate in scripture from the University of Aberdeen; another was three years into a doctoral programme at Marquette University, Wisconsin; another has an American MBA. When added to the competence of the others – like Bishop Peter Kwesi Sarpong, Oxford-trained anthropologist and author of several works on the Akan – the Catholic leadership has attained a quality that no other church can match.

The Catholic Church has frequently spoken out, in memoranda, communiqués and pastoral letters. Some of this has been quite brave. In a 'Statement on the State of the Nation' of 11 November 1982 the bishops were fiercely critical of the PDCs and WDCs. 'No clear thinking' had gone into the question: 'In many instances these committees have become instruments of terror, division and antagonism in our society. [...] The condition of the ordinary Ghanaian has worsened since the "revolution". [...] Atrocities of all sorts have been committed against innocent civilians [...] Wanton killings, senseless beatings, merciless molestation and general harassment continue without the government showing any willingness or ability to do anything about them. The sordid lawlessness of our nation reached a climax in the outrageous abduction and subsequent abhorrent, cold-blooded, cowardly murder of three judges and an ex-army officer.' In an historical retrospect, they admit that none of Ghana's previous regimes were very good, but 'We have to face the truth. The "revolution" is not producing the anticipated effects.' They went on to make recommendations: to hand over to a representative government; to set up a constituent assembly to decide the best form of democratic government; to declare a political amnesty.

A reading of their statements since then is instructive. Some of them deal with Catholic preoccupations – for example, condoms are not the

---

the Afrikania Movement', Ph.D. thesis, University of Leeds, 1995. In May 1990 Afrikania renamed itself Godianism, and joined with the Godian Movement of Nigeria, which itself seems in no better health; see A.U. Ihedinma, 'Towards the Return to Traditional Religion among the Elite of Igboland, Nigeria, with Special Reference to the Godian Religion', M.Phil. thesis, University of London, 1995.

[11] Paul Jenkins, 'Christianity and the Churches in Ghanaian History: a Historiographical Essay' in J.O. Hunwick (ed.), *Proceedings of the Seminar on Ghanaian Historiography and Historical Research*, Legon: University of Ghana, 1977, 267.

solution to the AIDS crisis. Some of them refer to Catholic institutional interests, like the right to run their own schools, to teach religion. Others deplore government measures adversely affecting the church's hospitals and clinics. However, by far the greater part of these statements address issues of general concern – depredation of natural resources, ethnic conflict, the condition of roads, drug smuggling, the effects of structural adjustment. Some intervention is quite specific: to resolve a strike action, to withdraw a bill attempting to curb NGOs. It is hard to assess the effectiveness of such pronouncements. Perhaps the tone of the earlier statements did not help, nor the fact that in early years the statements were signed by Bishop Sarpong of Kumasi, as chairman of the Catholic Bishops' Conference. Bishop Sarpong, as both an Ashanti and the person in charge of the Justice and Peace activity of the church, particularly drew the fire of Rawlings (in June 1985 Rawlings actually broke off a speech commissioning the Ghana Broadcasting Corporation's new transmitters to heap personal abuse on Bishop Sarpong, much to the consternation of the media crews covering the ceremony[12]). Perhaps the bishops' tone has become more conciliatory and complimentary towards the government (for example, for introducing a new voter registration exercise and with- drawing VAT in 1995) since the advent of the Fourth Republic, when the bishops' chairman was an Ewe like Rawlings. Relations are outwardly civil, but it was noteworthy that at the ordination of the five new Catholic bishops in May 1995, although the printed programme billed Rawlings as taking part, he was out of the country when the ceremony took place. Perhaps this was unavoidable, but at least one newspaper ran a banner headline: 'Catholics Not Happy.'[13] The strained relations are well known.

The Catholic Church has long been heavily involved in services of education and health, and increasingly in development and relief. Throughout the disaster years of the 1980s Catholic Relief Services was one of the major players in relief. The Catholic Church undoubtedly owes much of its standing to its international character, and to the human and financial resources it can therefore command.[14] These resources mean that Catholic involvement in many areas can rival or even surpass the government's. Certainly no other denomination can match it; perhaps all the other denominations put together cannot. Not all its array of projects

---

12 Shillington, *Ghana*, 137-9.
13 *Independent*, 31 May-6 June 1995, 1.
14 In 1983 Ghana had 244 local and 248 expatriate priests; 249 local and 278 expatriate sisters, and 44 local and 78 expatriate brothers. In 1995 Ghana had 665 local and 176 missionary priests; 465 local and 243 expatriate sisters; 113 local brothers and 57 expatriate brothers. Thus the missionary component is less both proportionately and in absolute terms, but in the mid-1990s the numbers of missionary priests and sisters were again increasing, with new congregations coming from the Philippines, India and Eastern

are successful, and not all are perfectly administered.[15] The Catholic Church is involved in other areas as well: in 1995 the Departments of Religious Studies at Legon and Cape Coast were headed by Catholic priests, and Divine Word missionaries run the Tamale Institute of Cross Cultural Studies, an influential educational centre. The church can also boast an educated and articulate laity.

Yet, notwithstanding its prominence, the Catholic Church has obvious weaknesses. Despite the statements of the bishops, its Justice and Peace Commission is only a shadow of what it could be. It is filled with people who are not particularly interested, just appointed because they are important or deserving – the bane of so many African organisations – and there is little effort to involve the grassroots. Also, a really independent newspaper committed to analysing what is happening in Ghana today could make a significant contribution; but the Catholic *Standard* ceased production because of lack of funds only a year after Rawlings lifted a two-year ban on publication. Catholic seminaries have several deficiencies. Despite the highly-trained Ghanaian personnel who staff these seminaries, a truly Ghanaian theology is not likely to emerge in the near future. A visit to the libraries of these seminaries shows the relatively low academic commitment. A working document prepared for the First National Catholic Pastoral Congress from 7 to 14 April 1997 reveals both the strengths and the weaknesses of the Catholic Church. The book is beautifully produced, with sections on Christianity's bearing on Ghanaian cultural practices, justice and peace, development, African traditional religions, the environment and Christian-Muslim relations. It is strongly affirmative of Ghanaian cultural practices like veneration of ancestors, and encourages Catholics to become chiefs (traditionally a great problem in Ghana) and even take part in ceremonies honouring tribal stools (or thrones); in all this the influence of anthropologist Bishop Sarpong is acknowledged.[16] It is equally positive on African traditional religion, whose conventional description 'as paganism, heathenism,

---

Europe (*Catholic Yearbooks*, published by the Catholic Secretariat, Accra). Although Ghana in 1995 had 300 major seminarians in training, recruits for religious orders had fallen slightly.

15 See the comprehensive evaluation, CoratAfrica, *The Socio-Economic Department of the National Catholic Secretariat, Ghana: Final Report*, Nairobi: CoratAfrica, 1993. Besides the National Catholic Secretariat, each diocese has its own development department. See, e.g., Kumasi Catholic Diocese, *Agricultural Possibilities for Small Scale Farmers in the Ashanti Afram Plains within the Framework of Environmental Conservation: an Evaluation Report*, June 1993.

16 Catholic Bishops' Conference, *Ecclesia in Ghana: On the Church in Ghana and its Evangelizing Mission in the Third Millennium: Instrumentum Laboris*, Accra: National Catholic Secretariat, 1997, 59-66. For the present-day problem of Christians becoming chiefs, see Richard Rathbone, *'Have you Heard my Message to my Fathers?' The Private Consciences and Public Lives of Two Remarkable Africans*, London: SOAS, 1996.

fetishism, animism, idolatry, polytheism is totally unjust to it'. It claims that 'Traditional Religion can enrich our belief as Christians and Christianity can uplift Traditional Religion to a height that by itself it could not attain.'[17] On Christian-Muslim relations, it recognises that both Christianity and Islam have greatly influenced modern Ghana: 'It is imperative that we recognise both religious heritages and uplift them for the development of our nation.' It hopes that 'the sons and daughters of Ishmael and Isaac will one day embrace one another with humility and love.'[18] It is doubtful whether any other church could produce such an impressive discussion document, and commit itself to such an impeccably liberal theology. Yet, with the Latin title *Ecclesia in Ghana*, the subtitle *Instrumentum Laboris* on the cover, and its generous quoting of Vaticanese from Popes and Councils, it is obvious that its primary audience is religious professionals rather than the grassroots. Also, the section on 'the sects' seems to be dependent on an article written by the present author; but whereas the latter article highlighted four particular churches as examples of a widespread phenomenon, this working document seems to think that these four are the only such churches in Ghana.[19] For all its attention to the world around it, the Catholic Church manifests some amazing blind spots. Possibly not a single expert responsible for drawing up this document has set foot inside one of the new churches mushrooming everywhere around them and drawing off so much of their membership. The Catholic Church sometimes seems so locked into its own agenda that it is genuinely ignorant of what is happening under its very eyes on the wider religious scene.

Although at the time of the creation of five new dioceses it was claimed that this was required by the growth of the church, it may be that the Catholic Church is not growing but in fact losing members. The Ghana Evangelism Committee surveys showed that attendance decreased by 2% between 1986 and 1993 (the director of the survey, in part explanation of this fall, claims that in the disaster years of the mid-1980s so much relief was being distributed through Catholic channels that the attendance figures then were artificially high). So although the significance of the Catholic Church cannot be denied, it is also true that its growth is not unchecked.

The Protestant Churches

Ghana's historically important Protestant churches are the Methodist, the Presbyterian (the Basel Mission church), the Evangelical Presbyterian

---

[17] *Ecclesia*, 148-9.
[18] *Ibid.*, 154.
[19] *Ibid.*, 138. See Paul Gifford, 'Ghana's Charismatic Churches', *JRA* 24 (1994), 241-65.

(the Bremen Mission church) and the Anglican.[20] These have been crucial
to the history of Ghana, and their contribution is well documented. Their
influence has been exerted not least through their great schools like the
Anglican Adisadel and the Methodist Mfantsipim which, along with the
non-missionary but very Christian Achimota, were instrumental in creating the Ghanaian élite, which had influence all over Africa. By the 1980s
these churches no longer had the field to themselves, and they were rather
disoriented, even defensive.[21] However, their social involvement and influence are considerable, as even a cursory glance at newspapers or radio
and TV news would show.

Since much of these churches' public activity is directed through the
Christian Council of Ghana (CCG), we will consider it in more depth.
The CCG was founded in 1929, and includes fourteen churches. It is not
just a centralised body, but comprises regional councils of churches. Its
centralised structure enables it to act and comment just like the Catholic
Church.[22] It too can be quite combative. In a June 1992 'Memorandum
to the PNDC Concerning the Transitional Arrangements for the Return
to Civilian Constitutional Democratic Rule', it drew attention to 'a number
of anomalies and irregularities...in the current political and constitutional
development in our country'. It called for the repeal of all laws which
violated fundamental human rights, the release of all political prisoners,
an unconditional amnesty for political exiles and the disbanding of all
CDRs, People's Militias and other paramilitary organs assumed to be 'integral levers' of the PNDC revolution. It queried the impartiality of the Interim Electoral Commission, and offered for consideration the proposal that
the PNDC government should resign in favour of interim government by a
Presidential Commission, consisting of a former Chief Justice, the speaker
of the dissolved Consultative Assembly, and the 'Head of a Religious
Body such as the CCG and the Catholic Bishops' Conference'.

More frequently, the CCG has operated in concert with the Catholic
bishops. The National Catholic Secretariat and the Christian Council
jointly issued a memorandum to the Armed Forces Revolutionary Council on 12 June 1979. They expressed deep regret that there was so much

---

[20]   For history of these churches, see F.L. Bartels, *The Roots of Ghana Methodism*, Cambridge
       University Press, 1965; Noel Smith, *The Presbyterian Church of Ghana 1835-1960*,
       Accra: Ghana Universities Press, 1966; J. Kofi Agbeti, *West African Church History:
       Christian Missions and Church Foundations 1482-1919*, Leiden: E.J.Brill, 1986.

[21]   For example, the pastoral letter of the Anglican bishops of August 1992 was very defens-
       ive in tone. The Bishops invite help in seeking answers to the questions: 'Why do you feel
       unfulfilled in the Anglican Church? What changes would you like to see in the Church,   and
       in what specific areas?' The Anglican Church, though privileged in colonial times, is the
       smallest of these mainline Protestant churches, and only two of its seven dioceses are viable.

[22]   For much of what follows, see Kwesi A. Dickson, 'The Church and the Quest for
       Democracy in Ghana' in Gifford, *Christian Churches*, 261-75.

violence. They welcomed Rawlings' statement that the coup was a moral revolution to restore human values to this country. They noted that 'This can be God's hour, a moment in our national life when as a nation we turn our backs on a sordid and disgraceful past, and set out together to build a great future. We can do this only on the basis of mutual trust and respect and constitutional legitimacy.'

The churches' opposition reached its peak in the blank refusal to comply with the government's June 1989 demands that all churches be registered with the Ministry of the Interior, so as to make them 'accountable' to the government. In a joint letter from the Catholic bishops and the Christian Council, dated 14 Nov 1989, they stated that 'in its present form PNDC law 221 constitutes an infringement of the fundamental human right of the freedom of worship. [...] Consequently we cannot in conscience register under PNDC Law 221 *as it now stands.*' The law was too draconian, and it was unacceptable that a bureaucrat intrude into places of worship. They stressed that they were not, however, 'opposed to legislation which affects worship generally in matters relating to law and order, and which protects the citizenry from exploitation. But it is our view that the current laws of the nation are adequate for that purpose.' The statement was fairly eirenic. They asked for prayers that their stance would not be misunderstood in any quarter, but the bottom line was a direct refusal to comply. The government refused to back down, and many non-mainline churches complied, but the mainline ones (Anglican, Presbyterian and Methodist, together with the Catholic) simply let the deadlines pass. The friction remained until with the coming of the Fourth Republic the proposed law simply lapsed.[23]

The Council and the Catholic bishops have continued to issue joint memoranda to government. Together they mounted a campaign (successful by 1995) for religion to be part of the school curriculum. They issued a joint pastoral letter, 'A Call to all Citizens of Ghana', dated 25 September 1992, to be read in all congregations just before the presidential election of October 1992, calling all to vote responsibly, to transcend revenge and refrain from violence, ethnic intolerance and intimidation. They also sent a joint message to Nelson Mandela on his release from prison.[24] In November 1995 they jointly held a seminar, 'Ghana's Economy: Which Way Forward?', producing a communiqué very critical of government, parliament and the Bank of Ghana.[25]

23 See *News from Africa Watch*, 18 May 1990, where it is noted that 19,000 registration forms were purchased by various religious bodies, and the Pentecostal Association of Ghana and the Organisation of Independent Churches wrote to affirm their support for the registration exercise.

24 *Christian Messenger*, Feb-March 1990, 1.

25 *Ghana Chronicle*, 27 Nov 1995, 1, with headline: 'Government is Responsible for Economic Mess – Churches'.

The two bodies thus readily cooperate in all sorts of activities, and genuinely enjoy working together. When relations between the Ghana Registered Nurses Association and the government broke down in June 1992, the CCG and Catholic bishops together successfully negotiated a settlement. They later spent four hours with striking university teachers trying to resolve their dispute with the government.[26] The two bodies met with the Council of State in May 1995, expressing their preparedness to play this role again.[27] This practical ecumenism is characteristic of Ghana.

The statements of the mainline churches have received great publicity – in the independent press and, above all, in the three main Christian newspapers, the *Methodist Times*, the (Presbyterian) *Christian Messenger*, and the (Catholic) *Standard*. These three are like many Ghanaian independent papers, run on a shoestring, often not appearing on deadline, and heavy on comment and analysis. Not only do they print and comment on statements of the CCG and Catholic bishops (each, very ecumenically, often leading with material from other churches), but they have provided many sermons and articles about political issues and human rights, and even many articles very critical of the government. For example, the *Messenger*, the *Times* and the *Standard* all gave ample space to one of Rawlings' greatest critics, the American-based Ghanaian economist George Ayittey, the latter two even provocatively entitling articles 'How to Topple a Military Regime in Africa'.[28] The *Standard* frequently led with aggressive anti-government headlines, and regularly ran a satirical column which was witty, sophisticated and full of classical and biblical allusions, gently ridiculing Rawlings.[29] Reading these newspapers, one finds not only dissemination of official church statements critical of the government, but also negative and even openly contemptuous comment.

Any discussion of the churches' role in Ghana must take account of Ghana's élite.[30] The split between the élite and the populists goes back to Nkrumah, who with his 'Verandah Boys' took power in the place of Danquah's élite. Rawlings took power as the ultimate populist, with nothing but contempt for the bankers, academics, doctors, lawyers, journalists, wealthy farmers and large entrepreneurs whose regimes of cronyism and aggrandisement had brought Ghana to its knees. It is that class to

---

26 *Daily Graphic*, 23 May 1995, 1.

27 *Daily Graphic*, 20 May 1995.

28 *Standard*, 30 Jan-5 Feb 1994, 3; 6-12 Feb 1994, 3; *Methodist Times*, May-June 1994, 3; July-Aug 1994, 3; see Ayittey's other articles in *Methodist Times*, March 1994, 3; Oct 1994, 3; Feb 1995, 3; April 1995, 3; *Christian Messenger*, vol. 7, no. 2, 1994, 7. See George B.N. Ayittey, *Africa Betrayed*, New York: St Martin's Press, 1992.

29 These were the work of Professor P.A.V. Ansah until his death in mid-1993; see *Ghanaian Chronicle*, 28 July 1993.

30 Ghana's élite co-exists with what may be 60% functional illiteracy (*Wall Street Journal*, 26 Jan 1994, 1).

which the higher clergy belong. This has undoubtedly lessened the socio-political influence of their public statements. They come from the same educated classes that Rawlings has demonised as responsible for Ghana's collapse. For their part they look at Rawlings and his disregard for individual liberties, freedom of the press and the right to form political parties and find him sadly wanting. Rawlings, authoritarian by temperament, is not going to be corrected by anyone, much less by members of what he considers an arrogant, self-seeking élite who used politics to plunder the country.[31] Here is a total non-meeting of minds. Rawlings' antipathy to the higher clergy was probably the main reason for his 1994 invitation to Louis Farrakhan, leader of the Nation of Islam, to visit Ghana.[32]

The Christian Council was thoroughly involved in the whole process of return to democratic rule, not just peppering the government with memoranda, but producing discussion material, holding workshops in all major centres, and printing reports and reflections.[33] This activity is

[31] Kwame Ninsin refers to 'the open and rancorous agitation against the government that emanated from the non-state political institutions that the ruling class dominated, namely the Christian Churches, the bar and bench, the independent press, and professional associations': 'The PNDC and the Problem of Legitimacy' in Rothchild (ed.), *Ghana*, 52. Likewise: 'Like many left-wing intellectuals inside Ghana, I treat the churches as an integral component of the established order' (Paul Nugent, *Big Men, Small Boys and Politics in Ghana: Power, Ideology and the Burden of History 1982-1994*, London: Pinter, 1995, 9). For a discussion of the different ways of conceiving human rights, see Jeff Haynes, 'Human Rights and Democracy in Ghana: the Record of the Rawlings Regime', *African Affairs* 90 (1991), 407-25; for the popular as opposed to élite support that Rawlings commands, see Richard Jeffries, 'Urban Popular Attitudes towards the Economic Recovery Programme and the PNDC Government in Ghana', *African Affairs* 91 (1992), 207-26.

[32] Farrakhan celebrated 'Saviour's Day' in Ghana on 6-9 Oct 1994, and was welcomed by Rawlings and government ministers. Many Christian organisations (like Women's Aglow) and even some Muslim groups opposed the visit. Rawlings took the opportunity to chide Christian leaders: 'Those little minds who express thoughtless contempt for any belief different from their own only expose their own bigotry.' Rawlings, at the official opening of the convention, entered into the spirit of things, telling how he had refused to have his last two children baptised if he had to submit to giving them European names. A crowd of 30,000 (including 2,000 visiting African-Americans) gathered in Black Star Square to hear Farrakhan deliver an address, based not on texts from the Koran but on Ezekiel and the parable of the Prodigal Son, on Pan-Africanism and on resisting the pervasive ideology of white supremacy. The address was beamed by satellite to twenty-three venues in America. It was not permitted to be screened in Britain, where Farrakhan has been banned since 1986. The visit to Ghana seemed to have no long-term effects. For the whole incident, see *The Final Call*, 2 Nov 1994.

[33] See *The Church and Ghana's Search for a New Democratic System*, Accra: CCG, 1990; *Christian Council Response to Ghana's Search for a New Democratic System*, Accra: CCG, 1990; *The Nation, the Church and Democracy*, Accra: CCG, 1992; *Report of the Church Leadership Seminar on the Church, Ecumenism and Democracy*, Accra: CCG, 1993; *Report of the Workshop on the Role of Local Councils of Churches in the Promotion of Ecumenism and Democratic Culture in Ghana*, Accra: CCG, 1993; *Report of the*

not restricted to the capital, but reaches out to the regions. The CCG is consultative and participatory, for many of its pronouncements arise from its workshops; in this it is different from the Catholic interventions, which tend to be *de haut en bas*. We meet other Christian Councils in the following chapters, but with this wide-ranging and professional involvement, the CCG is among the most impressive Christian Councils in sub-Saharan Africa. It is worth looking deeper at the theology behind this, most evident in the writing of Robert Aboagye-Mensah, who wrote much of the CCG material as well as a more theological work precisely on the role of the church in democratisation. Its real concerns are: Should the church be involved? Can African tradition contribute anything? Are ethnic considerations a hindrance? These issues are relevant, but it must also be said that his approach is essentially individualised and exemplary; more and more people living good Christian lives will bring about a good society. 'The mission of the church has direct and indirect impact on inward transformation of the individual which results in "social rehabilitation". Social transformation is inevitable because of "wide diffusion of better principles" which leaven society.'[34] Likewise, he writes that in the nineteenth chapter of Leviticus 'all the basic virtues required of the people of God to make a positive impact on social and political structures are highlighted.'[35] There is no reference to anything structural at all; no allusion to economic forces, wider systems, social structures. Aboagye-Mensah's approach is more akin to the Anglican missionary John V. Taylor's in the 1950s rather than to that of the German political theologians Jürgen Moltmann and Johann Baptist Metz or the Peruvian exponent of Liberation Theology Gustavo Gutiérrez.[36]

Ghana's mainline churches are linked to the World Council of Churches

---

Follow-up Workshop on the Church, Ecumenism and Democracy, Accra: CCG 1993 (the last three edited by David Dartey, Robert K. Aboagye-Mensah and B.D. Amoa). See also the study booklet, *Democratic Culture, Constitution and Free and Fair Elections: Study Material for Christians,* Accra: CCG, 1995. The CCG also commissioned two more substantial books: J.N. Kudadjie and R.K. Aboagye-Mensah, *The Christian and National Politics,* Accra: Asempa, 1991; J.N. Kudadjie and R.K. Aboagye-Mensah, *The Christian and Social Conduct,* Accra: Asempa, 1992. Aboagye-Mensah looks at the role of the CCG in 'The Church and Democracy in Africa: the Case of the Christian Council of Ghana' in *Evangel,* summer 1996, 55-9.

[34] Robert K. Aboagye-Mensah, *Mission and Democracy in Africa: the Role of the Church,* Accra: Asempa, 1994, 46. The quotations are from Lamin Sanneh and Livingstone.

[35] *Ibid.,* 133 (see also 52). Also, 'Leviticus 25 offers a Christian alternative to modern forms of structural adjustment programmes' in his 'The Stuctural Adjustment Programmes and the Christian Faith' in *Report on EATWOT's Seminar on the Structural Adjustment Programme and Christian Faith, Friday 8 October 1993,* Accra: CCG, 1993, 32.

[36] John V. Taylor, *Christianity and Politics in Africa,* London: Penguin, 1957. Dickson, himself one of Africa's foremost theologians, comments that there is 'little theological analysis' in this CCG literature ('Church', 273). 'It is difficult to locate anything comparable to liberation

(WCC), but they can hardly be said to represent any WCC Christianity. They are not 'liberal churches' in any Western sense, even to the degree that the Catholic Church so appears in its *Ecclesia in Ghana* document examined above. Most of them could best be described as Evangelical. The Western division between mainline and Evangelical is not so important here. The head of the Evangelical Association of Ghana has remarked: 'I work for two Evangelical groups; I exercise charismatic gifts both privately and publicly; I worship in a Methodist church where I am a lay preacher. I am a typical Ghanaian Evangelical.'[37] In Accra, there is a central ecumenical church, shared jointly by Anglicans, Methodists and Presbyterians. In February 1994 notices were displayed in the foyer advertising a Catholic function, the Campus Crusade training centre, the Sudan Interior Mission's Bible College, and an Anglican crusade billed in the following terms: 'Let Jesus take over your problems; let your business be revived; let your joy be restored; let your marriage be healed, as you become a brand new person in Christ Jesus.' A Bible study that month, led by the Anglican pastor, was quite fundamentalist: 'If you are a wife you know your level, that you are to succumb [*sic*] to your husband.' The sermon that day, delivered by another Anglican, was on the importance of the Bible: 'Let's forget this tradition business. Only Jesus; only Jesus; only Jesus.' In the course of his sermon the Anglican preacher introduced the notion of 'the rapture', an element of premillennialism more normally associated with American fundamentalists. The same Theological eclecticism is evident in the library of the mainline ministerial college, Trinity College near Legon. Throughout 1994 and 1995, among the few new acquisitions on display were books by the American charismatics Charles Swindoll and John Wimber. The Christian Leadership College in Kumasi, an extremely well-run theological college, is operated by the Methodists, Presbyterians and Evangelical Presbyterians; its whole ethos is thoroughly Evangelical. The Akrofi Kristaller

---

theology in the Ghanaian case. The mainstream churches have tended to concentrate on constitutional affairs rather than on trickier issues of social justice' (Nugent, *Big Men*, 9); the same author notes that the demands of Ghana's students and Bar Association and churches were 'virtually interchangeable' (*ibid.*, 196). Emmanuel Martey, *African Theology: Inculturation and Liberation*, Maryknoll: Orbis, 1994, provides an overview of African theology, without any particular application to Ghana; equally general are his articles 'African Theology and Latin American Liberation Theology: Initial Differences within the Context of EATWOT', *Trinity Journal of Churh and Theology* 5, 1&2 (1995), 45-63, and 'The Church's Doctrine of the State: Theological Investigations of Augustine of Hippo, John Calvin and Allan Boesak', *Trinity Journal of Church and Theology* 6, 2 (1996), 26-46. Another Presbyterian lecturer at Trinity College, a self-styled 'Apostle of Nkrumahism' has written several papers of theology in the service of Nkrumahism, even concluding the introduction to one manuscript 'Yes, Come Nkrumah!', an allusion to the conclusion of the New Testament: 'Come Lord Jesus' (Rev 22:20).

[37]   Interview, 9 Feb 1994.

Memorial Centre is a Presbyterian theological centre, yet its significant links are mainly to Evangelical (i.e. non-World Council) bodies; that is the theology it best represents.[38] An Anglican priest writes a book on the prosperity gospel; another writes the preface to a book on witchcraft. *The Christian Messenger*, produced by the Presbyterians, carries speeches of both Emilio Castro, then head of the WCC, and Rev. Bob Jones, America's archetypal fundamentalist. It is sometimes said that this eclecticism shows that Africa is transcending the historical theological divisions of the West. But it could equally indicate that theology does not matter greatly. Everyone in Ghana uses the word evangelisation, but it seems that almost all subscribe to the idea of evangelisation of AD 2000 and Beyond, or the church growth school that underpins it. Both view Muslims as children of Satan. Many Ghanaian Presbyterians and Methodists adopt this position; the WCC to which they are affiliated would not. If Muslims, like Christians, are children of the one God, one particular set of consequences follow; if they are on the contrary the children of Satan, other consequences follow. Few in Ghana seem particularly interested in thinking through that issue.

The Evangelical Presbyterian Church was founded among the Ewe by the Bremen Mission in 1847. All through the 1990s it assumed a very public profile, by dint of internal splits and lawsuits. In the mid-1990s it seemed to have solidified into two almost equal blocs, and the division was hardening. The split began as a challenge to the moderator, who had assumed a third four-year term in office. A group took him to court for contravening the constitution. The church set up a settlement committee to resolve the issue out of court. This committee exposed a constitutional nightmare. It disclosed that since 1974 a Pastors' Union had arrogated to itself the right to present officebearers, because (as the Pastors' Union minutes put it) 'it was felt that pastors could make better nominations of candidates for election than the masses.' This 'most irregular and unconstitutional' procedure had been allowed to continue for years. But besides the constitutional issues, the committee investigated the other grievances behind the split, which it listed as: finances, nepotism (and its opposite, official victimisation), the rise of the charismatic movement and other groups within the church, ethnic tensions, the use of a 'Guidelines Committee' to predetermine discussions at synod, and the *melagbe* theology of the moderator. The committee found much to support many grievances, and noted: 'There is a revolt in the EP Church from sections of both laity and clergy.' It nevertheless recommended that the moderator should complete his third term of office, as it was 'not in the interest of the Church to create a vacuum in administration.'[39] This committee's report is of some interest for us, for it will be noted that

---

[38]   The bi-annual newsletter *Akrofi-Christaller Centre News* (from Box 76, Akropong-Akuapem) discloses these Evangelical networks.

[39]   *Report of the Settlement Committee on the Constitutional Matters of the EP Church*,

several of these issues – the circumventing of the constitution, financial unaccountability, favouritism, ethnic friction and blocking of open discussion – are no different from the issues bedevilling Ghanaian society at large. The presumption that churches with participative democratic structures serve to foster democratic virtues is not borne out here.

However, events overtook attempts to settle out of court. The initial legal ruling in early 1990 was that the moderator's extra term was unconstitutional. However, the high court overturned that decision, saying that the constitution which he was judged to be flouting had in fact lapsed in 1978; as the church legally had no constitution, he could not be in contravention of it. This decision led to a split into two churches, the new one calling itself the 'EP Church of Ghana', the original the 'EP Church, Ghana' (their members generally known as 'ofs' and 'commas' respectively). All through the 1990s the Christian Council and the Bremen Mission tried to heal the breach. In April 1993 a memorandum of understanding was negotiated between the warring factions, which among other things committed both parties to withdraw all lawsuits. This agreement remained a dead letter, and sixteen lawsuits were still outstanding at the end of 1995 (most concerning the ownership of land and buildings, one bearing on the right to use the EPC name). The division was also hardening.

In this split some other things are of interest to us because they will recur below. The first is the use of authority. The EPC was effectively a dictatorship which ignored or bent the constitution, and survived through patronage. Also significant was the rise of charismatic practices – in effect the breakaway group assumed a decidedly more charismatic ethos. Equally significant is the role of external funds. The Bremen Mission had long before taken a decision not to use funding as a means of pressure. However, eventually they ceased to pay the money for many of the church's commitments (dues for Trinity College, for the Christian Council) to the church's headquarters, but paid it directly to the Christian Council. Without these funds, the church nearly collapsed. Equally, the viability of the breakaway group was enhanced when a former regional director of World Vision was able to obtain a salary for breakaway pastors as World Vision

---

Ghana, 1989. *Melagbe* (from Ewe 'I am alive') theology was devised by the Moderator as an attempt to break away from 'alienating and irrelevant Western-oriented Christianity' and to Africanise the gospel (N.K. Dzobo, 'The Relationship between the Gospel and Culture in *Melagbe* Theology', paper delivered at 1986 Africa Consultation, Birmingham, 15-17 April 1986). It had as its main focus the affirmation of abundant life. The Moderator used to wear insignia symbolising this, for example a snake encircling a cross. Although this theology was not the central objection to his remaining Moderator, it became an important issue. The group opposing him commissioned an inquiry which criticise it harshly; see Elom Dovlo, *A Review of Prof. N.K. Dzobo's Melagbe Theology commissioned by the 50th Synod of the Evangelical Presbyterian Church of Ghana*, n.d., available from headquarters. (It is not irrelevant that the author is the son of the former Moderator succeeded by Dzobo.)

workers. The Bremen Mission declined to contribute to the breakaway group, on the grounds that this would legitimise it; however, the Church of Scotland has in a small way funded both.[40]

It is noteworthy that two smaller members of the CCG have also experienced splits in recent years. In 1986 the Baptist Convention split into two factions over the authority of the Convention's President, the attempt to reduce the autonomy of the local churches, the resort to government forces and lawsuits to resolve church problems, and, not least, the rise of charismatic practices within the church. The Southern Baptist Mission, founders of the church, supported (some would say created) the group which fought against the Convention President's arrogation to himself of greater powers, and opposed the growing charismatic ethos. Reconciliation talks took place between 1989 and 1992, and in 1992 unity was restored. Put bluntly, the innovators won and the missionaries lost, and the majority of Baptist churches now seem little different from Pentecostals. Worship at the Calvary Baptist Church in Accra resembles that of any of the new Pentecostal churches mushrooming in the city. It sponsors crusades jointly with Pentecostal churches.

The Evangelical Lutheran Church (founded by the Missouri Synod) split in January 1995 essentially over issues of leadership – the church President had been in charge for nearly twenty years. This split too led to public lawsuits.

New churches

Of the specifically Pentecostal denominations, two are dominant: the Assemblies of God and the Church of Pentecost. Both registered considerable growth over the five years monitored in the GEC's surveys, and the Church of Pentecost now boasts, after the Catholics, the biggest attendance in the country. The CoP has a totally different structure from the churches previously discussed. Because local churches cannot pay for a full-time pastor, each local church is run by a presiding elder. About thirty of these churches fall under a district pastor or overseer. Church authorities claim that the church has thrived on local leaders and the devoted attention of the local people. Others say that one of the reasons for the CoP's growth is its lack of any educational requirements, which enables anyone wanting to begin a church to do so on behalf of the CoP. Certainly, the lack of educational requirements does bring its own problems, which we will return to below. However, I will not analyse the CoP in great detail here.[41] I will approach Ghana's Pentecostal sector through some examples of the newer autonomous churches, whose rise has been

---

40   See *Christian Messenger*, Feb-March 1990, 1; *Daily Graphic*, 16 Feb 1995, 6.

41   For the Church of Pentecost, see Emmanuel Kingsley Larbi, 'The Development of Ghanaian Pentecostalism: a Study in the Appropriation of the Christian Gospel in 20th Century

the most significant development in Ghanaian Christianity in recent years, and which have influenced, I would argue, older churches like the CoP and Assemblies of God.

One of the most high-profile charismatic churches is Christian Action Faith Ministries (CAFM) International, founded in Accra by Nicholas Duncan-Williams, the son of a politician-diplomat, (after his parents separated, he was brought up by his mother, a nurse, who worked in Wa and Bolgatanga). According to Duncan-Williams his youth was rather wild – twice he stowed away on ships to Europe. About 1976, while in hospital after something of a breakdown, he was converted and joined the Church of Pentecost. In that year he went to Nigeria to the Bible College of Benson Idahosa, completing the course in 1978 and founding his own church in 1979. In the space of a few years Duncan-Williams has become a major figure in Ghanaian Christianity.

In 1995 his church claimed about 8,000 members. Its headquarters is still in the middle-class residential area near Accra airport, but services take place at the grand new complex where the church's buses transport members each Sunday. There is only one service on Sunday morning, lasting four or five hours. It is in English, with translation into Ewe and French provided to one side. The service is made up of two main parts: music ('praise and worship') and the sermon. Although choirs and soloists participate, the singing normally involves the entire congregation, led by a Mr Ola Williams, and backed by a ten-piece band. It is exuberant and exhilarating. The songs – normally in English, sometimes in Akan – do not require books, for the words are simple and repetitious, and one hymn can be repeated for up to twenty minutes. Without doubt this music is a significant element in the whole experience. It was noteworthy that at a national thanksgiving service in 1994, sponsored by the Christian Council and Catholics as well as others, it was the CAFM team which led the congregational singing. In Accra it seems widely accepted that for music no other church can rival CAFM.[42]

Membership in the church involves much more than merely attending Sunday services. Everyone is expected to attend the Wednesday teaching service. The church also provides numerous activities, run by its vari-

---

Ghanaian Setting with Particular Reference to the Christ Apostolic Church, the Church of Pentecost and the International Central Gospel Church', Ph.D. thesis, University of Edinburgh, 1995.

[42] The CAFM music team was singled out for its contribution to this service in *Standard*, 6-12 Feb 1994, 8. Similarly, Ola Williams and the team provided the music for Canadian Peter Youngren's Accra crusade, 22-26 Feb 1994. For almost one and a half hours he led the enormous crowd in dancing, handkerchief waving and congas round the field. Such is the appeal of this music that even market women, not part of the crusade but within range of the public address system, were swaying and singing along.

ous departments or ministries – of welfare, youth, children, prayer, outreach to prison or hospital, counselling and music – and the professionals' and women's fellowships. Almost every evening there are meetings: zonal, departmental or sectional, or prayer meetings for specific groups. The most basic activity is the cell ('homecare') group. These Friday meetings are deliberately limited, as near as possible, to about an hour. They take the form of praise and worship for ten minutes, Bible study for thirty minutes, and prayer (including testimonies) for twenty minutes. The leaders and assistants of each of the sixty groups also meet the previous Monday to prepare the Friday meeting.[43] Since January 1993 it has been compulsory to attend these 'homecare' meetings. Failure to attend means, in the words of an official directive, that 'the Premarital Department will not accept you for counselling for marriage in this church. The Pastoral Team will not approve your wedding in the [church]. Outdooring and dedication of your baby will not be carried out by the Pastoral Team ... In case of death of any member of your family or relative the Church will not be under obligation to respond and assist ... Students on campus must demonstrate adequate proof of regular homecare attendance during vacation.'[44]

The church's theology is the Faith Gospel of success, health and wealth. This is spelt out in Duncan-Williams' book, *You are Destined to Succeed!* From Genesis 1: 29-30 we 'find out that God never planned for [us] or any of mankind to have sickness, fear, inferiority, defeat or failure.'[45] In this way he interprets the whole Bible: 'The Word of God is a tree of life that will produce riches, honour, promotion and joy.'[46] In his support he quotes all the high priests of the faith movement: Robert Schuller, Oral Roberts, Casey Treat, John Avanzini, Kenneth Hagin, T.L. Osborn, Paul Yonggi Cho, and his own mentor, Benson Idahosa.[47] Duncan-Williams considers that being created in the image of God (Gen 1: 26) refers to success; he quotes Casey Treat: 'In all truth, God is the most successful Being in the universe. He's the only One who's never had to cut back, lay people off, take out a loan or a lease, and has never rented

---

43   Interview with Homecare Coordinator, 2 March 1994. The material used in the Monday meetings is basically Paul Yonggi Cho's six-volume study guide, and similar material. The coordinator gave as the aims of the groups, to provide evangelism in the community, and to provide care for a growing church.

44   *Action Newsletter*, vol. 1 no. 1 Jan-Mar 1993, 4.

45   Nicholas Duncan-Williams, *You are Destined to Succeed* , Accra: Action Faith, 1990, 102.

46   *Ibid.*, 58.

47   In February 1994, his bookshop stocked only thirty titles. Five were by John Avanzini, six were by Lester Sumrall, and of the nineteen others, three were by Reinhard Bonnke and one each by Paul Yonggi Cho, Maurice Cerullo, Watchman Nee and Robert Schuller.

anything. God is successful.'[48] His understanding is that prosperity
inevitably accrues from the inexorable application of spiritual laws; he
quotes John Avanzini ('an acclaimed authority on Biblical Economics')
in support: 'God did not predetermine who would be rich and who
would be poor. He simply created His spiritual laws and freely gave them
to everyone. Every person then has a choice – to implement the laws of
poverty, or to implement God's spiritual laws of prosperity.'[49] Duncan-
Williams holds himself up as an example. He interprets Joshua 1: 8 in
this way: 'God implied that if Joshua would do these three things,
success and prosperity would be guaranteed ... What God told Joshua
is what He told me. What worked for Joshua, has worked equally
well for me. It will produce the same result in your life if you follow His
word.'[50]

'The traditional and orthodox churches we grew up in held many views
which were diametrically opposed to God's word. [...] They preach a
doctrine which says in essence – poverty promotes humility. But you all
know this is not true. [...] The missionaries erred tragically by not teaching the Africans God's Word and laws regarding sowing and reaping.'
This is perhaps understandable; missionaries were given all their resources
by churches and Christians overseas, so they felt they could not preach
'the full counsel of God regarding prosperity through giving, sowing and
reaping.' Also, Africans considered every white man affluent, and 'this
atmosphere produced guilt in the minds of those who have tried to preach
the full gospel. [...] Thank God, He has called us to declare his full counsel to our generation. I preach and teach prosperity like any other doctrine of the Bible.'[51] This last section of the book is shaped and given
some bite by the public opprobrium directed at Duncan-Williams for allegedly accepting a Mercedes from someone reputed to be a drug dealer.[52]
He defends owning a Mercedes by arguing that it is through his full gospel that so many of his flock have come to riches: 'Society provides the
best for its leaders to show them forth as examples ... God help me to be
a good and worthy example of the standards of God's word.'[53] He concludes: 'It does not matter what you think: God's Word stands. I believe
that God has raised me as a leader and example to my generation about
His goodness, mercy and prosperity.'[54]

A similar church is the International Central Gospel Church (ICGC),

48   Duncan-Williams, *You are Destined*, 72.
49   *Ibid.*, 139.
50   *Ibid.*, 74.
51   *Ibid.*, 145-50.
52   *Ghanaian Chronicle*, 3-9 May 1993, 3.
53   Duncan-Williams, *You are Destined*, 144.
54   *Ibid.*, 155-56.

founded by Mensa Otabil, also in Accra. Otabil, a former Anglican, set up ICGC in February 1984. In its earliest days particularly, it was distinguished for its evangelism. Those attending the second service would conduct a coordinated evangelism programme beforehand; those attending the first service would conduct a similar exercise afterwards. Through such methods, Otabil claims, the church increased in April 1987 from 700 to 1,500 in one week. By 1994 it drew about 2,200 to its first service and nearly as many to its second. Those who could not fit inside the rented hall, an overflow of about 1,200, participated with the help of closed-circuit TV outside.

Here again music is a crucial part of the service. Again the singing is mainly in English, thoroughly prepared, and involves the total participation of the congregation. There is always a short time for a choir, soloists, mime or drama – all of considerable quality. The whole service is remarkably professional: the logistical feats of organising back-to-back services for such numbers, and of taking offerings during them, are accomplished by armies of stylishly uniformed ushers. The church's myriad activities are advertised, financial matters are disclosed, including the takings of the previous Sunday (in March 1994 nearly 1.5 million cedis, then about US$1,800). The service remains extremely personal; newcomers are welcomed, at various times members of the congregation are asked to greet or hug those close by, individuals like recently engaged couples are introduced, ministers have birthday greetings sung to them. ICGC also has numerous ministries – for children, youth, students, 'family enrichment', the annual camp meeting, publishing and recording, missions and church planting – and an almost endless round of activities. One cannot become a member without following a course which terminates in a graduation ceremony. It, too, is built up on cell ('Covenant Family') groups, 115 of them by February 1994.

This is another Faith Gospel church, or recognisably comes from that stable. For example, Otabil began his sermon on 2 May 1993 by saying: 'God blesses us according to our deposits. If you haven't deposited anything, you have no right to ask for anything. [...] People think that you should give so that the church has money. No. The main purpose is that you enter into a covenant so the God of Abraham, Isaac and Jacob will meet all your needs.'[55]

Otabil's book *Enjoying the Blessings of Abraham* exemplifies this Faith Gospel. He writes: 'When you go through life and you have done all that is naturally needful, like having all your pay packet spent at the end of the first week of the month, what would you do? That is when you have to let the blessing of Abraham operate in your life and live by divine

---

[55]   The service on 6 February 1994 began with an hour of singing songs like 'The Lord can make your way prosperous', 'Jesus is the Winner Man', and 'I'm a winner'.

provision. [...] The natural is limited but God is unlimited and he will bring divine provision your way to pay for your school fees. He will bring divine provision to help you settle that account, to pay that debt, to get that shoe, shirt, car, land.'[56] It is simply not possible 'for the person that operates under the blessing of Abraham to get poorer.'[57] Otabil builds on the standard biblical texts of the prosperity gospel: Gen 22: 13-14; Gen 26: 12-24; Dt 28: 15-22; Gal 3: 13-14.

However, one does not have to attend very often before one notices real differences between Otabil and Duncan-Williams. Otabil's message is one of success: 'Every problem is temporary, every problem can be solved. [...] God did not create you with failure in mind, but with success.' But his is a different path to success. For Duncan-Williams success is achieved inexorably through the immutable laws of sowing and reaping. For Otabil it is reached through self-confidence, pride, determination, motivation, discipline, application, courage – and by skills and techniques that Otabil sets out to teach. Otabil has established what he calls 'The Winners' Club', which has seminars in Accra's Novotel (one of the city's most expensive hotels, in early 1994 charging $160 a night). Announcing the next meeting of the Winners' Club, a church official stated that it was for 'highly motivated and dynamic achievers in fields of business, law, commerce, accountancy, who seek to use biblical and secular principles to affect society – it is for anyone who believes he wants to be someone, that is an achiever.' An analysis of the talks Otabil gave to the Winners' Club in 1993 shows that among the key concepts are vision and imagination. One whole talk was centred round the idea of 'script'. A script is what determines the actions of all the players in a drama. Life is a drama, but normally the script has been written by others, and the unthinking person just plays out his role according to the script prepared for him. The secret is to take control of one's own life, and write one's own script for one's own circumstances. This involves rising above the dictates of tradition and the ancestors: 'We must be radical and new.' Equally central to his thinking is the notion of choice. The accepted wisdom that 'Every action has a reaction' must be changed to 'Between every action and every reaction there is a choice.' We can choose our reaction by using our imagination. And we must use the gift of choice to rise above any constraints of circumstances. Otabil finished one talk with these words: 'I hope by this short time we've had together that you have been challenged enough to desire a change, to rewrite the script by which you've been acting your life, to explore new areas in your life for your own business, and to make a decision to choose your reactions.'

---

[56]   Mensa Otabil, *Enjoying the Blessings of Abraham*, Accra: Altar International, 1992, 19-20. Altar International is Otabil's own imprint.

[57]   *Ibid.*, 24.

The same message of his sermons and lectures is found in Otabil's book *Four Laws of Productivity: God's Foundation for Living.* The book is an exhortation to self-improvement. Otabil finds four laws in God's first command to men: 'Be fruitful, and multiply, and replenish the earth and subdue it' (Gen 1: 28). In a somewhat forced exegesis, Otabil's theme is: 'If you believe God, no matter the colour of your skin, the country you are from, or the economy of your country or the world, you can still believe for a big God to give you a big ability to achieve big things for his glory.'[58] His roots are obviously in the faith movement; he takes as his starting point the Faith Gospel's key concept of 'seed', but he changes this to mean a talent within every person. Since all have some talent, all can succeed. One must find one's own special talent, protect it, then use it. One must use it with diligence, without envy or fear, with self-confidence, with courage to go beyond tradition or the average or the norm; with readiness to learn, analyse, invest, study. One must not hoard, must manage well, control expansion, and retain overall responsibility. 'God has put much into us, so do not underestimate, undervalue, underuse what you have. Do not cry, pity, or fear using what you do have.'[59] Aim high, for 'Apart from your tombstone, you should have a legacy to leave to the world.'[60] The book is basically a 'how to succeed' manual, written to foster personal effort.

This message strikes a very responsive chord among Accra's educated, English-speaking, upwardly-mobile youth. There *are* opportunities to be grasped in Ghana, now that the World Bank and the IMF have adopted it as their own. For those in a position to avail themselves of these opportunities and resolved to rise above their circumstances, this church encourages ambitions and goals, gives direction and discipline, fuels the desire to get ahead. Not surprisingly, then, the congregation at ICGC is slightly different from that at Duncan-Williams' CAFM. They seem younger, overwhelmingly between eighteen and thirty-five. They also seem better educated; there is no need for translation here, for all are familiar with English. They also appear more middle-class, or would-be middle-class, as the advertisements in Otabil's church magazine suggest – for evening wear, world travel, foreign exchange bureaux, computers and TV advertising.[61]

There is another important element in Otabil's theology. He never misses a chance to instil black pride. He has written a book called *Beyond the Rivers of Ethiopia: A Biblical Revelation on God's Purpose*

---

[58] Mensa Otabil, *Four Laws of Productivity: God's Foundation for Living* , Accra: Altar International, 1992, 134.

[59] *Ibid.,* 62.

[60] *Ibid.,* 96.

[61] *Green Pastures,* 27 Feb 1994, 8.

for the Black Race. Otabil is convinced that the Bible has been misinter-
preted by whites. He returns to the Bible to solve the question: 'Did God
ever use black people? Are we on God's agenda?'[62] He confronts the
question: 'Is the black race cursed?' (Gen 9: 25). He answers no, Ham
was blessed (Gen 9: 1). Numbers 23: 20 shows that such a blessing cannot be reversed. Cush the son of Ham was never cursed; he received a
double blessing as firstborn. 'He was father of the black races of the
world, and he was never cursed. Full stop.'[63] After the flood, the leaders
of the world were Cushites; Nimrod (a black) was 'the first governmen-
tal leader and motivator mentioned after the flood'.[64] Otabil admits that
Abraham's Cushite children were disinherited, but shows how they were
subsequently restored to their inheritance, for they remained faithful. One
of them, Jethro, was a priest before Aaron was. It was Jethro who taught
Moses all that he needed to lead the Israelites from Egypt. He knew all the
law before Moses; in fact, 'He was law-giver to Moses.'[65] It was this same
Jethro who invented grassroots organising: 'When you understand that Jethro
was of the Cushite or black race then it makes nonsense of the assumption
that black people cannot govern themselves. The nation of Israel and for
that matter all nations owe this black priest an honour for being the ves-
sel through whom principles of local government administration were
established.'[66] Hobab, Jethro's son, by acting as a scout for Israel, won
back their inheritance for Abraham's Cushite children (Num 10: 32).

One part of the inheritance of Judah (Judah means 'Praise') is this
ministry of praise, which involves music and dance; this is why blacks
everywhere have rhythm naturally.[67] The New Testament equally
shows blacks in key roles. The Magi were blacks (Mt 2: 1-12), Simon
of Cyrene carried Christ's cross to Calvary (Mt 27: 32), and the first
to hear the gospel was the Ethiopian eunuch (Acts 8: 26-40). Of the
three who commissioned Paul and Barnabas, two were black (Acts 13:
1-3), and Paul reported back to them after each of his journeys. So
much for the idea that mission boards must be made up of whites!
Blacks must take control of their own churches, and stop subscribing to white stereotypes of them. This is the age of the black church;
the time of the whites is gone. God will bring this about miraculously.[68]

[62] Mensa Otabil, *Beyond the Rivers of Ethiopia: a Biblical Revelation on God's Purpose
for the Black Race*, Accra: Altar International, 1992, 18. The cover carries this
endorsement from the Dean of Students, University of Ghana: 'A remarkable venture in
liberation theology that can lift the soul and leave it buoyant'.

[63] *Ibid.,* 38.
[64] *Ibid.,* 39.
[65] *Ibid.,* 48-9.
[66] *Ibid.,* 51.
[67] *Ibid.,* 50.
[68] *Ibid.,* 87.

Otabil's attempt to re-evaluate the role and worth of blacks has enormous appeal.[69]

There are countless other new charismatic churches throughout the country. The best known in Accra after Otabil's and Duncan-Williams' are Redemption Hour Faith Ministry, International Bible Worship Centre, Victory Bible Church, Faith Evangelical Church and Living Waters Ministry, but all regional centres have them too. Such churches might have begun in the urban areas, and indeed it is conditions in the cities that explain their rise.[70] However, although the distinction between urban and rural Pentecostalism is important and must be borne in mind, it should not be taken too far, because these churches have massive evangelisation programmes, and consciously target the rural areas. And these pastors and ministries are rapidly becoming almost paradigmatic. Otabil and Duncan-Williams are the most high-profile and successful exponents of the new wave. Other pastors, especially those of struggling churches all over the country, even within the CoP and the Assemblies of God, look to them as exemplars and models. Both Otabil and Duncan-Williams have daughter churches around the country, but in many ways the branches are incidental. The church leaders exert their greatest influence through networks of pastors which are not formally linked. Duncan-Williams has his Council of Charismatic Ministers, which is attempting to establish regional branches,[71] and Otabil has the Charismatic Ministers' Network. It is widely said in Ghana that that these two networks exist merely because neither Otabil nor Duncan-Williams is prepared to cede overall hegemony to the other. However, the view taken here is that each has an agenda sufficiently different from the other to make an independent stance understandable.[72] Through such networks these pastors do not exercise the obvious formal authority of, say, an Anglican archbishop, but in the circumstances of Ghana today their influence may be even greater.

It is obvious that throughout the 1980s all these churches could be characterised as Faith Gospel churches. In this they were recognisably of the same stripe as so many other churches in Africa – indeed, around

---

[69] 'The motivation to lift up the image of the black man' is said to be 'the thrust of [Otabil's] message' in *Green Pastures,* 27 Feb 1994, 7. This church newsletter and his group notes group notes in the 'Biblical Black Heritage' section, (available from Box 7933 Accra North) is peppered with words like leadership, potential, self-confidence, destiny, self-image, dignity, identity, purpose, positive, determination and talent.

[70] For the range of churches possible, see Margaret Peil with K.A. Opoku, 'The Development and Practice of Religion in an Accra Suburb', *JRA* 24 (1994), 198-227.

[71] Duncan-Williams also belongs to the Ghana Pentecostal Council, founded in 1981 (although it grew out of the Ghana Evangelical Fellowship formed in August 1971).

[72] An important network to which both Otabil and Duncan-Williams belong is the Charismatic Churches Football Association, comprising fifteen major charismatic churches which, besides its regular competition, on 5 March 1994 held a gala competition at Accra sports

the world from Latin America to the former Eastern bloc. Basically the message was that faith will bring you health, success, plenty and power.[73] The same phrases were used ('Believing on Jesus for', 'seed faith'), the same biblical texts were utilised (Dt 28-30; Phil 4: 19; 3 Jn 2; Mal 3: 8-11; Mk 10: 29-30; Mk 11: 23-24), the same stress was laid on tithing as the prerequisite for prosperity and on the automatic application of spiritual laws (of faith and giving). Indeed, the same combination of faith gospel and fundraising techniques has been widely observable in Ghana. On 4 June 1995 the speaker at CAFM called forward everyone prepared to 'stand alongside' Duncan-Williams to the extent of delivering 50,000 cedis to his office by 5 p.m. the next day. About 150 came forward, their names were taken, and they were promised God's abundant return on their investment. Then the same speaker asked all those who would like to have a copy of his recent book but who could not afford to buy it to come forward. About 200 moved to the front. One might have thought that he was about to donate them a copy, but no; he then asked all those in the congregation who could afford to buy the book for another to stand, promising an appropriate reward for thus 'sowing into the lives of others'. Two hundred who could afford the book then joined the 200 who could not, and they went off in pairs to buy it, while the rest of the congregation joined in praising God. In this way, the speaker sold 200 extra copies of his book in the one service.

When we consider the direct political involvement of these new churches, we see an enormous difference from Ghana's mainline churches which we examined above. Some would teach that a Christian has no concern with politics. But it is more likely that they subscribe to a political theology expressed in terms like the following.

The Bible reveals that God Himself is the greatest politician ... He gives positions to whom He wills [Dan 4: 25]. If His people are ready, God will prefer to give [power] to them. If they are not, He will give it to somebody [else] because there must be a leader anyway. Normally, when God is dealing with a rebellious people, He gives them a leader who will execute His judgement upon them. But when He is dealing with a repentant people He gives them a considerate leader who becomes His instrument of peace and mercy. I believe it is God's pleasure to give us the Kingdom now so as to show us His prosperity and mercy.[74]

The evangelist Owusu Tabiri expresses the same point: 'Ghana will not experience the Glory of God until the leader becomes a Christian. I

Stadium for Help Age Ghana. This league is a sign of the vitality and self-confidence of the new charismatic churches.

[73] Power is a very Ghanaian preoccupation. Guinness, the Irish brewers, advertise in Ghana in print and on TV as 'Guinness – the Power', which they do not in Ireland or Britain.

[74] *Watchman*, 5/1991, 8. Much the same is expressed in the editorial of another Christian newspaper, *Integrity*, 23 July 1994, 2.

have asked the Lord to intervene to give us [in the next election] his own choice.'[75] This idea that a 'God-fearing leader brings his people prosperity' – basically the theme of the Books of Kings – leaves these churches wide open to cooptation by a leader who claims to be God-fearing.

Soon after the 1992 elections Rawlings called on the Christian churches to hold a service of thanksgiving. The mainline churches refused to oblige, seeing this as an attempt by Rawlings to manipulate them into giving him their blessing. The Pentecostal churches, however, willingly conducted such a service, on 31 January 1993, praying for and over Rawlings – in effect, legitimising him.[76] All branches of Christianity – Protestant, Catholic, Pentecostal and Independent – held a national thanksgiving service on 30 January 1994 to mark the first anniversary of the inauguration of the Fourth Republic, attended by President Rawlings, his wife, the Vice-President, the cabinet, parliamentarians, the chief justice, judges, diplomats, chiefs, and an estimated crowd of 21,000. The churchmen leading the service were the Catholic Archbishop and the Anglican Bishop of Accra – and Duncan-Williams, whose equal billing with the two prelates would have been unthinkable even a few years before. The mainline churches were determined that this would be a thanksgiving for a year's democracy and not a celebration of President Rawlings. The Anglican bishop in his sermon, and the Catholic archbishop in his prayers, did not even mention Rawlings by name. In his sermon the Anglican bishop acknowledged 'a certain measure of success in our experiment in democracy', but attributed the stability to adherence to the constitution, stating that 'as long as we respect and obey it to the letter, we are bound to succeed.' The Catholic archbishop, in his prayers, spoke of respect for the constitution and law, of justice and mercy and service, and of 'the preservation of peace and the promotion of happiness', the 'increase of industry, sobriety and useful knowledge', praying for 'the blessings of equal liberty and justice'. Duncan-Williams, however, sounded a very different note: 'The leadership needs to be commended for turning to God and allowing the Christian community to thank God,' he proclaimed. 'There is an invisible hand over the nation holding back bloodshed. [...] Pray that this invisible hand may remain on our leaders.' The link between President Rawlings, Ghana's relative stability and God's favour was a theme which Rawlings himself gladly developed.[77] Understandably, the state-owned *Daily Graphic* gave Duncan-Williams more

---

[75]   Interview, 21 May 1995.

[76]   *Afroscope*, March 1993, 14.

[77]   For this ceremony see *Daily Graphic*, 31 Jan 1994, 8-9; *Ghanaian Times*, 31 Jan 1994, 1; *Statesman*, 13 Feb 1994, 6; *Christian Messenger*, vol. 7 no. 2 1994, 1 and 5 (Bishop Thompson's sermon is printed in full on p. 5); *Watchman*, 3/94, 1; *Ghanaian Democrat*, 7-13 Feb 1994, 5; *Standard*, 6-12 Feb 1994, 1. If most press comment was critical, one Christian newspaper had the headline: 'President Gives God Glory' (*Watchman*, 3/4, 1).

coverage than the other speakers, and the state-owned television in its extensive coverage (6 Feb 1994) also gave him considerable exposure. Some saw the whole ceremony as Rawlings' manipulating the churches into legitimising him. The *Free Press* protested that 'the National Day of Thanksgiving was meant to serve Rawlings not God', and criticised the mainline churchmen for being 'dragged by the nose into an unholy affair' and savaged their 'veritable culture of sycophancy'.[78] Closer analysis would show that the mainline churchmen studiously avoided sycophancy; it was Duncan-Williams who did not.

In 1995 the national thanksgiving service was held at Koforidua. It was Duncan-Williams who preached the sermon, against the sin of jealousy. The government press reported: 'He said those in authority should not fear anything if they believe that God put them in their places.'[79] The independent press was very critical. One commentator referred to the 'travesty in Koforidua called the Day of Prayer'.[80] Another paper, under the headline 'NDC Rally on Church Platform', claimed that it was 'organised solely to boost and glorify the image of Mr Rawlings and his wife', that the funding and organising was all done by the NDC, and that most attend such services grudgingly 'apart from die-hard sympathisers of the NDC, and some pentecostal and charismatic churches who in an apparent struggle for recognition would show enthusiasm about any such national programme.'[81] Another paper in an editorial railed at the Pentecostals for 'providing a thanksgiving service for Rawlings and his family who have survived another year of plundering the nation.' It deplored the 'thousands of Pentecostals – all innocent victims of political chicanery, ... hoodwinked by hired agents disguised as church leaders'. They do not 'see the abyss into which they are being misled by satanic agents in pastors' robes, ... by brokers hiding in pastors' garb.' The editorial concluded: 'Now we invoke the curse of God upon the leaders of the Pentecostal churches responsible for such blasphemy.'[82]

The uncritically supportive attitude of Duncan-Williams and other pastors towards the Rawlings regime is not to be explained through any conspiracy, but through something far more pragmatic – the desire for the respectability conferred by government recognition, and for the material rewards a well-disposed President can dispense.[83] But it is also to be linked with their particular theology. This situation, however, is not

78 *Free Press*, 25 Feb-3 Mar 1994, 4.

79 *Daily Graphic*, 3 April 1995, 1.

80 *Statesman*, 14 May, 1995, 6.

81 *Voice*, 23 March-2 April 1995, 1.

82 *Free Press*, 31 March-6 April 1995, 2. One commentator hinted that Duncan-Williams was being subtle, attacking Rawlings for envy and jealousy (*Chronicle*, 24-26 April 1995,3).

83 In this it is very similar to the attitude towards government historically displayed by the

uniform, nor is it static. Otabil has begun to introduce very different considerations. In a key address at his camp-meeting for the New Year of 1994, he spoke on 1 Sam 13: 16-22, a passage which describes how the Philistines kept the Israelites in subjection by ensuring that the only black-smiths in the region were Philistines; as a result the Israelites had to go to the Philistines every time they needed ploughs or utensils sharpened, and when they went to war they had neither swords nor spears. Otabil developed this as a metaphor for the Third World. 'When I read this verse I looked at the world and I saw it happening plain on the world arena.' The powers of the West play such 'political and industrial games' with Africa, ensuring that 'we will always be running but never catch up.' 'I get amused when we talk of breaking the yoke of colonialism and still use the blacksmith called IMF or World Bank to sharpen our tools to go and kill him.' He lambasts 'these World Bank consultants, these white people'. He insists 'our political leaders are selling us for generations yet to come', incurring debts that cannot be paid. Africans have to go to the West for everything they need to run Africa: 'We see the sons and daughters of Africa roaming the streets of Europe crying for crumbs from the master's table. [...] In our generation let us develop blacksmiths, people who will sharpen us, set us ablaze, equip us right here in our land.' This vision is not only for Ghana, but for 'the blacks in America [who] are totally lost. It is not only for Africa, it's about black people everywhere. [...] My ambition is that a generation will be prepared to fulfil a destiny. God is asking for blacksmiths in Israel!' There was very little narrowly spiritual content in this lecture; it was a cry for political and economic self-determination. Otabil seemed aware of this: 'You want me to speak about how Jesus heals and delivers. You know all that. Don't only know that, know other things too....' The word 'blacksmith' has since become almost a catchphrase summing up the mission of Otabil's church. Otabil is stronger on the general picture than on details of how it might be achieved, but this crusade for Africans to take control of their own political and economic lives is something he can be expected to pursue. Given the charismatic networks and Otabil's status as a role model for many pastors, this thinking can be expected to spread.

In accounting for the growth of these churches, there is no single explanation; there are several relevant factors. It is obvious that these are youth churches – as it is equally obvious that the congregations of the mainline churches are correspondingly older. In the mainline churches leadership positions are the preserve of the older generation, who cling to them and try to keep the youth in their place. To some degree these

---

non-mainline churches in Ghana (John S. Pobee, *Religion and Politics in Ghana*, Accra: Asempa, 1991, 80-98; Gyimah-Boadi, 'Associational Life', 128-31) and by the classic AICs generally; see Sundkler, *Zulu Zion*, 89.

charismatic churches can be seen as the young creating their own space where they can exercise some responsibility. But there is another sense in which these new charismatic churches are youth churches, one which does not imply any oppositional stance towards the older generation: these churches address the preoccupations of youth. Consider the most obvious issue, that of marriage. The young who attend Otabil's church are beautifully dressed, groomed and made-up. The preacher's first words on coming to the microphone on 3 May 1993 were 'My! you look beautiful this morning! Turn to the person next to you and say, "You look beautiful this morning." ' At the evening Bible Study two days later the preacher told members to hold the hand of the person alongside, to look into his or her eyes and repeat: 'You are nice. You look nice. You are in the image of God. You were made for love.' It is obvious on Sunday mornings that some of the girls have been up for hours styling their hair. Young people looking for a partner and one with similar goals, ambitions and aspirations who will help them get ahead receive considerable help here. In a city like Accra, where traditional ways of arranging marriages are breaking down, the church fulfils an important role. It oversees this whole procedure. Youth must register for 'singles activities' (these are closely supervised; it was announced at one Sunday service that at beach parties girls must wear t-shirts over swimming costumes). They must take courses on courtship and relationships. Once friendships are formed, the pastors must be notified so that appropriate advice can be given. One cannot be married in the church without going through all preliminaries. Couples married in the church on Saturday dress in their wedding finery the following day, and process out at the end of the service. This matchmaking function is openly admitted: 'The Ministry foresees future healthy marriages beginning from Christ-centered partnership before marriage and has thus begun fostering these.'[84] One of Otabil's assistant pastors, when asked about the glamorous appearance of the young women in the church, replied: 'It is part of our message. For those who are not married we teach them that life is not finished [i.e. they can still find a husband]. They have to look their best; they feel better in themselves.'[85] Similar attitudes are evident at other such churches. As the resident pastor at Tamale's World Miracle Bible Church (in a remarkable inversion of 1 Cor 11: 13) remarked, 'We don't want our girls to wear headscarves to church. If they wear headscarves, how will the young men see their beauty and love them?' He went on to say that he had met his wife through the church, as had one of the other pastors.[86]

Another factor to explain the rise of these churches relates to their

[84]   *Green Pastures*, no. 1, 1992, 7.
[85]   Interview with assistant pastor, 5 May 1993.
[86]   Interview, 20 Feb 1994.

worship. Most of these churches begin with a long session of 'praise and worship', much of which is participatory, and which is exhilarating in a way that the mainline churches cannot match. The contrast is particularly evident in Methodist and Anglican churches, where it is possible not to sing any hymns composed this century. Naturally some of the older generation, graduates of the college at Mfantsipim for example, who owe everything to their Methodist upbringing, prefer this kind of service, but such fierce denominational loyalty means little to the young (and significantly, over half Ghana's population are under twenty years of age). But it is not just that charismatic worship is more lively. In these socio-economic circumstances, these churches are creating a new expression of culture. Most young people have no money to go to night clubs, discos or concerts for their entertainment. The churches provide a new forum for a parallel music scene (one Christian magazine actually has a section entitled 'Christian Showbusiness').

This usually works in the following way. Every Sunday, in the major centres, at least one church will stage an evening which is part concert, part service. Performing will be its own best choirs or soloists, along with four or five of the new professional gospel artists. The professionals are paid, but they too in introducing their numbers invariably do a little preaching. Some of these are merely very good; most are superb. Their cassettes are well known, and they have only to begin and the audience/congregation are on their feet dancing. Some of this gospel music is Western, or heavily Western-influenced, like soul or rap, and performed in English, but much is genuinely Ghanaian, in the local Fanti, Ga or Twi languages, or even pidgin. The rhythms are local. This 'gospel' has become a significant expression of Ghanaian culture, not in any fossilised sense but in a contemporary form, in contact with the modern world and the West. This gospel music is widely played on radio, sold in markets and commented on in magazines and newspapers, and indeed it underpins an entire recording business. This is a remarkable social and cultural phenomenon, and these new churches are an integral part of it. In the face of this the deficiencies of the mainline churches are obvious, as was starkly evident at the elaborate ceremony consecrating the five new Catholic bishops in 1995. The stage was far from the congregation. Little of the ritual could actually be seen. The sound system was poor. Conventional hymns were sung, with little participation; only at the offertory did things liven up and in any way approximate to the vibrant participation of any normal charismatic service. All those in the congregation that day – as opposed to those religious professionals who planned the service – would have had experience of the lively gospel music of crusades and revivals. Long before the end people were drifting away.

This new sector of Christianity is distinguished for its media awareness and its use of technology. The first thing a new church will save for is its public address system. In a country like Ghana, quite an industry has grown up importing these systems, which are almost exclusively for new churches. One Bible school in Ghana, in its prospectus, lists among courses like 'Faith', 'Bible Knowledge', and 'Demonology', one labelled 'Electronics'; it is judged just as important for a pastor to know how to operate his public address system as about faith. Almost immediately, a new church starts recording and selling the pastor's sermons. After audio cassettes, they graduate to video cassettes. There can be few charismatic services in Ghana's major centres which are not now videoed.

There are a whole range of socio-economic factors that help explain the rise of these churches. We have mentioned the message of ambition, achievement and opportunity, directly geared to the upwardly mobile. There are opportunities to be grasped in Ghana. Those who are in a position to avail themselves of these opportunities here receive support and have their determination increased, incentives raised and ambition sharpened. Indeed, churchmen like Otabil regularly present themselves as entrepreneurs who have developed a successful enterprise, and thus as models for enterprising businessmen.

But socio-economic factors are important in another way. There is a whole range of economic opportunity that has been opened up by this charismatic explosion. Most obviously, these churches need a team of pastors, many of them ten or twenty. An entire new industry of Bible colleges has developed. The Ghana Evangelism Committee, the conduit of church growth thinking into Ghana, notes that 3,262 churches were planted in Ghana between 1986 and 1992. That means 3,262 pastors, or the creation of 3,262 new jobs over the five-year period, in a country where according to some estimates 300,000 jobs had been cut through government retrenchment. And the growth is expected to increase. The Baptist Convention had 300 Churches in 1990 and is planning for 2,000 by the year 2000; this means that the Baptists alone will create 1,700 new jobs in the decade. Sometimes one catches a glimpse of these dynamics in testimonies – like the Liberian studying at the Christian Service College in Kumasi who spoke of his leaving a Liberian refugee camp and finding it impossible to find a job: 'And then someone told me about this college.' All these new churches have building programmes; indeed both Otabil and Duncan-Williams have enormous structures on the way to completion. Otabil has begun building a university. All churches buy public address systems and video and recording equipment, which need servicing. Many buy vans or buses which transport members on Sundays but during the week function as income-generating projects; they are readily recognisable by the wording painted on the sides. All this economic activity is generated by churches. These churches, in contrast to the mainline ones, all insist on tithing, and some of the resulting income is circulated in relief projects. Besides churches, private individuals can cash in on this Christian revival too. On public transport going any distance, it is normal for someone to stand up at the front preaching, and then ask for a contribution. Others distribute literature on buses and ask for a donation. There is quite a trade in Christian literature, with entrepreneurs following crusades and church functions with their cases of Christian books and magazines.

There is an international dimension to much of this church activity. The economic collapse of Africa has meant the withdrawal from the continent of many multinationals. Despite the World Bank's and IMF's drive for private investment, it does not seem that this process has been reversed in the case of Ghana (apart from notable exceptions like Ashanti Goldfields). Thus linking with overseas institutions and benefiting from such contacts is harder than ever. Moreover, in the 1990s Western governments have become particularly restrictive in issuing visas even to those who can afford to travel, for they know full well that a good number of those leaving Africa have no intention of ever returning. For this reason, a visitor is now likely to be asked not so much for financial assistance to visit the West, but for a letter of invitation that could be used to influence an embassy. In the face of this increasing marginalisation, churches provide one of the remaining arenas for international contacts. This, presumably, is the reason for the word 'International' or 'World' in the titles of so many churches. Hints of this international preoccupation can be glimpsed everywhere in Ghana (even Pepsodent advertises its toothpaste in Ghana as 'New Pepsodent International', which it does not need to do in the West). Internationalism is particularly emphasised in these churches. A preacher is introduced as 'just flown in today', or 'leaving soon' for the United States or Britain. Bible schools list among their teachers anyone from overseas who has visited them, and give ordination certificates or accreditation from institutions in Britain or the United States. It is a particularly desirable feature that a church has branches in Britain, Germany or the United States. The well-known evangelist Owusu Tabiri frequently mentions that he has preached in the United States, Britain, Canada, Germany, France and the Netherlands, stresses his assistance to whites, and calls for testimonies from people who have themselves been overseas. One crusade preacher, in recounting the marvels God has worked through his ministry, frequently ends with: 'He [or she] was completely healed and has now gone overseas.' This final phrase indicates a special mark of God's favour.

Much of this international linking has an economic side. Visiting evangelists like Angley, Youngren or Newberry need committees to organise their crusades, and they pay in hard currency all the costs incurred in preparation. But as a more illustrative example, consider Bishop Samuel Addae of Shiloh Church in Kumasi. He was a Presbyterian lay preacher who while teaching physics in Nigeria met a Bishop Ramsey of Shiloh United Church, London. Bishop Ramsey invited Addae to London, where he did a one-year Bible course. After his return to Ghana he founded his church, a branch of Bishop Ramsey's Shiloh United Church, in 1985, and by 1995 it had grown to 400 members. One of his council members went to America, where he met Dr G.L.Williams of New Directions Ministries, North Carolina, and wrote back to Addae encouraging him to invite Williams to Ghana. Williams has come each year since for a convention, paying most of the funds for all the pastors who care to come. Addae explained to Williams his scheme to educate the independent pastors of the area. Williams put him in touch with a Bible Training Centre for Pastors (BTCP) scheme, which donates packages of materials to be sold in Addae's Bible school, and lets the local director set his own fees and keep the profits. In 1995 Addae had twenty-five students in the morning and twenty-one in the afternoon on this course, each paying 100,000 cedis ($100) for the year's materials and tuition. From fees Addae was thus collecting nearly $4,000, out of which he had to pay customs dues on the materials, find his teachers, and provide desks, chairs and so on, but the remainder provided an income which is not negligible in today's Ghana. Such a system has proved very popular. Addae's is only one centre in Ghana using this BTCP scheme; between 1994 and June 1996, the number of Bible schools operating this system increased from two to twenty-three.[87]

Note how these international links are established. Often the contact is initiated from overseas. For example, a British evangelist writes in July 1994 to Christian Hope Ministry outside Kumasi: 'This letter is an exploratory note to seek guidance as to a possible ministry visit to your ministry.' He goes on to list his activities in other countries, and furnishes testimonials. Christian Hope Ministry readily agrees to the visit, because the visitor will foot all bills, and, as they readily admit, a visitor can draw crowds and ensure some profit which it can put towards its extensive building programme. Often trips are to be arranged, paid for by international church growth bodies, to conventions like the Pan-African Christian Leadership Assembly in Nairobi in 1994, or the one in Seoul in May 1995. Individual contacts can lead to grants – like computers for Addae Mensah (see below) donated by Kingsley Fletcher, a prominent Caribbean evangelist. Study at an overseas Bible college can create contacts that bring support in later years. It is obvious that this kind of Christianity has spawned entire new areas of economic activity.

[87]   In mid-1996, BTCP had 104 centres in twelve African countries; details available from Dr D. Mock, 745 Peachtree St NE, Atlanta, GA 30365.

When added to the jobs made available in the development work of the Catholic and mainline Protestant churches, there is some truth in the claim that Africa's real 'parallel economy' is now that created by Christian activity.

The kind of Christianity associated with the new charismatic churches is fostered particularly through new parachurch organisations. The most obvious example of this is the Full Gospel Businessmen's Fellowship International (FGBMFI). In Ghana, the FGBMFI is more evident than in any other African country. Indeed Ghana now has an international vice-president overseeing the work in Africa. This is Kwabena Darko who, through his poultry farms, is one of Ghana's most successful business-men, and was even the New Independence Party's presidential candidate in 1992 (when he proved unable to deliver a 'Christian vote' in the way some expected).[88] Darko readily talks of an outbreak of disease among his chickens, which, when he laid his hands on them and prayed over them, God healed.[89] He preaches that the same success is open to any believing businessman. The FGBMFI has a large following in Ghana, and boasts over 100 chapters and 3,500 members. It also has its affiliate, Women's Aglow, of which Darko's wife Christiana is the national direc-tor for West Africa and serves on the international board. These organi-sations utilise lively charismatic worship at their breakfasts and dinners, and preach success and prosperity. They merit attention for the role they play as further conduits in channelling charismatic ideas into mainline churches, from which the majority of those who attend the breakfasts and dinners have come.

Consider this 1994 FGBMFI breakfast at Accra's exclusive Golden Tulip hotel. At a top table sat lawyers, finance directors, factory owners, consultants and a retired colonel. The main speaker gave his testimony for over an hour. He explained his rise and rise; from university, where he studied architecture and law, through broadcasting to a general managership in a multinational, to consultancy in advertising, marketing and public relations. The gist of his talk was: 'Promotion doesn't come from the East or the West; it comes from the Lord.' And, 'As the Lord did unto me he will do unto you.' 'It has not been by my effort but by the shed blood of the Lord.' God was a talisman more powerful than any rival. Indeed at one stage he said, 'Before you leave here today make sure you have Jesus in your pocket, in your heart.' He gave examples of Jesus getting him visas to the United States and Britain. It should not too readily be presumed that this message of Jesus bringing riches is par-ticularly African, for it is also propagated by the FGBMFI universally. The founder, Demos Shakarian, tells in his autobiography how God made

---

[88]   For his story see Kwabena Darko, 'Piercing the Darkness', *Voice*, no. 6, 1994, 3-8.
[89]   Interview, 19 May 1995.

him the biggest dairyman in the world.[90] What God did for Shakarian in California with cattle he has done for Darko in Ghana with chickens.

This charismatic explosion has taken place at the expense of the other churches. This is particularly true of the classical AICs, which seem to be in headlong retreat before the charismatic advance, as is evident from the figures of the Ghana Evangelism Committee's surveys. Attendance at the Apostles Revelation Society decreased by 17% between 1986 and 1991; over the same period the Church of the Lord family of churches decreased by 21%, the Musama Disco Christo Church by 17%, the Cherubim and Seraphim by 24%, the African Faith Tabernacle by 23%, and the Twelve Apostles Church by 22%. This reinforces some of the observations above, because the reasons adduced for the advance of the charismatic churches are also the areas where the AICs are weakest. The educated and enterprising youth have not been accommodated by the power structures of the AICs; in fact, in many instances the normally rather uneducated leadership would prefer to drive out the educated youth than have them mount a challenge, thus really signing their own death warrant. The AICs provide few links with the outside world. Nor are they engaged in redefining Ghana's contemporary culture. The 'African culture' that these AICs championed in the 1950s and 1960s is no longer at issue; as the head of the Musama Disco Christo Church said at the Good News Training Institute in 1995, '90% of what my grandfather [the church's founder] wanted to do, even the Methodists are now doing.' In this he was referring to using the vernacular, dancing, drums, and so on.[91] The Good News Training Institute just outside Accra (since 1995 the Good News Theological College and Seminary) was set up with Mennonite and Lutheran support to educate AIC pastors. Lecturers there claim that the AICs, forced to take stock especially in the area of theological education, have now stabilised and halted their decline. Whether they can claw back any headway in the face of the charismatic onslaught remains to be seen. Even the AIC pastors appear increasingly to be trying to model themselves on Otabil, Duncan-Williams and the like. By a process of natural selection they are forced to transform themselves to survive.

But the charismatic explosion has not only spawned a raft of new churches and decimated the AICs. It has had an enormous influence on the mainline churches too, over and above taking their members. As has been said, in one form or other the impact of charismatic thinking split the Baptist Convention in two between 1984 and 1990, and was a key

---

[90]   D. Shakarian as told to J. and E. Sherrill, *The Happiest People on Earth: the Long-awaited Personal Story of Demos Shakarian*, Old Tappan, NJ: Spire Books, 1975.

[91]   Interview with head of Good News Training Institute, 2 June 1995.

factor in splitting the EP church permanently.[92] It has impinged on the others too. The Anglicans and the Methodists have both tried to incorporate charismatic elements into their services. The Methodists in some parishes even have special youth services, and the youth will invite the charismatic gospel artists to their youth festivals. But it is the Catholics and the Presbyterians who have been influenced the most. The Catholics had a Charismatic Renewal Movement of over 1,000 groups in 1996.[93] The Catholics in Ghana even stage crusades almost indistinguishable from Evangelical revivals. A priest will call for clap, wave, or shout offerings to Jesus. Some priests conduct healing sessions.[94] At the 1995 pre-Pentecost novena devotions in Accra, the ceremony ended each night with the recitation of a prayer applying the most un-Catholic of concepts, the blood-covering of Jesus: 'I now cover myself with the Blood of Jesus Christ. I cover my mind, body, soul and spirit with the Blood of Jesus. I especially cover my thoughts, emotions, reactions and my attitude. I cover my spouse, all my children and their Christian spouses, all my grandchildren and the seed of all future grandchildren in the Precious Blood of Jesus. I cover my home, my property and all my possessions with the Blood of Jesus.' The attempts to accommodate charismatic pressures within the mainline churches cannot be said to have succeeded; for the most part they are inadequate and do not compare with the real thing available in the charismatic churches, and have not stopped the haemorrhage.

[92]   See Birgit Meyer, 'Translating the Devil: An African Appropriation of Pietist Protestantism: the Case of the Ewe in Southeastern Ghana 1847-1992', Ph.D. thesis, Amsterdam, 1995.

[93]   Information available in their newsletter *Charisnewsletter*, and their quarterly *New Breath of the Spirit*, and in an explanatory booklet, *History of the Catholic Charismatic Renewal in Ghana* (1986), all available from headquarters, Box 870, Kumasi.

[94]   A missionary priest wrote to the Catholic *Standard* deploring the healing activities of some priests, insisting that healing practices 'must conform with Catholic doctrine', and that 'self-made rites and self-claimed "gifts" can never have the support of the church.' A Ghanaian priest quickly replied that 'Until the local church comes out with some guide lines about healing services, "self-made rites" will continue to be popular with the faithful. [...] Until then, some of our faithful will continue to drift to the other Christian denominations ... or attend their healing services and Bible classes, consult spiritualists, mallams and fetish priests'; see *Standard*, 27 June-3 July 1994, 4. Also *ibid.*, 11-17 July 1994, 4. The Ghanaian priest has tried to promote awareness of these issues; see Henry Frempong, 'Helping Catholics Remain in the Church', *Standard*, 17-23 Oct 1993, 5; *ibid.*, 24-30 Oct 1993, 2 and 6. See also Henry Frempong, 'Resisting the Powers of Darkness', *New Breath of the Spirit*, no. 23, 12-14. Some of the issues involved here are touched on in Abamfo O. Atiemo, *The Rise of the Charismatic Movement in the Mainline Churches in Ghana*, Accra: Asempa, 1993; Cephas Omenyo, 'The Charismatic Renewal Movement in Ghana', *Pneuma* 16, 2 (1994), 169-85; Cephas Omenyo, 'The Charismatic Renewal Movement within the Mainline Churches: the Case of the Bible Study and Prayer Group of the Presbyterian Church of Ghana', M.Phil. thesis, Legon, 1994.

Deliverance

This charismatic explosion has been complicated by the development of the 'deliverance phenomenon'. The world-view behind this underlies much traditional thinking, but in the 1990s this thinking has ceased to be latent, and has assumed a remarkable prominence. The basic idea of deliverance is that a Christian's progress and advance can be blocked by demons who maintain some power over him, in spite of his coming to Christ. The Christian may have no idea of the cause of the hindrance, and it may be through no fault of his own that he is under the sway of a particular demon. It often takes a special man of God to diagnose and then bind and cast out this demon. Thus, in the mind of many of its exponents, this deliverance is a third stage, beyond being born again and speaking in tongues.[95] A favourite text is Jn 11: 1-44, in which Lazarus is called forth to life, but is still bound and must be 'let go' (Jn 11: 44). There is some difference of opinion as to whether it is a strictly 'necessary' stage.[96] Some seem to say yes, but Ghana's most celebrated deliverance exponent Owusu Tabiri cites in explanation another biblical passage, that of Dives and Lazarus (Lk 16: 19-31): in that story Lazarus reaches heaven, but Abraham, who receives him, had been blessed and powerful on earth (Gen 24: 1) whereas Lazarus had led a miserable life. All Christians are meant to be like Abraham; deliverance will transform the earthly life of a Lazarus into that of an Abraham.

A clear and systematic exposition of this deliverance thinking is to be found in a popular book, *The Package: Salvation, Healing and Deliverance,* written by Aaron Vuha, a member of the Evangelical Presbyterian Church of Ghana. Demons are former angels, disembodied beings, who when they come to earth 'find themselves rivers, mountains, rocks, trees, humans etc. to dwell in'.[97] We are most conscious of what is happening in this spirit world when we are asleep, in dreams. Activities of demons prevent humans from enjoying the abundant life that Jesus came to give. Some effects of their activities are phobias, complexes, allergies, chronic diseases, repeated hospitalisation, repeated miscarriages, non-achievement in life, emotional excesses, and strikingly odd behaviour. In discussing the work of demons Vuha gives special place to the inability to contract or maintain a happy marriage. The cause of this is a prior 'spiritual marriage' to a 'spiritual spouse', which is often manifested through dreams of sexual intercourse with this person. These spiritual marriages are often contracted when people are dedicated to family gods, stools or

---

95 M. Addae Mensah, in *Step*, 4, 5 (1992), 12.

96 Abamfo Atiemo, 'Deliverance in the Charismatic Churches in Ghana', *Trinity Journal of Church and Theology* 4, 2 (1994-5), 41.

97 Aaron K. Vuha, *The Package: Salvation, Healing and Deliverance*, Accra: EP Church of Ghana, 1993 , 36.

shrines. Spiritual marriages are detected by a lack of desire for marriage, the cessation of monthly periods, impotence, the end of a marriage (a spiritual spouse can kill rivals), childlessness, or an unsatisfactory sexual life. Demons enter human beings through 'doorways' or openings, such as ancestral gods, traumatic childhood experiences (such as sexual abuse or an accident), curses (not only on an individual, but on one's family or clan), covenants (agreements 'made on behalf of a family or clan members with shrines or gods or stools are binding on all members whether they actively took part or not'), involvement in 'wrong churches' (which include any using candles, incense and so on), Eastern cults, sex ('Satan has agents around seeking to deposit demons in people. Sex with such an agent lets in demons'), sin, names (demons associated with names 'make good' the meanings of the names), pornography, addiction, and contaminated objects (one should avoid the rings, earrings, clothes and shoes of others). One can expel demons oneself, or they can be cast out by another. The demons must first be identified (by discovering the names of shrines or stools, by noting effects in one's life like sickness or poverty, by noting the doorways opened to them), and then Vuha gives an elaborate procedure for casting them out, involving exhaling slowly. Sometimes this will be accompanied by yawning, coughing, spitting, vomiting or convulsions. Even a born-again believer is never perfectly delivered: 'No matter your spiritual standing, you are under constant attack and demons often make incursions into you only to be thrown out', although (confusingly) Vuha can also write that 'demons cannot come back unless you positively invite them back or you go back into the very sins you confessed which amounts to reopening the doors.'[98] The book is full of testimonies of casting out demons of childishness, divorce, sleep, sadness and poverty.

As an illustration of a specialised deliverance ministry, consider the Christian Hope Ministry, just outside Kumasi. This is not a church, and all activity ceases on Saturday morning after Friday's all-night session. Here about 5-10,000 people come every week, with about 2,000 attending the Thursday afternoon deliverance session. Those who come each day are divided into four groups according to whether their problems are to do with marriage, sickness, general (normally financial) constraints, or deliverance. Those with marital problems fill in a separate questionnaire. All others fill in a questionnaire which, after personal details and Christian affiliation, asks the petitioners whether they have attended a spiritual or Aladura church, 'palmist, fetish priest, card reader, dwarf worship or witch doctor'; have ever been given any ring, amulet or talisman for protection; have been bathed by a prophet or prophetess, malam or fetish priest; have had any incisions, and how many, on what part of

98   *Ibid.*, 82 and 95.

the body; have undergone puberty rites; have slept with anyone they have never seen afterwards; maintain a stool or seat or shrine in the family; have been adopted by or named after any river, god or tree; have made any covenant with a 'secret society, transcendental group, lodge, Buddhism, Krishna'; have received beads, ornaments or chains from anyone; experience excessive or useless dreams or nightmares; experience 'invisible presence'; easily lose personal property or money; hear voices; feel heaviness or a burning sensation; have had sex with any family member; have had an abortion; have had an 'enema with any native medicine' from a fetish priest; have applied nasal drops or concoctions from a malam or fetish priest; have made a vow to any object besides God; have taken a spiritual bath with the blood of a dove, sheep or animal; have had sex with any spiritual adviser; have excessive menstrual pains, or are addicted to alcohol, drugs, sleep or food. The answers to this questionnaire enable the full-time team of sixteen to establish whether the problem is demonic and, if so, to identify the demon.[99] In a special building with a sunken floor the patients (overwhelmingly women) lie fully clothed on tables, and those involved in the deliverance ministry, amid praying and shouting and often physical pummelling, drive out the demon.

This deliverance thinking has led since about 1993 to the emergence of institutions which promote and cater for the needs it addresses. The first of these institutions is the deliverance or prayer camp. Five major camps have appeared, all of them run by lay members of the Church of Pentecost: they are at Edumfa (Cape Coast), Sunyani, Sefwi and (in Accra) Macedonia and Canaan.[100] Macedonia began in March 1993, and by mid 1995 it held four days of revival near the beginning of each month, which about 10,000 attended. Also, every Saturday about 5,000, overwhelmingly women, attended a deliverance session. At these sessions women came out to the front where either they told or, more usually, had drawn from them the nature of the demonic blockage afflicting them. These sessions could be quite physical, with women speaking in the name of some demon and rushing around the open space, sometimes pursued by a team of about twenty fit men who physically restrained them. The evangelist often indulged in almost lighthearted banter with the spirits,

---

99 Similar questionnaires, with only minor variations, are used by Gospel Light International Church, and the Fountain of Life International Church in Accra.

100 Bethel and Macedonia both produce magazines of testimonies: *Bethel News* and *Macedonia News*. The testimonies tell of cures from barrenness and all kinds of sickness, obtaining visas and green cards, and often involve dreams, Muslims, fetish priests or false churches. *Bethel News* places great stress on overseas visits, and selling cassettes and raising money, and one can sense the tension between the camp and the Church of Pentecost. For the importance of overseas connections for these camps, see Rijk A. van Dijk, 'From Camp to Encompassment: Discourses of Trans-subjectivity in the Ghanaian Pentecostal Diaspora', *JRA*, 27 (1997), 138-59.

speaking through the women, before casting them out. Besides these camps, special deliverance ministries have appeared, such as the Christian Hope Ministry outside Kumasi described above. These institutions have grown up to cater for this development; others have changed their nature to cater for it. For example, crusades have moved from occasions for making a decision for Christ, or a combination of that and healing sessions, to fully-fledged deliverance rituals. In Koforidua, Evangelist Tabiri's May 1995 crusade was advertised as deliverance. The charismatic churches have also in general moved in this direction – even those which initially resisted deliverance. Thus by 1995 both Otabil and Duncan-Williams had deliverance teams alongside all the other groups that characterise their churches. Deliverance thinking has now come to dominate many of these churches, reshaping the Faith Gospel, which throughout the 1980s was their characteristic theology.

The origins of this outbreak of deliverance are complex. Matthew Addae-Mensah, the pastor of Gospel Light International Church in Accra, claims that he brought this thinking to Ghana in 1986 after attending Idahosa's Bible school in Benin City, Nigeria, and then pastoring churches for three years in Nigeria. When he returned to Ghana he began a deliverance outreach, which attracted considerable criticism from most, including Otabil and Duncan-Williams. There was quite a split in charismatic-Pentecostal Christianity. It was a visit to Ghana by Florida's Derek Prince that 'salvaged my reputation'. Many began to say, after Prince had conducted a seminar on deliverance: 'Now we understand what that young man is saying.' Addae-Mensah had 'feared persecution', and he told people coming to him to stay in their own churches. It was almost by accident that he founded his church. He had been operating his deliverance ministry in the Achimota forest on the northern outskirts of Accra, and crowds would be gathering at 2 a.m. awaiting his arrival at 7 a.m. This was a time of political insecurity, and the security services became alarmed; it was also the time when the government was trying to get churches to register, so mainly to protect himself he officially established a church and registered it. Addae-Mensah has photo albums of people delivered through his ministry: a deaconess whose father had been an occultist and who was tormented at times of worship for thirteen years; a pastor with an uncontrollable sex urge, caused by 'a lady who planted a seducing spirit in his food'; another pastor troubled by a demon also entering through food, which gave him a chronic cardiac problem; a man whose wife was possessed by a witchcraft spirit and spurned the pastor's offer of deliverance (she 'went home and died within three days, and the young man is now a big success in America'); a woman pregnant for four years, who gave birth two weeks after deliverance. He talks of demons operating in his own family, which have caused none of the males to live beyond the age of fifty and caused every woman to have at least one divorce.

Addae-Mensah speaks both of Nigeria and Derek Prince; both influences are important. There has been a spate of Nigerian literature on demons, the most famous individual book being Emmanuel Eni's *Delivered from the Power of Darkness*. In this Eni, who is from the Assemblies of God, recounts how he dropped out of school and took up with a young woman, ostensibly an accountant in a bank but who at night could change into a boa constrictor or make her body totally transparent like cellophane. One day, after she had gone to work, he searched the flat and found refrigerators full of skulls and skeletons. He realised then that she was from the spirit world. She eventually drew him down into this life, and soon he was with her plucking out the eyes of children, slaughtering and eating them. He was taken to India for further initiation. He became part of the spirit world and could travel at will to any part of the globe. One day a beautiful woman took him to a city beneath the sea. She revealed herself as the Queen of the Coast, and gave him powers to change into all kinds of animals, including hippopotamuses, boa constrictors or crocodiles. In this city under the sea scientists were working in laboratories developing all sorts of inventions like flashy cars to distract men's attention from God – under the sea, too, was a special TV which revealed the whereabouts of born-again Christians. When he returned to Lagos, the Queen of the Coast gave him assignments to kill various people, which he did in the company of other people who lived mainly in the sea (that is to say that they were really from the underwater spirit world). He even had a conference with Lucifer himself, and was given more powers to change into a woman or beast or bird or cat. He also used instruments for detecting born-again Christians. As an agent of Satan he killed people by causing natural disasters like the collapse of buildings or road accidents. He performed his task so well that Lucifer made him chairman of wizards. Eni describes in detail the difficulties he had in attacking born-again Christians, for so long as a Christian 'remains in God and does not get entangled in the affairs of this life', the devil can never touch him. In 1985 Jesus appeared to Eni and saved him. Satan's agents battled to take him back and tempted him with bribes, but with God's help he remained faithful.[101]

---

[101] Emmanuel Eni, *Delivered from the Powers of Darkness*, Ibadan: Scripture Union, 1987. Among the African books and booklets on demons widely available in Ghana are Kaniaki and Mukendi, *Snatched from Satan's Claws: an Amazing Deliverance by Christ*, Nairobi: Enkei Media Services, 1991; Symons Onyango, *Set Free from Demons: a Testimony to the Power of God to Deliver the Demon Possessed*, Nairobi: Evangel, 1979; Victoria Eto, *Exposition on Water Spirits*, Warri: Shalom Christian Mission, 1988; E.O. Omoobajesu, *My Experience in the Darkness of this World before Jesus Saved Me*, Agege (Lagos State): Omoobajesu World Outreach, n.d.; Zacharias Tanee Fomum, *Deliverance from Demons*, Yaounde: IGH (Box 6090, Yaounde), n.d.; Kaluy Abosi, *'Born Twice': From Demonism to*

However, as Addae Mensah indicated in acknowledging his debt to Derek Prince, that is not the full story. We noted the resistance he experienced until Derek Prince came to Ghana on a lecture tour; only then were others prepared to accept deliverance – in the words Addae Mensah attributed to them: 'Now we understand what that young man is saying.' It was the same with Tabiri. When I asked him if his preoccupation with spirits and demons was derived from local African conceptions, he demurred, saying he got it all from American authors Derek Prince, Marilyn Hickey and Roberts Liardon, whose books he promptly fetched from his bedroom: 'I got the foundation from them. I develop it in the light of experience, as I go round, to African conditions.'[102] The dynamic here is perhaps similar to that which Cox has detected in Korea: 'Korean Pentecostalism has become a powerful vehicle with which hundreds of thousands of people who might be embarrassed to engage in the "old-fashioned" or possibly "superstitious" practice of shamanic exorcism can now do it within the generous ambience of a certifiably up-to-date religion, one that came from the most up-to-date of all countries, the USA.'[103] A similar process is suggested by Max Assimeng, Professor of Sociology at Legon. 'Things are truer if un-African, so we quote Americans. It is traditional, but projected in modern dress. The more foreign, the more serious, true, powerful it is.'[104]

In fact, it is noteworthy that many Ghanaian church leaders, including Addae-Mensah, reject Eni as dangerous. When Joseph Anaba, pastor of Broken Yoke Foundation in Bolgatanga, told me that his particular charism was demonology, I asked, encouraging him to elaborate, whether his demonology was something like Eni's. I was surprised by the force and speed of his reaction: 'No, I don't have that attitude so much.' He

Christianity, Benin City: Joint Heirs Publications, [1990]; John Cudjoe-Mensah, *Satan and his Tricks*, Kumasi: St Mary's, 1989; Sunday Adekola, *Understanding Demonology*, Ibadan: Scripture Union, 1993; Victoria Eto, *How I Served Satan Until Jesus Christ Delivered Me: a True Account of My Twentyone Years Experience as an Agent of Darkness and of my Deliverance by the Powerful Arm of God in Christ Jesus*, Warri: Shalom Christian Mission, 1981; Heaven U. Heaven, *How to Cast out Demons or Evil Spirits: a Practical Guide to Deliverance*, Lagos: Heaven and Blessings Books, 1985; Iyke Nathan Uzora, *Occult Grand Master Now in Christ*, Benin City: Osabu, 1993; Nathaniel O. Adekoba, *Fundamentals of Deliverance Ministry*, Ikeja: Highways Publications, n.d.

102 Interview, 21 May 1995. Marilyn Hickey, *Break the Generation Curse*, Denver, CO: Marilyn Hickey Ministries, 1988; Roberts Liardon, *Breaking Controlling Powers*, Tulsa: Harrison House, 1987. Tabiri also brought Kwaku Dua-Agyeman, *Covenant Curses and Cure*, n. p., 1994. The latter had been an Anglican priest, but in 1995 was with Rhema Temple, Kumasi.

103 Cox, *Fire*, 225.

104 Interview, 26 May 1995. He continued: 'In the eyes of many, "African Christianity" is offensive, a denigration of the real thing. Not many want it.' See also J.M. Assimeng, *Salvation, Social Crisis and the Human Condition*, Accra: Ghana Universities Press, 1995.

criticised the general Nigerian tendency to attribute everything to demons, and by name; understandably, his training as a pharmacist made him less ready to attribute every illness to demons. He listed the people who best expressed his understanding of demons as the Americans Lester Sumrall, Kenneth Hagin and Gordon Lindsay. Not long afterwards I had the opportunity to ask the resident pastor at World Miracle Bible Church in Tamale whether his demonology was anything like Eni's. Again, a rather similar answer was forthcoming: 'No, some of those Nigerian books are not well based, frightening. Some are so weird and exaggerated. We don't take them as true, especially Nigerian books. We just concentrate on Frank Hammond's book.'[105] Even Addae-Mensah himself distances himself from Eni as 'extreme'.[106] American charismatic Christianity has a strand which gives enormous prominence to demonic beings. This has been evident in Paretti's best-selling novels, Wagner's *Territorial Spirits* and in books like Rebecca Brown's – at the beginning of 1995 Rebecca Brown and the equally demonic Mark I. Bubeck were the fastest-selling authors in Accra's Evangelical Challenge Bookshop.[107] American demonology also gives great stress to the sexual, and to child murders and cannibalism. These two strands – the African and the Western – reinforce one another, even feed off one another, and in certain circles tend to coalesce.[108]

We outlined above Vuha's 1993 book *The Package*. At the end of 1994 Vuha published a sequel, *Covenants and Curses: Why God does not Intervene?*, to address the question why deliverance does not solve all medical, emotional, spiritual and financial problems. The answer is

---

[105] Frank and Ida Mae Hammond, *Pigs in the Parlor: a Practical Guide to Deliverance*, Kirkwood, MI: Impact Books, 1973.

[106] Interview, 30 May 1995.

[107] Atiemo, 'Deliverance', 39. For further illustrations see Gifford, 'Ghana's Charismatic Churches', 241-65.

[108] Thus a Christian magazine, in advertising a forthcoming conference, could categorise Rebecca Brown and Eni as the same thing. It states simply: 'The evangelist Emmanuel Eni and Rebecca Brown, *who were Satanists before converting to Christ*, are scheduled to attend.' Among the Western books and booklets on demons widely available in Ghana are Frank E. Paretti, *This Present Darkness*, Wheaton, IL: Crossway, 1986; Frank E. Paretti, *Piercing the Darkness*, Westchester: Crossway, 1989; Rebecca Brown, *He Came to Set the Captives Free*, Springdale, PA: Whitaker, 1989; Rebecca Brown, *Prepare for War*, Springdale, PA: Whitaker, 1990; Bill Subritsky, *Demons Defeated*, Chichester: Sovereign World, 1986; Lester Sumrall, *Three Habitations of Devils*, South Bend: LeSea Publications, 1989; Stuart Gramenz, *Who are God's Guerrillas?*, Chichester: Sovereign World, 1988; Stephen Bransford, *High Places*, Wheaton, IL: Crossway, 1991; Elbert Willis, *Exposing the Devil's Work*, Lafayette, LA: Fill the Gap Publications, n.d.; John Osteen, *Pulling Down Strongholds*, Houston, TX: John Osteen Ministries, 1972; Frank and Ida Mae Hammond, *Pigs in the Parlor*; Lester Sumrall, *Alien Entities: Beings from Beyond*, South Bend: LeSea Publications, 1984; and the pamphlets of Kenneth Hagin and Gordon Lindsay.

that covenants and vows 'seemingly tie up God's hands'.[109] Someone vowed to a demon (even by parents, or before becoming a Christian) would be affected: 'God is powerful enough to set [the person] free but would not, since the demons have a "legal" right to oppress him'.[110] Likewise blessings and curses affect us, according to Dt 28-30. 'Those who qualify for curses cannot escape or avoid them. They would suffer setbacks, failure, no reproduction, defeat in all spheres of life, a life that can simply be described as a life of frustration.'[111] People come under curses through things like inheritance (up to the fourth generation, Ex 20: 5), worship of idols, murder, wrong worship, sexual sin, divorce, robbing God (not paying tithes, Mal 3: 8-10) and cursing Israel (Gen 12: 1-3). Vuha writes: 'Nobody comes under a curse unless he/she deserves it', yet (confusingly) also writes: 'He is also under a curse, if he belongs to a nation that is under a curse, or lives in an area or home whose inhabitants have been cursed.'[112] The way out is to examine one's life: 'If there is a curse or if there is a covenant entered into against the will of God, or if there is a broken covenant or if a bad seed is sown or if any of the above is inherited from ancestors, unless they are revoked or cancelled they will each run their full course of consequences.'[113] Curses or covenants must be identified and revoked, and Vuha gives prayers which achieve this.[114] The theological ideas contained here can also be found in, for example, Derek Prince.[115]

Ghana's parachurch institutions have played a large role in spreading this teaching. Scripture Union organises two separate programmes every year to train people and to enable those involved in deliverance ministry to share experiences. Their first in 1984 attracted about fifty people. In 1992 eighty-four teams participated in the programme at Aburi, and in the same year 1,244 participated in their Kumasi meeting.[116] The FGBMFI has begun to promote this too. At a meeting at the Labadi Beach Hotel

[109] A.K. Vuha, *Covenants and Curses: Why God does not Intervene*, Accra: EP Church of Ghana (1994), 3.

[110] *Ibid.*, 31.

[111] *Ibid.*, 54.

[112] *Ibid.*, 55 and 57.

[113] *Ibid.*, 67.

[114] This second book contains much anti-Catholic material, proving that 'Mary' and the saints are spirits that need exorcising. They enter at Catholic baptism or on Ash Wednesday, or through anointing with oil (79-83). Another Ghanaian book which illustrates the whole deliverance phenomenon, but written by a Catholic, the founder of Christian Hope Ministry outside Kumasi (discussed above), is Francis Akwaboah, *Bewitched*, London: Christian Hope, 1994.

[115] Derek Prince, *Blessing or Curse: You Can Choose*, Milton Keynes: Word Publishing, 1990.

[116] Atiemo, 'Deliverance', 39; Paulina Kumah (ed.), *Twenty Years of Spiritual Warfare: the Story of the Scripture Union Prayer Warriors' Ministry*, Accra: Scripture Union, 1994.

on 27 May 1995 ($212 a night at that time), a pastor of one of the new deliverance churches was the guest speaker. He had begun his church in 1992 and by mid-1995 had over 1,000 members. He found spirits responsible for all kinds of rejection, including 'societal machinery of rejection', by which he meant continually being passed over for a top position: 'Find the root cause; there must be a spiritual reason.' He could identify spirits responsible for recurring conditions in families: if everyone is poor (he assured his listeners 'Today you can reverse that'); if many are divorced; if many of the women have difficulty in childbearing; if many in the family have mental or emotional illnesses; if there has been a history of suicide. The bulk of his address was on curses. He insisted that when a superior person (a pastor, teacher, husband or parent) pronounced something over you, 'it will come to pass, unless you walk under the blood of Jesus.' He cited as biblical evidence the story of Jacob and Laban; Jacob's innocent statement that the guilty person 'shall not live' (Gen 31: 31) had to be fulfilled, and thus Rachel had to die in childbirth. In many of his examples spirits came to enjoy sexual intercourse with women at night, thus causing them to be barren or to have difficulty in bearing children. In another, an eight-year old boy was paralysed and prayer could achieve nothing. Then the pastor had asked the boy's name. He asked his mother what the name meant. Even the mother had no idea. 'I discovered it referred to a spirit, and cast it out. Then I told him to walk, and he is perfect now.'

It is possible to view the rise of deliverance theology as a response to or mutation in the face of the shortfall of faith preaching. Faith preaching in so many cases cannot be said to have worked. Faith did not bring about all that was promised. Deliverance still allows the emphasis on success, as long as something more than faith is added. The FGBMFI speaker just referred to actually quoted the standard Faith Gospel text, Dt 30: 28, but this time added a crucial rider. Yes, he said, there are some curses that are purely a result of your choice (according to the Faith Gospel, you *choose* whether to receive blessing or curse.) But he went on to say that there is another set of curses that comes not a result of choice but from other sources, namely demonic influences. It has not been difficult to combine the two strands. A visiting speaker at Duncan-Williams' church did just that. He spent the first part of his workshop dealing with deliverance, but then, with all demonic influences destroyed, his hearers could 'speak things into existence'. Speaking things into existence is pure Faith Gospel.[117] Again, this deliverance gospel has influenced the mainline churches, as the Faith Gospel did before it. A ministry like Christian Hope

---

[117] Among the persons he claimed to help by deliverance and faith was one 'going to the embassy this week to get a visa. God will go before you. What they demanded from you before, they will forget. [Cheering.] Speak it into existence.'

near Kumasi receives letters from all the mainline churches inviting the team to conduct deliverance sessions for them. A June 1994 letter from a Kumasi Methodist church invited the team to 'help revive our church' by running four all-night sessions and three revival weeks for them; the letter ended with a reference to Acts 16: 9, 'Come to Macedonia and help us.' Another letter from a superintendent of a circuit invited them to run a 'deliverance and healing service' at a camp meeting which 5,000 were expected to attend. The ministry receives regular letters from Catholic churches inviting them to run deliverance session or revivals. The ministry says it will accommodate all requests except those from 'spiritual churches' (AICs) or Jehovah's Witnesses (though requests from the latter are not very likely). The Catholic Charismatic Renewal in its 1995 pre-Pentecost novena in the Holy Spirit Cathedral, Accra, ended each night with a prayer from which I have already quoted. It continues:

I bind [Satan] and all his demons and I pull down every satanic stronghold over me and my family in Jesus' name. I strike them dumb and strip them of their power to manifest against me and my family in any way. [...] I ask you, Father God, to assign four warring angels to come against every demon that has been assigned to my family and me today.

This novena ended with an all-night deliverance session. Between 1 a.m. and 3 a.m. on the Saturday morning a young local priest conducted a deliverance session largely indistinguishable from those at Bethel or Macedonia prayer camps. The cathedral was full with about 1,000 people. The books on sale outside were the same as were on sale at the deliverance camps.[118] Surrounded by his deliverance team of about thirty, he called those afflicted to the altar. Among the categories of afflicted persons, he mentioned those whose parents had taken them to a fetish priest for protection. 'Don't be ashamed. It's not your fault, your parents took you. It is not your fault. You didn't know.' He told them: 'Come out now, don't pray, don't speak, every power, every spirit, I bind you.' He repeated endlessly the phrases: 'Break loose, Every power, out, out, I instruct you, break lose, by the blood of Jesus, the blood, I touch you. Destroy them. Be subject. The power ... Break them in Jesus' name.' He breathed over those afflicted. Other spirits he mentioned by name were those which prevented women from marrying by coming at night in sexual dreams; spirits that continually spirited money away, even when it was safely hidden; and demons inciting to fornication. Each group could be around the altar for about thirty minutes, while he shouted his invocations

---

[118] Included was a book by a Nigerian Catholic priest and seminary lecturer, Stephen Uche Njoku, *Curses: Effects and Release*, Enugu: Christian Living Publications, 1993. His acknowledgement to Derek Prince and his wife is significant: 'Their video tape recording on "Release from the Curse" provided the initial tonic I needed to write this book. Their format helped me to put together more clearly what I had been doing in an unclear manner' (iv).

and walked among them laying on hands. Many women would fall at his touch, and they would be carried out (some resisting strenuously) to a hall beside the cathedral when more of the team would pray over them. After three such episodes, he said that he would 'put an end to deliverance; now we will have physical healing', and called up those who suffered from asthma, hypertension and similar illnesses, and (again breathing over them) and repeating 'receive it', he administered physical healing.

Birgit Meyer has shown well the centrality of the concept of Satan for the Ewe Christians of the EP Church. She argues that the missionaries brought the concept of Satan and identified it with Ewe traditional religion and all its evil spirits, witches and powers. 'By conceptualising the pre-Christian religion as diabolical it was rendered negative, but it nevertheless became a basic ingredient of Ewe Christianity.'[119] Thus although the missionaries intended to abolish the old religion, they had made it indispensable to demonstrate the meaning of Christianity. Personal sin was downplayed; all attention was given to Satan and his minions. Witchcraft was virtually identified with Satan. Through the equation of Satan and witch, 'witchcraft belief becomes part of Christian ideas', indeed a structural element of their Christian faith'.[120] Meyer shows that although witchcraft was denied and dismissed as superstition by the church leaders of the EP Church – and by Western theologians too – this is the basic belief of the rank and file. Church leaders will not preach about it, but for the majority of church members this is the central reality. Only the Bible Study and Prayer Fellowship (BSPF), in which 'the ideas of the congregation are taken seriously, helps them to protect themselves and offers spiritual healing.'[121] Meyer is writing specifically of the EP Church but her remarks have a wider application. For most Christians in Ghana, witches and Satan are integral to Christianity. Yet Satan has all but dropped out of the discourse of the leaders of the mainline churches, especially of the Catholics, whose missionaries do not talk about Satan or witchcraft. Nor are these topics covered in the seminaries, or mentioned in the communiqués of the bishops. And in accounting for the rise of deliverance theology, most see a direct link with the country's desperate socioeconomic conditions. With so little available, people will turn to anything to try to better their lot, or to discover why they are faring so badly. Ritual murders and the lynching of alleged witches persist in Ghana.[122] One may point to deliverance as a relatively harmless way of dealing

---

119 Birgit Meyer, ' "If you are a Devil, you are a Witch, and if you are a Witch, you are a Devil': the Integration of "Pagan" Ideas into the Conceptual Universe of Ewe Christians in Southeastern Ghana', *JRA* 22 (1992), 109.

120 *Ibid.*, 119.

121 *Ibid.*

122 *Ghanaian Times*, 30 May 1995, 1; *Daily Graphic*, 27 May 1995, 1.

with this problem; to pray over a witch is less socially disruptive than lynching her.

By mid-1995 deliverance had grown to such a degree that there was widespread alarm, mostly on the grounds that Satan had become more central to Christianity than Christ. Otabil privately expressed concern – privately because he preferred to use his influence to moderate excesses rather than lose all influence by denouncing it openly. His concern arose for a characteristic reason: that because in practice deliverance bears on idols, local spirits, ancestors, stools and face markings, it hardly applies to whites and is really tailored for blacks, and is thus one more way of alienating blacks from their culture.[123] Even Addae-Mensah was trying to set up a fellowship of deliverance pastors 'to regularise, to bring sanity'.[124] The Catholic Charismatic Movement in 1996 produced a 'Training Manual' for deliverance, with a theology not noticeably different from the examples considered above.[125] Obviously the Catholic authorities are monitoring the situation, but are very reluctant to drive people out by reacting too forcefully; they seek to control the development rather than split the church. This was the message behind the theme of the 1995 Pentecost novena: 'Preserving Unity through the power of the Holy Spirit.' Bishop Sarpong of Kumasi in July 1995 invited one of the two official exorcists of London's Archdiocese of Westminster to come to Ghana to assist in the whole matter of exorcism. He came in late 1995 to conduct seminars with the local clergy in Kumasi, Tamale and Accra. Yet this is a living issue in Africa in a way that it cannot be in the West, where for the last few hundred years the idea of being the plaything of malignant fates has receded right to the periphery, to such a degree that evil spirits have become in most mainline churches a purely residual or formalised doctrine. It is perhaps Ghanaian Christianity's most pressing issue, and it is striking that the Catholic authorities show a real reluctance to face the issue directly, in its African particularities, from their own resources.

The Church of Pentecost, the church most closely associated with the prayer camps, became seriously alarmed. Deliverance became a serious source of tension within the church, all the more so because, with its traditional lack of interest in theology, it has difficulty in deciding the

[123]   'African Christians especially, still carry the spiritual influence of their cultural practices most of which are steeped in idol ancestral worship' (Atiemo, 'Deliverance', 41). Rebecca Brown, in addressing an almost entirely Black church in London, expressed it thus: 'You folks are under even greater attack than other cultures, because your cultures [are involved in demon worship]. A hundred percent of your background is involved in demon worship ... In the USA there is a mass movement for Africans to go back to their roots, but their roots are demon worship ... Almost every single thing done in African culture is to do with demon worship' (London's First Born Redemption Church of God, 14 Dec 1995).

[124]   Interview, 30 May 1995.

[125]   *Healing and Deliverance Training Manual*, available from Box 99, Kumasi.

issue one way or the other. At the same time as the church authorities moved to regulate the practice, the five principal prayer camps announced that they would begin a nationwide crusade, conducted by the five camp directors, in Ghana's largest cities. Tabiri in particular had become too big for the CoP. His wealth became a matter of comment in the national press. For his part, he attacked the CoP leadership,[126] and in October 1995 split from the Church of Pentecost to found Bethel Prayer Ministries International.

Civil society

Our discussion has shed considable light on the churches as institutions of civil society. In the hard sense, as bodies independent of and making demands on the state, the CCG and the Catholic bishops are obviously key components of Ghanaian civil society. In an excellent study of just these points, Gyimah-Boadi argues precisely that whereas the Ghana Bar Association and the Association of Recognised Professional Bodies could not hold out against the hegemonic instincts of the PNDC, the Christian Council and the Catholic bishops generally succeeded 'in maintaining their autonomy and integrity in the face of government hostility.'[127] Considering churches in the looser sense – not in relation to the government at all but as organisations in themselves empowering and advancing their members –it is staggering to witness what is done in the context of church bodies: in choirs, synods, sodalities, fraternities, youth or prayer groups, Bible study fellowships, cell groups – the list is endless.[128] All of these provide opportunities for leadership, organisation, planning, discussion, budgeting and every sort of activity. There is no need to make unrealistic claims for these bodies or to overlook the obvious and frequent shortcomings in their operations. There are many well-publicised instances of abuses; we saw some in considering the split in the EP Church, and in May 1995 the Presbyterian Moderator even had to issue a pastoral letter deploring the abuses of pastors: 'The Presbyterian Church of Ghana, [formerly] the champion of moral excellence, is now being ridiculed for moral decadence.' But for all that, churches and their related bodies must be the most obvious places where people are able to take some control over their own affairs, and their success is even more marked when compared with the Committees for the Defence of the Revolution, and later

---

[126] *Free Press*, 20 Oct 1995, 3.

[127] Gyimah-Boadi, 'Associational Life', 143.

[128] 'Participation in religious organisations is the most prevalent form of associational life in Africa today', Naomi Chazan, Robert Mortimer, John Ravenhill, Donald Rothchild, *Politics and Society in Contemporary Africa*, Boulder, CO: Lynne Rienner, 2nd edn 1992, 94. In Ghana 'the only truly significant societal organisations that women report they belong to are religious organisations (24.1 percent)' (Herbst, *Politics*, 172).

the District Assemblies, institutions the government attempted to establish to put people in control of their own affairs, and which are generally seen to have been ineffective.[129]

One other aspect of the civil society debate is relevant here, the claim that the organisations of civil society foster a culture of tolerance, respect and compromise. Historically, Ghana has been characterised by inter-religious harmony. However, in the mid-1990s incidents of intolerance became increasingly frequent. Christians are increasingly seen as in conflict with traditional religions and Islam. The first conflict stems largely from Christian intolerance. Traditionally chiefs have proscribed drumming at a certain time of the year. Increasingly Christians repudiate the chiefs' right to make such demands, and refuse to abide by them, claiming 'We must obey God rather than men.' This has led to violence and arson. Above all, however, friction is becoming evident between Christians and Muslims. Muslims have traditionally constituted little threat to Christians, being far fewer and much less educated. The mainline churches in their relations with the government have sought to include and cooperate with Muslims, and even though the Muslim Council refused to collaborate (largely out of a desire not to offend the government), the Ahmadiyya Council and the Christian bodies cooperated very amicably. Although the present rise in tension can be attributed in some measure to the harsh economic conditions, it is also due to the paradigm of Christianity embodied in the Pentecostal and newer churches, for whom evangelism is the essence of Christianity and the only thing to be done with a Muslim is to convert him. Here too, to some degree, a particular understanding of Christianity becomes a cause of the friction.[130]

Ghana's ethos is recognisably Christian, and still identifiably Protestant, even though the Catholics, because of the resources available to them, have become Ghana's largest single Christian body. These mainline churches have attempted to provide moral leadership and direction. The country's mainline Protestant churches have attempted to involve themselves directly in political affairs, normally through the CCG, and their intervention is articulate, sophisticated, professional and peristent. Protestant leaders cooperate very amicably with their Catholic counterparts

[129] Michael Oquaye, 'Decentralisation and Development: the Ghanaian Case under the Provisional National Defence Council', *Journal of Commonwealth and Comparative Politics* 33 (1995), 209-39.

[130] The bi-weekly *Watchman* illustrates this intolerance almost every issue; against traditional religion, especially its toleration by the government, which is regarded as the source of the nation's ills (*Watchman* 2/1994, 1), and against Islam (*Watchman* 4/1995, where it states explicitly that Islam is satanic). The *Watchman's* regular feature 'News from the Christian World' is dominated by reports of persecution and imprisonment and torture of Christians.

since they share the same class interests. Precisely because this church leadership is identified with Ghana's powerful élite, it has tended to be dismissed by Rawlings, avowedly a populist, who resents advice from such quarters. He has a personal antipathy towards them and they for their part have never forgiven his unconstitutional acts of lawlessness. Church leaders seemed genuinely astounded in 1992 that a majority of the population could vote for Rawlings.

Other churches have mushroomed in recent years, in an enormous variety. Most have preached a Faith Gospel, which in the mid 1990s is being supplemented or overlaid by deliverance thinking, which although growing out of traditional conceptions is expressed in standard Western Pentecosal idioms. These new churches have tended to be coopted fairly easily by government, and their Faith Gospel, their nearly exclusive emphasis on church growth, and the increase of deliverance thinking combine to prevent them from challenging the government, or from even seeing that as their task. This may be changing, at least for some like Otabil. These newer churches have seriously depleted the membership of both the mainline churches and the AICs, but also, through their intensity and through institutions like crusades and revivals, have had a more diffuse pentecostalising influence on all churches.

4

UGANDA

The peoples making up present-day Uganda formed different kinds of political units, some of which were strong centralised monarchies. The biggest of these became the kingdom of Buganda, and there were other much smaller and more egalitarian polities. Muslim traders and slavers reached Buganda by the mid nineteenth century, and Islam had taken root in the country by 1860. Kabaka (King) Mutesa I admitted the explorers Speke and Grant in 1862. When Henry Morton Stanley followed in 1974, Mutesa displayed an interest in Christianity, and it was Stanley himself who asked for missionaries to evangelise the kingdom in a famous letter to the *Daily Telegraph* of 15 November 1875. Anglican missionaries of the Church Missionary Society (CMS) arrived in 1877, to be followed two years later by the Catholic White Fathers. King Mwanga of Buganda, who succeeded his father in 1884, originally welcomed them both, although he was baffled by the rivalry between them. Buganda religion was more secular than that in many other places in Africa; the Kabaka was not a sacred king providing the link between his people and the gods, as the king of Ashanti was considered to be. Thus Mwanga could experiment with both Islam and Christianity without subverting his entire state.[1]

Both Anglicans and Catholics stayed near the court, where there was considerable interest on the part of young courtiers. The erratic Mwanga turned against the young Christians (known as 'readers', indicating the importance of the new bureaucratic skills Christianity was introducing) and murdered nearly 200 – these were later known as the Uganda Martyrs. Mwanga did not have the power to deport the missionaries, but he tried to reduce the influence of all three groups, whereupon the Catholics, Protestants and Muslims joined forces and overthrew him in 1888. The alliance then quickly fell apart, and soon afterwards the Muslims staged a coup and installed a new Kabaka, and Catholic and Protestant missionaries fled. Now the Catholics and Protestants joined with the exiled Mwanga again, and in 1889 overthrew the Muslim regime and restored him. However, Mwanga's power was now circumscribed, and henceforth real power was to lie with Protestant and Catholic chiefs. In 1892 the

---

[1]   J.D.Y. Peel, 'Conversion and Tradition in Two African Societies: Ijebu and Buganda', *Past and Present* 77(1977), 108-41.

Uganda

two groups, Catholics and Anglicans, declared war on each other.

This remote part of Africa's interior had long remained relatively unaffected by European interference. It was Germany's interest in East Africa – it took control of Tanganyika in 1885 – that led Britain to arrange for the Imperial British East Africa Company (IBEAC) to assume control in Uganda, and in 1892 Captain Frederick (later Lord) Lugard arrived as the Company's agent. In 1892 when the war broke out between the Catholics and Anglicans, Lugard naturally sided with the Anglicans; they were British, whereas the White Fathers were French. National allegiances of the missionaries were so evident that the Anglicans were known as the *Bangereza* (the English) and the Catholics the *Bafaransa* (the French). Lugard's intervention ensured victory for the Anglicans, although they were the weaker side, against the king and the Catholics, something which has affected the religious makeup of the country ever since.

In 1892 also, the IBEAC experienced financial difficulties, and threatened to withdraw from Uganda. The CMS missionaries and their supporters in Britain led the campaign to persuade a reluctant British government to step in and assume control; at least in part this was to preserve the privileged political position the Anglicans had won in the civil war. The campaign was successful and in 1894 a Protectorate over Buganda was declared in which Bunyoro, Toro, Ankole and Busoga were included in 1896; in the late 1890s treaties were also made with chiefs to the north of the Nile. By 1919 Britain had taken control of the whole area of modern Uganda, but only with difficulty and with Baganda coope-ration.Through collaborating with the British in this conquest the Baganda gained themselves a privileged position (and much new territory), but also the resentment of many of the other groups, which has lasted till this day. The relationship between the Baganda and the other groupings constitutes, after religious division, the second enduring tension in Ugandan politics.

In the Protectorate the missions continued to exert enormous influence. All education was in their hands; only in the 1950s did the administration decide to open its own schools. Here again, the two separate and competing school systems reinforced the divide between Catholics and Anglicans. Here, unlike in Ghana where the élite readily identify as a class, a division along religious lines was built into the élite from the beginning.

Within the Protectorate, Indians – normally called 'Asians' and originally brought in to build the East African railway – were encouraged and assisted to engage in business and trade; Africans received no such assistance. Asians were given a place on the Legislative Council, something denied to Africans until after the Second World War when

Britain had accepted that decolonisation was inevitable. Regional allegiances militated against any nationwide nationalist movement. In 1952 the first nationalist party was founded, the Uganda National Congress, but it was plagued by factionism. In 1954 the Democratic Party (DP) was established, which was indeed nationwide, but its aim at that time was to promote the interests of the Catholics against the Anglican ascendancy. In 1959 the Uganda Peoples' Congress was founded, which the following year, uniting with a section of the older UNC, became the Uganda Peoples' Congress (UPC) led by Milton Obote, a Lango. In the run-up to independence, the rise of any properly nationalist movement was hindered because the Baganda, seeking a separate state, refused to countenance any proposal which treated Buganda as an integral part of greater Uganda. In the event, in the elections just before independence, a coalition of the UPC and an exclusively Baganda party, the *Kabaka Yekka* (the King Alone), defeated the incumbent DP. So Uganda came to independence in October 1962 with Milton Obote as Prime Minister. In 1963 it became a republic with Kabaka Mutesa II as federal President. This attempt to address the problem of the dominance of Buganda by giving it federal status foundered in ethnic conflict, epitomised by that between Prime Minister and President. In February 1966 Obote staged a coup against Mutesa, who fled into exile, and in April Obote made himself Executive President. In September 1967 he abolished the four kingdoms, bringing Buganda directly under the central government of Uganda, and introduced a new constitution. In 1969 he banned all opposition parties.

Obote was overthrown in January 1971 by Idi Amin, who assumed full executive powers. In 1972 Amin, as part of an 'economic war', expelled all Asians, which at a stroke destroyed a great part of the country's economy. His regime became a byword for brutality and savagery, particularly though not exclusively gainst the Acholi and Lango. Intellectuals were murdered or fled, the infrastructure crumbled, institutions collapsed. Only Uganda's fertility prevented starvation. In 1978 Amin tried to annex the Kagera salient, part of Tanzania, and in retaliation the Tanzanian army, along with the Uganda National Liberation Army (UNLA), composed of exiles, invaded Uganda and in April 1979 took Kampala. A provisional government was established and in December 1980 held elections, won by the UPC, so Obote returned from exile to become President a second time. The elections were widely deemed to have been rigged, and opposition groups took to the bush to fight Obote's regime. The most important of these groups was Yoweri Museveni's National Resistance Army (NRA). The Obote government responded by torturing and murdering of thousands of civilians. As the war escalated, Obote was overthrown in 1985 by the army, which established a Military Council, promising elections one year later. All opposition movements reached agreement with the Military Council, except for the NRA, which took possession of Kampala in 1986 and dissolved the Military Council.

Museveni formed a cabinet with representatives of all groups, even three from the previous administration. A National Resistance Council (NRC) was established, and in place of a legislature Museveni introduced a system of Resistance Councils (RCs) to oversee local affairs. He encouraged guerrilla forces to join the NRA, and has been quite successful in this, although in 1996 there are still dissident forces, particularly in the north, most notably the Lord's Resistance Army built on the remains of Alice Lakwena's Holy Spirit Movement, which was crushed in 1987 with considerable loss of life.

In 1989 Museveni held local elections and set in train the writing of a new constitution. He also prolonged the government's term of office for another five years, and reimposed his ban on party political activity, which he sees as the cause of the divisions which have wrought such devastation on Uganda. He has invited all former resident Asians to return, pledging restoration of their property, and has also permitted the restoration of the ancient monarchies, but only as symbols and ceremonial leaders. The Kabaka was restored in March 1993, and the Kings of Toro and Bunyoro the same year; only Ankole (Museveni's own region) has opted against restoration. In March 1993 the draft constitution was published, which provided for a continuation of Museveni's non-party 'Movement' government and banned party political activity for a further seven years. In 1994 elections were held (with candidates standing as individuals, not as party representatives) for a Constituent Assembly whose task was to finalise and enact the new constitution. This Assembly had a working majority of Museveni's supporters. The constitution was promulgated in October 1995, and in the May 1996 presidential elections, with candidates standing as individuals again, Museveni won 70% of the vote in a poll judged to be free and fair.[2]

Museveni took control of a country that was in ruins, with no functioning institutions, which he has tried to rebuild. He has adopted IFI structural adjustment, reduced the manpower of his army by nearly half, preached reconciliation and tolerance, encouraged exiles to return (even personally welcoming former opponents at the airport), and tried to include in his National Resistance Movement (NRM) people from all groups and parties in the country. He has tried to decentralise, through his system of Resistance Councils and Local Defence Units. Museveni seems respected and popular, though there is considerable corruption among top officials, and despite his repeated denunciations of this

[2] For many of these issues, see Holger Bernt Hansen and Michael Twaddle (eds), *From Chaos to Order: the Politics of Constitution-making in Uganda*, London: James Currey, 1994.

corruption, he has not moved rigorously against it. Although one cannot downplay Uganda's enormous problems, especially the social disruption caused by the AIDS epidemic, the spiralling cost of living, the brutality of the insurrection in the north, and the hardship of ordinary people as they struggle to pay for schooling or health care, there is in a great part of Uganda today an almost palpable spirit of optimism.

Outside Uganda, Museveni receives a remarkably good press, with both Britain and the United States particularly strong supporters. He has been the recipient of considerable aid money, and in 1995 had 67% of Uganda's bilateral debt cancelled as a reward for his good economic governance. He is often presented as the most remarkable of a new breed of leader, a military commander with a relatively disciplined army, with a cause to fight for and totally contemptuous of the generation that took Africa to independence. He is frequently seen as the dominant figure in the region, with friends and disciples adopting his policies in Eritrea, Ethiopia, Rwanda and Zaïre. Museveni is frequently hailed as a ray of hope on the continent.

Church-state relations

The churches in Uganda have traditionally been the Catholic and Anglican, the latter normally called the Protestant Church, or the Church of Uganda (COU), since the British government did not encourage other groups, and Amin's edicts in 1973 and 1977 outlawed all churches except the Catholic, Anglican, and much smaller Orthodox.[3] The Anglican and Catholic churches are an essential part of the social fabric, and have become fused at a deep level into political, social and cultural life. The most salient feature still is the rivalry between the Anglicans and the Catholics. This stems from religious wars in the nineteenth century, and became institutionalised in different parties. The UPC was linked

---

[3]   For their history, see M. Louise Pirouet, *Black Evangelists: the Spread of Christianity in Uganda 1891-1914*, London: Rex Collings, 1978; John V. Taylor, *The Growth of the Church in Buganda: an Attempt at Understanding*, London: SCM, 1958; Tom Tuma and Phares Mutibwa (eds), *A Century of Christianity in Uganda 1877-1977*, Nairobi: Uzima Press, 1978; Yves Tourigny, *So Abundant a Harvest: the Catholic Church in Uganda 1879-1979*, London: Darton, Longman and Todd, 1979. The founder of the Orthodox Church was originally an Anglican, who in 1929 was rebaptised by Greek Orthodox from South Africa. In 1995 a Ugandan was created metropolitan. The church claimed in 1995 to have 50,000 members (this figure may be considerably inflated). Church leaders are all trained in Greece and adhere to a Byzantine liturgy, but many youth prefer Western music and are leaving in large numbers. The church is trying to modernise by becoming development-oriented. In 1989 it embarked on a Rehabilitation and Development Programme 1989-91, which attracted some $750,000 over a period of about five years. In 1993 it adopted a new $2.5 million plan, most of which is pledged from the USA (interview with Secretary General, 27 July 1995).

to the COU, and the DP to the Catholic Church, although as we shall see a too simplistic identification should be avoided.

There are far fewer Catholics in top political positions. This is a matter of genuine resentment. The Catholics consider that they were cheated out of political power in the pre-independence elections of 1962, not just by politicians who happened to be Anglicans but by the Church of England itself; the Catholic leader of the pre-independence government laid a good deal of the blame for his defeat in the 1962 elections on the Archbishop of Canterbury himself.[4] In 1980 as well, the DP (though in this case it was supported by Anglican Baganda too) considers itself to have been robbed of victory. This has led to what one Makerere professor refers to as 'the Catholics' chronic sense of grievance'. This feeling of discrimination lasts up to the present day. As one rural Catholic told me: 'When an Anglican bishop is ordained, Museveni gives him a [Mitsubishi] Pajero. When a Catholic bishop is ordained, he gets a cow.' The political significance of this division between Catholic and Protestant is probably the main reason why AICs have never taken root in Uganda; it was simply too important for one's identity to be either a Catholic or an Anglican.[5]

The COU has been intimately tied to the state. It was a 'quasi-establishment' during the colonial period, and has tended to cling to this position since independence. Ward remarks that the Catholic sense of being deprived of their rightful position made the Catholics 'a powerful critical voice *vis-à-vis* the state'.[6] But this critical voice has not been very evident since independence. Louise Pirouet remarks that 'as elsewhere in Africa, the churches were extravagantly deferential' to the independent government.[7] She lists matters on which the churches 'should have raised their voices'. The erosion of civil liberties in independent Uganda long antedated Amin's coup. Detention without trial came into use in 1965; a year or so later two men were detained for writing an article critical of the government: 'Once again the churches made no protest – neither of these men was a Christian, but that should be beside the point.'[8] She writes:

---

4   See Ben Kiwanuka, 'How Ben lost the '62 Elections', written soon after losing that election, and reproduced in *Veteran Yearbook*, Jan-April 1994, 3-15. Kiwanuka claims the DP was fighting not just the UPC, but three other forces, viz. the Church of England, the British government, and the expatriate civil service.

5   Peel, 'Conversion and Tradition', 140. 'Control of the traditional political order by the Christians gave them great power: the only road to office and place for everyone else, lay through joining one of the Christian parties' (D.A. Low, *Religion and Society in Buganda,* Kampala: East African Institute of Social Research [1958], 16).

6   Kevin Ward, 'The Church of Uganda amidst Conflict', in Holger Bernt Hansen and Michael Twaddle (eds), *Religion and Politics in East Africa* (London: James Currey, 1995), 72.

7   M. Louise Pirouet, 'Religion in Uganda under Amin', *JRA* 11(1980), 15.

8   *Ibid.*

'Why did the churches do so little when the security forces themselves harassed the people and threatened their civil liberties? [...] It seems a fair question to ask.'[9] She suggests several reasons. First, it was easy to take for granted a certain amount of violence because it was part of the pattern of life in Uganda. The churches became so 'preoccupied with trying to maintain their position and privileges without realising that the wider threat should also concern them.'[10] They were pressurised in various ways: there was talk of expropriating church land; the Department of Religious Studies at Uganda's university was branded as 'useless'; the churches were 'continually upbraided for fostering disunity'.[11] The Anglican Church was weakened by internal division between the Baganda and the rest; the Catholic Church was still associated with the opposition, and the large numbers of Catholic missionaries in the country had the effect of making it seem foreign, and it was thus difficult for it to protest in any way.[12]

Even under Amin's wild excesses the churches could not easily transcend their history. A good many churchmen actually welcomed Amin's coup. The Catholic Bishop Adrian Ddungu of Masaka made a speech hailing Amin as a liberator – which apparently anyone who overthrew the Anglican Obote and his 'socialism' had to be. Likewise, Baganda Anglicans welcomed Amin: Bishop Tutaaya of West Buganda diocese is reported to have hailed him as 'our redeemer and the light of God'.[13] The Baganda were preoccupied with getting the body of the Kabaka who had died in exile returned to Uganda, in the hope that the Kabakaship would then be restored. The Langi and the Acholi were extremely apprehensive and lay low. Others displayed fatalism about the likely consequences of a military coup. Others were fooled by Amin's continual references to God. For whatever reasons, Pirouet remarks: 'No one demanded just government.'[14] At the expulsion of the Asians in 1972, 'The Churches simply stood aside.[...] The Makerere [University] students put up a rather better show than the churches: they marched into the town in protest when the expulsion order was extended to citizen Asians.[...] Over the expulsion of the Asians, the churches reached their nadir.'[15]

While all this is true, it has to be said that once the Amin regime was in power, 'many of the classic forms of protest against oppressive regimes were hardly viable options.' 'Totalitarian' is hardly the adjective to describe Amin's regime; rather it was arbitrary, whimsical and anarchical.

9   *Ibid.*, 16.
10   *Ibid.*
11   *Ibid.*
12   *Ibid.*
13   Cited in Ward, 'Church of Uganda', 79.
14   Pirouet, 'Religion in Uganda', 17.
15   *Ibid.*, 18.

To protest was not necessarily to advance any cause or serve any purpose; or to risk a definable punishment which could be calculated in advance. It was to risk unspecified ills involving looting of property, torture, imprisonment and death, not to mention reprisals on one's family or tribe. And trivial unintended offences could meet the same response as some great stand on matter of principle. For those who escaped into exile there was the possibility of some constructive opposition, but inside Amin's Uganda silence and ironic humour might be the only means of survival.[16]

Individual Christians did offer opposition to Amin. This was inevitable, if for no other reason than that the vast majority of Ugandans are Christians (Barrett's figure for the mid-1980s is 78.3%). Likewise, probably more persistent opposition came from Catholics, if for no other reason than that there are considerably more Catholics than Anglicans in the country (49.6% to 26.2%[17]). Certainly churches became full as they never had been before; they came to provide 'alternative structures and foci of loyalty at a time when most structures had broken down.'[18]

As the Amin regime continued, the churches were forced into some form of opposition. Partly this resulted from Amin's apparent drive to Islamisation. By late 1976, particularly after Muslim-Christian violence in Ankole in August, the COU archbishop and the cardinal decided that insecurity had reached such a point that action had to be taken nationally. They invited all bishops and senior Muslim leaders to meet near Kampala in September; the Anglican Archbishop Luwum was elected chairman. The meeting expressed deep concern about the state of the country and the indiscipline of the security forces, and amounted to a wide-ranging denunciation of the regime. Amin, when he obtained the minutes of this meeting, was furious, and also nervous lest the religious leaders should unite against him.

Amin was also angered by the plans of the Anglican Church to celebrate its centenary in 1977. In addition, it was collecting funds to build a church headquarters in Kampala's city centre. Amin was always nervous about the churches' collecting money, fearing that they might use it to fund opposition to him. This particular project, though, was especially infuriating to him, because his much-touted Muslim Cultural Centre had never eventuated, and the large sum donated for this by Saudi Arabia had simply disappeared. Archbishop Luwum was also actively canvassing abroad for help for Ugandan refugees in Kenya. On 25 January 1977

---

[16] Ward, 'Church of Uganda', 83.

[17] David Barrett (ed), *Encyclopedia of Christianity* (Nairobi: OUP, 1984), 686.

[18] Pirouet, 'Religion in Uganda', 19. Ward writes of the churches at this time: 'It was the corporate strength of the churches which was seen as such a threat - their immovable presence when all other institutions (parties, judiciary, press etc.) had collapsed' ('Church of Uganda', 83).

there was an attempt to assassinate Amin, almost certainly Acholi-led. He probably concluded that the church leaders were to blame; soldiers raided the archbishop's house on 5 February. The cardinal immediately visited the archbishop to discuss what needed to be done, and joint action was decided on. Eventually, perhaps because they believed they were under more immediate threat, the Anglicans felt they could not wait to be as cautious as the Catholics would have liked. They went ahead to write a courteous but firm letter to Amin along the lines agreed at the conference the previous September, and more recently with the Catholics. Archbishop Luwum was murdered on 16 February.

The Anglican response to the death of Luwum was to elect Silvanus Wani, a kinsman of Amin, as the next archbishop. By the time Wani came to retire, Amin had been overthrown and Obote had returned to power, whereupon the church elected a prominent Obote supporter, Yona Okoth, to succeed Wani. This pattern has manifested, according to one observer, 'a tendency to elect men who were not necessarily popular to the believers but simply because they were in the good books of the government in power at the time'.[19] This perception is widely held, so much so that the COU newspaper, in an article in May 1994 speculating on the successor to Okoth, could ask without obvious irony, in the light of established procedure, since Museveni was now in control: 'Is it possible to have an NRM Archbishop?'[20] Likewise, an APS news bulletin could end a report on Uganda's archiepiscopal succession: 'Since independence it has been the practice to elect an archbishop who had a working relationship with the country's incumbent head of state. If this tradition is to be followed to the letter, Ugandan Anglicans would be having an archbishop from the western Uganda kingdom of Ankole where President Yoweri Museveni hails from.'[21] However, it is too simple to see these elections as manifesting just an uncritical deference to the rulers of the day and a servile attempt to side with them. Luwum was killed as a representative of the Acholi, whom the increasingly despotic and arbitrary Amin wanted put in their place. A good case could be made that Wani might have been able to stand up to Amin, who claimed to respect him as an elder – at least Amin could listen to him, without immediately suspecting subversion. Moreover, Wani had been an army chaplain in the Second World War, and was popular with the ranks of Amin's army. Since the army was rapidly becoming a mob terrorising Ugandans, Wani more than any other candidate might be able to urge restraint without being eliminated forthwith. The choice of Wani could

---

[19]   Quoted in Ward, 'Church of Uganda', 83.

[20]   *New Century*, May 1994, 3. The article answers its own question: 'Some have suggested that the NRM functionaries have nothing at stake in the Church of Uganda to invest any resources to ensure selection of "their" choice.'

[21]   *APS Bulletin*, April 25, 1994.

thus be defended as an attempt to preserve the church and Ugandans from senseless attacks from an increasingly embattled Amin and an increasingly lawless army.

A similar defence could perhaps be made of the next choice, for when the new archbishop came to be appointed the situation had changed dramatically: Obote had returned to power, and Amin's army and the tribes that had dominated it were being victimised by the new army, the UNLA. Wani's close connections with the old army, dominated by his own West Nilers, made it virtually impossible to establish a working relationship with the UNLA. In October 1981 the UNLA devastated Wani's home district, and as a Kakwa he found it difficult to protest publicly and lacked the influence with those in power to make his voice heard effectively. His inability to moderate the government's tough stance and the contempt in which he was held by the army meant that it might be better to appoint an archbishop who had the confidence of the government and the army and who might be listened to. Even granting these good reasons, however, the twists of Uganda's recent history have ensured that the COU leadership has been prevented from playing any significant prophetic role. For just as the tide turned after the overthrow of Amin, leaving Wani as an anachronism, so Obote was removed only a few years after Okoth's election, making Okoth too an anachronism for almost a decade of Museveni's rule. He held on, to some degree ignored by Museveni and not widely respected by Ugandans, who knew that his greatest qualification for the job was his close link with Obote, the evils of whose regime are widely remembered.[22] As we shall see, the 1995 election of his successor also complied with government wishes. The COU at the very top level has thus not been able to fill any role of conscience of the nation, or moral commentator on national issues.

The Catholic leadership, too, has not been able to transcend its history. Their 'sense of grievance' has not encouraged them to confront governments. Also, as Pirouet has written, after the death of Luwum it was difficult to establish the same liaison between Catholics and Anglicans. Catholics are said 'to have felt that the Anglicans acted precipitately and unwisely and so brought the archbishop's murder upon themselves, and

[22] 'Local residents had claimed that Archbishop Okoth had been assisting the rebel groups waging war against President Yoweri Museveni in order to return to power former President Milton Obote now exiled in Zambia. It was further alleged that the archbishop was a friend and close confidant of the exiled leader' (*APS Bulletin*, 25 April, 1994). Such sentiments are often heard. For example, a report on the Rwandan catastrophe in 'The Indian Ocean Newsletter' claimed that Museveni was high on the list of France's enemies; comment on this states: 'The news communiqué comes from a group of very marginal Ugandan political opponents [of Museveni] which include Bishop Okoth [and others named].[...] It reflects their bitterness at having been once again and still more pushed aside by the Ugandan elections of March 28' (*New Vision*, 6 June 1994, 4, and *Citizen*, 2-8 June 1994, 8).

endangered the Catholic centenary celebrations held in 1979.'[23] Their centenary seemed to matter more than the socio-political chaos developing round them.

Since Museveni's accession to power, church-state relations have been of less importance. Museveni himself (unlike Rawlings) has no particular animus against the churches. He states publicly that while still a schoolboy he left the *balokole* (or Anglican revival) movement because of its refusal to take a stance on Ian Smith's declaration of independence in Rhodesia in 1965. As one observer quite wittily describes him: 'He neither drinks nor smokes and he quotes the Bible like a very good Christian to make up for his not going to church.'[24] Seeing party politics as the bane of Uganda historically, and knowing the denominational element within the parties, he keeps a critical distance from the churches. In his early years there were reports that some of the NRM 'political schools' set up to educate people about its aims were denouncing religion, but when the churches protested Museveni moved to stamp that out. He is more than prepared to attend religious functions and to speak most generously of the churches' work. His wife is born-again, even speaking at crusades, and her patronage is eagerly sought for Christian activities.

 A word should be said about Islam. The Muslims lost the religious war in 1889, and have since remained peripheral to Ugandan life. In the Amin years they took a higher profile, though it is wrong to say that these years witnessed an Islamic revival. Museveni's bush war was largely funded by Libya, although Museveni quickly returned to the Western camp after taking power - indeed, Muslim 'fundamentalism' from the Sudan is now a serious threat, and relations between the two countries are fraught. Today there are some signs of Muslim activity within Uganda - trucks pass with legends like 'Islamic Medical Association of Uganda' and 'Islamic African Relief Agency', and in 1988 the Muslims founded their own university in Mbale. Some Christians can be heard claiming that Muslims have increased to about 10% from about 4% twenty years previously. Barrett claims that Uganda in the mid-1980s was 78.3% Christian and 6.6% Muslim, so such talk of the 'Muslim threat' seems tendentious.[25] Moreover, the Muslims in Uganda are characterised by fierce divisions, and in the early 1990s there were occasions when troops had to storm mosques, with some loss of life, to separate feuding factions.[26]

23 Pirouet, 'Religion in Uganda', 26.

24 *Monitor*, 10-12 July 1995, 3.

25 Barrett, *Encyclopedia*, 686. It is often argued that the Sudan government has an interest in destabilising Uganda; see *National Analyst*, 11 April-10 May 1995, 16-18. In November 1996 Museveni claimed that over 100 Muslim fundamentalists (Salaf Tabliqs), Ugandans trained in the Sudan and invading through Zaïre, had been killed in a fierce battle near Kasese (*APS Bulletin*, 25 Nov 1996).

26 Again in 1996; *Sunday Vision*, 3 Nov 1996, 1.

The internal ordering of the churches

In accordance with the aim of examining the churches' role in promoting civil society, I will concentrate here on questions relating to their internal ordering. During the 1990s there have been major crises in both the Catholic and the Anglican churches which have thrown into high relief their internal functioning. Both have received extensive publicity.

The Catholic example is the diocese of Kabale, on the borders of Rwanda and Zaïre, which was established in 1966, being carved out of Mbarara diocese. The Bishop of Bukoba in Tanzania was initially appointed apostolic administrator of the new diocese, and in 1969 Barnabas Halem'Imana was appointed its first residential bishop. The people in this area are Banyarwanda (both Hutu and Tutsi) and Bakiga; in 1995 there were five Kinyarwanda-speaking parishes, and twenty-two Bakiga-speaking ones. Bishop Halem'Imana is a Munyarwanda, which immediately caused some resentment among the Bakiga. He did not handle this tension very well, although there were no serious problems for several years. All agree, however, that the bishop was no administrator. He was a great advocate of development and self-sufficiency, but projects like buying motels and land were so badly administered that they made no money for the diocese. And when his troubles escalated, this inevitably gave rise to accusations of corruption. The diocese had a synod in 1985, at which all sorts of things were agreed. It was the bishop's failure to implement the synod's decrees that seems to have triggered serious conflict at the next diocesan synod in 1990. Shortly after, in October 1990, the Tutsi Rwanda Patriotic Front (RPF) invaded Rwanda from this part of Uganda. Halem'Imana is a Tutsi, and by all accounts he closely identified with the RPF, and used diocesan development funds to assist them. As one observer commented, 'His development director might well be in uniform.' His house was very near the road to the border, and many speak of the RPF officers calling on him on their way through. This led to the final break with most of his priests, of whom about half rebelled against his authority; another quarter supported him, and a quarter tried to remain neutral. He excommunicated the rebels, but they simply ignored the ban, and carried on as normal. The bishop had very close links with Ugandan security forces, which by now were thick in the area (even though Museveni continually denied it, the NRM obviously supported the RPF) and by all accounts the bishop used his links with the security forces to harass his priest opponents, and even have them arrested – whenever the security forces raided rebel priests' houses, there was considerable destruction.[27] The Bishop could not enter eight or nine parishes without threat of serious violence. The entire diocese became polarised and, when all church groups ceased to exist, effectively collapsed.

[27] *New Vision*, 7 May 1994, 24; *Topic*, 26 May 1994, 6.

The media covered all this very closely. The Archbishop of Kampala, with the heads of the men's and women's associations of religious orders, attempted to mediate, but with no success. In 1994 the Uganda Bishops' Conference appointed a commission to look into the problem. The investigation was conducted by three canon lawyers (two bishops, and a professor of canon law at one of the national seminaries), which led some to complain that as far as the authorities were concerned the case concerned canonical niceties rather than substantial issues, but this approach received approval from others because the problem was being resolved through proper procedures. In mid-1994 the report was completed, and outlined four options. It was considered at a plenary meeting of the Catholic bishops, and Halem'Imana himself chose the option that he resign (technically, therefore, he was not dismissed).

The Catholic Church was fortunate in that it had in Uganda a former Superior General of the White Fathers, someone with a long history of dealing with bishops and wide experience of Africa. As a French Canadian he was totally outside local politics, but he had the added advantage that he had begun his missionary life in that area, and spoke Bakiga. Within days of Bishop Halem'Imana's resignation, the Apostolic Delegate had asked the missionary to take over, and within three weeks he was installed. Appointed initially as an administrator, he occasioned little resentment among the local clergy. Moreover, he possessed considerable human skills, and for four months said nothing; he just listened to the stories of everyone involved and asked for advice about how to resolve the problem. In this way he was able to get all eight lawsuits pending at the time of his arrival withdrawn. He lifted the excommunication on the rebel priests – after a decent interval, to avoid claims that the rebels had 'won'. Quietly he redeployed the clergy of almost half his parishes. Tension was quickly reduced, and when the diocese had a feast on 27 July 1995 to celebrate the first anniversary of his arrival, all except one of the 27 parishes took part, and it was even possible to have Bishop Halem'Imana listed on the programme as one of the speakers. (He did not in fact attend, but only because President Museveni was visiting his home town on the day of the feast.)

The COU crisis occurred in the diocese of Busoga, with its centre in Jinja. This example can be dealt with at more length because the issues here have received enormous publicity. The crisis began on 20 August 1992, with the resignation of the dean of the cathedral, an engineer who had been ordained late in life.[28] He was considered to be a close friend of Bishop Bamwoze, but his resignation statement, which was really a

---

[28]   As Engineer Zikusoga, a prominent Anglican layman, he had been used by Amin to resolve the Baganda/non-Baganda split in the COU in 1971; see Ward, 'Church of Uganda', 80.

letter copied to all relevant parties, listed his grounds for resignation: the total ignoring of the dean and chapter and their rights and responsibilities; the woeful state of the cathedral, which the bishop would do nothing to repair; the economic plight of the clergy; the bishop's neglect of parts of the diocese, including Sigulu Island which he had never visited in twenty years; the abandonment of several diocesan projects; and the Multi-Sectoral Rural Development Project (MSRDP) which in many ways had become more important than the diocese.

Although there had been widespread but unfocused dissatisfaction with the bishop for many years, this resignation triggered a concerted revolt.[29] On 6 September local Christians met at the cathedral and passed a vote of no confidence in the bishop. The meeting acknowedged the truth of the dean's complaints, and in a letter to the bishop elaborated on some of the complaints; for example, that the laity had been prepared to collect funds for the repair of the cathedral but had been actively stopped from so doing by the bishop; that the bishop had abandoned his official residence near the cathedral and opted to reside in his home area; and that his abandonment of his own children showed that he was no longer fit to run the diocese (referring to 1 Tim 3: 1-7 and Titus 1: 5-9). This statement was signed by 149 people. On 22 September a similar meeting was held at St James Church, Jinja, attended by over 1,500 people, which also passed a vote of no confidence in Bishop Bamwoze.

On 1 October the Busoga Diocese Steering Committee, which had been established to oversee opposition activity, sent a letter to all the Anglican Christians of the diocese which outlined the reasons for deposing the bishop. An even wider range of charges were listed under the headings of spiritual bankruptcy, lack of development and mal-administration. The letter then claimed that biblically the incumbent bishop had forfeited any right to remain in his post, and called for all to support the move to change the leadership. 'We have no room for filth and trash.[...] Reject him by the normal but effective non-violent means.' On the same day the steering committee wrote another letter to Archbishop Yona Okoth, the Archbishop of Uganda, outlining the lack of constitutionality of everything in the Busoga diocese, listing the decisions taken so far, outlining under fifteen points the reasons for dismissing Bamwoze, and asking Archbishop Okoth to appoint a caretaker bishop to oversee the diocese before a substantive bishop could be elected; to effect a constitution 'in line with the dictates of present Uganda'; to freeze all diocesan bank accounts 'for obvious reasons'; to initiate an audit of diocesan assets; and to tell Bamwoze not to try to visit any church in the diocese. This letter too was copied to the office of the President, the

---

[29] Ward deals with an attempted breakaway movement in the Iganga part of the diocese since 1983, 'Church of Uganda', 95.

Minister of Internal Affairs, the Inspector General of Government, local administrators and police commanders and civic officials. During most of these events the bishop was outside the country on an extended tour. On his return a group of fifty supporters met him at the airport, and took him back to the cathedral where they could not hold a service because his opponents had securely locked the doors.[30]

The Archbishop of Uganda had taken advice and had decided to request the party that made the allegations to support or substantiate them and the party against whom they had been levelled to concede or refute them. On 25 January 1993 the Secretary of the Province of the Church of Uganda wrote to both parties, asking for a response within a week of receipt to sixteen questions; for example, whether or not the diocese had a diocesan chancellor and a diocesan constitution, whether or not the bishop had good reasons for deserting his official residence, for not repairing the cathedral, for removing cattle from the project round the cathedral to his home region, and so on. On 4 February 1993 the steering committee replied to the sixteen points, dismissing two of them as irrelevant (whether or not Bamwoze was the only signatory to diocesan bank accounts and whether the diocese should be divided), but attempting to substantiate all the others.[31]

On 5 February 1993 the House of Bishops met near Kampala and issued a statement deploring the conflict in Busoga, reminding all that the 'the Church resolves conflicts through established organs of the church', upholding Bishop Bamwoze 'as the rightful Bishop of Busoga Diocese', and announcing that it had 'set up a committee to look into the situation.' This committee of four bishops travelled round the diocese collecting opinions, but alleged that it could not attend a diocesan synod scheduled for 21 June 1993 because of a warning that its members would be killed if they attempted to do so. The steering committee denied it had ever made such threats, and for its part alleged that a pro-Bamwoze priest was terrorising the opposition group with gangs of armed thugs.[32]

On 13 July the four bishops comprising the investigating committee published their report. In this they listed all the reasons advanced for or against removing the bishop, and tried to arrange them in some sort of order. This report seemed to support the bishop, but in its recommendations seemed to acknowledge the basic justice in the rebels' cause. The first of these recommended that the diocese be split into three new dioceses; and the second that Bamwoze remain as diocesan bishop if requested to do so by any of the three new dioceses, or take early retirement within one year of the acceptance of the report. This report,

[30]   See report and interview with Bamwoze in *New Century*, Nov 1992, 1 and 8.
[31]   Bamwose's reply is found in the report of the House of Bishops special committee.
[32]   See *New Century*, July 1993, 1 and 3.

however, solved nothing, because when Archbishop Okoth on 10 August visited the diocese to communicate the recommendations of the committee, the anti-Bamwoze faction refused to meet him in a hotel and assembled at the cathedral instead. The archbishop refused to speak to the crowd assembled inside on the technicality that he could not enter a cathedral in his province without the consent of the local bishop, and offered to address the crowd outside the cathedral. The 'mammoth gathering which had now turned into a mob' insisted that he address them inside the cathedral, and began dragging him there. It was only with considerable difficulty that the archbishop reached his car, and managed to drive off, the 'rear window smashed by stones thrown by the wild crowd'.[33] On 27 August Bamwoze himself was subjected to similar physical violence at Batambogwe.

On 27 September 1993 the pro-Bamwoze faction held a synod election in those churches which it controlled, and the anti-Bamwoze faction held its own elections in its areas. After the House of Bishops meeting 11-12 January 1994, the bishops issued a press release announcing that Bishop Bamwoze would be given a year's sabbatical leave, to begin in April 1994, and in his absence the Archbishop of Uganda would take over the diocese of Busoga. They also noted that in his attempt to implement some of their recommendations, Bishop Bamwoze had not complied with the proper procedure. The House of Bishops therefore dissolved the synod elected on 27 September, and called for new elections on 10 April. It also deplored the physical attacks on Archbishop Okoth and Bishop Bamwoze, and called for calm from all parties.

In a letter to Archbishop Okoth of 14 February, the steering committee rejected the proposal to hold elections on 10 April, arguing that this date gave Bishop Bamwoze time to fix the poll before leaving for his sabbatical. It also called for a constitution, the election of a substantive bishop for Busoga, and the appointment of a substantive chancellor, before any attempt to elect a synod; the committee expressed itself as being 'determined never to return to vague systems of leadership'. It went on to say that if the House of Bishops was not willing to comply with 'the people's wishes', the diocese would 'arrange a formal farewell to the Church of Uganda' and secede as the 'Anglican Church in Busoga'. Although the steering committee had seemed originally quite prepared to accept Archbishop Okoth as caretaker bishop,[34] this rapidly changed, and on 3 April it wrote to the archbishop (as usual, the letter was copied to central government representatives, district and regional police

---

[33]   *New Century*, Sept 1993, 1 and 8.
[34]   *New Century*, Feb 1994, 3, quotes the chairman of the steering committee as not op-
         posed to Archbishop Okoth's being a caretaker bishop as the House of Bishops had
         originally recommended.

commanders, and regional special branch) accusing the archbishop of fueling the crisis 'using your highest office, with high level gimmicks', regretting his resolve to proceed with 'sham elections' on 10 April, deploring Bishop Bamwoze's escape 'scot-free', and accusing the archbishop of 'canonising crimes of a fellow bishop'.[35] On the day of the proposed elections, the anti-Bamwoze faction instead introduced its new bishop-elect, a priest from Busoga who had for some time been working in Kampala as a prison chaplain and who had an M.A. in theology from the University of Michigan. Archbishop Okoth's subsequent defrocking of the bishop-elect was simply ignored by the anti-Bamwoze faction, and he took up residence in the bishop's house vacated some years before by Bishop Bamwoze.[36] The Church of Uganda tied to evict the anti-Bamwoze Christians from the cathedral and the bishop's house through the high court by filing title deeds to the land. However, on 19 May Archbishop Okoth and Bishop Bamwoze had the humiliation of having their new title deed ruled invalid by the Commissioner of Land Registration. Because Bishop Bamwoze had never attempted to regularise the land titles before, and had done so with irregularities on this occasion, they were rejected.[37]

On 13 June 1994 the steering committee wrote to the Archbishop of Canterbury asking him to employ some mediator like Archbishop Tutu, and emphasising its wish to retain links with the Anglican communion. It repeated its resolve to go through with appointing a new bishop on 2 October. In fact, however, it did not. After mid-1994 tension was reduced somewhat, as Archbishop Okoth approached retirement and both sides waited to see what a new archbishop might do. The election of Archbishop Nkoyooyo was generally welcomed by both parties, who gave him some breathing space before demanding a resolution. The new archbishop spoke to both parties separately, and then in July 1995 met both together. This meeting was reported in the national press at considerable length. Unfortunately, there was no agreement over what had been decided.[38] The archbishop tried to get Bamwoze to agree to a year's sabbatical, beginning February 1996, and in July 1996 the House of Bishops decided that Bamwoze should take early retirement at the completion of the sabbatical. (According to Bamwoze's supporters, the archbishop's zeal to oust him was fuelled by obligations he had to Bamwoze's opponents who helped raise him to the archbishopric.) Bamwoze has rejected this procedure as totally improper. At the time of writing, the dispute

---

35 Similar sentiments are expressed in another letter to Archbishop Okoth dated 10 April 1994.

36 For the defrocking, see *New Vision*, 24 May 1994, 28.

37 *New Vision*, 1 June 1994, 18; *Daily Topic*, 25 May 1994, 5. The steering committee insisted on calling this title deed a 'forgery'.

38 *New Vision*, 21 July 1995, 1; *New Vision*, 25 July 1995, 1.

continues, with the Busoga diocese threatening that it will leave the COU.

It is almost impossible for an outsider to assess the charges against the Bishop of Busoga. When given the chance he has defended himself eloquently. In his eyes the problem arose from the money he had been able to bring into the diocese through his Multi-Sectoral Rural Development Programme (MSRDP). Most of the leaders of the rebel faction were insiders, and knew the amount of money in question. According to Bamwoze, 'They wouldn't be Ugandans if they didn't vie for the money', and ' "The politics of eating" affects all aspects of Ugandan life.' Personal ambition is another factor: the engineer who began the revolt wanted to take over as bishop. Also, the bishop would argue that state politicians, including Museveni, must have been involved, because to run the opposition campaign would have cost more than could be raised locally. He claimed that some politicians' vehicles had been seen transporting participants in various skirmishes. When asked why politicians would be so involved, Bamwoze refers to the conscientisation he has been able to achieve through his MSRDP. He describes the politicians' attitude as 'While Bamwoze is in charge, we cannot influence [i.e. dupe] the people'. Also, since Bamwoze would have been one of the serious candidates for the archbishopric in 1995, they set out to discredit him before he could become a player on the national stage. In this task, the politicians co-opted his fellow bishops; Bamwoze considers the support he received from the other bishops as halfhearted at best.[39]

For its part the steering committee, at the time of writing, was led by educated and significant people. One leader (till his death in 1995) was a former Ugandan ambassador to Paris, another a former government minister and ambassador to Britain. The co-chairman was the mayor of Jinja, and of a high rank in Museveni's system of Resistance Councils, the most prominent politician in the city. They did not see their campaign as an attack on the Church of Uganda, but claimed to be fuelled by disgust and shame at what the COU has descended to. It is said that on one occasion Museveni gently chided the mayor of Jinja for embarrassing him by getting involved in this distasteful affair; the mayor quickly replied that, if Museveni wanted it he would resign his political office, but he would not give up his efforts to reform the Anglican Church. This mayor of Jinja talks at length of his debt to the COU. From a peasant family of twenty-one children, he is one of only two to receive an education; he received it because he was taken up by a CMS missionary, who even gave him employment in his house during the holidays so that he could continue his education. When he had to leave school, it was this missionary who drummed into him that there were no limits to what he could achieve if he applied himself. He has gone on to success in

[39] Interview, 13 July 1995.

horticulture, printing and brick-making. He repeats that all his wealth and position, everything he has, he owes to the CMS.

It is not evident that the opposition to the bishop is overtly political, or political in any stronger sense than everything is political in the public affairs of the COU. For his critics the bishop is pro-Obote, as was his friend and protector Archbishop Okoth. The steering committee may exaggerate this link: for them Bamwoze was still (in 1995) in charge of collecting funds to bring Obote back to power. And they credit him with playing a considerable role in bringing Obote back in 1980. The money that the Archbishop of Canterbury gave towards building the Bugembe cathedral (or alternatively towards a memorial for Bishop Hannington, murdered in 1892 on his way to Buganda) was in fact (they say) diverted to acquiring arms for Obote; in gratitude, when he returned, Obote built the cathedral at Bugembe. All the steering committee make much of links with Obote, alleging that Archbishop Luwum was murdered by Amin not because he was a Christian, but because he genuinely was gun-running for Obote. Okoth, then Bishop of Bukedi on the Kenyan border, would bring the arms across the border and take them to Kampala, relying on the relative immunity of a bishop at roadblocks. According to the steering committee, guns were truly found at Namirembe. One of them asserted: 'Amin was right to kill Archbishop Luwum.'[40] This emphasis on links to Obote is stressed to explain how Bamwoze was able to remain immune for so long, through connections with all branches of the security apparatus in the area. It is through these top-level links with the security apparatus that critics explain the elimination of opponents of Bamwoze, and because of these supposed links the steering committee continually asks that the security forces stay out of the 'purely ecclesiastical' Bamwoze affair –

---

[40] This issue is hardly resolvable now, because it is so closely tied up with present-day politics. Ward judiciously writes: 'It was because he was an Acholi rather than because he was a Christian that Luwum was murdered in 1977. It seems certain that there was a plot to overthrow Amin and that Acholi were involved. As an Acholi "elder", Luwum may have known something about what was going on; though as a church leader he is unlikely to have been directly involved. His strong *balokole* commitment, undoubtedly the mainstay of his spiritual life, makes it extremely unlikely that he would directly involve himself in conspiracy' ('Church of Uganda', 84). Ward also notes that 'Luwum was and is the victim of the persistent force of ethnicity in Ugandan life.' He remarks of the far from enthusiastic celebration in 1987 of the tenth anniversary of Luwum's death: 'The time was not ripe for a jubilant celebration of the memory of Archbishop Luwum. It was only a year since Obote's second UPC administration had been violently overthrown after a five-year civil war in which Kampala and Buganda had suffered tremendously. People were in no mood to remember events in any way connected with what could be seen as a plan to restore Obote and the UPC to power' ('Church of Uganda', 85). The Busoga steering committee have no room for Ward's nuances; for them, Bamwoze's sympathies with Obote and UPC can be used as ammunition.

and it is to keep them informed that they copy all relevant correspondence to all the security officials in the area.[41]

The charges are usually grouped under the headings 'spiritual bankruptcy', 'lack of development' and 'administration'. However, the important thing is no longer whether these wild accusations are true, but that they are widely believed, and the belief itself has become a fact of considerable social importance. For many in the diocese no charge is too outrageous to be believed. The widespread coverage in the media is, if anything, deliberately restrained. As an article in the COU's own newspaper *New Century* remarked:

Talking to the Christians of Busoga Diocese in private one learns that there is much more these Christians hold against their shepherd which they have withheld from the public especially from the press but which according to one prominent university don from Busoga 'are known even by every Musoga child'. They withhold the complaints because it is very dirty linen which cannot be washed in the open and because religious ethics requires that at least they give some respect to their bishop as well as protect the image of their church and its leadership in general. The stories about their bishop's life and conduct are some of the most staggering in our time.[...] Just give an audience to anyone from Jinja, Iganga or Kamuli, and what you hear will stagger you to the hilt.[42]

In Uganda, no less than elsewhere, 'development' is a key criterion in assessing any church leader.[43] It is seen as part of a bishop's job to attract funds, begin projects, provide employment, and above all to have buildings to show for his efforts. Many would argue that Bamwoze's record in this regard is not negligible. His Multi-Sectoral Rural Development Project (MSRDP), until it effectively collapsed in 1995, had many successes to boast of. He established the Busoga Trust in London in 1982. This trust has as its priority to support the water and sanitation sector of the MSRDP.[44] However, in his diocese Bamwoze is criticised fiercely in this area of development. Dean Zukusoga's letter which triggered the whole rebellion has a whole section on the MSRDP. His complaints centre on the need 'to dispel ignorance and suspicion on terms, conditions, mode and dispersement of donations' and to place 'diocesan Christians in a position of shared responsibility'; both accountability and shared responsibility

---

41   Ward notes a case in West Ankole where politics were deeply mixed in church affairs: 'The chairman of the UPC wanted the church building to stop.[...] In the next few months a number of those who had been active in the fund raising were shot in mysterious circumstances' ('Church of Uganda', 91).

42   Sam Tumwesigire, 'Who will redeem Busoga Diocese', *New Century*, March 1993, 3.

43   For a general treatment of all religions in development, see Syed A.H. Abidi (ed.), *The Role of Religious Organisations in Development of Uganda*, Kampala: Foundation for African Development, 1991.

44   1994 newsletter and other material available from the Busoga Trust, St Margaret Pattens, Eastcheap, London EC3M 1HS.

are, it is alleged, markedly absent. Bamwoze is 'director, manager, monitor and financial controller'. Zukusoka continues: 'MSRDP is the darling of the diocese'; it is seen as a parallel, even more important and better-funded institution, paying 'attractive salaries in the ranges of 7,500-172,000 shillings per month compared to 3,772-27,000 shillings per month for the clergy, who sometimes are not paid for several months.[...] It is so easy to understand why MSRDP is a lot more attractive, especially as it provides additional facilities and advantages such as motorcars, motorcycles, bicycles, housing, food and other forms of allowances.'

The dissatisfaction is expressed more trenchantly in the steering committee's letter to all Christians of the diocese of 1 October 1992: 'The so-called MSRDP, with its dubious employees, is a personal enterprise for his ends and that of his close henchmen.' This letter goes on to list many deficiencies in the realm of development. It is obvious that the state of the cathedral brings particular shame to the anti-Bamwoze faction. Its wide glass frontage on two sides is blown out, the glass dome is destroyed, and its general condition is lamentable.[45] The anti-Bamwoze group note that the local Christians have twice tried to do something about this; in one scheme seven Christians contributed one million shillings each in an attempt to lead other Christians to follow their example, but Bamwoze vetoed the entire scheme and had the money returned to the donors.[46] His critics are not agreed as to why the bishop would want to keep the cathedral in its current state; some claim that he finds it easier to get money overseas when he can present himself as so poor that he cannot even repair his cathedral, others that if overseas donors learnt that locals could raise such sums themselves, much of the bishop's fundraising would be undermined. (Both explanations reveal the extent to which local activities are influenced by regard to overseas donors.) This issue of development is further complicated by his Catholic counterpart in Busoga being Dutch. It is a sad fact of church life in Uganda that just by dint of being white the Catholic bishop is immune from the charge of embezzlement. The very fact that Bamwoze's achievements are regarded as deficient by comparison reinforces the belief that he must be embezzling.[47]

Probably the main charge is that of bad administration. The point is continually stressed that there is no constitution of the diocese, there are

---

[45]   The appalling state of the cathedral is described in *New Century*, Nov 1993.
[46]   Letter of steering committee to Provincial Secretary, 4 Feb 1993.
[47]   It must be said that Busoga Christians when speaking of Catholic development refer primarily to the new religious houses (buildings again!) of the White Fathers, Combonis, Mill Hills and Brothers of the Holy Cross who have moved to Jinja to establish a philosophy centre. The fact that the Holy Cross Brothers' new buildings border on the Anglican cathedral property, and that they allegedly expressed an interest in buying Anglican land, reinforces Anglican fears that they are losing out to the Catholics.

no organs of governance or control that Bamwoze accepted; the draft constitution that was never taken beyond its preliminary stage in 1972 leaves everything to the bishop 'as he sees fit'. There are no checks and balances. No one has had any share of responsibility, and there are no channels through which contributions could be made, suggestions offered, or redress sought. The bishop was literally a law unto himself, and accountable to no one. This is therefore much more than a personality clash. At root there is a rejection of the entire system of unaccountability, autocracy and despotism.

Ethnic issues

Uganda has its own intractable forms of ethnic division.[48] There is the major divide between the Bantu, Nilotic, Nilo-Hamitic and Sudanic peoples. Some of Uganda's constituent peoples are centralised monarchies, and others are acephalous. Even the kingdoms are not of the same power or influence, and the dominance of Buganda has proved intractable; it is the fact that Christianity is such a part of Baganda identity that makes ethnicity such an issue for the churches. In Uganda's history accidental divisions too have developed, such as the difference in educational levels between the Baganda and the Karamajong to the east. Also, different callings have come to characterise different tribes; most notably, the northerners came to dominate the army. Even here things are not static; the West Nilers and Sudanese were dominant in Amin's army, the Acholi in Obote's, and now the southerners (even Banyarwanda) in Museveni's. Such differences are significant today, with the north seeing itself as benefiting less from the Museveni regime than the south.

It must be said that the churches in Uganda are seriously affected by these tribal divisions. As Ward has said, 'The Church of Uganda has reflected – or, rather, embodied – the tensions and conflicts operating within state and society.'[49] The most obvious problem is that between the Baganda and the other groups that make up Uganda. This has frequently led to a movement for the Baganda to form their own separate ecclesiastical province. The 1961 church constitution created a Province of the Church of Uganda, with five dioceses from the old diocese of Uganda, and three from the diocese of Upper Nile. The archbishop was to be elected from the diocesan bishops and would retain his own diocese. However, in 1965 Erika Sabiti, the Bishop of Rwenzori, was elected archbishop. The Baganda were outraged that the first African archbishop was not a Muganda, and the other tribes were even more outraged that

---

48 Of relevance here is D.W. Waruta, 'Tribalism as a Moral Problem in Contemporary Africa', in J.N.K. Mugambi and A. Nasimiyu-Wasike, *Moral and Ethical Issues in African Christianity: Exploratory Essays in Moral Theology,* Nairobi: Initiatives, 1992, 119-35.
49 Ward, 'Church of Uganda', 73.

the Muganda Bishop of Namirembe took the former Bishop of Uganda's house, with the Archbishop of the Province relegated to the guest house – the 'boys' quarters', as it was dismissively called. When in 1967 Obote introduced a new national constitution and abolished the old kingdoms and any trace of federalism, the Baganda Anglicans became even more intransigent and determined to retain their cathedral and keep the 'Province' in its place. This made Archbishop Sabiti's task extremely difficult, since he came to be seen as an Obote man. As it became evident that it was impracticable that the archbishop be based outside Kampala – in Sabiti's case, in Fort Portal – the realisation grew that the church constitution had to be changed. But Obote's 1967 national constitution, with its stress on the unitary state and the powers of central government, made the Baganda all the more determined to cling to their institutions and traditions, not least in the church. In 1970 a draft church constitution recommended that a new diocese of Kampala, carved out of the Namirembe diocese, be created as the archbishop's see; that the archbishop's powers be strengthened; and that Church Commissioners be established to administer all land held by the Church of Uganda. Most of the church land was in Buganda, much of it given under a 1900 agreement or by individual Baganda landowners, and the plan would alienate the land of Buganda. This 'Obote constitution', seen as a 'UPC blueprint' for the church, was strongly resisted by the two Baganda dioceses of Namirembe and West Buganda. At the provincial assembly in Mukono in 1970, when they were unsuccessful in modifying it, the Baganda dioceses walked out, and openly talked of seceding from the ecclesiastical province. A synod of Namirembe diocese on 23 January 1971 voted to secede, but this event was rapidly overshadowed less than twenty-four hours later when Amin's coup deposed Obote. In the aftermath Archbishop Sabiti was accused of being behind Obote's 'master plan' to control and manipulate the churches, and was even denied entry to Namirembe cathedral on 31 January 1971. The Baganda pointedly denied him any official role in the ceremonies connected with the interment of the Kabaka's remains in April. Amin set himself to heal this division within the church, and at a conference held in the International Conference Centre in Kampala on 25-29 November 1971 he forced the reluctant Baganda to agree to the new church constitution. The desire of the Baganda to secede and set up their own province has never disappeared - just as the non-Baganda Anglicans have persisted in their determination to keep the Baganda in the one nation-wide province. In the 1990s this has been a live issue,[50] running simultaneously with the

---

[50] See *APS Bulletin*, 25 April 1994; a columnist writes of the need 'of making the next Archbishop a Muganda in order to forestall Buganda declaring a Province of their own' (*Sunday Vision*, 29 May 1994, 9).

debate on Buganda's becoming a self-governing but 'federal' state.[51]

This fissiparous tendency has long been evident in the COU. There has been an impulse towards an ethnically homogeneous diocese, with a local man, of that tribe and area, as bishop. In the debate before the adoption of the 1972 church constitution the idea was floated that the episcopate should not be tied to a particular locality and ethnic group; bishops should not be 'tribal' but should represent the whole church and be available for transfer to any part of Uganda. At the time the Baganda were violently opposed to this, for it smacked of Obote's policy of 'mobilisation' – the creation of a political core of civil servants and politicians responsive not to factional and regional divisions, but to national priorities as formulated by the central organs of party and government.[52] This thinking received its *coup de grâce* in 1981, when a reshuffle of bishops occurred in which a number (as part of the normalisation process after the overthrow of Amin) returned to their home areas as bishop, and in their places new bishops were created from those localities. (Obote, in power again at this stage, criticised this as creating a 'tribal church', again advocating his 'mobilisation' concept by which bishops would be appointed by a central secretariat of the church.[53])

The tendency to create these local dioceses has continued apace; thus the Bakonzo campaigned successfully for a separate diocese (against Toro domination) and in 1984 were given their own diocese of Rwenzori South. Another case is the eastern district of Mbale. In 1981 the archdeaconry of Bugisu, an area known as Buhugu, broke away from the diocese of Mbale and insisted that it be made its own diocese. Behind this lay longstanding rivalries with the other group in the diocese, and resentment at a somewhat autocratic bishop from that group. This breakaway area in no way met the COU's own criteria for erecting a diocese. However, the breakaway people persisted, and on 26 March 1992 the House of Bishops gave in and announced the establishment of the diocese of North Mbale and named the new bishop. Just a few days before this announcement (probably as part of the deal) the caretaker bishop of Mbale had convened a meeting of all the clergy of the seceding archdeaconry and their wives, at which they 'acknowledged their sin of rebellion and asked for forgiveness from Mbale diocese, the House of Bishops and the entire Church'. This meeting was said to have 'brought about the healing among the clergy who had stayed out of church discipline since their breakaway in 1981'. At this meeting the caretaker bishop effected some changes. The former archdeacon who had been dismissed by the people in Buhugu

---

[51] See the headline: 'Federalism: Would Buganda survive as an Integral State?', *New Vision*, 10 June 1994, 4 and 25.

[52] Ward, 'Church of Uganda', 78.

[53] *Ibid.*, 94.

because of his faithfulness to Mbale diocese administration was reinstated. The canon who had assumed the post of bishop was asked to step down, and was then appointed vicar of the central church. 'In reconciliation to one another, they regretted having been divided among themselves and acknowledged the importance of unity and team work for effective service to God. Then Bishop Okile prayed to God to forgive them.'[54]

As if this were not enough, the archdeaconry of Sebei also broke away from Mbale diocese in October 1990, claiming it had been 'oppressed administratively', and demanded a diocese of its own. The 'committee for the sought diocese' told the House of Bishops they would never return to the Mbale diocese, and would deal only with a bishop or some other person 'who goes to them as an Archbishop's delegate', and no one else. The area seeking to become its own diocese comprised seven parishes. This area had become an administrative district in 1961, but 'although this led to great strides in education and agriculture the same cannot be said for the church.' No church buildings had been put up for thirty years, and the centre of the archdeaconry had a hut for a church; church numbers had steadily declined with the youth leaving for new Pentecostal churches; health and educational involvement was minimal; and 'while the population at large has generally become more educated, the church continues to be manned by people with very little education. The one or two with some education are normally put in a position where they cannot influence the direction of the church.'[55]

Such fissiparous tendencies were deplored by President Museveni himself when he spoke at the consecration of another bishop; he deplored the division created in the church through the creating of such 'unwarranted small dioceses', and called rather for the strengthening of existing dioceses. The COU newspaper addressed this phenomenon in an editorial in May 1992. It acknowledged that since the 1960s the COU had broken up into small dioceses 'some of which have been created out of tribal and dialectical sentiments.' It recognised that 'administrative wrongs' often lay behind the splits, but that in permitting the establishment of the new dioceses, the church was addressing the symptoms rather than the cause of conflicts. It called for the revising of the COU constitution to give sufficient power to the central leadership 'to demand reasonable administrative accountability within the structures.' The editorial lamented that without such accountability – presumably of local bishops in their dealing with minority groups in the diocese – 'many archdeaconries will become dioceses.'[56]

---

54 *New Century*, April 1992, 1.

55 *New Century*, Sept 1992, 2.

56 *New Century*, May 1992, 2. Frank Rwakabwohe calls for the amalgamation of COU dioceses, because 'there are quite a number that are not viable economic and spiritual enterprises' (*New Century*, Aug 1991, 4).

Ethnicity is a problem for the Catholics too, as we have seen from the problems in the diocese of Kabale, which became racked with ethnic tension. However, the Catholics seem to have a very different approach from that of the COU. They have decided against a 'tribal church'. This is not Obote's 'mobilising' idea debated by the Anglicans before 1972 and then so positively repudiated in the reshuffle of 1981. The Catholics have no centralised authority in Uganda for deploying personnel: whereas the Anglican Archbishop of Uganda has some responsibility for the whole country, the Catholic Archbishop of Kampala has no authority at all outside his own diocese. The Catholic bishops elect the head of the episcopal conference for a term of two years, and even then he has just a coordinating role. Whereas a COU diocese submits to the House of Bishops two names (both inevitably from that diocese), Catholic bishops are not nominated by the local diocese but are appointed by Rome on the advice of the Apostolic Delegate (purportedly after wide consultation). In 1995, eight of the sixteen Catholic dioceses had bishops from outside the local area. In Fort Portal the bishop was a Muganda, who had previously been the Bishop of Moroto; by all accounts he is well accepted and respected. He has been helped in that previously he had been the rector of a national seminary, where many of his priests had already known him. In Gulu in the far north the bishop, himself a Munyoro, was given an auxiliary from West Nile. The latter was accepted so long as he was an auxiliary, even for two years as Apostolic Administrator, but when in February 1990 he was appointed the substantive bishop, there was considerable opposition, not so much from the people as from the clergy who tended to see the appointment of an outsider as a slight on them. (Indeed, many Catholics in Uganda, in discussing this issue, will readily say precisely that 'No priests in Gulu are suitable', presumably alluding to the issue of celibacy.[57]) According to many, the consecration was approached with considerable apprehension for what it might lead to. In the event it went off well enough, and the bishop has struggled on, with some difficulty. (Referring to this affair, one news bulletin states: 'The Vatican put its foot down and the Acholi Christians from Gulu had to accept as a bishop a person who was not from their own community.'[58] There is no doubt that its authority structure enables the Catholic Church to attempt what the Anglicans would never contemplate.) In Moroto and Kotido, the two Catholic dioceses of Karamoja, both bishops are outsiders, from Masaka and Tororo respectively. In these areas, both extremely undeveloped, the problems of acceptance are not so great. Even in Kampala, the archbishop since 1990, though a Muganda, is not from the

---

[57] The Gulu priests' observance of celibacy is questioned in *Monitor*, 31 May-3 June 1994, 5.

[58] *APS Bulletin*, 20 Dec 1993.

Kampala Archdiocese but from Masaka. He became the first Bishop of Kiyinda-Mityana in 1981, and moved to Kampala in 1988. Here he was initially received with some coolness, but after a short period of treading carefully succeeded in winning genuine acceptance.

It seems to be the policy of the Catholic Church that, where practicable, bishops should be made as trans-tribal as possible. In its final message the 1994 African Synod in Rome made much of the image of Church-as-Family, transcending 'ethnic exclusivism' which was characterised as a 'deceit of the devil'.[59] Even many Anglicans would applaud this Catholic approach; the COU provincial secretary has stated: 'It would be a very good thing if we could get them [bishops] from everywhere.'[60] However, there is another school of thought that would oppose it, saying that the local community is the local church, so it should have its own language, liturgy and leaders. In a country like Uganda where any sense of national identity is so undeveloped, no such identity will develop until each constituent people feels equal. This means that it must be taken seriously, which includes providing its own leaders. If, as in the Anglican church, this means that people can be bishops without much education, certainly without the university degrees that the Catholic Church seems to demand, this is far better than bringing in outsiders. The very Catholic Masaka area has fifty priests who could become bishops throughout the country; but the slightest hint of Baganda imperialism would destroy the fragile stirrings of national unity. The smaller tribes will feel they belong to Uganda only when they are taken as equals. In the words of one Catholic academic, 'The Anglicans have understood this much better than us Catholics.'

A related issue which further illustrates these different approaches is that of the training of clergy. The COU has Bishop Tucker Theological College (BTTC) at Mukono, but it also has six regional colleges, and some even more informal schemes of training clergy. In fact BTTC seems under some threat, and the roll was down from 140 to 106 in 1994 and 107 in 1995. Several reasons are suggested for this decline in the standing of BTTC. First, the regional colleges cost much less to run, and secondly, they provide a much lower standard; furthermore, many bishops find less educated clergy easier to deal with. Thirdly, the informal schemes of education enable the bishops to promote whomsoever they like with a minimum of fuss. Consequently, it is possible to find COU dioceses with not a single graduate among their clergy.[61] None of these reasons reflects particularly well on the motives of different bishops, and any policy that

---

[59]   Message of 6 May 1994; the *APS Bulletin* picked this out as the most important point in the statement.

[60]   Interview, 30 May 1994.

[61]   See *Uganda Confidential*, 16-23 May 1994, 10-11.

so downgrades education must be thought rather shortsighted.

The Catholics, by contrast, have four national seminaries.[62] They have consciously rejected any regional system of education, and adopted a policy that staff and students must be totally mixed. New students are distributed in such a way as to preserve an ethnic balance. This policy is possible because the Catholic bishops seem able to think far more nationally than their Anglican counterparts; one has only to visit the two shrines of the Uganda Martyrs at Namugongo to see that the Catholics give an importance to theirs that the Anglicans obviously do not. The Catholics can find money to maintain something that belongs to the church as a whole, which the Anglicans evidently cannot. The remarkably good physical condition of the Catholic seminaries in comparison with BTTC seems to indicate the same thing. The Catholic system of national rather than regional education is not unconnected with the greater funds available to the Catholic Church, which is prepared to incur the greater expenses involved, of transport costs for example; Rome contributes $600 annually for every student in training.

Some would claim that the Catholic policy is less than spectacularly successful; the students at the seminaries tend to break up into language groups with great readiness. But others claim that though it is bound to take a long time, signs of progress exist. They cite examples of priests who choose to spend their holidays in other areas of the country, with friends they made during seminary years. In the early 1990s at Ggaba seminary, certain tribal groups banded together to fix the elections of the student president. The staff seized on this as an opportunity for education, and met with all groups of students to air all the issues involved openly. Nobody claimed transcending tribalism would be achieved overnight.

A comparison of the COU and the Catholic Church

Both churches are big institutions with established structures, large grassroots membership and solid traditions, but there are obvious differences between them. The Anglican Church is smaller, but is much more powerful politically. All Uganda's heads of government (except Amin) have come from an Anglican background. This proximity to power has compromised it; as already noted, the COU has had only a weak prophetic voice because history has seen it elect its archbishop in the light of political reality, only to see that reality change with the archbishop left out of events. This was the case even in 1995. The Baganda dioceses of the COU were threatening to secede and create a province of their own unless they were given the archbishopric. They demanded a Muganda archbishop. These demands were parallel to a movement among the Baganda generally to

---

62   The Archdiocese of Kampala also has its own seminary for older candidates.

establish a federal (effectively an autonomous) state for Buganda. According to one bishop, the outgoing Archbishop Okoth was told by the government, desperate to hold the church together, that the new archbishop was to be the Bishop of Mukono, a Muganda. Okoth then dutifully canvassed for Mukono among the other bishops, and Mukono was duly elected. When I remarked to my informant that this government interference in church elections seemed like history repeating itself, he replied that the pressure was more severe this time. 'On previous occasions we were told "We don't want Kivengere; if you can't give us Okoth, at least give us Dunstan Nsubuga." This time we were given no room to manoeuvre at all.' It is necessary to add that the new archbishop is widely recognised as a good choice, but this account of government interference bears some semblance of truth, for if the Baganda provinces had seceded from the ecclesiastical province, it could well have increased the momentum for Baganda federalism, to which Museveni is strongly opposed.

But even apart from political interference, the COU bishops have not enhanced their church's standing. They are widely seen as unaccountable, dictatorial and autocratic. This, rather than the nature of any specific accusations, is the lesson of the Busoga crisis. The style of leadership that has brought the Bishop of Busoga into such strife is widely seen in other dioceses too. Busoga was the flashpoint in the 1990s, but the problem is far deeper and wider. The Busoga steering committee claimed to have received letters of support and offers of prayers from all over the country, from people watching the outcome, for if the revolution succeeded in Busoga, there were many other dioceses where the same approach would be adopted. Equally, it was widely claimed that the other bishops' support for the Bishop of Busoga arose from the realisation that if he were unseated, many of them would soon be challenged. This was the way the steering committee reacted to the report of the House of Bishops. The report was widely thought to be almost exclusively the work of Bishop Kamanyire of Rwenzori, and the steering committee's letter to the bishops' special committee included this sarcastic aside: 'We would like to praise our fellow laity in Rwenzori Diocese for having put up with you for 12 years and continue to hold you in high esteem, yet you are no less a replica of Bamwoze in the Rwenzoris ...'[63] This perception is commonly encountered across Uganda. As a columnist in the *Sunday Vision* expressed it, 'If the Archbishop was to set a precedent and withdraw Bamwoze, wouldn't the Christians in Fort Portal also throw out Bishop Kamanyire, and then Bishop Bamunoba in Bushenyi, and then the Catholics throw out Bishop Halem'Imana from Kabale in sympathy with their brothers in the Church of Uganda? Where would matters end?'[64] Another report

[63]   Letter of Isabirye Mula, coordinator of the steering committee.
[64]   *Sunday Vision*, 29 May 1994, 9.

critical of Bishop Bugimbi of Luwero, accusing him of falsifying his age and driving out opponents in the ranks of the clergy ('including the only graduate clergyman in the Luwero diocese') and laity, concludes: 'Some Christians are already warning that if Bugimbi fails to retire peacefully, Luwero may become another Busoga.'[65] This is what the anti-Bamwoze faction are aware of when they repeatedly claim: 'Nothing will be the same in the Church of Uganda after our revolution.'

The Busoga crisis is intimately linked with a crisis of credibility in the leadership structures of the COU. The dissatisfaction is widespread. In June 1994 *Uganda Confidential* carried an article about the then Bishop of Namirembe, accusing him of numerous charges:

Nepotism, sending only relatives for further studies abroad and leaving others to struggle on their own. Retrenching staff under the pretext of lack of funds and their places being immediately filled in by his relatives. Promoting unfit relatives to high positions of responsibility and allowing his brothers and sons to misuse diocesan cars when other members of staff are not allowed to drive them.[...] The bishop has allegedly conspired with his brother, Canon A. Musiwufu, to sell off the diocesan land at Mbuya and most of the 'buyers' have been the bishops children and immediate relatives who have acquired that land under pseudo-names. Although formerly the proceeds from the sale or leasing of church land were meant to develop the estates department, today the money has reportedly been diverted to the bishop's personal bungalows at Lungujja, Nsangi and Muyenga....

The synod hall and the bishop's personal houses are said to be under construction by the same builders, who alternate between the sites, but all labour charges are met by the synod hall committee. This 'was carefully organised through his brother Musiwufu who was recently forcefully made canon contrary to the advisory committee's recommendation.' A German NGO which had been providing the Namirembe diocese's support for over 500 orphans had recently found that much of their money had been diverted 'to the construction of his third bungalow at Nsangi'. The Germans had recently given the bishop four months' grace to rectify the finances. When this did not happen, the NGO transferred its money from Namirembe diocese to the Uganda Protestant Bureau. Escalating unpaid bills have meant that the Namirembe diocese students at theological colleges are behind in paying their fees to the tune of 14.5 million shillings. Yet the bishop's personal account in London (the number is given) 'has continued to swell, thus ranking the bishop among the richest Ugandans.' 'When the bishop went to the USA last year the friends of the diocese donated two computers. Although they were meant for the diocesan office, one was installed in the bishop's residential office while the second has gone missing.'[66] Although there were some who claimed that this article was

---

[65] *Uganda Confidential*, 16-23 May 1994, 11.

[66] Bishop Kauma was reported as responding in tears to these accusations at a COU church

unfairly slanted, few denied that there was truth in the allegations. Earlier the same publication made similar and equally detailed accusations against the Bishop of West Ankole.[67]

However, whether or not such accusations are true has ceased to be the important point. The significant point is that this is what is widely said and widely believed. The bishops are part of a system that is unaccountable, self-serving and lacking in transparency. It is this whole system that is being rejected. Busoga's steering committee continually refers to the 'colonial legacy' of the Church of Uganda. 'The church law, the entire administration are naturally colonial and not any different from standard dictatorship. The system is too obsolete to promote the church any further without putting Christianity to the risks of oblivion.[...] The relics of colonialism [must] be discarded completely and [we must] try to forge an acceptable and tenable church system.'[68] The bishops had fortified 'themselves against constructive criticism as this would otherwise dislodge them from the house of eaters. Some "protectors" have translated the scriptures in eating ways that favour their firm entrenchment and perpetual stay in their imperial sees.' It is the Bishop of Busoga who 'is the chief cause of the sorry state [of Busoga] in addition to the impact of the colonial legacy which has obstructed modernity and transparency.[...] Be it reiterated here that we are just church reformists, and we hanker for an acceptable church system that marches abreast of democratic governance, transparency and modernity. We are not anti-Bamwoze per se, nor are we anti-people, but we are anti-bad system, anti-poor leadership, anti-dictatorship.' The document calls for a code of ethics or conduct, like those for doctors, teachers or accountants.

Any member of these professions who behaves or acts in breach is subject to disciplinary action. What happens in the ministry of God? Do all those who profess knowledge, feign piety and divine inspiration as 'called' to serve in the ministry of God take trouble to observe strictly their code of conduct as provided for in the Holy Book, the Bible?[...] It is incredible for a bishop to fail for 21 years to establish essential organs in the diocese such as a diocesan constitution, synod, chancellor, commissary.[...] Christians are further unhappy over [the bishop's] failure to put in place people and machinery for the proper spiritual growth and general development in the diocese [in order that he might] ensure his perpetual stay unchallenged.[...] Some Christians, notably those protective of their stakes, have questioned our capacity, asserting that we had no right to challenge the bishop, but this does not hold substance.[...] Days are gone when bishops were unquestionably held as

---

in Mutundwe. The report also notes that when the congregation was allowed to ask questions, it expressed considerable concern at what was happening, and seemed unconvinced by his answers (*Daily Topic*, 30 May 1994, 1 and 4).

67   *Uganda Confidential*, Feb 1992, 7.

68   The document later repeats that bishops have used as their cover 'the colonial legacy and canon law'.

sacred, untouchable, incorruptible, above open criticism. If Presidents have been criticised, and others removed, what is special with Bishop Bamwoze?

The document goes on to assess the campaign's success to that date. 'We have weakened the shackles of the colonial church system, including the stability of some bishops whose probity has been in question in their respective dioceses. Bishops like Bamwoze and his replica in the Rwenzoris are in the mire. More are likely to be unveiled and shaken up [if] they stand against transparency under the guise of "canon law".' It notes that as a result of its activity the House of Bishops has initiated 'some positive steps towards reformation' by recommending a code of conduct for all COU members, up to and including the archbishop, the enactment of conditions of service for all in the COU, and enactment of diocesan constitutions. 'These are good gestures of positive response towards church reformation. This is what we long to have, and continue to exist for.'

The self-styled reformers keep repeating that Uganda has changed; under these changed conditions, the former kind of leadership will no longer be tolerated. According to this way of thinking, the Busoga crisis is a sign of hope. Ordinary people, the rank and file, will no longer put up with a system that was formerly taken for granted. It is evidence of a real democratisation at the grassroots. However, it has to be said that it provides scant support for the theory that it is the churches that are influencing the exercise of political leadership in the nation generally. The influence seems to flow the other way. In Uganda today it is the political leadership, notably Museveni himself, who is seen to stand for democratic leadership. He has promoted local involvement through the Resistance Councils, fostered decentralisation, denounced abuses of authority and demanded accountability. It is the experience of Ugandans in the political sphere that has made Christians no longer prepared to put up with what they have been offered in the churches. The *Sunday Vision* columnist referred to above describes people saying of Busoga: ' "Uganda is a democratic country", they say, "why should people be forced to keep with a bishop they don't want?" '. Another letter in the *New Vision* ends: 'It is worth remembering that the democratic wind of change blowing over cannot by-pass religious institutions.'[69] The Busoga steering committee's stocktaking at the end of one year's activity spells this out too:

The Church of Uganda owes its origin and operation to the Church of England, which in the mid 1960s granted us independence by change of colour of the leader but not the church system. Since then nothing has changed despite our changing Uganda society in which the church operates ... Museveni took to the jungle and fought for our liberty for five years. A lot of anomalies have been put right in

[69] *New Vision*, 2 June 1994, 5. The writer concludes: 'So clergy, time is running out!' This letter in fact deals primarily with the Catholic crisis in Kabale.

the political, economic and social sectors. Ugandans are aware to some extent now, under the able leadership of President Museveni, and we cannot afford to continue operating under church systems which are suppressive, with untouchable leadership. [We must have] a new chapter in the church governance with genuine machinery to solve conflicts when they arise... [The colonial system must] be changed to befit modern Uganda under the NRM'.[70]

Many of the COU's problems stem from lack of financial resources and its (as it currently operates) very great needs. One result is that many of the clergy transfer to parachurch or similar organisations offering better remuneration.[71] Another is that the church will take money from anyone and everyone. Some of these links are formally organised; England's diocese of Winchester has each of its deaneries twinned with a diocese of Uganda, and within these Winchester deaneries, parishes are twinned with a parish or archdeaconry in Uganda. The diocese of Bristol functions in the same way.[72] The diocese of Mityana has formal links with Winchester's Whitchurch deanery, with a Canadian diocese, and with a Swiss Reformed body, Action Swiss Return. This last is significant, for the COU will form links well beyond the Anglican communion; Britain's Ichthus Fellowship, Australian Baptists, American Presbyterians, New Zealand Pentecostals, all are involved in teaching, supporting, aiding, the COU. These links bring not only money; personal exchanges lead to wider benefits, like the daughter of a rural pastor boarding with a Bristol family to attend school there, or a village headmaster taking courses in America. One of these links is more significant. Since 1984 conservative American Presbyterians have been involved in an enormous educational mission to the COU, by the 1990s bringing several teams each year, up to forty people in all, for weeks of workshops and seminars in all COU dioceses. The Americans, not all of whom are pastors, pay their own way. Some return year after year. The dynamics of these workshops are worth exploring. There may be a six-day seminar for COU clergy and wives. The clergy willingly attend; this may be the first time they have eaten meat for a considerable time. The Americans meet all the costs; as some of them are prepared to admit, if they are billed $4,500 for such a workshop, they know full well that the real costs may be considerably lower. The difference is kept by the individuals or the community organising the seminar. There is another question worth pursuing: what

[70] Isabirye Mula, 'Busoga Crisis: Feature on One Year of Active Engagement', a document prepared for the executive of the Busoga Diocesan Steering Committee, dated 9 October, 1993.

[71] African Evangelistic Enterprise (AEE), for example, runs an extensive child adoption scheme for over 5,000 Ugandan children with a German donor body. The Germans send 44 DM per month per child; of the nearly fifty full-time administrators of this scheme in Uganda, many are COU priests.

[72] *New Century*, March 1992, 1.

is happening to any specifically Anglican character of the COU as the result of year after year of workshops run by conservative Presbyterians? The Americans see themselves in the role of Wesley and Whitefield reviving the Anglican Church of the eighteenth century. But for the COU personnel, in their crushing poverty, the financial considerations seem to override any theological considerations.[73]

Kevin Ward's study of church-state relations in Uganda ends with this paragraph:

The NRM has undoubtedly brought many advantages to the greater part of Uganda in terms of peace and stability, local democracy and a disciplined army. The idea of the accountability of government officials, civil servants and the armed forces is beginning to be applied in the life of the church also. Popular pressure is mounting for the church also to practise a self-critique of its standards of public morality and administrative practice.[...] Increasingly it has been felt that the church also has shared in the corruption of national life, and that it is facing a severe moral crisis which will erode its credibility if the issues are not tackled urgently. Financial accountability, especially in the use of foreign funds, a clerical preponderance in church life, nepotism in the training of ordinands, episcopal autocracy – these are some of the issues still requiring attention from Anglican leaders.[74]

Here again we meet the explicit admission that the new thinking comes from the political sphere and is flowing from there into the churches.

There is a genuine feeling that the COU is facing a crisis. If it does not surmount this, it may even disappear. As one supportive letter to the Busoga steering committee expressed it, 'If you fail, then our whole church is gone.' The *National Analyst* paints the COU as 'collapsing slowly'.[75] There is no doubt that its perceived deficiencies are major reasons for the great defection to newer churches. As the COU *New Century* openly admits, 'We all know that the young generation these days does not think much of the Church. The Church of Uganda has recently launched a campaign to attract the youth back.'[76] The members of the steering committee at Busoga will not leave the COU, because they are all of an age to remember, with enormous gratitude, the CMS

---

[73] In 1994 one of the American team centred his teaching around New Tribes Mission videos; Anglicanism in most of its forms would have little in common with this ultra-fundamentalist mission.

[74] Ward, 'Church of Uganda', 102-3. Waliggo also sees the influence moving from national politics to the church: John Mary Waliggo, 'The Role of Christian Churches in the Democratisation Process in Uganda 1980-1993' in Gifford, *Christian Churches*, 223-4; also *New Century*, May-June 1991, 4; *New Century*, July 1993, 4; *Uganda Confidential*, 6-13 Sept 1993, 7.

[75] Kesi Kanyogonya, 'Corruption and Tribalism besiege Nkoyooyo', *National Analyst*, 4 May-1 June 1995, 30-32.

[76] *New Century*, May 1994, 3; for admission of Catholic losses, see *Citizen*, 9-15 June 1994, 6.

missionaries. And they are of that generation that were educated by the church, and have owed their subsequent success to that education. But the young do not share those loyalties. And the drain of youth from the Anglican Church, and from the Catholic Church also, is considerable. 'Youth Exodus from Big Churches', proclaimed a *New Century* headline.[77] Masaka church leaders told a delegation of COU bishops: 'The massive desertion was so alarming that checking measures should be taken.'[78] As we have seen, the steering committee makes much of the need to change 'colonial structures'. By this they mean the element of dictatorial control which characterised the colonial church. Yet, paradoxically, their insistent cry is 'We want the CMS back'. At every turn they deplore what has happened to the COU since the missionaries left; the 'bishop-elect' of Busoga told me that as soon as he took control he would write to the Archbishop of Canterbury to ask for missionaries. The church experience in Busoga, then, has not been an empowering one, or led to self-esteem, self-confidence and self-determination. It has led many Christians of Busoga virtually to despair of their ability to run the church. This reinforces the view that the state is in a far healthier condition than the church, for no one is asking the British to return and run Uganda; it is only the church that the *Wazungu* (foreigners) are required for.[79]

The Catholic Church, for its part, is considerably bigger than the COU. Yet the COU has twenty-seven dioceses to the Catholics' sixteen, and considerably more parishes and priests, but these figures hide a significant structural difference. An Anglican priest often has the position and duties of a senior Catholic catechist, and many Anglican parishes are the

---

[77] *New Century*, Sept 1990, 1 and 8. For the Catholic awareness of the problem, see Simon Peter Kasumba, 'The New Evangelical Church Sects in Kampala City, with Reference to Kabowa Redeemed Church of Christ and El-Shaddai Ministries, Kawempe: their Challenge to the Catholic Church', Dip.Theol. thesis, Makerere University, 1990; Mubiru Bernard Patrick Kasambeko, 'The New Christian Religious Movements in Jinja Diocese', Dip.Theol. thesis, Makerere University, 1992.

[78] *New Century*, Sept 1992, 2.

[79] No account of the COU would be complete without a mention of African Evangelistic Enterprise (AEE), not unconnected with the *balokole* movement (see below), whose aim is given as 'to evangelise the cities of Africa through word and deed in partnership with the church.' It is part of Michael Cassidy's African Enterprise (AE) of Pietermaritzburg, South Africa, although in Uganda it is the creation of the late Festo Kivengere, the remarkable and charismatic Bishop of Kigezi (1972-88). For Kivengere, see Anne Coomes, *Festo Kivengere*, Eastbourne: Monarch, 1990. Under Kivengere's leadership, while maintaining its evangelistic thrust, it broadened out to include leadership, management, stewardship and family life training, schemes of integrated community development, and conflict resolution. In the 1990s AEE has acted to bring reconciliation to COU disputes in Lango, Bunyoro and West Ankole. Opinion differs as to whether AEE is best seen as part of the COU or as an independent ministry. Its activities are chronicled in its bimonthly newsletter *Hope Bulletin*.

equivalent of 'mass centres' in the Catholic system. Despite the numerical superiority, the Catholic Church has never had the political importance of the COU. But if it is weaker in political influence, as a social force and agent of development it is far stronger. One has only to visit the Catholic diocesan headquarters in major cities like Kampala, Kabale, Fort Portal, Jinja or Soroti, usually just outside the city, to see the schools (primary and secondary boarding, often special and technical schools), offices, hospitals, seminaries, convents and mechanical workshops. Of course the COU is involved in development too. Its Planning, Development and Rehabilitation (PDR) department is a giant NGO – compare the computers, offices and vehicles of the PDR with those of the COU itself.[80] But it cannot compare with the Catholic involvement.

For the purposes of our present study we must mention two qualities that make the Catholic Church different from the COU: external ties and considerable funds – the two are not unconnected. The external ties are obvious everywhere. The crisis in the Catholic Diocese of Kabale which we discussed earlier was resolvable because eventually Rome will remove a bishop who is judged to be doing substantial harm to a local church. (Even though the Kabale bishop technically resigned, there is little doubt that Rome would have acted had he declined to go voluntarily.) There is no equivalent Anglican mechanism for external agents to resolve the Busoga crisis. Catholic bishops are appointed by Rome, through a process that is not very transparent. This is how non-locals have been appointed bishops in so many Ugandan dioceses, and it is also the reason why the government would find it very difficult to interfere in Catholic episcopal appointments. Because of these links to a centre outside Uganda – 'foreign control' some would call it – many Anglicans make the distinction: 'We are the Church *of* Uganda, the Catholic Church is the Catholic Church *in* Uganda.'

The external links are most obvious in the missionary religious orders which almost institutionalise internationalism. Although these are nearly all Africanising, some new missionary orders are still being brought in. The Bishop of Hoima brought in a group of American sisters in July 1995 to run a school – a newspaper report notes that they built the school themselves 'and the rectory'. This not only suggests succinctly why bishops seek missionaries so assiduously, but also hints at the connection between external links and financial resources. The Catholic Church has enormous resources it can draw upon. These are not only, not even primarily, from Rome. Through the department of Propaganda Fide Rome does provide some funds, for example \$35,000 annually for

---

[80] The PDR instituted a \$6 million Grassroot Development Programme in 1993; unfortunately, its implementation proved, for various reasons, something of a disappointment; Church of Uganda, *Detailed Grassroot Development Programme 1993-94*, Kampala: PDR Department, 1992; Church of Uganda, *PDR Annual Report 1993*, Kampala: PDR Department, 1994.

the running of every diocese, and although every bishop will stress how inadequate this is, it is $35,000 more than many COU dioceses have access to. Propaganda Fide also supports all four major seminaries, and provides about one-third of the costs of all the minor ones. But most Catholic funding comes from the big agencies like Misereor or Missio in Germany, Caritas International and countless smaller ones like Miva (which provides vehicles for Catholic institutions). Some bishops, when asked, admit that they have no idea of the total funds coming into their diocese – so much of it comes through channels like religious congregations who are not directly under the bishop. Catholics have recently begun twinning dioceses and parishes as well. In mid-1995 the parish of Hoima twinned with the German parish of Würzburg, and other parishes of the Hoima Diocese are seeking links with other German parishes. Such links are extremely beneficial. The Catholic Diocese of Tororo even has a house in the United States, and sends about three priests there every summer for fund raising. This not only brings money into the diocese, but it also works wonders for the financial security and morale of the priests. A priest can usually make sufficient contacts over that time to provide for himself for the rest of his life. (Those lucky enough to study overseas can look forward to a life of assistance from friends made then, and even holidays abroad.)[81] The problem, of course, is that the church becomes dependent on this foreign money, and is reluctant to do anything for itself, and even incapable of it. Thus the Fort Portal diocese set up a Justice and Peace Department in early 1994. The first thing it did was to send an application for $27,000 to Misereor to fund a series of seminars. Because no agreement had been finalised by mid-1995, the department had done absolutely nothing in its first year of existence. While the structures of dependence may not then be so very different between the Catholic Church and the COU, there is so much more money coming through the Catholic system that it is spared some of the more glaring problems of the Anglicans. A patronage system needs cash to function; when the cash flow is diminished, the inadequacies loom larger.

The Catholic Church – not so politically compromised, more disciplined, better ordered and (crucially) better funded – functions with reasonable efficiency. Catholicism is obviously an integral part of the identity of countless Ugandans - one has only to join the hundreds of thousands each year at the Uganda Martyrs Shrine at Namugongo to be reminded most forcefully of that. (And again, to reinforce much of the foregoing argument, the Catholic shrine and ceremony are so much more impressive than the Anglican, although admittedly devotion to martyrs is more a Catholic than an Anglican concern.) But it cannot be said, to

---

[81]   In the mid-1990s the Catholic clergy negotiated a salary of $60 a month from the bishops; up till then their remuneration was on a far more casual basis.

adapt Douglas Hurd's image of post-imperial Britain, that Uganda's Catholic Church 'punches its weight'. It can hardly be said to provide moral leadership to the nation. It has no great history of involvement in or concern with public life. The Catholics have not shown any inclination to produce sociopolitical statements like the church in Ghana. It has produced rather infrequent pastoral letters, namely *With a New Heart and New Spirit* (June 1986), *Towards a new National Constitution* (March 1989), *Let Your Light Shine* (October 1992), and *Political Maturity: Consolidating Peace and National Unity in Uganda* (1995).[82] The Catholic bishops seem so grateful to Museveni for finally halting Uganda's spiral of violence that their attitude is one of profound gratitude. They would find it hard to challenge him, and basically they support his programme.[83]

The Catholic Church is also not grappling with the issues facing the church itself. Doornbos outlines many of the issues which the church will confront in the near future, for example the decline in missionary numbers, and concludes that none of them is being addressed.[84] Kassimir refers to the questioning of the 'moral authority of priests'.[85] Here presumably he is referring to the matter of clerical celibacy, a question the official church refuses to address, apparently on the reasoning 'Because the issue shouldn't arise, therefore it doesn't arise.' The

[82]   The earlier letters are discussed in Waliggo, 'Role of Christian Churches', 205-24.

[83]   In their statement 'The War in the Northern Part of Uganda and the Search for Peace: an Open Letter of the Catholic Bishops of Uganda to the Government Leaders and People of Good Will' (issued 28 August 1996) the bishops obviously are more open to a negotiated settlement than Museveni, who opted for a military solution. The same openness is gently suggested in the statement of the Uganda Joint Christian Council 'Peace for the North' (of 1 June 1996).

Catholic reflection on socio-political issues are found in the proceedings of the 'Uganda Theological Weeks'. The fourth, held in 1988, focused on integral development; the proceedings are published as J.T. Agbasiere and B. Zabajungu (eds), *Church Contribution to Integral Development: Fourth Uganda Theological Week: African Theology in Progress*, vol. 2, Gaba: AMECEA (Spearhead 108-9), 1989. The fifth, July-Aug 1990, focused on 'The Church's Contribution to the Making of a New National Constitution for Uganda'. The sixth, August 1992, focused on 'The Church and Education for Leadership in Uganda'. See also the Catholic Archbishop Joseph Kiwanuka memorial lectures: J.M. Waliggo's 'Archbishop J. Kiwanuka and the Vision of Integral Development' (1991), M. Semakula's 'The Christian Church and Promotion of Human Rights' (1992), and Vice President S.B.M. Kisekka's 'The Christian Challenges of Leadership of Society' (1993). The Anglican equivalent is the Festo Kivengere lectures; see Dean Michael Senyimba's 'Bishop Festo Kivenjere: the Man and his Legacy' (1991), Canon John Bikangaga's 'Justice and Reconciliation in the Context of Uganda Today' (1992), and Dr Tom Tuma's 'The Church-State Relationship in post-Independence Uganda' (1993).   ·

[84]   Martin Doornbos, 'Church and State in Eastern Africa: Some Unresolved Questions' in Hansen and Twaddle, *Religion and Politics*, 260-70.

[85]   Ronald Kassimir, 'Catholics and Political Identity in Toro' in Hansen and Twaddle, *Religion and Politics*, 129.

haemorrhage of Catholics to newer churches is admitted, but there is no attempt to analyse or even understand the phenomenon. It is celibacy (observed far more in the Catholic heartlands of the south-central region than elsewhere) or the failure of many Ugandan Catholic priests to live up to it, rather than power or money, that Catholics have in mind when they adduce the hypocrisy of the clergy as a reason for joining new churches. The Catholic Charismatic Renewal, which might conceivably be one way of meeting the challenge posed by the newer churches, struggles on, with little support or encouragement from bishops or local priests. In theory Uganda's Catholicism, like that in other East African countries, is distinguished for Small Christian Communities, the grassroots cells into which a parish is divided. Although some missionaries have attempted to introduce them, most people are prepared to admit that rarely in Uganda do they function with any success (we will mention below the remarkable exception of Kampala's Kamwokya parish). Kassimir claims the Catholic lay associations in Toro 'speak less to the needs of new generations'.[86] One wonders what the pious European sodalities of previous years contribute to Uganda today – especially the new right-wing ultramontane organisations whose literature is frequently found in Uganda. Such literature was particularly linked to a spate of visions of the Virgin Mary allegedly occuring in the south from November 1987. The local bishop, Adrian Ddungu of Masaka, declared in a pastoral letter of 31 May 1989 that the supposed apparitions lacked all authenticity and forbade further gatherings at Mbuye, the centre of a burgeoning cult. Preoccupation with these visions seems to have decreased as the area gradually returned to normal after the traumas of the 1980s.[87]

The real strength of Uganda's Catholic Church may turn out to be the congregations of sisters, which are attracting candidates in considerable numbers, and which have always been important for Ugandan Catholicism.[88] The sisters are increasingly well trained, and their training is so unclerical that they are less concerned with status than with service. They have a certain independence and are beginning to organise themselves into an articulate group within the church. The moral leadership that is not coming from the official Catholic Church may eventually come from this quarter. Significantly, the communiqué after a study conference of religious sisters in August 1995 in Kampala contained a commitment to leadership training, dialogue with Muslims, and 'reading the signs of the times in the light of the Gospel through social analysis'.[89] The change

---

[86]   *Ibid.*, 137.
[87]   For these 'visions', see Paul Gifford, 'Mary's Message for Africa', *Tablet*, 29 Feb 1992, 270-1.
[88]   See Richard Gray, 'Christianity' in A.D.Roberts (ed.), *Cambridge History of Africa* 7:*1905-40*, Cambridge University Press, 1986, 165-6.
[89]   AMECEA Doc. Service 449, 10 Jan 1996; see also *New Vision*, 1 Aug 1995, 2.

in the general status of Ugandan women that Museveni promotes is having its effect on the church too.

There is little ecumenism in Uganda. A Uganda Joint Christian Council (UJCC) exists, made up of the COU, the Catholic Church and the small Orthodox Church. This was founded in 1964, but it has attempted very little over the subsequent thirty years. However, the Christian Council did involve itself in preparing for the 1994 elections for the Constituent Assembly with a programme of civic education and by monitoring the election process on the day itself. The civic education prepared monitors and community leaders, and at the grassroots focused on salient issues of the draft constitution, the functions of the Constituent Assembly, and voting procedure. UJCC monitors monitored the nominations, checked the rolls, observed candidates' meetings and conduct of campaigns, and on 28 March 1994, polling day, 15,802 UJCC monitors were deployed throughout the country. At each step of the way monitors had assessment forms to complete. The whole exercise cost US$536,642, provided largely by the EU, assisted by USAID, the Canadian government, the African American Institute, and the World Council of Churches. Despite acknowledged shortcomings, this exercise was a new thing for Ugandan churches, the first such attempt at cooperation.[90] Just a week before the elections the heads of the three UJCC churches issued a rare joint statement, stressing that the Christian values of justice, peace, equality, freedom and leadership as service were the cornerstones of democracy, calling on all sectors of society to ensure that the elections were successful.[91]

However, it must be said that, election activities apart, the UJCC functions in name only. One has only to visit its offices to see that no one expects it to achieve anything. It is, admits one Catholic bishop, 'largely window dressing'. It is not like the Ghana Christian Council, which we saw in the preceding chapter, or the Christian Councils of neighbouring countries like the Sudan, Kenya and Tanzania, which are enormous bodies employing numerous staff in a wide range of departments. In Kenya it is one of the most high-profile NGOs in the country, while the Christian Council is probably the most important social body in the Southern Sudan. Uganda has no wish to go down that road. It was Cardinal Nsubuga who refused to countenance employing any more staff. It is important for the Catholic Church that there exists a Uganda Joint Christian Council, but the Ugandan Catholic leadership, very hierarchical and clerical, have little interest in any organisation they do not control. The Catholic Church has invested so much in defining itself

---

[90] UJCC, 'Interim Report of the UJCC Monitoring Team, on the Constituent Assembly Elections', Kampala: UJCC, 8 April 1994.

[91] UJCC, *Participation is the Sure Road to Democracy in Uganda*, Kampala, 16 March 1994.

against the COU that anything along the lines of ecumenism that might blur the distinction is not encouraged. Probably the same thinking explains the lack of interest in 'inculturation'; a few missionaries provide the only voices calling for it. The established practices are what have traditionally distinguished Catholics from Anglicans; that is all the justification they need.

The Pentecostal churches

As noted above, Uganda effectively had only the two major churches and virtually no AICs; in this it was very different from Ghana. Yet within the COU was a remarkable phenomenon that had many qualities of a Pentecostal church, namely the *balokole* movement, the revival movement of the 'saved', which began in Rwanda in the 1930s and spread in waves throughout East Africa. It was essentially a lay community of prayer and fellowship, very unclericalised, uncompromisingly rejecting any assimilation between the church and the world, and between Christianity and African custom, which it deemed to be happening among the mass of lukewarm Christians. There are different assessments of the qualities the *balokole* movement has brought to COU public life. Some claim that it has led to an element of exclusiveness or intolerance: 'Compromise was alien to *balokole* vocabulary.'[92] At the same time, it is also said to have fostered 'a culture of honesty, openness, accountability, and restitution.'[93] Undoubtedly it did both, as Hastings notes: 'If the Revival brought a much needed new outburst of commitment to the confession of faith and high moral standards, an intense personal loyalty to Christ which would prove decisive for many in moments of crisis, it also brought conflict, narrowness, spiritual arrogance and near schism.'[94] Some schisms were real, like that of the *Abazukufu* (the 'reawakened') which began in the 1960s as a result of the perceived laxity of the saved. Even though the revival persists in the 1990s, it is nothing like the force that it was.[95] It seems to have run out of steam during the Amin years, and several reasons are given for this. First, the movement was based on the concept of equality, yet about this time several *balokole* became COU bishops. The movement was disoriented by this infusion of episcopal authority,

[92] Ward, 'Church of Uganda', 74.
[93] Apolo Nsibambi, interview, 26 May 1994. For the history of the *balokole* movement, see Max Warren, *Revival: an Enquiry*, London: SCM, 1954; F.B. Welbourn, *East African Rebels*, London: SCM, 1961; C. Robins, '*Tukutendereza*: A Study of Social Change and Sectarian Withdrawal in the *Balokole* Revival of Uganda', Ph.D. thesis, Columbia University, 1975; Kevin Ward, ' "Obedient Rebels" – The Relationship between the early "Balokole" and the Church of Uganda: the Mukono Crisis of 1941', *JRA* 19 (1989), 195-227.
[94] Hastings, *History*, 53.
[95] The movement 'in many respects ... has stagnated and is no longer an agent for change in the church'; from a statement of foreign missionaries working with the COU and meeting at Mukono, April 1995.

not to say authoritarianism. Likewise, a movement built on unity now developed different centres of power. Secondly, some of the bishops who laid claim to the label *mulokole* seemed in their conduct anything but 'saved'; such discordance caused some crisis of identity. Thirdly, under Amin, the moral map changed; uncompromising truthfulness simply could no longer work in circumstances where one could survive only by operating on the black market. Fourthly, the exclusively personal or individual ethics of the movment had little to offer in circumstances where some social theology was demanded. For all these reasons, the movement had run out of steam by the mid-1980s when Museveni restored some sense of normalcy, and before it could re-establish itself new churches were appearing with a different appeal, one far more attractive to the young. Thus it is possible to see the full-blooded Pentecostal churches so visible today as something other than a revival of the *balokole* movement. Obviously the new churches fulfil part of the role played by the movement formerly, but we shall analyse them as part of a wider Pentecostal phenomenon rather than in terms of the particularities of Central Africa which threw up the *balokole* revival.

Since about 1986 when Museveni restored order, enabling Uganda to rejoin the international community and most Ugandans to resume their lives, new churches have appeared, with an enormous increase in the numbers of Christians. This is evident far beyond the bounds of Pentecostalism. The Seventh Day Adventists had been present in the country since 1927, as part of the work in Kenya. Up till 1987 they enjoyed gradual growth, but after that they mushroomed. In 1987 they had 220 churches and 42,358 members; by 1994 they had 460 churches and 91,052 members. The Adventist Development and Relief Agency (ADRA) was established in Uganda in 1991, and by 1995 employed about 70 people, building schools, digging boreholes, and running clinics and child survival programmes (funded by USAID). The Mormons are another group gaining a high profile in Kampala and environs to the East. They began in Uganda in 1989, and by 1995 had about 40 missionaries (full time church workers), of whom about 30 were non-Ugandans. Kampala alone had 24. They were planning for 67 by 1996, so that Uganda would become an independent mission.[96]

[96] In the early 1990s there were also twenty-five Presbyterian churches, of five different groups, each of the five relating to different mother bodies. Moreover, Korean Presbyterians have opened a Bible school near Kampala. In 1994 and 1995 American Presbyterians were holding a convention of all branches, trying to form them into one denomination. The United Methodist Church has also appeared, started by a former Elim pastor who studied in a Methodist College in the United States. In 1994 an American UMC couple settled in Jinja to run his Bible college, and to coordinate short visits of American Methodist teams who come on construction and church-planting trips. Some of the new imports seem quite dubious (for the Church of God of East Africa, see *Uganda Confidential*, 1-14 April 1993, 14; *ibid.*, March 21-28 1994, 5). Robby

It should be said immediately that new missionary groups are not permitted to enter Uganda just to evangelise; they have to be involved in development as well. Thus much Christian development work is not the result of any theology but simply needed to enable Christian groups to enter the country. These activities have taken on an added importance as the Uganda government has reduced its activity, both as a result of the general IMF-World Bank philosophy of rolling back the state, and also out of reluctance to squander scarce resources in poorly supervised projects.[97] As the central government has withdrawn, NGOs (especially churches) have moved into the vacuum – and the functionaries who once made their living from government activity are now forced to do so from NGOs and churches. Right across the board this phenomenon has to be allowed for; churches in Uganda are increasingly tied up with the survival, jobs, health, schooling, prospects, travel and advancement of countless Ugandans. Any discussion of conversion or the increase of Christianity in Uganda that leaves these considerations out of account fails to do justice to Uganda's changing social reality.

It is the rise in Pentecostalism that is giving Christianity its high profile today. One can hardly enter a taxi or a lift without being greeted with 'Praise the Lord'. Of course, some of this might be linked to the *balokole* movement or to the Catholic Charismatic Movement, which had in 1995 an estimated 5000 adherents in 300 prayer groups throughout the country.[98] But most of Uganda's new churches are surely best seen as examples of the new pentecostal phenomenon – they are very similar to the churches we found in Ghana, and have arisen quite independently of the *balokole* revival. Most of them would distinguish themselves from the *balokole* movement quite sharply – in just the same way as in Ghana the new charismatics distinguish themselves from the Independents – and even attack it publicly (the *balokole* all-night prayer sessions, with their real or imagined abuses, seem a particular focus for attack).

The Pentecostal sector of Ugandan Christianity has had a most artificial existence, for under the British Protectorate such churches were positively

---

Muhumuza, 'Weird Cults Storm Uganda' (*National Analyst*, 6 July-3 Aug 1995, 10-12) extends the discussion to groups like Hare Krishna, Transcendental Meditation and the Branhamites.

97　'The Government has been reluctant to dish out money in bogus development projects where corrupt civil servants used to help themselves freely' (editorial in *New Vision*, 17 June 1994, 4).

98　Interviews with director, 24 May 1994, 26 July 1995. Uganda's Catholic Charismatic Renewal has produced its own newsletter, *He is Alive*. The Renewal is linked to four Emmaus Pastoral Workers' communities. As one might expect, in Uganda there seems far less contact between the Catholic Renewal and Pentecostalism generally than in Ghana.

discouraged. Even so, some denominations did take root. The biggest by far of the pentecostal denominations is the Pentecostal Assemblies of God, a fellowship of autonomous churches founded in Uganda in 1935 by missionaries of the Canadian Assemblies of God. They are strongest in the East, having arrived as a spillover from Kenya. By 1995 they had about 2000 churches, with five missionary couples.

The Ugandan Assemblies of God (UAOG), founded by the American Assemblies of God, was always much smaller. Their last missionaries left in 1985, at the height of the chaos under Obote's second government. The total collapse of the denomination came five years later after the disgrace of Jimmy Swaggart, whose financial assistance had effectively kept the local church functioning. With no more funds for housing and vehicles, only a few congregations proved self-supporting. At this stage they invited the Calvary Charismatic Centre (CCC) of Singapore to take over the denomination. The CCC has been involved in church planting in Uganda since 1985, and by 1995 it had one American and 14 Singaporean couples working in Uganda, with effectively two distinct roles: to found their own CCC churches (nine by 1995) and to reestablish the UAOG (54 churches, with a goal of 30 new ones a year).[99]

Another major Pentecostal denomination is Elim, an offshoot of Elim of Lima, New York. This was founded in East Africa by two brothers in law – Bud Sickler, who stayed in Kenya, and Arthur Dodzeit, who moved to Uganda in 1962. They both used the same techniques, which are of some importance for any understanding of pentecostal statistics in East Africa. They established a system whereby Americans like Gordon Lindsay, T.L. Osborn and David Nunn provided a salary for two years for local pastors while they were establishing their church. Understandably, the number of Elim congregations – in Kenya the Pentecostal Evangelistic Fellowship of Africa (PEFA), in Uganda the Elim Pentecostal Evangelistic Fellowship of Uganda (EPEFU) – increased enormously. When the two year period was drawing to an end, the pastors resorted to all sorts of ploys to maintain their salaries: leaving their earlier church to establish an entirely new one, not minding whether the old one survived or not; moving their members to another location and giving it a new name, or simply staying where they were but renaming the old church. Because of such tactics the statistics for pentecostal Christians have always been questionable. The Elim church in Uganda had the misfortune to have its headquarters adjacent to Kampala's notorious Lubiri barracks, and this meant that Elim was the first church to be proscribed by Amin in 1972. During the subsequent Amin years Elim existed

---

[99] The CCC has its own mission strategy, applied all around the world: a team of about five missionaries does church planting intensively for nine months in a particular place, then pulls out, leaving one of their number as the pastor.

underground but with little supervision and when it resurfaced in the 1980s it was almost destroyed in messy leadership struggles. It had certainly lost all pretensions to be a loose fellowship, and the leadership was arrogating to itself considerable power. In 1987 the son of Arthur Dodzeit came back as pastor to the flagship church in Kampala. As an American with access to funds, he set up a feeding programme, a primary and a secondary school (under a separately registered organisation, with his wife the head of both), even a television studio. By comparison, the rest of the denomination was able to attempt very little, and he effectively became more powerful than the denomination itself. This has led to all sorts of conflicts in the church, some of which have been particularly unedifying.

The other major Pentecostal denomination is the Full Gospel Church, founded in 1962 by a missionary from Vancouver (who had originally been with Elim). He too was deported in the Amin years. There were about 200 churches when the missionaries left, but these had grown to about 400 when the missionaries were allowed back in the mid-1980s. By mid-1995 there were 700 churches. Thus we have a repeat of the phenomenon we encountered above with CCC; in these days of church growth strategies, a single church in the West can create an entire denomination in Africa. Glad Tidings Church in Vancouver, with a mere 500 members, 'oversees' 700 churches in Uganda (together with 50 in Taiwan and 12 among the Eskimos). The Taiwanese churches are now self-supporting, but this is not the case in Uganda. The Canadian parent supports the Uganda Glad Tidings Bible School, among other things, and has even set up (with resources from World Vision and UN agencies) Child Care International which has considerable involvement in the Rakai district, where there is a large concentration of its churches. The organisation even established a community radio station in the area. All these activities bring the Full Gospel churches considerable prestige, besides employment for their pastors supervising the water projects and orphanages. The Deliverance Church is another Pentecostal denomination that should be mentioned here; like the Full Gospel Church, it also can be considered a derivative from Elim.

All these denominations were founded under overseas influence, and are still assisted with overseas funds and personnel. They have a fairly long history in Uganda, even if this has been somewhat chequered, given the opposition from the British authorities and open persecution from Amin. Besides these, there are other Pentecostal organisations which have arrived since the stabilisation effected by Museveni. One of these, Chrisco, founded by Harry Dass, an Indian now based in the United States, has grown considerably in East Africa, and his Ugandan churches around Mbale, Mbarara and Kampala are effectively a spillover from his much more extensive operations in Kenya. Then there are the New Life Churches founded by Victory Christian Church, an Assemblies of God church in Auckland, New Zealand. (This church was linked with the CCC, for at one time the same man doubled as pastor both in Auckland and Singapore. The New Zealand involvement began as part of the Singapore mission, but since early 1995 the two thrusts have been completely independent.) This is yet a third example of a single Western church creating an entire new denomination, such is the imbalance of power and resources between the West and parts of Africa. Uganda had 14 Victory churches in mid-1995 – in Lira, Kampala, Kabale and Mbarara. The Auckland church funds the missionaries and the Ugandan pastors and their Bible school in Mbarara, and in 1995 was considering investing in tea and banana plantations and taxis as income-generating projects.

There is thus considerable variety even within the externally influenced pentecostal churches. But by far the most interesting are the homegrown pentecostal churches. These are mushrooming in luxuriant fashion. Kampala alone has a large number of new churches, with names like the Namirembe Christian Fellowship, the Rubaga Miracle Centre, El Shaddai Ministries, the Kampala Pentecostal Church, the Redeemed Church of Christ, Prayer Palace Christian Centre, Victory Christian Centre, the Church on the Rock, and Abundant Life. Similar churches have appeared in all the major centres – in 1996 there were eleven in Mbarara and an estimated fifty in Soroti; some of these, like Dickson Lubega's Kabarole Christian Fellowship in Fort Portal, are major players on the local scene. Nor should churches of this type be seen as an exclusively urban phenomenon – all are aggressively involved in church planting in the surrounding rural areas, spreading their particular brand of Christianity. To give some impression of the variety in question here – a variety that the simple label 'pentecostal' hardly does justice to – we should look in some detail at four examples within Kampala.

First, consider the Kampala Pentecostal Church, known locally as KPC. This is a church of the Canadian Pentecostal Assemblies of God (PAG). It is distinguished for its lively worship, but the latter is exuberant rather than unrestrained; for example, no trance-like states would be encouraged. Here, participation is complete, the English hymns are led by a five-piece band (electric guitars and percussion, with the pastor's Canadian wife on the electronic keyboard.) The services are a blend of testimonies, choir singing, and will even include healings, but these are neither emphasised nor flamboyant. The essence of the service is the sermon, delivered whenever possible by the Canadian pastor. The message is fundamentalist – in mid-1995 the church hosted visiting millennialist Barry Smith – and is influenced by the faith movement. Thus the pastor preached in July 1995 about 'the law of harvest'. He claimed that 'God is not more inclined to bless an American than a Ugandan.[...] When walking in God's favour, God blesses us. If we are faithful, abundance will continue to flow'. As an example he said that 'I believe God loves me enough to give me a new Land Rover Discovery. I've already seen it [in faith], and God has provided most of the money... It will happen. I haven't got it registered yet, but I've seen it in faith'. However, it would be misleading to suggest that the church's incessant preaching was one of prosperity. This sermon was one of a series on the miraculous, and in this same sermon the pastor actually said: 'You know my life, you know I don't preach this every week'.

This is not a personal church. The pastor is important, but in no way is this his church. He is highly respected, but if he were shifted tomorrow it would make no great difference to the church (in fact, the pastor went back to Canada for a year, and claims the church progressed in his absence). He is one of a team of five pastors, whom he trains on the job, and he gives great emphasis to leadership training. This is the only way in which the message could be construed as political; the church stands for the reform of Uganda through total personal integrity on the part of Christians who take on positions of leadership.

The church's most obvious characteristic is its professionalism. Services begin and end on time. Choirs are well rehearsed, and take their assigned place in a planned programme. Hymns for congregational singing are projected on a giant screen. Sermons are meticulously prepared and skillfully delivered, with points clearly made, and fréquent recapitulations and summaries. The office staff are stylishly dressed, competent and obliging. The church has a wide range of activities (for youth, for mature youth, for women, with nearly a hundred cell groups), all conducted exactly as advertised. The church building is a former cinema in central Kampala, and the church owns the entire block of about twenty shops, all of which have been extensively renovated, making this some of the most desirable real estate in the area. The church is heavily in debt because of this development, mainly to the Canadian Assemblies who advanced most of the money, but this investment should in time provide a considerable income. There is absolutely no suspicion of financial irregularity or personal enrichment – essentially because the pastor is white and therefore trusted totally. The entire business operation is managed by another Canadian missionary.

The church has grown enormously; it began at Easter 1984, and by mid-1995 had about 5000 people attending its three Sunday morning services – obviously it would soon require a fourth. To convey some idea of this achievement, this number is already more than those attending the Catholic Cathedral at Rubaga, and more than those attending all the services at both Kampala's Anglican cathedrals. (Some suggest that much of the KPC membership formerly belonged to the congregation of the nearer Anglican cathedral.) But numbers alone do not convey the church's impact in the city. The pastor recounts that in 1984 the newspapers would not advertise a pentecostal service; he could not even borrow the Campus Crusade 'Jesus Film', because 'We don't lend to Pentecostals'. Initially there were all sorts of problems with parents refusing permission for children to attend KPC. Now, however, important people are openly grateful for the church's effect on their children. The church's members are educated (services totally in English ensure that), and many are well off, obvious from the expensive cars in the parking lot. The church has its own strategy of church planting. KPC aims to create city churches and to branch out from there. Each year since 1994 it has targeted three cities where the PAG has no presence – thus largely in the south and west. Teams of about 25 people, trained in personal evangelism, spend two weeks in the chosen city. In the first week they engage in personal evangelism; the second week they follow up the contacts from the first week. Then a pastor from Kampala is left in charge of the new church. Through this method, in 1994-5 the KPC founded strong churches in Mbarara, Kabale, Masaka and Fort Portal; the centres for 1996 were Masinde, Luwero and Hoima. These churches are thus daughter-churches of the KPC rather than part of the general outreach of the PAG. KPC is thoroughly North American, with all that that means in terms of professionalism, presentation, planning, marketing and customer satisfaction. This Western element is no doubt a big part of its appeal, and there is no doubt that the effect of all its activities is Westernising.

Secondly, consider Namirembe Christian Fellowship (NCF), an autonomous church begun in 1977 by Simeon Kayiwa, a young art graduate and teacher. This is Kayiwa's church. He could not be transferred; it is his church or, more properly, the church is him. He personally has attracted a large following, for whom he is 'a mighty man of God, with an overflowing anointing'. His were the gifts that brought the church into being, and preserve it. These gifts are particularly evident in healing, and now it is for his claim to heal AIDS that Kayiwa is known. By November 1994 he claimed to have healed over 30 AIDS patients. Newspapers suggest that although he trains others in a healing ministry, the ability to cure AIDS is special to him.[100] But his gifts go further than healing AIDS. He can perform spectacular miracles, and he will readily recount how in 1982 the girlfriend of a witchdoctor in Hoima came to him. Kayiwa told her not to go back to the witchdoctor, so she stayed with him for six weeks. 'The witchdoctor said he was going to kill me within a week if she did not go back'. Kayiwa, unafraid, sent the witchdoctor a message that he himself must come to Jesus. 'That very

---

[100] A cutting on NCF notice board, cut from a Dubai newspaper, obviously dependent on a news conference arranged for Kayiwa by *Miracles* magazine (see below).

day fire came from heaven and killed him.' He tells how a woman was attacked by fire for a month. The fire would hover in the house, burning various things, like children's toys. 'The burnt spots in the house are still evident'. 'The Anglican clergy went, but they couldn't do anything. It got worse. I went into the compound and it stopped immediately. It stopped because of the anointing I have, and because of (my) faith.' In recounting his exploits he frequently refers to the role of dreams. Services at NCF are not as organised as at KPC. It is often clear that they have not been planned, and sermons tend to be repetitious and rambling. The preacher can even arrive late. The social status of those attending is not as high, and the numbers are in the hundreds, rather than thousands.

Although NCF is obviously a local church and belongs to no Western denomination, international links and overseas recognition are a key element in its dynamics. In Kayiwa's case the external connection comes in the form of a new British magazine on the paranormal, *Miracles and the Extraordinary*, which promotes him as a miracle-worker. 'This man routinely reverses nature.'[101] It runs features on the Ugandan AIDS patients he has cured, and refers to the Cambridge economics lecturer he cured and to the English stroke victim who regularly telephones him for prayer and 'is now playing the piano for the first time in many years'. But it highlights more than his special healing powers. It recounts the story of John Buyinza who 'brought a Ugandan banknote, the equivalent of a pound, to Pastor Simeon ten years ago. He prayed over it and now John lives in a 250,000 pound house.'[102] The magazine has also taken Kayiwa to Britain and America (where he claims he had eleven and eighteen radio interviews respectively), and even to Hollywood – the magazine ran a feature on him and the star Steven Seagal. The magazine carries advertisements for trips to Uganda for a week with Simeon Kayiwa, a week which includes 'healing seminars, private counselling and classes on spiritual growth, prayer, psychology and relationships', along with excursions to the source of the Nile or the Mountains of the Moon.[103] The magazine has pledged 10% of its profits to Kayiwa's ministry.

It must be said that *Miracles* promotes claims that seem wildly improbable. It claims that Kayiwa has 2,000 churches, and 2 million followers. This claim could be true only if Kayiwa is considered the father of the entire Pentecostal movement in Uganda. Kayiwa sometimes argues in that way – in 1977 no similar churches existed; his was the first, and

---

[101] *Miracles*, May-June 1995, 10 (available from 157 Gloucester Road, London SW7 4TH).

[102] *Miracles*, March 1995, 26. The articles on Kayiwa are in *Miracles*, Nov 1994, 8-19; March 1995, 22-27; May-June 1995, 10-14.

[103] *Miracles*, March 1995, 49. One of those who came returned with plans to set up a bus company, with a percentage of the profits for Kayiwa's ministry (interview, 26 July 1995).

therefore every Pentecostal believer in Uganda today stems from him. There are pastors who readily acknowledge Kayiwa as their spiritual father. At other times Kayiwa talks of all the churches that directly stem from him, but insists that he has no interest in keeping them tied to him; on the contrary, he encourages them to stand on their own when they are self-sufficient. The claims of *Miracles* seem mainly for external consumption.

Kayiwa's standing in Kampala is not as high as the KPC pastor's. Kayiwa has undoubtedly followers, and even a certain preeminence among a group of born-again pastors; he is the president of the Fellowship of Born-Again Churches and the United Reformed Council. But many of the general public regard him with some suspicion. In fact he seems remarkably casual in his attention to his church. In 1995 he enrolled for an MA in International Relations at the American International University in Nairobi, and spends months at a time in Kenya.

Thirdly, consider the Abundant Life Church, which was founded by a black Canadian, Handel Leslie, in Kampala in October 1989. It began meeting in Kampala's Sheraton Hotel, but in January 1991 moved to a spectacular hilltop site 9 km. along the Entebbe Road. Free buses are provided every Sunday to transport worshippers to the church (at a weekly cost to the church of 500,000 Ushs, or $500). In October 1992 the present building was opened, which holds about 1200. This building will become a mothers' hall when the proposed domed 15,000-seat cathedral is completed, at an estimated cost of $1.5 million, '90% of which will come from local people'. The pastor is from an adventist-pentecostal background, and studied 'at Church of God and interdenominational seminaries in the States'.[104]

This church is totally personal. If Pastor Handel Leslie left, there would be nothing. He is the prophet, he is the pastor, he is the anointed man of God. This is a faith church – the pastor is a member of the International Convention of Faith Ministries – but the general faith doctrine has here taken its own path. If Kayiwa's church focuses on healing, Abundant Life, though not ignoring healing, has relegated it to the very periphery to focus almost exclusively on success. And success is understood mainly in terms of becoming a successful businessman. We have seen this development in Ghana in Mensa Otabil's church, and Leslie shares another thing in common with Otabil, the denunciation of working for the

---

[104] When asked the reasons for the growth of the church, he explains: 'We seek to motivate people to be involved in the community. We place an emphasis on work, and the success principles of scripture. We foster self-image, for God puts potential in people. And we teach that Jesus still heals today, is a healer and provider.[...] People flock here because this is practical for their lives, God is doing things for them here. There is also a dynamic sense of worship, and people are given an opportunity to flow with gifts of the spirit.[...] When people experience something in their lives, they spread it [i.e. the church's reputation]' (Interview, 7 June 1994).

government as a waste of time. One must have one's own business; even if one is a lawyer or doctor, one must create a business, perhaps run by others, which will be the main source of revenue (this represents a complete change from the days of African independence when to have a government job was to be one of the chosen). But whereas Otabil teaches that success comes from skills and training, for those at Abundant Life it comes from the quasi-magical gifts of the pastor – or more correctly, through his anointing, and through the inexorable working of the spiritual law of sowing. (There is a slight tension here; success is to come through the automatic application of laws, and yet it needs the pastor's influence.) Both aspects of this message call for some exposition.

On 29 May 1994 in the course of the service he claimed: 'I feel anointing in my left hand. All those who want a job within seventeen days come out'. About 120 came out to the front, and he touched their hands with his left hand, saying: 'Receive jobs in Jesus' name. I command these jobs to come, I command these jobs to come (repeated ten times). Seventeen days will not pass without a job. Come, in Jesus' name (six times). I break the spirit of joblessness in Jesus' name. I decree those jobs to come. Jobs, I command you to come. And I speak of the highest and best jobs'. At another time, he interrupted his talking to point to a woman near the front and say, 'Sister Elise, do you need that car? Do you need that car?' He called her to the front, and he laid his hand on her forehead: 'Let it happen, let it be a sign'. At another time he broke into his sermon to say: 'Doctor, come here. I've seen all you've done for the church. In the next ninety days God will give you a vehicle'. All these blessings are to come solely through the special gifts of this pastor, through his special anointing.

The second aspect of the message is the law of sowing and reaping. In the course of one service the pastor held three separate collections. He called all those who were jobless but hoping for a job to come forward to pledge 10% of the salary they were hoping for, the pledge to be paid within the following ten days. As soon as the jobless came forward, ushers distributed pens and paper for them to write their names and the amount. Then at the end of the service he told of a revelation he had the previous Friday night. He called out all those who would pledge 8,000, 80,000 or 800,000 shillings (US$8, $80, or $800) within the following ten days. Again the sanction of God was invoked: 'Obey the urging of the spirit'. About 120 came forward, and paper and pens were immediately distributed so that they could write their names and the amount. He told them: 'You are doing this for yourself, for your business, your promotion.'

The following Sunday he preached on the gift of prophecy, and had no hesitation in describing himself as a prophet. The latter part of the sermon dealt with supporting the prophet. 'Whenever you meet a prophet you should not meet him empty-handed. Because usually something happens.' He told the story of Elijah taking money from the widow (1Kings 17: 7-16), and how every time she went to her store it increased. 'You cannot give to a prophet and become poor. God will never decrease your supply, he will increase it'. He told the story of Saul's consulting a prophet about his missing asses (1 Sam 9: 3-8). In commenting on verse 7, he said: 'It is important to bring the man of God a gift. Yet there are people who don't think to give a prophet anything. The way to get more out of a prophetic anointing is to bless the prophetic anointing'. In the course of an exposition he commented on Naaman the leper (2 Kings 5):

You cannot merchandise the annointing... When you give to a prophet you are not paying. It is a prophetic principle, he who gives to a prophet will not go empty. You should not wait for any special announcement to bless the Man of God. When you get a job, just come and bless the Man of God.[...] Some of you are such [in financial difficulties] because you are rebelling against what God is saying in this church.[...] Some say "Why does he preach so much about money?". You are the greatest blocking to your own blessing.[...] If you don't receive, it's nobody's fault (but your own). When you obey a prophet, you receive a prophet's reward. If we had a visiting pastor, and I asked you to bless him, you would. Well I want you to give like that today.[...] I don't have any specific need today, but God has great plans. Don't give to a servant of God what is left over. When you come to church you should not come empty-pocketed, you should not come empty-handed. I will give you two minutes to get ready. If you need to write a cheque, do so. You're giving to a servant of God. You must realise where most of your blessings are coming from. [He prays.] Lord, I'm speaking double blessings this week. I command prophetic blessings on their storehouses, bank accounts, supernatural blessings, and this week, so that they may know that (these blessings have come) by what I did on Sunday.

After this nearly three quarters of the congregation went forward to give an offering to the pastor, who collected it personally in his own hands saying 'God bless you' to each donor, and then placing it in baskets by his side. If 800 people gave an average of 500 shillings, this would come to 400,000 shillings (about $US 400).

During the service on 16 July 1995 he said that God had revealed to him that there were sixty-seven people in the church whom

... I will launch into their own businesses. Some are already in business, but not at full capacity. Let these people trust me, and give me 120,000 shillings ($120) in the next seven days. Listen to me, the prophetic anointing is at work. God says if you will trust me for 120,000 shillings in 7 days [you will prosper].[...] Some professional man, God is going to launch you in a side business. Some are working in an office; you'll never be a millionaire working in an office. Stand in two lines. Some of you are schoolteachers, you are not receiving anything. I hear God saying you are going to do better. A woman wants to open a pharmacy but does not have the capital. I hear God saying if you will obey today, you will see his glory. Someone needs a pickup [truck]. I see a new brand of pickup. A businessman – if you will obey the prophetic word of God today, you will see the outpouring of God in your business. [Then he asked his assistants how many had come forward.] Forty-five? God says there are sixty-seven. [He continues.] One wants to do importing from Japan. I hear the Lord say, if you will release it today, you will see wonders. If you take a step of faith, you will be surprised what God will do for you and your family. This money will come to you unexpectedly. When it comes, you'll say "I don't believe this". You'll remember these words. There are still seven women, the Lord says, sitting here, that if you will obey the word of the Lord today, you will be surprised. There's a woman working in the President's office. The Lord says I want to promote you. Don't deny the promotion. [Again he asks his assistants how many have lined up before him.] Sixty-five people? Two are not listening. One of them is a businessman. The Lord tells me that your business needs rejuvenation. If you obey today, you will see signs and wonders. Some of you say, "I've given before and nothing has happened". As I stand here under the anointing, I tell you prophetically, the Lord says there is coming a turning around. I see great favour coming to some of you, an unprecedented favour. I hear the Lord say that he wanted to make you rich in the past, but you were not ready for it. You put yourself first. As you rearrange (your life, this will change). [His assistants tell him that the required sixty-seven have now come forward.] Lift up your hands. I release an impartation in their lives of success in whatever they do. I say that they will succeed and not fail. I decree the doors of God have opened. I decree that the word spoken over you today will come to pass. Let it happen. [He lays hands on each one.] I desire to make you a financial pillar in my Kingdom. The contracts are so many, coming from every side. They are coming, says the Lord. The spirit of greatness is coming on you in Jesus' name. I hear God saying there is an open door. I command those blessings in Jesus' name. I decree it... I command you to prosper in Jesus' name. I hear the Lord say, every limitation is being removed. Lord, I create into her life the ability to prosper. I hear that someone will literally bring you the money you need.[...] There are times God speaks and it does not come to pass in the person's life, because you have nullified God's word.[...] If you obey in the time [the seven days God has specified], it will come to pass. Whatever God told you to do, you must do it within seven days.

On this day, he called for five separate offerings. First, there were the sixty-seven who pledged 120,000 shillings each. Then there was the ordinary collection of tithes and offerings. (These are different things; tithes are placed in an envelope, with the name written on the outside, to stop people handing in empty envelopes. The offerings are over and above the tithes, and must be held above the head, the notes unfolded so everyone can see the amount.) Fourth there was an opportunity for a 'Gideon offering' (sometimes called the 'fleece test'), based on Judges 6: 36-40 where Gideon challenged God to confirm his promises; in a Gideon offering, one gives a certain amount to God, challenging God to multiply it. And finally there was a 'prophetic offering', in which the congregation was invited to make a contribution to the prophet, on the understanding that 'he who makes a gift to a prophet will receive the reward of a prophet' (Mt 10,40).

The worship here is lively, with English hymns, a band with electric guitars and keyboards, a choir who perform two or three numbers every service, but the service is almost exclusively focused on the pastor, although his wife will sometimes play some part in the proceedings. The members are well off, young and beautifully dressed. The members seem very westernised, with the women in stylish fashions and hats – there are few in traditional attire or *gomesi*. There are numerous expensive cars in the car park, some with the legend 'World Bank' or 'Office of the President' on the doors. There are sometimes visiting speakers (like Nicholas Duncan-Williams of Ghana) and the pastor will frequently travel outside Uganda 'for courses', but the dynamics here are essentially intra-Ugandan. The message is for local people, and the money is (as we have seen) raised locally. The church has political aspirations, to influence Uganda through the economic power and importance of its members.

It is difficult to monitor the appeal of this church, because extraneous factors have intruded to distort its growth. In early 1995 *Uganda Confidential* targeted the pastor, denouncing him as a homosexual, a diamond smuggler and general racketeer.[105] *Uganda Confidential* is an interesting publication, devoted to exposing corruption in government and the civil service, and depending in large measure on leaks of official documents. It draws occasional libel suits, including one for a story linking Mrs Museveni to a murder. (Some cite this as illustrating Museveni's new Uganda; such an accusation was met with a lawsuit rather than closure, torture or death.) There is no doubt that the editor of *Uganda Confidential* regards Leslie as a total charlatan and is out to discredit him. The effect on Abundant Life Church is hard to measure.There is no evident decrease in numbers. Some members say that it is all a plot, either of other pastors to destroy Leslie because he is so successful, or of Abundant Life's junior pastors to enable them to take control of such a profitable enterprise. By late 1996 Leslie seemed not only to have weathered this storm, but to have gained important institutional support. Four Nigerians of Winners' Chapel, Lagos, had opened a Bible school in central Kampala which drew up to 300 students to its evening courses. The Nigerians, closely linked with Abundant Life, were preaching the same unnuanced message as Leslie.

Fourthly, consider the Holy Church of Christ. This church looks back to the Ghanaian prophet John Obiri Yeboah, who lived in Uganda in the 1970s but returned to Ghana when Amin moved against pentecostal churches. He returned to Uganda in 1986, before dying in 1987. This Prophet John is an important figure in current Ugandan Christianity, for several churches are descended from him, and he established the first association of pentecostal churches, called the National Fellowship of Born Again Churches and United Reformed Council, in 1986.[106] During his brief second stay in Uganda, he allegedly singled out a woman and

---

[105] *Uganda Confidential*, 11-18 May 1995, 16; 13-20 July 1995, 16; 20-27 July 1995, 1.

[106] For this church, see Robby Muhumuza, 'The Church with the Spirit of Obiri Yeboah', *Involvement*, Dec 1994-March 1995, 7-13. The Redeemed Church of Christ (in fact, all

made her a prophetess. She was an ordinary woman before this (and according to her critics, the prophet John promoted her well beyond her capacities), but in the light of Prophet John's anointing, she and her husband Sam, both in the mid-1990s in their early thirties, have gone on to establish their church, in which he is the pastor and she the prophetess. This is a truly joint operation.

Services last from about 10am till about 5pm each Sunday, and are attended by about 1200. The congregation seems to come from all classes. Much of the service is spent in healing, which both the pastor and his wife perform. The church has a most distinctive character, for Prophet John had been a Catholic, and candles, incense, water and oil are everywhere in evidence. As the long lines move to the front for healing, bottles of olive oil and buckets of water from the spring under the church are utilised – the oil is even rubbed on women's stomachs. At the end of the service everyone is not sprinkled but thoroughly dowsed with holy water. There is no choir at these services. This was a deliberate choice; for both pastor and prophetess, choir practice and fornication are almost synonyms, and they insist that it blocks the working of the Holy Spirit to have such dubious people standing near the pulpit. There is surprisingly little singing, although occasionally the pastor or the prophetess will break into a few verses of some old favourite, which an electronic keyboard will take up. There is no attempt to involve anyone beside themselves. The service is essentially them, although there are frequent testimonies, with the microphone passed to people clamouring to testify, nearly all of whom speak in local languages, translated into English. Most of these testimonies focus on what the pastor or the prophetess has done for the testifier.

These services have a much more African feel than those of the other churches we have noted – indeed, in many respects this church could well be viewed as a late-begotten classical AIC, new to Uganda, but passé in Ghana where its origins lie. The prophetess can fall into a trance and lie apparently senseless on the steps. There are periods of uninhibited and unrestrained worship, with women shouting and whirling and requiring restraint to prevent harm. It is also quite relaxed – at times the couple's young children wander up to their mother, to be given a coke or something to eat. The service is the major church activity. There are no cell groups or Bible studies for members, and there is no mission strategy.

Uganda's various 'Redeemed' churches) stem from him; so too the very high profile World Evangelical Redeemed Church of Archbishop David Makumbi, and the Namirembe Christian Fellowship of Pastor Simeon Kayiwa, and Prophetess Viola Katusabe's Church on the Rock, Najjanankumbi. See Kasumba, *New Evangelical Church Sects*. For more on the Church on the Rock, see *Involvement*, Dec 1994-March 1995, 22-3. There is even a 'St John Obiri Yeboah Primary School' in Mpigi district (New Vision, 16 June 1994, 3).

During office hours on weekdays the church functions as a clinic – this is the word the couple choose to describe their church – with at any time up to 20 waiting their turn to see one or the other.

If the service involves (besides the sermon) mainly healing, the testimonies and prayers focus on jobs and money. Again, there is a heavy accent on success, and here too success comes not so much through faith as through the gifts of the couple. Because they have the anointing of the Spirit, they can do more than any witchdoctor could through his satanic wiles. And there is an acceptance of African reality not found in most other churches; frequently the testimonies repeat: 'I went to the witchdoctor to no avail; then I came to the prophetess and I was cured [or found a job, or made some money].' Going to the witchdoctor is not denounced; it is just pointless when one has the opportunity to come to the prophetess or pastor and be helped by Jesus himself. The pastor can be unashamed in his pitch for money; on 12 June 1994 he asked everyone to line up and bring him 15,000 Ushs ($15) to complete the roof of the church, and told them that they should bring 20,000 Ushs ($20) the following week. The element of success and prosperity is prominent here, the pastor told me: 'I used to be poor and sick. But we built a house in six months, we built a church in six months. Our God makes us able'. And while proudly showing me round their buildings, both kept repeating: 'Can the devil do this?' During a service, the prophetess prayed: 'Jesus has put down our enemies; we shall never be poor'. The banner across the front of the church in 1994 read 'The first day of the major economic recovery', meaning that to come to this church is to reverse any economic decline.

This is less the unadulterated Faith Gospel of Hagin and Copeland, and has more of a local flavour. They have heard of the American proponents of the Faith Gospel – in Uganda's charismatic churches today it would be hard to be uninfluenced by them – but not really read them. They do not have visiting speakers or go overseas for courses. They are not funded from overseas, although they are seeking links. They are both remarkable people, very intelligent, with an impressive knowledge of the Bible, though lacking the education or formal training of someone like Kayiwa. Yet they have thought deeply about Uganda's situation. They repeat Museveni's theme that 'We need job-creators, not job-seekers'. They claim that the problem in Uganda is not illiteracy but the number of educated people with no jobs. And poverty is not the problem. 'There is money here, you in the West have been misled. The problem is not poverty; it is lack of trust, of knowledge, of organisation'. Again, 'The problem is not poverty, it is guidance, mobilisation, trustworthiness and organisation'. So they have set themselves to create wealth, motivate their members, and witness to accountability and skill in organisation. They have embarked on an impressive building project involving pastor's house, church, and a bakery. The bakery, which opened in late 1994, produces 60,000 loaves 'of European bread' a day. The couple have calculated the demand, given their advantageous position between Makerere University and Mulago hospital, and talk of 100 agents, 200 retailers, and a profit of 12 million shillings a week. This business is a key part of their vision. It will enable the church to flourish; the agents and retailers will tithe and this will bring in a million shillings a week. They see this as an integral part of preaching the gospel: 'You can't convince people unless you have done things', which in Uganda primarily means erecting fine buildings. Also, after and because they have done things, they will be able to find overseas partners and get assistance, which will help them complete their project of a radio station and a conference centre. The radio station will be for all the born-again churches, and would have half its programming local, half from overseas. The proposed conference centre, with elaborate plans drawn up by a Kenyan architect, is also seen as a business venture. Although costing $1.5 million, letting sixteen rooms at 30,000 shillings a night will bring in over 3 million shillings a week. Much of their service is spent praying for jobs and promising jobs, but they have a genuine economic vision and a GOP (Get Out of Poverty) plan to achieve it; there is less supernaturalistic agency than at Abundant Life, though they do not promote the practical training in skills of Otabil in Ghana.

The socio-political role of Pentecostalism

As in Ghana, there is obviously great variety within Ugandan Pentecostalism. Most of the newer churches seem to be similar to the Ghanaian ones, but, as remarked above, some exhibit qualities which in Ghana are characteristic of older churches which are tending to be superseded – ecclesiastically, Uganda lags behind Ghana. Obviously the Faith Gospel has reached Uganda and is strengthening its grip. But churches like the Holy Church of Christ promise blessings and abundance more directly in terms of traditional beliefs than of the teachings of Hagin or the Copelands. Uganda does not (or not yet) have the deliverance ministries so prevalent in West Africa. Part of the reason for this might be the 'strikingly less "magical" ' character of traditional Ganda religion.[107] Nor are Uganda's pastors so insistent on writing books.[108] We noted in Ghana the tendency for what makes most sense in an urban context to fan out into districts and then rural areas, through extensive evangelism. This is

---

[107] Peel, 'Conversion and Tradition', 118-19.

[108] Though Robert Kayanja of the Rubaga Miracle Fellowship has written: *Power Words* and *Thousandfold Increase*, both n.d., available from Box 1680, Kampala. These are basically faith gospel; see in the latter the claim that with this Christianity one will 'need more pockets' (13) and his claim that through giving away an older car at God's command, he received a new one (27).

true in Uganda as well. For example, in Fort Portal, Pastor Dickson Lubega, himself a disciple of Kampala's Simeon Kayiwa, has begun his own pentecostal church, the Kabarole Christian Fellowship. Lubega claims to have established 180 churches in surrounding villages by 1995, and although this number seems highly exaggerated, there is no doubt of the church's intense evangelistic effort.[109]

In accounting for their rise, some reasons are obvious and valid in both Ghana and Uganda. First, the lively worship, especially when compared with the traditional worship of the COU, although the COU has tried to meet this issue, making one Sunday service at Namirembe cathedral and one at All Saints as charismatic as they can. (It must be said, however, that neither remotely rivals in enthusiasm or participation the services of, say, Rubaga Miracle Centre or KPC.) Secondly, the element of intensity or seriousness. Most do not simply *attend* these churches; they come with Bible and pen and paper, and throughout the sermon copy references and take notes frantically. This element of seriousness in these churches is (even more than in Ghana) contrasted with the supposed lack of seriousness of those who attend the mainline churches – establishment people, 'political' people, the great and the good who are there out of social duty or political necessity or tradition. This attitude to Uganda's mainline churches (which explains both why one leaves the mainline churches and why one turns to the new pentecostal ones) extends to disgust at the way some of the mainline churches are run. Another important consideration is the impoverished circumstances in which Ugandan Christians find themselves. Western (usually American) missionaries wanting links in Uganda have no shortage of eager applicants. Churches and missions coming from overseas needing local representatives, office staff and evangelists are inevitably providing jobs, funds, vehicles, housing, position, opportunities, a livelihood.[110]

I have noted some of the claims made for these churches. There is no doubt that these churches do serve many of these functions. There is no doubt, for example, of what they can do by way of personal reformation. This is linked to the element of intensity just mentioned. Every evening one can see hordes of youths listlessly gathering around Kampala's taxi park or sports stadium, an easy prey to drink, drugs, sex, and crime. The

---

[109] Interview, 24 July 1995.

[110] Musana Paddy, 'The Pentecostal Movement in Uganda: Its Impact with Specific Reference to Kampala City' (unpublished M.A. thesis, Makerere University, 1991) has a section on 'Reasons why people leave Institutional Churches to join Pentecostals' which collates the results of a questionnaire (225-8). The reasons given include: (no.4) 'hypocrisy in the institutional churches', (no.10) 'opportunities to use talents', (no.12) 'most leaders in institutional churches do not show moral examples', (no.16) 'to obtain recognition', (no.19) 'to obtain sponsorship to study abroad', (no.23) 'to obtain foreign aid'.

aimlessness of this existence leads to enormous frustration. In the circumstances of the current AIDS epidemic in Uganda, it can also lead to a far more serious fate than frustration. All churches in theory could lift people from this life, but in fact it is the intensity of the born-again experience which has proved that it can take people on to another plane. This fervour has some relevance in Museveni's Uganda. Museveni is creating a new country from the ashes of the old. As he has repeatedly claimed, 'This is not a changing of the guard; this is a new dispensation'. And for many at least he is winning. The two established churches were part of this old dispensation, and they too have to be transcended. This sentiment is everywhere heard in the vocabulary of the born-agains: words and phrases like 'victorious', 'breaking through', 'climbing over', 'creating a new order'. Their hymns express this victory, this unstoppable surge, this wave carrying all before it. But it is only the religious side of a more widespread enthusiasm. The born-again movement is part of Museveni's movement of reconstruction, in a dynamic not so evident in Ghana. Frequently people claim that Museveni is surrounding himself with born-agains. In 1994 a Senior Principal Revenue Officer told this writer that 273 employees had recently, as part of a rationalisation of the civil service, been retrenched from the tax department. Beforehand, corruption was rampant - in his language, 'Spirits controlled the tax office'. It was his job to select those to be made redundant, and he made sure that no born-agains were dismissed. As a result, in the month before the dismissals, the office collected 21 billion shillings; the month after, they had collected 59 billion. In his language, 'God is working miracles, we shall claim the place in Jesus' name.'[111] In Museveni's Uganda, to an extent not possible in much of Africa, Pentecostalism need not be an opting out, it may be an opting in.

We have referred to the personal transformation made possible by churches in the face of the AIDS epidemic. In parenthesis we must refer to two programmes launched by churches to combat AIDS, the Catholic 'Youth Alive' programme and the Baptist 'True Love Waits'. The Catholic programme was drawn up by an American missionary sister from an American counselling model of behavioural change. It began in the early 1990s with 'Education for Life' seminars, within a group providing support.[112] It has led to a network of 'Youth Alive' clubs which both involve youth in AIDS prevention programmes and encourage creative activities diverting youth from a way of life that would lead to AIDS. A key element is 'fulfilling one's dream', or raising ambitions which careless premarital sex might imperil. The programme historically was linked to both the Catholic Charismatic Renewal and the cell-like Small Christian

[111]   Interview, 9 June 1994.
[112]   Kay Lawlor, *Education for Life: a Behaviour Process for Groups*, Entebbe: Ministry of Health, 1989.

Communities (SCCs). It is gradually being modified away from these Catholic institutions to broaden its appeal to other denominations. In Kampala's Kamwokya area, where the programme has its headquarters, it is still closely linked with a thriving set of SCCs which are geared not so much to social analysis as to community care. This care embraces those suffering from AIDS and orphans, but includes many other activities besides: baking, shoemaking, sewing, and even a clinic and a library.[113]

The Baptist 'True Love Waits' programme was brought to Uganda from the USA. In Uganda it has been modified somewhat. (Not the least interesting modification sheds significant light on the dynamics of Uganda's current Christianity. In America the pledge to abstain from pre-marital sex is made in church in the company of one's parents; in Uganda this element could not be preserved because, in the words of the programme's director, 'In the new churches we work with, their parents are all Anglicans and Catholics'.) The team travels around schools, asks for a four- or six-hour session, at the end of which it calls for a pledge to abstain from pre-marital sex; often a 10-20% response is claimed. In the presentation great use is made of the 'dream' idea borrowed from the Catholic programme. Heightening aspirations which casual sex would endanger is necessary, according to the director, because ambitions are generally so low. The director himself is prepared to state that many of his family and all his school friends are dead already; if he had not become a Christian he would be dead too: 'Christianity is needed here to stay alive'.

Another claim made for these newer churches is that they provide scope for leadership to a much greater degree than the traditional churches, where a trained class occupy leadership positions and professionally manage all aspects of church life on behalf of members. In Uganda, however, the pentecostals have no monopoly on leadership opportunities. Almost every night the TV news reports courses in personnel management, leadership training, resource management, and all sorts of administrative skills, and most of these courses are run by NGOs or by churches. In Uganda, leadership training is a priority of *all* churches, almost part of the essence of Christianity. Thus the Catholics' sixth theological week was devoted to 'Education for Leadership in Uganda'. Their annual September Tribune had in 1994 the theme 'Christ the Model for Good Leadership'. The Catholic Comboni missionaries produce an attractive bi-monthy periodical entitled simply *Leadership*. The COU's Planning, Development and Rehabilitation Department devotes enormous resources to numerous projects in leadership training. African Evangelistic Enterprise has as one of its objectives training for leadership, management and stewardship.

---

[113] See *The Youth Alive Newsletter*, and Glen Williams and Nassali Tamale, *The Caring Community: Coping with AIDS in Urban Uganda*, London: ActionAid/Amref, 1991.

The American Presbyterians who run workshops for the COU have in their seminars lectures on leadership and management principles. Some of the pentecostal churches do this particularly well. For example, the pastor of the Kampala Pentecostal Church made leadership his special focus in 1994. The sermons deal with biblical personages, from Genesis to Revelation, from the angle of leadership. Its Thursday lunchtime meetings are all on leadership: topics include 'setting goals', 'un-reliability', 'handling crises', 'the Christian at the workingplace – his/her fruitfulness', 'cross-cultural interaction', 'friendship', 'money in biblical perspective', 'handling conflicts', 'singlehood – how to cope', with biblical studies on leaders like Melchisedech, Darius, Elisha, Paul, Daniel interspersed . It is true that the accent is on managing one's personal life by means of life skills and integrity, but even within the church there are about 200 in leadership roles and they meet every two weeks in a 'Harvesters' Fellowship' for special training. The pastor gives these sessions great importance. This church is perhaps a perfect example of a church fulfilling the functions that theorists of civil society would have it play, except that finances are in the hands of the Canadian missionaries of the Pentecostal Assemblies of God, so that financial accountability is one skill not learnt, or at least not yet. (Nor does the church hold elections; office-holders are appointed.) Many of the leadership skills learnt in churches might be specifically directed at leadership in ministry (for example the Baptists' six week ministry practicum in April and May 1994 with units like 'What really changes people', 'What is effective ministry', 'Knowing your full potential', 'Know your gifts and skills', 'The potential of small groups' and 'How to deal with conflict in ministry'). This emphasis is understandable, for many people will explain that there is today such a revival occurring in Uganda that the only brake on it is the lack of personnel to manage it. Nevertheless, the skills taught in this personal or family or church area are then available for application in the wider sphere. In Uganda today all the churches seem to view this leadership training as among their most pressing priorities.

However, some of the claims for these new churches need more study. Not all obviously promote brotherhood or equality, for there is in many a considerable element of totalitarianism. Consider the ideas of the founder of Abundant Life on the role of the pastor, a topic he returns to frequently. There is no idea of brotherhood here.

'One of the most difficult things in the body of Christ is to be submitted to each other. You need to know you don't call your pastor 'brother'. Not brother, he's a pastor. Call another brother your brother, *he*'s not your brother, he's your leader.... Pastor means a shepherd, a leader. Sometimes people will say, 'May I see you, brother?' I look at them [as if to say] 'Who are you talking to?' I do not allow people to call me by my first name, except my wife. Every church in the USA that has spiritual authority does not allow the pastor to be called 'brother'. In the kingdom of God you need to know what to do. You need to identify who exactly your pastor is.

In another sermon he glorifies his own role as pastor: 'Some might ask, "What kind of a pastor are you?" I am the pastor God wants; if there were more like me we wouldn't have the troubles we do.'[114] He has given the pastor a status that not many archbishops would claim; and he is not hesitant in appropriating it for himself. The whole church is focused on him. The activities of this church are basically his preaching; surprisingly for such a church, there are not even cell groups.

Consider his teaching on the nature of a prophet, another subject he is prone to return to. 'The Bible says God will do nothing without revealing it to prophets. Which of you has a right to tell the President how to run Uganda? None of you. Yet God tells leaders what to do. It's for spiritual leaders to talk to other leaders. I tell you this so you can understand how prophesying about nations works'. In a democracy, the people *do* have a right to tell Museveni how to run the country; he is accountable to them. But this pastor teaches that only a spiritual leader particularly blessed by God can do this; he does it by virtue of the fact not that he is a citizen of the country but that God reveals his plans to certain specially chosen and anointed servants, among whom he is fortunate to be numbered. Again, 'Many things I could say about the problems of Gulu [viz the insurrection in the north]. The Lord tells me'. By implication, those who cannot lay claim to the special revelation of God cannot have much to say about the problems of Gulu. A divine sanction is invoked to elevate his views to a totally different plane; they are given a status that makes them by definition unchallengeable. Few archbishops would make such claims.

Nor is there necessarily any accountability. Again, consider Abundant Life, admittedly an extreme case. We have described its aggressive fund raising. It is not clear how much is collected, nor what it is spent on. The fundraising allows no scrutiny. The pastor claims that anyone who is a member of the church and is faithfully tithing could ask to see the accounts of the church, but it is doubtful if any avail themselves of this right.[115] Even if all the money raised was spent on the construction of the new church, it still has to be said that the vision of a 15,000 seat domed cathedral on the top of this hill is very much the pastor's own vision. The people had no say in this decision or in planning it. It is a case of 'his vision, their resources'. But it is not presented as his vision but as God's will.

Also, it must be said that this church is hardly calculated to develop

---

114 He continued: 'Some of these pastors in town have made themselves into little Gods. [People say] If we could just touch the hem of his garment." I never want to reach the stage when people worship me. They started to do that in Kenya. The Lord told me "Don't go to Kenya too often".'

115 Interview, 7 June 1994.

any critical awareness. In one sermon the founder of Abundant Life said:

'The greatest thing for the future well-being of Uganda, it is when Uganda establishes relations with Israel openly. A nation that blesses Israel is blessed, a nation that curses Israel is cursed (he cites Gen 12,3). It's coming, links are slowing returning. That's why the economy in Uganda has started to revive. When that relationship is established publicly, northern Uganda will come to peace, the fighting will subside. Who ran the Israelites from Uganda? [The congregation shouts 'Amin'.] Yes, a northerner. God will heal the North when the Israelites come back.'

Then to show that this was not just his private opinion, he declared solemnly: 'Thus saith the Lord'. (Israelis had been involved with Uganda's security forces from 1964 until April 1972.) The pastor had already said in the same service: 'Any President with any sense would welcome born-again churches. We pray more for them. The people who keep Museveni in power are the born-again Christians. The people who keep Chiluba in power in Zambia are the born-again Christians. The people who keep Moi in power in Kenya are the born-again Christians. Those who keep Moi in power are not the Catholics. Moi told me this himself. So pray for our leaders.' Anyone with awareness of Kenyan politics in the 1990s would realise that 'keeping Moi in power' is perhaps not something to boast of. In this Christianity, however, a Christian's duty is simply to support a President, particularly one who promotes evangelism.

In July 1995 a visiting 'biblical expert', Barry Smith, conducted a three day seminar at KPC. About 1200 attended and heard him explain that Matthew 24: 34 referred to 1948 (the establishment of Israel, the beginning of European Union and the founding of the World Council of Churches, all of which the Bible supposedly regards as great evils); that Revelation 13:16-18 foretells the computer chip, and that 'this word of God will soon be fulfilled when we have computer chips implanted in our right hands or foreheads'; that 2 Peter 3:8 shows that the world will end in AD 2000; that Revelation 13:5 proves that the Antichrist will be revealed when Syria signs a peace treaty with Israel; that 2 Thessalonians 2: 7 foretells the new world order and privatisation. He insisted that privatisation is evidence of the advent of the anti-Christ, even though this is what Museveni, in his economic restructuring, has been attempting. Smith insisted: 'The people who are doing this sincerely believe this is the best way to go. Don't criticise people doing this.[...] God allows it to continue so he might show his power'. He told his audience: 'You needn't worry; Jesus is in charge.[...] In spite of the things taking place around us, our citizenship is not here.[...] Don't you worry about the new world order, worry about the coming of Jesus'. This does not prove that millennialism is a major theme in Ugandan Christianity – it is not; but it illustrates something else. At one stage Smith, in displaying his biblical erudition, pronounced the Greek letter 'xi', rhyming it with 'see', and a considerable number of people in the audience began softly correcting him with 'sigh'. They had obviously conducted hours of Bible study, so that they could recognise Greek letters. But the same study had not taught them anything about the nature of apocalyptic literature and how one might use it. It had not equipped them to evaluate Smith's lectures as a farrago of nonsense.

Another characteristic of so many Pentecostal churches calls for some comment. As we have seen, the theorists of civil society put great stress on tolerance and compromise. It is true that there is an extended fellowship of 'born-agains' that transcends individual churches, but at the same time an enormous intolerance exists in these circles. For example, the pastor of Abundant Life spends a good deal of time denouncing the Holy Church of Christ; some denunciation appears in every sermon. This particular church (again betraying its Catholic origins) gives great veneration to the Prophet John Obiri Yeboah. His portrait is prominent around the church, his name is invoked frequently, and many members wear T-shirts bearing his portrait and inscriptions like 'Faith can move Mountains, Prophet John says', and even 'There is only one Jesus and Prophet John is his Messenger'. This veneration of a founder is savaged by Abundant Life. Similarly, although the Abundant Life pastor is convinced he is a prophet and extols the gift incessantly, he is equally convinced that the Prophetess is a false prophet. Likewise, the Holy Church of Christ makes much of the healing powers of the holy water flowing from the spring under its church; every member of the congregation brings plastic containers to the services to replenish the stocks at home. The pastor of Abundant Life denounces this, poking fun at 'jerrycan' churches. The Holy Church of Christ is less denunciatory of other churches, but it certainly acts as a source of division and friction in the born-again community. The meeting that the Holy Church of Christ couple convened to offer other born-again pastors a stake in their proposed radio station, degenerated into an attack on them for their candles, incense, water and oil, and broke up in disarray.

The government has become alarmed by the intolerance between churches. Pentecostal churches used to be able to broadcast their own TV and radio programmes; Simeon Kayiwa of the Namirembe Christian Fellowship and Robert Kayanja of Rubaga Miracle Centre were two who did so. However this was all stopped in 1990.[116] Kayiwa ruefully says of this: 'Perhaps we made mistakes. Maybe one of us criticised the big religions. The government depends on the missionary hospitals and schools of these churches, so they stopped the programmes.'[117] This lesson appears to have been learnt. It is noteworthy that the pastor of Abundant Life will criticise the Holy Church of Christ for using water,

[116] *Weekly Topic*, 22 June 1990, 16.
[117] Interview, 11 June 1994.

candles, oil and incense, but he is adamant: 'We do not criticise the Catholics here'. Kayiwa says that government ministers have been 'appalled by the infighting' between the born-again churches, and that these fear they may be banned or 'told to go back to your mother churches. The government cannot understand why we don't'. This intolerance seems to be growing because of the increasing importance given to Satan and demons in this Christianity (although in Uganda this development has not hitherto given rise to the deliverance thinking and institutions of Ghana). In this thinking others come to be seen not as different groups with their own interests, which call for compromise and negotiation, but as agents of Satan to be vanquished, eradicated and even annihilated.

The best example of this is not from one of the Pentecostal churches, but from Kampala's COU All Saints Cathedral, which has itself become very pentecostal, to the disquiet of some of its own members. In May and June 1994 a part-time curate there, also assistant dean of the Faculty of Education at Makerere, gave a series of talks on 'Idol Worship, the Occult, Sorcery and Divination'. In the course of these he denounced Allah as a demon, and explained the 200 deaths in an accident at Mecca a few months before as the regular sacrifice Satan demands each year. He then went on to denounce 'certain elements of Catholic practice' as witchcraft. 'The rosary is a piece of witchcraft. So is the crucifix. We worship a living Christ, therefore the cross must be empty as his tomb is empty.[...] The devil wants to be worshipped. The moment you begin worshipping (any sacred) object, the devil comes and occupies it. Roman Catholics who worship the rosary, immediately the devil enters it, and the rosary becomes witchcraft and they practice witchcraft.[...] It is the same with the communion wafer. They worship the host. The host is not Christ. People who can see in the spirit see demons there....'[118] The following week he continued: 'Allah is not God; he is a demon'. He proceeded to argue that the Baha'i religion was satanic (particularly its perverted appropriation of the Christian symbol of the dove: 'The devil is using this to take people from Christianity'), the Unification Church, the Mormons, Freemasons (whom another All Saints pastor had received in the cathedral: 'This church needs deliverance'), the Jehovah's Witnesses ('If you belong to this church I pray that you leave. They have written their own Bible, to include all Satan's words'), the Church on the Rock, and Prophetesses. And these views are expected to lead to action; in his concluding prayer he reminded God: 'You are giving us this knowledge so that we may fight a war'. (Compare this intolerance with the inclusiveness Museveni tries to foster; he accepted allcomers in his NRA during the bush war, and afterwards was prepared to negotiate with any bandits ready to join him. Addressing a service in this same All Saints

118   Talk, 30 May 1994.

Cathedral, Museveni once actually urged church leaders to 'promote peace and stop creating problems for the people of Uganda').[119] The demonising of the Catholics is more than the traditional antipathy felt towards them by Anglicans and the demonising of the others is not traditional African thinking; the speaker, in expounding these views, frequently acknowledged his indebtedness to California's Peter Wagner.[120]

In discussing the Pentecostal churches, we must consider the pheno-menon of crusades. These are frequent and, as in Ghana, attract a bigger crowd if conducted by a foreigner, but they are less exuberant because Uganda does not have anything like Ghana's highly developed gospel music business. Consider the evangelist Ernest Angley of Akron, Ohio, who in June 1994 held a three day crusade in the centre of Kampala. The dynamics of this crusade are worth considering, for they illustrate some of the points made above, not least that Christian missions are now perhaps the biggest single industry in Uganda. Many of Uganda's pastors had been in contact with Angley over several years, and it was through them that Angley proposed that he come for a crusade. These pastors called a meeting of the National Fellowship of Born Again Churches and United Reformed Council (which really exists only to coordinate such crusades), who agreed to invite him and established a committee to coordinate the crusade. Angley sent one of his team for three months' preparation. As part of the total mission, his television programmes were screened on Ugandan TV on two evenings each week; this required negotiations with the television service, legal local representatives, and an office which could handle the letters and enquiries after the programmes and provide the follow-up. Angley provided all the necessary money, and several Ugandan pastors were given funds, employment and status. In Uganda's current situation the material benefits accruing from staging crusades are crucially important. In this case the local representation became permanent, for Angley returned the following year for crusades in Kampala and Jinja, and his programmes have become a regular feature on Ugandan television. If that is the dynamic on the side of the Ugandans, Angley too benefits from this arrangement. Three Americans accompanied him on the platform for his crusades, videoing everything with cameras that made those used by the Uganda Broadcasting Commission look primitive. The Uganda crusade furnishes the raw material for the programmes on his television stations in America, and for others screened overseas. This factor surely explains the grossly inflated size Angley claimed for the crowd on the final night: 'We must have 200,000 here,' he proclaimed. In fact, it would not have been more than 30,000 at the most (the unseasonably rainy weather kept many away), but viewers watching this on television around the world

---

119   See *APS Bulletin*, 5 July 1993.
120   C. Peter Wagner, *Territorial Spirits*, Chichester: Sovereign World, 1991.

would have no way of challenging these figures, for all they could see were rows of faces extending as far as the lights allowed.

It has to be said that Angley's Christianity reinforces some of the points made above. We are not saying that Ugandans are bound to absorb everything said at these crusades[121] – Kayiwa implied that he had some reservations about the evangelist – but there are considerable pressures reinforcing this Christianity. The day before the crusade began, Angley invited all pastors to a workshop at Kampala's Sheraton Hotel, Uganda's best. Included in the advertisement was the information that free books would be distributed. A huge crowd attended, all receiving a copy of Angley's latest book. Many of these pastors had little theological education, and might possess no books at all. Therefore *faute de mieux* Angley's presentation becomes the source of unlimited sermons.[122]

We spoke above of the authoritarian rather than egalitarian nature of some Pentecostal Christianity. Consider the following prophecy which Angley made over himself at this meeting for pastors:

Yea, says the Spirit of the Lord, I have sent my holy prophet among you, I have sent my messenger among you. If you seek to hinder my power, I will push you out of the way and never deal with your spirit again. I will let you go with your arrogance, and fear will be your companion. I will not grieve for you, my servant will not grieve for you. I have sent you one that will give my truth. I have called him to deliver my word. In the services I have ordained through him, I will set you free. I know your ways. I know everything that is right and everything that is wrong. I have brought my servant to help you. I am giving you *my* message, not the message of my servant. Take heed, or die in bondage, says the Lord, and be forever damned in time and eternity.

This is not calculated to promote rationality or critical evaluation. Noone can dissent in any way from anything the evangelist might go on to say without opposing God himself.

Angley also manifested the divisiveness discussed above. This seems to be almost inevitable. When there is such a plethora of crusaders passing through, there is considerable pressure to distinguish yourself from all the others, to show that you are still necessary because in some important way the others were all deficient. Angley did this by claiming that many preachers have a wrong view of baptism in the Spirit. Those who claim that they can pray in tongues 'at will' or 'that you can speak in tongues any time you want to' are wrong. That teaching is not of God. On the second night he repeated: 'The Lord himself visited me and told me it is

[121] On the day the crusade began, the *New Vision* carried a sustained attack on Angley across its centre pages; Paul Kurtz, 'Journalist Doubts Faith Healing', *New Vision*, 10 June 1994, 14-15.

[122] Ernest Angley, *The Deceit of Lucifer*, Akron: Ernest Angley, 1989. He had distributed the same book in Ghana during his visit there.

not true that people can talk at will. He told me its not his baptism. With some people its just flesh, but in other cases a demonic spirit got in and was doing the speaking'. His claim was that he could deliver the 'real Holy Spirit', as opposed to what others had been offering.

Angley also manifested the magic supernaturalism mentioned above. He claimed that on the final night he would heal everyone afflicted with AIDS. That night, in a state of trance, he proceeded to give the numbers of those cured during the crusade, numbers that 'an angel standing beside me' was revealing to him: 64,574 had been baptised in the Holy Spirit during the crusade; 7,547 cured of hip complaints, 14,341 of nervous disorders, 59,443 of troubles in the mind, 41,607 of fear, frustration and despair, 829 who 'needed your heart recreated', 19,207 of 'diseases, I am not talking about AIDS, which doctors were not able to cure', 21,864 of blood condition, 24,605 of stomach problems, 10,177 of bad kidneys, 15,477 of arthritis, 16,214 of back condition, (inaudible) of bowel condition, 31,027 of 'a special burden', 41,117 of a damaged brain, 17,503 of crossed eyes. These claims are by definition unchallengeable, being revealed by God himself.

Uganda's Christianity has a very different composition from Ghana's; the country, almost since its birth, has been a duopoly of Anglican and Catholic Churches, with no significant AICs. These two churches are part of the social fabric for most Ugandans, less in terms of ethos (as in Ghana) than institutionally; Catholics and Anglicans have traditionally been linked with different political parties. Both Ghana and Uganda were forced to their knees about the same time, the early 1980s. In Ghana the collapse was primarily economic, in Uganda economic collapse went with total anarchy and savagery. In those years of chaos, Uganda's churches offered shelter and survival to their members, perhaps all that could reasonably be expected in the circumstances.

Since then, as in Ghana, a military leader has attempted to rebuild the country, and similarly swallowed the IMF medicine. In the place of collapse, Museveni has introduced a new dispensation. The COU is still resolving its stance towards Museveni's NRM government, because traditionally allied to the UPC which Museveni overthrew, and is therefore not well placed to act as conscience to Museveni. The leadership of the Catholic Church is grateful to Museveni for halting the chaos, and has long been rather turned in on itself, given that the public arena was so monopolised by Anglicans closely linked to the COU leadership. The Catholic Church thus feels little need to advise Museveni, much less to challenge him in the way the Catholics in Ghana challenge Rawlings. The Ugandan Catholic Church in effect busies itself with its enormous involvement in development. There is no output of church statements issued by the churches either separately or together. For historical reasons there is no ready cooperation; their leaders do not naturally see themselves as belonging to the same class, espousing a shared viewpoint. Neither church has leaders of the stature of some churchmen in Ghana.

Museveni's advent has affected the churches in another way. Museveni, much more than Rawlings, is something of a visionary with an agenda for Uganda (some say all Africa) involving grassroots participatory democracy, accountability, transparency. The churches had formed part of the previous political culture, more autocratic, hierarchical, unanswerable. The churches are finding it hard to adapt to the new dispensation, and it is Museveni who is challenging them to do so. Their difficulties in adapting have been evident in some spectacularly malfunctioning dioceses.

Uganda's new Pentecostal churches are just as visible as those in Ghana; perhaps it is even more evident in Uganda that they are growing less through a movement of mass conversion than through a haemorrhage of nominal members from the two historic churches. There is considerable variety among Uganda's newer churches. Some manifest elements associated more with AICs in Ghana, and which in Ghana seem superseded. Although the deliverance mentality is undoubtedly not far below the surface, there is no public evidence in Uganda of Ghana's 'deliverance' phenomenon.

5

ZAMBIA

In its present form Zambia is a creation of Cecil Rhodes' British South Africa Company, and its strange shape is evidence of its artificial composition. The BSAC concluded treaties with most of the Zambian chiefs in the 1890s (before 1969 Barotseland in the west had a special status within the country), and administered the area till 1924, when control was transferred to the British government (the company retained mineral rights up till the 1960s). The Protectorate of Northern Rhodesia, as it was called, had a substantial number of white settlers; in 1952 there were about 43,000, some in commercial farming, but most associated with the mines of the Copperbelt along the Zaïre border. These mines drew workers from far and wide, and have made Zambia among the two or three most urbanised countries in Africa. Today about half its population live in a narrow strip along the line of rail or on the Copperbelt. The mines both disrupted village life by drawing men away for work and provided an arena for struggle for workers' rights through unions. During the 1950s the movement for Zambian independence was launched by the African National Congress (ANC) and taken up shortly after by the slightly more radical United National Independence Party (UNIP). In 1953 Northern Rhodesia merged with Southern Rhodesia (now Zimbabwe) and Nyasaland (now Malawi) to form the Central African Federation – a merger partly engineered by the settlers of Southern Rhodesia to enable them to profit from Northern Rhodesia's mineral wealth (it is no accident that the giant Kariba dam, built during Federation on the Zambesi between Northern and Southern Rhodesia, has the power station on the southern side).

Because of the resistance of the African peoples of both Northern Rhodesia and Nyasaland, who saw the Federation as a threat to their rights, it was dissolved in 1963, and the next year Northern Rhodesia became the Republic of Zambia, with UNIP's Kenneth Kaunda, a teacher, its first President. Independence thus came after a relatively bloodless though persistent struggle. Like Nkrumah, Kaunda, as the most prominent nationalist leader and already head of the transitional government, came to power with considerable legitimacy. Because of the hopelessly inadequate nature of its educational and social institutions, Zambia could not boast the educated élites of either Ghana or Uganda; at independence in 1964 it only had 109 university graduates and 1,200 with secondary school certificate. This relative lack of human capital has been an enduring problem throughout the years of independence.

For Zambia's first ten years the high price of copper ensured considerable prosperity. After 1975, however, copper prices plummeted. The country had not diversified, and thenceforth the economic decline was to be substantial, since even in 1991 copper accounted for 93% of foreign exchange earnings. Agriculture had been neglected; even in the 1990s it accounted for only about 10% of GDP, with a few commercial farms producing most of Zambia's agricultural output. Kaunda's principled stand against neighbouring Rhodesia and South Africa added to its economic woes. Radical economic reforms, especially to remove subsidies from food staples, were continually blocked by urban protest – in 1986 food riots had to be put down with the loss of at least fifteen lives, after which Kaunda capitulated again. He had declared Zambia a one-party state in 1972, but his UNIP government was genuinely inclusive (although the Bemba are the most numerous of the seventy-odd language groups with about 18% of the population, Zambia has no bloc as dominant as the Ashanti in Ghana or the Baganda in Uganda). Nor was Kaunda's rule a tyranny, although his nationalisation of so much of the economy after 1969 gave enormous scope for corruption among government officials. As the economic decline continued, protest mounted. In July 1990 the Movement for Multi-party Democracy (MMD) was formed, which Frederick Chiluba, the leader of Zambia's trade unions, quickly came to lead. A great many elements soon united under the MMD umbrella, and their combined pressure forced Kaunda to agree to a new constitution, a multi-party election, and even overseas observers to monitor them.

In the elections of 31 October 1991, Chiluba received 76% of the vote to Kaunda's 24%, and in the parliamentary elections MMD secured 125 of the 150 seats; UNIP took the other twenty-five, with four other parties failing to obtain a single seat. Kaunda immediately ceded office, something almost without precedent in independent Africa, and Chiluba was sworn in on 2 November. However, by mid-1992 there was widespread opposition to the government's policies, especially the rigid implementation of structural adjustment. There was also a common perception that the government included several corrupt ministers, and in local government elections in November 1992, 90% of registered voters abstained, presumably out of disillusionment. Chiluba briefly declared a state of emergency in March 1993, on the grounds that elements in UNIP had attempted a coup; three of Kaunda's sons were arrested. After this, relations with Iran and Iraq were severed, due to their allegedly having funded the plotters. Soon afterwards fifteen MMD government members resigned from the party, claiming that the government was protecting corrupt ministers, and formed the National Party. Opposition increased in the face of

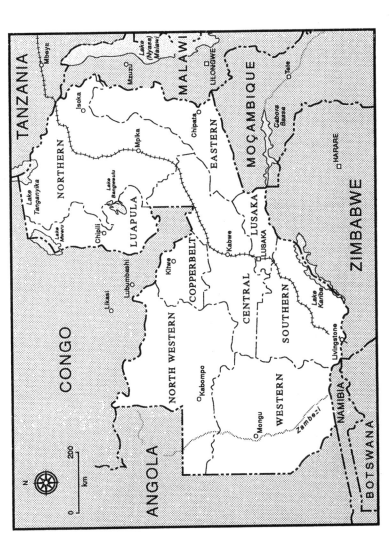

Zambia

increasing social and economic hardship, unbridled corruption and the lack of any perceived sense of direction. In May 1996 Chiluba shamelessly changed the constitution to bar Kaunda from challenging him for President. UNIP and other parties boycotted the November 1996 presidential elections, which Chiluba duly won with 70% of the vote, although turn-out was only 40% of those registered, which was in turn only about 60% of the number estimated eligible to vote. We will have occasion below to fill out some of these details.

The churches

Zambia has its own unique configuration of churches. The country is about 75% Christian, 1% Muslim and 24% traditional believers; the Catholic Church by far the most influential denomination. Like Uganda, where different areas are dominated by the Mill Hills and White Fathers, Zambia has been divided geographically into Jesuit, White Fathers and Franciscan areas. Zambia's Anglicans (like Ghana's but unlike Uganda's) are Anglo-Catholic or high church, but they are relatively few in number. The United Church of Zambia (UCZ) is a remarkable ecumenical venture that is almost unique in Africa. It began on the Copperbelt, where Christians moving to the mines found no church to receive them and various Protestants formed the Union Church of the Copperbelt. Later this group, together with the Free Church of Scotland and the London Missionary Society from the Northern and Luapula Provinces, formed the Church of Central Africa. The Methodists in the south and the Paris Mission to Barotseland in the west joined in 1965, and a new name was adopted – the United Church of Zambia – along with a new constitution. The Reformed Church in Zambia (RCZ) is the daughter church of the Dutch Reformed Mission from South Africa. The Anglicans and the UCZ are the most important members of the Christian Council of Zambia (CCZ). We will have occasion to say more about all of these churches when discussing political developments, but first it is necessary to mention other important churches which do not feature below.

First, the AICs. These are no longer so prominent, although two de-serve mention for their historical importance. The Lumpa Church was founded in the 1950s by Alice Lenshina, a peasant woman who claimed to have died and risen again. She recounted her experience to the Free Church of Scotland missionaries at Lubwa mission near Chinsali. They encouraged her to revive the faith of the people, and with their blessing she began preaching. In time she became independent and met with enor-mous success, and the Catholic and Presbyterian missions nearby were amazed at the defection of their adherents. She built an enormous church, but at its opening Jesus failed to appear as promised, and her decline began from about that time. The church was finally destroyed as a result of clashes in 1963 with supporters of UNIP; the latter was at that time busy eliminating possible alternative centres of allegiance. Sporadic clashes became an open war, in which the official death toll was 1,111, although it was probably much greater. The crackdown was ordered in 1963 by Kenneth Kaunda as the Prime Minister of the new transitional government, and the tragedy was given some piquancy because both his mother and his older brother had joined Lenshina. Up to 30,000 survivors fled to Zaïre, whence many were tempted back in the early 1990s, although Zambia's new government was determined that remaining adherents be dispersed throughout the country and not allowed to settle back around Lenshina's village of Kasomo, where her carefully tended tomb is to be found in the ruins of her church. Lenshina is an important figure in Africa's Christian history, but we will not devote more time to her here, in the conviction that the dynamics of Zambia's Christianity today have moved on.[1]

The other independent church of some historical importance was the 'Catholic Church of the Sacred Heart of Jesus', founded by Emilio Mulolani at the same time as Lenshina founded hers, and in the same area; indeed both can be seen as responding to the same social pressures that built up in the nationalist period. Mulolani's church still exists (often called the Mutima Church) but is now fairly insignificant – Mulolani discredited himself by advocating such practices as mixed nude bathing, to manifest natural innocence. Catholics today tend to view his work quite sympathetically, acknowledging his gifts and zeal, and regret that structures in the 1960s were not able to accommodate him.[2]

Zambia currently has two other churches that demand comment. One is the New Apostolic Church, the third most numerous church in Zambia. On 1 January 1982 it had 194,195 members; by 30 June 1994, 704,838; and by June 1996, 793,934, an increase of 409% in fourteen years. Yet for all this, the church remains almost unknown. Partly this is its own wish, for it joins with no others, and cooperates in nothing. The New Apostolic Church had its origins in Britain in the first part of the nine-

---

[1]   For Lenshina, see Andrew Roberts, 'The Lumpa Church of Alice Lenshina' in Robert L. Rotberg and Ali Mazrui (eds), *Protest and Power in Black Africa*, New York: OUP, 1970, 513-68; Wim M.J. van Binsbergen, 'Religious Innovation and Political Conflict in Zambia: the Lumpa Rising' in *Religious Change in Zambia: Exploratory Studies*, London: Kegan Paul, 1981, 266-316; Brian Garvey, *Bembaland Church: Religious and Social Change in South Central Africa 1891-1964*, Leiden: E.J. Brill, 1994; H. F. Hinfelaar, *Bemba-Speaking Women of Zambia in a Century of Religious Change 1892-1992*, Leiden: E.J. Brill, 1994, 73-100; At Ipenburg, *'All Good Men': the Development of Lubwa Mission, Chinsali, Zambia, 1905-1967*, Frankfurt: Peter Lang, 1992.

[2]   Garvey, *Bembaland Church*, 159-71; Hinfelaar, *Bemba-Speaking*, 101-25. See also Louis Oger, *'Where a Scattered Flock Gathered': Ilondola 1934-84*, Lusaka: Missionaries of Africa, 1991, 148-55; also *Times*, 18 May 1994.

teenth century in the Catholic Apostolic Church, often called 'Irvingites' after Edward Irving (1792-1834), their best known preacher though never their leader. In 1832 in London a man called Cardale was accepted as the first 'new apostle', and by 1835 all twelve apostles were named. In Britain the last of these apostles died in 1901; all had refused to ordain successors. It was left to the branch in Germany to fill the depleting ranks of apostles, a step they first took in 1863, thus effectively breaking with Britain and beginning the New Apostolic Church. The church came to Northern Rhodesia from South Africa in 1928, and experienced steady growth till the 1980s, since when it has increased enormously.[3]

Several reasons could be adduced in part explanation of its rapid growth. The first is its professionalism. Buildings, furniture, vehicles and equipment all testify to that. Its headquarters are far more impressive than the offices of the Christian Council or the Catholic Secretariat. Statistics are compiled for every service, and national statistics every few months; in the mid-1990s all records were being put on computers. Each Sunday all the church's services around the world deal with the same topic, with different sermons laid down for evening and morning services. Literature is prepared in five different languages for Zambia, on their own printing presses. A colour magazine, *Our Family,* is produced in South Africa and trucked to a wide circulation in Zambia. This is an impressively efficient operation.

Secondly, considerable funds are provided; all the professionalism and competence in administration have to be paid for. Most of this money is available from abroad, and Lusaka's magnificent headquarters, the principal churches (indeed, a good part of the cost of all churches) and the vehicles are all funded in this way. The church has no formal training institutions, but the frequent seminars and workshops are paid for too. Besides, the church has a considerable relief budget; this goes primarily to its own members. Thus part of the dynamic operating here is related to Africa's extreme dependence. (Critics in many African countries claim that the church gives handouts of clothes and food to prospective members, though this is denied.) The importance of overseas links is suggested by the fact that Zambia's twenty apostles were in 1995 learning German.

Thirdly, although as mentioned above there is no formal theological education, there is enormous scope to hold office, and a great chain of command along which aspirants are able to progress. Its ranks, with the number holding that rank in Zambia in 1996 in brackets, are District Apostle (1), Apostle (20), Bishop (12), District Elder (167), District Evangelist (297), Shepherd (967), Community Evangelist (1,357), Priest

---

[3]   New Apostolic Church, *A History of the Kingdom of God,* Dortmund: New Apostolic Church, 1991; for Zambia, see their *Jubilee Year* booklet, Lusaka, 1982.

(6,624), Deacon (5,184), and Subdeacon (4,984).

Fourthly, this professionalism, participation and achievement is espe-cially evident where music is concerned. Music is linked to evangelisation, which is pursued in imaginative ways. On 7 August 1994 the New Apos-tolic churches in Lusaka held a 'Guest Service and Choral Singing'. The choirs were spectacular. The singing was totally Western, as were the Christian Rock concerts that another church was offering in the capital at the same time, but whereas the latter were evidence of American pop culture, this New Apostolic service drew on the very different strand of Europe's musical heritage. The choirs of Lusaka's New Apostolic churches, accompanied by a full string orchestra, sang polyphonic motets and oratorios by Bach, Handel and others, with baritone, tenor, soprano and contralto soloists at microphones Not since the British governing classes ruled Zambia, and perhaps not even then, would such a concert have been heard in Zambia. Again, the excellence and professionalism spoke for itself, and the Western tradition that this all tapped is obviously of great appeal to many. At the service, the preaching was directed straight at guests. Such evangelism is linked to an enormous stress on literature; the magazine *Our Family*, available in several Zambian languages, is widely distributed.

Sometimes the impression is given that a 'Pentecostal explosion' is taking place in Africa. This church proves that there is far more going on than that, for a church less Pentecostal would be hard to imagine – which is rather unexpected, since prophetic utterances were a key feature of the original 'Irvingites'. We will not linger further on the New Apostolic Church, for their direct public role is quite limited; they will have nothing to do with politics.

The other church that must be mentioned is the Jehovah's Witnesses, whose early incarnation through Central Africa as the millennialist 'Kita-wala' movement has been well documented.[4] Henkel says that the Jehovah's Witnesses are the biggest church in Zambia after the Catho-lics, giving a figure of 800,000 in 1984.[5] This is incorrect; their official figures for 1994 were 83,000 members in 2,000 congregations. It must immediately be said that the JWs calculate their members in a unique and quite restrictive way, but even on a loose evaluation – like the Catholics' – the number would still not exceed 300,000. This still gives Zambia a higher proportion of JWs than any country other than a few Pacific micro-states. They are increasing, and have built an enormous headquarters just south of Lusaka with a sweeping drive-way and landscaped

4   Karen E. Fields, *Revival and Rebellion in Colonial Central Africa*, Princeton University Press, 1985.

5   Reinhard Henkel, *Christian Missions in Africa: a Social Geographical Study of the Im-pact of their Activities in Zambia*, Berlin: Dietrich Reimer Verlag, 1989.

grounds including lawn sculptures. The reception area is like that in an expensive hotel. About 140 live there, with rooms serviced like a hotel, each room with its own microwave oven – for Zambia, a remarkable luxury. Behind the living quarters are a floodlit swimming pool and floodlit tennis court. Another wing of the complex houses the facilities for translation: the *Watchtower* and other publications are translated into ten languages by a local team supervised by expatriates. This church too has an enormous concern with literature. The 140 living here are not paid but merely given an allowance; this means that although some are married – the two-room flats are adequate for a couple – when children arrive, families have to leave. Any contribution to political developments in the country is indirect; JWs are not interested in these, and refuse even to vote. However, for all that, their indirect influence is not negligible. All over the country JWs benefit from the stress on literacy and training in public speaking and verbal advocacy. Many outsiders comment on the cleanliness and honesty that seems to derive from their sectarian intensity. Besides these qualities of a personal kind, others point to more social effects. Among Zambia's matrilineal societies, there is often confusion between the roles of father and maternal uncle in bringing up children. Of all groups, the JWs are said to have taken most strongly to 'modern' or 'Christian' marriage involving equality between the partners and mutual support, thus tending to change traditional patterns.

For the sake of completeness, we should mention the Seventh Day Adventists (SDAs), who between 1990 and 1994 increased from 102,000 members to 229,000. They attribute their growth to lay involvement and their focus on youth.

There is no nationwide survey of Christian attendance as there is for Ghana, but under the influence of the Ghana Evangelism Committee the Evangelical Fellowship of Zambia (EFZ) has begun similar research. By mid-1994 it had completed the survey only of Lusaka. This showed that Catholic attendance on a Sunday was 102,065 (10.39% of Lusaka's total population). Attendance at churches belonging to the Evangelical Fellowship of Zambia was 37,563 (3.61%); at Christian Council churches 16,582 (1.66%);[6] for the SDA 12,183 (1.24%); for New Apostolic Church 25,882 (2.63%), and at Independent Churches a mere 5,939 (0.58%). There is another category of 'Sundry Churches' which originate from or are related to overseas churches, with attendance of 12,192 (1.24%); presumably this consists mainly of JWs. Thus Catholics are by far the most

6 EFZ, *Exposing the Unevangelised Localities/Townships and People in Lusaka Urban*, Lusaka: EFZ, 1994. Six churches belong both to the EFZ and the CCZ. In this survey, the numbers of these six churches are included in the EFZ. If the procedure were reversed and their numbers were included in the CCZ and deducted from the EFZ, the attendance figures would be 29,113 and 25,032 respectively.

dominant – the survey administrators admitted that they were surprised by the following of the Catholics, just as they were surprised and disappointed with the mere 37,563 that attended born-again churches.

If we consider Zambian Christianity in general, perhaps the most significant feature is the genuine ecumenism that is so evident. Zambian Christianity is always spoken of in terms of three 'mother bodies'. the Catholics (referred to as the Episcopal Conference of Zambia or ECZ), the Christian Council of Zambia (CCZ), and the Evangelical Fellowship of Zambia (EFZ); the last-named was begun by Baptists for evangelical churches in the traditional sense; in recent years its constituent churches have almost without exception become very Pentecostal. It is not essential to belong to one of these three bodies to enter the country or be registered as a society, but in fact most Protestant groups do belong to one of the latter two, some to both of them. Obviously the three bodies are not of the same kind, since the ECZ comprises the Catholic Church alone, whereas the CCZ and EFZ are associations of thirteen and twenty-four churches respectively. The ECZ is able to act with a speed and resolution (when desired) that the other two could never match. The constituent churches have varying degrees of commitment to the two Protestant organisations, which consequently have a rather unwieldy structure. The three bodies have tended to cooperate closely since 1969, when the government was threatening to introduce Scientific Socialism. In response to that threat, they produced a joint statement entitled *Marxism, Humanism and Christianity*, and the success of their combined resistance gave them the incentive to cooperate further.[7] They have continued to do so, with a readiness that makes Zambian Christianity, in this regard, virtually unique on the continent. We saw that in Ghana the Catholics and mainline Protestants cooperate closely, but in Zambia the cooperation includes Pentecostals.

It can be said, however, that the cooperation is frequently on Catholic terms. This is because, as noted above, the ECZ is a unified entity in a way that the others are not, and because the Catholic Church in Zambia has a missionary component that is highly qualified and experienced. Thus the Catholic education director in the Catholic Secretariat handles education-related matters with the government on behalf of all the other churches, including the SDAs – and by all accounts, meetings of the officials from these various churches are genuinely pleasant. However, Zambia's ecumenism shows both the possibilities and limitations of ecumenical cooperation in Africa. For one thing, it is largely functional; the churches unite to do specific things. Nor are the Catholics eager to be hampered by the organisational difficulties of cooperating with the

---

7   See also Clive Dillon-Malone, *Zambian Humanism, Religion and Social Morality*, Ndola: Ndola Mission Press, 1969.

unwieldy Protestant bodies. There are jointly controlled organisations in Zambia which clearly show the limitations. Multimedia, the Mindolo Ecumenical Foundation and the Africa Literature Centre are long-established ecumenical institutions, but they limp along, functioning at a fraction of their potential, precisely because they are ecumenical. Part of the reason is that the Catholic Church will not commit itself to them in the way it commits itself to its own institutions. Because it does not have total control or power, it has little incentive to make them work. Multimedia (which we consider in more detail below, because of its weekly *National Mirror*) is sponsored by so many different churches, each of which wants some of its members to work there, that it is overstaffed and inefficient. For that reason it has over twenty directors, far too many to function with any clear purpose.

Traditionally and most obviously, the churches have an enormous social involvement. This is particularly evident in traditional areas like schools and clinics. Although primary schools were taken over by the government after independence, secondary schools were left with the churches. In mid-1994 there were still forty-one church secondary schools, twenty-seven run by Catholics, five by the UCZ, four by the Brethren in Christ, two by the Anglican Council, and one each by the Salvation Army, the Reformed Church in Zambia, the SDAs, the Evangelical Church in Zambia, and another autonomous church body. On 11 March 1993 a statute gave churches even more control: for example, now both the principal and the deputy principal must belong to the church which runs the school. Thus churches have a far greater control of their schools in Zambia than in most African countries. These church schools have considerable prestige; in the 1995 public exams, while the pass rate nationally was 59.6%, that for the Catholic schools was 85.4%.[8] The structurally-adjusting government has also offered to give back many primary schools, though only the Catholics are beginning to take up this offer.[9] The church contribution to clinics and hospitals is just as considerable.

Before concluding these introductory remarks, something must be said about Zambia's Muslims. They are insignificant in numbers (perhaps under 1% of the population, compared to perhaps 16% in Ghana and 6% in Uganda). Most are Asians, who dominate Zambia's trading sector. There is considerable tension between the Asian and Zambian Muslims, most of which arises over control of resources.[10] Additionally, in recent years a note of tension has entered Christian-Muslim relations. A 1995 notice at Lusaka's Abundant Life Church, where the pastor is a key figure in

---

[8]   See *Impact*, May 1996, 9.

[9]   *Ibid.*, Oct 1996, 1.

[10]   *Times*, 1 June 1994; 4 June 1994, 1, and letters following.

the EFZ, called for prayers 'against the spirit of Anti-Christ – Islam, Spiritism, Satanism etc.' Christians now frequently talk of 'the Muslim threat'. The usual complaint is that the Asian traders are going into the villages with food and clothing and effectively 'buying' converts; those who make this accusation seem undecided whether the money is the Asians' own, or whether it comes from Arab states. Certainly Chiluba has established links with Israel and closed the embassies of both Iran and Iraq amid accusations of activities unbecoming diplomatic status (it is common enough to hear the 1993 plane crash which killed Zambia's soccer team called an act of terrorism, related to the expulsion of these diplomats).

The rise of Islam is taken far too seriously in some circles. Indeed, the dean of the Anglican cathedral in Lusaka has set up a 'Muslim Desk' at the cathedral, ostensibly a project run jointly by the ECZ, CCZ and EFZ. The dean has announced that the Shi'ites in Zambia had claimed that 15% of the Zambian population were now Muslim and that the Sunni Muslims in Zambia had recently stated that there were half a million Muslims in the country. He called these statistics 'alarming', and referred to Islam's 'aggressive' and 'underhand' methods.[11] It may well be that this 'Desk' is no more than a private crusade, with the CCZ and ECZ quite embarrassed by the whole thing but not prepared to say as much publicly. Obviously many Christians in Zambia are alarmed by such surveillance and policing in the matter of religion, and the increasing intolerance it represents.[12]

The churches' role in Zambia's change of regime

Kaunda's regime began with considerable promise, largely because of the resources available from copper exports. However, since the mid-1970s, the decline has been catastrophic. Many factors were responsible for Zambia's economic performance – falling prices, the transport problems of a landlocked country, South African destabilisation – but the most significant factor was the inexperience, incompetence and increasing corruption of the members of the Kaunda government. Kaunda's final years saw the country brought to its knees.

[11] *Times*, 10 May and 16 May 1993.
[12] Editorial in *Times*, 19 May 1993; a letter on the same day calls the Desk 'outrageous'; another letter in the *Times* of 8 June 1994 deplores the 'divisive evil of religion'. It is not uncommon to read Evangelical denunciations of Islam in the media; for example, Rev. Francis Lumba wrote: 'Islam in particular has nothing to offer to Zambia and the whole world except confusion which leads to bloodshed. The behaviour of Moslems in the world makes very sad reading' (*Times*, 7 June 1992). There was an eirenic editorial entitled 'Our Brothers the Muslims' in the Catholic monthly *Impact*, August 1993, 2. The Catholic editor of *Icengelo* was said to fear that an 'Islamic Invasion threatens Zambia' in *Mirror*, 2-8 June 1996, 1. He immediately responded, claiming that this was a total distortion of his views (*Mirror*, 23-29 June 1996, 10).

Christianity was always a factor in Kaunda's regime. It played a large part in conferring legitimacy on Zambia's first government, and Kaunda clearly used it to this end. He made great play of the fact that his father was a pioneer missionary (and at the end of his life a Presbyterian pastor), and often referred to his Christian roots. He used Christian rhetoric to project an image of compassion, uprightness and integrity, and made political capital from his image as a Christian gentleman.[13] However, in his last years considerable tension arose between Kaunda and the churches, on several scores. One of them was that Kaunda had the misfortune to label his political philosophy 'humanism', meaning perhaps a rather idealistic and utopian combination of Christianity and traditional African values.[14] But for anyone familiar with American Evangelicalism, the word 'humanism' carries the worst of connotations. As the head of the EFZ has written in reference to the 1991 election, 'The political ideology of humanism was attacked by the church as a philosophy which puts man at the centre of society, instead of God. This never works. Humanism is a disaster.'[15]

Another reason for tension was the perception that Kaunda had not only forsaken true Christianity, but had fallen under the sway of Eastern gurus. Long interested in Indian spirituality, in the 1980s he became linked with a Dr M. A. Ranganathan and established his David Universal Temple at State House. To many this was 'tantamount to blasphemy. [...] Dr Ranganathan's practices are not from God but from the devil.'[16] The Maharishi Mahesh Yogi also joined with Kaunda in a project to make Zambia 'Heaven on Earth', and a TV programme on this bizarre scheme was screened just a few days before the 1991 election. These links with 'occult spiritual powers' alarmed many born-again Christians, who claimed that the devil had 'mobilised his forces of darkness to fight against, and perhaps destroy, the nation of Zambia'.[17] Just before the

[13]   This point is well made by Harden 'The Good, the Bad and the Greedy', in his *Africa*, 217-70: the Good is Kaunda, the Bad is Liberia's Doe, the Greedy is Moi of Kenya; Harden's point is that it is the 'Big Man' model of leadership that is so detrimental, even if adopted by a 'kindly and idealistic' man like Kaunda.

[14]   Kenneth Kaunda, *A Humanist in Africa: Letters to Colin Morris from Kenneth D. Kaunda*, London: Longmans, 1966.

[15]   J. Imakando, 'The Role of the Church in the Democratic Process in Zambia' in *Civil Society and the Consolidation of Democracy in Zambia*, Lusaka: Foundation for Democratic Process, 1992, 3. Compare this with Falwell's statement that 'humanism has its origin in man's attempts to place human wisdom above divine revelation' (Jerry Falwell, *The Fundamentalist Phenomenon: the Resurgence of Conservative Christianity*, Garden City, NY: Doubleday, 1991, 199), and Robertson's that America's decline has come about through society's 'putting man at the centre of the universe' (Pat Robertson, *America's Date with Destiny*, Nashville, TN: Thomas Nelson, 1986, 175).

[16]   *Mirror*, 28 Oct-3 Nov 1991, 5.

[17]   *Mirror*, 6-13 Oct 1991, 4.

election, a group of pastors in Ndola denounced these links as 'demonic', and deplored the fact that the government 'had banned the registration of more churches but permitted occult systems to enter Zambia'. One of these pastors, Bishop Danny Pule, was reported to have called on Christians to 'pray sincerely for a peaceful transition and demolish "demonic" strongholds by divine power. Some presidential and parliamentary candidates [Pule claimed] were relying on witchcraft and demonic power to win the election, which invited spiritual darkness into the land.'[18] It was not hard to decode this message and work out whom Pule was supporting – and indeed he was subsequently appointed Assistant Minister of Finance when Chiluba came to power.

A far more important reason for tension, however, was the general perception of the churches as standing in the forefront of the opposition. One sign of this was the high profile of the Christian media. The national dailies in Kaunda's Zambia were the *Times of Zambia* and the *Daily Mail*, the former owned by the party, the latter by the government (the distinction between the party and the government was imperceptible). Needless to say, neither paper published much that was critical of the government.[19] In this vacuum the church media played a crucial role. Most prominent (initially unique) was the weekly *National Mirror*, owned jointly by the CCZ and the ECZ through their company Multimedia. During 1990 and 1991, in contrast with the national dailies, it offered, besides extensive coverage of religious news, a wide range of background articles on African leadership, Africa's economic collapse, university students' grievances, donors' reluctance to lend to Zambia, interviews with former detainees and, not least, full-page advertisements for MMD and extensive interviews with Chiluba. It has to be said that the decision to play such a role was largely an editorial one, made without extensive hands-on direction from the board. The second example is the Catholic Bemba-language monthly *Icengelo*, edited by an Italian Franciscan priest. The UNIP government fiercely attacked this for its extensive political coverage, and after it printed Amnesty International reports on Zambia, and compared Zambia's situation (unfavourably) to that of South Africa, the editor was in 1989 and 1990 subjected to extensive interrogation by government ministers and security officials, who accused him 'of being an agent of some power trying to destroy the peace in the country'.[20] He refused to change his stance, published the first interview with the then largely unknown Chiluba, and thereafter gave Chiluba space whenever

---

[18]   *Times*, 17 Oct 1991, 1.
[19]   Before the elections an 'independent' body was set up to oversee both in an effort to counter the perception that both were run by Kaunda. This effort had little effect on the bias of either paper.
[20]   *Mirror*, 13 April 1992, 5.

he requested it. *Icengelo* increased its circulation – in November 1990 it was 65,000 copies, by December 69,000 copies.[21] The third publication that exerted considerable influence was the monthly *Workers' Challenge,* likewise Catholic and also produced on the Copperbelt. These church publications undoubtedly played a real role in articulating opposition to Kaunda and driving a wedge between him and the churches.

While the tension between Kaunda and the churches was growing, Chiluba had quickly risen to head the MMD, the umbrella movement for all opposition currents. Chiluba was not only a devout churchgoer, a member of a UCZ church on the Copperbelt, but also 'born-again', experiencing a conversion while briefly imprisoned by Kaunda for his trade union activities in 1981. He later received the gift of tongues at a crusade in Malawi preached by the German Reinhard Bonnke. Thus, as Kaunda came to be increasingly regarded as a renegade Christian presiding over a corrupt and oppressive government, Chiluba stressed (and his supporters stressed even more) his impeccable credentials as a true spirit-filled believer. Christian motifs were introduced into the political struggle – the diminutive Chiluba being frequently referred to as David challenging Goliath, and even more frequently being portrayed as Moses, about to bring his people to freedom after almost forty years of fruitless wandering in the wilderness.

In his last years in power, when shortages and riots and an attempted coup were indicating that the *status quo* could not continue, and he was losing general support, including that of the churches, Kaunda became desperate – 'like a wounded bull', in the words attributed to the Catholic Archbishop Elias Mutale. Mutale, an impressive man who as Archbishop of Kasama had doubled as the Administrator of Lusaka for nearly two years in the late 1980s, was killed in a mysterious car accident in February 1990. Rumours circulated that he had been killed by the government's security services – he had in fact just come from a meeting with Kaunda. Nothing was said officially until one day Kaunda himself made an outburst on national television that the Catholic Church was accusing him of murdering the archbishop. He claimed some years later that he even wrote to the Pope about it.[22] Another public outburst of rage and frustration with the churches occurred at a 1990 conference called for all branches of Christianity by World Vision. Kaunda opened the conference, and in the midst of proceedings he departed from his text to lash the churches; he said he was 'shocked to see the collapse of the Christian spirit', especially in Zambia which had enjoyed such good church-state

---

[21] *Mirror,* 20 May 1991, 4.

[22] Rumours have persisted that the archbishop was murdered. See the headline in the *Weekly Express,* 15-21 Aug 1994, 'How Archbishop Mutale was killed'; the article talks of his 'assassination', as does the editorial that day.

relations. The country was witnessing 'for the first time messages of real hatred preached from the pulpits in Zambia. Spiritual leaders wrote messages of such anger and hatred as if they had never known what we stand for.' He expressed his shock that Christian leaders could allow what was being published in *Icengelo* and the *National Mirror*, and referred with particular bitterness to the aftermath of an attempted coup. One night not long beforehand a Lieutenant Luchembe had taken over the national radio station to announce that the government had been toppled. There had been widespread rejoicing, but the 'coup' quickly proved to be a one-man operation, and normality was soon restored, although not before some churchmen (notably Bishop John Mambo, the overseer of the Church of God) had spoken to foreign radio services welcoming the coup. Kaunda attacked the clergy in his audience publicly: 'Do you know what would have happened if Luchembe and his colleagues had succeeded? What happened nearly brought another Amin, and we all know what took place in Uganda, even priests were not spared.'[23] His outburst was such that soon afterwards church leaders met him at State House 'for consultative talks' to re-establish harmony. At this meeting Kaunda reviewed the traditionally close relations between the church and the state, calling the church one of the five special pillars of the nation (along with the press, the judiciary, the legislature and the executive), and hoped that it would remain 'as unshaken and firmly in position as it was during the liberation struggle and through the first and second republics.' He went further to say that the church was 'not only a pillar but also the mirror of society and the very conscience of the people.'[24]

During his last months, with his support visibly ebbing, Kaunda did all he could to use Christianity to prop up his tottering regime. On 7 November 1990 he hosted a Prayer Breakfast at Lusaka's Intercontinental Hotel. Invited were Pik Botha, Foreign Minister of South Africa, President Museveni of Uganda, President Masire of Botswana, President Chissano of Mozambique, Prime Minister Lekhanya of Lesotho, President Buyoya of Burundi, Prime Minister Dhlamini of Swaziland, President Holomisa of the Transkei, Namibia's Labour Minister, and ANC Secretary General Alfred Nzo. The meeting was to enable leaders to meet 'in the spirit of Christ', and the focus was on 'Peace and Reconciliation'. President Museveni preached forgiveness, and said that 'he had been approached by American priests [*sic*] to hold the prayer breakfast in Uganda, but suggested President Kaunda be the host because of his Christian faith.' Earlier, President Chissano (who also was facing elections) was quoted as saying: 'A good Christian ought to be a good revolutionary, standing

[23] *Times*, 31 Oct 1990, 1.
[24] *Times*, 27 Nov 1990, 1.

for justice, freedom and equality, all well tabulated in the Bible.' Even Dhlamini (who, coming from an absolute monarchy, had no need to court voters) had 'urged African leaders to follow the teaching of Jesus Christ if unity is to prevail on the continent.' Kaunda was quoted as saying: 'When people were bound to God in peace they were bound to each other in peace.'[25] This breakfast is significant in portraying the way that Christianity is seen in some parts of southern Africa – as something totally good, which enhances the standing of all associated with it.

Kaunda preached the same message of peace in July 1991 at an ecumenical service at Lusaka's Anglican Cathedral, called by the churches to pray for a peaceful transition to the Third Republic. He preached: 'Nothing can be more important than love, the more we love the more we are bringing God's kingdom nearer.'[26] Likewise, in officially opening the Reformed Church in Zambia's synod in September, he urged the church to pray for peace; 'The peace that the Almighty God has given us for the last twenty-seven years must be sustained through solemn prayer.'[27]

Such efforts did bear some fruit. In September 1990 a Seventh Day Adventist delegation met him for prayers at State House, and one pastor said Kaunda's installation as President was not 'a miracle' but God's design. 'I know that my God has this land in his hand. No one can take it away,' he said.[28] The pastor of a UCZ congregation in Lusaka in June 1991, during a service attended by Kaunda, was reported to have 'reminded the nation that the present UNIP leadership had scored much success, including the upkeep of peace. [He then referred to the fierce criticism of Kaunda being voiced at this period.] It was not surprising that people were despising the leadership. Even in biblical times Jesus was despised and crucified for doing good. The Bible admonishes people who opposed their authorities because the attitude was tantamount to rebelling against God.' The same report notes that Kaunda donated K25,000 for the new church.[29] The Apostolic Faith Church of Livingstone also offered considerable support.[30]

By July 1991 the political situation had deteriorated considerably. A new multiparty constitution had been written in response to popular pressure, but it had been drafted by a UNIP team, with the result that MMD

25 *Times*, 8 Nov 1990; 10 Nov 1990.

26 *Times*, 29 July 1991, 1.

27 *Mirror*, 2-8 Sept 1991, 4. He also asked for prayer for 'all those who were in politics so that they did not mislead others by projecting false promises which would never be fulfilled.'

28 *Times*, 18 Sept 1990, 1.

29 *Times*, 24 June 1991, 1. It is impossible to give US dollar equivalents accurately; the exchange rate of the kwacha with the dollar slipped from 2:1 in Oct 1985 to 21:1 in Jan 1987 and to 670:1 in Feb 1995.

30 *Times*, 30 Aug 1991, 1.

was refusing to accept it.[31] Besides, the election date was not clearly set, the official registration lists had yet to be published, the state of emergency had not been lifted to allow for free campaigning, and the public media were still manifestly partisan. In these circumstances, fearing that the situation might spiral out of control, the churches met Kaunda and offered to set up a meeting between him and the MMD. This took place at Lusaka's Anglican cathedral, and successfully resolved a good deal of the tension.[32]

In the few months before the elections, the churches made probably their greatest contribution to a peaceful transition. They joined to form the Christian Churches Monitoring Group, which then became a major force in the formation of the Zambia Elections Monitoring Coordinating Committee (ZEMEC), which set out to train a grassroots army to observe procedures at all polling stations on election day. It also set out, in the time available, to provide some voter education. This education stressed 'electoral principles' – every citizen has a right to vote, a candidate must exhibit proper credentials, all must accept the outcome, and elections are for the common good of the entire nation. They offered guidelines on responsible voting, explained the documents necessary for voting and the procedures to register as a voter, and urged voters to avoid bribes, intimidation or disruption, to attend rallies to form an opinion of the candidates and parties, and to cooperate fully with law enforcement agencies. They also called for a day of prayer on the Sunday preceding the elections.[33]

At the time of the October 1991 elections, then, Christians generally were perceived to be against UNIP and favouring MMD. There were reports of some UCZ pastors openly campaigning for MMD from the pulpit.[34] Many were more subtle. A pastor at a Ndola seminar on 'Church and State' said that the church should not support 'corrupt political leaders or dictators ... [or] any ideology or philosophy that opposes God'.[35] The same pastor, in another seminar on 'The Church in Plural Politics' held the month before the election, urged Christians not to vote for 'people whose character is questionable. Their families don't give a good example. They are involved in scandals. They are dictators. They hold on

---

[31] The EFZ at its AGM, 7-8 June 1991, urged that this 'UNIP constitution' should be rejected because it was drafted by only one political party (*Mirror*, 10 June 1991, 4).

[32] It appears that the Catholics were mainly responsible for arranging this meeting, but the Catholic bishops were still so cautious that they made certain they were not around to host it.

[33] See, for example, their advertisement in *Mirror*, 21-27 Oct 1991, 14. The role of ZEMEC is very positively assessed in Eric Bjornlund, Michael Bratton and Clark Gibson, 'Observing Multiparty Elections in Africa: Lessons from Zambia', *African Affairs* 91 (1992), 405-31.

[34] *Mirror*, 23-29 Sept 1991, 1.

[35] *Times*, 9 Dec 1990.

to power. They have wrong motives. They may even kill everybody who opposes them.'[36] In Zambia's context, it was not difficult to see this as directly referring to Kaunda. The born-again churches particularly were thought to be on the side of Chiluba and the MMD.[37]

On election day, 31 October 1991, Chiluba and his MMD won in a landslide and, to his immense credit, Kaunda departed quietly. The role of the churches in making the elections possible, but also in gently promoting Chiluba, has not been sufficiently recognised. One cannot ignore the role played by labour unions (Chiluba came to prominence because he was the head of the unions, not because he was a Christian), women's groups and the international community, or gloss over the fact that the populace was generally alienated from UNIP by shortages. However, the churches played a considerable role in the change. It was often said that Chiluba's victory was an answer to Christian prayers.[38] The three Christian bodies – CCZ, EFZ and ECZ – combined for what was almost a coronation service for Chiluba in Lusaka's Anglican cathedral. The Anglican archbishop anointed the new President, charging him to 'Be strong and show yourself a man, keep the charge of the Lord your God, walk in his ways, keep his statutes, his commandments, his precepts and his testimonies as it is written in the first and second testaments.' He was reported as telling the congregation that they met 'to covenant with the Almighty God to anoint the President of the Third Republic according to the Word of God, trusting that he will grant grace, wisdom and knowledge to enable President Chiluba to execute the duties entrusted to him according to God's blessings.'[39]

'A Christian nation'

On 29 December 1991, only two months after the election, in a ceremony at State House broadcast on television, Chiluba proclaimed Zambia a Christian nation. He claimed that 'The Bible, which is the Word of God, abounds with proof that a nation is blessed, whenever it enters into a covenant with God and obeys the word of God.' He quoted 2 Chronicles 7:14: 'If my people who are called by my name will humble themselves and pray and seek my face and turn from their wicked ways, then will I

---

[36] *Times*, 14 July 1991.
[37] Although some high-profile charismatic preachers may have been seen as campaigning for Kaunda; see a letter in *Times*, 22 Nov 1991, accusing Pastor Sexton Chiluba of City Community Church of campaigning for Kaunda.
[38] Thus, 'So in the scramble for Zambia, Christians prayed, and satanists meditated, and prayed, suspended in mid-air. At the end of the day, Christ's forces prevailed against the kingdom of darkness' (Ronald Mwale, 'Zambia returns to God', *Mirror*, 18-24 Nov 1991, 5).
[39] *Mirror*, 11-17 Nov 1991, 2.

hear from heaven and forgive their sin and will heal their land.' On behalf of the people of Zambia, he repented of 'our wicked ways of idolatry, witchcraft, the occult, immorality, injustice and corruption'. He then prayed for 'healing, restoration, revival, blessing and prosperity' for Zambia. 'On behalf of the nation, I have now entered into a covenant with the living God. [...] I submit the Government and the entire nation of Zambia to the Lordship of Jesus Christ. I further declare that Zambia is a Christian Nation that will seek to be governed by the righteous principles of the Word of God. Righteousness and justice must prevail in all levels of authority, and then we shall see the righteousness of God exalting Zambia.'[40]

Following the announcement, there was a general euphoria on the part of many born-agains, but the elation was not universal. The Catholics and the Christian Council were not consulted before the declaration, and even the EFZ seems not to have been consulted as a body. It appears that the idea was either Chiluba's own or urged on him by Brigadier General Godfrey Miyanda, soon to be appointed Minister without Portfolio, and then in 1994 Vice-President. Influential too were Danish missionaries of the Apostolic Church on the Copperbelt. Chiluba may have contacted the officials of the EFZ, who no doubt were reluctant to bring in the other bodies because they saw this as their hour, having in the past felt themselves slightly overshadowed by the ECZ and CCZ. This lack of consultation, even if unintended by Chiluba, somewhat marred the event; even some who wholeheartedly approved of the idea seemed somewhat put out at not being consulted.[41] However, the reaction of the rank and file within the born-again community was fairly euphoric: 'Zambia has been declared a Christian nation. We can only praise the Lord', enthused one. 'Sunday December 29 shall surely go down in the history of the country as the day when the nation of Zambia entered into a covenant with God.'[42] Old Testament theocratic ideas, based on the books of Kings and Chronicles with their linking of a godly ruler and national prosperity, were evident in these statements.[43]

---

40   Chiluba referred to 2 Kings 23: 3; Jn 14: 6; Lk 22: 20; Jer 7: 23; Prov 29: 4; Rom 13: 11. Extracts cited in *Times*, 20 Feb 1994.

41   See headline in *Mirror*, 30 Dec 1991, 1, 'Chiluba Ruled Offside'. Among those who approved of the principle were the director of the World Baptist Evangelistic Association, the moderator of the UCZ, the director of the AME Church, the Deputy Minister of Information (Rev. Dan Pule), and the director of the Reformed Church in Zambia (Rev. Foston Sakala).

42   Chishala Kateka of Bible Life Ministries, 'Chiluba's Proclamation, God's Plan', *Times*, 12 Jan 1992.

43   A letter from the director of Charity Christian Ministries in Luanshya in the *Times* captures much of this well: 'I am one Christian who has been so excited about the declaration of our nation a Christian nation. I have been so excited that sometimes I

Other opinion, however, was scathing. An editorial in the *Times* described as 'ominous and very unsettling' this 'sudden preoccupation with the non-issue of whether or not Zambia is a Christian country ... there can be very little at the end of [this road] except a polarised society and the gnashing of teeth.'[44] Muslims reacted quite cautiously, asking for clarification on the position of minorities. Such caution brought them only angry condemnation from the born-again sector, one Assemblies of God pastor accusing Muslims 'of trying to take advantage of Christians who were peaceful, because Islamic teachings were based on violence.'[45] The Christian churches (again, all three bodies) reacted officially on 16 January in a press statement drafted essentially by the Catholic Secretariat. This cautious response praised the declaration as a statement of intention to conduct the government according to the very highest Christian ideals, but warned against interpretations which could only compromise social cohesion and the nature of Zambia as a secular state.[46]

About the same time, on 25 December 1991, Chiluba established diplomatic links with Israel. This seems to have stemmed from Chiluba's Christian Zionism, a form of thinking widely shared in Zambia's evangelical churches. Christian Zionism links several supposed biblical

---

feel like I should jump and fly into the air because of excitement ... In Bible history, whenever there was such a move it was the will of God and it happened for a purpose. We read about these situations especially in the books of Kings, Chronicles, Nehemiah and Ezra. God could touch the heart of a king and unexpectedly a king would exalt God in his nation, or give an encouragement to the work of God, or make a decree in favour of the children of God as in Esther 8,1-7. I have a feeling that our present Government is not there by accident. As I have been closely looking at and examining our situation with the Word of God I have discovered that our Government is a blessing from God and it is actually in need of a lot of help from us Christians, as we read in 1 Timothy 2, 1-4. Therefore there is need to enlighten Christians and every Zambian to bless the Government to allow God to fulfil his will for our nation. I am appealing to you, fellow Zambians, Government, the church, companies and other organisations to help me launch a programme on television so that I may be sharing what I feel will help the nation spiritually at this time. I believe God has something for us'(*Times*, 14 Jan 1995, 4). This letter illustrates the Old Testament underpinning of the declaration: the understanding that it demands wholehearted support for the government, and then the realisation that there is possible employment in it.

44 *Times*, 31 Dec 1991, 1.

45 *Times*, 1 Jan 1992.

46 The communications officer of the Catholic Secretariat, a White Father, wrote a letter to the *Mirror* in which he said: 'I still feel that the declaration of Zambia as a Christian Nation was unnecessary, ill-timed, poorly thought-out, and unfortunately framed in a covenant ceremony which made President Chiluba look like the new Moses of modern times. The televised show did and does contain, for him, the seeds of possible political embarrassment in the future' (*Mirror*, Feb 1992, 10). Just how prescient he was remained to be seen.

prophecies to the modern state of Israel, and leads to uncritical support for its policies. Four pastors prominent in the EFZ had all argued on ZNBC TV that the Gulf War was linked to biblical prophecies, and that 'since the Israelis were God's chosen people all world affairs were supposed to be centred around Israel.' They argued that the Middle East problems could not be solved by the United Nations but 'through religious means'.[47] The EFZ issued a press release on 7 February 1991 stating that 'The Bible is clear that God will bless those that bless Israel. This may imply that those who oppose Israel can only expect the wrath of God. Some of the present difficulties experienced in our country can be attributed to a direct result of rejecting Israel.' Another born-again pastor wrote: 'We know that our nation will only prosper if it changes its stand against Israel.' Writing just before the election, he stated that Christians 'shall only vote for a party whose foreign policy would strive to promote Zambia's relations with the international community. [...] This shall include a diplomatic relationship with Israel above all.'[48] Zambia's high-profile evangelist Nevers Mumba called for the review of Zambia's Middle East policy – all on grounds of Christian Zionism.[49] In a later article, Mumba wrote: 'Zambia has cursed Israel in both word and attitude and we are still reaping the curse on our nation. God's word is final. By being against Israel we are standing up against God and his will ... No wonder we lack progress.'[50] Another pastor set the establishment of diplomatic links with Israel as the first priority of any new government.[51]

Such Christian Zionism, which is widespread in Zambia's Evangelical churches, goes largely unnoticed by Catholics and the CCZ, who seem totally unaware that such views are possible. Yet, because these views are so important in the born-again camp, it seems likely that before the election Chiluba made them the promise that he would restore such links with Israel, perhaps also break them with Iran and Iraq (which he later did). In these circles this was bound to be a great vote-winner, and would have had the effect of distinguishing clearly between Chiluba and Kaunda, who in these same circles was considered to be too close to the Arabs. Israel has increased its influence in Chiluba's Zambia. It may be that

---

47   *Times*, 3 March 1991; the pastors were Sexton Chiluba of City Community Church, Ernest Chelelwa of Assemblies of God, Helmut Reutter of the Apostolic Faith Mission and Gabriel Schultz of Abundant Life. See also *Mirror*, 16 Mar 1991, 4.

48   Rev. Mpundu Mwape, 'Church lobbies for Israeli Ties', *Times*, 6 May 1991. In this article he writes, 'The West as well as the East Bank belongs to Israel historically' (thus ceding Gaza and the Golan Heights to Israel).

49   'Zambia faces Religious Invasion', *Times*, 24 Feb 1991.

50   *Times*, 13 Oct 1991. He deduces his Zionism from Mal 3: 6; Dt 28: 64-67; 2 Chron 7: 19-22; Is 43: 5-7; Mt 24: 32.

51   *Mirror*, 30 March 1991, 5

Zambia is one country for which Christian Zionism is a key determinant of foreign policy.[52]

On taking office, Chiluba appointed born-again pastors to government posts – most notably, besides some governorships of provinces, the Minister and Assistant Minister of Information. The minister was Rev. Stan Kristafor, Zambian-born but of East European immigrant stock and a wealthy Copperbelt businessman. Kristafor soon banned Muslim programmes on radio, a ban that the Vice-President had to lift on the grounds that Muslims had freedom of worship by the constitution. Kristafor also banned the television shows of a Zaïrean artiste on the grounds that they were pornographic, another ban that subsequently had to be lifted. (Kristafor was later dismissed for the allegedly racist manner in which he treated employees.) There was a subsequent argument about pornography in general. Under Kaunda there had been strict controls on it, as on much other literature. The relevant minister lifted the ban as part of a general liberalisation, but after a massive outcry on the part of the churches, Chiluba reimposed it.

Chiluba continued Kaunda's practice of attending and speaking at church functions; in Zambia, it would be hard for a President to do otherwise. He is invited to churches of all kinds. For example, he opened the EFZ headquarters in January 1993.[53] On such occasions he uses Christianity to his own political advantage. For example, while preaching at a UCZ fundraising dinner in Kitwe in October 1992, he could state: 'What I want [to be] one of the biggest differences between my government and the previous regime is the significant shift of focus in that under humanism man was at the centre of all human activities, while we [MMD] search for divine truth about God's Kingdom as manifested in his creation.'[54] At other times he is the recipient of Christian homage that translates into political advantage. For example, when Chiluba visited an interdenominational conference for pastors in Lusaka, the president of the Institute for Church Growth in Zambia said, according to a

---

[52] In July 1994 Chiluba made a state visit to Israel, which was dealt with as a pilgrimage in a TV programme screened on ZNBC TV on 2 Aug 1994. Besides the state functions, Chiluba visited Bethlehem, the Garden Tomb, the Temple of Solomon, Galilee, Capernaum and the place of the baptism in the Jordan. All the footage of these scenes was accompanied by appropriate biblical references. The increasing Israeli involvement in Zambia was deplored in *Mirror*, 3-9 Dec 1995, 14. In April 1996 Chiluba called clergymen to State House to pray for Israel on the grounds that 'All who curse Abraham will be cursed; all who bless Abraham will be blessed.' An AME pastor attacked Chiluba for not understanding that Israel's fate is clearly laid out in the Bible, and cannot be changed (*Mirror*, 28 April-4 May 1996, 6).

[53] *Times*, 31 Jan 1993, 1.

[54] *Times*, 11 Oct 1992. He could add that 'his government had seen the power of God given to man during creation abused by supreme parties that reigned and rode rough shod over man, dehumanising and perverting things in life.'

newspaper report, that 'the church would back the President who he described as God-sent', and the founder of the institute warned that 'disrespect to President Chiluba was disrespect to God who put him there.'[55] In this Chiluba is merely repeating what Kaunda did before him, and utilising Christianity for the legitimacy it can confer.

However, Chiluba has gone further, almost co-opting Christianity. As in so many African countries, crusades and revivals are a continual feature of Zambian life. Zambia differs, however, in that the President himself invited the preachers. It is the American Ernest Angley who focused attention on this issue, and so gave the question of miracle crusades a prominence it never had before in Zambia. It is unclear how the acquaintance between Chiluba and Angley was made; some say they started to correspond when Chiluba was in prison in the early 1980s. There is no doubt that it was at Chiluba's invitation that Angley first visited Zambia. Chiluba asked the local Evangelical churches to host the crusade, which they did. He invited Angley to State House, and hosted a reception for him. Chiluba spoke at the closing Angley service in Lusaka's Matero stadium saying that 'By declaring Zambia a Christian country we want to show the Lord that we are clearly for him. Zambia is ready to be put to the use of God, the beacon of light shall rise from here. We are ready to go out and evangelise our neighbours and the rest of the world.' He said that the world was now in the end times, and it was henceforth important to put together all forces to carry on the fight against Lucifer: 'This is no time to quarrel. This is the time to unite.' And Angley, for his part, described Chiluba as 'the dearest man he has ever met in world politics, saying that in him Zambians have not only a remarkable President, but a God-fearing preacher as well. "I know that you are chosen by God, ordained by God, to lead this great nation. This is just the beginning. God is going to bless this nation", Rev. Angley said with an arm around President Chiluba.'[56]

However, Angley is not one of America's most uncontroversial evangelists, as we noted above in discussing Uganda. His crusades drew enormous criticism, mainly because of supposed cures which did not bear investigation, and because his preaching was centred so much on himself.[57] Yet Chiluba invited him again the following year. This time the Evangelicals who in the previous year had agreed to form the organising committee declined to do so, and another group had to be found. This time the crusade began very inauspiciously: the television advertisements showed a man being cured in the previous year's crusade, but shortly after they were screened the man announced that he had not been cured

55   *Times*, 18 May 1994.
56   *Mirror*, 7-13 June 1993, 4.
57   *Times*, 5 Jun 1993.

at all.[58] Nevertheless, during Lusaka's 'Zambia for Christ' crusade in June 1994, Chiluba again hosted a reception for Angley at State House. This time Chiluba was more defensive, and was reported as saying 'that Christians should soldier on because disseminating the word of God was not a crime. As leader of Zambia, he had a responsibility to show the nation God's ways to avoid misleading people. The peace and tranquillity in Zambia was God's wish and Zambians should give themselves to Him. Rev. Angley praised Mr Chiluba for withstanding criticism since he took office.'[59] Angley's second visit, too, produced a very negative reaction. The *Post* savaged Chiluba in an editorial: 'It is unacceptable for a President of this country to use the taxpayers' money to fulfil his personal religious dreams. [...] Chiluba's commitment to born-again fanaticism is personal. He is not in it for the good of all the citizens of this country. [...] It is necessary for all Christians to stop this religious madness. Fundamentalism and its excesses and selfishness will eventually undermine Christianity in this country. Chiluba's religious fanaticism is ... dangerous to the good democratic governance of this country. [...] Chiluba should concentrate on addressing the political and economic ills of this country and tackling the corruption of his government.'[60]

Hardly had the Angley crusade finished when it was announced that Richard Roberts, son of Oral Roberts and president of Oral Roberts Ministries, would be visiting Zambia for crusades. Once again, it was discovered that the invitation to Roberts was from President Chiluba himself. This caused considerable reaction on the part of the churches. Church leaders argued that invitations to foreign evangelists should be made through the churches, not the government. The protests were not so much from the Catholics and the CCZ but from within the born-again fraternity itself, thus lending support to the idea that part of the objection was that established Evangelical pastors were being ignored.[61] The committee

---

[58]   *Times*, 1, 2 and 5 June 1994.

[59]   *Times*, 5 June 1994.

[60]   *Post*, 12 Aug 1994, 2. Also: 'How can Chiluba justify spending even one ngwee of taxpayer's money on Ernest Angley? Or the use by Angley of taxpayers' money? Or Chiluba's own use of taxpayers' money to travel across the country to attend Angley's crusades? Moreover, Chiluba is employed on a full-time basis by the taxpayer to manage the affairs of government and state and not to go around the country praying with useless preachers like Angley. [...] Chiluba is busy wasting valuable working hours following religious fanatics like Angley. There is no serious work he is doing in State House to inspire Zambians to work. [...] Christianity was not brought to this country by rich television preachers. It was brought by men and women who were prepared to suffer and sacrifice.'

[61]   *Sun*, 29 Aug-5 Sept 1994, 1. The CCZ General Secretary refused to comment in this article, although the General Secretary of the ECZ said that religious affairs were best left to the church, and the director of communications of the ECZ had criticised Chiluba for inviting Angley in 1994 (*Post*, 7 June 1994, 2).

sponsoring Roberts' crusades was headed by those Evangelicals who currently had the President's ear. But these crusades, too, brought considerable ridicule. Much was made of a boy who had been cured at Roberts' Mufulira crusade, and was presented to President Chiluba on the night he attended. But the Italian Franciscan editor of *Icengelo* tracked the boy down and interviewed his mother and other relatives, who were insistent that the boy had not been healed at all: the mother was reported as saying: 'They are just playing with our suffering. [...] As for the miracle, it is just a big lie.' The article publicising all this, mischievous where it was not totally contemptuous in tone, was directed at the President: 'So they have also fooled the President on TV! That is absolutely disgusting!' It ended: 'Please, Mr President, stop inviting these fake evangelists. We are much better off without them.'[62] The third high-profile American evangelist invited to Zambia was Benny Hinn; the invitation was extended by the Deputy Minister of Finance, Rev. Dan Pule, and given great prominence on Hinn's television programme. Hinn came for various crusades in 1994 and 1995, and in turn pledged to raise money and campaign for Chiluba's re-election.[63]

Chiluba can take advantage of Christian conventions too. In August 1994 the present writer attended a convention staged in Lusaka by Nevers Mumba of Victory Ministries (to be examined below in detail.) Not only did Chiluba give the organisers and speakers a reception at State House (the visiting speakers and selected local pastors held a 'political summit' with Chiluba one afternoon), but Chiluba himself officially opened the convention, when Mumba delivered a long address to the President, and then the President preached. Mumba's address praised Chiluba for establishing links with Israel (remarks that drew the crowd to their feet), and denounced media reports critical of the government, which he attributed to evil spirits. 'We are going out of this conference not believing reports of newspapers but the reports of the Lord!' He then gave reasons to support Chiluba, including: 'Chiluba is part of the household of faith. His victory is our victory. His success is our success; if he fails we fail [and then people will say]: "Let's get a Muslim and see what he can do." ' Chiluba in his sermon insisted that when he made mistakes true believers should not try to remove him but pray for him. The prayers of Christians had brought him to power without violence. Subsequent problems had arisen because Christians had stopped praying – he thereby implied that Zambia's difficulties were their fault, not his. 'With your prayer and fasting, we will manage. The greatest problem is when you grumble. God says grumbling is like lack of faith.' He then told the story of Moses delivering Israel from Egypt, effectively identifying himself

[62]   *Times*, 17 Sept 1994, 4.
[63]   *Mirror*, 3-9 Dec 1995, 14.

with Moses. He was careful to suggest that God had appointed him to the leadership, also identifying any talk of re-electing Kaunda with the cry to return to Egypt which was so offensive to God. It was a virtuoso performance for which he was cheered to the echo; it was also a shameless piece of electioneering, utilising Christian rhetoric to the full. Besides the ideological onslaught in his set talk, the President also took the opportunity to greet several born-again pastors from the platform by name – a deft political touch which would have repaired some of the bridges which had become rather rickety over the previous several months. As if Chiluba's sermon were not enough, however, Mrs Chiluba came to the convention another night. She sang – and brought their erring son Castro, whose misdemeanours had frequently been in the headlines, and who was welcomed with a special cheer. On the final night Vice-President Miyanda attended, and he also sang and spoke. There is little chance that any of the thousands attending would have voted for anyone other than Chiluba and Miyanda, and their understanding of Christianity would be a decisive factor in their decision.

Chiluba takes every opportunity to utilise Christian discourse to his own benefit. In April 1993 the national football team all perished in an air crash near Libreville, en route to Senegal. The event was a national tragedy. At the state funeral Chiluba spoke: 'I rededicate this nation and submit it to you. [...] No king appoints himself. No one is born President. You alone appoint and remove. [...] We are here because you have given us to do your will to your people. You are king and the ruler of this nation. [...] You brought me in in order to proclaim your name as our God.' Moreover, at Christmas in 1994 a huge banner 'Zambia for Christ' adorned the gates to State House. Chiluba can even respond to critics; 'Judge not, and you shall not be judged.'[64] In a part of the Pentecostal sector, this Christian rhetoric seems to work.[65]

A corrupt and uncaring Christian nation

As early as 1992 it was obvious to all that operationally the MMD government was very little different from the UNIP government it replaced. The similarity extended to personnel. Many of the members of Chiluba's government had actually held office under Kaunda. Some had been dismissed, some may have left in disillusionment, but a good number had rather opportunistically seen the writing on the wall and changed horses while there was still time. To some degree this was obvious even before the 1991 elections. Some of the least impressive rejects of UNIP

64   Programme 'Churches and Democracy', ZNBC 29 July 1994.

65   Thus at Lusaka's Jesus Worship Centre the pastor can say in his sermon: 'It is not often that we have godly kings as we do today.' Therefore, 'If we are going to do anything for this nation we must raise people to obey' (services, 24 July 1994).

had become key financial supporters of MMD, including some who had been implicated in drug smuggling; indeed some wits, even before the 1991 elections, were claiming that MMD stood for 'Mass Movement for Drug Dealers'. By mid-1994 the same corruption that had distinguished the worst of the UNIP era was flourishing in MMD. In early 1994 Western donors, offering more than $600 million in badly needed balance of payments support, demanded and received the resignation of Foreign Minister Vernon Mwaanga, Social Welfare Minister Nakatindi Wina and her husband Sikota Wina, the Speaker of Parliament, because of their reputed drug dealing. Then in July 1994 Vice-President Levy Mwanawasa resigned, alleging that Chiluba's government was corrupt; in particular, he claimed that Health Minister Sata was unfit to hold office. Then Chiluba dismissed Legal Affairs Minister Ludwig Sondashi after the latter accused him of receiving money from a drug fund managed on his behalf by Health Minister Sata.[66] In Zambia one of the quickest ways to make big money is by drug smuggling, since its uncontrollable borders with eight countries and its air links with South Africa and Europe have made it a transit point for channelling cocaine, heroin and mandrax. Fears were expressed that the proliferation of indigenous banks in Zambia was related to laundering drug money.[67]

Rumours of all sorts of corruption were plentiful. It was often said that since many of the government officials did not really expect to be re-elected in 1996, they were determined to make as much money as they could while they had the chance. Hence yet another meaning of the letters MMD was said to be 'Make Money and Depart'. A much publicised case was that of a deputy minister accusing the Minister of Finance of corruption in allocating Japanese aid. In mid-1994 Minister of Finance Ronald Penza was publicly said to have made millions of dollars from a 'dry port' customs facility near Lusaka.[68] His role in the collapse of the private Meridien BIAO Bank was also subject to speculation. Yet another case was the fiasco of the privatisation of the Zambia Consolidated Copper Mines (ZCCM). The government had commissioned a feasibility study of the way to privatise ZCCM, and the report recommended not selling the five copper mines and auxiliary units as one, mainly because whoever owned such an entity controlling 90% of foreign exchange earnings would effectively control Zambia's economy and its government. The government vacillated, first rejecting the report,

---

[66] See *Economist*, 16 July 1994, 56; *Guardian*, 30 Aug 1994, 8.

[67] *Times*, 13 Feb, 1995, 6; *Post*, 14 Feb 1995, 6, 10-11. At the launching of Aero Zambia, an airline bidding to replace the defunct Zambia Airways, the Minister of Transport spent some time urging the new airline not to indulge in drug trafficking, thereby tending to confirm rumours (*Sunday Times*, 12 Feb 1995, 1).

[68] *Post*, 26 July 1994, 1.

and then establishing another commission. At the height of this debate some ministers went public, charging that a clique of politicians and businessmen were derailing the privatisation for their own ends. Chiluba dismissed two government ministers for making these accusations.[69] At about the same time Zambia Airways was liquidated, and the private media speculated that a few ministers had in effect sold the airline to themselves, at a discount, and then with South African expertise relaunched it on its profitable routes as a new private airline. And Chiluba himself had been accused of maintaining his secretary in luxury accommodation at the taxpayers' expense, and of squandering more public money in taking a twenty-two-person delegation to a Christian revival in Sweden. As structural adjustment caused untold suffering to ordinary people, Mwanawasa admitted that as Vice-President he had lived 'in a ten-bedroomed house, with wall to wall carpet, two Mercedes-Benz to myself and two for my wife, four land cruisers, a Toyota Corolla for the children and a vanette at my kitchen door.'[70] By mid-1994 public feeling was running so strongly against the MMD government that a group of younger politicians, labelled the Young Turks, were publicly advocating that some of the more notorious of the old and tainted figures of MMD should be dropped if the government was to survive.

If the politicians were enriching themselves, the ordinary people were becoming desperate. For them the decline was catastrophic. From a baseline index of 72 in 1980, average real earnings fell to 44 in 1986, 30 in 1991 and to a low of 21 in 1992. Average life expectancy in Zambia fell from fifty-four years in 1990 to forty-eight years in 1993. The under-five mortality rate rose from 150 per 1,000 live births in the 1980s to 202 in 1992. In addition, 40% of children under five were stunted. Furthermore, gross enrolment in primary schools fell from 92% in 1983 to 84% in 1993. Outbreaks of water-borne diseases such as cholera and dysentery were frequent as services collapsed; in mid-1994 only three of Lusaka's twenty-two garbage collection trucks were functioning.[71] Unemployment was increasing as firms went into liquidation, or as multinationals like Colgate, Johnson and Johnson, GEC and Dunlop scaled down their operations or moved to South Africa or Zimbabwe. In many areas transport ceased to exist as the national bus company collapsed.

---

[69]   *ANB-BIA Supplement*, 15 Dec 1994, x-xi.

[70]   *Sun*, 18-24 July 1994, 3. For Zambia's political culture, see Bratton, 'Economic Crisis'; Michael Bratton and Beatrice Liatto-Katundu, 'A Focus Group Assessment of Political Attitudes in Zambia', *African Affairs* 93 (1994), 535-63. The importance of regional variations is well portrayed in Wim van Binsbergen, 'Aspects of Democracy and Democratisation in Zambia and Botswana: Exploring African Political Culture at the Grassroots', *Journal of Contemporary African Studies* 13 (1995), 3-33.

[71]   National Commission for Development Planning, May 1995, cited in *Impact*, Aug 1995, 19.

Cases of witchcraft multiplied, often an indicator of social stress.[72]

MMD was effectively replicating UNIP rule.[73] One bizarre similarity between Kaunda and Chiluba was often noted. Kaunda's son was arrested for shooting a girl dead outside a nightclub, and after a long legal process, he was finally freed when Chiluba came to power. But in 1994 Chiluba's own son Castro was involved in a similar incident, shooting a girl (this time not fatally) and also being taken to court. There were other similarities. The judiciary were intimidated, and dirty tricks were used to discredit opponents. The media speculated that Chiluba was involved in a car accident that killed the president of the National Party.[74] In mid-1994, the MMD provincial elections were characterised by acrimony and accusations of vote-rigging. Some outspoken journalists were ordered to be imprisoned indefinitely, not by the police or the courts, but by the Speaker of Parliament.[75] By May 1996 tension was such that there were terrorist bombs exploding near key locations.

As the situation deteriorated, the three church bodies (ECZ, CCZ and EFZ) issued a joint pastoral statement, declaring a 'Year of Political Responsibility'. This praised some improvements effected by the new government; deplored the intolerance of politicians; drew attention to the need to support the poor under structural adjustment; emphasised the importance of agriculture in Zambia; called for groups like the Electoral Commission and the Human Rights Commission to remain free from political interference; called for the promotion of justice, peace and development and community; deplored public apathy; and urged that political life be guided by 'Gospel values of respect for human dignity, human rights, common good, and social justice, solidarity, integral development, special concern for the poor and and non-violence in resolving conflict.' They outlined programmes that churches could adopt in the coming year, mainly dealing with raising political awareness.[76] They even organised a service in April 1996 at the Anglican cathedral (the normal venue, despite the small numbers of Anglicans, because of its size and location) during which leaders of the political parties recited a pledge in which they committed themselves to a peaceful, non-violent electoral campaign later in the year; to seek reconciliation and understanding; to

---

[72] In Chiawa near Lusaka fifteen died in witchcraft rituals in early 1995: see *Sunday Times*, 12 Feb 1995, 1; *Times*, 22 Feb 1995, 3.

[73] The continuity between the UNIP and MMD regimes is the theme of Jan Kees van Donge, 'Zambia: Kaunda and Chiluba: Enduring Patterns of Political Culture' in John A. Wiseman (ed.), *Democracy and Political Change in Sub-Saharan Africa*, London: Routledge, 1995, 193-219.

[74] *Mirror*, 10-16 Sept 1995, 2 and 11; *Mirror*, 8-14 Sept 1996, 1.

[75] Some churches were vociferous against the arrest; *Mirror*, 10-16 Mar 1996.

[76] *Mirror*, 12-16 Nov 1995, 8-9.

cooperate with anyone wishing to enhance the democratic process; and to dialogue.[77]

The election monitoring group ZEMEC had decided after the 1992 elections to remain in existence as the Foundation for Democratic Process (FODEP), both to monitor subsequent elections and to educate about democracy. The ECZ and the CCZ remained perhaps the key players in the new body, but at this stage the EFZ withdrew, mainly because it was uneasy with other members like the women's lobby. Confusingly, however, the two spokesmen for FODEP remained Evangelicals: Rev. Foston Sakala of the Reformed Church and Bishop John Mambo of the Church of God, members of FODEP in their personal capacity. Both have frequently been called on for media comment, but (as we shall see) sometimes their comments have appeared unconsidered and they have been thought to have their own agenda.[78]

Meanwhile, after renouncing the UNIP presidency in 1992, Kaunda had retaken control of the party in June 1995, and was moving around the country, obviously preparing his bid to return to power in 1996. Although a Kaunda victory did not appear likely – the people had not forgotten their plight during his rule – his appeared the most formidable challenge to Chiluba. So Chiluba moved to have him deported, on the grounds that his parents were not Zambians but Malawian. This met widespread denunciation, even ridicule, so Chiluba prepared a new constitution requiring any presidential candidate to have parents born in Zambia. (There was some irony in this, for it is uncertain that Chiluba can prove he was not born the other side of Zambia's most artificial border with Zaïre). Many churchmen protested and called for a special assembly to discuss and approve any new constitution, rather than the totally MMD-dominated and subservient parliament.[79]

In the preamble to the new constitution, too, Chiluba proposed to include the declaration of Zambia as a Christian country. The review

---

[77] *Mirror*, 7-13 April, 1996, 8-9.

[78] Jérôme Lafargue ('Surveiller et Socialiser: l'Action de la FODEP en Zambie', paper delivered at Table Ronde, 'Mouvements religieux et débats démocratiques en Afrique', Pau, 8-9 Dec 1994) sees the inadequacies of FODEP, but does not seem aware of its make-up (to call Mambo *'évêque de EFZ'* is confused). FODEP's statements are often *'malhabile'*, but Lafargue seems to equate the spokesmen with *'les réseaux religieux'*. Within these religious networks there are different theological currents, and Lafargue seems unaware of political theology of the last three decades. He seems quite amazed that statements contain no (or in another case only one) *'référence religieuse'*; therefore they are *'politique'*, not religious. He sees these statements as evidence of 'tactique' or *'stratégie ecclésiastique d'entrée politique'*. The political theology of say, the Jesuit Centre for Theological Reflection (whose influence is detectable behind not a few of FODEP's considered statements) can distinguish several senses of the term 'political involvement', and displays a subtlety far beyond the extempore remarks of FODEP's spokesmen.

[79] *Mirror*, 5-11 Nov, 1.

commission preparing the new constitution had in fact argued that this
was not wanted by most Zambians, and that 'the rights of Christianity or
any other religion could be safely secured without any form of
declaration.' The government overruled this and wanted it to be inserted
that Zambia was a Christian nation. This reawakened the whole debate.
The CCZ and the ECZ issued a joint letter in November 1995 in which
they called for wider debate and consultation on the proposed constitution,
and then at length argued against including any declaration of Zambia as
a Christian nation. They conceded that most Zambians are Christians,
but argued that the constitution belonged to all citizens, not just to those
who profess Christianity. 'No loophole should be left which might, at
some future date, lead to non-Christian Zambians being regarded as
second-class citizens, or even excluded from public office.' They warned
of a danger of division in a nation 'when specific religious beliefs are
accorded privileged status or preferential treatment.' They claimed that
'authentic religious practice will not be fostered by this declaration. It
could lead to the abuse of religion for purely political ends, and even
bring discredit on the name "Christian".' They claimed that if Zambia was
to be a Christian state, this would come about not by reason of a declaration
but by reason of Christians living their faith. They ended: 'The Christian
Church will promote the democratic institutions of our government and
support the building up of a genuinely democratic spirit throughout the
country. This will contribute greatly toward ensuring that Christianity
remains a living reality in Zambia, and does not simply become a political
slogan or a religious motto.'[80] Chiluba was to ignore this, and much other
comment, and sign the new constitution into effect. Since the clause re-
stricting the presidency to citizens of Zambian parentage was widely seen
as a blatantly undemocratic move to forestall any challenge from Kaunda,
the governments of the United States, Britain, Norway and France immediately declared that they would reconsider their aid to Zambia.[81]

In all this there is evident a yawning divide within Christianity itself.
On political matters the Catholics and the Christian Council could speak
as one. In many things they were joined by the Evangelicals, or a sector
of them – but by general admission this Evangelical sector was motivated
by the belief that it had not received what it considered its rights from
the 'Christian' government. Another sector of the Pentecostals, though,
had been thoroughly co-opted. This sector centred on the Pentecostal

---

[80]   *Mirror*, 10-16 Nov 1995, 6. Note also the Catholic Bishop D. de Jong's expression of
similar sentiments, and his presuming to speak on behalf of the CCZ as well (*Mirror*,
16-22 June 1996, 8-9). However, the outgoing UCZ General Secretary supported the
inclusion of the declaration (*Mirror*, 16-22 June 1996, 6). The Law Association of Zambia
resolved that including the declaration in the preamble was 'discriminating, contentious
and unacceptable' (*Mirror*, 18-24 Aug 1996, 10).

[81]   *Mirror*, 9-15 June 1996, 2.

Assemblies of God, to which Miyanda belonged and with which Chiluba was increasingly associating himself. Indeed, the pastor of Lusaka's PAOG flagship church had actually supported the indefinite arrest of the three journalists referred to earlier.[82] It was this division within the churches that led both sides at inter-party talks in mid-1996 to refuse to have the meeting brokered by the churches: one side thought the mainline churches were allied with the opposition, while the other thought some prominent Pentecostals were in the pocket of Chiluba. In a rebuff to the churches most unusual in Zambia, they preferred the Law Association of Zambia to mediate instead.[83]

In the face of this perceived corruption at the top, and increasing desperation, disillusionment and apathy among the people, the Catholic Church voiced its criticism of the government's performance, particularly the structural adjustment programme, through pastoral letters and statements. On 23 January 1995 the Catholic Commission on Justice and Peace (CCJP) released a statement denouncing the government's political shortcomings, corruption, intolerance, encouragement of violence and the lack of public scrutiny. The statement deplored the way that the country was being run for the benefit of the banking sector and traders, and indeed 'speculators and profiteers, some of whom are senior government officials'.[84] Statements from the Justice and Peace committees (local, regional, national) of the Catholic Church became more frequent and more critical until a group calling itself the Alliance for Concerned Catholics published advertisements denouncing these committees for 'preaching violence and linking up with opposition parties'. Then the Catholic bishops responded by publicly announcing that they 'fully recognise, support and stand by' the CCJP.[85]

Tension between church and state was increasing generally, and reached occasional flashpoints. In December 1994 the Christian Council had a day-long seminar during which the General Secretary, the Rev. Violet Sampa-Bredt, was fiercely critical of the government. She denounced the 'massive and deplorable starvation' and other social evils

---

[82] *Mirror*, 21 Mar-6 April 1996, 2. The PAOG had earlier disagreed with the other churches and sided with the government in arguing that the new constitution be adopted by parliament (*Mirror*, 12-18 Nov 1995, 1) and that the Christian nation clause be included (*Mirror*, 15-21 Oct 1995, 7); and supported Chiluba when he drew almost universal ridicule by revealing the existence of security bunkers under State House, attempting to portray them as Kaunda's 'torture chambers' (*Mirror*, 17-23 Sept 1995, 7).

[83] *Mirror*, 12-18 May 1996, 2.

[84] *Mirror*, 29 Jan-4 Feb 1995, 1; *Post*, 17 Feb 1995, 2; *Post*, 21 Feb 1995, 2; officials of the CCJP repeat these charges in interviews and lectures (see *Mail,* 16 Jan 1995, 3; *Post*, 14 Feb 1995, 3), and opposition politicians use such statements for their own purposes (*Post*, 21 Feb 1995, 2).

[85] *Mirror*, 31 Dec-6 Jan 1996, 1; *Impact*, Feb 1995, 7. The various statements of CCJP are to be found in successive issues of *Impact*..

created by government policies. She called the privatisation programme a 'rip-off exercise'. 'Even if we need the structural adjustment programme, we certainly do not need it in its present form, where corrupt activities have been reported to occupy centre stage.' She claimed that 'The economy has been plundered by politicians and is on the brink of collapse', called the declaration of a Christian nation 'now empty', and ended by saying that the CCZ would aim in 1995 to target 'our membership and civil society in general to take a much more pro-active role in the governance of our country'.[86] The CCZ Secretary then left for Europe. While she was out of the country, the government accused her of denouncing the government before the Swedish media. When she returned she strongly repudiated these accusations, and then, flanked by the General Secretary of the Catholic Secretariat and officers of the EFZ, held a press conference at which the chairman of the CCZ, Anglican Bishop Clement Shaba, further denounced the government.[87] This was given considerable publicity, and drew an official press statement from State House which acknowledged the concerns of the churches; reaffirmed 'the imperative of dialogue between government on one hand and the emerging civil society especially the church on the other'; corrected the view that erroneously interpreted dialogue as frequent sojourns in State House; and urged anyone with evidence of corruption to contact the anti-Corruption Commission rather than seeking to involve the President himself.[88]

While opposition politicians tended to support the church spokesmen, government members rallied to the government's defence.[89] The government media reacted to the churches' press conference sharply. (The MMD had gone back on its manifesto to sell off the public media, which had by now become mouthpieces for the MMD as they had been for UNIP in the previous dispensation.) The *Sunday Mail*, under a headline 'Church Plot!', claimed that the church 'casting aside its religious robes' had initiated 'an unprecedented but orchestrated inter-denominational onslaught on the three-year-old MMD government'. The *Daily Mail* editorial denounced church leaders who 'in their fight for dominance

---

[86] *Mirror*, 18-24 Dec 1994, 1 and 8-9.

[87] See *Mirror*, 22-28 Jan 1995, 8-9; note in Bishop Shaba's statement the major concern that the church was being ordered around by government, a view that was repeated by Bishop John Mambo, Foston Sakala, and Joe Imakando (*ibid.*, 1, see also 3).

[88] *Daily Mail*, 18 Jan 1995, 3.

[89] For the opposition, see *Mirror*, 22-28 Jan 1995, 1; one government minister, speaking at the launching of a Bible translation, called on the church to stop attacking structural adjustment (*Mirror*, 5-11 Feb 1995, 8). Reverend Peter Chintala, the Deputy Minister of Youth, Sport and Child Development, as well as President of the Free Baptist Church of Zambia, expressed sadness over the church criticisms, saying that 'the church and government should be co-partners in development ... as is evidenced in the Bible which says that any government instituted on earth is God given' (*Mirror*, 19-25 Feb 1995, 5).

over others, are turning more and more to politics to gain support' and called it unchristian 'for church leaders to lie and exaggerate to win support'. It denounced church leaders' preaching 'how to do to the government what was done to the UNIP government in 1991... It appears that some churches, especially those opposed to charismatic ones, have mounted a war against the government which they perceive to be biased against their church. [...] Some of them are truly bent on bringing down the government.'[90]

This was still in the air when a television talk show featured Fr Umberto Davoli, the editor of *Icengelo*. Before a studio audience, and in the face of hostile questioning from the presenter, he denounced government policies for their effects on the poor, criticised the declaration of Zambia as a Christian nation (on the grounds that the people were not consulted and that it discriminates against non-Christians) and attacked the born-agains. The programme was actually filmed some weeks before it was screened, and in those weeks the government media attacked him for the views expressed.[91] It was broadcast to enormous publicity, and drew widespread comment, most of it decidedly supportive of the priest.[92] In an unguarded moment during the programme Fr Davoli implied that he had someone in mind to take over from Chiluba as President. This lapse enabled MMD officials to attack him for directly interfering in politics. They suggested that the Catholic Church was grooming its own candidate

[90] *Sunday Mail*, 15 Jan 1995, 1; *Mail*, 16 Jan 1995, 1; the *Sunday Mail* editorial comment also implied that the root cause was 'what some faiths deem are alleged biased tendencies by government where the leaders are giving more favours to born-agains than the rest of the faiths' (*Sunday Mail*, 15 Jan 1995, 1; see also *Sunday Mail*, 19 Feb 1995, 1). An attack on 'the so-called spiritual counsellors to the President who spend most of their time hanging around State House' is found in *Mirror*, 22-28 Jan 1995, 3. The CCJP expressed concern over the 'sponsorship of a particular brand of Christianity' (*Mirror*, 29 Jan-4 Feb 1995, 1), and the executive secretary of the CCJP complained that 'one brand of Christianity has become state religion', only to be rebutted by the PAOG General Superintendent (*Post*, 17 Feb 1995, 3).

[91] See *Weekly Express*, 25-31 Jan 1995, 1; *ibid.*, 1-7 Feb 1995, 1.

[92] E.g., *Post*, 17 Feb 1995, 5 and 7; *ibid.*, 21 Feb 1995, 5-6 and 9; *Times*, 17 Feb 1995, 5; *Sun Times* 19 Feb 1995, 3 and 5. Fr Davoli further publicised his criticisms at a day seminar 'Should the Church participate in Politics' held at Mindolo Ecumenical Foundation in Kitwe, 11 Feb 1995. In this talk he hammered SAP as a poor instrument of development; insisted that the free market be subject to some kind of social control; pilloried the government for taxing the low-waged; called on the government to initiate labour-intensive enterprises; denounced the disproportion between the burden imposed on those who were already suffering too much and the privileges enjoyed by leaders and government officials; and demanded that the priorities be the real needs of the people. He insisted that concern for all these issues was demanded of the Christian, citing Is 1: 13-17; 56: 10-57:1; 58,6; Amos 2: 6-7; 5: 11-15; 5: 22-3; James 1: 27; Jer 7: 6; Ez 18: 12; Mic 2: 2; Zac 7: 10; Lk 1: 51-3; 4: 18; Mt 25: 35-46. (Some of this talk is covered in *Mirror*, 19-25 Feb 1995, 1). He repeated similar ideas addressing the Ndola Press Club on 21 February (*Times*, 23 Feb 1995, 3).

to supplant the non-Catholic and born-again Chiluba.[93] The Catholic Secretariat immediately released a statement reaffirming the guardedly supportive Catholic position on Zambia as a Christian nation, asserting Fr Davoli's right to speak out against abuses even though he was not an official spokesman of the Catholic Church, and dissociating itself from any 'personal speculation' about individual candidates, such matters being not the concern of any church but of political parties only.[94]

In this rather charged atmosphere of friction between the government and the churches, many repeated the observation that it was the churches that had brought down Kaunda and his UNIP government. In an editorial the *Mirror* concluded that the state should beware of a fight with the church. 'If that is what they are spoiling for, then we earnestly beseech them to look upon the political tomb of Kenneth Buchizya Kaunda (1964-1991) and tremble. He tried to wrestle with *Icengelo* and the clergy and where did he end up? What about Malawi's Kamuzu Banda? He tried to wrestle with the Catholic bishops after a controversial pastoral letter. Where is he today?' The *Sun* remarked that Kaunda 'could teach the MMD a lesson or two on how the church literally brought down his once indomitable UNIP empire.' And the *Sunday Times* repeated: 'It is known to all Zambians that the Catholic Church sunk its teeth deep into the one-party system and refused to let go until the structure fell.'[95]

Because of the intense interest in these issues, within two days of the interview with Fr Davoli another programme was screened, an interview with the Vice-President, with no studio audience, on two of the issues raised by Fr Davoli—the declaration of Zambia as a Christian nation and that of the born-agains. Miyanda presented the declaration as 'an act of faith, a commitment, a public pronouncement to say that this is the way we are going to govern our nation'. He rejected the idea that Chiluba should have consulted the people: 'I reject that. If you've accepted Jesus, you follow his teaching.' Later he repeated that he found it 'outrageous coming from Christians' that Chiluba should have asked the churches whether Zambians should accept Jesus. He claimed he was unable to understand why the issue of the declaration was being discussed again, implying that 'there must be some reason other than the question of the declaration.' When it was gently suggested that the conduct of leading government figures might call the declaration into question,

---

93   See *Mail*, 13 Feb 1995, 1; *Times*, 14 Feb 1995, 5; *Daily Mail*, 14 Feb 1995, 1. A letter in the *Times* (15 Feb 1995, 5) wondered if the Catholic candidate was Henry Mtonga, retired Inspector General of Police, whom a Catholic television programme had featured some weeks before.

94   *Mail*, 20 Feb 1995, 8; *Mail*, 21 Feb 1995, 7; *Mirror*, 19-25 Feb 1995, 8.

95   *Mirror*, 29 Jan-4 Feb 1995, 2; *Sun*, 30 Jan-5 Feb 1995, 11; *Sunday Times*, 19 Feb 1995, 3.

Miyanda replied that if ministers fall short, they should be challenged, 'But why attack the declaration ... why attack Jesus? That's what is happening when you attack the declaration. [...] Any Christian who condemns the declaration, I question whether they are for Jesus.' He claimed that 'the declaration is the best thing that ever happened to this country', because there was revival everywhere, more choirs and young people who understood the Bible. The advantage of the declaration was that the time of bribery and corruption was over; the declaration would help to change attitudes. He insisted that Christians should not be publicly criticising the government: 'The President is a Christian; his Christian brethren must [telephone] him ... But you can't start condemning [him] in the paper – that's unbiblical.'

The next Saturday, Miyanda met about 250 'church leaders' in a closed meeting designed to repair the rift between church and government. The 250 were mainly Evangelicals, with only three Catholics and about fifteen from the CCZ churches. Despite the composition of the meeting, the Secretary General of the Catholic Secretariat was made chairman and he and the Secretary General of the CCZ (again working together) ensured that no communiqué be issued. In the course of the meeting almost all possible interpretations of the declaration were expressed: that Christian ministers should now have positions in government; that churches should be given land to build on; that the current religious education syllabus in schools be set aside and replaced with the Bible; that the building of mosques in Lusaka be halted. Miyanda in his lengthy speech apologised for the lack of consultation that marked the original declaration. On their side, all the church leaders said that they accepted the declaration. A five-person committee was then appointed to plot a future course of action, a committee made up of the General Secretaries of the EFZ, CCZ and ECZ, with the head of the SDAs (as not represented in those bodies) and one other.

The confrontation between the missionary-editor and the Vice-President showed that there was no common ground between them. The priest spoke as a rather typical Western liberal Christian, for whom the separation of church and state constituted an immense advance, and the declaration of a Christian nation was a retrograde step. For the Vice-President (who is widely regarded as a politician of integrity), to question the declaration is quite simply to question Jesus. That the Vice-President may genuinely not understand the theological viewpoint of the opposing group was indicated at the meeting with churchmen. Nevers Mumba stated that the declaration had to be seen in terms of evangelism; the General Secretary of the CCZ disagreed, saying that it must be related to the church's 'holistic' ministry. Miyanda immediately interposed that they were in agreement; one was talking about evangelism, the other about 'holiness'.

He genuinely may be unfamiliar with the use of the word 'holistic' in the discourse of the General Secretary, which embraces things like access to education and health care.

We have referred to a split in the ranks of the Evangelicals. Many EFZ officials and pastors had also expressed their embarrassment at this so-called 'Christian government', because scorn for the 'Christian government' tended to be extended to them as well. For example, a statement in his own defence issued by the dismissed Minister of Legal Affairs made much of chicanery in the Office of the President, 'a place which is supposed to be the fountain of justice, a place from where the doctrine of "national Christianity" for Zambia evolved'. He noted tartly that his 'culture and [his] Roman Catholic faith' would not permit him to be part of such corruption, and concluded: 'People who are privileged to hold the office of President should learn to tell the truth.'[96] All the talk about corruption in government led to the accusation that the government was 'putting on the veil of religion to hide its misdeeds'.[97] Opposition politicians accused Chiluba of 'trying to politicise Christianity and use it as a decisive campaign tool. [...] Last time our country was proclaimed a one-party state. Now it is a one-religion nation. Who knows, next it could be another dangerous clown proclaiming a one-language country, or a one-race country.'[98] Such sentiments had a sobering effect on many Evangelicals.

But there was something else behind the general Evangelical dissatisfaction. This was the feeling, on the part of many Evangelical ministers, that 'their government' had not brought them the access and influence they had expected, even demanded as of right. Many Christians thought that the MMD owed them some gratitude, either in the form of a Ministry of Christian Affairs, or a number of pastors among the ten MPs whose nomination the constitution left to the President, or at least unlimited access for pastors to State House and a President willing to accept Christian advice.[99] This Evangelical sector of Christianity does not really

[96]   Full-page advertisement in *Sun*, 18-24 July 1994, 12.

[97]   *Post*, 3 Jan 1995, 3. Sometimes this sentiment could be expressed with considerable scorn: 'Zambia seems to be one of the few truly Christian nations of the world where one can get away with any crime. Coup plotters are freed to become top government officials, thieves are promoted to top government jobs in the hope of reform, corrupt ministers and members of parliament are paid highly in the hope of stopping corruption. Those with drug-trafficking accusations are defended and sent to parliament. What crime can't one commit and be forgiven in this holy land? It now seems easy to understand why President Chiluba declared Zambia a Christian nation - to blunder and be forgiven infinitely' (*Post*, 17 Feb 1995, 6).

[98]   A. Mbikusita-Lewanika, formerly of the MMD but then of the National Party (*Post*, 3 Jan 1995, 3).

[99]   See *Mirror*, 16-22 Nov 1992, 6-7.

have a theology of good government; for them all that is needed is to have Christian leaders (frequently themselves) either in positions of influence or as advisers to those who hold such positions. Thus the David Livingstone Memorial Presbyterian Church of Southern Africa said that Zambia 'can only be a Christian nation if religious leaders take up active positions in the running of the country's affairs'. The spokesman continued: 'The Presbyterian Church wants to show the world that Zambia is for sure a Christian nation and in practical terms, the solution is to have church leaders elected to decision making bodies of the government.'[100] Bishop John Mambo approved the idea of a churchman being nominated as an MP (not discounting the suggestion that it might be himself), on the grounds that the church had an important role in influencing political decisions or change. He added that the person thus selected by the three mother bodies should also be the President's adviser and chaplain at State House.[101] The same Bishop Mambo was later unsubtly to claim: 'The state and church are partners in terms of governance in any democracy. In England they share power – the Archbishop of Canterbury has a seat in the House of Lords.'[102] Continually quoted in the media, he persisted that only Christians should be in parliament, and that 'pagans should not be voted for in the 1996 general elections ... The Church must move in and run the affairs of this country.' Mambo added that although not yet ready for a political position, 'he would not hesitate to go for one when need arose.'[103]

The pastor of Livingstone Future Hope Church and the Southern Province FODEP chairman was also reported as saying that 'Government should among other things see to it that church leaders are seconded to parliament specially to represent the Church.'[104] Resentment at being excluded had surfaced as early as 4 January 1992 when a circular from the President's office restricted the clergy's access to the President; henceforth applications to see him were to go through the three church

---

[100] *Mirror*, 29 June-5 July 1992, 4.

[101] *Mirror*, 3 Feb 1992, 1

[102] *Sunday Times*, 19 Feb 1995, 3. On another occasion the same Bishop Mambo expressed his regret over the way Kaunda had run his government: 'How can a leader survive when he ignores clergymen and wholly relies on the special branch to run a country?' The report said that Mambo 'called on the government to grant express communication with the head of state and ministers so as to enable the church to take an active and major role in the running of the country's affairs.'

[103] *Mirror*, 27 Aug-2 Sept 1995, 1. Also *Mirror*, 18-24 Dec 1994, 6.

[104] *Mirror*, 3-9 Aug 1992, 4. He also recommended the formation of a 'Ministry of Christian Affairs so that the Church could have representatives both in parliament and cabinet.' Finance Minster Emmanuel Kasonde rejected this saying that the church already had enough representation in government: 'I am a staunch Catholic believer and I took to politics not for anything else but to represent my church in government' (*Mirror*, 24-30 Aug 1992, 4).

bodies to Brigadier General Miyanda, at that time Minister without Portfolio. The Moderator of the Reformed Church of Zambia, Rev. Foston Sakala, rejected this, saying: 'The new arrangement is not acceptable to us because any church leader in this country has the right to see the President directly on any urgent problem.' In the same report, Bishop John Mambo was just as adamant, and he gave his reason: 'President Chiluba and his fellow leaders should bear in mind that there is no wise person in the country who should claim that he defeated the previous UNIP government. It is God who came to the rescue of the oppressed Zambian people.'[105] He implied that God acted through his anointed church leaders. The same thinking lay behind the anger of the high-profile Pastor Sexton Chiluba, who accused the MMD government of 'being uncooperative with the church and ignoring the power of God'. Politicians were trying to solve things 'without turning to God for guidance'. If this state of things was not changed immediately, it 'will contradict President Chiluba's declaration of Zambia as a Christian state'.[106] Part of the resentment stemmed from the way President Chiluba seemed to change his confidants among the clergy as it suited him. The EFZ leadership came to be marginalised, and other pastors took their place as the Christians with immediate access to the President. This did not help the disposition of those clergymen who thought they were more deserving.

Before the 1996 election, Kaunda's UNIP and six other parties opted for a boycott, and tension again increased. On 28 October church leaders from the CCZ, ECZ and EFZ attempted to mediate. They tried to persuade Kaunda to call off the boycott, and to get Chiluba to postpone the election until 'the ground was level' for all contestants. Chiluba accused the church leaders of being 'too sympathetic to Kaunda', but did promise that he would meet opposition leaders to iron out disagreements. It was a promise he did not keep.[107]

The churches tried to provide guidance for the elections. The CCJP, for instance, produced a set of sermon notes. These materials urged all preachers to be non-partisan, but encouraged them to promote proper conditions for the elections:

We need responsible citizens who choose good leaders who will really serve the people. We can decide who the best candidate is by looking at the qualifications, the past records, and the programme that the candidate offers ...[A good candidate must display] a commitment to social justice and a special concern for the poor, professional competence that includes a deep knowledge of our problems and a balanced judgement in proposing solutions. Moreover, the candidate must be open to dialogue, to criticism, to teamwork, and to accountability. A desire to

---

[105] *Mirror*, 1 June 1992, 4.

[106] *Mirror*, 22 June 1992, 1.

[107] *Post*, 13 Feb 1997, 1; *Sunday Times*, 9 Feb 1997, 1.

serve the nation must be first, not an ambition for personal power and self-enrichment ... For a Christian the choice must not be on the basis of tribe, religion, friendship or even simply party...voting in this way is not only a *right* but a *duty*.

On the other hand, a section of Evangelical Christianity rallied to Chiluba. The day before the elections the *Sunday Mail*'s regular 'Words of Faith' (attributed simply to 'The Evangelist') came out for Chiluba: 'The country has been given in covenant to God and its leadership must forever remain in the hands of men and women who live in fear of the Lord and confess Christ as the Lord and Saviour of this land.' It then provided a chart showing the differences between MMD and the other parties contesting the election: the National Party, Zambia Democratic Party, Agenda for Zambia, and Movement for Democratic Process. On the issues of 'Accepting God (Ex 20, 2-3)', 'the market economy (Is 65, 21)', 'food security (Gen 6: 21)' and 'Bible education (Dt 6:5-8)', it marked the MMD positively and all the others negatively. As for the only other issue on the chart, only the MMD would preserve Zambia as a Christian nation. In the light of this chart, it was 'obvious that the party for any Christian to support is the MMD'.[108]

On election day, with UNIP and six other parties persisting in their boycott, Chiluba won handsomely, and his MMD took 131 of the 150 parliamentary seats. Election monitors tended to regard the actual voting as free and fair, although some observer bodies (and donor countries even more) expressed serious misgivings about the constitutional blocking of Kaunda's candidacy, the fairness of the voters' roll, and the use of state apparatus for MMD campaigning.

The internal ordering of the churches

We have described the economic and social collapse of Zambia in the 1990s. This has led to desperation – and determination to tap into the resources of the West. This is obviously one reason for the mushrooming of NGOs; it is acknowledged that entrepreneurs rush to establish them to fit in with the preferences of likely Western donors – AIDS education, gender issues and civic education, the last of these having been particularly successful in attracting funds. Thus institutions like Baton Rouge's Southern University have established themselves in Zambia, with USAID money, to promote democratic governance. Not only does the office employ nearly twenty people, but it funds local counterpart NGOs in all

---

[108] *Sunday Mail*, 17 Nov 1996, 3. The following Sunday the same column claimed that 'November 18 was a day of the Lord. [...] It was a victory of the Lord over Satan, a victory of light over darkness, truth over lies, peace over violence, love over hate, joy over sadness. [...] Those who have eyes to see have surely seen the hand of God in directing the affairs of Zambia in the last few weeks resulting in ... the glorious victory of President Chiluba and MMD in the election' (*Sunday Mail*, 24 Nov 1996, 3).

kinds of civic action. The Federation for the Democratic Process (FODEP), whose core is the churches, is part of this dynamic. Thus Bishop Mambo of the Church of God hoped for computers, and to be enabled to print literature in many local languages.

This background cannot be ignored in discussing the internal dynamics of churches. Churches provide avenues of accumulation, too. Thus Ernest Chelelwa, the pastor of Jesus Worship Centre which Miyanda attends, was appointed to Zambia's Human Rights Commission and in 1995 went on a month's fact-finding tour of four European countries. The perfectly legitimate expenses provided for this would constitute an enormous addition to his income. Nor is the money thus generated necessarily used only for the personal projects of the recipient. A group of nine young men, the Zambia Capella, began in mid-1993 a ministry of singing and testifying in American schools; by January 1995 they hoped to have 2,000 Americans sponsoring students in Zambia; by 1996, they planned for 10,000. World Vision runs an enormous child sponsorship scheme in the west of the country, with Western donors providing $120 a year, of which half goes to the child and half to sustain an enormous network of projects and numerous support staff.

The economic situation relates intimately to the life of churches and Christians. In February 1995 this author met outside a Bible college a student who explained that he had worked in purchasing and distribution for Reckitt and Colman, while his wife had been a teacher at a Ndola primary college. Both had given up these jobs to come to this Bible school. His brother had been head of Solwezi secondary school, and had given that up to enter another Bible school. The brother's wife was a nurse, and had given that up to study at yet another Bible school. All this makes considerable economic sense. Between 1982 and 1995 the buying power of a teacher's salary fell by 80%, and nurses probably fared even worse. These are the educated and trained professionals, and they are desperate to find something better. It is obvious that there are far more opportunities as a pastor or – particularly – the employee of an overseas-based parachurch organisation than as a teacher or nurse, or even as a qualified factory worker, as this informant was. He also said that he intended to go to another diploma-conferring Bible college after his present one, and then hoped to study overseas. He had already received an offer from Oral Roberts University which would give him four years' study and then two years bonded to the local American church that would pay for him, but he considered that six years away from his family was too much. He hoped to get a better offer when he had finished his course and this would enable him to take his family.

Zambia has a particular make-up that gives the churches a special importance. The manufacturing sector is controlled almost exclusively by expatriates, most of whom are South Africans, while the trading sector is dominated by Asians. In a sense, the only sectors open to Zambians are politics, the civil service and the church. Hence the importance of church organisations. And often the one adopts the culture of the others. It is part of Zambia's political culture that a leader should provide for his dependants. For their part, followers seek a patron, and hold on to him. It has long been a tradition that politics provides avenues of accumulation for oneself and for one's family, relatives and region; over the last thirty years this has been accentuated and has come to be accepted; no one ever seems to be prosecuted for using office in this way. This mode of operation has affected the churches greatly.

Within the denominations there have been several well-publicised struggles for resources. Zambia's Apostolic Faith Mission (AFM) was part of a South African outreach, but after Zambia's independence in 1964 the South Africans discreetly left and handed their work over to the Velberter Mission from Germany, on the grounds that Germans would be more politically acceptable than apartheid South Africans. The Zambian members of the church always resented the fact that the land was not given to them. In 1992 the local church expelled the head of the Velberter Mission, hoping thereby to take the land themselves (the expelled German remained to establish his own Gospel Outreach Fellowship, which includes many from the AFM). The Pentecostal Assemblies of God experienced much the same problem; the local church did not think that the handover of leadership and assets to them was rapid enough. They accused the Canadian missionaries of refusing to train local leadership in order to continue their control.

Zambia's biggest group of Baptists were embroiled in lawsuits in the mid-1990s. The Southern Baptist Convention, the biggest sender of Protestant missionaries in the world, never submits its missionaries to the local churches they serve, as many other bodies do. Thus the Baptist Mission of Zambia, comprising the Southern Baptist Missionaries, was a legal entity separate from the Baptist Convention of Zambia, the administrative arm of the Baptist churches founded by these missionaries. The two bodies worked in partnership, and much of the funding for the convention came from the Mission, but there were properties, vehicles and farms that legally remained within the control of the Baptist Mission, and would remain so until the local church was totally self-sufficient, at which time the Southern Baptist missionaries would leave and begin work elsewhere. However, in the early 1990s the president of the convention was a professor of law at the University of Zambia and she set about taking control of the Baptist Mission as well (she had been a Catholic until a few years before and some consider that her model of authority is that of a Catholic archbishop, not the president of a Baptist convention).

Her first step was to write to the Minister of Immigration asking that no visas for Baptist missionaries be granted or renewed unless the request came through her as president of the convention. The Baptist Mission challenged this in court, although it attempted to restrict the publicity to a minimum. On 8 February 1995 a judge accepted the mission's contention that this was an internal matter, to be resolved by the Baptists. He gave them time to do so, and ordered that in the mean time temporary work permits be given to missionaries. But such is the influence of the convention president over the Ministry of Immigration that the ministry continued to refuse visas, and even to deport missionaries whose visas were expiring. In the convention's meeting in November 1995 the executive refused to allow discussion of the president's letter to immigration authorities. In the following months about 130 of the 550 convention-affiliated churches seceded over this issue and formed the Baptist Fellowship of Zambia, which was officially established in August 1996. It is this fellowship that now cooperates with the Baptist mission; the convention executive threatens with summary dismissal any churches of the convention that maintain fellowship with the mission.

It was widely accepted among Baptists that the convention president's agenda was to take control of the Baptist mission's assets. Some claimed that the convention was attempting to drive the American Southern Baptist missionaries out in order to bring in a new group of European Baptist missionaries, with whom the convention would negotiate a new relationship, more to their advantage. In all this 'the convention' effectively meant a few individuals on the executive; the majority of the churches that made up the convention had little idea of what was being done in their name. The crucial point is that, far from the Baptist polity being a classroom for democratic virtues, the economic realities of Zambia's political world have permeated church structures.[109] Because of this fact of life, many Western donors in effect take control of their own funds. Thus the Reformed Church is given funds for relief by the Canadian church; but the Canadian church sends its own administrator along with the funds. This is resented by the Zambian church.

The UCZ, which for thirty years has been an experiment almost unique in Africa, has begun to experience tension. Splits are appearing along the lines of the original churches, which correspond to ethno-regional divisions. Some of the Lozis of the west broke away in March 1994, and in 1995 the former Methodist areas in the south pulled out, too. Many reasons were given. The letter notifying the UCZ authorities of the southern secession, dated 25 September 1994, cited constant scandals of financial mismanagement and lack of seriousness in the leadership. But,

[109] The chief immigration officer decreed in 1996 that since it is government policy to issue work permits to missionaries, he would be issuing them for Baptist missionaries.

for our purposes, just as significant was the letter's claim that the seceding members were repossessing all the moveable and immovable assets of the former Methodist Church. These included church buildings, mission stations, and some very profitable land along the Kafue river where there is potential for tourism. The secessionists immediately moved to acquire the services of a distinguished legal firm in Lusaka to fight for these assets – a difficult task given the provisions of the original agreement that all assets would remain in the UCZ in the event of one of the constituent bodies breaking away.[110] In fact, the western splinter group was unsuccessful in its attempt to obtain legal title to UCZ property, which seems to have brought caution to the southern group in its attempts to acquire church assets. The economic context is an important factor in both splits.

The Anglican Church is quite small, far smaller than one would expect in a former British colony. It is growing, as are all churches, but could hardly be called flourishing. When the northern diocese needed a new bishop in 1987, it could not agree on any candidate. As a result, the election was taken out of its hands and the bishops of the province (comprising Botswana, Zimbabwe and Malawi besides Zambia) made the decision when gathered at Lambeth; they chose a Malawian because a man from outside the system was more acceptable to the various factions in the diocese. A fourth diocese was created for Zambia's Eastern Province in 1995, and a New Zealander with many years experience in southern Africa was named the first bishop. The Anglican Church has very few trained clergy – in Lusaka there are two full-time priests for thirty-one communities. The expatriate dean of the Lusaka cathedral gave an insight into the dynamics of the Anglican Church in an interview broadcast on the BBC. Asked about the desirability of missionaries, he said:

'The missionary society has been saying for the last ten years that missionaries should go home. The church has been left to flounder on its own.[...] People long for the good old days of missionaries where there was the commitment, the love, the devotion, tremendous pastoral care, great teaching, and people are saying 'We wish this could have carried on a bit longer.' Of course, we would all prefer a situation where the local congregations would take the wheel in their hands and steer the vehicle of the church and keep this going and expand things on their own, but it isn't happening. To me it seems that the price we are paying for a principle, for a bit of romantic thinking, saying 'All missionaries out' ... is enormous, in terms of failed church work. When we look at the quality of the local clergy – forgive me for saying this but I am the vicar general of this diocese, so all cases of indiscipline, corruption and immorality and what have you on the part of the clergy do come also to me not just to the bishop – the overall picture is *grim*. I want to add immediately that if I were living in the conditions these clergy are living [in], I wonder how I would be behaving. So this is no judge-

[110] *Times*, 15 Feb 1995, 1; *Times*, 20 Feb 1995, 1.

ment, no reflection on them. I'm just saying that you see a picture of general disintegration and poverty and loss of morale, and loss of morale is only a small step to loss of morals. I'm afraid that this is what we are seeing. I think certainly the Anglican Church, I cannot speak for the other churches ... made a colossal mistake in pulling out the missionaries so quickly, and it would have been a tremendous help to the local church and to Christ's work in Africa to have had a couple of decades more of this kind of work.[111]

There, in all its political incorrectness, is a glimpse of the internal dynamics of a church without missionaries and, of course, without the resources they bring.

Only the Catholic Church receives sufficient resources to be able to maintain its institutions, and therefore preserve discipline and function with reasonable efficiency. The Catholic Church's most salient feature is the number of expatriate missionaries: in 1991 572 priests, of whom 429 were expatriates (in 1987 the corresponding figures were 560 and 446); 174 religious brothers, of whom 130 were expatriates (189 and 131); 1,020 religious sisters, of whom 464 were expatriate (932 and 485).[112] These missionaries are generally qualified, experienced and – most important for our purposes here – able to conjure up considerable funds by the very fact of being expatriates. Thus the Catholic Church is in a position to act in all sorts of ways denied the other churches. The Catholic Secretariat is dominated by whites in a way that would not be tolerated for a moment in Ghana or Uganda. Although in 1996 there was only one white missionary in the hierarchy (before 1995 there was none), behind the scenes much of the direction is provided by expatriates. It is relevant to the missionary dominance that some of the generation of local priests who might now be running the seminaries and wield influence in the Catholic Secretariat were either dismissed or eased out in the early 1970s because of their perceived assertiveness. Thus the first attempt at Africanisation can be said to have been largely aborted. Their dominance is not flaunted by the white expatriates, but it is of some significance and indeed determines much of Zambian Catholic life.

If proof of the significance of missionaries is needed, compare the two missions of Lubwa and Ilondola. Lubwa, the historic seat of Protestantism – where UNIP, Kaunda, his friend and subsequent political opponent Simon Kapwepwe and the Lubwa Church all originated – is now a ruin, the fine brick houses where the illustrious Scottish missionaries lived are derelict, and the hospital is given over to the government. Only 30 miles away, in an even more isolated spot, the old Catholic mission

---

[111] 'The Reckoning', radio programme made by Colin Morris, broadcast on BBC Radio 4, 30 April 1993. On this 'programme Rev. Merfyn Temple, a former Methodist missionary to Zambia, stated: ' "We want the missionaries back" means "We want the money".'

[112] *Zambia Catholic Directory 1991*, Ndola: Mission Press, 1991.

of Ilondola boasts a beautifully restored cathedral, its interior decorated in local motifs, and the priests' house is sound, enclosed in walled gardens and boasting a fine library, with rooms for the renowned White Fathers' Bemba-language course. The whole place is staffed by missionaries. The contrast could not be more stark.[113]

Some argue that the Scottish mission saw this coming. It was able to let go of the mission and adopt another model of small churches among the people. In that case, it can be said that the Catholics have not yet been forced to change their model; they can still struggle on with their institutions. And it must be said that adopting this new model has not been without problems. Thus a large part of the case of the UCZ's southern secessionists was that the old missionaries adopted a fourfold mission: spiritual, educational, medical and agricultural. In the UCZ in the 1990s there is only the spiritual; the other three have fallen into ruin. Those on the periphery readily accuse the leadership of eating the money that could prevent this. This may not necessarily be the case; it is simply beyond the church's capacity to maintain the institutions the missionaries bequeathed to it, and it has either (making a virtue out of necessity) consciously opted not to try, or failed in the attempt. There is no doubt, however, that the old system is what the people prefer. In frustration the southern sector seceded, hoping (incorrectly) that the Methodists in Britain would support them, sending back missionaries to restore and revitalise hospitals and schools. (The secession may have been resolved by the 1996 church elections, in which the church, dominated by the Bemba and educated urban groups, for the first time displayed the sensitivity to elect someone from the allegedly neglected south to national office.)

It is in the field of development that the Catholic Church stands out. Each area is different, with the dioceses functioning independently, but in areas of the north-east, for example, there are still more hospital beds available in Catholic hospitals than in government ones. Even in agriculture the Catholic involvement is so formidable in comparison with other churches and even the government that some government officials suspect the church of ulterior motives. Most of this involvement is made possible only by the missionary presence and foreign funds.

But in the 1990s the Catholic involvement is ranging increasingly wider than schools and clinics, and here we find a more direct political input. The bishops have spoken out on various socio-political issues, but other Catholic bodies make statements as well – Justice and Peace Commissions, the Development Programme, the youth – and they do so on topics as diverse as land reform, agriculture, structural adjustment, and inflation.[114] Zambian church statements display an economic awareness that equiva-

---

[113] Ipenburg, *'All Good Men'*; Oger, *Scattered Flock*.

[114] Pastoral letters are 'Economics, Politics and Justice' (July 1990); 'You Shall be my

lents in Ghana and Uganda lack. This quality is probably attributable to the Jesuit Centre for Theological Reflection, which has even taken to pricing a basket of staple goods (grain, cooking oil, sugar, salt etc.) each month, and calculates the cost of living for a family of six. This calculation runs as a monthly feature in the *Post* and is widely discussed. These calculations show more clearly than government figures the rise in the cost of living, and also the near impossibility of survival for the ordinary wage-earner (thus in May 1995 the minimum required was K145,000; a schoolteacher then earned about K60,000).[115] And the influence of this Jesuit Centre is wider. It is used by the Christian Council, by FODEP, and even by many of the Evangelicals, some of whom would not venture to speak publicly before checking their statement with the Jesuits.[116]

Catholic missionary institutions range from *Icengelo* to the AIDS-related Kara Centre, run by both Jesuits and Franciscans. (More recently, other missionaries have brought to Zambia the 'Youth Alive' project we met in Uganda.[117]) It is mainly missionaries that are behind the attempts to establish 'Training for Transformation' groups, similar to Latin American base communities, concerned with conscientising and confronting the local situation, and often attempting small projects like credit unions, building dams or making bricks; these groups are increasing, mainly around Monze.[118] There are also Justice and Peace groups, as we have seen, at local, regional and national levels, and their statements are often found in the newspapers. However, it is clear that these are hardly a priority for the church as such, more the projects of missionaries.[119] The Catholics moreover have several expatriate missionaries teaching

---

witnesses' (July 1991); 'The Future is Ours' (Feb 1992); 'Pastoral Statement on Drought and Famine' (June, 1992); ' "Hear the Cry of the Poor": a Pastoral Letter on the Current Suffering of the People of Zambia' (July 1993); 'A Call to Love and Care: a Pastoral Letter on the Family' (Oct 1994); 'Building for Peace: a Pastoral Letter in view of the 1996 General Elections' (Oct 1996). Other statements include: ZEC, 'Zambia's Inflation: Some Social-Ethical Reflections' (Jan 1993); The Catholic Agricultural and Rural Youth Movement, 'Land Tenure in Zambia' (Jan 1993); *id.*, 'Towards a Better and More Productive Life in our Villages' (April 1993).

115 *Jesuit Centre for Theological Reflection Bulletin*, April-July 1995, 27.

116 Its approach is found in Joe Holland and Peter Henriot, *Social Analysis: Linking Faith and Justice*, Maryknoll: Orbis, 1980; Peter Henriot, Edward DeBerri, Michael Schultheis, *Catholic Social Teaching: our Best Kept Secret*, Maryknoll: Orbis, 1985. The Jesuit Centre also publishes a regular *Bulletin*.

117 *Mirror*, 23-29 June 1996, 13.

118 'Participatory Evaluation, the National Development Education Programme ... Training for Transformation, March-November 1991', Lusaka: Catholic Secretariat, Summary Report, 21, admits that 'the programme has on the whole not had a big perceived impact on people's lives.' One handicap has been the 'lack of interest and participation on part of some priests, indifferent to a lay-dominated TFT programme' (24).

119 Fabian J.M. Maimbo and Jo Kollmer, *A Participatory Evaluation of the Justice and*

Religious Studies and Education at the university, and others in the Inspectorate for Religious Education.

The expatriate contribution does cause tension with the local clergy, but it must be said that it is not enormous. Resentment against the missionaries did flare up in the wake of the Zambian Catholic Church's greatest recent trauma, the 'Milingo Affair'. Emmanuel Milingo was made Archbishop of Lusaka in 1969. In 1973 he became aware that he possessed healing powers, and conducted healing and exorcism sessions which drew great crowds until friction with his fellow bishops and with the missionaries of his own archdiocese led him to abandon public services. Controversy continued, however, and Rome sent two Kenyan bishops to conduct an investigation in 1981, with the result that in 1982 Milingo was summoned to Rome where the following year he was forced to offer his resignation as archbishop. In Zambia, his removal caused an outcry from his many supporters, harshly critical of 'white missionaries' and even of his fellow Catholic bishops. Rome has never made public the reason for its intervention, although the other Zambian bishops were eventually forced, in their own defence, to issue a pastoral letter in December 1982 which shed a little light on events: *A Letter from the Members of the Zambia Episcopal Conference to the Catholics of Zambia on the Recent Events in the Archdiocese of Lusaka*.

All sorts of reasons, personal, administrative and even political, have been suggested, but it is probable that the main one was the fundamentalist and anti-scientific theological position underlying Milingo's explanations of healing. It is significant for our purposes that no purely 'African' explanations on Milingo's part exist; Milingo had already become firmly linked to the Western charismatic movement before he began writing his accounts of possession and deliverance. Later works from his base in Rome, though very Catholic with their references to saints and popes, acknowledge their dependence on sources like Derek Prince, John Wimber, Arthur Lyons, Trevor Dearing; indeed, the stories of satanic activity and rituals which characterise his books are remarkably similar to those of Rebecca Brown which we encountered in discussing Ghana. We have seen a somewhat similar dynamic in Ghana.[120] Ten years after his

---

Peace Programme, Lusaka: Social Education Department, Catholic Secretariat, April 1993.

[120] See, e.g., Emmanuel Milingo, *Face to Face with the Devil*, Broadford, Victoria: Scripture Keys Ministries, 1991. For the Africanness of Milingo, even while in Zambia, see in their different ways: Aylward Shorter, *Jesus and the Witchdoctor: an Approach to Healing and Wholeness,* London: Geoffrey Chapman, 1985, 187-90; Adrian Hastings, 'Emmanuel Milingo as Christian Healer', *African Catholicism: Essays in Discovery,* London: SCM, 1989, 138-55; Hinfelaar, *Bemba-Speaking*, 170-78; Gerrie Ter Haar, *Spirit of Africa: the Healing Ministry of Archbishop Milingo of Zambia*, London: Hurst, 1992, esp. 134-64.

removal the damage and divisions seem largely healed, not least through the obedience and loyalty displayed by Milingo himself; resentment and resistance on his part might easily have caused a major schism. (We return to the issue of Vatican intervention below in discussing Cameroon.)

The lack of animosity towards missionaries is one more area in which the church mirrors society, for race relations in Zambia have been generally quite relaxed – not least because outstanding Protestant missionaries like Colin Morris and Merfyn Temple admired and supported Kaunda in his struggle. For Kaunda nationalism was never opposition to whites but to the colonial system.[121] However, there is no denying that tension does exist. For example, in the Mbala diocese the bishop is a local Zambian, but the key positions – of pastoral director, director of the leadership training centre and financial controller – are all in the hands of whites. This, of course, makes sense for the bishop: all of these can independently lay hands on funds that even he could not tap, and which local Zambian priests certainly could not, and which he needs to preserve the enormous development activity of the diocese. But many local clergy feel somewhat frustrated.

It has to be said that the Catholic diocesan clergy receive substantial criticism. They are educated to a level no other church can match, but this education brings its own problems, for it confers status and provides an avenue to relative wealth. Consequently, according to many, the Catholic clergy are more interested in power, money and status than in the people they are theoretically trained to serve.[122] The crucial distinction here is probably not between local clergy and expatriate clergy, but between diocesan and religious clergy. The diocesan clergy are normally placed on their own, without great support, and are subject to strong pressures from their extended family and culture. There have been well-publicised problems of celibacy in Mbala, Mansa and Ndola dioceses; in 1995 newspapers drew attention to the fact that several diocesan priests had to be dismissed in Ndola diocese, and gratuitously named several others who might well have been dismissed also. However, the priests belonging to religious orders are given support, live in community, have opportunities for further training, and participate in determining their congregation's direction. All this provides a greater morale, fosters idealism, and sustains dedication. It is noteworthy that the last Zambian named to the hierarchy was a Jesuit. For the same reason, many insist that Catholic sisters are infinitely more impressive. To some degree, this

---

121   Merfyn Temple (ed.), *Black Government? A Discussion between Colin Morris and Kenneth Kaunda*, Lusaka: United Society for Christian Literature, 1960; Kenneth Kaunda, *Zambia Shall be Free: an Autobiography*, London: Heinemann, 1962; Colin M. Morris, *Kaunda on Violence*, London: Collins, 1980; and see note 14 above.

122   Because of the growing number of candidates a fourth seminary was being mooted in 1996 (*Impact*, Oct 1996, 1).

is merely the churches mirroring society again, for as many also point out, women do most of the work and take most of the responsibility in Zambia anyway. Nuns are committed to and responsible to their religious community, which makes them far more selfless and dedicated.

The Catholic Church doubtless has its internal problems. The Catholic Secretariat's refugee department was asked by the UNHCR to be the implementing agency for the enormous refugee camp at Maheba in the north-west, near the borders with Zaïre and Angola. This 'camp' is in fact an area of 780 square kilometres, comprising seventy-five villages housing up to 27,000 refugees, and it has been in operation for over twenty years. Of course, corruption in all refugee camps is a fact of life, given the enormous sums of money involved, the crushing poverty, and the likelihood that they are in fairly lawless areas. This Catholic operation was marked by corruption at every level, conspicuous in which were the local bishop and his family. After complaints from the UNHCR, and its refusal to continue funding an operation so poorly managed, the Catholic refugee department was closed down. The Catholic Church tends to handle these issues with considerable discretion; little is made public, no enquiries are held, and normally nobody (certainly no priest, much less a bishop) is disciplined. This bishop's unaccountability was so notorious that the *Pastoral Statement on Drought and Famine* could not be signed by all the bishops, since with his signature on it the section on 'favouritism and corruption in the distribution of assistance' would have been seen as the height of hypocrisy. (This bishop died in 1992, and – as in Uganda's Kabale diocese – Rome immediately named a white missionary as administrator, who in 1995 became the new bishop.) But the general secretary of the secretariat, after penning an editorial of *Impact* calling for loyalty and a halt to rumour-mongering, was quietly removed under something of a cloud, and given a job back in his home diocese. The oversight of the camp was given to the Lutheran body CARE, but the Catholics had so successfully minimised publicity that the Lutherans promptly reestablished the whole corrupt network. The Jesuit Refugee Service entered as a support NGO to CARE, the implementing NGO, but its attempts at community development, involving conscientisation, rapidly led to tensions with the profiteers, who had the deputy minister of the Province, an AME pastor himself, ban the Jesuits in early 1994 on the grounds that they were there illegally, and working beyond their mandate. They were allowed to come back in 1995, although with a circumscribed mandate.

Paradoxically, although we have been talking of priests and bishops and sisters, the Zambian Catholic Church is much more a lay church than may appear, or than the authorities may wish. The big mission stations are typically enormous concerns, with seventy or even 100 'centres' or communities which effectively run themselves. Many of these see a priest only twice a year, and for the rest of the time, they organise and conduct their own services, elect their own church councils and prayer leaders, and manage a whole range of activities. They send representatives to a higher level of sub-parish, which in turn sends representatives to the parish council. There is no need to over-romanticise these communities; only a fraction may function with any great efficiency. But over and above the scope offered here for participation, personal development and leadership, there is something else happening. The Catholic Church in Zambia is characterised by a great proliferation of what are called 'movements' or Catholic societies like the Banazareth, womens' groups, the Pioneer Total Abstinence Society, the Legion of Mary, St Vincent de Paul Society, Franciscan Tertiaries (including in non-Franciscan mission areas) – and even choirs could be considered in this way. Often the emotional attachment is to one particular movement – in some cases the attachment to the movement has been known almost to outweigh the attachment to the Catholic Church. Sometimes individuals belong to more than one of these organisations. These not only exist at a central mission station, but tend to do so in the centres as well. These movements organise themselves, and organise events for groups of centres, and for deaneries, dioceses and even at national level, all with only very loose supervision by the clergy. Again, they function with varying degrees of efficiency, but they illustrate that while the Catholic Church presents itself as a pyramidal or hierarchical structure, in many ways it can equally well be seen as a vast array of interlocking networks which often depend in no strict sense on the bishop. Bishops are said to support all these networks, but they may not quite realise that the result may be to lessen their own position and authority.

Small Christian Communities (SCCs – the equivalent of the 'Base Communities' of Latin America) are not characteristic of the Catholic Church. They were theoretically introduced throughout East Africa from the 1970s, but have had considerable problems gaining acceptance as more than just one other 'movement'. For this reason it was forbidden, in the diocese of Ndola for movements to meet on Thursday nights; that night was to be left free for SCCs. Another factor militating against any system of SCCs is that, at least in the rural areas, they have no natural place in the structures as they currently exist. The 'centres' are their own SCCs, and any attempt to introduce them additionally is unnecessary and simply confusing. Thus they have not become a significant part of the Catholic dynamic.[123]

[123]   Joseph Komakoma, 'Towards a Relevant Pastoral Approach: Pastoral Ministry on the Copperbelt Region of Zambia', Mémoire for Licentiate, Catholic University of Louvain, 1990.

The Catholic bishops in Zambia are not as significant as those in the other countries under consideration, which is perhaps surprising given the strength of the Catholic Church. In Zambia today, after the removal of Archbishop Milingo and the death of Archbishop Mutale, no Catholic bishop is a national figure. Historically, few bishops were trained overseas. The newspapers hardly ever mentioned the Archbishop of Lusaka, Adrian Mungandu, in the years leading up to his retirement in 1997. When Catholic statements are made, they have almost always been elaborated within the Catholic Secretariat, and are issued in the name of its General Secretary.

In one particular way the Catholic Church does not exemplify the accountability and transparency so beloved of the civil society theorists. Bishops have access to considerable funds. Many go for trips abroad every year, at least partly to raise funds, but no one knows how much they collect; no one knows how decisions are reached on how to spend it. In Kasama Archdiocese, for example, enormous effort was put into building a pastoral centre, but the archbishop effectively bankrupted the arch-diocese in building it. Similarly, the Bishop of Mbala decided to shift his seat to Mpika; admittedly it was far more central for him, but the cost was enormous at a time when 70% of Zambians were living below the poverty line. Both might be able to defend their decisions, but currently there is no need for that; both are 'big men' and are accountable to no one. In a fine statement on democracy, the Catholic bishops demanded of the new government transparency in raising money, in spending money and in decision-making. It was not lost on many observers that they them-selves are totally unaccountable in all these areas.

The changing born-agains

Many new churches have been founded in Zambia in recent years. Some are local, many others are founded by groups moving in; clearly it would not do for the 'Christian nation' of Zambia to be seen to create difficulties for missionaries. (By contrast, neighbouring Zimbabwe in 1994 refused to admit new missionaries or renew the visas of incumbent ones, not necessarily as a statement about Christianity, but as a judgement that the missionary influx was getting out of hand and Zimbabwe had sufficient pastors of its own.) In Zambia new groups do not have to engage in any development activity. The new missionaries are not of the charismatic sector only. The new Orthodox Church in Lusaka caters for Copts, Ethiopians and all Eastern European Orthodox as well as locals. There are some new groups like the Independent Faith Mission which came to Zambia in 1993 and is positively anti-Pentecostal (this is not a 'faith church' in the way we have been using the term, being the mission agency of America's independent Baptist churches). Others like the Liebenzell

Mission International are equally anti-Pentecostal. Not all the emergent Bible schools are Pentecostal, but most are, and a real shift has been observable in just a few years. A large sector of the Evangelical fraternity has become Pentecostal, often influenced by student bodies like the Zambian Fellowship of Evangelical Students (ZAFES), Scripture Union, and the Nurses' Christian Fellowship. The Brethren Church (CMML) has split over this, with one wing linking with Britain's Covenant Ministries International, run by the charismatic Bryn Jones. The Zambia Baptist Association, comprising the mainly Lamba-speaking churches founded by South African missionaries, has also experienced great strain, and one group opposing the encroachment of Pentecostalism has formed the Reformed Baptists, adopting a 17th-century statement of faith as its constitution. Most famously, in 1993, a part of the UCZ youth wing broke away in a dispute over Pentecostal practices, to become Grace Ministries Mission. The launching ceremony drew 3,500 people. Opinion varies over the wisdom of the UCZ leadership in handling the demands of the youth. Lutherans, Anglicans, even Catholics have been able to accommodate charismatic sectors in their denominations. Not so the UCZ. 'The new ideas of worship which they are talking about are quite contrary to the teachings of the Bible,' stated the church's Moderator, in justifying their expulsion.[124] There has been a shift in the status of Pentecostals too. As one speaker at Victory '94 (see below) expressed it, five years previously it would have been an embarrassment to admit to being born again; by 1994 it was not. It would be wrong to oversimplify the diversity between these proliferating Pentecostal groups, but we can make the following generalisations.

First, these churches expound the so-called Faith Gospel. The faith paradigm has become as widely accepted as Christianity, and is the staple fare on Zambia's television. On Sundays there can be seven successive Christian programmes, almost all foreign products, including 'the 700 Club', 'Benny Hinn', 'Praise the Lord', 'Ernest Angley Ministries' and (from South Africa) 'Rhema Church Hour' – all Faith Gospel. The literature available is overwhelmingly Faith Gospel too – the EFZ bookshop is awash with it. It appears that Chiluba himself subscribes to this theology. At the annual conference of Swedish Pentecostal churches in 1994 he told the congregation: 'Give one tenth of your money to [God] and see returns on your capital. [...] The benefits you will receive will astound you.' He takes it somewhat further; if you give to God, you will experience not only personal prosperity, but national prosperity. During

---

124 *APS Bulletin*, 1 Nov 1993; also *Mirror*, 16-22 Aug 1994, 4. By 1995 the church was thoroughly Faith Gospel. The pastor travels to Benny Hinn conventions. In a testimony on 7 Aug 1994 a woman claimed that she had her car stolen only to get it back a month later with the door handles fixed and painted a shiny metallic red; 'so now when I drive along people say the Lord is blessing her.'

the ceremonies celebrating the fourth anniversary of the declaration of Zambia as a Christian nation, he actually said that 'because Zambia had entered into this covenant with God, God is blessing this nation to the point where we shall stop borrowing. We shall lend instead.'[125]

In discussing Ghana and Uganda much space was given to individual charismatic churches. It is not necessary to repeat this for Zambia, where the new churches are not noticeably different in their theology or mode of operation from their equivalents in Ghana, even if they are as yet smaller. Also, as in Ghana, traditional AICs seem to be losing out heavily before the onslaught of the newer charismatic churches, even away from the cities (admittedly this judgement is fairly impressionistic, since Zambia lacks the statistics available for Ghana). Rather than discussing individual churches, we will instead focus here on an important element in Africa's charismatic explosion, the convention or conference phenomenon. Conventions serve to internationalise and homogenise the movement, both within Africa and across the world; they are the main instrument creating out of allegedly independent autonomous bodies what is becoming in many respects a super-denomination. We will illustrate this with reference to the Victory '94 convention of the Copperbelt evangelist Nevers Mumba, held at the Mulungushi Conference Centre, Lusaka, on 7-13 August 1994.

We have mentioned Mumba at several points above. He is the founder of Victory Faith Ministries in Kitwe on the Copperbelt. In 1981 he was an interpreter for Reinhard Bonnke on his crusades in Zambia, and Bonnke arranged for him to study at Christ for the Nations in Dallas, Texas, between 1982 and 1984. This Bible school supported him to the tune of $100 a month for some years after his return. He began his church in 1984, and started a Bible school in 1985. He has continued conducting crusades, has founded his network of Victory Bible Churches from these crusade converts, and has had his own television programme. He had a high profile in the Christian nation debate, passionately promoting the declaration as a defence against what he sees as 'the Muslim threat', and on the Old Testament reasoning that a righteous king brings national prosperity.[126] In 1993 Mumba held his first convention, inviting overseas speakers, the main speaker being Bonnke. Mumba is in the vanguard of the

---

[125] *Times*, 11 Dec 1994 (where headline reads: 'Faith Key to Success - Chiluba'); *Mirror*, 7-13 Jan 1996, 2.

[126] Nevers Mumba, *Integrity with Fire: a Strategy for Revival*, Tulsa, OK: Vincom, 1994; see his quarterly *Victory Report*; also *Mirror*, 22-28 Jan 1995, 7. Mumba sees three 'levels' of Christian nation: where a declaration is made (e.g. Zambia), where there is great awareness of Christ although no declaration (e.g. Ghana [*sic*]) and where a nation is founded on biblical principles (e.g., United States); see *Mirror*, 22-28 Jan 1995, 7. Mumba is frequently attacked in the Christian press for his politics: *Mirror*, 14-20 Aug 1994, 2; *ibid.*,14-20 Aug 1994, 11.

charismatic push in Zambia – it is partly because he can stage such conventions, packed with international speakers, that he stays ahead. The convention is both a sign of his hegemony and a reason for it. Many other pastors cooperate and participate; it raises their profile, but at the price of appearing subordinate to Victory Ministries

There are all sorts of things going on at a convention. This one was first of all a lecture series. The message centred round personal problems of sex, marriage and work. Much of the preaching was church-centred, calling for integrity on the part of pastors, efficiency, evangelisation. There was much advice for running a credible ministry. The exhortation was often to take the nation for Jesus, but there was very little preaching that dealt with Zambia's socio-political context and a Christian's responsibility in that field.

The convention was also part rock festival, with a judicious blend of soloists, groups and community participation. The music varied from soul and spiritual to disco, rock, heavy metal and rap (all Western; it would be hard to find anything specifically African in the music at all). The choirs and soloists were superb, and had obviously practised at length. As one would expect from the music, the conference was patronised predominantly by the young – but also by the hopeful, the English-speaking, the upwardly mobile. The superior international-standard venue is therefore important. It is not only the music that makes entertainment a key category through which one has to analyse such a gathering, for the preachers were at the same time comedians and actors, media personalities as well as lecturers. Given Zambia's dearth of other entertainment and even the lack of exciting television, the element of showtime increases in importance.

And there were other functions as well. It was noticeable how beautifully dressed and groomed the youth were, particularly the women – who wore high heels, even if they had to walk back several miles to their homes afterwards. The choir, dominated by about eighty young women, wore clothes of a different colour every day (which again reinforced the impression that this was a gathering of middle-class people). Several times during the week, in various contexts but particularly that of prayer, it was remarked that many of the young women in the choir were looking for husbands. That these conventions provide a forum for young men and women to meet and develop friendships seems unquestioned. Partners discovered at such a convention can be presumed to be sincere, motivated and ambitious.

Besides an opportunity for entertainment and beginning friendships, this particular convention provided occasion for emotional release. At Victory '94, the first speaker was Nevers Mumba himself, preaching on the text 'My tears have been my food day and night' (Ps 42: 3). The theme was heartfelt contrition for iniquity. At the end Mumba paused, and people responded appropriately by wailing, shrieking, even banging heads against walls. This response was expected – one could even say orchestrated. But the speaker immediately after this was the American Paul Grier, known for his 'Intoxicated with New Wine' sermon, in which he argues that joy is the special characteristic of the Christian. Near the end he normally throws in a little ditty: 'Ho ho ho hosanna, Ha ha ha leluia, He he he he saved me, I've got the joy of the Lord.' He paces his sermons so that the element of mirth gradually develops throughout. Paul Grier had attended Victory '93 the previous year, and had already been in the country a month preaching on the Copperbelt, so most of those present knew his general thrust. As a result, before he had gone very far, it was difficult to hear him for people shrieking (with laughter now), rocking in their seats, even collapsing in the aisles and rolling on the floor. In many cases these were the same people who half an hour before had been overcome with grief. This is something more than spontaneous relief; these manifestations were to a large degree consciously orchestrated, as was the very decision to run these two particular sermons back to back. This behaviour would have alienated many Catholics and mainline Protestants, and not everyone at Victory '94 was impressed either. This was something more than unrestrained dancing or singing or the exuberant exercise of tongues, and highlights the value many place on uninhibited displays of emotion in a more or less controlled setting.

So there are many things happening at such a convention. It is at the same time religious worship, a lecture series, a rock concert, a marriage market, an opportunity for emotional release, a rekindling of ambition, an experience of community and mutual encouragement. (As we saw, on the evenings of visits from the Chilubas and the Vice-President, this convention was a political rally as well.) But we will concentrate on this convention as disclosing the mechanism through which diverse and autonomous churches are moulded into a recognisable unity, and through which certain individuals assume roles of oversight, in a strand of Christianity that would claim to have no truck with popes, patriarchs, bishops or even moderators. Thus these gatherings function like synods or councils in the older traditional denominations. It is also arguable that they can perform a richer function, as a means through which genuine change is effected in the movement. Thus we will discuss Mumba's Victory '94 as illustrating both stability and change within African Pentecostalism, or as both reinforcement and modification of a theological paradigm.

Most obviously, Victory '94 was a celebration of the Faith Gospel. Nearly all these preachers, notably the Americans, preached a version of it, as featured prominently in the wide advertising campaign that preceded the convention. The literature was overwhelmingly Faith Gospel. The

African Christianity

convention, besides the other things, was also a book fair, with stalls selling a wider range of books than can normally be found in Zambia. A few of these were local products, but most were American, often imported via distributors in South Africa, something made possible through the liberalisation of Zambia's economy. Many of the speakers, notably Enock Sitima of Botswana and David Newberry of the United States, sold their own tapes and literature, along with those of others. The authors on sale were overwhelmingly the Copelands, Kenneth Hagin, Casey Treat, Jerry Savelle, Norvel Hayes, Charles Capps, Fred Price, John Avanzini – all the big names of the faith movement. The books that did not sell during the conference were sold at a discount to local bookshops (which offers another insight into how this faith gospel literature has become so pervasive in Africa).

In the course of the week there were some classic expositions of the Faith Gospel (not least from Billy Lubansa, whom we meet below in Cameroon). Nevers Mumba himself, for example, taught at some length the principle that material goods will follow you if you order your priorities correctly and put God first. And on one evening he even encouraged people to give him the car they came in ('When Jesus lays his hand on it, let it go'), reminding his listeners: 'You only receive by giving.' If charismatic pastors in Zambia have at times expressed concern for the poor, there was no sign of this at this convention. The focus on the upwardly mobile was obvious. For example, Nevers Mumba himself, on the night Chiluba attended, enumerated what to him were the successes of the Chiluba administration to date. One of these was economic liberalisation, but the reason he gave for this was revealing – he praised it not for any good it brought to the country or ordinary people, but because 'This is the only country in the region where you can go to the bank and get foreign exchange in minutes, and then fly to New York.'

However, and here appear the pressures for change, two of the main preachers did not fit easily into this picture. First was Musa Sono, pastor of Grace Bible Church in Soweto. He called on people to think ('One of the things we Pentecostal charismatic Christians are not famous for is reasoning'). But more important for our purposes, he effectively destroyed the Faith Gospel. 'In South Africa if you were white you always had more than a black man. [...] Most white people were making it, and not because of faith, but because of being advantaged economically.' In another talk, he said:

'We need to change our thinking on money. When you grow up and things don't work, you have two options. You can pretend all is right, or you can admit they are not and start thinking. I know some things are to do with faith [but] certain sectors of our community were more advantaged than others. They were prospering, but we from disadvantaged sectors were not prospering. In church, they said the way they were prospering was because of faith, but in all honesty, one thing was very obvious, it had nothing to do with faith. It had something to do with being advantaged economically.'

He concluded: 'We have to change our thinking. It [faith] works in certain parts of the world because they have certain advantages. In Soweto it just doesn't work.'

More important, consider Mensa Otabil of Ghana (significantly, Sono admitted that he had only begun to think this way after he had heard Otabil when both were visiting Botswana). We have already met Otabil in Ghana, but here we see him operating internationally, building up his authority at the continental level. He had met Nevers Mumba in February 1993 at a 'Faith Summit' in Zimbabwe organised by Ezekiel Guti, founder of the Zimbabwe Assemblies of God Africa (ZAOGA). Otabil had invited Mumba to his campmeeting at Christmas 1993, and this was Mumba's return invitation.[127] Otabil dominated Victory '94 in Lusaka with his imposing presence, eloquence and striking west African robes, which he changed for every appearance. Otabil had three prongs to his message – black pride, structures and tilling one's own vineyard – and they can be considered in some detail here because of their novelty for Zambia and because of their impact.

His most important message was black pride. 'Look around the continent, the situation seems almost hopeless. It seems one big continent of war, strife, hunger, malnutrition, pain, famine, killing, ignorance. If you look at CNN it seems all the bad news comes from Africa. [...] When you look at yourself as an African, it is easy to think that God has cursed you.' Consequently Africa's biggest problem now is its inferiority complex: 'We are a people who feel inferior and wallow in our own inferiority.' We have mentioned Otabil's black reading of the Bible in discussing Ghana. In his talks in Zambia, he repeated his general thrust, though with some refinements. After proving that blacks were never under a curse, he moved to the privileged position of blacks in the plan of salvation. Abraham had Ishmail by Hagar and Isaac by Sarah, but after Sarah died Abraham married Keturah, by whom he had six children (Gen 25: 1-6). Thus the majority of Abraham's descendants are in the line of Keturah. Among Keturah's descendants were Sheba and Dan, who were Cushites (Gen 10: 7), so she must have been Cushite herself. Thus Abraham had six black children. This is why blacks are never called 'Gentiles' in the Bible; they are the seed of Abraham in the dispersion. In the story of Moses, too, blacks were crucial. Moses dwelt in the land of Midian. This Midian was one of the children of Abraham and Keturah.

---

[127] Otabil had already visited Zimbabwe at the invitation of Andrew Wutawunashe's Family of God. Ezekiel Guti was also in Zambia for Victory '94.

The reference to Jethro 'the priest of Midian' (Ex 3: 1) shows that at a time when there was no priesthood in Israel, and no one in Israel knew God and no Israelites were worshipping God, there was only one priest who knew the true God. God therefore took Moses out of his people for forty years and sat him at the feet of the priest Jethro. So a black priest taught Moses for forty years (we can be sure Jethro, the father-in-law of Moses, was black, because in Numbers 12: 1 Miriam and Aaron murmured against Moses' 'Ethiopian wife'). So it was a black man who taught Moses about God. In fact, Jethro knew all the law before Moses: it was he who gave the law to Moses. Later, when Israel was in danger of disintegrating, it was Jethro who came to Moses and taught him how to govern Israel (Ex 18: 13-26). Jethro was thus the first person to set up local government administration. The first to establish government in Jewish society was a black: 'Who told you we cannot organise – we were the first to do it! Without Jethro the people of Israel would have perished in the wilderness. Thank God for the black priest Jethro!' Later still (Numbers 10: 29-32) Moses needed Hobab (a Midianite, and therefore a black) to show the Israelites the way to the Holy Land. Moses promised that if he would act as guide, his people would receive the same reward as the Jews, the children of Israel (10: 32). He obviously did so, for Judges 1: 16 shows that Hobab's descendants had settled in Israel. And, very significantly, these black people were situated within the tribe of Judah. Thus blacks were given an inheritance among the tribe from which the Messiah was to come.

Otabil claimed that two races have been persecuted without cause: Jews and blacks. In both cases it is to do with the coming of the Messiah. 'We have not been persecuted because of colour: we are persecuted because we bruised the heel of the serpent. [...] The nations have been blessed because of us; and we have been hated for this.' So blacks must not blame their persecutors. Moreover, God is going to revive the land of Africa. From Africa God will send out ambassadors to the rest of the world. After 400 years of slavery in Egypt, the Jews were delivered; for 400 years blacks have suffered under slavery, but that era ended on 27 April 1994 with the South African elections. Now the time of the blacks has begun, and the era of the whites is over.[128]

---

[128] For Otabil's book *Beyond the Rivers of Ethiopia* see pp. 82-3 above. Otabil's influence has come to Zambia in other ways. On p. 88 above we discussed his 'blacksmith' campmeeting sermon on 1 Sam 13: 16-22. Mumba was a visiting preacher at this campmeeting, and he brought this message back to Zambia. In February 1994, on two successive weeks, he preached this 'blacksmith' sermon on his programme on Zambia's one TV channel. Mumba is a less commanding figure than Otabil, and Zambia has a far larger white population than Ghana, and its churches many more missionaries. The programmes created quite an outcry. Although some letters to newspapers praised him for 'urging Africans to be proud of what they are', and for his call for 'renewed confidence in blackness', others denounced him for being 'unbiblical' and 'irreligious', and accused him of racism and preaching a message of hate. One who claimed to be

Otabil himself is not so much anti-white as determined to lift the self-esteem of blacks. 'Am I saying that blacks are better than others? No, I'm just tracing [the role of] blacks, because I am black.' And again: 'Am I saying other nations are not blessed? No, we have an inheritance, and other nations will rejoice because we are coming into our inheritance.' He can inculcate black pride with considerable humour, as when he gently chides the black women in his audience for succumbing to white ideals of beauty and straightening their hair. 'I love my flat nose ... God gave me a double portion of the British nose. God loves me so much that I can breathe double the air.' 'You think I'm proud? No, I'm a very humble man – a very *confident* humble man.' And again, to applause: 'Proud? No, I'm just an African being the way God intended us to be.'

It would be hard to overestimate the significance for those who consider themselves the wretched of the earth, despised for their colour, of a message that glories in blackness. Its appeal is wide. The thousands that heard him in Zambia responded to his preaching with undisguised excitement, relief and gratitude. As one girl, in considerable awe, was heard to tell her companion at the end of an Otabil sermon, 'This man certainly has the message for all Africa.'

The second strand to Otabil's preaching was the notion of structures. This is a recent element in his thought. As late as 1992 he could write: 'The world, particularly the part called "the third world", is looking desperately for a better economic system. All they have to do is learn God's system for the whole world to prosper.'[129] 'God's system' here is obviously the laws of sowing and reaping that the Faith Gospel advocates. Again, 'Most of the time, the reason people are poor is because of lazi-

---

a grandson of one of the last converts, in 1873, of David Livingstone himself, expressed his 'disgust'.

Another preacher on Zambia's national radio in July 1994 argued that the pointers in Genesis 2 prove that the Garden of Eden had been in Africa: 'There is no other place on earth where these factors combine.' Bathsheba was black (Sheba, he explained, means 'black'). Solomon was therefore Coloured. The Bible tells us that he was not liked by his brothers (1 Kings 1: 19): 'I believe that was because of the colour of his skin.' The fact is undeniable: 'One of the greatest kings of human history actually came from Africa.' Solomon himself fell in love with the black Queen of Sheba, 'because he recognised [in her] someone of his stock.' All these points have been made at other times by Otabil, although it is unclear whether this particular preacher was dependent on Otabil or whether they are both dependent on black American or Caribbean literature. However, this preacher was clearly addressing the same issue as Otabil: 'You who are listening, perhaps you have an inferiority complex. Perhaps you think that you have only been educated in your own or neighbouring countries. I tell you tonight you are worth it. God chose Africa initially. [...] You don't have to sit with a psychological problem, an inferiority complex. God chose you right from the beginning. You are very, very special ... you have been in the Bible from the start.'

[129] *Four Laws*, 101.

ness.'[130] But by mid-1994, all this had changed. At Victory '94 time and time again he stressed 'structures':

'We can get everyone in Africa saved, but that won't solve our problem. The root of our problem is not [that] we are not saved. The root of our problem is man-made. I do not believe that just believing in Jesus Christ is the end of life. Jesus must do something about our poverty. [...] Jesus must help overcome our ignorance, our superstition. The poverty in Africa is not spiritual. [...] Poverty is physical. Poverty is a social condition. You can bind it, it won't be bound. You can claim it, it won't be claimed, because it is not spiritual; poverty is physical. [...] When I was growing up, I was told there was only one solution: 'Give and it will be given to you.' I did this and I got poorer. The preacher said 'Give and God will give to you.' It didn't happen. [...] If you are in a poor nation, you will be poor. You can't be richer than your country. So your personal individual prosperity is tied up with the prosperity of the nation. [...] We have to think structurally, to think about the economy of the nation. You can't preach in Africa and not be political. [...] If a nation is poor, its people will be poor. If a people are not part of the mainstream of society they will be poor. [...] Christians can't say "Let's leave politics to politicians." No, if wrong policies are made, you can pray all you want, and you won't have [anything]. In South Africa, God has changed the situation. They have a black President – thank God for that – but 98% of the wealth in South Africa is in non-black hands. So you can have a black President (but what's different?). [...] Christians have the faith, non-believers have the money. We [this is a direct attack on faith-gospeller John Avanzini, many of whose books were on sale at Victory '94] try to claim *their* money with *our* faith. [...] You can't claim anyone's money by faith – it's illegal. If you want to have money, there is only one way. It's work. [...] On 6 March 1957 [Ghana was] the first nation to get independence. But the economy is not controlled by Ghanaians. The economy is controlled by multinationals. We worked for them to create wealth for them to take it out of the country. We were hewers of wood and drawers of water for them. I prayed to God to prosper me [but] we have to change economic structures, we have to change social structures. If I don't have that opportunity, I can pray all I want and I'll still be poor. When we were colonised, structures were built in our nations. The British came not because they thought we needed the gospel; that's not why they came. They came because they wanted raw materials. [They take untreated raw material] then bring it back [treated] and impoverish you. You can pray all you want, but it won't help. [...] We have to start looking at the structures of our nations. You have an opportunity to do this here in Zambia, it's the only nation with a President who acknowledges Jesus as Lord and the Bible as the Word of God. We pray for your success here, but having a Christian President is not the end of it. You can have a Christian President or whatever, but that may not change anything, because poverty is not spiritual. You can have a Christian President, Vice President, Minister of Finance, whatever, the dynamics of prosperity are not spiritual. [...] We have to change the structures that govern our nation. We have to build new structures to empower you. God is helping us as a people to look where we come from. Colonialism – we have to mention these words in church – neocolonialism – a very tricky word

[130] *Ibid.*, 95.

this – the people don't come, he stays where he is, but sets up structures so that he controls you by remote means. We have to understand these structures.'[131]

Almost all of this is a frontal attack on the basics of the Faith Gospel. To the significance of this we shall return, but note Otabil's claim that having a 'Christian President' means nothing of itself. Here, with his emphasis on structures, he went considerably beyond all those Zambian Evangelical pastors who talk in terms of 'Christian leaders'.

The third strand in Otabil's message was tilling one's own vineyard. This is closely linked to his preaching on black pride; indeed he led into it from his text of Song of Songs 1: 5: 'I am black but beautiful.' The very next verse states: '[Because of the colour of my skin?] they have made me keeper of the vineyards, but my own vineyards I have not kept.' This, claimed Otabil, reflects African conditions: 'We have become keepers of other peoples economies. Our economies supported Europe. [The British] trained us to be good administrators, but never to change things – that's the point of an administrator.' Otabil told his audience that he had taken a drive around Lusaka, and asked who owned the shops he saw. He was told 'Indians'. He asked his driver if he knew any African who owned a shop, and was told 'No'. Then Otabil pointed to the little market stalls on the side of the road, and asked who owned them; the reply was 'Africans'. He told his audience: 'I see Zambians moving to Botswana, to South Africa. While Zambians are moving out, Indians are moving in.' Otabil was specific that he was bringing a message of prosperity, but prosperity would not be caused by faith or deliverance.

He proceeded to give a remarkable exegesis of Malachi 3: 10-12, one of the key texts for the Faith Gospel. This text is normally taken to prove that if you tithe you will be blessed abundantly. But Otabil claimed that the blessing is specified as 'rebuking the devourer so that it will not destroy the fruits of your soil'. Otabil pointed out that this means that before you can be blessed you have to own your own land: 'Whoever owns the fruit of your ground is the one who receives the blessing from your tithe. Because you tithe the devourer is stopped, but because of your tithe the owner gets the blessing. So [in the Zambian situation] the Hindu man [sic] who doesn't know God is the one who gets the benefit of your tithe. [...] They use your money to go and build mosques!' Otabil interpreted the story of Jacob to show that while Jacob worked for Laban (whom on another occasion Otabil had called the 'Father of the Lebanese') 'Jacob was the one tithing, Laban was profiting. Laban was the owner, Jacob the caretaker. It was Laban who was blessed.' ('Twenty years working for Laban, just children he couldn't look after. Twenty years, and all he

---

[131] Otabil's sermon, 9 Aug 1994. Note also another talk on the reasons for poverty: 'It's not because the demons are there, but because the conditions don't favour you. It's not the demons, it's conditions.'

had was an overpopulated family. That's like Africa, so much work, and just people we cannot feed.') That was why Jacob said to Laban, 'Give me my own land.' Then 'All the profit came to Jacob, because he was the total owner.' Then Otabil addressed his audience:

How come you [live] in your own country, and you don't own anything? The only thing left is to run to Botswana and South Africa. The tragedy of African governments is that they keep their own people poor, and keep foreigners rich. [...] You don't own anything, any businesses, and you don't even know how to run one. When the British colonised us, they trained us to look after the structures they set up. They made us lawyers, administrators, civil servants. Lawyers with funny white wigs! We say we are independent, and wear white wigs! Lawyers and judges with wigs, that's how they trained us! They trained us to be nurses, teachers, civil servants, to run the colonial machine. While you are running the colonial machine, others came in and took the land and sell things to you. You have nothing! How is the Lord going to bless you? [...] The only way to earn is through goods and services that are marketable. Not signing civil service files for the rest of your life. I've never seen any civil servant get rich. [...] That is not the way. [...] You can be free for thirty years, but you are still wearing wigs and own nothing! All our people here [in Africa] became labourers, farm workers, mine workers. Who owns the mines? The Bible says, 'People of Africa, lift up your hands.' We have lifted up our hands to everyone, to the British, and they impoverished us. To the Russians, with their socialism, and they destroyed everything. Now it's to America, Taiwan, Singapore. The key is not in America. [...] The key lies in a work-conscious, ownership-conscious, skilled populace. Don't think, 'Who can give me a job?' Think, 'When can I start a business?' Look at us preachers. We didn't work for missionaries. We started our own ministries.

Then he addressed the great obstacle facing Africans, which again linked with his theme of black pride:

Look how our people behave when they see a white man. They look as though they've found a gold mine. [Laughter.] Stop laughing; it's not funny. They start behaving weird. Go to a village. If a white man comes everyone runs. When the white man says, 'Raise up your hands', it's not Christ they are receiving, it's aid. How can people develop or achieve with that mentality? We have to cure this disease.

Then he added a lengthy discussion on the role of whites in Africa's problems; at one point he actually turned to the white Americans sitting beside the platform: 'You feel we are preaching against you. Well, some of your governments and some financial institutions in your countries are part of this problem.' Again, this message about entrepreneurship was clearly a revelation to the Zambians attending the conference. These Christians had never heard this message before, and it was received with excitement and obvious exhilaration.

Otabil's three emphases are of considerable importance, and were a serious innovation in Zambia's evolving charismatic Christianity. It should not be thought that Otabil has thought all this through consistently. Some confusion is apparent. For one thing, all his stress on owning one's own business leaves aside the difficulty, within present structures, of getting enough capital or training to begin a profitable business – also the particular problem for Zambia of manufacturing anything that cannot be undercut by traders importing from South Africa. Furthermore, for all his seeming awareness of the way colonial and neo-colonial structures have negatively affected Africa, he never mentions the role that Africa's own élite have played in bringing the continent to its knees; to dwell on that would not fit very well with his emphasis on black pride. Nor, for all his insistence that the Faith Gospel is no help in Africa, has he totally transcended it to become some kind of Latin American liberation theologian. He has little theology of a just society. His denigration of lawyers and civil servants suggests that he does not truly appreciate what a properly functioning state might look like. His theology in no sense constituted any 'preferential option for the poor'. Occasionally he let slip that he was preaching the way to acquire what he called 'serious money'. 'Prosperity is when you have breakfast in Zambia, lunch in Britain, dinner in America, and it doesn't affect your finances because you are flying in your own plane. Let's have some mighty Christian businessmen! That's going to come when we are tilling our own vineyard.' (However, it would not be fair to build too much upon rhetorical flourishes like these.) He also shares the faith gospel view that all this money is for evangelisation.

However, this discussion of Otabil (and to a lesser degree Sono) shows the tensions within this brand of Christianity. The Faith Gospel, which is almost axiomatic for so many of Africa's charismatic churches, was at Victory '94 virtually said to be useless. Not that this was adverted to by the other speakers, even by Nevers Mumba himself; he seemed quite able to praise Otabil for his stimulating message, and then go on to preach a full Faith Gospel himself. And it was noteworthy that many of those who applauded Otabil then went out to buy the books of Avanzini and Copeland that he had so effectively demolished. The seeds of change were not sown by a Zambian; it is doubtful whether Zambia's charismatic sector has any figure who could have independently articulated any one of Otabil's themes: black pride, structural reform and entrepreneurship – Zambia's charismatic sector does not possess the creativity of Ghana's. It has been argued elsewhere that the Faith Gospel has little to contribute to Africa's development.[132] But this convention is proof that the churches where it has been the staple diet are not static, and in this forum Zambians were repeatedly exposed, in Otabil's numerous lectures, to entirely new

[132] Paul Gifford, 'African Fundamentalism and Development', *Review of African Political Economy* 52 (1991), 9-20.

ideas. Nobody who was present could doubt the enormous impact Otabil made. Pastors, keen to imitate such a successful role-model, returned to their churches with Otabil's tapes to preach from; it remains to be seen just how the tensions he exposed will be resolved.[133]

Christianity has played a unique role in Zambia. Under Kaunda it was acknowledged to be one of the pillars of the nation. Political rhetoric took on a Christian flavour; Christian motifs characterised public discourse. Christianity came to permeate the national culture, as in Ghana, but Nkrumah used Christian metaphors in his political rhetoric because that was the air he breathed; Kaunda, in expounding his humanism, used Christian discourse out of some personal conviction. Thus there developed no defensiveness on the part of Christian spokesmen, or any great fear that they would be harassed; indeed they had ready access to State House. The various branches of Christianity developed a habit of working together, the leaders united not on any basis of class but through experience of successfully arguing their case. It was this sense of power, which they first experienced through opposing the introduction of 'scientific socialism', and the immunity that they enjoyed in such an avowedly Christian order that led them to play an important role in the 1991 transition: through brokering meetings between the parties, using church print media openly to press for change, and training and deploying an army of election monitors at polling stations on election day.

Since 1991, under Chiluba, Christianity has been raised to an entirely different plane and given a formal rather than an informal constitutional status. This has come about through Chiluba's declaration of Zambia as a Christian nation. With this declaration, Chiluba (aggressively born-again in contrast to the nominally Catholic Rawlings and the nominally Anglican Museveni) has made Christianity a crucial element in public life. This has not worked as Chiluba probably intended. The Catholics and the Christian Council have become more and more critical of his labelling as Christian a regime so obviously corrupt and incompetent. In Zambia the churches can be far more forthcoming than they are in Uganda; accustomed – even encouraged – to speak out, Zambia's mainline churches have been allowed, through this declaration, to conduct the debate on their own terms. Chiluba has given them an entire set of criteria by which to find him wanting. Even the Evangelicals (which in Zambia effectively means Pentecostals) have found fault with Chiluba, many of them admittedly on the purely self-interested grounds that his declaration

---

[133] One of the American speakers at the convention later wrote to Nevers Mumba about Otabil, denouncing him as merely promoting a 'social gospel', and advising Mumba to have nothing further to do with him.

of Zambia as a Christian nation has not brought them the influence and rewards they anticipated. On the other hand, there are Pentecostal groups which blindly support Chiluba on the grounds that a Christian President must be supported, or that declaring Zambia a Christian nation warrants unquestioning support.

The Pentecostal or born-again churches are numerically not so dominant here, nor do they have the creativity of Pentecostal churches in Ghana, but they have a remarkably high profile because this is the sector to which Chiluba and Vice-President Miyanda belong. Their support gives this sector of Christianity an artificial salience. Zambia shows that such churches are not necessarily to be understood in terms of the 'exit option', or 'walkout', for under Chiluba these churches have become – even more than in Uganda – part of the establishment, and a possible route to power, status and reward.

Unlike both Ghana and Uganda, Zambia was a settler colony. Because of its small local élite and the mines' need for specialist skills and technology, there was long a demand for expatriates. Within the churches, too, the relatively small élite and (just as important) the support of prominent Protestant missionaries for the nationalist cause have ensured that there has been little anti-missionary sentiment. Missionaries play a much more obvious role in Zambian Christianity than they do in Ghana or Uganda. This is particularly true of the Catholic Church. It is this unashamed drawing on missionaries' expertise that gives to Zambian church statements an awareness of the economic dimension that is not so evident in either Ghana or Uganda. And within the born-again sector, Zambia has far more whites in positions of influence than Uganda and (particularly) Ghana. Because after the declaration of Zambia as a Christian country missionaries have been granted open access, this influence seems unlikely to diminish in the immediate future.

6

CAMEROON

Cameroon is the shape of a long tapering triangle on a relatively short base, situated to the east of Nigeria. Its borders divide peoples in a totally artificial way; the Nigeria-Cameroon frontier divides fourteen recognisably distinct cultural groups. Northern Cameroon is mainly savannah or relatively open hill country where contact is easy, far different from the south where the 'Peoples of the Forest' are isolated and separated by rivers and dense tropical jungle. The formation of political units is thus very different in the two areas. In the south education and industry are much more developed .

Modern Cameroon has emerged from a colonial tradition different from the countries we have considered so far. The greater part of Cameroon began its colonial existence in 1884 as Kamerun, Germany having staked its claim five days before the British arrived.[1] The Germans were not particularly interested in their new colony (Bismarck was mainly determined that the British would not have it) and hardly developed it at all. Large tracts were given to two German companies to exploit the tropical forest, and Africans suffered greatly from forced labour. In 1911 Kamerun was considerably enlarged when the French gave Germany some strategic adjacent territory to the south and east in return for Germany giving France 'a free hand in Morocco'. After the First World War, when Germany lost its colonies, the area was split into the protectorates of French Cameroun and a much smaller British Cameroons, this status being confirmed by the League of Nations in 1922. These areas became UN trusteeships in 1946. On 1 January 1960 French Cameroun became independent. In February 1961, after a UN plebiscite, the northern sector of British Cameroons opted to join Nigeria but the southern sector, fearing domination by the Igbo, who through their party the NCNC were the dominant force in the adjacent Eastern Region of Nigeria, opted instead into a Federal Republic of Cameroon, with a guarantee of a separate parliament and its own British-derived systems of law and education. In 1972 the francophones abolished this federal system and changed the name to the United Republic of Cameroon, which in turn was changed in 1984 to the Republic of Cameroon.

Cameroon came to independence against the background of a fierce

---

[1]   Pakenham, *Scramble*, 200.

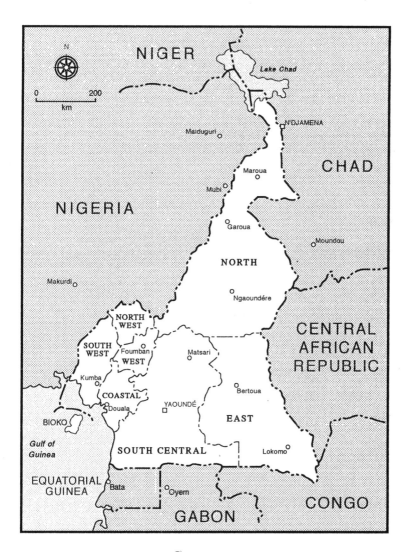

Cameroon

nationalist struggle waged by the Union des Populations du Cameroun (UPC), headed by Reuben Um Nyobe (1913-58). The French were not prepared to cede to the UPC, fearing the repercussions for their territories in North Africa and South-east Asia. Therefore they opposed the nationalists with considerable ferocity, especially after the UPC took up guerrilla operations in December 1956 (French forces remained in Cameroon to lead the struggle against the UPC at least five years after independence). The French handed power to their puppet, the northern middle-ranking Muslim politician Ahmadu Ahidjo, who was content with independence with strong ties to France. Without great legitimacy, Ahidjo set about establishing a presidential system of total control. With the rationale of national unity, he forced all opposition groupings into his one party, and destroyed most elements of civil society. Coming from the north, he feared the political implications of the south's wealth. Thus until the mid-1980s there was no paved road linking the nation's two biggest cities, Douala and Yaoundé, or between Yaoundé and the rich agricultural Western Province.[2] However, he needed the support of the more educated, more developed and wealthier south, so could not marginalise any one group.[3] In 1982, in a surprise move, he ceded control to his protégé Paul Biya, and the following year, after falling out with Biya, withdrew to France. Biya, a Catholic from the south, promised a more open dispensation but in the event has entrenched one-party rule. He surrounded himself with barons who have ruled both incompetently and exclusively in their own interest. Government in Cameroon is essentially an exercise in group aggrandisement – '*la politique du ventre*' is a traditional Cameroonian expression which Bayart gave more general circulation. And whereas Ahidjo had revenues sufficient to fuel a patronage system, Biya has had to make do with dramatically reduced income. Between 1980 and 1991 Cameroon had negative growth; its GNP per capita fell over that period by almost 1% annually. Tensions built up all through the 1980s, and after Africa's democratic opening in 1989 they could no longer be contained.

Dissatisfaction with Biya solidified around the anglophone John Fru Ndi and his Social Democratic Front (SDF). The anglophones have become particularly strident in their denunciation of Biya's government, which they tend to dismiss as totally corrupt and incompetent. Their contempt has grown in tandem with a curious romanticising of their British colonial legacy. The anglophones of the western region now argue that they were given structures of law and justice, and systems of education and administration which could have been used to develop the country.

---

[2]   Van de Walle, 'Neopatrimonialism', 141.
[3]   See Richard Joseph, *Gaullist Africa: Cameroon under Ahmadu Ahidjo*, Enugu: Fourth Dimension Publishers, 1978.

The francophones are not interested in any of these things, but only in self-aggrandisement, and the British legacy has been gradually destroyed by the vindictive, corrupt and incompetent Biya (or alternatively the Beti, the francophones generally, or just *La République*).[4] The anglophones are merely 20% of the population, but in their opposition they were joined by a large part of the francophone Bamileke – referred to as the 'Anglo-Bami' bloc. (Since the colonial and therefore linguistic divide was artificial, the northern anglophones of the grasslands round Bamenda, where Fru Ndi comes from, are Bamileke also; conversely, the coastal forest anglophones are quite different from their anglophone neighbours to the north.) The Bamileke, whose heartland is the Western Province, are the biggest grouping within Cameroon, probably the most enterprising and certainly the most prosperous. The spectre of a Bamileke takeover of the country has long loomed large in the nightmares of Cameroon's other groups.

In pursuit of their political goals, basically a national conference, the SDF initiated a programme of non-cooperation, culminating in a project of '*villes mortes*' or closing down all commercial activity. Since

---

[4]   In Buea 5,000 people gathered on 2 and 3 April, 1993, and produced the 'Buea Decla-ration'. This document refers to the 'intolerant and hypocritical attitude of our francophone brothers' who believe in 'torturing, maiming and assassinating dissent-ers', have looted and demolished the flourishing economy of the region, shut down the airports and sea-ports, 'destroyed the system of local government and of community development which we had instituted in anglophone Cameroon', 'destroyed the roads', attempted 'long-term control of our natural resources for the benefit of France', and discriminated against anglophones in education. In view of the francophone government's 'propensity for evil, corruption and manipulation', the declaration calls the 1972 imposition of the unitary state unconstitutional, and commits all anglophones to the restoration of a federal constitution. Of particular interest is the pervasive tone of finding francophone ways 'alien to us'. Thus military checkpoints are 'strange to anglophones'. 'Before reunification we were certain of the protection and enjoyment of our individual and civil liberties. One could not be arrested and left to languish in prison without being charged. It was unheard of for people's private premises to be searched without a warrant. The police did not carry guns everywhere.' Government interference in the judiciary is 'unknown to us anglophones'. Before 1961 'we had been practising parliamentary democracy in a politically pluralistic society which was far more developed that what obtains in Cameroon today, three decades later.' Anglophones then had a 'system of public accountability'. The first government had organised a general election in which it was defeated, and 'in keeping with the anglophone conception and practice of democracy', the government stepped down.

In the words of one intellectual, 'three decades of reunification' have brought for anglophones 'feudal oppression, mountains of suspicion and hate, retrogression, ... pauperisation, and resentment' (Bate Besong at First Anglophone Cameroon Literature Conference, 18-21 Jan 1993, quoted in George Ngwane, *Bate Besong*, n.p.)

Of course, the claim that to be anglophone is to be ordered and disciplined is rhetori-cal rather than empirically descriptive, as a quick look over the border at Nigeria might indicate; but Cameroon's anglophones do not let the chaos in Nigeria influence their claims.

the heartland of the SDF – the North-west, South-west, West and Littoral Provinces –is also the area where oil, bananas, cocoa and rubber (i.e. nearly all Cameroon's exports except timber) are produced, and includes Douala, the country's biggest city and only port, Cameroon's economic life came to a shuddering halt. This went on for two years. The economy had had negative growth during the 1980s; now it collapsed altogether. By the end of 1991 the state may have collected as little as 15% of the previous year's revenues.[5] But Biya did not give way, and responded with great brutality. For example, in response to some restlessness among the students at the university, a huge and costly wall was built around the perimeter of the campus, so that in the event of disturbances the students could not flee the soldiers sent in to deal with them – and this in a university which cannot afford books or lecturers' salaries. Opposition demonstrations were crushed with some loss of life.

In 1992 elections were held. The SDF boycotted the parliamentary elections in March; even so, Biya's Rassemblement Démocratique du Peuple Camerounais (RDPC) scraped home by the narrowest of margins. The presidential elections were in October. Despite considerable harassment of the opposition, doctoring of electoral rolls and government control of the media, John Fru Ndi, it is widely agreed, won the presidential elections. However, Biya had gone too far to give way now. He announced that he had been re-elected by a narrow majority, and on 27 October 1992 introduced a state of emergency, placing John Fru Ndi under house arrest. In March 1993 gendarmes fired on peaceful demonstrations in Bamenda, killing several and wounding more, and beating and torturing demonstrators (in November 1992 security services had tortured a protester to death). So Biya and his clique maintained their power, at enormous cost to the economy and social cohesion. Since 1993 the economy has started operating again and some of the heat has gone out of things, although the most important anglophone bodies, including the SDF, have gone beyond calls for a return to a federal system to press for total independence.[6] There is a certain circumscribed freedom of the press; new newspapers come and go. The security services are not quite as obtrusive as they were. However, robbery and violence are everyday occurrences. Education continues to disintegrate. The destruction of the forests goes on unabated. The infrastructure deteriorates, with roads even within the cities impassable at times during the rains. Services are

[5]   Van de Walle, 'Neopatrimonialism', 146.
[6]   Cameroon was admitted to the Commonwealth on 16 Oct 1995, an event that the government hailed with euphoria, trumpeting it as recognition that Biya was a true democrat ('Cameroon is thus to sit with some of the most civilised nations of the world', *Cameroon Tribune*, 20 Oct 1995, 5). The anglophones regretted that the Commonwealth had not demanded more from Biya in terms of democratisation (*L'Expression*, 20 Oct 1995; *Herald*, 19-22 Oct 1995).

neglected, and rubbish piles up within the cities. Those on fixed wages, like civil servants, teachers and nurses, have been harshly squeezed: having already suffered a drop in salary (up to two-thirds in some cases), they were further squeezed when Cameroon's currency was devalued by 50% in January 1994. The state newspapers and media are blatantly misused; the same footage showing a march in support of Biya can be repeated on TV news for several days. Government funds are used for narrowly political purposes, like the extraordinary congress of the RDPC of October 1995. Corruption goes unchecked and unpunished – like the scam whereby the Minister of Sport tried to restructure the administration of the game to enable him to cream off gate takings. Only the prospect of having Cameroon banned from all international competitions – Cameroon had performed with great distinction in both the 1990 and 1994 World Cups, amid national euphoria – forced him to give way.[7] Biya pursues a policy of divide and rule, especially in the anglophone region; between April and June 1995 thirty-three were killed in various land clashes in the North-west Province.[8] Division cripples the opposition; by the end of 1995 Cameroon had 117 registered political parties.[9] The country's decline continues apace.

In this dynamic the role of France is very important. France has considerable commercial interests in Cameroon. The currency (as for most of its former territories) is the franc of the Communauté Financière Africaine (CFA franc), pegged to the French franc. This locks France into the economics of all these countries (in January 1994 France devalued the CFA by 50%). In return, however, this linked currency gives France extensive control of its former colonies, and some French politicians have lucrative links with African leaders. Elf Aquitaine is the major oil company in Cameroon. Renault was able to prevent Volkswagen opening a factory there. French logging companies – with directors like Jean-Christophe Mitterrand (director of the Elysée Africa desk 1986-92) and Valéry Giscard d'Estaing – are unchallenged in exploiting Cameroon's tropical forests. But the interest extends far beyond the mere business realm; France has a real political concern. It has thought that it needed francophone Africa if it is to remain a world power.[10] Many would argue that one of the key factors in Biya's retention of power in 1992 was the refusal of France to allow an anglophone to assume power in what it regards as its sphere of influence. It was the French acceptance of the election results which

---

[7]   *Star Headlines*, 20 Sept 1995, 2.
[8]   This phenomenon illustrates both the venality and the incompetence of the ruling clique: one article blames local government officers who 'get money from both disputing parties, play for time, and wait for their transfers' (*Effort*, 4 June-7 July 1995, 4).
[9]   *Effort*, 7-20 Oct 1995, 8.
[10] Joseph, *Gaullist Africa*, 4-7.

enabled Biya to override the charges of vote-rigging; the German and American observers had left before the elections, claiming that the voting could not be free and fair.[11] The opposition newspapers (not generally known for their subtlety) sometimes delicately make their point by inserting, without comment, a photograph of Mitterrand (or subsequently Chirac) alongside a story about Biya or his RDPC.[12] Among Cameroonians it is not only the anglophones who readily talk of 'the totally pernicious influence of the French'.[13]

The Catholic Church

There is no agreement about the numbers adhering to different religions. Baur claims that Cameroon is 23% Muslim, 65% Christian, and 10% traditionalist; Barrett's figures for the mid-1980s are 22% Muslim, 56% Christian and 22% traditionalist; Médard writes that 10-20% are Muslims, and 20-30% Christians, leaving over 50% traditionalist.[14] The truth depends on where one draws the line distinguishing nominal Christian (or Muslim) from traditionalist. Some of the main churches have had a complicated history, because British missions had to give way to German, which in turn had to give way to others from France. Apart from the Catholic Church, churches have tended to be geographically delimited; thus, for example, the Eglise Presbytérienne Camerounaise is centred among the Bulu around Yaoundé, the Union des Eglises Baptistes Camerounaises around Douala and the Littoral Province, and the Lutheran Church (ELCC) around Ngaoundéré. However, throughout the 1980s this was slowly changing, for two reasons: most churches were actively bent on planting churches in other areas, and churches spring up when functionaries and businessmen move to other areas and bring their church with them. Most of the major churches can now be found in nearly all provinces, but that does not alter the fact that churches have centres of gravity in the areas where they first took root. We will encounter the persistent claims of these core groups again and again.

The major churches are all now active in the north too, but Christian involvement there is quite recent. The Germans, and then both the French and the British discouraged Christian missions there. This policy was carried

---

11   The very same consideration is said to have been behind the French involvement on behalf of Habyarimana's Rwandan government, and then opposition to the RPF which is largely anglophone (Clapham, *Africa and the International System*, 93).

12   Biya initially backed Balladur rather than Chirac for France's 1995 presidential elections, so his relations with Chirac were initially somewhat strained.

13   'Mitterrand et l'Afrique', *Politique Africaine* 58 (1995).

14   John Baur, *2000 Years of Christianity*, 468; Barrett, *Encyclopedia*, 208; Jean-François Médard, 'Identités et politiques: le cas des églises protestantes au Cameroun', paper delivered at Table Ronde: Mouvements religieux et débats démocratiques en Afrique, Pau, 8-9 Dec 1994.

on by Ahidjo, who fostered the impression that the north was thoroughly Muslim. This was never the case. The north was dominated politically, but not numerically, by the Fulbe Muslims who had invaded part of the north in the nineteenth century. Their control was strengthened by the colonial administrations and then by Ahidjo. Under him there was even discrimination against the *Kirdis* ('pagans' from the Islamic viewpoint) and pressure on them to convert. There was even some persecution of the churches. All this changed after Biya's accession to the presidency, especially after the suppression of an attempted coup in 1984 by the basically northern (and Fulbe-officered) presidential guard. The Fulbe have had their power curtailed considerably, and the churches now enjoy freedom to evangelise in the north.[15]

The churches in Cameroon bear marks from French colonial history; thus categories like '*laïciste*', '*cléricaliste*' and '*intégriste*' have some application. But the more recent past has also affected the churches. Although Ahidjo did not seek an all-out war with the churches, his drive for unity under an all-powerful presidential system led him into conflict with them over schools and hospitals. One sector of his administration would have preferred Cameroon without schools than with ones run by churches, or even by the people themselves. (Independent Cameroon has been characterised by an indifferent or even fiercely anti-Christian élite, even though almost all are mission products – a result of French metropolitan culture with no equivalent in the other countries we have studied.[16]) Even church women's or youth groups or trade unions were absorbed or eliminated – tolerated only if they did not threaten the party equivalents. Funds which the churches derived from overseas were closely monitored. The religious press was worn down after a long struggle. The Christian reaction to all this was enormously complex. Some sectors resisted, others tried to collaborate. Even among those resisting there was no uniformity. For some the resistance was on ethnic grounds; others saw behind Ahidjo a determination to Islamise the country; others resisted for reasons of political liberties; others cited their 'prophetic mission'. The collaborators argued that the churches could cooperate without losing their identity, and indeed harmony would see their work prosper. The Protestant churches probably preserved better relations with the government over these first years of independence.

The possible permutations of these attitudes were myriad. Thus within the Catholic Church alone, Archbishop Jean Zoa of Yaoundé was in favour

---

[15] This is well treated in Médard, 'Identités', 13-14.

[16] The role of the Christian missions has been the subject of more debate in Cameroon than in the other countries we have considered; see Mongo Beti, *The Poor Christ of Bomba*, Heinemann, 1971 (French original 1956), and Kenjo Jumbam, *The White Man of God*, London: Heinemann, 1980.

of a lay church and cooperation with the regime. Mgr Ndongmo of Nkongsamba was just as favourable to a lay church, but adopted an attitude of confrontation to what he considered an Islamising government. Mgr Mongo of Douala was a clericalist, but shared Mgr Ndongmo's oppositional stance. The expatriate clergy were divided between those guided by notions of social justice, and those who were largely indifferent to such considerations; both were very different from the local clergy, particularly the association of local priests in the Bamileke areas who were nationalists, and hostile (even racist) towards the expatriate clergy. These nationalist priests, of course, were in strong opposition to the hierarchy which had committed the Catholic Church to oppose the nationalists, seeing them as communists.[17] Traces of this diversity, even disunity, linger into the mid-1990s.[18]

The Catholic Church is today the only truly national church in Cameroon, which was entrusted to the German Pallotine Fathers in 1890. The northern region was separated in 1912 from the south and given to the German Sacred Heart Fathers of St Quentin, centred on Kumbo. During the First World War, all German missionaries were expelled, and the Holy Ghost Fathers (or Spiritans) took charge of the southern part in place of the Pallotines. The Sacred Heart Fathers merely replaced their German personnel with French, who in time shifted their headquarters from Kumbo to Nkongsamba. The western part of German Kamerun, by now a British protectorate, was in 1923 entrusted to the Mill Hill Fathers, centred on Buea. Much later, in 1946, the provinces of the far north were entrusted to the Oblates of Mary Immaculate.

By 1995 the Catholic Church was divided into twenty-two dioceses, and perhaps 30% of the population identify themselves as Catholics. The distribution is not uniform. In the southern provinces over 50% claim to be Catholic. The densely populated western areas are about 25% Catholic, and the vast but often thinly populated northern areas less than 5%.

The Catholic Church reflects the same deep and pervasive divisions as the country at large – in many ways it holds up a mirror to the nation. To illustrate this, we consider three different cases, the first of which is one of the most significant events in Cameroon's recent history, and indeed one of the most bizarre in the history of the Catholic Church in Africa, namely the Ndongmo affair.

---

[17] Louis Ngongo, *Histoire des forces religieuses au Cameroun: de la première guerre mondiale à l'indépendence 1916-1955*, Paris: Karthala, 1982; Richard A. Joseph, *Radical Nationalism in Cameroon: the Social Origins of the UPC Rebellion*, Oxford University Press, 1977, 258-61.

[18] For all these points, see Jean-François Bayart, 'La fonction politique des églises au Cameroun', *Revue française de science politique*, 33 (1973), 514-36; Jean-François Bayart, 'Les rapports entre les églises et l'état du Cameroun de 1958 a 1971', *Revue francaise d'études politiques africaines* August 1972, 79-104.

The Ndongmo affair. Albert Ndongmo was the first local bishop of Nkongsamba, appointed in 1964. At this time the diocese of Nkongsamba covered all the Bamileke area. Beginning in the 1950s, the UPC conducted an armed uprising against the French, from whom it elicited a brutal response. – it was the era of the uprising in Algeria, and the French were in no mood to compromise. But even after Cameroon's independence, the UPC continued its revolt against Ahidjo, whom it regarded as a usurper, left by the French to perpetuate French control.[19] Ndongmo claimed that he was asked by Ahidjo in 1965 to see if he could mediate with Ouandié, the last rebel leader still at large, in an attempt to conclude hostilities. His instructions were uttered in front of witnesses, important functionaries whom he named. Over the next few years he had several contacts with the rebels; then, after a time of little contact, it seems that in 1970 the government was closing in on Ouandié, who notified Ndongmo that he was in danger where he was. Ndongmo therefore transported the rebel leader, in his own car, to his seminary about 30 km. from Nkongsamba, even keeping him a few nights in his own house. Ndongmo managed to leave the rebel leader in a place where he felt he would be safe.

Ndongmo claimed that all this was in terms of the remit granted him by the President, but he was from that area and, according to later statements, all his sympathies were with the rebel cause. 'The struggle was just. If the end sought was truly what he claimed, namely to make Cameroon a modern, developed country, and Cameroonians a blessed people who are not governed from abroad. He did not want us to have our feet in Cameroon and our heads in Paris or London or wherever.' When his interviewer remarked 'Clearly you chose one side, the rebels', he replied: 'The side, yes, but not necessarily the methods.'[20] He was a controversial character, although no one doubts his exceptional gifts. He had preached against government brutality towards the local people, and even gone so far as to threaten that he would urge the people of his diocese to refuse to pay taxes. As two authorities on Cameroon euphemistically put it, '*[son] comportement personnel ne manquait pas d'être jugé quelque peu baroque par de nombreux catholiques.*'[21]

After taking the rebel leader to his safe place, Ndongmo had to leave for Rome, summoned there to explain how he came to own a plastics factory in Douala. Ndongmo had explained that 'I did not depend on the

---

[19] For UPC uprising, see Joseph, *Radical Nationalism*.

[20] Quotations from Ndongmo are from an interview in *Jeune Afrique Economie*, October 1991, 119-48 (present author's translation, as throughout this chapter). See also Bayart, 'Rapports', 101-3.

[21] J.-F. Bayart and Achille Mbembe, 'La bataille de l'archidiocèse de Douala', *Politique Africaine* 35 (1989), 82.

Vatican economically, because I took initiatives on the diocese's behalf. I thought – I still think – that it is absolutely humiliating for African bishops to go all over the West begging on their knees to get money. One should be able to set up some self-financing structures, and that's what I had begun to do.' He added: 'But I was denounced by some "colleagues", by one bishop in particular, whom I will not name.'

Ndongmo took nearly three weeks to return to Cameroon, and on his arrival at Douala airport he saw a newspaper headline announcing that a new apostolic administrator had been named for Nkongsamba, *sede plena*; in other words, he remained bishop, but Rome had taken the administration of the diocese from his hands and given it to another (who had been ordered to sell the plastics factory). But Ndongmo had had no time to think of this, or even to learn that while he was away Ouandié had been discovered and arrested, for he had immediately gone to see the Archbishop of Douala and had been there only a few minutes when the telephone rang and the governor told him that a car was being sent to fetch him. In fact the car was already there, and Ndongmo was taken to the notorious military prison in Yaoundé. He was interrogated for months, and then tried for treason in January 1971. This was a military trial, and the judges 'did not know' that President Ahidjo had commissioned him to search out Ouandié with a view to bringing about peace. Years later, when asked if he had told the court that Ahidjo had entrusted him with this task in front of witnesses, Ndongmo replied: 'There are some things that a chief does not say in public, and I am a chief myself. I simply said that someone would be able to tell them better than I why I had gone to see Ouandié, namely the President of the Republic Ahmadu Ahidjo. I suggested that they should ask him if he knew anything, yes or no.' Ndongmo was found guilty of treason, and sentenced to death by firing squad, but this was commuted to life imprisonment. He was sent to a notorious camp in Tcholliré, where he had no radio and no newspapers, and was kept away from other prisoners. He had a few visits from the papal nuncio (the Pope sent him some seeds for his garden), but he had little support: 'After my arrest, a bishop – what am I saying, an archbishop – went to tell the Head of State that the measures were quite correct, and that I should be punished.'

After five years, Ndongmo was freed – just before an election, which enabled Ahidjo to present himself as merciful. The release was part of an agreement with the Vatican, according to which Ndongmo was to leave Cameroon for Rome. Ndongmo insisted on seeing Ahidjo before he left, but the meeting seemed to resolve nothing. Although Ahidjo said that his exile in Rome would be for only a few years, Ndongmo moved to Canada and lived quietly there as a Canadian citizen for the rest of his life. He returned to Cameroon with Pope John Paul II on the occasion of

the papal visit in 1985, and again in 1989 in connection with the establishment of a Catholic university in the country. He remained a figure of
controversy and to the end of his life he would speak of his own principled
stand, comparing it with that of others: 'I opted to defend the people. I
struggled, and I always had the people behind me. But at that time, some
other bishops had only one aim, to appear favourably in the President's
eyes, with whom they would sip champagne.' Indeed, on his 1989 visit
the Archbishop of Douala was reluctant to have him as a guest. Within
UPC circles some have even suspected that Ndongmo might have played
some role in betraying Ouandié to the security forces.[22] In later years
Ndongmo was dismissive of Biya, claiming that Ahidjo had deliberately
picked him as his successor, knowing full well that he would destroy
Cameroon; in this way Ahidjo would have proved that he had been
indispensable. Yet Ndongmo continued to offer himself as someone
capable of reorganising the country politically, even as president of a
national conference. He died in Canada in 1992, and his body was brought
back to Cameroon, to be buried with some pomp in his dilapidated
cathedral at Nkongsamba.

The account of this incident highlights some motifs we will meet again:
the wish to be independent of foreign control, both political and
ecclesiastical; financial dealings which are less than totally transparent;
close identification with the political aspirations of one's own ethnic
group; and deep episcopal disunity. The archbishop that Ndongmo
declines to name but constantly disparages is, as everyone knows, Mgr
Jean Zoa, who was still in 1996 Archbishop of Yaoundé.[23]

The battle for the Diocese of Douala. The same motifs are just as evident
in a second significant episode, which has been called 'the battle for the
Diocese of Douala'.[24] The Archbishop of Douala, himself a Bassa, had
since 1981 asked Rome for a coadjutor bishop. Instead, in 1987, he was given
two auxiliary bishops, one Bassa and the other Bamileke. On 16 March
1987, fifty-one (out of eighty) Cameroonian priests of the Douala
archdiocese wrote a memorandum to Rome entitled 'Some new light on
the situation currently obtaining in the Archdiocese of Douala'. The
memorandum was headed 'confidential', but it was given wide publicity
in Cameroon, and indeed elsewhere. It purported to expose a plan of
'Bamilekisation' pursued by expatriate clergy, the papal nuncio and
foreign interests, and noted the parallel between the ecclesiastical project
and the general attempt of the Bamileke to take political power. The
authors referred to the stated objective of Mgr Ndongmo to set up four

---

[22] See *Jeune Afrique Economie*, March 1992, 117.
[23] Bayart and Mbembe, 'Bataille', 81.
[24] *Ibid.*, 77-84.

ecclesiastical provinces, one of which would comprise the dioceses of Douala, Nkongsamba and Bafoussam. The bishop of any one diocese could become metropolitan, and Ndongmo thought it entirely normal that a Bamileke should become Archbishop of Douala. They conclude: 'An auxiliary bishop from Bafoussam, a Bamileke, has just been named in Douala. Mgr Ndongmo's dream has in 1987 become reality.'

The authors parade their statistics: of the twenty bishops in Cameroon ten were Bamileke, five Beti, two Bassa, and the others expatriates; they concluded that the Bamilekisation of the hierarchy was already far advanced. They outlined the reasons advanced by the church's decision-makers in support of this course of action: the Bamileke were hard-working and dynamic; they were used to a hard life, so they were less prone to breaking the obligation of celibacy; they were a very religious people, and thus ready to accept and live the gospel; they were a people used to obeying, and therefore equipped to lead. These alleged reasons were refuted one by one. The real reasons for the promotion of the Bamileke, the memorandum insists, were economic and political. Economically it enabled European businessmen to ally themselves with rich Bamileke. 'The marriage the Europeans have made with the Bamileke is not a love match, but one of self-interest. To better exploit, then to dominate, Cameroon's weak and poor, they must forge an alliance with the economic force that the Bamileke are.' And since the economically powerful need political power, they need to take over the strategic national areas. 'This Bamilekisation of the hierarchy naturally tends to the taking of political power. The north is effectively conquered, as is the west, the east too. There remains only the Littoral, namely Douala, and the buckle is fastened.' The authors quote remarks attributed to missionary priests: 'The Bamileke, an industrious, enterprising and numerous people, will take over the country sooner or later. They already have economic power, they will soon have political power. The church must not be left behind.' The authors imply that this course of reaction could plunge Cameroon into a situation reminiscent of Europe fifty years before: 'The pro-nuncio, in discovering in the Bamileke tribe the virtues of the Aryan race, is surely reviving a particular history?'

Besides the economic and political reasons there were human ones too. As early as 1970 the previous Archbishop of Douala had resolved on building a seminary. The missionaries (Jesuits, Spiritans and Dominicans) had opposed this, even denouncing the bishop to Rome. The bishop, Mgr Tonye, 'had to thump the table with his fist to get the [expatriate] financial controller to withdraw some money to begin the building'. The seminary had gone ahead and now, with local clergy being trained, the missionaries were afraid. The missionaries needed their man as a coadjutor bishop:

'Either Mgr Tonye will send us packing, or we will send him packing.' But instead of a coadjutor, Douala had been given two auxiliaries, one an outsider, and the list sent to Rome had included no name from outside the diocese. The outsider named as auxiliary was not known in the diocese and could speak none of its languages. Moreover, he had been associated with attacks on the Archbishop of Douala, and was even a signatory of a letter accusing him of attempting to embezzle from the funds for the building of the seminary. That alone disqualified him from sharing leadership with the archbishop. And why was there so little regard for Douala's own clergy? Douala is the primatial see of Cameroon, and '*Prima sedes a nemine judicatur* [Let the prime see be judged by no one].' The relative autonomy of the churches of Brittany, Alsace and Corsica was relevant. The memorandum concludes: 'We repeat that to surrender economic, political and religious power to a single tribe is to run the risk of a totalitarian regime in Cameroon.'

This document drew a reply from the priests of the Assemblée du Clergé Indigène du Diocèse de Bafoussam (ACIB) on 22 June 1987, which refuted point by point the charges of the Bassa priests of Douala.[25] They drew attention to the massaging of statistics (for example, a retired Bamileke bishop was included, but a retired non-Bamileke was not), and the simplistic identification of the West Province with the Bamileke (ignoring non-Bamileke like the Bamoun, Tikar and Mbo). They dwelt on the 'anti-gospel and anti-ecclesial nature of the memorandum'. They agreed that the document was essentially political:

It is an appeal to national mobilisation against the Bamileke.[...] For the political theorists [*politòlogues*] of the memorandum, you do not avoid dictatorship by separating and balancing the three executive, legislative and judicial powers, but by distributing between different tribes the economic, political and religious power. Since the Bamileke have the economic power, we must make sure they never get political power, by depriving them of religious power.

They concluded by showing how this agenda was contrary to the national task set by President Biya.

This high-profile struggle was apparently ethnic but actually much more. The ethnic element was essentially 'shadow theatre' and hid '*la politique du ventre*'; this was basically an intra-Bassa struggle for spoils.[26] This reading was vindicated when Archbishop Tonye was removed in 1989. His involvement in petrol stations and hotels had effectively bankrupted the diocese, and reduced it to chaos. Indeed, the above struggle

---

25   'Point de vue de l'Assemblée du clergé indigène du diocèse de Bafoussam (ACIB) sur le Mémorandum des prêtres autochtones de l'Archidiocèse de Douala intitulé: Un Eclairage Nouveau', *Politique Africaine*, 35 (Oct 1989), 97-104.

26   Bayart and Mbembe,'Bataille', 79-80; also Mbembe, *Afriques indociles*, 159-60.

was an indication of the advanced state of the chaos, and resentment at an outsider being sent in (at least partly) to monitor developments. Tonye departed on a Friday, and Cardinal Tumi, then Archbishop of Garoua, was enthroned in Douala within ten days. Cardinal Tumi, although Banso and anglophone, was accepted because of his status as a cardinal, and because of his own undisputed moral authority. His task, however, has been far from easy. We must note that such a public spat among the Catholic clergy is unthinkable in the other countries we have considered.

Bishop Nkuissi. A third case, given just as much publicity, involved Nkongsamba again. It should be recalled that Ndongmo had been summoned to Rome about a plastics factory, and removed from administering the diocese even before his arrest. After he resigned in 1973, he was replaced in 1979 by Thomas Nkuissi (in 1970 part of the original diocese of Nkongsamba had been split off as the diocese of Bafoussam). Nkuissi always claimed to be motivated by a desire for Africanisation – in later years he used the word inculturation. This avowed obsession was the localisation of the church, in pursuit of which he was led to set up his own religious orders. He established four. It appears that in building up these orders, he was interested in numbers, and was prepared to take even those rejected by other congregations and to use diocesan funds to compensate the families of those willing to provide candidates. Priests received no set remuneration; one in an administrative job in the city could receive 60,000 CFA a month; another in a remote rural parish as little as 2,000 CFA. Many went into business, some even failing to arrive for services on a Sunday if business called. It has been claimed that Nkuissi used diocesan funds to favour a small clique from his own region; even if this was not so, it is true that a certain group of priests were able to travel to Europe regularly, and were commonly said to keep wives and families there. His policy of Africanisation, as implemented by him, had the effect of marginalising (if not driving out) the missionaries, and of course the systems and structures that the missionaries could have maintained gradually ceased to function, as indeed did the diocese.

The episcopate of Nkuissi culminated in what has been euphemistically called '*une fin de règne tumultueuse*'.[27] In 1991 the Catholic Church celebrated its centenary in Cameroon. Various ceremonies were held around the country (not least because the divided hierarchy could not agree on any central celebrations). At the centenary ceremony in his diocese on 17 February, Nkuissi preached a sermon which was, not surprisingly, a plea for Africanisation, inculturation and indigenisation. This was the time of the Gulf War, and Nkuissi began by referring to the

[27]   *Effort*, 24 June-7 July 1995, 15.

'tons of destructive bombs ... dropped for the avowed aim of showing Western solidarity and of safeguarding the interests of the West. A pretext is advanced, but trouble is taken to explain that, even without that, sooner or later this had to happen, for a great power was establishing itself in the region, which is against Western interests.'[28] The same Western solidarity that was bombing Iraq was responsible for the pittance paid for Africa's primary produce. 'The effectiveness of the actions of Western solidarity is guaranteed by multinational corporations, either economic or religious, which aim to keep the rest of the world in passivity and mediocrity.' Thereafter Nkuissi concentrated his fire on the religious multinationals within the Catholic Church. He noted that one of the preparatory documents for the forthcoming African synod had enquired whether there might be too many diocesan religious congregations in Africa. Nkuissi said that he had done some research and found that there were 400 religious congregations in Central Africa, but of these 371 were foreign and only twenty-nine were African diocesan congregations. 'Three hundred and seventy-one foreign congregations in just half of Africa! This is saturation to the level of nausea, this is suffocation to the level of asphyxiation, this is spiritual sterilisation, this is cultural robbery!' Far from the need to reduce local African congregations, there was a need for a religious life which could meet 'the needs of Africa and of Africans, and not those of Western solidarity'. He continued:

'Obviously with twenty-nine against 371 we are discouraged and inclined to surrender, since all these powerful foreign congregations descend from heaven and wash over us. But it falls to us to engage in earthly combat where we will be invincible. For we are masters of the terrain, the terrain of language, the terrain of culture, the terrain of traditions, the terrain of customs, the terrain of poverty and of heritage.'

This sermon, televised nationally, caused consternation among missionaries, many of whom complained to the papal pro-nuncio.

Five months later the funeral of Mgr Ndongmo took place. The body had been brought back from Canada and his people wanted to take it to their village, but Nkuissi refused and ordered that it be guarded by soldiers. Besides this, a disaster tragedy was only narrowly avoided during the funeral, when banks of seating erected for the occasion collapsed, seriously injuring several people. All this lost Nkuissi the support of many local people, who revered Ndongmo and considered him a figure of international standing. The accident showed the incompetence, perhaps the venality (had the money for proper seating been siphoned off privately?) into which the diocese had descended.

---

[28] This sermon is found in Thomas Nkuissi, *Dernières paroles d'évêque diocésain* (Nkongsamba: the author, 1993), 9-22.

A month later Nkuissi was embarrassed when Rome stopped him ordaining seven of his eleven candidates for the priesthood. Bishop Nkuissi preached about the campaign of 'informing and slander' against the diocese; he called for legality in the church, and then applied to his own case the high priests plotting against Jesus (Mt 26: 3f), the Jewish leaders plotting against Paul (Acts 23: 12-16) and Micah's curse on leaders plotting evil (Mic 2: 1). Evil and hypocritical religious leaders were trying to crush God's agent, but they would be thwarted.[29]

On 12 December he preached at the funeral of a priest of his diocese, and in the course of the sermon he explained that the priest had '*un problème de cohérence de la personne*', and had been led to believe that he was a messiah.[30] Many of the priest's family were so incensed that they tried to attack the bishop even during the ceremony. Soldiers were required to maintain order.

At the midnight mass of Christmas 1992, Nkuissi again preached on the forces of darkness operating in the diocese, but by then Rome had moved. The papal pro-nuncio had telephoned him on Christmas Eve, asking to see him on Boxing Day. He was gone by 31 December, leaving a letter to be read from the pulpit on 10 January, which for all its brevity opens a window on how Rome operates in these matters.

Dear Brothers and Sisters,
On Christmas Eve the pro-nuncio called me on the telephone. The day after Christmas he came to the diocese. He spoke of my resignation. I asked if he had a form to sign. He gave me a page with two lines printed on it. I signed. Then followed a commentary – in the background was my sermon of 17 February 1991. We chatted, we ate, he left.[31]

It is clear from the preface and postscript to Nkuissi's printed sermons that he justified everything on the basis of his policy of Africanisation. The prologue of his *Dernières Paroles* assembles the statistics to show what he had achieved. In 1971 the diocese had forty-nine priests, twenty-eight expatriates and twenty-one locals; by 1991 there were sixty-one – eight expatriates and fifty-three locals. In 1971 there were twenty-five brothers, all expatriates; by 1991 there were seven – one expatriate and six locals. In 1971 there were fifty sisters – thirty-five expatriates and fifteen locals (of a congregation belonging to another diocese); by 1991 there were still fifty sisters, but by now only fourteen were expatriates and thirty-six were locals, two-thirds of them from Nkongsamba. And so on. He concludes: 'This is Africanisation of personnel. This allows indigenisation of structures, which permits true inculturation.'[32] But, no

---

[29] *Ibid.*, 37-43.
[30] *Ibid.*, 49-52.
[31] *Ibid.*, 63-64.
[32] *Ibid.*, 5-7.

matter what his intentions, no matter how idealistic his goals, his diocese, through his managerial neglect or incompetence, had descended into chaos by the end. For him Africanisation meant taking control of everything. He marginalised all missionaries and the skills they might have contributed, and neglected any procedures or systems or structures that might have brought order to the diocese. In this the diocese mirrored the country. The absence of any system, the lack of will to put rational procedures or structures into place, enabled a group to plunder and enrich themselves at will. Like the state, the Catholic Diocese of Nkongsamba was strong on high-sounding rhetoric, but short on any effective or transparent structures that could deliver on the rhetoric.

The end was not just chaos but bankruptcy – with the result that even one of the much-vaunted local sisterhoods had to resort to prostitution to survive. In the subsequent investigation into the affairs of the diocese, Rome dismissed the four leading figures of this congregation, including the woman who had been its co-founder, not just from their positions of authority within the order, but from the order itself. The Bishop of Bafoussam, the neighbouring diocese, also chairman of the Bishops' Conference and himself a Bamileke, was put in charge as apostolic administrator, and he dismissed other church workers and tried to discipline priests. Those who had profited from the old system formed a 'Front for the Liberation of the Diocese', which blamed 'one faction of the diocesan clergy, manipulated by the Sacred Heart Fathers'.[33] After two years a new bishop was appointed in 1995, choosing as his motto 'That they may be one' (Jn 17: 11). He has set about trying to introduce systems, even as basic as filing cabinets for the piles of documents that cluttered the diocesan offices, and among his first appointments were expatriate Sacred Heart Fathers as his health director and deputy finance director. But he has enormous problems: the diocese has been plundered, his cathedral is crumbling (the brochure for his consecration includes a plea for money for its restoration), and discipline and morale are low.[34]

Although the Nkuissi case can hardly be called typical, it was not an isolated case either. The Bishop of Doume Abong-Mbang 'retired' in mid-1995, and at the time of writing it is widely believed that at least one more francophone bishop will also retire shortly.

Let us now turn to the other major division of the country, the anglophone area of the North-west and South-west provinces, which the Catholic Church has divided into three: the Archdiocese of Bamenda, and the

---

[33] Announcement dated 22 Jan 1993.
[34] One priest he attempted to discipline sued the bishop (*Soleil d'Afrique*, 53 (Oct 1995), 5.

Dioceses of Buea and Kumbo. Here too the Catholic Church mirrors the country. We mentioned above that the anglophones in general consider themselves to be characterised by order, structure, and discipline. It is widely admitted that the Catholic Church in the Bamenda ecclesiastical province (where Catholics number 21% of the population) is far more unified and disciplined, and has far better trained clergy than anywhere else in Cameroon. Consider the Diocese of Bamenda, presided over since its creation in 1971 by Archbishop Verzdekov, an anglophone Banso like Cardinal Tumi. Here there are systems, procedures and an attempt to address problems. One of the most divisive of these is the gulf between missionary and local clergy in all the countries we have considered. Missionaries have access to resources which most African clergy do not. Bamenda has met this problem by instituting a car-pool system, in which no one owns a vehicle individually; all belong to the diocese, for the work of the diocese. So if a missionary's congregation or relatives or friends buy him or her a vehicle, it belongs to the archdiocese and remains at its disposal. Also, the user of any vehicle pays so much per mile to the diocese for the use of the car (the rate increases for trips outside the archdiocese in order to discourage private trips), with the result that by the time the car needs replacing the archdiocese has built up a sizeable sum towards its replacement.

Such financial arrangements are handled from a superbly organised secretariat, which operates effectively as a commercial bank. All Catholic organisations and individuals in the diocese (and further afield) lodge their money not with Cameroon's notoriously suspect commercial banks (the collapse of the Meridien BIAO bank in mid-1995 cost the Cameroon Baptist Convention and missionaries over 2 million CFA) but with the secretariat. Funds are kept overseas in foreign currencies, which meant among other things that all diocesan funds avoided the 50% devaluation of January 1994. Although the secretariat is not advertised as a bank for the general public, many in fact use it as their way of remitting funds overseas for school fees and the like; it is far more reliable.[35] Diocesan salaries are fixed. Priests are paid 100,000 CFA a year, which is said to be adequate, since board and lodging are taken care of, but in 1995 the clergy were negotiating a revision of their estimates. Priests are forbidden to involve themselves in business, and are moved around with some rapidity. The diocese puts aside into a retirement fund 1 million CFA for every priest. Parishes have to send in to the secretariat full accounts of their monthly income and expenditure, and every year a budget is agreed for each one; failure to keep to this results in the secretariat freezing parish

---

[35] The financial theory and practice of the Bamenda archdiocese are found in Erwin Hain, *Financial Self-reliance within a Self-reliant Church*, a booklet published by the archdiocese in 1979.

accounts. Diocesan balance sheets are opened to the priests each year, and annual diocesan accounts are sent to Rome.

When asked why this ecclesiastical province should be so distinguished for these systems, most suggest two reasons; a particular form of colonialism and the founding missionaries. The first reason alludes to the increasingly widespread perception among the anglophone élite that British administration was marked by law and structures and systems. The belief in the beneficent nature of the structures introduced by Britain is probably greater within the Catholic Church than in the population generally, because of the British attitude to confessional schools. In 1989 the Catholic bishops of Cameroon, both francophone and anglophone, produced a pastoral letter on education, in which they noted that the Catholic Church is involved in education as a service. They continue: 'We must recall that the school system in the British tradition which obtained till 1976 in the present ecclesiastical Province of Bamenda (administrative provinces of the North-west and South-west), was the perfect answer to this notion of service.'[36]

Under the British, any 'voluntary agency' which could show that it was not a business enterprise, adhered to the agreed educational policy and could ensure the proper training of teachers had a legal right to receive state grants. These covered all teachers' salaries and national insurance contributions, the running of the schools, grants to teacher training colleges, improvements and repair of buildings, and medical assistance to the schools. Teachers in agency schools were paid according to the same scale as operated in government schools. Besides the provision of aid, religion could also be taught in these schools. The British attitude was pragmatic – the missions could provide education far more cheaply than the administration.[37] The French attitude was more ideological: in a lay state, mission schools should receive no state subsidies, and religion had no place in a lay curriculum. This British system, the 'perfect answer' in the opinion of the Catholic bishops, both anglophone and francophone, has gradually been whittled away, and from about 1991 the state has been remiss in its agreed subvention – which reinforces the anglophone conviction of the corruption, incompetence and vindictiveness of *La*

---

[36] CENC, *Pastoral Letter of the Bishops of Cameroon about Catholic Education,* January 1989, 9; note that the moderator of the anglophone Presbyterian Church in Cameroon has a similar view of the British colonial attitude to church schools; see his preface to Nyansako-ni-Nku (ed.), *Cry Justice: the Church in a Changing Cameroon,* Buea: PCC, 1993, i.

[37] The bishops note that in 1925 the British government asked for 'all primary education to be entrusted exclusively to the Christian missions. This came about because it had been proved that the same amount of money which was meant to run one government school – namely 1,000 pounds –was used to run twenty denomination schools, when it was handed to the Christian missions' (10).

République, and fuels their own feelings of superiority and their desire to secede.

Besides a particular colonial heritage, many explain the order of the anglophone dioceses by the policies of the congregation that planted the church here, namely the Mill Hill Fathers. The order was established in 1866 by the future Cardinal Vaughan of Westminster and named after the North London suburb where their headquarters is, although its missionaries have been Dutch or Irish as much as English. In establishing the church here, they identified totally with the local church, making no distinction between their property and that of the local diocese. Thus when local Cameroonians took on the administration of these dioceses, the Mill Hill missionaries handed over everything, and stayed to assist in whatever way they might be asked. There was thus little resentment towards the missionaries on the part of the emerging local clergy. (Some have pointed out that the problems in Nkongsamba may have their origin partly in the policies of the Sacred Heart Fathers who, when a local administration was established, kept a sizeable block of the church compound for themselves, and then tended to stand back to observe and criticise.)

The generally positive perception of both the colonial power and the missionary founders has led to there being little antipathy towards expatriates and their ways. Quite the contrary. The structures the Mill Hill missionaries established were taken over and preserved. The car-pool system, for instance, was devised by Mill Hill missionaries before independence. Indeed the missionary who set up the financial structures in the 1970s was still controlling Bamenda's archdiocesan finances in the 1990s. A Cameroonian has been associated with this task for several years, so by 1995 it was more correct to say that the system was jointly administered. After this thorough apprenticeship, the Cameroonian was perfectly ready to assume full control when the white missionary stepped aside. Already the day-to-day functioning of what is effectively a major bank is in the hands of totally competent local sisters. (It may be noted that the financial oversight of all three anglophone dioceses was in the early 1990s still in the hands of white missionaries. Only illness caused oversight in the diocese of Kumbo to be transferred to a Cameroonian in 1993.) There seems little impatience with this arrangement; structures are considered to be important, and jobs must be given to the competent. The result is that far from these dioceses being bankrupt, all books are balanced (although breaking even is, of course, achieved thanks to funds from overseas). The books are not only transparent but open for inspection.

Archbishop Verdzekov, far from having anything against missionaries, positively touts for them. For some time he had a standing arrangement with the papal pro-nuncio, if he ever found missionaries interested in coming to Africa, to act on his behalf. Nor has he ever attempted to establish his own diocesan congregation; he says he has no gift for that. In the early 1990s several congregations were coming to work in his archdiocese: Calasanctians, Kiltegans, Claretians, Conceptionists and Capuchins. They are attracted by the structures and predictability – and the appreciation given to their services. Although they do not have to, almost all choose to opt into schemes like that of the car-pool. Archbishop Verdzekov defends his stance theologically, that the local church needs the charisms of such missionary congregations, and of course it suits him practically; he has only four parishes in the city of Bamenda, and would like ten. Missionaries also bring resources; for example the arrival of the Spanish Calasanctians linked the archdiocese with Spanish aid networks that it had no access to before. Missionaries also bring skills. Sacred Heart College in Bamenda, long run by English Marist Brothers, has long been one of the premier schools in the country. When the Marist Brothers insisted on pulling out in 1993 to redeploy elsewhere, Verdzekov was most reluctant to see it happen, as were most parents, thinking that standards would fall. The three diocesan clergy put in to run the school in 1994 in fact maintained the 100% success rate in exams. Some argue from this that Archbishop Verdzekov is excessively hesitant to Africanise; to others it shows that Africanising pragmatically rather than ideologically enables the highest possible standards to be maintained.

It is not argued that these anglophone systems are perfect – for example, most priests seem ready to disconnect the milometers in their vehicles, so that the mileage eventually submitted to the secretariat is considerably massaged. Equally it would be a mistake to exaggerate the uniformity of these three anglophone dioceses: Buea is not so welcoming of missionaries, and although Kumbo is welcoming, the bishop is not skilful in handling them. They also have policy disagreements; for example, on the status of pidgin as a proper liturgical language. But although they do not solve all problems, all anglophone dioceses are marked by procedures and structures.

The northern ecclesiastical province, comprising the four dioceses of Garoua, Ngaoundéré, Yagoua and Maroua-Mokolo, is a totally different reality. Here Catholics make up only 5% of the population. In Catholic (as opposed to Protestant) thinking, it seems to be assumed that establishing the church here can only be accomplished by expatriate missionaries. In these dioceses – and to them we could add the south-eastern ones of Yokadouma and Batouri – the majority of new bishops are expatriates, and from religious congregations: a Polish Oblate was appointed to Yokodouma in 1991, a French Scheutist to Batouri in 1994 and a Belgian of the Little Brothers of the Gospel (a congregation stemming from Charles de Foucauld) to Maroua-Mokolo in 1995. By 1995 five of Cameroon's twenty-two dioceses were headed by an expatriate. (The other recent appointment in the north was, significantly, of an anglophone from Bamenda as Bishop of Yagoua in 1993.) Such appointments reveal an attitude which would hardly be tolerated for a minute in the other countries under consideration. Some diocesan clergy do grumble among themselves, but it is remarkable how little protest there is. In Catholic thinking it seems agreed that the establishing of these new churches needs Western money, and only religious congregations can provide the personnel.[38] Surprisingly, among the few prepared to express reservations about the policy were the religious orders themselves. At the 1995 meeting of the heads of religious orders, in discussing the appropriateness of appointing expatriate bishops in the new dioceses, they (still overwhelmingly expatriate themselves) wondered: 'Is this not just a solution for the short term?'[39]

In the north the activity of the Catholic Church is different from that in the rest of the country. It basically looks after those who have come from elsewhere. It is evangelising, but not the Islamicised tribes, and restricts its activities to the marginalised tribes among whom some success is expected. This is very different from the church growth thinking that influences most of the Protestants. Catholics are also involved in education and development of all kinds. The personnel are basically missionaries but not necessarily European; some are from African countries like Zaïre.

Given the history of Cameroon, it is unrealistic to expect the Catholic Church to speak in unison or to produce the agreed statements that characterise, say, the Catholic Church in Ghana. Generally, in this society, the bishops are identified with their own regional interests. The Beti bishops of the south are regarded as friends of the regime. One attended minor seminary with Biya, but all have links of patronage with him. Archbishop Zoa has long been considered sympathetic to the regime, even if in the mid-1990s he was also thought to be establishing more

---

[38] For an outstanding example to the contrary, see Jean-Baptiste Baskouda, *Baba Simon: le père des Kirdis*, Paris: Cerf, 1988; *Kudumbar: journal du foyer des jeunes de Tokombéré*, Oct 1995. The Catholic parish of Tokombéré is twinned with St Germain-des-Près in central Paris. In October 1996 the French parish was raising 200,000 francs ($30,000) for school fees for 200 in Tokombéré. That donation alone, not particularly significant for the middle class parishioners of St Germain, makes the Catholic parish of Tokombéré a major centre of development.

[39] Minutes of Religious Superiors' meeting of 8-10 March 1995. Many maintain that whites are more accepted in Muslim areas.

independence. On the other hand, Cardinal Tumi and Archbishop Verdzekov are inevitably seen as opposed to the regime. Both have spoken out on issues of public concern, but their impact is lessened because (this being Cameroon) the very fact that they are anglophone means that they are seen as opposition figures. When someone from his area was tortured to death in police custody, Verdzekov issued a pastoral letter denouncing the torturers, and a few days later repeated his charges on Radio France Internationale. For this outspokenness, he was pilloried by the government.[40] Cardinal Tumi is undoubtedly the moral leader of the church. He has been a bishop in three different sees, and was already a cardinal as Archbishop of Garoua. Although an anglophone, he studied in France and is perfectly bilingual. Even outside the Catholic Church he exerts considerable moral authority. When other francophone countries were holding national conferences, chaired in many cases by Catholic bishops, expectation was high that Cameroon would have such a conference, and it was assumed that Cardinal Tumi would chair it. His comments are given great publicity; he gave a celebrated press conference in June 1990, in which he answered questions on the country's problems.[41] He gave an equally wide-ranging and celebrated interview in *Jeune Afrique Economie* in 1990.[42] He issued his own pastoral letter 'To All Christians and Men of Good Will' on 2 September 1992, outlining a Christian's obligations just before the presidential elections. In October 1994 he was summoned to the presidential palace for an hour's meeting with President Biya. This was the first item on TV news that evening, and 'Biya Receives Tumi' was the headline in several newspapers the following day.[43]

Individuals like Verdzekov and Tumi have undoubted moral authority, but the Catholic Bishops' Conference of Cameroon is not widely regarded as a player on the national scene. The conference has made strides towards unity, and in 1996 it even produced a pastoral letter 'Against Tribalism'.[44] Paradoxically, though, for a church which has such obvious problems, Cameroon's Catholic Church has leaders of continental stature. Verdzekov was one of the ten secretaries of the Synod of Bishops for Africa; Tumi was one of its three presidents, and president of the Symposium of

40   *Cameroon Tribune*, 9 Dec 1992, 1. At this the Catholic hierarchy *en bloc* (at the instiga-
      tion of the apostolic delegate) rallied to his defence and published and distributed his
      letter throughout the whole country.
41   Published as Cardinal Christian W. Tumi, *Texte Intégral de la conférence de presse donnée
      à Yaoundé le 11 Juin 1990*, n.p.
42   *Jeune Afrique Economie*, August 1990; another interview, *Herald*, 31 Oct-2 Nov 1994,
      3.
43   See, for example, the *Herald*'s headline 'Biya Receives Tumi! Has Dialogue begun? Or
      Will Tumi Chair Constitutional Talks?', *Herald*, 31 Oct-2 Nov 1994, 1; also *Messagère*,
      31 Oct 1994, 5; *La Nouvelle Expression*, 1-7 Nov 1994, 4-5.
44   *Effort*, 30 Nov-13 Dec 1996, 9-10.

Episcopal Conferences of Africa and Madagascar (SECAM) until the Synod, and thereafter a vice-president, having declined to stand for the presidency again. He is also something of a troubleshooter, being sent by Rome to resolve problems in other African countries. Thus of Africa's handful of internationally renowned Catholic bishops, two come from remote Cameroonian villages just a few miles from each other. To these two should be added Archbishop Zoa of Yaoundé, who achieved prominence at the time of the Second Vatican Council (1962-5), when he was effectively spokesman for Africa's francophone bishops. However, shortly after this the Ndongmo affair occurred, in which Zoa was perceived by Rome to have sided with the state against his fellow bishop. For not using his influence to mitigate the effects of this crisis, it is thought that he was subsequently marginalised by Rome. Certainly he is not the international figure that he looked like becoming in the 1960s.

Besides these, it must also be said that Cameroon is distinguished for its radical thinkers in a way that our other countries are not. Cameroon has produced Jean-Marc Ela, the former Jesuit Fabien Eboussi Boulaga, the Jesuits Englebert Mveng and Meinrad Hebga – all francophones, which leads some to claim that if the francophone sector is more undisciplined, it also has more scope for creativity and initiative. In some ways the situation is reminiscent of the Catholic Church before the Second Vatican Council; continental Europe produced independent thinkers in a way that ultramontane Britain, Ireland and the United States never did. Jean-Marc Ela is the nearest Africa has come to a liberation theologian in a Latin American sense, and indeed he is often cited to show that Africa does produce liberation theology. His books are published in the West, even translated into English, and he lectures regularly in Europe and Canada. He is an advocate of Christianity as humanisation, which influences his whole understanding of the role of the church. This strand of his thought is caught in a quotation like the following:

The human condition in today's Africa is characterised on the one hand, by the imperialism of the developed countries and the cultural and technological domination of the West, and on the other hand, by injustice and oppression, in all of its various forms ... ultimately, the denial to millions, individually and collectively, of their basic human freedoms, at the hands of bureaucracies that are rotten to the core.[...] The cry of the African – of the African human being – ought to move the churches to question themselves as to what they are, what they are saying, and what they are doing in Africa.[45]

For all his *réclame* in the West, it must be said that Ela has been totally

[45]   Jean-Marc Ela, *African Cry*, Maryknoll: Orbis, 1986, 137-8; also 'How can the African human being attain to a condition that will enable him and her to escape misery and inequality, silence and oppression? If Christianity seeks to be anything more than an effort to swindle a mass of mystified blacks, the churches of Africa must all join to come to terms with this question'(*ibid.*, vi).

marginalised (*'pas bien integré'* is the standard euphemism) in the Catholic Church in Cameroon. In the early 1990s he used to celebrate mass every Saturday evening in a parish near the University of Yaoundé, to which students would flock in their hundreds. This mass was quite an event, being marked both by liturgical inculturation and radical, socially aware sermons. Ela taught at the University of Yaoundé and at the Faculté Protestante, but not at Yaoundé's Catholic University. He was in Rome at the time of the 1994 Synod of Bishops for Africa, not as part of the official Cameroon delegation, but invited by an alternative group. When one enquired why he was so marginalised, different answers were given: that he is just writing for the West and what he writes has no bearing on the life of people in the villages;[46] or that he is a sociologist, not a theologian. The Catholic University insisted that it had nothing against him, and the students were free to invite him for occasional challenging talks, but it is another thing to entrust him with a sustained and coherent course of lectures extending over an entire academic year.

Eboussi Boulaga, also, is a thinker of some international reputation and considerable independence. For instance, after the Pope's visit in 1995, when everyone seemed to agree that 'inculturation' was the message of the African Synod, he wrote that he personally never used the word. It implied that culture was a static thing, which it is not; it was invoked for all the wrong reasons, like explaining (for as long as politicians could get away with it) why multi-party democracy is foreign to Africa; and the appeal to African cultures reached its *reductio ad absurdum* in the *authenticité* of Mobutu's Zaïre. It is human beings who produce cultures, and human beings of freedom and integrity should be the focus of the church's concern, not their cultural products.[47] Mveng in the field of culture and history and art, and Hebga in spirituality (most notably traditional healing) have both made sizeable contributions to the intellectual life of the Catholic Church in Africa.[48]

The Catholic Church is easily the biggest organisation in the country apart from the state itself. Even with its divisions, it has real leaders of considerable moral stature and intellectuals whose analyses carry weight. In some areas (most notably Zoa's Archdiocese of Yaoundé) it is involved

---

[46] However, see his *Les villages de la périphérie de Yaoundé en agonie? une église s'interroge*, Yaoundé: the author, 1991.

[47] *Messagère*, 4 Oct 1995, 7; Mbembe adopts the same view in *Afriques indociles*. Eboussi Boulaga has written extensively on inculturation: see his *Christianity without Fetishes*, Maryknoll: Orbis, 1984. Just as negative about 'inculturation' is *Herald*, 5-8 Oct 1995, 6.

[48] If the above-mentioned theologians are radical, Cameroon also has an articulate group of fiercely loyal academics too; see 'Lettre des Intellectuels et Universitaires Chrétiens à Sa Sainteté le Pape Jean-Paul II' delivered before the Pope in Yaoundé cathedral, 4 Sept 1995; in this they undertook to translate papal documents into local languages.

in combating oppression and injustice. For all these reasons it has constituted something of a threat – sufficiently to attract harassment from the state. The state in 1994 tried to set up a 'Tumi Affair' to discredit the Cardinal.[49] Catholic institutions have been the target of many suspicious physical attacks. Above all, priests and sisters have been murdered in mysterious incidents, most notoriously Mgr Yves Plumey, the retired Archbishop of Garoua, whose body was found in his house at Ngaoundéré on 4 September 1991. Since then twelve others have been murdered, including in mid-1995 Fr Mveng (a few weeks later Jean-Marc Ela fled into exile in Canada, alerted to probable attempts on his own life). All these murders remain unexplained; indeed there has been no real attempt by the authorities to solve them. It is widely believed that at least some are the work of government hit-squads, and part of a project to intimidate that element of the church that might threaten the state.[50]

In analysing the dynamics of Cameroon's Catholic Church we have given some importance to the missionary connection. We noted that in areas like the northern provinces, for example, the Catholic Church is effectively a missionary enterprise (in a way the Protestants would not contemplate). There are new forms of missionary involvement – the Focolari, the Emmaus Community, Pain de Vie and the Italian NGO Centro Orientamento Educativo.[51] Still, however, most missionaries belong to religious congregations, and, if not to those that established the church here, then to newer ones from Europe, from the former Eastern bloc, India, Latin America or other African countries. If some dioceses have marginalised them, many positively seek them, for all the skills,

---

[49]   Cassettes were circulating of phone conversations between the security services and a boy who was to plant arms in the Cardinal's house, to cause an incident that would force Rome to withdraw Tumi as it had Bishop Ndongmo in the 1970s.

[50]   The Cameroon Episcopal Conference issued a declaration dated 29 April 1995 on the death of Mveng, in which they claimed that lack of interest in solving any of the murders of Catholic personnel 'raises doubts' about the ability and goodwill of the authorities, hinting very bluntly about government connivance (*Cameroon Panorama*, June 1995, 2-3). The Pope on his September 1995 visit referred to this publicly, and the diplomatic temperature dropped considerably (see *Effort*, 23 Sept-6 Oct 1995, 11). The Pope's visit was fully covered in *Nleb Ensemble*, 1 Oct 1995; *Star Headlines*, 20 Sept 1995, 1 and 8; *Ouest Echos*, 21 Sept 1995, 6-7; and *Herald*, 21-24 Sept 1995, 4. The government tried to turn the visit to its advantage: see the RDPC party paper *L'Action*, 21 Sept 1995 and the government's *Cameroon Tribune*, 15 Oct 1995. Others sensationalised it: *Le Nouvel Indépendant* (18-25 Sept 1995, 10-12) saw an agenda of promoting Opus Dei, and claimed that Tumi and (prominent conservative Catholic) Mendo Ze were Opus Dei members, and that it had been behind the assassination of Mveng. *Hebdo* (9 Oct 1995, 4-5) saw the Pope coming to reform a church in chaos. For background to Mveng's murder, see *Le Nouvel Indépendant*, 25-31 Oct 1994, 4; *Africa International*, June-Aug 1995, 30-2.

[51]   For the Focolari in Cameroon, see *Appel*, 27 (1994), 31; for Pain de Vie, see *Effort*, 21 Sep-4 Oct 1996, 14.

resources and contacts they can bring. In 1993 Cameroon had nearly ninety women's congregations, with about 1,400 workers, of whom 800 were expatriates; and over thirty men's congregations, with 750 workers, of whom 560 were expatriates.[52] The Archdiocese of Yaoundé in 1995 had forty-four women's and twenty-nine men's congregations, the number increasing every year.[53]

The process of Africanising these congregations is evident in Cameroon no less than in other places. The phenomenon is most evident around the new Catholic University in Yaoundé: just off the campus, on adjoining properties, are new seminaries of the Marists, Oblates, Saints Apôtres, Pallotines, Missionaries of the Sacred Heart and Claretians. Within a few miles are other seminaries of the Vincentians and the Sacred Heart Fathers (of St Quentin). All cater for an average of thirty or forty students. Most are situated here to benefit from what the University has to offer, but these religious orders have also jointly established their own place of academic formation nearby, the theological school of St Cyprian. Not all their students are from Cameroon; many of these houses have candidates from other countries of the region, if not further afield. And normally the full training involves time elsewhere too.[54]

This phenomenon at Yaoundé is a good example of what is happening elsewhere on the continent – at Ibadan, at Jinja (as we have already noted), in Butare (before the destruction of Rwanda) and – most spectacularly of all – outside Nairobi, near the Catholic University of Eastern Africa. What we have just described is most obvious in the case of men's congregations, but the same is happening in congregations of women. However, since women's education has not been as advanced in Cameroon, their training houses are not near the University; up till now fewer of their numbers could profit from the opportunities the University offers. Most of these congregations are in the process of establishing themselves, and in no way constitute an independent pressure group within the church, much less *vis-à-vis* state or society – as they can be considered in some countries of Latin America or the Philippines.

We have here a great example of the way in which church organisations –

---

[52]   Statistics furnished by president of Religious Superiors, 11 Oct 1995.

[53]   Of the 464 religious in the archdiocese, 133 were Cameroonian, 85 French, 51 Italian, 42 Canadian and 38 Spanish (Annex to minutes of Religious Superiors' meeting, 8 Mar 1995).

[54]   For example, the Marists study theology in Yaoundé, but only after completing their philosophy in Senegal. The Capuchins do their novitiate in Madagascar. The Missionaries of the Sacred Heart do their novitiate in Zaïre, their philosophy in their home countries, their theology in Cameroon. The Sacred Heart Fathers (of St Quentin) study philosophy in Zaïre and theology in Cameroon. The Mill Hills do their philosophy in Uganda, their theology in London. The Pallotines do their philosophy and novitiate in Rwanda, their theology in Cameroon. The Marist Brothers after postulancy in Bamenda go to Ghana for novitiate and Nairobi for general academic studies.

here the religious congregations of the Catholic Church – provide new international networks and opportunities in the way suggested by Bayart's concept of extraversion. International networks are made possible by foreign funds, and introduce Africans to international travel, opportunities and international standards. Even in these seminaries students become used to private rooms (sometimes with ensuite bathrooms), hot running water, regular and substantial meals (sometimes including wine), private transport. This can give rise to considerable anomalies; congregations can spend up to 700,000 CFA per year on the training of an individual student, while their houses are situated among people who cannot find the 20,000 CFA a year to send a child to primary school. This discrepancy seems far more of a problem to congregations in Latin America than in Africa.

Mention was made above to Yaoundé's new Catholic University, more properly l'Université Catholique d'Afrique Centrale (UCAC), established in 1991 by the forty-two bishops of the six countries of the region.[55] As tertiary education has collapsed in Africa, Catholic universities have appeared at several places on the continent; by 1996 there were seven or eight, and others in various stages of planning. It cannot be said that they have proved a great success, with the exception of this one in Yaoundé, unquestionably the most professional of all. In 1996 it comprised two faculties, one of social sciences and management, and the other of theology. The former is entrusted to an international team of Jesuits. Besides the key posts in that faculty, the Jesuits hold the positions of vice-rector and librarian. All are men of considerable experience and competence. The expatriate vice-rector has a network of contacts, through which he has been able to raise funds in Europe; in 1995 he had sufficient funds, through an organisation 'Friends of UCAC' that he had established in France, to provide at least partial scholarships for 55% of the students, necessary if the University is not to become an enclave of the rich. Through other contacts he can arrange exchanges and links with European and Jesuit universities worldwide. His determination to relate the University to the reality of Cameroon is evident; in 1993 he co-founded a human rights research group, which in 1994 held an important colloqium on human rights in the region and published the proceedings speedily and professionally.[56] The theology faculty, by contrast, is in the hands of local clergy and is considerably less successful. One has just to visit the library and compare the periodicals in the two faculties to see the difference. UCAC illustrates so many of the points made above: as a

[55] ACERAC (Association of Episcopal Conferences of Central Africa), comprises Cameroon, the Central African Republic, Chad, Congo, Gabon and Equatorial Guinea.

[56] See Denis Maugenest et Paul-Gérard Pougoué, *Droits de l'homme en Afrique centrale. Colloque de Yaoundé 9-11 Novembre 1994*, Yaoundé/Paris: UCAC/Karthala, 1995.

university it scores so highly where it unashamedly draws on the skills, resources and networks provided by missionaries.

We have argued, in this discussion of Cameroon's Catholic Church, not that it is a foreign church, but that its external links are an integral part of its dynamics. Those foreign links, which no other churches can match, give it a particular character, for they give it access to personnel, many of whom have great education and skills, and to funding unavailable to other churches. In today's economic straits, patronage systems are collapsing all over Africa; here is one that can still function.[57] The question that inevitably arises here is that of the independence of the Catholic Church. It is clear that it enjoys no absolute independence. When abuses become particularly evident (or when Rome judges them so), Rome will eventually intervene. In Cameroon, it must be said, this intervention has been evident quite frequently, but even leaving aside dramatic cases where it has occurred, Rome has ultimate authority. Cardinal Tumi is effectively the head of the Catholic Church in Cameroon. He did not rise to that position in any of the ways Cameroon's other church leaders rose. He was appointed – because he was competent, certainly, but also because his loyalty is to Rome; his project is Rome's. This right of ultimate oversight is not to be underestimated, and as Cameroon's case shows, it can constitute an important act of political engineering. The most senior Catholic churchman had been Archbishop Zoa, often perceived as close to the regime. To make an anglophone both Cardinal and Archbishop of Douala, Cameroon's most important city, was to alter the whole perception of the Catholic hierarchy. Strictly Cardinal Tumi has no authority outside his own diocese, but his moral authority is so great, he personifies the Catholic Church in Cameroon. That some external agency can determine who should wield this authority is remarkable.

But equally remarkable is the use he can make of this authority. Cardinal Tumi was appointed not just because he was competent, but because he had shown integrity, accountability, leadership and vision. Manifesting these qualities further, he has been elected president of SECAM and one of the three presidents of the 1994 Pan-African Synod of Bishops. There are very few international Catholic donor agencies that would question requests from someone of that prominence; thus he can garner considerable resources. As an example, consider the Catholic newspaper *L'Effort Camerounais*. This began publication in 1955, and raised its voice

---

57   This is glimpsed in the following tribute to Bishop Cornelius Esua of the (anglophone) Kumbo Diocese: 'The multi-purpose modern complex structure acting as the Bishop's House: the many beautiful churches in almost all the villages: plans to renovate the Kumbo Cathedral before the year 2000, are all works of Bishop Esua which have earned him the title "Beggar". He usually asks for asistance from his friends in Germany and Italy as well as from his Christian community' (*Effort*, 2-15 Nov 1996, 14).

most courageously in the face of Ahidjo's attempt at total control.[58] It was forced to close in the period 1975-87, and again in 1992-4. Cardinal Tumi resurrected it in 1994, with the help of an Italian lay missionary movement. He put a missionary couple in charge, with the husband running the finances and the wife as editor-in-chief. Under their direction it has become a first-rate paper; educating, explaining, analysing. Through the networks of this missionary movement, *L'Effort* has been able to acquire the redundant presses of *L'Eco* of Bergamo, Italy. This is just a small example of the way missionaries and their resources make the Catholic Church a very different animal from Cameroon's Protestant churches, the most important of which we will now briefly consider.

The Protestant churches

We have already referred to the complicated histories of some Protestant churches, as missionary societies changed with British, German and then French rule, mentioning their 'centres of gravity' in the region and among the people where a mission began. The Eglise Presbytérienne Camerounaise (EPC) was founded in 1879 among the Bulu in the south by Americans of the Presbyterian Church of America, before the amalgamation of the American Presbyterian churches into the PCUSA; at that time American Presbyterian missionaries were allotted mission fields on the grounds of theological compatibility, and Cameroon was a mission field of the fundamentalist wing of the church. In the case of the EPC, links with the founding church have persisted unchanged. At one time there were over 100 American missionaries in Cameroon. Now there are only a handful. The church has officially about 100,000 members, although the numbers could be nearer 200,000 (because the church taxes parishes according to its numbers, the numbers tend to be underestimates[59]). The church has been described as '*indisciplinée et desordonnée*', a judgement which is perhaps somewhat lenient.[60] In 1996 the three most recent general secretaries had been dismissed, even defrocked, the second of these escaping to France with what were estimated to be millions of CFA. Lawsuits are in train against him, in an effort to recover some of this money. In the mid-1980s the church had over a billion CFA in the

---

[58] For its early history, see Jean-Paul Bayemi, *L'Effort Camerounais ou la tentation d'une presse libre*, Paris: Harmattan, 1989.

[59] In 1992 the official communicant members were 109,821, an increase of 3,820 on the previous year. but the report of the statistics committee notes that only one of the four synods filed returns, and the committee worked out the statistics for others. So the figures are 'quelques approximations, qui reflètent la place négligeable qu'occupent les statistiques dans notre église' (Minutes de la 35e Assemblée Générale, Ma'an, 22-29 Jan 1992, EPC, General Secretariat, Yaoundé, 1992, 193-94).

[60] *Appel*, 15 (1991), 19.

bank, but by 1994 not only had these funds disappeared but the church owed so much that if the EPC were to open an account in any bank the funds would be seized. Many claim that the church has been so riven by factions – mainly the ethnic groups of the Bulu, Bafia and Bassa – that it was close to splitting apart. But, as we have indicated in other instances in Cameroon, this charge of 'tribalism' may not be the fundamental issue. Consider the following case.

In the 1980s it became apparent to all that the EPC was slipping behind the Catholic Church and the Eglise Evangélique Camerounaise in evangelisation. In 1988 the EPC General Assembly set up a commission to study the evangelisation of Cameroon's major cities. In 1989 it recommended establishing parishes on the outskirts of major cities, and noted that no effort was being made along those lines in Yaoundé. In 1993 the General Council (the church's executive organ between General Assemblies) noted that despite the enormous growth of Yaoundé, the minutes of the EPC's Consistory there showed no serious involvement in evangelisation. At this time Yaoundé had over 1 million inhabitants, and the EPC had only six parishes. By contrast, in Douala, where it is only a minority church and a latecomer (this being the stronghold of the Eglise Evangélique and the Baptists), it already had fifteen parishes. Likewise, in Yaoundé, which was historically EPC territory, the Eglise Evangélique had already nine parishes (and the Catholics nearly fifty). The General Council therefore took the decision to take the city of Yaoundé out of the hands of the Yaoundé Consistory and entrust it to all four synods and nineteen consistories of the EPC. This recommendation, accompanied by strong criticism of the Yaoundé Consistory, was confirmed by the 37th General Assembly of January 1994, which proclaimed Yaoundé a 'mission field [*champ d'evangélisation*]' open to all consistories. The Yaoundé Consistory objected that this plan would lead to duplication, overlapping and chaos. So the General Assembly asked a *Comité de Stratégie* to partition the city into zones, a task which it had completed by March 1994. According to this plan, the city centre was left to the Yaoundé Consistory, but the suburbs were distributed among the four synods.

Meanwhile, on 18 February the Yaoundé Consistory had written to the General Council expressing its submission to the will of the General Assembly. However, it continued, the General Assembly should take account of the disorder that would follow the application of the plan. The Consistory 'officially and publically disclaimed all responsibility if tribal and sectarian infiltrations brought disturbance and disorder to Yaoundé as in the past.'[61] This may have expressed just a fear, but many understood it as a threat, especially as the Consistory went on to say that

---

[61] All Yaoundé's newspapers covered this in some depth. The quotations here are taken

it would keep its territory ('land belongs to its first occupants'), and copied the letter to the security services.

In April 1994 the General Secretary invited the synods to begin activity in their new areas despite what he called threats of destabilisation made by elements within the Yaoundé Consistory. In July the first service conducted by a synod from outside Yaoundé was broken up by security forces. A few days later the provincial governor summoned a meeting of the General Secretary and representatives of the Yaoundé Consistory, and asked the General Secretary to delay the implementation of the General Assembly's strategy. Many claim that the governor uttered this injunction at the bidding of the powerful political forces who are elders in the Yaoundé parishes and close to the pastors. This was the understanding of the General Secretary, who declined to comply, arguing that the state had no right to interfere in the affairs of the church.

On 7 August various pastors of external consistories held a public service around the headquarters of the EPC to deplore the attitude of the Yaoundé Consistory and denounce 'the involvement of civil servants and politicians in the internal affairs of the EPC'. The tension came to a head in October 1994 when security services used tear-gas and clubs to disperse worshippers at a service conducted by a pastor from an outside consistory. Several needed hospitalisation, and one pastor lost an eye. The Yaoundé Consistory blamed the General Secretary for summoning the military; he in turn insisted that the Yaoundé pastors themselves had summoned them.[62] Even before this the General Council had condemned the Yaoundé Consistory, and denounced seven pastors and an elder to the Permanent Judicial Commission of the EPC for involving government authorities in the affairs of the church, something forbidden in the EPC constitution (citing 1 Corinthians). The Yaoundé Consistory in its turn rejected the competence of the Judicial Commission to judge them.

The Judicial Commission was due to give its decision on 27 October 1994 at the EPC headquarters. The Sunday before, the Yaoundé pastors had asked all their Christians to assemble around the headquarters on the day of the verdict (the most obvious explanation of this is that, fearing the decision would go against them, they wanted to intimidate the commission). However, at 1 a.m. on the morning of 27 October the provincial governor issued an edict forbidding until further notice any meetings of the General Assembly, General Council or Permanent Judicial

---

from two 'dossiers' in *Kunde Mensuel*, Nov 1994, 6-7, and *Génération*, 2-8 Nov 1994, 7-11.

[62] . The Executive Secretary of the Yaoundé Consistory certainly defended the soldiers' actions: 'There is a saying that the land belongs to those who occupy it first. What had to happen has happened; the vandals have been put in their place ... When the church disturbs public order, the man in charge has to exercise his responsibility' (*Kunde*, Nov 1994, 7).

Commission within the Central Province. About 2 a.m., solders took control of the entire area and turned back members of the Judicial Commission when they arrived to give their verdict. Thus the *status quo* was preserved, with the help of government forces.

In this incident, obviously, there is an ethnic element; this is sometimes alluded to. Cameroon is undergoing a process of urbanisation; people are flocking to Yaoundé from all areas, and when they arrive they gravitate to areas settled by kinsfolk. This is why the committee that drew up the areas of demarcation stipulated that services must be in French as well as a vernacular language; they did not want a parish becoming purely ethnic. But, this said, ethnicity is not the basic issue. The basic issue is '*la politique du ventre*'. There were six big parishes in Yaoundé, with considerable institutions. This gave the pastors of these parishes status, position, wealth and access to power – prizes to be held on to. By the same token, those seeking to come in were not motivated entirely by evangelisation: in the words of one of Yaoundé's most prominent pastors, 'This business is about money. They say that Pastor Moubitang has a Mercedes, Pastor Azambo has a car, the pastors in Yaoundé are rich, and they want to come to Yaoundé themselves to get rich too.'[63] Basically, this is a struggle for spoils, and by and large it is seen as this: 'God's Dollars [*Les Dollars de Dieu*]', was the heading of one newspaper account of this affair. In this same account one pastor described it as 'a business about livelihood and resources'. Another pastor is quoted as saying: 'I would much prefer to be an assistant pastor in a good parish in Yaoundé or Douala than in charge in Babimbi where the Sunday offerings hardly reach 700 CFA.' This article describes the EPC's two kinds of pastors – country and city – and continues (quoting the Cameroon proverb that Bayart has popularised): 'Undoubtedly in the EPC a pastor grazes where he is tethered. So you can understand the determination of small rural pastors to tether themselves elsewhere.' It outlines the benefits of being a city pastor, particularly one of those 'who administer the aid coming from American missionaries, and especially those who manage all the economic structures like schools, hospitals, and property'.[64]

This general perception that the EPC is driven by '*la politique du ventre*' is perhaps the greatest reason why American missionaries have left. They are embarrassed by its greed and mismanagement. They, unlike Rome, cannot interfere. On the contrary, sensitive to charges of racism or neo-colonialism, they have painted themselves into a corner with the vocabulary of 'partnership'. The Americans had taken this to the lengths of ceasing to send money designated for scholarships for ministerial

---

63   Quoted in *Génération*, 2-8 Nov 1994, 8.
64   *Ibid.*, 10. Another account notes: 'There is a strong smell of money in the city parishes of Yaoundé' (*L'Express Plus*, 28 Oct 1994, 8).

students, on the grounds that it was not for them to lay down what their aid should be spent on. Thus what used to be specially designated scholarship money was simply included in their general grant. As a result, students who used to be assisted financially are no longer, and what the former scholarship money is now spent on no one knows. Other Protestant bodies (at least until about 1995) have adopted the same approach. The Executive Committee of the World Alliance of Reformed Churches was hosted by the EPC in mid-1995, but would not take it upon itself to comment on the internal disorder of the church.[65]

There is another important point here. Obviously, as we have seen, in a hierarchical structure like that of the Catholic Church, a bishop is a law unto himself. This can lead to a situation like those in Douala in the 1980s and Nkongsamba, where eventually Rome intervened. And Rome is generally accepted as being unchallengeable; as we saw, the Bishop of Nkongsamba just signed the paper put in front of him and left quietly. Even in the cases of Cardinal Tumi and Archbishop Verdzekov, where no one implies that there is anything but strict probity in finances, there is no check on them. But in a Presbyterian system, it is sometimes said, we have something essentially different: here are elections, a constitution, committees, synods, assemblies – in a word, popular participation and legal procedures that must be followed at every step. But it has not worked like that. In the United States, whence the EPC was founded, a pastor is a teaching elder; the others are governing elders and the pastor is not in control. But the church in Cameroon was not established that way. Missionaries came and attempted to replicate their Presbyterian structures, but in fact the missionaries maintained control, and this was the lesson left to Africans. When this was added to the local conception of a chief, the pastors ended up in total control.

The case of the Yaoundé Consistory has many legal elements. In the opinion of many, even a church commission cannot resolve things because it is considered standard procedure to stack any commission from the outset.[66] Some argue that this whole matter has been handled uncon-

---

[65] The noble 'Yaoundé declaration' after this meeting of 26 July-1 Aug 1995 is found in *World Alliance of Reformed Churches Update*, Sept 1995, 4-6.

[66] Some hold that the establishment of parishes within the city which nevertheless do not belong to the Presbytery of Yaoundé but to presbyteries in other areas is against the church's constitution; to set up more parishes may indeed be the sensible way to go forward, but if so, the constitution should be changed first, rather than proceeding in violation of the constitution. Those holding this view would also say that the decision to establish these new parishes was taken at an illegal synod, the 1992 assembly having broken up after it was assembled and shifted to Yaoundé; according to the constitution a general assembly once convened must be concluded in the place of convening, and if such a transfer takes place, a new assembly must be constituted. Moreover, most espousing this view of unconstitutionality also hold that the Judicial Commission has

stitutionally all along the way.[67] Even the dismissal of general secretaries was not done through due process. Certainly the EPC has all those synods, assemblies, committees – in exactly the same way as the state has its judiciary, assembly and rights guaranteed by the constitution. The parallel is apt, because the EPC is just like the state, even a mirror of it – which in many respects is not surprising. A newspaper headline, 'The EPC – Colony of the Government?' ('*L'EPC – Colonie du Renouveau*?' where *Renouveau* signifies the RDPC government), gives the impression of two distinct if interlocking realities.[68] In fact the state and the EPC are just aspects of the same reality. The same personnel make up both. One account of this episode lists the state personnel who are elders in Yaoundé's EPC parishes: the head of the armed forces, the director of presidential security, the former acting general of the Sûreté Nationale, the former director of political affairs of the security services, and so on.[69] This is Bayart's rhizome state (see above, p. 7) in all its glory.

So can the EPC act as a challenge to, or as check on, the state? It is split into three groups, the Bassa, Bulu, and Bafia. Biya is of the Bulu group, and that group in the church is strong in his support. Some of the others are less warm, so the church finds it difficult to take a position on any public matter. In general however, it mounts no challenge to Biya. At its general assemblies it traditionally sends a message of support to the President. In 1985 this included: 'We promise you our total support for the realisation of the cultural and socio-economic programme for Cameroon.'[70] The 1992 message merits quotation at more length:

Given the respect for religious liberty and the lay nature of our state as envisaged by the constitution;
Given that according to its confession of faith, the EPC obeys state authorities and has the duty to advise them in the fulfillment of their delicate task;
Given that in this period of great political change, the government has not ceased to exert praiseworthy and charismatic efforts to increase public awareness of the trends to national unity and peace, an indispensable condition for the success of our struggle against the economic crisis and underdevelopment;
Given the consensus reached during the tripartite meeting in Yaoundé, thanks to

---

been stacked by the current General Secretary, himself from another area, who is determined to control the pastors of Yaoundé.

67   The account in *L'Express Plus*, 28 Oct 1994, 2 and 8, argues that the procedures against the Yaoundé pastors were 'unconstitutional'; disciplinary cases are outside the powers of the General Council, which can be invoked only on appeal, after due processes at a lower level.

68   *Génération*, 2-8 Nov 1994, 10.

69   *Ibid.*

70   Minutes de la 28e Assemblée Générale, 9-13 Jan 1985, EPC, General Secretariat, Yaoundé, 1985, 83.

which God has allowed Cameroon to rediscover its usual calm, and Cameroonians to resume activity interrupted during the ordeals and turbulence which have recently afflicted our country;
[The delegates] address to His Excellency Paul Biya, President of the Republic of Cameroon, their profound gratitude and encouragement.[...]
Assure him of the EPC's total and unconditional support in every struggle whose aim is to unite Cameroonians and to establish peace and social justice.[...]
May Almighty God bless you in the accomplishment of your difficult task.[71]

Given that this period of crisis was marked by the attempts of the opposition to force a national assembly, such statements are seen to be definitely partisan.[72]

Let us turn now to another Presbyterian church, the Presbyterian Church of Cameroon (PCC), founded in 1884 by the Basel Mission, with which it maintains strong links. Even though it became independent in 1957, its finances until 1993 were handled by a Basel missionary.[73] In 1995 it still had about twenty-five 'fraternal workers' (or missionaries). Most of the missionaries were from the Basel Mission, although it has others from other German sources – Dienst in Uebersee, Christoffel Blindenmission and Deutschentwicklungshilfe. Its official 1995 statistics claimed 235,000 members in 1,197 congregations. Its membership is almost entirely in the anglophone provinces. As remarked above, the anglophones are not a homogeneous ethnic group, and there is some tension between the people of the grasslands in the north and the coastal forest peoples to the south. The church has thus two different women's centres, and two different youth centres – even two different Bibles. Its constitution admits this tension in stipulating that the moderator and the synod clerk (or general secretary) 'shall not be indigenes of one and the same province' (no. 133).

The PCC illustrates a characteristic of Presbyterian churches throughout West Africa. In most of the founding ones the office of moderator is largely symbolic and ceremonial and for a very limited period, usually

---

71 Minutes de la 35e Assemblée Générale, Ma'an, 22-29 Jan 1992, EPC, General Secretariat, Yaoundé, 1992, 203.

72 In 1991, at the time of opposition strikes, the EPC issued a communiqué (undated) to the effect that (*'Fort de ce que l'EPC n'a jamais rien rapproché au gouvernement du Renouveau'*) during the period of strikes, any of its teachers who arrived late for work without a valid excuse would be considered to have resigned. Compare Joseph's very positive assessment of the EPC's role in challenging colonial structures: Joseph, *Radical Nationalism*, esp. 29-31, 133-4.

73 A good deal of PCC history can be found in its silver jubilee publication, Nyansako-ni-Nku (ed.), *Journey in Faith: the Story of the Presbyterian Church in Cameroon*, Buea: PCC, 1982. Its budget in 1994-5 was 456 million CFA (*Presbyterian Newsletter*, Oct 1994, 3); that for 1995-6 was 518 million CFA (circular of 28 April, 1995).

only one or two years. However, in West Africa in the 1960s a movement developed to give this office some power; the office of general secretary (or synod clerk) was shorn of some of its power which was handed over to the moderator. In this way the moderator of some of these Presbyterian churches has assumed some of the powers of an archbishop. Not only have his powers increased, but his term of office has been extended. A reluctance to step down has become evident. According to the PCC constitution, the moderator is allowed two terms of five years, with a third term permitted 'in exceptional circumstances' (no. 142). In 1994 the PCC moderator put himself forward again for a third term and was duly elected. Many are at a loss to discern the 'exceptional circumstances' that demanded this.[74]

The PCC has also involved itself in political debate, making statements and sending open messages to the President, Prime Minister and other authorities on public issues, which have been collected in a single volume. These interventions are respectful, well expressed, and often quite brave – calls for a national forum, an electoral code, an independent electoral commission, and so on. However, never far from the surface are signs of the specifically anglophone complaints of exploitation, dispossession, discrimination and benign neglect, and specifically anglophone demands for a proper bilingualism, a federal structure and the British-derived education system. Protests about torture and firing on peaceful demonstrators are not about torture and demonstrations in general, but about particular cases which happened in anglophone provinces, to anglophones. And the statement before the presidential elections in which the leaders state that 'our duty is not to direct anybody who to vote for' seems a little disingenuous. They claim impartiality and urge readers to vote for the candidate who fits certain criteria: 'Who do we trust has the integrity to stop the massive corruption and institutionalised looting of public funds, which is now common practice in our country? Who do we trust can turn this rapidly declining economy around? Who do we trust can ... make every Cameroonian really feel at home here?' The answer to such questions could not be President Paul Biya, who over ten years has been responsible for all these evils. Since the only other genuine candidate was John Fru Ndi, it had to be him. And since he happened to be an anglophone (even a member of the PCC, and reputedly a friend of the leadership as well) it is not surprising that these statements have been taken by others as partisan. Probably this was unavoidable. The PCC is a regional church, and its leaders bravely and eloquently articulated the preoccupations of the members. That needed to be done. But their sociopolitical involvement comes across as lobbying for particular interests, the sort of thing any other educated body like lawyers or academics or

[74]   Recall the case of the Ghanaian Evangelical Presbyterian Church discussed on pp. 74-6 above.

journalists could do, rather than – despite the odd reference to 'divine calling' or 'prophetic responsibility' and the occasional biblical text and the invariable final exhortation to prayer – any social or liberation theology of the kind Jean-Marc Ela has elaborated.[75]

After the bitter political confrontation subsided somewhat about 1992, the PCC developed another strong tension, which has threatened to split the church apart. This arises from 'revival' – essentially the Pentecostalisation of the PCC. In April 1994 the Synod issued 'guidelines' for revival, declaring that every church needs it, but PCC revival 'is not to be an imitation of Pentecostalism', nor would it 'adopt Pentecostal mannerisms', and no exclusive claims about baptism by immersion or glossalalia would be permitted. On 11 April the following year the Synod Committee (the Synod proper was unable to meet because of costs) issued another 'Special Statement on Revival'. This repeated that the PCC 'in principle' encourages revival, but resolved that 'Pastors, elders and other church leaders of the PCC who in the name of "revival" are engaged in doctrinal and liturgical practices which are not in consonance with those of the PCC, shall be asked to desist from such practices, latest December 31 1995.' Any who did not comply would be dismissed if they were pastors, and would lose their leadership position in the case of elders.[76] If they continued even in spite of these measures, they would lose their membership in the PCC. This caused quite a storm: the most high-profile offender publicly called the ban unconstitutional and demanded that the moderator and synod clerk be dismissed.[77] What the result of this tussle will be remains to be seen. But two things are important. First, Cameroon is still at that stage where a church can think it will win against Pentecostalisation (recall the Baptists in Ghana). Secondly and more important, the PCC is a disciplined, ordered and structured church which values those structures and insists on them. It is not accepted that anything goes. It has discipline and rules, and the leadership will (try to) enforce them. In this the anglophone PCC and the anglophone Catholic dioceses are similar, as distinct from the EPC and the francophone Catholic

---

75   Nyansako-ni-Nku, *Cry Justice*. The quotation is from the statement, signed by both the moderator and the synod clerk, 'Your Christian Conscience and the Presidential Elections', 35-8. The dean of the Faculté Protestante, also from the PCC, was a known friend of John Fru Ndi (see *Génération*, 2-8 Nov 1994, 11), who preached fiery denunciations of the government. Six days after the March 1992 parliamentary elections he preached in Yaoundé's main PCC church: 'The people spoke on the 1st of March. And it was God who spoke. The people said no to the Rosicrucian regime.' A short time before, in another sermon, he had preached: 'God is telling the Rosicrucian mafia with its ringleader, the time has come for me to rescue the peoples of this nation and I have already chosen someone I will use'; in the context the someone chosen by God is obviously Fru Ndi.

76   Statement dated 11 April 1995. Other statements dealing with this problem are dated 12 Jan 1993; 26 Sept 1994; 24 April 1995; 20 Sept 1995.

77   *Herald*, 13-15 April 1995, 1; *Herald* 17-19 April 1995, 1.

dioceses. However, there is a big difference between the ways the Catholic and the PCC churches (the two most affected so far) handle this issue. The Catholics have done everything they can to prevent its becoming an issue; the PCC has met it head-on.

The Eglise Evangélique Camerounaise (EEC) is the biggest of all Cameroon's reformed churches, with between 500,000 and a million members.[78] Its origins are complicated. The activity of Alfred Saker's (London) Baptist Missionary Society (1843-84) was taken over by the Basel Mission (1886-1914) when Cameroon became a German colony. When the Germans were expelled the Paris Mission Society took their place (1917-57). The church became independent in 1957, and for most of its independent life it was run by a rather charismatic but very dominant President, Kotto. He had two qualities of some importance for the church. He came from a very small ethnic group, and therefore (like Ahidjo on the national scene) had no choice but to involve all the others. Secondly, because he was prominent in the international ecumenical world and trusted entirely by European missionary agencies, he could attract immense resources. He used this patronage quite even-handedly, and the church grew greatly. The EEC's main groups are the Bamileke and the Bamoun, although it has sizeable minorities like the Duala. In the early 1990s Kotto was moved aside in something of a coup, and before long the Bamileke were seen to be in control, raising again all the fears of a takeover by them. This has led to great tension within the church, many claiming (especially among the Duala) that all the spoils – the resources, jobs, scholarships – are going to that group. The conflict came to a head at the church's 41st General Synod in early 1997, which was wrecked by the two groups fighting for control of the church. First, the treasurer drew attention to the financial deficit incurred in 1996, and the flouting of the constitution by the office holders. Then the financial commission reported that it had not been able to complete its work because of the lack of key documents (this, as the church's own magazine states, may have been true, or may have been an electoral ploy on the part of the office-seekers to discredit the incumbents). The Synod descended into such spectacular

[78] Besides the EPC and the PCC which we have described above, there are the Eglise Protestante Africaine (EPA), and the Eglise Presbytérienne Ortodoxe (EPO). The EPA was formed by Kassio people who broke away from the predominantly Bulu EPC in 1934, chiefly because they had long been thwarted in their demands for preaching in their own language. It is a narrowly ethnic church, with about 7,000 members in 1995. (See *Appel*, Nov-Dec 1992, 26). The EPO is found mainly in the south of the country. It too has ethnic origins. Many Bulu considered the EPC a Bulu church, and when a Bassa was elected general secretary, they broke away to form the EPO.

disorder that no elections were possible; eventually a compromise was reached under which the five office-holders were to remain in office for a period of two more years while problems were addressed, after which they could not be re-elected. The church's own publication acknowledged sadly that in so publicly fighting for spoils the church had 'forgotten that it was the body of Christ'.[79]

The Union des Eglises Baptistes Camerounaises (UEBC) too traces its origins back to Saker and the Baptist Missionary Society and subsequently to the Basel Mission (and the Baptist Mission of Berlin) and then the Paris Mission Society. The church in 1995 had about 70,000 members, and has spread far beyond its heartland; it has had foreign missionaries in the north since 1954. All churches want German links; the UEBC has a historical claim to them, and its Secretary General since 1972, himself trained in Germany, has developed these considerably. He has been something like a favourite son of German agencies, although relations cooled somewhat in the mid-1990s mainly because of the size of the new headquarters he built. Like the Presbyterian, the Baptist polity is strong on democratic participation. But the General Secretary has trained a successor in Germany. If the networks and resulting aid are to be maintained, his candidate effectively becomes the only serious contender to succeed him.

When the Basel mission ceded control to Cameroonians in 1957, it left its institutions – schools, hospitals, printing press and land – jointly to its two daughter churches, the EEC and the UEBC, to be administered by a joint board CEBEC (Conseil des Eglises Baptistes et Evangéliques du Cameroun). For the first ten years this board functioned quite well, but since about 1967 there have been enormous problems. These basically concern resources, because institutions bring money. The Basel missionaries had preferred the highlands of the interior to the heat of the coast, and consequently most of their institutions are to be found inland, in the EEC heartland rather than in the UEBC heartland nearer Douala. The EEC wants to dissolve CEBEC and let the local churches assume responsibility. They argue that CEBEC has become a 'super-church', and the doctors, nurses and teachers think they are employees of CEBEC rather than attached to an individual church. But they also think that geography favours them and that by liquidating CEBEC the EEC will gain possession of most of the institutions. The UEBC realises full well

[79] The synod is covered at length in *Appel*, March-Apr 1997. The reason given for reforming financial controls was not surprisingly 'to gain the greater confidence of our partner churches' (*ibid.*, 7). EEC is prominent in the Communauté Evangélique d'Action Apostolique (CEVAA), the body of churches associated with the Paris Mission (see esp. *Appel* 36 (1995). The church makes much of its involvement in ecumenical bodies, and in 1995 had about ten missionaries or *coopérantes*.

what is at stake (as one Baptist leader bluntly put it: 'The Bamileke [his label for the EEC leaders] want ...'). The UEBC say they have no objections to winding up CEBEC, but in that case the constitution is quite clear that the institutions must be distributed between the churches equally. The result is an impasse.

Besides the UEBC, there is another Baptist Church prominent around Douala, the Eglise Baptiste Camerounaise/Native Baptist Church (EBC/NBC). As noted above, the Baptists were the first missionaries in Cameroon, but when the Basel Mission took over their work in 1884, they attempted to restrict the substantial autonomy of the local churches. This led to a rupture in 1888, when the NBC constituted itself an independent church. The Basel Mission protested to the German colonial authorities, who banned the NBC from competing in the Basel Mission's area of activity. This has restricted the NBC to the area around Douala. The NBC sets great store on African culture. They do not forbid polygamy, and are said to include many who have close links with the local pre-Christian religion of the area.[80] Services are in Duala, with no translation; those which this writer has attended have always stressed the motifs of resisting colonisation and remaining true to themselves; invariably they have compared their triumphant struggle for cultural authenticity to that of Nelson Mandela (although this area is francophone, they set great store by the word 'Native' in the rather cumbersome title of their church). It is hard to find accurate statistics for the EBC/NBC; in the mid-1990s estimates range from 10,000 to 40,000 members.

The dynamics of this church shed light on those of contemporary African Christianity more widely. By 1990, for all its glorying in African culture and its independence, the church was clearly dying. Its poverty was obvious, the services were lifeless, with no instruments to accompany the choirs. The flagship church in Douala had been under construction for years, and remained an uncompleted shell. Even the graves of Lotin Samé and other founders had fallen into disrepair.[81] It had only one trained Cameroonian pastor, and was led by an old man, poorly educated, speaking only Duala. Without French or English he could not take part in Cameroon's ecumenical meetings, much less join the international bodies from which the benefits flow. Thus in the early 1990s a small group led by the only trained pastor (he was part-time since he also worked for Elf Aquitaine) realised that the church would have to

[80]   For a fascinating view, almost an insider's, of the traditional religious world of Douala, see Eric de Rosny, *Healers in the Night*, Maryknoll: Orbis, 1985.

[81]   For the church in its prime, see Richard A. Joseph, 'Church, State, and Society in Colonial Cameroun', *International Journal of African Historical Studies* 13 (1980), 5-32.

change or die. Pastors would have to be trained. Development projects would have to be undertaken. There was no hope of change under the old leader, who refused to step down, arguing that by doing so he would lose his livelihood. He had some support, due to members showing respect for their elder. The reformers mobilised for the 1995 church elections, and their church coup was successful. The new president immediately began to work for membership of the World Council of Churches, gaining admittance in September. Then he set off to Britain to establish links with the Baptist Missionary Society there, and sought similar links elsewhere. He tried to make the coup as painless as possible, even giving the former president the title 'President Emeritus'. But the crisis could not be avoided; older pastors who supported the old man were cast aside. At the time of writing, the church is on the verge of splitting.

The NBC gloried in its autonomy and championing of local culture for 100 years. But there is no mileage in that now. In Africa's current circumstances the church was falling further behind others, and in real danger of disappearing. Hence the ecclesiastical coup. In confirmation that a key dynamic in Africa's churches is finance, in the 1980s the EBC/NBC had formed a 'federation' with the UEBC (theoretically established to seek union, but nobody realistically expected that). In the federation constitution it was noted that the federation would operate without prejudice to the external links 'already entered into by the individual churches'. This meant that the EBC/NBC had no claim on the links the UEBC had formed already. But the new head of the EBC/NBC has quickly attempted to change this.[82]

Finally, there are two smaller churches, which both confirm the importance of extraversion and provide a slight variation. First, the Lutheran

---

[82] The third Baptist church is the Cameroon Baptist Convention (CBC), centred on the Grasslands of the North-West Province. It too sees its origins in Saker and the BMS, but its growth came after the Second World War (see Lloyd E. Kwast, *The Discipling of West Cameroon: a Study of Baptist Growth*, Grand Rapids: Eerdmans, 1971). It became independent in 1954 with 218 congregations and 18,000 Christians. In 1994 it claimed 745 congregations and 70,000 Christians (although others would give half this figure). In recent years they attempted to open a mission field in Equatorial Guinea, but had to close it from lack of funds. The church is assisted by the North American Baptist Convention, the Baptist General Conference, and Regions Beyond Missionary Union. About 95% of the CBC's budget comes from the United States. The NAB and BGC have involved themselves with institutions like hospitals and the seminary, but are talking more now about leaving the institutions to the nationals, and moving into other things – like converting the Fulani. The RBMU has come most recently, to work among the Fulani and the Pygmies of the South-east. As observers note, it is highly unlikely that the CBC would have opted for either work; these are basically American interests, which the church acquiesces in because of the benefits arising from the missionary involvement.

Church in Cameroon (LCC).[83] In 1995 this numbered about 1,700 members in about twenty communities organised in five parishes. This is not a mission-established church. The head was a pastor in the Full Gospel Church (see below), who fell out of favour with his leadership. He came to Kumba where, because of the Nigerian Civil war, a group of Nigerian Lutherans of a church founded by the Wisconsin Synod had settled. They needed a pastor, and he had had some training, so he took the post. For fifteen years Americans of the Wisconsin Synod came to give annual seminars to prepare candidates for ordination. Over several years, an arrangement was reached whereby the Cameroonian Lutherans became part of this Wisconsin network. Wisconsin paid $2,000 a month, and in 1994 two Americans arrived in Cameroon to establish a Bible school. The school, offering a five-year course, opened in 1995 with fifteen students. Because of the small membership of the church, naturally most of these students were not life-long Lutherans; for geographical reasons nearly all were former Catholics and Presbyterians. The church requires that they be Lutherans for two years before they can be admitted to the school.[84] The Americans are 'partners', but are aware that providing 99% of the church's finances means that their control is hardly likely to be challenged.[85]

Exactly the same dynamic exists in the even smaller United Pentecostal Church (UPC). It too is not a mission church, being founded by a Cameroonian who was likewise a former Full Gospel pastor. He had gone to Nigeria for a T.L. Osborn crusade in 1974. There he came within the orbit of Nigeria's UPC church, and eventually returned to Cameroon and established the church there. In 1993 an American missionary joined the Cameroonian UPC headquarters in Bamenda. This American link has enabled the church to open a Bible school, the funds being provided by an American women's group. Here too nearly all the students were former Catholics and Presbyterians.

---

[83] There are two much bigger Lutheran Churches in the north. First, the Eglise Evangélique Luthérienne du Cameroun (EELC), founded in 1960 from the Norwegian and American Lutheran missions, and centred on Ngaoundéré; in 1995 it numbered about 115,000 members. For the EELC's dependence on external funding and its role as a vehicle for Gbaya ethnic interests, see Philip Burnham, *The Politics of Cultural Difference in Northern Cameroon,* Edinburgh University Press, 1996, 85-91. Second and further north, the Eglise Fraternelle Luthérienne au Cameroun (EFLC), founded by an American mission in 1918, becoming autonomous in 1964.

[84] The Lutheran missionaries seem aware that there is no reason why young Cameroonians should trouble themselves greatly about sixteenth-century divisions in Europe, or even twentieth-century intra-Lutheran American splits.

[85] Kumba is also the centre of Cameroon's Anglican Church, essentially a church of Igbos from Nigeria. The province of West Africa is raising it from a missionary district to a missionary diocese, even though it comprises only six churches, and despite border tension over the disputed Bakassi peninsula in 1995 which led many Igbos to return home.

The LCC and UPC cases are similar in that their financial help is not from a major agency with open-ended commitment and relatively inexhaustible funds. The Lutheran venture is a five-year contract. The Americans will continue this link only if the Cameroonians of the LCC take up the challenge. If they do, the Americans will continue to help. If they do not, at the end of that time the Americans will withdraw. They will also withdraw if the LCC seeks links elsewhere (as it did surreptitiously in Germany). The exercise is a 'short sharp shock' treatment in taking responsibility and owning the whole enterprise. Similarly with the UPC. The American missionary has made himself extremely unpopular by refusing to deliver substantial resources. He insists that the Cameroonians should stand on their own feet, but they insist he is demanding too much of them too quickly. He refuses to compromise.[86] In both cases the outside connections will make them independent and responsible or will cease. Obviously this is exactly what is not the case with so much mainline church assistance.

The born-again community

There are two born-again churches which are fairly strong and can be regarded as established, though neither is in the same league as any of the mainline churches discussed above. One is the Apostolic Church, of British origin, which came to Cameroon from Nigeria and is now a presence in the anglophone area. In Cameroon the church had in 1995 a handful of Swiss missionaries.

The second is the Full Gospel Church. In 1931 a handful of Pentecostal churches in Germany joined in a body called 'Vereinigte Missionsfreunde' (United Mission Friends) for involvement in foreign missions. They began in China, but the Second World War destroyed their efforts overseas. In the late 1950s missionaries were again sent out, this time to Australia and Africa. One of those sent to the Cross River area of Nigeria made exploratory trips across to Cameroon which he thought was ripe for Pentecostal evangelism. In 1961 he established a mission station at Mutengene, not far from Limbe, and involved Nigerian assistants. Great emphasis was put on evangelism from the start. In 1969 the church was legally established. In 1970 a permanent Bible school

---

[86] The UPC General Secretary feels responsible for his pastors: 'Other Churches can give their pastors medical benefits and pensions. I can do nothing.' He has been forced to look elsewhere for assistance, but as a Jesus-only (or non-Trinitarian) Pentecostal, this is difficult. 'If I was a Trinitarian, I could have found it already.' A South African has made overtures to assist, but the general secretary (a man of some principle) does not want to be disloyal. However, 'If I found an opening, I would welcome it.' The general secretary's position is made more difficult because one of his pastors left to join the Apostolic Church, and quickly moved to Europe on a scholarship; the other pastors 'are all talking about this'.

was established at Bamenda. The Germans were helped by English missionaries and from America by missionaries of the Assemblies of God, who worked with the Full Gospel Church rather than beginning a church of their own. The church runs two health centres and a home economics centre, but the primary emphasis is still evangelism. It has always been strongest in the anglophone area – there are nine churches in Bamenda city alone – but from 1970 it also had a presence in the francophone region. In 1995, of the first-year students in the Bible school, seven were anglophone and twenty francophone. This opening to the whole nation was symbolised by moving the national headquarters from Bamenda to Douala in that year. The missionary founder is still in the country, but a Cameroonian has been General Superintendent since 1986. The church was quite small until about 1990, since when a minor boom has taken place. Some of their authorities attribute this to the politico-economic upheavals in the area over this period. In the words of one official, 'Politics lead nowhere, there is no way out. As in the time of Jesus they were expecting deliverance from the Romans, and had to turn elsewhere.' Such a boom leads to a situation in which, of the twenty-seven first-year Bible School students, only three came from Full Gospel backgrounds; the others were mainly former Catholics or Presbyterians. In 1995 the church comprised about 280 churches, with five missionaries.[87]

Cameroon has hosted revivals of the kind we have met frequently in Ghana or Uganda. Bonnke held crusades in Kumba and Bamenda (both anglophone cities) in the early 1990s. And Benson Idahosa of Nigeria, probably the best-known church leader the Pentecostal explosion has produced in Africa (and who is frequently to be found on American platforms), held a three-day conference in Douala in May 1993. His teaching is worth referring to, because if the Faith Gospel is fairly pervasive in African Pentecostalism, Idahosa is prepared to take it to lengths dared by few others. In the course of one sermon in Douala,

---

[87] Historical details are found in W. Knorr, *A Short History of Full Gospel Mission, Cameroon*, Bamenda: Gospel Press, [1986]. Another church which might be mentioned here is the Vraie Eglise de Dieu du Cameroun, begun by Pastor Nestor Toukea in 1959, which in 1994 claimed 204 churches in Cameroon, ten in the Central African Republic and sixteen in Chad. A 'holiness' church, it keeps to itself, and is more African than the born-again churches considered above. In 1995 it was intermittently publishing the newspaper *La Foi qui Sauve*. For the sake of completeness we should also mention the Summer Institute of Linguistics, whose 200 missionaries are heavily involved in Bible translating and literacy. For the latter they work closely with the government and with the Linguistics Department of the University of Yaoundé I; all these joint projects are dependent on SIL-acquired funds. SIL is a conservative body whose members claim to keep well out of the political sphere; its work leads it to stress cooperation with national governments. In Cameroon it is not engaged in church planting, but associates with various churches, in Bamenda with the Full Gospel Church. For details, see SIL, *Rapport Annuel 1993-94 Cameroun*, SIL, BP 1299, Yaoundé.

Idahosa claimed that his faith had brought him so many clothes he did not know he had them; a car that even Nigeria's President Babangida could not match ('When my car passes in Nigeria, people gape'), so much food that he simply collapses. In a final session, an associate (who later admitted that his only theological training was in Kenneth Copeland seminars) invited the crowd to come forward to receive a special 'anointing', which he promised would change their lives as it had his. He explained that before his anointing he used to travel economy class, but afterwards always travelled first class; before the anointing his wife and he had always had to go without food if they had guests but since then, whenever a guest came, he could afford to kill a cow; after the anointing he got a better car, with air-conditioning and a chauffeur, and expected to have a Mercedes 500 Concorde before November. Before his anointing he had a three-bedroom house, now he had a seven-bedroom house, but was expecting to have twelve bedrooms by the end of the year. It was clear that for Idahosa and his team the agenda was fund-raising. He explained: 'God has told me to start the first Christian university in Africa. Wouldn't you like in the future through Nigerians to have a Christian university in Cameroon?' Then he gave his hearers the chance 'to sow'; for thirty minutes he lined up those who wanted to do so: first 10,000, then 5,000, then 2,500, then 1000 CFA (at that time, US$1 was worth about 270 CFA), insisting 'God will bless every seed sown', and 'I wish I were you, so that I could sow and expect a miracle'. Immediately afterwards, he invited everyone to come forward to buy a book he had written and a magazine 'for only 1000 CFA'. It should be said that nearly everyone present took part in both of these exercises. Of course there has been no accounting for any of these funds.

However, such conferences and crusades have not produced the plethora of new churches so obvious in the other countries we have studied. Driving around Cameroon, it is remarkable how few churches – comparatively – one sees. The explosion has not happened yet, and this despite the fact that everyone talks interminably of the advent of '*les sectes*' – the mainline Protestants here generally adopting the Catholic terminology.[88] The reason for this is basically the fairly brutal social control used by the state for so long. The political repression in force

---

[88] Even in the early 1970s Bayart was writing 'Les sectes pullulent' ('Fonction politique', 534), but he was referring to groups like the Jehovah's Witnesses. In the 1990s there are many pamphlets and articles about 'the sects': Tatah H. Mbuy, *Sects, Secret Societies and New Religious Movements in Modern Cameroon*, Bamenda: Neba Publishers, 1994; *Connaître Marie*, Oct-Nov 1995, 9-12; the Archdiocese of Yaoundé's 1992 publication, *Dieu des ancêtres, Dieu révélé en Jesus-Christ: Catéchèse pour les classes de premiere et terminale*, 11-16. See also the Minutes of the Religious Superiors, 8-10 March 1995. The Catholic discussions have generally little merit, being totally undiscriminating between groups, and showing little sociological understanding.

right up to 1992 discouraged, to put it mildly, the formation of any form of association.[89] There were two aspects to this, sometimes not easily separable. State security was particularly brutal in denying freedom of association; this also applied to religious associations. But there was also the use of the state security by already established churches to prevent any challenge being made to their privileged position. In this there was an element of collusion; in return for the churches not challenging it, the state was prepared to guarantee their hegemonic control. This still continued in the mid-1990s, as we shall see.

State interference to block new churches has given rise to some peculiarities. The process of legal registration was difficult and lengthy and not to be undertaken lightly – this is the reason why the US Assemblies of God chose to work under the Full Gospel Church rather than attempt to found a church of their own. But there have been some interesting attempts to circumvent this registration process, as in the case of the United Pentecostal Church (UPC), a white oneness (or non-Trinitarian) Pentecostal church from America, brought to Cameroon via Nigeria in 1976, as mentioned above. As required, the founder, a Cameroonian returning home after some years in Nigeria, applied for permission to function as a church. The first step was to get a permit for activity in some restricted area; the security services could monitor its progress closely as well as get reports on the organisation in other countries. After a couple of years, the Minister of Territorial Administration refused a permit for the church, rather strangely since in his decision he referred to the 'benevolent' security report. The church leader then went looking for an already existing church he could affiliate with, and he approached two very small and static mission churches in the area, Global Frontiers in Kumba, and the World Wide Mission which has a school nearby. Cameroonians in the World Wide Mission were willing, but the missionaries vetoed the move. So he approached the Cameroon Church of Christ (CCC), a small splinter from the PCC which numbered only about 200 after twenty years' existence, and reached an agreement with it in 1983. Thus there arose the anomaly of an essentially Presbyterian church united to a oneness Pentecostal church. In time the UPC grew – it numbered about 700 members in 1995 – with the CCC restricted almost to a single village. It is noteworthy that now, when restrictions have been relaxed and the UPC could register on its own, the UPC leader, out of loyalty, has refused to break the link and still pays what he calls a 'monthly royalty' to the CCC (realising rightly that the minuscule CCC would suffer without it).

Since 1992 and the political thaw, the situation concerning Pente-

---

[89] 'The state destroyed them [civic associations] all in the first two decades after independence', Van de Walle, 'Neopatrimonialism', 151.

costalism has changed. Indeed, one can observe changes occuring before one's eyes. There are interesting aspects to this belated Pentecostal flowering. First, the phenomenon has a clear Nigerian element – to such a degree that the Synod Clerk of the PCC can dismiss the whole development as the work of 'commercial Nigerian preachers'. It is true that many of Cameroon's less established churches started as spillovers from Nigeria – we have already noted this in the LCC, the Apostolic Church, the Full Gospel Church and the Church of Christ – and the same tendency is observable in many emerging charismatic churches or ministries. However, it is remarkable that Cameroon's preoccupation with security has had the effect of choking off a whole generation of Nigeria's independent churches. The Aladura churches – like the Christ Apostolic Church, the Church of the Cherubim and Seraphim, the Celestial Church, the Church of the Lord (Aladura) – are hardly to be found in Cameroon. And it is not they which are now arriving as part of a new wave, but the next generation of churches like the Deeper Life Church and newer charismatic ministries. It is understandable that the entry point into Cameroon is often through the anglophone area which abuts Nigeria and has a common language. Secondly, the growth of new ministries and churches in Cameroon is subject to very real constraints; to some degree it is controlled or at least obstructed by the Apostolic and Full Gospel Churches. The latter (and they have tried to involve smaller ones like the Vraie Eglise de Dieu) have attempted to form an Association of Pentecostal Churches. The stated aims of this association are to manage any Pentecostal explosion – to regulate divisions within the born-again sector, and to prevent members from switching between one church to another. New bodies attempting to plant churches experience this association as something more sinister.

Consider the case of the Nancy Porter Memorial Bible School in Buea. This is one of Cameroon's few examples of a phenomenon we found everywhere in the other countries we have studied. Nancy Porter, an American who had worked for thirty years in Africa, spent the 1980s in Nigeria. She was funded by a group which she had established in Phoenix, Arizona, called Harvest Heartbeat Ministry. In the late 1980s she met a young Nigerian named Justice Sunday who had been for four years a pastor in Nigeria's Christ Deliverance Church.[90] They came in July 1992 to Cameroon, with a two-pronged plan; to establish a Bible school and a church, the latter beginning from house prayer groups. Nancy Porter rented a house for the pastor, and paid him 10,000 CFA a month. The young Nigerian set about creating his housegroups, while the American tried to establish the Bible school. Unfortunately Nancy Porter died suddenly in

[90] Founded by Rev Moses Ewoh, of Ahoada Town, Rivers State.

1993; the Nigerian pastor handled her funeral arrangements so devotedly that Harvest Heartbeat Ministry in Phoenix told him not to return to Nigeria but to remain in Cameroon, with their financial support, and complete Nancy Porter's vision. Very soon he encountered difficulties in establishing his church. He received such harassment from the security services – he insists this was at the instigation of the Apostolic and Full Gospel Churches – even being arrested twice, that his American backers eventually told him to give up any ideas of establishing a church and to restrict his goal to building up a Bible school. Linked to and using the material of Vision Christian College, California (with which Phoenix had made the contact), he set up his Bible school named in memory of Nancy Porter. It opened in January 1995, with twenty students paying 20,000 CFA a year for a three-year course leading to a diploma given by Vision Christian College.[91] Most of the students were already elders or pastors of some kind in churches like the Apostolic, the Full Gospel and Deeper Life, and in ministries like Power Evangelism Ministry and the Christian Missionary Fellowship. Since many were working, the classes were held on Friday afternoons and all day Saturday. The young Nigerian employed two other teachers (pastors in the Apostolic Church and the Christian Missionary Fellowship) at 20,000 CFA a month, all money coming from Phoenix (in the first few months he lost one teacher who claimed the Americans were sending more and that the Nigerian was eating some of what was his due; he left to found his own 'bilingual' Bible college). The school director has also had problems from others who think that because he is 'working with whites' he has access to considerable funds. (In fact, Harvest Heartbeat Ministry is five women, some of them widows – further evidence, in Africa's current economic crisis, of the enormous influence a little Western input can have.) He was building up a sizeable school library by writing to Ernest Angley (who had donated cassette sets as well), Marilyn Hickey, Norvel Hayes, Chuck Swindoll, the Copelands, Kenneth Hagin and Gordon Lindsay's ministry –all of whom readily responded with free literature.

In all these details this Bible school is the replica of countless others all over Africa. However, the point to note here is that this Nigerian had to give up trying to establish a church. From his experience he insists that there is no possibility of establishing new churches in settlements like Buea, an administrative rather than a commercial centre, with an established population. The only chance in Cameroon, he claims, is to begin in a commercial centre like Mutengene, Kumba, Limbe or Tiko, where Nigerian traders provide a large part of the population, and where, because of the floating business population, the control of the Full Gospel

---

[91]   Another Bible school in Yaoundé independently operates on almost the same basis, with this link and material from Vision Christian College.

and Apostolic Churches is much reduced. These two churches think any revival in Cameroon is their responsibility. The Bible school director claims that whereas in Nigeria born-again churches will support and encourage any similar church, these two, in their born-again duopoly, will fight any rival, even utilising the security services. Thus in Cameroon a new church will be opposed, in his nice phrase, 'by both the dead and the living churches' (the former are the Catholics and Presbyterians, the latter the Apostolic and the Full Gospel Churches). He has resigned himself, at least temporarily, to the role of introducing revival by influencing the Apostolic and Full Gospel churchmen who attend his Bible school, though he resents the control that these two churches are able to exert in Cameroon.

There is a more significant example. When discussing Zambia we mentioned as a speaker at Nevers Mumba's Victory convention Billy Lubansa, a Zaïrean on the staff of the Pan African Institute of Development (PAID), a position which gives him diplomatic status. When he was at the Zambian branch of the institute, he attended Reinhard Bonnke's 1986 Fire Conference in Harare, and there had an experience that led to his establishing Flaming Fire of God Ministries and a church in Kabwe, and becoming an important figure in Zambia's revival. In 1990 he was transferred to the Institute's West African branch in Buea, Cameroon. Having already established his own flourishing church in Zambia, one suspects he would have liked to establish one there, but he very quickly discovered that that would not be possible, since the Apostolic Church and the Full Gospel Churches would not permit it. He thus changed tack. In comparison with Zambia, he found Cameroon's Pentecostal churches dead. He attended the Full Gospel church but 'I got nothing, I felt so dry.' He attended an Apostolic church where the sermon lasted a mere ten minutes. 'Then I saw why God brought me here.[...] My mandate was to get the local churches out of the doldrums.' He started mixing with pastors, and organised crusades 'with signs and wonders'; the Cameroonians were amazed, because 'they believed only whites could do that.' He preached at conventions, and above all organised his own big conferences: the first, at the University of Buea in 1992 with the theme 'And Fire Sat Upon Them', drew 2,000; the second, at Limbe in 1994, with the theme 'Armed for Action', drew 4,500. To these conferences Lubansa invited international speakers – Musa Sono and Nevers Mumba (both of whom were speakers in Zambia); Tim Salmon of South Africa; Chikwanda Matthews of Zambia; Muligwe of Venda; Makandla of Zimbabwe; Arthur Mentis, a white South African; Dave Bailey of Canada; Robert Dion of Ivory Coast; and David Demola of the International Pastors and Ministers Conference, New Jersey, which Lubansa attends every year. Expenses are considerable. The first cost

10.2 million CFA, of which Lubansa himself paid 3.8 million; the second cost 7.2 million CFA, of which he paid 2.1 million.[92]

Lubansa makes no secret of the fact that he is trying to change the ecclesiastical face of Cameroon. He does this with some sensitivity. For example, the Full Gospel, Apostolic and Deeper Life churches all require women to be veiled. Lubansa brought his choir from his church in Zambia for his 1992 conference, and had to warn them (as well as the white South Africans) to be sure to bring hats. He considered Cameroon's Pentecostals extremely closed: 'They received from the missionaries the idea that they have the whole truth, they can't learn from anyone.[...] I showed them that they are all one church.' Thus he introduced the crucial new idea of 'interdenominational'. 'Stop preaching the gospel of condemnation, I told them; preach grace, peace, reconciliation.' He taught them 'the Power of the Word; to believe'. Thus he personally has played a large role in introducing the Faith Gospel to Cameroon (he gives as his 'spiritual mentors', Ray McCauley, Reinhard Bonnke, Kenneth Copeland, Kenneth Hagin and R.W. Shambach). He explains that the people of Cameroon have not been taught about giving:

At the offering they would give brown coins [5, 10, or 25 CFA]; 'God would not mind', the pastors used to tell them. *I started breaking that teaching.* I gave a seminar 'Being delivered from the Power of Poverty' [for which he used the books of Copeland and Avanzini]. An Apostolic Church pastor told me that the missionaries had told them, 'You don't need education, or big churches, because you are going to heaven.' This was implanted in them. *We have to uproot all those things.*[...] They used to preach 'Blessed are the poor'. [They must change] to 'Jesus came to bring abundant life, prosperity.' They taught that money was evil. We need to have it to spread the Kingdom.

This uprooting he accomplishes through his own conventions, and by being invited to speak at Apostolic Church and Full Gospel conventions. It has been hard – he claims that two things have been blocking the revival in Cameroon, first a 'religious spirit' ('the majority are Catholics'), and a 'tradition spirit', referring to veneration of ancestors. However, he claims he has had considerable success in his educative mission. When the headquarters of the Full Gospel Church was shifted from Bamenda to Douala in December 1995, Lubansa was guest speaker at the Bamenda farewell. This constituted a 'mighty breakthrough'. He spoke at a 1995 Full Gospel convention 'Crossing over to the other Side', which was all about 'getting out of the doldrums, coldness, tradition'; a Full Gospel missionary was heard quoting him the next day. Lubansa claims that the

---

[92] Because of his status and connections Lubansa can tap other sources; one individual contributed a million CFA to the first conference; a woman gave 400,000 for the second. He also tapped firms, on the grounds that 'we were working for the Cameroonian nation'; CDC gave 100,000 CFA to the second; Del Monte gave 15,000; the Cameroon Brasseries and Guinness donated drinks. Each participant paid an entry fee of 1,500 CFA.

current leader of the Apostolic Church is 'a transformed man; always in my house'. By 1995 Lubansa had his own radio programme on local radio. For his 1996 convention, with the theme 'O God, Restore and Revive Us', he set up grassroots committees to cover the whole of Cameroon, francophone as well. In this way Africa's new Pentecostalism is rapidly coming to Cameroon.[93]

As well as this conscious re-education of Cameroon's existing Pentecostal churches, there are other processes afoot. New Pentecostal churches are arriving. The Nigerian Assemblies of God, in Cameroon calling themselves Pentecostal Assemblies of God (but not linked with the churches of that name we met in Uganda and Zambia, which are founded by Canadian missionaries), came to Bamenda in 1987. After about seven years there, the Cameroonian pastor and his Nigerian wife had a church of only about sixty – though they attributed the slowness of its growth not to any hegemonic control of the born-again sector by the Full Gospel and Apostolic Churches, but to both the 'religious spirit' of the strongly established Baptists, Presbyterians and Catholics who 'think they are Christians and don't realise they need something more', and to the strength of their local African culture (it will be remembered that these are exactly the reasons Lubansa gave for the weakness of revival in Cameroon generally). They moved to Douala, and among the transient and uprooted urban dwellers have had much more success (again we recall the opinion of the Buea Bible school director that in Cameroon such conditions were indispensable for establishing a church). Besides these churches in Douala and Bamenda, they had also opened another, pastored by a Nigerian missionary, in Yaoundé. Although the Douala church claims to be bilingual, it seems primarily English-speaking. There is almost no evidence of local languages or rhythms or instruments. Even though the pastor claims that only half the members are Nigerian, one forms the impression that the fraction could be much higher. All seem young, many being Nigerian youths importing goods on their own behalf or for others. Certainly the message seems geared to such people. In mid-October 1995 the pastor preached on 'Determined to Change', from the text Daniel 1: 8. Determination was the motif throughout:

If you are determined to come out of poverty, work. And work can be anything, even selling plantains, and God starts blessing you. Your business can be cleaning floors. God does not bless empty hands.[...] Determination leads to action.[...] Determine ... do everything to become rich. Do everything God says you should do and become rich.[...] You go to a night club all night, and you are too sleepy

---

[93] He travels widely on the continent, and even has an office with four full-time workers in Lubumbashi, Zaïre. Billy Lubansa in 1995 expressed the view that his role was finished in Cameroon; he intended to resign and return to Zambia to pastor his church and conduct crusades across the continent.

the next day. You have a new girl every day, what is your gain? You have a bottle of beer every day, what is your gain? You have a stick of cigarettes every day, what is your gain? Say 'I'm determined to change today.' When you turn to Jesus, Jesus walks in with salvation, forgiveness, prosperity, blessing, anointing, the presence and power of the King of Kings.

Thus Christianity helps you get on: 'I refuse poverty, for from today Jesus is my saviour.' This is a very practical message for these young Nigerian traders who, if they avoid the obvious traps of night clubs, girls, drink and cigarettes, stand a good chance of outperforming those who succumb. In this church there is no stress on healing; it is prosperity, or getting on in the world, that is important. As might be expected, this message is linked with the other means of getting on, namely giving: 'In the international community people say "Nigeria is finished". No, Nigeria is not finished. Nigerians prosper more than others because they *give*. They have discovered God's secret. The USA is not great because of anything particular.[...] America has discovered the secret, they *give.*'

If the message is fairly predictable for such a church, so is the aggressive evangelism. October in particular is 'increase month'. Every member is enlisted: notices on the church door tell members that in October, 'Voyages outside your vicinity are cancelled'. There are prizes for bringing most visitors to services, giving the most, or arriving earliest. Members are recommended to hire buses and place them, decked with banners advertising the church, at significant points around the city, to bring new members to worship. The month ends with a crusade, to which every member is expected to bring at least five people.[94] Notices and fliers state that the church should increase two or threefold in the month. By October 1995 the church attracted about 600 to Sunday services.

So far, Cameroon has no big new churches of the type we saw in all our other countries, those of Otabil, Duncan-Williams, Leslie or Nevers Mumba. The relative insignificance of the Pentecostal Assemblies of God merely serves to emphasise this fact. Nor has the literature that we found everywhere in these other countries made its appearance. The books we commented on in Ghana and Zambia are simply not here. The Christian bookshops mainly contain English speaking Evangelical material, and material by the same authors translated into French. These are overwhelmingly authors like Billy Graham, John Stott, C.S. Lewis, Watchman Nee and Charles Spurgeon. Original Protestant material written in French is scarce. But the literature of Copeland, Hagin and the like is simply not evident in the bookshops. It is only to be found in the private collections of those who have written for copies.

---

[94] The crusade was widely advertised in this way: 'Come for your miracles, healings, deliverance from barrenness, sleepless nights, ill luck, demonic oppression, etc.'

The churches' role in society

Turning to the churches' wider role, we must consider their function as the leading institutions of civil society. First, there is little evidence that they provide a lead in transcending regional or local boundaries. There is little ecumenism in Cameroon, perhaps even less now than in the early 1970s.[95] Catholics and Protestants are seldom in contact with each other, although in July 1994 Catholic bishops and Protestant leaders met in Yaoundé, and jointly wrote to Biya requesting an interview; Biya did not deign to reply. The division is evident even on formal occasions like the Pope's visit. A leader of a major Protestant church replied, when asked if he had attended the ceremony for the Pope's visit in 1995: 'Why should I? Cardinal Tumi wouldn't come when the General Secretary of the WCC visited Cameroon, so why should I go when the Pope comes?' (The same church leader, on another occasion, dismissed the anglophone Cardinal Tumi as a 'front for Nigeria'.) Another important Protestant churchman, when asked the same question, replied that he was pleased he was out of the country at the time, as it saved him from declining the invitation. In 1995, on Reformation Sunday, the day the mainline Protestant churches in Yaoundé come together to celebrate their Protestant identity, the Presbyterian preaching provided a fairly traditional attack on Catholicism. 'Several people who call themselves Christians bow down to idols and adore humans whom they call saints,' he said, concluding: 'If you give yourself to a religious system, you are bound for hell fire.' For their part the Catholics just go their own way, remarkably uninterested in what Protestants are doing. Some of this unfriendliness is directed from Rome. There is a convent of Presbyterian nuns in Bafut near Bamenda. The Catholic religious congregations meet every year, and in 1995 invited these Presbyterian sisters to their meeting, only to receive an injunction from Rome informing them that the Presbyterian sisters 'would be quite out of place in such a gathering'.[96]

But even among the Protestant churches themselves there is little cooperation. Some even refused to attend Reformation Day in 1994 because it was being celebrated at one of the EPC churches which was considered to be responsible for much of the EPC strife. Even within the one strand of Protestantism there is a remarkable spirit of non-cooperation. The three strong reformed churches (EPC, EEC, PCC), because they are doctrinally identical, began discussions about unity, but the negotiations foundered eventually because, as the leaders are perfectly frank in acknowledging, no one leader was prepared to give up his post. In the

[95] Bayart ('Fonction politique', 521) notes that after independence Archbishop Zoa would sometimes act for the Protestant churches.

[96] Minutes of Religious Superiors' meeting, Yaoundé, 7-8 March 1995. For this Presbyterian community, see *Appel*, 29 (1994), 30; *Appel* 8 (1997), 13-14.

current arrangements, there are three general secretaries; all fear losing out if these pasts are reduced to one. It was proposed as early as the 1960s to establish a joint seminary for these reformed churches. The land was bought but just lay idle because nothing could be agreed. In the early 1990s the land was being partitioned for individual churches to use for their own purposes.

Cameroon has no Christian Council, although it does have a Fédération des Eglises et des Missions Evangéliques du Cameroon (FEMEC), brought into existence by the government, which prefered to deal with one body rather than with many. It has not been a great success. FEMEC cannot speak in the public domain. The division between the Beti and the 'Anglo-Bami' bloc is as evident here as it is in the political sphere, and this means that it restricts itself to the lowest common denominator. One official founded in 1993 a Cameroon branch of ACAT (Action by Christians for the Abolition of Torture), which limps along but is hardly a force in the country.[97] FEMEC has had a development department, which has been far stronger than FEMEC itself, but even this has fallen on hard times. European donors have, according to the normal euphemism, 'lost confidence' in FEMEC, and its funding has been drastically reduced.[98] The director had to resign in 1992.

There are several headings under which the churches' role in society can be considered, of which four are salient. First, because it is probably the most obvious, is the role of education. In parts of the north, church educational activity is particularly evident, and particularly important. In some villages the number of school-age children attending school is as low as 2%. The local Muslim leaders do not value education since their feudal position depends on keeping their (largely non-Muslim) subjects illiterate. The government, dependent on local leaders for their own conti-nuance in power, is happy to preserve this situation. It is this educational involvement, even more than strictly evangelistic activity, that constitutes the biggest Christian threat to Muslim control in the north. Many of the major churches have a considerable investment in education, but the Catholic involvement is enormous. One Catholic source gives the relevant statis-tics in 1993 as 1.7 million pupils in public schools and 800,000 in Catholic

---

[97] This is an ecumenical body, with Archbishop Verdzekov and a Lutheran pastor as co-patrons. The international body (FIACAT) planned to hold a training session on human rights at Yaoundé's Catholic University in 1997.

[98] Cameroon's Protestants (like its Catholics) paradoxically provide some of the continent's most prominent ecumenical figures. The development officer of FEMEC is one of the seven Vice-Presidents of the World Council of Churches, where a defrocked secretary general of the EPC is also a Vice-President. The EPC head of education is one of the Vice-Presidents of the AACC. Such representation is much greater than that of any other of the countries we are considering.

schools. The same source gives the teacher-pupil ratio as 1:150 in public schools and 1:50 in Catholic schools.[99] Of course, the current economic situation has precipitated an enormous crisis for church schools. In 1982 the state began a system of paying subventions for them, but through the 1990s these payments have become very intermittent and partial; between 1989 and 1991 there were none at all. Some say that this is due to more than the country's economic straits coupled with the general greed and incompetence of the ministry. One opinion is that some functionaries, having studied in France, are genuinely convinced in principle of the necessity of a secular education. Others claim that the government, especially the Rosicrucian element within it, is determined to destroy the system of church, and especially Catholic, education.[100] In the face of rising financial difficulties, some churches have had to close their schools. Thus by the end of 1992 the PCC had closed ninety primary schools.[101] The ELCC has also had to close them – a policy supported more by their American than their Norwegian missionaries. Catholics have done all they can to avoid this step. It is widely recognised that this dependence on government subventions has enabled the state to exert considerable pressure over the church. When Cardinal Tumi was called to see President Biya in October 1994, at least one commentator wondered in print whether he had done a deal with the President in order to secure the government subventions of which Catholic schools are in such need.[102]

This kind of involvement, secondly, extends to development generally. Most of the churches work in clinics and hospitals and primary health, literacy, women's projects and agriculture. The relatively small Cameroon Baptist Convention, for example, is involved in two hospitals, thirteen health centres and twenty-four primary health posts. That sort of activity is characteristic of all the major churches.[103] One aspect deserves special note: education in the area of justice and peace. This education is not

99   *Peuples du Monde*, Nov 1993, 21.
100   The role of the Rosicrucians in Cameroon is the subject of much debate. In April 1986 FEMEC issued a statement that one could not be Christian and Rosicrucian: for this text, see Michael Bame Bame, *Jesus Christ and the Rosicrucians*, Yaounde: Society for Christian Growth, 1992, which actually labels Rosicrucianism 'Satan worship'. See his statements in note 75 above. Cardinal Tumi also has said that a Christian cannot be a Rosicrucian (*Effort*, 6-19 July 1996, 3) where he claims that the Rosicrucian Grand Master had assured him, contrary to much speculation, that President Biya was not a member.
101   Moderator's Message, on 35th Presbyterian Church Day, 15 Nov 1992.
102   *New Expression*, 2-8 Nov 1994, 11.
103   Mention should be made of the independent NGO (although Catholic-founded and in-spired) INADES-Formation, operative in ten African countries, and in Cameroon since the 1960s, with offices in Bamenda, Yaoundé and Maroua. Its involvement is consider-able in agriculture, rural self-development, women and development, preventive medi-cine and environmental protection.

characteristic of the churches generally, but some sectors of the Catholic Church in particular are beginning to take it seriously. Archbishop Verdzekov organised week-long justice and peace seminars for all his church workers in October 1995, and the religious orders have attempted to make education in this area an integral part of the training of all their recruits.[104] Most impressive of all is the system of grassroots justice and peace committees established in the Catholic Archdiocese of Yaoundé. This system began in 1988, and thirty-three out of the 100 parishes had such a committee by 1995. The committees involve themselves in local issues: in the notoriously corrupt prison services, on behalf of people who have been put away for reasons of convenience; in reconciling conflicts in villages; in resolving problems arising from polygamy; in issues of witchcraft; and in land rights.[105] The committees comprise volunteers from the local community, but the archdiocesan offices, directed by an expatriate sister, establish the committees and then provide an extensive educational and support service.[106] Such involvement can hardly be called typical, but the dioceses of Bafoussam and Bertoua are attempting to follow the lead of Yaoundé.

Thirdly, the churches provide opportunities for countless people to learn and practise all the skills required in associational life: planning, public speaking, discussing and debating – not just for dignitaries and leaders in assembles and synods, but for everyone in the countless small groups that make up church life. In these smaller groups the most ordinary people can participate and even provide leadership. Almost every church at every level has men's groups, women's groups, groups for youth, students, pupils and mothers. And of course even the smallest church has one choir, if not several. All these groups organise themselves, elect officers, run meetings, arrange activities – some of them quite ambitious.[107] The Catholic Small Christian Communities are not prominent here, but even in the Catholic Church there is a vast array of organisations (with names like the Legion of Mary, the Sacred Heart, the

---

[104] See the minutes of the Religious Superiors' meeting 8-10 March 1994, on the theme 'Promotion of Justice and Peace: its Implications for Formation'.

[105] An example of witchcraft: a soldier had taken his new car to his village to show his relatives how he had made good. On the way back to Yaoundé, he was involved in an accident which destroyed his car, although he was unhurt. He accused nine people from his village of having used witchcraft to destroy his car. They languished in gaol for nearly a year, receiving forty-five lashes a month, until Yaoundé's archdiocesan Justice and Peace Committee took up the case. Archbishop Zoa willingly appeared in court on the accused's behalf, and eventually the case was dismissed.

[106] All committees have the same composition: besides the president, secretary and treasurer, two counsellors 'of the Word' (i.e. catechists), two of the '*loi écrite*' (i.e. lawyers), and two of '*tradition*' (i.e. experts in customary law).

[107] For example, Catholic women's groups, especially in anglophone Cameroon, seem particularly strong. They hosted the WUCWO (World Union of Catholic Women's

Good Samaritans, the Catholic Women's Association) that provide many of the same opportunities for participation and involvement. Again, for some people involvement in these groups is primary; they belong to the wider church through membership in the smaller group.

A problem can often arise because these groups tend to form along linguistic lines. In Ngaoundéré, where functionaries have come from many parts of the country, the central Catholic parish has sixteen distinct linguistic groups, and eight choirs could be vying to perform at one mass, especially for feasts like Christmas. The parish priest has tried to make choirs an opportunity not to divide people but to bring them together: only one choir performs at each mass, but it sings hymns in four or five languages. This is an example of a church group addressing the ethnic question. (We have already met the problem of ethnic parishes in the EPC's strife in Yaoundé.)

Fourthly and finally, we can mention a conscious political theology. We distinguish this from the kinds of protest against abuses or exhortation to good government which could come from any concerned, informed and articulate group like lawyers or journalists. Many churches in Cameroon have protested and exhorted. The statements have tended to be in line with the centre of gravity of the particular church, as we have seen: the EPC has tended to support the government, the PCC has articulated the concerns of the Anglophone community, the EEC is seen as expressing the perspective of its Bamileke majority. The Catholics are the only truly national church, and they have been limited in their clear and unambiguous political guidance for the same reason. The rise to eminence of Cardinal Tumi has meant that the church is no longer seen as the ally of the government; but his utterances, no matter how appropriate they may be, are apt to be dismissed by some as the typical response of an anglophone.

If Ghana and particularly Zambia have been infused with a palpably Christian ethos, Cameroon is markedly different. Colonisation by a statist, centrist and lay power militated against official sympathy for Christianity, and provided little encouragement for Christianity's involvement in health and education. This tendency was heightened after independence by a Muslim head of state, aware of his own lack of legitimacy and bent on eliminating alternative centres of allegiance. These policies have persisted under the allegedly Catholic Biya. If in Zambia it is expected that churches contribute to national debate, in Cameroon such intervention would not

Organisations) Africa Regional Conference in September 1989, on the theme 'The Vocation of the African Woman for all round Development in Church and Society Today' (see WUCWO *Final Report*).

be welcomed. We noted that its élite is very important in the analysis of Ghana, and that the relative lack of one is important in Zambia. In Cameroon the élite is just as important as in Ghana, but it is an élite of a very different kind. Ghana's is educated, ostensibly Christian, Westernising; Cameroon's is more obviously parasitic, often anti-Christian, hell-bent on enriching itself. The self-serving use of power or *'la politique du ventre'* constitutes the ethos or culture into which the churches are inserted; they tend to replicate that model of society, being corrupt and malfunctioning, even to the extent of protecting their own hegemony when they sense it is threatened by new churches.

The country is racked with divisions, and the churches mirror these. For this reason the Protestant churches cannot even establish a Christian Council, much less produce agreed statements as in Ghana or Zambia. Even the Catholic Church, unique in being a national church in the strict sense, is split; this is why it has produced nothing like the pastoral letters or statements we have encountered in our other countries.

The country's divide between anglophone and francophone regions highlights the split within Christianity. The Anglophone churches function far better as structures, which as we have seen is not unconnected with leaving the finances in the hands of missionaries, who by definition lie outside Cameroon's élite culture. If the francophone churches function less satisfactorily institutionally, in some cases spectacularly less so, they have nevertheless thrown up individuals that our other countries cannot begin to match. In the area of theology, particularly political theology, francophone Cameroon has produced more significant thinkers than our other three countries.

Like Ghana, Cameroon has a large Islamicised area, which is largely unevangelised. Whereas Ghana's Protestants have devised a concerted strategy of evangelisation, Cameroon's are unsurprisingly much less organised. The north highlights the different Catholic approach to founding churches, which is essentially to leave it to expatriates with the necessary resources and personnel. The Catholic Church's efforts lie less in planting new churches than in planting religious orders, which is not so much an activity of the Cameroonian church as of the expatriate orders.

Cameroon's Pentecostal sector is very different from that in the other countries we have studied. For decades the Cameroonian state rigorously discouraged all gatherings of any size. However, since 1992 Pentecostal growth has gathered pace, and the new churches emerging seem similar to those we have met elsewhere. This is hardly surprising, since their emergence tends to be shaped by similar transnational factors.

Ghana and (particularly) Uganda currently seem to be involved in a process of national reconstruction or reform. Since this is the milieu in which the churches operate, it has affected their agenda, hopes and strategies. By contrast, Cameroon seems rudderless, locked into a system which does not permit reform. That is the public culture in which the churches are enmeshed.

7

THE CHURCHES' PUBLIC ROLE

Although there is no intention to repeat the points made above, we will briefly recapitulate before proceding to some general conclusions. Of our four countries, the first, Ghana, was created in its modern form by the early Protestant missions, and this has given it a Christian ethos to this day. After independence, it suffered a catastrophic economic decline, reaching its nadir in the early 1980s, since when Rawlings has implemented IMF remedies. Throughout these years the mainline Protestant churches have attempted to exert moral influence, particularly through the Christian Council. The Catholic Church, now the biggest single denomination, has done the same, either through its own channels or in conjunction with the Christian Council. Both groups work well together, for church leaders are from the same class; it is basically those Western, liberal, middle-class values of order and rule of law that they have promoted, rather than any strict Liberation Theology. During these years, the nature of Ghanaian Christianity has subtly changed. Proportionately, Ghana's mainline churches, according to reliable surveys, are losing members. Spectacular real growth lies with newer Pentecostal churches; these must be distinguished from traditional AICs, which are themselves suffering a far greater decline than the mainline churches. The Pentecostal explosion has not only taken members from the mainline churches, but Pentecostalised these churches themselves. The new churches stand for a Faith Gospel focusing on this-worldly blessings, and increasingly for a deliverance theology which, though built on African traditional conceptions, is expressed strongly in terms of modern Western charismatic thinking. Some of the most educated and articulate new church leaders display considerable creativity, and are relating this Pentecosal Christianity to Ghana's particular circumstances.

Uganda in the 1970s spiralled to greater depths than Ghana. Since then it too has struggled to reform, achieving some success. Uganda has a totally different religious geography from Ghana, for the Anglican and Catholic Churches have historically constituted a duopoly. Both were present at the birth of modern Uganda, and have become part of the social fabric. The two churches have tended to define themselves over against one another, and this persisting opposition is evident, for example, in the lack of ecumenical cooperation. Other churches have had only limited opportunity to establish themselves – in colonial times because of British restrictions, and since independence because of the chaos into which the country descended. Since the advent of Museveni in 1986, newer churches have proliferated, many because of new missionary links and what these can mean to Ugandans attempting to improve their situation. Museveni, to a degree which has brought him recognition as something new in Africa, seems genuinely to have the country's best interests at heart, which has led the churches to attempt less in the way of moral comment and to restrict themselves to cooperating through development work. Both historic churches are somewhat bewildered by the mushrooming of the newer churches.

Zambia constitutes yet another politico-religious mix. It cannot boast an élite like Ghana. Here there was white settlement, and the mines have effected considerable urbanisation. A leader of considerable legitimacy presided over economic success for some years after independence, only for the copper price to plummet after 1975. That began a decline which led to a widespread movement for change in the elections of 1991. The change has not proved adequate to halt Zambia's decline. Unlike in Uganda, there have traditionally been many churches in Zambia. In a remarkable experiment, some merged at independence into a United Church, a union brought about mainly through particularly far-seeing missionaries. The churches after independence had a particularly warm relationship with government because Kaunda, the son of a pastor, made Christianity a pillar of his dispensation. The Chiluba government has tried to raise these informal links on to a higher and structural plane, by declaring the country a Christian nation. Zambia's Pentecostal flowering assumes a higher profile because it is this sector of Christianity that is associated with the Chiluba government. Christianity has become an integral part of the political debate here, and not the least interesting part of the dynamic is the 'Christian' government's corruption and incompetence. The missionary influence is more evident in Zambia than in Ghana and Uganda.

Cameroon is the only (mainly) francophone country we are considering. Here the Catholic Church is the largest denomination, although French lay and statist administrations and then a Muslim President determined to eliminate all forms of civil society have curtailed its influence. Here there was nothing like the cosy church-state relationship of Zambia. Cameroon's governing élite have been particularly self-serving, and have beggared the country in pursuit of their own gain. These attitudes are at least partly shared by the church élite, and many churches, too, are characterised by *'la politique du ventre'*. Since civil society was till the early 1990s very circumscribed, Pentecostal churches have not had the opportunity to grow in the same way as in Ghana and Zambia.

They have appeared even more recently than in Uganda, but now they are emerging, particularly through the anglophone corner adjacent to Nigeria.

Amid all these differences several similarities stand out. We will focus on some of the more significant, of which the first is well summed up in Bayart's concept of extraversion.

Extraversion

For all the talk within African church circles of localisation, inculturation, Africanisation or indigenisation, external links have become more important than ever. Through these links the churches have become a major, if not the greatest single, source of development assistance, money, employment and opportunity in Africa. These links – bringing ideas, status, power, structures and resources – operate for different churches in different ways, at different levels. We will summarise our findings.

We have seen that these links are most obvious in the case of the Catholic Church. The church has a strongly universalist strand in its theology, and the local church is incomplete in isolation – so the links are by definition constitutive. In the realm of ideas they ensure at least some exposure to theologies like those of Latin America. Practically, they are enormously significant too and have all sorts of consequences. External links preserve the church from becoming locked too narrowly or too exclusively into the local dynamic.[1] International structures ensure that leaders follow standardised procedures – they must do so under threat, in the last resort, even of dismissal.

It is worth stressing that these international links do not operate by virtue of the fact that the Vatican is considered legally a sovereign state.[2] The Vatican does have diplomatic relations with all the countries we have studied, but it would be hard to argue that these have any great bearing on the functioning of the local Catholic Church or on the way the government treats it. What matters far more is that the same diplomat who (as papal nuncio or pro-nuncio) has links with the host government is also the link man (as apostolic delegate) between the local and the international church. How he uses his power as apostolic delegate varies considerably. We have seen the delegate to Cameroon take his job very seriously – even inviting himself to visit the Bishop of Nkongsamba, and personally handing him a resignation form to sign. By contrast, the

---

[1]   To the evidence adduced above one might add that in Rwanda, where the Catholic Church was locked totally into the structures of power, it was Rome that forced the Archbishop of Kigali, Mgr Vincent Nsengiyumva, to resign from the MRND central committee in December 1989, and then sidelined him in favour of his namesake Mgr Thaddée Nsengiyumva. The belated attempt to disengage from the Habyarimana regime was thus instigated not by local leaders but by Rome.

[2]   Haynes, *Religion and Politics*, 63.

resignation of Uganda's Bishop of Kabale seems to have been engineered by the other Ugandan bishops acting in concert, and thus more a local than an external initiative, although admittedly the two are not mutually exclusive. Certainly appointing a foreign missionary to replace local African bishops in both Uganda and Zambia would have involved the apostolic delegate.[3]

A more significant form of external linking is the presence of Catholic missionaries. Nearly all Africa's Catholic bishops are African, but the level of middle management is often still dominated by missionaries. Missionary links do not all work in exactly the same way. We noted the differences due to the different religious orders; in Zambia alone there is a considerable difference between the areas of the Jesuits, with their stress on school education, and those of the White Fathers with their linguistic skills, closeness to village life and commitment to Africanisation. But the recent change in the general ethos of the Catholic missionaries in Africa has been enormous; from a most ultramontane influence right up to the 1960s, they have become overwhelmingly exponents of an 'enlightened form of Christianity'.[4] Catholic missionaries will oppose deliverance thinking, not because it is anti-Christianity (they are well aware that historically much European Christianity was intimately associated with such thinking), but because they consider such thinking a block to development. It is largely through its missionaries that the Catholic Church promotes its modernising agenda; for example, the Africa Faith and Justice Network, a lobbying organisation with permanent offices in Washington and Brussels, is not strictly a body of the African church, or even promoted by the African bishops, but more properly an operation of the various Catholic missionary orders which operate in Africa.[5]

Where the Catholic modernising agenda goes so far but no further is in the question of population growth. Africa, in the opinion of many, will have a very precarious future unless some effort is made to check it. Without such an effort, any meagre economic growth will be more than

---

3   International links also provide Catholic bishops with relative immunity from outraged Presidents. Here, too, it was not anything the supposedly sovereign Vatican state could do that kept, for example, the Archbishop of Monrovia immune from Doe's anger; it was the threat that if anything happened to the archbishop, American bishops would pressurise Washington to cut crucial aid to Liberia (Gifford, *Christianity and Politics*). Likewise, within hours of the leak that a meeting of Malawi's cabinet had discussed murdering the Catholic Bishops, the British bishops (in concert with other European church leaders) were mobilising in support and hinting of pressure on the European Union regarding aid to Malawi.

4   'Nowhere did the [Vatican] Council have a more startling effect than in the African missionary field' (Hastings, *Church*, 569).

5   It was obvious that the petition for debt relief circulated at the 1994 Synod of Bishops in Rome was largely a missionary initiative (see Africa Faith and Justice Network, *African Synod: Documents, Reflections, Perspectives*, Maryknoll: Orbis, 1996, 114-16).

neutralised, and the present collapse will continue. The Catholic bishops refuse to address this, but it must be said that this seems to arise from their Africanness just as much as from papal teaching. At the Synod of Bishops in Rome in 1994, it was obvious that the African bishops were instinctively supportive of the papal decision to oppose the consensus at the forthcoming UN Cairo conference; they saw this as the West imposing itself on Africa just as much as they saw it in religious terms.

External links also provide the Catholic Church with a network of regional and international associations and fora. It has a continent-wide organisation SECAM (the Symposium of Episcopal Conferences of Africa and Madagascar) with its headquarters in Accra, Ghana. By comparison with, say, its Latin American counterpart CELAM, it is remarkably ineffectual. It attempts very little, and keeps a remarkably low profile; its first foray into the explicitly political realm was a March 1993 letter, signed by its president, Cameroon's Cardinal Tumi, 'To the Heads of State of Africa and Madagascar'. A comparison with CELAM is instructive. The fact that CELAM has been so prominent and thus brought itself into conflict with the Vatican was one of the key factors that caused SECAM to be so unambitious; the bishops of Africa have no desire for conflict with Rome. Another factor, the bane of so many African regional bodies, is that to sit on such boards is often seen more as a reward than as a challenge; the people so appointed are also on other boards, and thus cannot do much for any particular one.[6] Africa's Catholic Church held a Synod of Bishops for Africa in Rome in 1994. This was the first time that the bishops – anglophone, francophone and lusophone – had ever met together. Although little of moment came immediately out of the synod itself, it stimulated considerable grassroots preparation in some areas, and has led to various follow-up programmes. It may yet prove to be something of a milestone.

Africa's Catholic Church is divided into nine regional bodies. These vary in importance, the most effective being the Nairobi-based AMECEA (the Association of Member Episcopal Conferences of East Africa), to which Zambia and Uganda both belong. This meets regularly for long and well-planned meetings and is a genuine market-place of resources and ideas. AMECEA must take a good deal of the credit for the Malawi bishops' pastoral letter in 1992, and it then kept encouraging the bishops when they lost their nerve somewhat due to the furore it provoked. AMECEA's analysis of the church's role in Rwanda was sobering, self-critical and instructive.[7] AMECEA has also cooperated with the Protestant

---

[6]   Clapham writes of Africa's regional boards: 'Virtually every commentary on them, in-deed, consists in little more than a recital of the failure of the institution concerned to work in the way that was ostensibly intended' (*International System*, 118).

[7]   Wolfgang Schonecke, *What does the Rwanda Tragedy Say to AMECEA Churches?*

All Africa Conference of Churches (AACC) – also based in Nairobi – in providing workshops for church leaders on democratisation.[8]

Overseas links, as we have stressed, bring resources,[9] and the Catholic Church has enormous resources available to it, so much so that it always seems to be presumed that money will come from external sources; it is rare in Africa to hear Catholic appeals for money. It is worth emphasising that most of the money comes not from Rome, but from foundations or agencies (often German or American) or from personal contacts. Here again the missionary element is crucial, for it is often through these contacts and networks that funds materialise. Such external links play a part in promoting the church's modernising aims. Many of the Western agencies have set their priorities in recent years; thoroughly Western and liberal ones like human rights education, education for democracy, election monitoring and grassroots empowerment, particularly of women. Even if the local church left to itself would not have given these priority, it is encouraged to do so by financial considerations.

The availability of funds is connected, too, to the relative discipline and unity in the Catholic Church (the phenomenon of two churches, 'progressive' and 'conservative', so evident in some Latin American countries, is much less significant in Africa). Resources help discipline in two ways. The first is that foreign donor funds must normally be accounted for, especially if one intends to obtain more. This encourages accountability, which brings its own reward. We have noted that those who have earned the complete trust of donor agencies by accounting for every cent can ask for a great deal more. Other places where the plant lies deteriorating are proof that nothing turns the taps off more certainly than failure to account for previous grants. The second consideration is perhaps more important. As resources have dried up in recent years, many African neo-patrimonial and clientelistic institutions, not least governments themselves, have fallen apart, for there is not enough benefit flowing down the system to keep the clients on board or in line. Inasmuch as the churches (taking their nature from surrounding culture) are clientelistic institutions, the Catholic Church is one that still attracts sufficient resources for it to function with some degree of cohesion. One other effect relevant to our concerns is that as Africa's economic collapse has continued, Catholic Church leaders have become less prone to

---

Nairobi: AMECEA Documentation Service, 1995.

[8] The proceedings of one is published as Hizkias Assefa and George Wachira, *Peacemaking and Democratisation in Africa: Theoretical Perspectives and Church Initiatives*, Nairobi: East African Educational Publishers, 1996.

[9] Martin identifies this as an important area requiring more research in Latin America, *Tongues*, 292.

co-option by governments; there is more to be gained from foreign church networks than from local African governments.

An obvious disadvantage of the access to resources is that the Catholic clergy are in danger of becoming a caste of functionaries whose privileged status marks them off from the people they theoretically claim to serve. Africa's economic situation has made of the church a road to status and professional or economic advancement. Of course this situation is no different from that prevailing in Ireland or certain of America's ethnic enclaves until quite recently, but in the West since the Second World War economic growth has caused the status and remuneration of the clergy to drop far below those of most other professions; in Africa, by contrast, the deteriorating conditions have meant the reverse by a large factor.[10] This question is not unrelated to the obligations of celibacy. Allowing for significant regional variations, it is commonly assumed that these are widely flouted.[11] There have been cases of clergy using their power to demand sex from those in no position to refuse. This has been a problem in areas where AIDS is prevalent, and particularly affects nuns in local sisterhoods. Only in the mid-1990s is this issue being openly addressed, and it still requires courage; as in one East African country where a superior general, protesting to an archbishop about the treatment of her sisters by his clergy, was summarily dismissed. There is general dissatisfaction in Africa with the entire selection and training of clergy. This was a major preoccupation of the 1994 Synod of Bishops for Africa, although little immediately came of it. In Kenya in 1992 an open letter was published by young Kenyans criticising the African clergy on some of these points, and comparing their commitment most unflatteringly with the dedication of the missionary clergy. This letter was subsequently reprinted in both Ghana and Zambia.[12]

The mainline Protestant churches are also, by definition, international organisations. All the questions just raised in regard to the Catholic Church arise here as well. However, in most of the points we have just considered, Protestant connections function less fruitfully than the Catholic ones. Structurally, many Protestants place their focus on the local congregation;

[10]   For the commercial interests of Africa's Catholic clergy, see J.F. Bayart, 'Les Eglises chrétiennes et la politique du ventre', *Politique Africaine* 35 (1989), 3-26; Mbembe, *Afriques indociles*, 92-4. It is claimed that in part of Tanzania the Catholic Church is primarily perceived as a business, inextricably dependent on foreign donors: see Maia Green, 'Why Christianity is the "Religion of Business": Perceptions of the Church among Pogoro Catholics in Southern Tanzania', *JRA* 25,1 (1995), 25-47.

[11]   In a background article on the 1994 African Synod, *Time* stated simply: 'Up to three-fourths of African priests are in effect married and raising children' (*Time*, 25 April 1994, 68). The *Independent* was even more sweeping: 'All African priests expect to have wives, or at least concubines, when they are ordained' (*Independent*, 19 Sept 1995, 2).

[12]   Printed in *Impact*, Aug 1993, 19-20.

they are not geared to coordinate themselves to speak or act as a unit or as a cohesive denomination. They do not have an internationally recognised supervisory body – Lambeth, for example, is not Rome, the Archbishop of Canterbury is not an Anglican Pope – and other mainline churches are even less structured. Also, this is the sector of Christianity that has come to talk of 'partnership', so the founding churches in Europe or America, ever conscious of charges of racism or paternalism or colonialism, are generally reluctant to interfere with their daughter churches. We saw how in Uganda both the Catholic and Anglican Churches have recently had spectacularly malfunctioning dioceses. The Catholic bishop was eventually moved out, but the Anglicans have no mechanism to do this, and the Anglican problem has continued, much to the detriment of the church's moral authority.[13]

The mainline Protestants have today relatively few missionaries. Africa's mainline Protestants called for a moratorium on missionaries in the 1970s, but even by then their flow of missionaries had contracted to a trickle. In finances, too, they are hard pressed. As economies have collapsed, the churches have been seriously affected. Those churches able to find external funds have sometimes found a genuine independence from local pressures, but those unable to do so have sometimes become even more dependent on the largesse of a President for their operation, or on their rich members, who tend by the nature of things to be linked to government.

The Protestant churches have their supra-denominational and supra-national associations too. We have seen the Christian Council in Ghana – one of the most effective on the continent – and in Zambia, where it finds it much harder to function effectively. In Cameroon ecumenical relations are so undeveloped that the Protestant churches cannot create so much as a council for themselves. (In Uganda, the largely symbolic council is a different body, uniting Catholics and Anglicans.)

These Councils associate in regions; Zambia's is a member of FOC-CESA (Fellowship of Christian Councils of Eastern and Southern Africa), which functions intermittently. Ghana's is a member of FECCIWA (Fellowship of Christian Councils in West Africa). These groupings, funded by German and Scandinavian agencies, are still rather embryonic. Africa's Protestants also have the All Africa Conference of Churches.

---

[13] In fact the Anglican Church in Kenya was in the early 1990s, by the admission of one of its own bishops, tearing itself apart (*Daily Nation*, 24 Sept 1994), with two, maybe three, messy lawsuits before the supreme court. This means that the Church of the Province of Kenya is seen to have little authority to challenge the government over tribalism, spoils politics, unaccountability, lack of transparency - so much so that some have suggested that its troubles have been fomented by security services precisely for this reason; see Njoya, *Option*, June 1995, 28.

The AACC has departments for development, refugees, women and external affairs, and has conducted seminars and workshops for its member churches on democratisation, peace and reconciliation. After the Rwandan crisis of 1994, the AACC went through a difficult time, for the tragedy split it profoundly. Its president during the first part of the 1990s was Archbishop Desmond Tutu, and indeed its leadership represents his kind of liberal, socially-involved, structurally-aware Christianity.

There is another continent-wide organisation, the Association of Evangelicals of Africa (AEA), based like the AACC in Nairobi, which was founded in 1966 as a conscious opposition to the 'liberal' churches of the AACC. This continental body is made up of national associations of Evangelicals. In Zambia the Fellowship of Evangelicals functions, but in Ghana it does not; in Uganda the sorts of churches that might belong barely exist as a conscious group. The Evangelical sector of Christianity shades into the Pentecostal, and by the late 1980s was losing out heavily to the burgeoning charismatic sector and its nascent structures, as we saw in Ghana. The Association of African Independent (or now, Instituted) Churches (AAIC), likewise based in Nairobi, functions fitfully.

Externality is not a feature only of the mainline churches. Of the Pentecostal churches we have considered, some have constitutional links in the same way as the mainline churches – the major Pentecostal churches in Zambia and Uganda, for example, are both daughter churches of the Pentecostal Assemblies of Canada. In Africa's current situation all churches see the range of benefits that come from overseas links.[14] The Ugandan Assemblies of God, for instance, when the American AOG could no longer support them, turned to the Calvary Charismatic Centre. Turning to overseas protectors is not new. However, such is the disparity of resources now that it is hard to maintain the pretence of equality or 'partnership'; as we noted, a single church in New Zealand or Canada can now create or sponsor an entire denomination in Uganda. To be sure, one can often hear from African churchmen a rhetoric of self-reliance, a call to stand on one's own feet and not to sell out to foreigners; indeed some such appeal seems obligatory at conferences and conventions. On his visit to Zambia described above, Otabil recounted (to great applause) his reply to an insistent American: 'If you must give me something, give me a printing press, and then go home.' Otabil is perhaps one of those who means what he says; he and his church are in a league where they can relate to overseas bodies from a position of some strength. But most seek some form of link, whatever the rhetoric. An observer of the African NGO scene has written: 'Many African NGOs, like the modern African Christian churches ... exist only to the extent that there is a donor

---

[14]	Discussed in Gifford, *Christianity and Politics*, 199-210.

somewhere prepared to fund their activities.'[15] This is a crucial element of Africa's contemporary NGO and church scene, and to neglect it is to give an incomplete picture of contemporary African Christianity. There is far more than a Pentecostal explosion occuring in Africa; the Ghana surveys of church attendance showed the other growth area was in what they called 'mission-related' churches. Growth in the latter arises from the assistance missions provide, as we suggested in discussing the amazing growth of the New Apostolic Church in Zambia.

In drawing attention to the fact that most, though not all, of these links are with American churches, we imply nothing sinister – we are *not* making the point that Africa's Christian growth is directed by the CIA as part of an imperialist plot to keep the continent subservient. It is true, as we have seen, that there is an increasing army of American missionaries on the continent, and it is probably true that a good many of them would broadly sympathise with what is known in the United States as the Religious Right. But in sub-Saharan Africa, especially after the Cold War, it is church growth thinking rather than the new economic realism which drives them. We have stressed throughout that Christian missions are now very important for Africa; perhaps the biggest single industry in Africa. But missions are an enormous industry in the United States as well. Colleges and seminaries offer courses in missions. Special ministries translate scriptures and provide resources, back-up, expertise and literature. Even where they are not planting churches, such transnational ministries help to establish the local Christian agenda and define what Christian commitment means – often enough with computer software. We have observed how even quite small American churches have their own mission outreach to plant or adopt daughter churches. For them, especially, part of the involvement is not specifically about Africa at all; it is the commitment to Africa that drives and focuses church activity back home. Here too the churches display the dynamic observable in the international aid community; the aid industry 'needs' Africa, as does the mission industry.[16]

As an illustration of the processes involved here, consider the organisation AD 2000 and Beyond, which in the 1990s has become very active in the Third World, with Africa divided into five regions (we encountered this body in Ghana, Zambia and Cameroon). AD 2000 does not set up new structures, but coordinates existing ones. Thus local churches, groups and people do not lose any obvious autonomy, but are

---

[15] S. Jamela, quoted in Matthias Schmale, *The Role of Local Organisations in Third World Development,* Aldershot: Avebury, 1993, 2. This tendency to be subsumed into North-South partnerships is one of the major themes discussed at a 1990 seminar of the University of Edinburgh's Centre of African Studies, *Critical Choices for the NGO Community: African Development in the 1990s,* Edinburgh: Centre of African Studies, 1990.

[16] Clapham, *International System,* 256-66.

nevertheless subjected to forces tending to homogenise them or make them part of a concerted strategy. AD 2000 would claim to be a network of partners, but by the nature of things it is more complicated than that. The key players are all American.[17] The entire ethos is also American; its stress on quantification, sophisticated software, programmes, planning, networks, reports, publicity, assessment – all are unthinkable outside its origins in the United States. It brings with it a discourse, a set of images (in our terms, a theology), diffused through workshops, conferences and literature. Here we must give full weight to the 'paradigm-enforcing power' we referred to earlier. The focus is totally on evangelism – and in one sense Christianity here is reduced to numbers, planning and marketing. This is the sector of Christianity with the crusading missionary thrust. It has given rise to a vast army of missionaries (at the Global Consultation on World Evangelism in Seoul in 1995, 60,000 students committed themselves to some form of missionary activity; the South African meeting in 1997 planned to send out a similar number). This Christianity, though not socially involved and not even particularly politically aware, necessarily plays a socio-political role in contemporary Africa, most notably through its targeting Muslims in what is traditionally considered Muslim territory. There is nothing strange in this. On one understanding of Christianity, zeal to convert the unbeliever is the most natural thing in the world, but it must be stressed that this is only on one understanding of Christianity. AD 2000 involves (perhaps 'operates through' catches it better) the Association of Evangelicals of Africa, but it is so dominant that it draws in as well the mainline churches, which many·observers might think represent another form of Christianity altogether. We saw the Presbyterians involved in AD 2000 in Ghana. An unsuspecting observer might assume that this is a WCC church with a WCC theology, but increasingly this cannot be presumed. This parachurch movement, because of its 'paradigm-enforcing power', has had an enormous effect on Africa's mainline sector as well.

Although the Christian evangelistic thrust is undertaken on purely religious grounds, its effects can be viewed in another light. In 1993 Samuel Huntington wrote a celebrated article entitled 'The Clash of Civilisations?' in which he argued that after the end of the Cold War the fundamental source of conflict in the new world order would be not ideological or economic but cultural; conflict will arise from the clash of whole civilisations, which he lists as 'Western, Confucian, Japanese, Islamic, Hindu, Slavic-Orthodox, Latin American and possibly African'. In what follows he totally ignores Africa, and in essence focuses on conflict between the West and Islam. He argues that to protect its interests

---

[17]　This is not to say that all these are identical - there is often tension between them, evident in a place like Nairobi where so many have their African headquarters.

the West must 'support in other civilisations groups sympathetic to Western values and interests'. A visitor from Mars, observing the forces that function to foster Western values and lock sub-Saharan Africa into Western networks, would very quickly fasten on Christianity. Of course, not Christianity alone; other forces are just as obvious, like aid, immigration, education systems, even national languages, but Christianity is perhaps as significant as any. The observer might further note that much of the Christianity spreading in Africa today has built into it a combative anti-Islamic stance (when he considers Zambia, he might also note how pro-Israeli the same Christianity is). We do not argue that this is a conscious US policy; indeed Huntington's article serves to emphasise, if emphasis is needed, just how marginal Africa is to US global thinking. Nor is it argued that missionaries are consciously engaged in any such role; the number of American missionaries subscribing to *Foreign Affairs* must be negligible. Nevertheless, no student of international relations could fail to observe how the enormous evangelistic thrust in Africa serves to hold sub-Saharan Africa in the Western embrace.[18]

From the African side, external links are the most natural thing in the world. The material benefits to African churches are obvious, but this is not the only consideration. In the post-Cold War world the United States is the only superpower. The status of superpower signifies far more than military might – it indicates a cultural appeal. Over much of Africa, the young listen to Michael Jackson tapes, watch Rambo videos, smoke Marlboro, drink Coca Cola, and wear Levis, NY Yankees baseball caps and Nike trainers (or imitations thereof). Even where the baseball caps and T-shirts are made in China or Korea, they will be printed with NY Yankees or Chicago Bulls logos because it is a large part of their appeal – Deng Xiaoping or Kim Il Sung T-shirts would not sell, while Michael Jordan or Magic Johnson shirts do. In Kisangani, in the wasteland that is central Zaïre, the only businesses still functioning in 1995 were diamond trading houses with names like Captain Bob, American Ninja and Delta Force. In this very obvious sense, President Bush was correct when he claimed in his acceptance speech at the 1988 Republican convention: 'We have whipped the world with our culture.'[19]

America is seen as the land of opportunity, the lodestone and cynosure. As the opportunities in Africa have continued to contract throughout the 1980s and 1990s, the attraction has increased. Here, no doubt, America's

[18]   Samuel Huntington, 'The Clash of Civilisations?', *Foreign Affairs* 72, 3 (1993), 23-49; quotations are from pp. 25 and 49 respectively. Of course, in the Europe of late antiquity missionary outreach (e.g. of the Franks to the Frisians and the Saxons) was often demanded by regional security. Huntington subsequently developed his argument in *The Clash of Civilisations and the Remaking of World Order*, New York: Simon and Schuster, 1996.

[19]   Cited in Martin, *Tongues*, 272.

black élite is of great symbolic importance. There is little popular anti-American sentiment on the continent. America was not included in the tirades against colonialism. In Africa, American economic involvement has never been the obtrusive factor that it is in Latin America – or as even French involvement is in Cameroon. Those suffering from the harsh medicine of the IMF and the World Bank do not see them as particularly American policy instruments.[20]

The cultural appeal of the English language is linked to America's appeal. The ambitious youth who masters English can dream of an American education – the ultimate goal of the young African. (In Equatorial Guinea, the only Spanish-speaking enclave on the continent and one totally lacking opportunities, some youths enrol in the American Pentecostal Bible school just to learn English. Pentecostalism, learning English and enhancing opportunity may not be very distinct in their minds.)

In this context we cannot ignore the image of America as Christian.[21] Indeed, it would be hard to ignore it, because for many American missionaries the essence of America is its Christianity. It is worth putting this in context, since so many Europeans find this easy identification of Christianity with America somewhat bizarre. For Eusebius, Christianity and the Roman empire were made for each other; Constantine's dispensation was providentially established by God for the spread of Christianity. Much nearer in time, the British Protestant in the Victorian age was convinced that his country was the apogee of human achievement, and that the reason was its Protestant faith. Even Queen Victoria had written to the chiefs of Abeokuta in Yorubaland that the greatness of England depended upon knowledge of the Bible.[22] This is another important parallel between what happened in the nineteenth century as local structures succumbed under Western impact, and what is happening today in a possibly greater collapse. The larger cultural package of the world's superpower is not to be ignored in assessing Christianity's appeal and increase.

Indeed, history indicates that the growth of Christianity in Africa was never unrelated to its relations with the wider world; externality has always been a factor in African Christianity. Much of the dynamic we are trying to analyse now is glimpsed in these remarks of Adrian Hastings on the end of the nineteenth century:

The organisation of large states, symbolised by government houses whose grandeur must have been quite astonishing to many who saw them, the railways,

20   Clapham, *International System*, 141.
21   Coleman concludes a comparison of the faith movement in Sweden and America: 'It is as though the symbolic significance of the United States is so powerful that it rivals even Israel in its exemplary implications' (Coleman, 'Conservative Protestantism', 364).
22   Hastings, *Church*, 274. For the importance of Protestantism in creating the United Kingdom, see Linda Colley, *Britons: Forging the Nation 1707-1837*, London: Pimlico, 1992, esp. 20-31.

the newspapers, the cathedrals, the sense of now falling beneath the authority of some remote potentate of seemingly infinite resource, the King of England or the Emperor of Germany, the sheer enlargement of scale, power and knowledge within a space of twenty years, and the very numerous possibilities of participation within this new system of things, inevitably precipitated a pursuit of new systems of meaning, truth, philosophy, and religion. The religions of tradition were not unchanging. They were not incapable of incorporating new elements and experience. But they were closely tied to relatively small-scale communities, and very often to authorities which had now been deeply discredited. They had been appealed to and had failed to halt the white invasion. The new school learning ignored or mocked them.

Despite all this, most people would for a time turn all the more fervently to the invisible powers they were familiar with, but a more reflective, modern-minded minority was no less bound to seek for spiritual and moral alternatives. All the conquerors claimed to be Christian, and at the end of the nineteenth century it seemed overwhelmingly obvious that power, riches, and knowledge belonged to Christian nations. It would have been very strange if Africans did not, in the situation of conquest, seek to share in the beliefs of their conquerors. If the process of Christianisation was now to be greatly accelerated, it was not just that there were vastly more missionaries about, with plenty of privileged opportunities for proselytism, it was because Africans themselves had been placed in a situation of objective intellectual unsettlement and were thoughtful enough to seek appropriate positive answers of a religious as well as a technical kind to their current dilemmas.[23]

African Christianity and its growth were thus always tied to relations to the wider world. Initially Christianity was a religion of ex-slaves and outcasts and refugees; only in the urban society along the West African coast and the ever-growing colonised areas of South Africa did Christianity make headway, and here the dynamics of traditional Africa had already broken down under Western impact by the mid-nineteenth century. By the end of the century the increasing impact of the West created an entirely new situation across much of the continent. 'It was the context of modernisation in latter-day colonialism which proved, in African circumstances, so enormously favourable to the spread of Christianity.'[24] Above all it was literacy that the missions brought: 'Master this and you could become teacher, clerk, or new-style farmer. The sky was the limit. And it went with lots of other quite secular things: elementary mathematics, hygiene, bicycles, things clearly linked with the still-greater mysteries of train, car, electric power.'[25] All the skills that Christians learned were by then becoming politically and economically valuable; they brought an automatic adjustment of status. The end of the twentieth century sees Africa in a crisis as great as that at the end of the nineteenth century.

23 Hastings, *Church*, 404-5. See also Mbembe, *Afriques indociles*, 80-91.

24 Hastings, *Church*, 550.

25 *Ibid.*, 458.

One method of surviving it is through 'extraversion'. External relations can create and sustain domestic African groups, not only churches, although churches furnish the most obvious examples. Realisation of this is crucial for any analysis of African society today.[26]

In Chapter 2 reference was made to Martin's study of the rise of Pentecostalism in Latin America. Martin's explanation is in terms of a shift in global forces, the triumph of the Anglo over the Hispanic. Pentecostalism is 'the third and latest wave in the successive socio-religious mobilisations which have affected the "Anglo" world, especially America.[...] Pentecostalism is also the first wave to cross the border from the Anglo to the Hispanic worlds on a large scale.'[27] His book is a celebration of the cultural creativity of the Latin Americans, but also an explanation of the cultural pull of the United States generally.

The religious influence is only one aspect of a broader influence, economic, political and cultural. The religious traffic moves alongside the economic traffic, sometimes with the religious slightly ahead of the economic, and sometimes vice versa; sometimes in cooperation, occasionally in antagonism. The two kinds of traffic will have a family likeness; perhaps similar economic and political assumptions, certainly similar ideas, ideals, language, techniques, know-how and forms of communication and self-presentation. Yet none of this flow from North to South in any way depends on the specifically religious bridge, even though the religious bridge provides a definite reinforcement. The sign and symbol of this reinforcement may be the US-style supermarket at one end of the boulevard and the US-style church at the other end.[28]

The mechanics of the process of globalisation are evident here. On one level, religious networks function in the same way as the new global industries like banking, law, health, sport, technology and science, or higher education. We have considered African Christianity as a means of

---

[26] The West has reacted to recent events in Africa with all sorts of structural adjustment, democratisation, development and aid programmes, and even armed intervention. 'All of these measures, while regarded externally as attempts to resolve the problems of African statehood (or to ease the sufferings of African peoples), may more accurately be treated internally as providing resources through which, following the processes of extraversion made familiar by Bayart, local actors can find some means to keep themselves going. The US intervention in Somalia, for instance, created a set of tactical opportunities through which each of the local factions could seek to increase its access to money, weapons or food. The concern of Western aid agencies to find counterpart African NGOs through which to manage their relief programmes immediately spawns a set of NGOs designed to meet the purpose. External actors readily find their presence perpetuating the very conditions which prompted their intervention in the first place' (Clapham, 'International Relations'). Before the Mozambican elections in 1995, the UN was offering considerable funds to political parties to help them compete, and many set up such parties (called 'Kombi' parties, because of the Volkswagen vans that came with registration) merely to collect the money.

[27] *Tongues*, 26.

[28] *Ibid.*, 280-1. For similar statements of powerful US influence, see Cox, *Fire*, 157, 225.

plugging into such global religious networks, all the more important since Africa tends to be bypassed by many of the others. The emerging global system both corrodes inherited or constructed cultural and personal identities, yet at the same time also encourages the creation and revitalisation of particular identities as a way of gaining more power or influence in this new global order. Religion has been and continues to be an important resource for such revitalisation movements. Thus Beyer explains the rise of Islamic fundamentalism – but also religious movements in places as diverse as Ireland, Israel, Iran, India and Japan. But the dynamics of Africa's burgeoning Christianity are somewhat different. Africa is not reacting to globalisation by revitalising African traditional religion; we saw that movements like Afrikania in Ghana (and Nigeria's Godianism) have very little appeal. Africa is responding to globalisation by opting into exotic religions. So much of Africa's mushrooming Christianity is closely linked with a particular religious expression in the United States. Africa's newest Christianity, while in many ways reinforcing traditional beliefs, also serves, as we have seen, as one of Africa's best remaining ways of opting *into* the global order.[29]

We have drawn attention to Western links as a significant factor within all branches of African Christianity. It must be stressed that such links are quite compatible with a considerable creativity on the part of African Christians. Indeed, for Bayart creativity is of the essence of extraversion; the central idea is that Africans consciously turn links to their own ends and purposes. Peel writes of Africa's 'active engagement' with external influences,[30] and it is widely acknowledged today that Africa's Christianity was always the creation of Africans rather than of missionaries.[31] The creativity is even greater with Africa's newer charismatic forms. Cox offers a suggestive image in his discussion of the parallels between Pentecostalism and jazz. These two elements share 'the near abolition of the standard distinction between the composer and the performer, the creator and the interpreter'.[32] We have argued that Africans in their current

[29] Peter Beyer, *Religion and Globalisation*, London: Sage Publications, 1994. It is another sign of the marginalisation of Africa that Beyer elaborates his globalisation theory without reference to the particularities of Africa. It is noteworthy too that Paul Kennedy's 1996 BBC Analysis Lecture 'Globalisation and its Discontents' (30 May 1996) was in reality elaborated in reference to all the globe except Africa; the lecture was really about incorporating Middle Eastern and Asian (and to a lesser degree Latin American) countries into the formerly overwhelmingly Western networks. The only mention of Africa was a passing reference to the 'hopeless countries of Africa'.

[30] J.D.Y. Peel, 'Poverty and Sacrifice in Nineteenth-Century Yorubaland: a Critique of Iliffe's Thesis', *Journal of African History*, 31 (1990), 484; see 482-4.

[31] 'The fate of Christianity depended upon its ability to be reread in terms and with implications for the most part unimagined by its propagators' (Hastings, *Church*, 306; see also 591).

[32] Cox, *Fire*, 157.

plight are being even more creative with Christianity – it is a sign of how deeply-rooted Christianity now is in Africa that it can be put to such myriad uses.

But this creativity should not be so emphasised that it glosses over the West's cultural significance. In Africa's current decline, one only has to visit the United States Information Service in Accra, the British Council in Kampala and Lusaka, or the Alliance Française and indeed even the Goethe Institut in Yaoundé to sense the cultural impact of such institutions. As bookshops fold and libraries deteriorate, these institutions assume incalculable importance as conduits of ideas and images. Their periodicals, films, educational documentaries and news summaries assume an importance they could not possibly have in the West, where other divergent voices obtrude. The same process is observable in Africa's cash-strapped universities. When, for example, the agricultural faculty of an African university forms a link with (say) Michigan State University, which then provides teachers, texts, resources and exchanges, it is un-realistic to ignore the 'paradigm-enforcing power' of the latter. Michigan State has fairly clear ideas on what constitutes the study of agriculture, and these are likely to cover things like free markets, private (as opposed to common) ownership of land, cash crops and exports. It is not 'agriculture' in some abstract or pure form that is being imparted. One might object to this, but to some degree that is the way of the world. To misquote Gellner, the shocking inequality of cultural forces is simply a fact of our time. It is surely valid to approach Christian institutions in the same light. Whatever else it is, Christianity is a cultural product, honed in the West over centuries. The format of Africa's crusades and services, the music, the use of the Bible and even the selection of texts continually suggest particular origins and betray particular roots. This is specially true of American Pentecostal literature, which has been abundant in Africa at least since the 1980s. In many places this abundance was matched by an equal dearth of any mainline Christian literature. As a result, one cannot uncritically speak of the 'orality' of Africa's Pente-costalism; even among illiterates the discourse is often derived from this ubiquitous literature, through the medium of more literate pastors. The formal effects of cultural links need to be studied in each particular case.

Islam, equally, is an African religion with cultural, economic and political baggage. Although not so obtrusively in the cases studied here, in many sub-Saharan countries it is a serious competitor, and where it competes it also does so not just as a religion but as part of a cultural, economic and political network. Peel describes the competition between Islam and Christianity for Yoruba favour in the mid-nineteenth century – an instance of some importance, for this part of Nigeria was one of the few arenas where the two new world religions competed on a relatively equal footing and with almost equal success. He outlines the special appeal of each. Islam's was its magico-spiritual techniques through prayers and charms; the prestige of its international networks and its political-military clout; and the social openness of Yoruba Muslims towards non-Muslims, which facilitated Africans' identification with the Muslim body. For Christianity the attraction was the appeal of Christ as mediator, and its association with the technological power of its European bearers, later to be diffused through the colonial order. (Peel highlights the resulting paradox. Christianity, which claimed to offer moral renewal and eternal salvation, was most respected by its rival for its accompanying material culture, which in its own eyes was purely secondary. The relative success of Islam was due to two things which missionary Christianity could not yet emulate: its magico-spiritual techniques and its social affability. Thus Islam was led to invoke in its own defence, in the face of superior European technology, an other-worldly dimension that was probably of little concern to its new Yoruba converts.)[33] A century later, the situation is no less complex and paradoxical, and the international cultural, political and economic links have not lost their significance.[34] International networks and political-military clout, as well as technology, now operate distinctly in favour of Christianity. And it is the particular contribution of the new Pentecostal Christianity that it offers magico-spiritual techniques equal to any in Islam.

The competition between the two religions can sometimes be driven by international links. In the particular countries studied here, the balance is one-sided; it is so obviously Christianity that links with the successful and profitable networks. However, the Sudan is a case where the geopolitical aspect of Christianity is plain. Thus African Rights, in attempting to account for the staggering rush to Christianity in the Southern Sudan since about 1992, suggest that as the Muslim Brotherhood in the North has increased its references to 'the Arab world', the Southerners have been 'invited to internationalise their ideology of resistance in a similar way' – that is, by opting into the Christian West.[35]

This is not to suggest that establishing external links is the only

---

[33] J.D.Y. Peel, *The Encounter of Religions in Yorubaland, 1845-1912,* forthcoming.

[34] Of course, links can work against a religion too, as has often been the case in the past. Becoming a Catholic or a Muslim in British Africa was a way of combining conversion to a world religion with distancing oneself from the colonising power. Becoming a Baptist or even more a Kimbanguist served the same purpose in the Catholic Belgian Congo. See Hastings, *Church,* 462. Hastings immediately goes on: 'The success of Harris or Oppong may be related to quite the same sort of logic. While the old gods which had failed were rejected, it was at the command not of a colonialist but of an African who was manifestly uncolonial. A " world religion" was accepted, but by no means in the form the conquerors provided.'

[35] African Rights, *Great Expectations,* 7.

significant activity in this religious area, or that such links are locking Africa into two hermetically-sealed blocks. This is obviously not the case, and other factors can counteract this tendency. For example, just after the execution of Ken Saro Wiwa in 1995, when Nigeria was being made the pariah of the international community, who should arrive in London as part of the charm offensive of the Muslim Abacha regime but Archbishop Benson Idahosa. Here other factors had obviously proved more important, and the Nigerian journalists attending Idahosa's press conference were fairly certain what these were; in their terms, Idahosa had been 'settled'.[36]

We have argued that the drive for overseas links has been greatly accelerated by the recent sociopolitical and economic collapse of Africa. Sometimes the stress on African creativity obscures the reality that in large parts of black Africa there is a mood of Afropessimism, not in the normal sense that foreigners are inclined to wash their hands of Africa as hopeless, but in the more important sense that Africans themselves have lost self-confidence. Some can still blame the current situation on the colonising powers, but far more are too young to have personally experienced discrimination at the hands of European imperialists. All they have known is oppression at the hands of their own élite. Many look at their own leaders and despair of African competence and integrity.[37] For many, self-esteem and self-confidence have been the first casualties of Africa's decline. We heard Otabil begin his preaching in Zambia: 'When you look at yourself as an African, it is easy to think that God has cursed you.[...] We are a people who feel inferior and wallow in our own inferiority.' It was this that led him to develop his theology of black pride.[38] If in Ghana and particularly Uganda there are signs of hope amid the grinding poverty – at least by taking the IMF medicine they are being integrated back into the world community – in Zambia and Cameroon, where the élites seem to have no idea how to arrest the steep decline (indeed no idea except enriching themselves), one can sense growing despair.

This mood has to be factored into discussions of developments within Africa's Christianity. After independence, in the euphoria of the 1960s and 1970s, many African theologians spent much of their time re-valuing African traditions. Now the growth areas of Christianity are those that demonise African traditions and culture. Around the time of independence

---

[36] *Guardian*, 16 Dec 1995, 6. 'Settled' is a term that developed in the Babangida era (1985-93) to refer to the co-option of political opponents and others by threats, bribes and other inducements.

[37] The crisis such leadership engenders is greater because traditionally a leader is not just a functionary, but a representative in a fuller sense; see John V. Taylor, *The Primal Vision: Christian Presence amid African Religion*, London: SCM, 1963, 135-53.

[38] This is not just an African issue; Edward Said has written of the 'self-hatred' of the Arabs, confronted with their powerlessness before Israel (*Guardian*, 25 April 1996, 15).

was the golden era of the AICs, the churches where African traditions were preserved and valued. But these are the churches, according to the Ghana surveys, whose appeal and membership are plummeting – in some other countries, apparently, the same thing is happening. It may be that the great exception to this is South Africa, where the latest figures indicate a flowering of independent churches.[39] This would seem to reinforce our thesis that the 1980s and 1990s have been for South Africa what the 1950s and 1960s were for Black Africa – years of increasing resistance, struggle, victory and elation. In the mid-1990s, under Mandela, the pride of South Africans is palpable, like the euphoria in Ghana in the first days of Nkrumah. But in Black Africa the euphoria has long gone.

Different Christianities

Our study has emphasised the diversity of Christianity. So much comment on Christianity in Africa makes the assumption that Christianity is Christianity, or that it is a single easily identifiable entity. We have not proceeded on this understanding, and have distinguished a wide range of Christianities, functioning differently.

One of the most significant issues here is well conveyed by this remark of Adrian Hastings, writing of the early Portuguese evangelisation of the Congo. He notes the similarities in worldview at that time of both the missionaries and the evangelised: belief in local powers, protective objects, holy places, an expectation of miracles and prodigies, an acceptance of spiritual causality. 'The religious sensibilities of 16th-century Iberians as much as of pagan Africans were absolutely pre-Enlightenment, and close cousins to one another.[...] The missionary and the African often understood each other better than most of us can understand either.'[40] Hastings is drawing attention to a change that has occured in mental framework that separates modern Europeans not only from many other cultures, but even from Europeans of two or three centuries ago.

Scholars have analysed what has happened to religion in the West as a result of the Enlightenment. Keith Thomas, in tracing the decline of magic in England between the Reformation and about 1700, notes that the link between misfortune and guilt was broken.[41] The hardships of life came to be attributed to impersonal social causes rather than to one's personal failings or those of other people. Theologians became quite ready to accept the frequency of unmerited suffering. Stoicism became the basic

---

39   This may not be so: it is not clear exactly how the new type of charismatic churches are distributed between categories like 'AICs' and 'Other Pentecostal Churches'; see J.J. Kritzinger, 'The Religious Scene in Present-day South Africa', in J. Killian (ed.), *Religious Freedom in South Africa*, Pretoria: UNISA, 1993, 2-4.

40   Hastings, *Church*, 75.

41   Keith Thomas, *Religion and the Decline of Magic*, London: Penguin, 1973, 713.

religious message for those in misfortune, and 'the prospect of material relief by divine means was only intermittently upheld outside sectarian circles after the seventeenth century.'[42] The 'animistic conception of the universe which had constituted the basic rationale for magical thinking' simply fell away, in the process of 'disenchantment' made famous by Weber, and was replaced by a conception of an orderly and rational universe in which effect follows cause in a predictable manner.[43] Accusations of witchcraft 'were thus rejected not because they had been closely scrutinised and found defective in some particular respect, but because they implied a conception of nature which now appeared inherently absurd.'[44] As the result, by the end of this period the nature of religion had changed. A distinction could be made between religion and magic, which would not have been possible two centuries earlier. As Thomas notes, 'religion which survived the decline of magic was not the religion of Tudor England.[...] The official religion of industrial England was one from which the primitive "magical" elements had been very largely shorn.'[45]

There are important differences in the roles religion plays in European countries, depending on whether Catholicism or Protestantism has been the dominant religion, and the way that either one allied with national élites in addressing the rise of liberalism and socialism. Further differences arise if religion has been called on to play a part in cultural defence (as traditionally Catholicism in Ireland) or cultural transition (as Afro-Caribbean Pentecostalism in Britain). But in all European countries, there has been a significant decline in the social importance of Christianity. Specialised roles and institutions have developed to handle various functions previously carried out by one institution. For example, specialist institutions have arisen to provide education, health care, welfare and social control, all of which were once in the domain of religious institutions. With economic growth there emerged an ever-greater range of occupation and life experience, which decreased the plausibility of a single moral universe or grand design. Besides this factor of 'social differentiation', close-knit, integrated small-scale communities were replaced by large-scale

---

[42]   *Ibid.*, 766.

[43]   *Ibid.*, 771 and 786.

[44]   *Ibid.*, 690.

[45]   *Ibid.*, 765-66. As Hugh Trevor-Roper concludes his *European Witch Craze*, the whole 'intellectual and social structure' which underpinned belief in witches had to be broken. 'In the mid-seventeenth century this was done. Then the medieval synthesis, which Reformation and Counter-Reformation had artificially prolonged, was at last broken.[...] Thereafter society might persecute its dissidents as Huguenots or as Jews. It might discover a new stereotype, the 'Jacobin', the 'Red'. But the stereotype of witch had gone' (H.R. Trevor Roper, *The European Witch-Craze of the Sixteenth and Seventeenth Centuries*, London: Penguin 1969, 122).

industrial and commercial enterprises, modern states co-ordinated through massive impersonal bureaucracies, and anonymous urban agglomerations. Society rather than the community has become the locus of the individual's life, and society now depends less on the inculcation of a shared religious or moral order than on the utilisation of efficient technical means and appropriate behaviour. In these circumstances changes are evident in the way people think. It is not just that the media and education diffuse an Enlightenment culture, or that the worlds of transport, medicine and business are increasingly dependent on high technology. In every sphere of life bureaucratisation, planning and regularisation are evident, which inevitably affects our understanding of causation, and of what constitutes an argument for a position or a reason for a course of action.[46] Some would claim that Christianity itself played a large part in this process, arguing that by its very nature it tends to desacralise. Thus Wilson can even refer to 'such a vigorously exclusivist and anti-magical religion as Christianity'.[47]

It is the internal transformation within Western Christianity rather than numerical decrease or decline in social importance that is significant.[48] The supernaturalistic has largely disappeared (we will use this term to distinguish the realm of demons, spirits, witches and so on from the supernatural – God, heaven, prayer, the resurrection of Christ, sacraments – which has largely persisted in Western churches).[49] In the West the worldview underpinning deliverance thinking has ceased to be culturally significant. Reality is generally not experienced in terms of witches,

---

[46]   'For every social problem, whether of economy, polity, law, education, family relations, or recreation, the solutions proposed are not only non-religious, but solutions that depend on technical expertise and bureaucratic organisation. Planning, not revelation; rational order, not inspiration; systematic routine, not charismatic or traditional action, are the imperatives in ever-widening arenas of public life' (Wilson, *Religion*, 176-7). See also Steve Bruce, *Religion in the Modern World: from Cathedrals to Cults*, Oxford University Press, 1996.

[47]   Wilson, *Religion*, 28.

[48]   What had been seen as a gradual numerical decline seems to be turning in the mid-1990s into a major cultural shift. By 1996 the Anglicans in Britain were losing 26,000 members a year and the Catholics 29,000; the yearly loss from all denominations was 74,300. The Methodists were losing twenty-six members a day, and admitting that they could be extinct in forty to seventy years. The fall-off among youth may be even more significant: Anglicans lost 34% of their fourteen- to seventeen-year-olds in the nine years between 1987 and 1996. See *Guardian*, 6 April 1996, 24; *Guardian* 11 April 1996, 9. Cox is at his weakest in detecting a religious renaissance in Europe (*Fire*, 185-211).

[49]   It is risky here to over-generalise. One cannot be too definite about what modern or Western man or woman can or cannot believe; as late as the 1950s it seems that a geography student at London University obtained a first-class honours degree without at any point in her exams being false to her conviction, held on religious grounds, that the earth is flat (Denis Nineham, *The Use and Abuse of the Bible*, London: Macmillan, 1976, 32). Rebecca Brown, a key figure in deliverance thinking, claims to be a medical doctor.

demons and personalised spiritual powers, and Christianity has changed to take account of this. Even in America, where church attendance remains high, the supernaturalistic has largely receded. America has seen a fundamentalist reaction, which would claim to be reversing the Enlightenment. However, much of this movement has its own particular agenda, and even the espousal of creationism appears 'to have no impact whatsoever on the assumptions on which the social system operates'.[50] We do not have to pursue this further here, and distinguish or justify 'enlightened versions of Christianity'.[51] The foregoing can be admitted, without in any way accepting the Enlightenment uncritically, or disguising the tremendous problems facing Western 'Enlightenment' societies at the end of the twentieth century.[52]

In Africa the religious situation is very different. For one thing, as African states collapse or withdraw, the churches are being forced to involve themselves in all sorts of activities from which they have long been displaced in Europe, and which even in Africa were being taken from them in the years immediately after independence. But far more important is the question of religious vision. In Africa most Christians operate from a background little affected by the European Enlightenment; for most Africans, witchcraft, spirits and ancestors, spells and charms are primary and immediate and natural categories of interpretation. For them religion 'is concerned with the explanation, prediction and control of space-time events';[53] it is primarily about power, or obtaining the good offices of supernatural forces – which, of course, as Thomas reminds us, was the primary concern of English religion too until the seventeenth century.[54] Most Africans have an 'enchanted' worldview. Yet most African Christians are members of mainline mission churches which 'officially' embrace a theology affected by the Enlightenment. African churches have Western missionaries, many of whom embody this Enlightenment and non-supernaturalistic theology. Many African church leaders have

---

And Derek Prince, the guru of Ghana's deliverance movement, was educated at Eton and Cambridge, and claims to have been a philosophy fellow of Kings College, Cambridge, between 1940 and 1949. There are still plenty of individuals who can live, or affect to live, in another world as well. Stephen King's novels reach the bestseller lists, and all the British tabloid newspapers have daily horoscopes. And out-and-out Faith Gospellers like Morris Cerullo or Kenneth Copeland conduct conventions in Britain (it is in the West that they earn their living), but one only has to attend these occasions to realise how 'counter-cultural' in a really hard sense they are, and how dependent on the immigrant population.

50   Wilson, *Religion*, 38; see also 43-4.
51   Martin, *Tongues*, 23.
52   Wilson, *Religion*, 88, Hobsbawm, *Age*, 562.
53   Robin Horton, 'African Conversion', *Africa* 41, 2 (1971), 85-108, and authors there cited.
54   Thomas, *Religion*, 27.

completed degrees in the 'internally secularised' theology faculties of the West. This gives Africa's mainline churches a rather ambiguous character. Their official theology and activity and public pronouncements tend to be of the Westernised kind, but most of their members have a very different understanding and widely divergent expectations.

The two strands have until recently coexisted reasonably successfully. For the most part, church authorities, at least publicly, discounted the popular or primal conceptions. There was faith in the modernisation or Westernisation process, and these mainline churches were agents of modernisation; they understood themselves in that way. But since the 1970s the modernising project has visibly run out of steam, and often been positively repudiated by the peoples who were supposed to be its beneficiaries. At the same time the Pentecostal churches have taken root. When a Pentecostal Christianity is preached that stresses the reality of demons or witchcraft, it has quite naturally evoked a powerful response from people with an 'enchanted' worldview. Pentecostal Christianity is answering needs left entirely unaddressed by mainline Christianity. For this reason, countless thousands are leaving the mainline to join new Pentecostal churches. This drift is not sinister; it is quite natural. Its rationale is detected in the reasons given for leaving the mission churches and joining the new churches. Mainline Christians are allegedly 'not biblical' because they do not take seriously divine and demonic interventions and apparitions that fill the Old Testament. They 'do not believe in miracles' because they regard the stories of Elijah, Elisha and Jonah as unhistorical, and do not seriously expect to replicate New Testament miracles today. Mainline Christians 'deny the supernatural' because they insist on explaining a child's death in terms of bacteria or microbes rather than witches or spirits. They are merely 'political', because they explain the state of the nation in terms of falling commodity prices, unequal trade flows or government mismanagement or corruption, rather than spiritual forces.

This drift from the mainline to the Pentecostal churches constitutes a significant realignment within African Christianity, and highlights what is surely a crucial point of the division between 'élite' and 'popular' Christianity. It was not that the church leaders addressed only their own needs (most of all their status and remuneration) and ignored the people. Though admittedly there has been much of this, in some cases leaders were assiduously addressing what they thought should have been the real needs of the people. It was the people who decided that their needs were totally different. Africa's mainline churches since the 1920s have been increasingly promoting a modernising agenda, with the stress on schools, clinics and, more recently, development projects. They tended to presume that this process would continue inexorably, to the glory of God and the betterment of everyone. The reaction against mainline Christianity or, better, opting when the opportunity presented itself for a Christianity that caters for completely other needs, has left many mainline churchmen bewildered. The churches that seem best able to surmount this challenge are those (like the Presbyterians and Catholics in Ghana) that have actually developed institutions to contain both tendencies.

The tension between the two Christianities, one expressed in terms of a primal vision, the other affected by the Enlightenment, is highlighted by Zambia's Archbishop Milingo now he is forced to operate in Europe. In 1996 Milingo was banned from holding services in the Archdiocese of Milan, precisely because of fears that he might have encouraged a 'credulity which explains all psycho-physical ills as due to the influence of the devil, and leads people to expect exorcisms, healings and miracles'.[55] Here the contrast is marked up boldly. Cardinal Martini of Milan, one of the Catholic Church's foremost biblical scholars, is simply not prepared to have Milingo's Christianity promoted in his diocese. For some, especially those influenced by cultural relativism, an 'African' theology such as Milingo's is to be encouraged. In Cox's perspective, the flowering of primal spirituality is a sign of hope, because Western liberal Christianity has run into the sand. Bediako for his part wants to desacralise without despiritualising. By this he appears to mean that he wants Weber's 'disenchantment', which would bring Africa technological and scientific advance, but that the primal mentality – awareness in daily life of ubiquitous spiritual forces working in the universe – should persist.[56] How these might be combined is arguably the biggest question facing Christianity in Africa; Bediako does not offer a solution.[57]

Others argue that the world as we have it is set up by the West; the West has laid down the principles by which it operates, and these are summed up in the one word, rationality.[58] If religion is to play any public role in this dispensation, it must take account of that. 'Only a religion which has incorporated as its own the central aspects of the Enlightenment critique of religion is in a position today to play a positive role in furthering processes of practical rationalisation ... [and] contribute to the revitalisation of the modern public sphere.'[59] This view involves an

[55]   *Tablet*, 20 April 1996, 525.

[56]   Bediako, *Christianity*, 212.

[57]   For insights here, see Richard Gray, 'Christianity and Concepts of Evil in Sub-Saharan Africa' in his *Black Christians and White Missionaries*, New Haven: Yale University Press, 1991, 99-117.

[58]   David S. Landes, *The Unbound Prometheus: Technological Change and Industrial Development in Western Europe from 1750 to the Present*, Cambridge University Press, 1969.

[59]   José Casanova, *Public Religions in the Modern World*, University of Chicago Press, 1995, 233.

unashamed value judgement that the Enlightenment was a watershed.

You cannot understand the human condition if you ignore or deny its total transformation by the success of the scientific revolution. [...] [This] has totally transformed the terms of reference in which human societies operate. To pretend that the scientific revolution of the seventeenth century, and its eventual application in the later stage of the industrial revolution have not transformed the world but are merely changes from one culture to another, is simply an irresponsible affectation.[60]

According to this view, all societies have had to make their peace with the Enlightenment; in doing so, some have retained more, some less, of their previous culture.[61] Bediako has not addressed this viewpoint.

Mihevc has written a combative rebuttal of the World Bank's activities in Africa, and the harm they are doing in Africa through the enforcement of structural adjustment. His is a liberation perspective, focusing on the political and particularly economic structures that cause such harm in Africa. However, he goes on to claim that what he describes is common in African churches, indeed almost representative of African Christianity today. Mihevc writes of a 'fundamental theological reorientation on the part of churches in Africa [evident in] the re-affirmation of liberation theology rooted in prophetic discourse condemning corrupt leaders and calling for elections. A key constitutive element in this re-orientation has been the churches' response to the effects of the debt and SAP crisis.'[62] He sees 'increasing attention being accorded to economic concerns, especially those related to the international financial system', and points to an 'explicit integration of a political economy analysis within a theological framework'.[63] This 'focus on the economy marks a significant theological movement.'[64] He claims that at various levels 'popular [theological] education materials are being produced which provide a comprehensive analysis of the root causes of the debt crisis.'[65] His examples, taken mainly from officials and activities of the All Africa Conference of Churches, are no doubt correct, but they are so unrepresentative as to give an overall impression that is quite misleading. From our case studies one would maintain that what Mihevc describes is precisely what African Christianity is *not* about. We have seen that in Cameroon and in Uganda there is little concern with structural matters. In Zambia some of these concerns are voiced by the churches, but the

60   Ernest Gellner, 'Anything Goes', *Times Literary Supplement*, 16 June 1995, 8.

61   Ernest Gellner, *Postmodernism, Reason and Religion*, London: Routledge, 1992, 61.

62   Mihevc, *Market*, 225.

63   *Ibid.*, 226.

64   *Ibid.*, 264.

65   *Ibid.*, 241.

source of this theology is mainly the Jesuit Centre for Theological Reflection, and cannot be said to be a preoccupation of the churches generally. The Christian Council of Ghana operated an extensive 'democratisation' programme, but even that was built on concerns quite different from Mihevc's; it addressed issues of a far more basic kind, such as whether a Christian should vote and, as we noted, its thrust was more gently Evangelical, claiming that a life of personal Christian integrity will lead to change in the nation. Mihevc's abstracting from personal activities and focusing on structural forces like the World Bank and IMF belongs to another level of discourse.

Most varieties of Christianity in Africa, judging from their preaching or literature, are not partners in Mihevc's discourse. African Christians ask the same questions as Mihevc: Why are Africans suffering? Where does evil come from? What might redemption or salvation mean in these circumstances? But their answers only very infrequently consider African political structures or Western influences like the international banking industry. Their principal answers are expressed in terms of lack of faith or blockages caused by demons. That this is understandable cannot be denied, and it makes 'a certain sense'. Most Africans manifest a 'primal' mentality, and we have shown that churches meeting these primal needs are understandably flourishing. Mihevc may be right in suggesting that African theology needs a stronger base in the Enlightenment; but he is surely incorrect in implying that such a theology is already flowering.

A strength of Mihevc's analysis is his understanding of power. He shows how the World Bank controls the discourse of development in Africa. In his words, the World Bank 'owns' the agenda for Africa's development in the 1990s.[66] Its resources ensure that its theorists provide the paradigm which determines how things are interpreted, and the narrative into which data are woven. With such 'paradigm-enforcing power' it is not surprising that they can neutralise or coopt any alternative discourse or agenda.[67] Africa's theological agenda is no longer immune from non-theological determinants. A primal discourse leads naturally to a theology of deliverance from demons. It is not quite so natural that it should lead to some of African Christianity's other dominant motifs. For example, the primal imagination would not lead automatically to evangelisation, or church growth, or 'taking the nation for Jesus' – emphases that come from organisations like AD 2000 and Beyond, which as we have seen are so dominant in this field that their paradigm is widely accepted, to the extent that any alternative is almost impossible. This paradigm has considerable socio-political effects, for it privileges

[66]   *Ibid.*, 132.
[67]   Clapham, *International System*, 168; Leys, *Rise and Fall*, 64.

evangelism almost to exclusivity. If evangelism is effectively all there is to Christianity, then Chiluba is a good President; and if promoting evangelism is all that is needed, Christians must fight to keep him in office. That is a far cry from Mihevc's discourse.

What we have said has a bearing on much writing on African theology. We noted this in the case of Bediako, whose analysis ignores much of what is happening in African Christianity today. It is even more evident in Parratt's survey of African theology. Parratt argues (against those who would say that South Africa's theology is largely political and that Black Africa's is largely cultural) that 'Theology throughout Africa finds its common ground in three basic elements – in the Bible and Christian tradition, in African culture and religion, and in the contemporary sociopolitical situation.'[68] If we alter his punctuation and consider the three elements as five, we see that only one is of marked significance in much of African Christianity today, and that is the Bible, treated in a very non-critical way. One forms the impression that at the level of church life Christian tradition is largely ignored and, where adverted to, probably dismissed as a distortion; African culture is generally very suspect, and African religion positively demonised; and the contemporary sociopolitical situation is dismissed as theologically irrelevant. This does not invalidate much of Parratt's fine overview of African academic theology; it merely serves to illustrate the gulf between élite academic theology and Christian developments in Africa today, and to show how marginal mainline academic theology is. It is done by Western-trained professionals, largely for Western consumption (the criticism often made of Ela's Liberation Theology in Cameroon) and seems sometimes quite unrelated to the significant developments afoot.

Africa's new Christianity

Cox makes a distinction between 'fundamentalism' and 'experientialism' in an effort to catch the essence of so many new religious movements without conveying the negative connotations of 'fundamentalism'.[69] For the same reason we have avoided the word 'fundamentalism' in this discussion. Emphasising a reactionary element, though it may capture a key aspect of partner churches in America, does not capture the key dynamics of Black Africa's new churches. In Africa the appeal is to a primal imagination, but this does not involve a positive repudiation of Enlightenment rationality in the way that is required in the West. Also, in much of the discussion of Western religion, fundamentalism connotes some stress on doctrine. This is not required in Africa, nor is there any

---

[68] Parratt, *Reinventing Christianity*, 27.
[69] Cox, *Fire*, 300-20.

idea of 'nationalism' – indeed, in a sense, there is nothing more transnational in Africa than the born-again movement. Nor is there any idea of repudiating the secular state; in much of the born-again movement there is little political awareness at all.

Similarly with the word 'sect'. Even though the word is so frequently applied to newer churches in Africa, the idea of turning one's back on the world is, as we have seen, rarely involved at all. Far from fulfilling any command to be separate (Lev 20: 24) these churches are one of the best available means of linking into the outside world. For this reason, too, we have not stressed the idea of 'exit option' or 'walkout', which might have been perfectly appropriate in analysing the role of groups like the Jehovah's Witnesses in Zambia in, say, the 1940s. Today, in Uganda and Zambia, becoming born-again actually brings one close to power; elsewhere, though it may indicate some turning against the political élite, it can be a way of linking into other material benefits.

We have felt justified in distinguishing between AICs and the newer churches. This is not to argue that all the new churches are identical, but they do appear to possess a set of family resemblances. We would further argue that these are tending to supplant the family resemblances formerly adduced to identify AICs. The newer churches, though they depend on primal conceptions like deliverance, do not represent a return to the past, or a bridge to traditional culture, in the way the AICs did. They are harshly negative concerning much of Africa's traditional culture – not just polygamy and (in Zambia) practices like the 'cleansing' of widows. They repudiate the veneration of ancestors. We have seen these new churches attacking 'spiritual' churches for precisely such things. The new churches reject all the ritual – candles, blessed water, white cloths, drumming, sacrifices – that has been associated with the AICs.[70] (An interesting boundary shift is observable here: many AICs began by denouncing the mainline churches as not Christian, but now the same accusation is being made against them.) Sacral robes are nowhere in evidence. Their worship is exuberant, but it is less and less characterised by the trances and possessions characteristic of the AICs (possessing 'the gift of tongues' is not 'possession' in the earlier sense). Dreams have given way to a much more direct form of divine communication. The new churches maintain a preoccupation with spirits, but in a markedly different way from the AICs. Miracles are performed without instrumentality. All their props are modern and sophisticated. Their language tends to be English or French and their music Western. They emphasise their links with the wider world. Culturally they play a role different from that played by the AICs.

The formal theology of the new born-again churches is essentially the

---

[70] Monica Wilson, *Religion and the Transformation of Society: a Study in Social Change in Africa*, Cambridge University Press, 1971, 73, 127.

Faith Gospel as outlined in Chapter 2. As an elaborated Christian vision this is an American development, linked in its origins to positive thinking. We have noted how well suited this was to the United States in the 1960s and early 1970s, when the economy was booming and there were countless opportunities to be grasped. It was also extremely functional for the televangelists who developed it; its stress on seed-faith or giving ensured the revenues they needed to build their media empires.

We have seen how widespread this prosperity theology has become in Africa. It is preached at length in the newer churches, and these beliefs are ritually enacted, with collections and offerings. They are reinforced by countless testimonies. Freston argues that the prosperity gospel is characteristic only of the third wave of Pentecostalism in Brazil (that is, of the churches of the 1980s); we have argued that in Africa it has spread even to earlier churches, like Ghana's Church of Pentecost, and even into the mainline churches. It has spread by various means: through the wide diffusion of literature, through organisations like the FGBMFI, through the burgeoning Bible schools and through the rise of 'pastors' conferences' that have increasingly become a feature of crusades (where formal training is so limited the impact of these conferences is considerable.) Above all it has spread through the paradigmatic ministries of such high-profile exponents as Ghana's Duncan-Williams, Zambia's Nevers Mumba, Uganda's Handel Leslie, and – the most high-profile of all – Nigeria's Benson Idahosa. Of course these are all middle-class religious entrepreneurs of the major cities, but the Faith Gospel is increasingly at home in rural areas. For church leaders this faith teaching is obviously very functional, for it brings in revenues that enable them to survive and flourish in a very competitive field. First and foremost, the teaching suits them, the pastors. That it should have won such a general acceptance in Africa's current situation is both quite natural and rather surprising. This calls for some comment.

It is natural that the Faith Gospel should be so prevalent, because Africa's traditional religions were focused on material realities. In the nineteenth century, Crowther wrote of the Yoruba religious search for 'peace, health, children and money'.[71] This preoccupation has been noted several times since.[72] Westernised mainline Christianity does not cater for this, so it is perfectly natural that the Pentecostal Christianity which

---

[71] Cited in J.D.Y. Peel, 'An Africanist Revisits Magic and the Millennium' in Eileen Barker, James A. Beckford and Karel Dobbelaere (eds), *Secularization, Rationalism and Sectarianism: Essays in Honour of Bryan R. Wilson*, Oxford University Press, 1993, 98, n. 15.

[72] Inus Daneel, *Quest for Belonging: Introduction to a Study of African Independent Churches*, Gweru: Mambo Press, 1987, 46; Monica Wilson, *Religion*, 37; Okot P'Bitek, *African Religions*, 62.

does should fare so well. It is also to be noted that the classical AICs, though focusing on well-being, did not place the emphasis precisely as it is placed now. Their preoccupation was predominantly health – understandable particularly in rural life, where sickness was the most obvious and recurrent trial. But the newer generations in the cities have slightly different needs; sickness has not lost its importance, but these are wage-earners (or would-be wage earners) whose concerns centre on employment, promotion, cash, accommodation, transport – which in rural areas, involved in agriculture within the extended family or kinship group, do not arise in quite the same way. We noted that in many of the churches under consideration, wealth has become far more important than health, though not entirely displacing it. If this prosperity message is most understandable in cities, it has moved deep into rural areas. Churches that began in capital cities began to plant churches in regional centres, and then district centres. Their dynamism, resources and techniques have spread the prosperity message, so appropriate for them, into areas where it is much less natural. This is not an entirely new phenomenon. As Peel demonstrated in relation to the Aladura, beliefs which started as dependent variables of a particular social situation have gone on to acquire an institutional framework transforming them into independent variables with their own power to bring about ideological and social change.[73]

But the prevalence of the prosperity gospel is also remarkable in view of the continent's state of visible collapse, in which the vast majority are inescapably caught up. It is sometimes assumed that these new churches will play the role some attribute to the Methodists in eighteenth-century England.[74] This is often said without adverting to the fact that their theology is so very different. For one thing, the world of witches, spells, curses and sorcery had already receded before Methodism made its contribution to the increasing rationality of English economic life. That is clearly not the context of the new churches in Africa. Yet there is an even more important difference between the theology of early Methodists and these new churches. The early Methodists preached hard work: Thompson argues that Wesley's teaching of conversion, conviction and grace meant that 'man or child only found grace in God's eyes when performing painful, laborious or self-denying tasks', that workers must endure their working conditions and be prepared to suffer; that was their vocation.[75] The theology fostered asceticism, abstemiousness, deferral

---

[73]   J.D.Y. Peel, *Aladura: a Religious Movement among the Yoruba*, London: Oxford University Press, 1968; R. Horton, 'African Conversion', 95.

[74]   This is the thesis of Martin, *Tongues*, where Methodism provides both the model and problematic for Latin American Pentecostalism (27-46). Peter Berger in his foreword seems to go further than Martin (9).

[75]   Thompson, *Making*, 409.

of gratification, and all of these led to investment. However, according to the Faith Gospel, one only needs belief, or belief and giving money, or belief and the special gifts of the pastor and God will do everything. Much of the Faith Gospel is well captured in this letter from a Zambian printed in Kenneth Copeland's magazine:

'I am writing to thank you for the two issues of the magazine you sent. Honestly, they have been revolutionary to me. I used to be a very negative person, but the articles in the magazines have had such an impact on me that the negativity is disappearing. I have a totally new vocabulary and it is affecting all those around me. Being raised in a poor family caused me to accept poverty as part of the 'package deal'. Now that has completely changed.[...] I now look at things differently as the mountain of lack has been commanded to be removed and cast into the sea, and I do not doubt in my heart. I believe the things I say will come to pass and they do. Just the other day a friend who did not know I had asked God for some money walked up and gave me K4,500. Praise the Lord – my needs are being met. The vibrancy and joy of living that eluded me so long have finally come to me. Thank you and God richly bless you.[76]

Here we find (besides the new paradigm or 'totally new vocabulary' encountered through foreign literature) the idea that faith will ensure that God intervenes to enrich the individual Christian. These new churches are not reinvigorating the Protestant ethic. On the contrary, Freston is surely correct when he writes: 'Prosperity theology represents an advanced stage of the decline of the Protestant ethic.'[77] Members of these churches may work very hard, but this is not the message they hear incessantly preached. Eighteenth-century Methodist theology led to investment, but the Faith Gospel places no emphasis on investment. The riches that it insists are the right of every Christian are not for investment but for evangelism. This is not to say that the proponents of the Faith Gospel do not become entrepreneurs – regarded from any social scientific perspective, this is exactly what its preachers are – but this is certainly not the message that is everywhere inculcated.

We return again to the question of wider networks. The faith theology that is heard so widely in Africa was not devised in Africa. (We have just said that it coalesces very well with the central preoccupations of much traditional African religious thought; but that, we maintain, is something slightly different.) It might be thought that Africa's circumstances might give rise to a theology that, for example, stresses redemption through suffering.[78] But this concept has almost been lost. Suffering has no place

---

[76]   *Believers' Voice of Victory*, Oct 1996, 13.

[77]   Paul Freston, 'Pentecostalism in Brazil: a Brief History', *Religion* 25 (1995), 131-32. He continues: 'It separates wealth and salvation, thus lacking the psychological mechanism (anguish about eternal destiny) which supposedly impelled the puritan in his rational search for prosperity.'

[78]   Mbembe, *Afriques indociles*, 105.

within the Faith Gospel, according to which the Christian should be healthy, rich and successful.[79] The Faith Gospel seems to be in conflict with the immediate experience of innumerable Africans. In that sense, it is difficult to see it as something developed in relation to African religious experience.

Compare this, for example with a genuinely (albeit now discredited) African theology, that of South Africa's Afrikaners. The Afrikaners drew on their Puritan emphases of election and ordination, and then added the motif of the Exodus from the experience of their own Great Trek in the 1830s, and the motif of the Covenant from their vow before the battle of Blood River (1838). A people largely illiterate, though steeped in the Bible, and cut off from other civilisations, developed these images into their foundational narrative or national myth. Later, to justify their relations with the Black population, they grafted on motifs allegedly drawn from the biblical texts of Genesis 1: 28 and 11: 1-9; Deuteronomy 32: 8-9; and Acts 2: 5-11 and 17: 26.[80] That is an example of theologising out of experience, in the light of particular needs and preoccupations. Yet from Zambia to Ghana, Cameroon to Uganda, the flourishing new born-again churches cite Deuteronomy 28-30; Malachi 3: 8-11; Mark 10: 29-30 and 11: 23-24; 3 John 2; and Philippians 4: 19. It is difficult to see this prosperity motif as reflecting common experience in any of these countries. Obviously the Faith Gospel's element of 'seed faith' has proved more functional for entrepreneur pastors than the theology has proved dysfunctional for their followers. It has thus made 'a certain sense' (to use Ranger's phrase again), but we have argued that because that sense has proved inadequate, at least in West Africa, there is now an evident move to transcend it.

We have argued that this is an area in which African creativity is most visible. It was precisely because in Africa's current circumstances, with people visibly getting poorer by the day, the emphasis is perceptibly shifting. We noted that some important voices, though coming from the faith stable, have left it far behind. Otabil, without an actual public denunciation, effectively denies it. He talks in terms of structures, for an individual cannot succeed if his surroundings do not permit. He has developed his own theology of entrepreneurship.[81] He is one taking this message across the continent – we witnessed its advent to Zambia. More

---

[79] In this regard, Freston describes prosperity theology as 'a religious discourse which rejects traditional Christian theodicy' ('Pentecostalism in Brazil', 132). Cf African Rights, *Great Expectations*, 7.

[80] W. de Clerk, *The Puritans in Africa*, London: Penguin, 1976; Douglas Bax, 'The Bible and Apartheid' in John W. de Gruchy and Charles Villa-Vicencio (eds), *Apartheid is a Heresy*, Grand Rapids: Eerdmans, 1983, 112-43.

[81] For similar ideas in Brazil, see Freston, 'Pentecostalism in Brazil', 132.

often, though, particularly in West Africa, the shift has been to stress deliverance. This theology attempts to explain that faith does not always bring its reward; sometimes one is blocked, but with deliverance one can obtain everything that faith promises. This second element, the deliverance that must be superimposed on faith, was also to be found in traditional African religions. Okot P'Bitek writes: 'African religions ... are concerned with the good life here and now, with health and prosperity, with success in life, happy and productive marriage etc. They deal with the causes of diseases, with failures and other obstacles in the path of self-realisation and fulfilment.'[82] But once again, this stress on demons is also an important strand in American Pentecostalism. We have argued that authors like Peter Wagner, Derek Prince and the Hammonds cannot be ignored in any discussion of the contemporary formulation and legitimation of Africa's contemporary deliverance theology.[83]

The prominence of the Faith Gospel and deliverance serves to emphasise how little millennialism there is in contemporary African Christianity. 'Millennialism' covers the ideas associated with the book of Revelation: dualism, the corruption of the present order, its inevitable destruction, the suffering of the elect in this order, and an imminent divine intervention to establish a totally new dispensation. Cox puts millennialism at the very centre of Pentecostalism, which he effectively defines as a 'millennial sensibility'.[84] Africa has had its millennialists: preachers like John Chilembwe and Elliot Kamwana in Central Africa, William Wade Harris and Garrick Braide in West Africa. It has also been exposed to the pre-millennial dispensationalism of John Nelson Darby which has been so important in American fundamentalism and which reached its apogee with Hal Lindsey's popular *Late Great Planet Earth*, which in the 1980s was America's best-selling non-fiction book (if such it can be called).[85] This book illustrated and catered for the American preoccupation with Russia and Israel. We have occasionally seen these ideas surface in Africa: Chiluba's preoccupation with establishing diplomatic links with Israel stems from this theology, and we heard echoes of it in Leslie's preaching in Uganda. Visiting speakers lecture on this in Africa, and the framework is widely known – when Barry Smith gave his seminars in Uganda, his assumptions and methods came as no surprise to his listeners. But this approach is not widely picked up. The popular Christianity we encountered was personalised, not cosmic. It was not concerned with a renewed order or any 'new Jerusalem', but with a job, a husband, a

---

[82]   Okot P'Bitek, *African Religions*, 62; Also Monica Wilson, *Religion*, 37.

[83]   Cox regards this Western deliverance strand as extremely dubious; *Fire*, 281-87.

[84]   Cox, *Fire*, 116.

[85]   Hal Lindsey with C.C. Carlson, *The Late Great Planet Earth*, New York, NY: Bantam, 1970.

child, a car, an education, a visa to the West. It was about succeeding in this realm, through faith or (increasingly, at least in West Africa) through faith and deliverance from satanic blockages. We saw in many cases that success has become more central than healing. On the face of it, it might be thought that there are millennial images that could resonate powerfully with Africa's truly apocalyptic plight – most obviously, the scourges of war, famine and disease (Revelation 6: 1-8), or (at least in the optimistic interlude of 1989-93) the imminent dethroning of evil powers and the dawning of a new order. But these images have not been widely developed. Daniel and Revelation have posed no threat to Deuteronomy, Kings and Malachi.[86]

Nor is there much stress on an otherworldly order, or much expectation of a reward in an afterlife. London's *Economist* has written of what it calls South America's 'sects': 'Mostly they offer political quietism, promising a reward in the next world for the miseries of this one.'[87] It is to be stressed that this is *not* the message of Africa's new churches, which is mainly one of fullness in this life, through faith or through faith and deliverance. We remarked that missionaries have been criticised for teaching Africans to endure hardship in this life in exchange for happiness hereafter. If the criticism was once valid, the missionary legacy has vanished with scarcely a trace, for it is terrestrial rewards that feature so prominently in African Christianity now.

Civil society

Having clarified the varieties of Christianity in Africa, we are better placed to address their multifarious public roles. The churches' public involvement has been glimpsed at many levels. We discovered little political theology, in a Latin American sense, except in Cameroon where it was totally marginalised.[88] This theology and its associated structures, the Small Christian Communities, have not taken deep root in Africa.[89] But, in a gently embryonic way, this kind of thinking is expressed in the Catholic pastoral letters and the statements of Christian Councils. Their ethos is roughly that of the Church of England's 1986 *Faith in the City*, or the American Catholic bishops' 1986 pastoral letter *Economic Justice for All: Catholic Social Teaching and the US Economy*, or the 1996 letter

---

[86] Mihevc, *Market*, 236-42, gives a rather different impression.

[87] *Economist*, 10 Feb 1996, 70.

[88] Parratt, *Reinventing*, 26-7, 124, 193-94, gives a somewhat misleading impression of the salience of socio-political issues within theology in Black Africa.

[89] Anne Hope and Sally Timmel, *Training for Transformation: a Handbook for Community Workers*, Gweru: Mambo Press, 1984, was developed in a church programme beginning in Kenya in 1974; training in the programme is conducted by the Christian Council in Zimbabwe and Catholics in Nigeria.

of the Catholic bishops of England and Wales, *The Common Good*. Such documents are normally drafted by committees which include academic sociologists and economists as well as theologians, and they embody rationality in advocating legislation or increased efficiency, control and supervision. The pronouncements of Africa's mainline churches approximate to this genre, although they can have a more Evangelical spin as well. As we saw in the case of Ghana, the Christian Council produces public statements, but its theological content is gently Evangelical, suggesting that if an individual adopts a life of personal integrity the country must follow.

The question of direct political involvement of the newer churches is more complex. Bayart is most unsatisfactory on this point – not least because times have moved so quickly that his 'contemporary sects' are really yesterday's, having been replaced by new born-again churches. Bayart generalises that 'the independent church fragments on the periphery and feeds social dissidence', and describes the Lumpa Church as setting itself up as 'a peasant counter-society'.[90] Bayart is describing a previous generation of churches. He claims that new churches, in an exercise of the 'exit option ... ignore rather than contest the state', as if these were the only two options. At least Zambia and Uganda offer a third option to the born-agains, which is to get as close to the state as possible. Africa's new churches have a rather different agenda, one element of which is to walk the corridors of power.

When the new churches do enter the political arena, although they certainly insist that corruption should cease, they hardly have a conscious social agenda.[91] In describing the situation in Brazil, where the born-agains have secured a sizeable representation in parliament, Freston notes that far from purifying a corrupt political culture, 'Pentecostalism has assimilated the political culture at all levels.' He argues that Brazil's Christian politicians are not so much corrupt as 'time-serving', which he defines as 'the art of keeping oneself close to power, regardless of ideology or principle, in order to receive benefits' – often for the church.[92] This is roughly the political agenda of the born-agains in Zambia, where the benefits that the pastors seek from their born-again President are that

[90] Bayart, *State*, 256-7.

[91] This qualification is missed in Haynes' remark (*Religion and Politics*, 199) that these churches seek 'social justice'.

[92] Freston cites a leading Pentecostal deputy as saying, at a time of debate about limiting the President's terms of office: 'If President Sarney offered me 100 radio stations in exchange for a term of office of 100 years, as long as the radios were for preaching the gospel, I would accept.' In other words, when compared with unrestricted evangelism, constitutional checks and balances count for little. See Freston, 'Popular Protestants in Brazilian Politics: a Novel Turn in Sect-State Relations', *Social Compass* 41 (1994) 563.

Zambia should be declared a Christian nation, that legislation be enacted against Islam, that churches be given government land, that they be chaplains to President Chiluba, that they have unlimited access to State House, that they be on national commissions, and that there be more evangelistic crusades. The thinking is essentially that pastors be given more recognition and a greater slice of the cake – for the purposes of evangelisation. Meanwhile, corruption and mismanagement bring Zambia to its knees.

Sometimes a misleading impression is given in discussions of the revival of political religion in the Third World, by lumping together Christian and Islamic fundamentalism. It is true that the latter has increased enormously in North African states at the same time as these new 'fundamentalist' Christian churches have proliferated to the south. Both may have similar causes, but in important respects it can be very misleading to treat them as parallel movements. Islamic fundamentalism of its very nature has a political agenda. It has a social blueprint – *Sharia* law – which it seeks to impose. In corrupt and incompetent North African states, this movement is obviously one of protest and destabilisation. What is called 'Christian fundamentalism', on the other hand, is a force for political stability in all the countries we have studied. This Christianity has no blueprint for society in any explicitly political sense.[93] At an indirectly political level, its effect is stabilising as well: they may refuse to pay bribes, but they inculcate prayer for leaders, obedience to laws and payment of taxes.

This question of the political role of churches is more often posed indirectly, in terms of civil society. In Chapter 1 we discussed this as one of the main concepts used in analysing Africa today – in political science, economics and development studies alike – and we accepted this as a useful concept in a study of the political impact of Africa's churches. But two remarks are in order. First, even though in Latin America it is normally the newer churches that are researched for their transformative internal dynamics, in Africa this approach has application to all. We have noted the importance of choirs in Protestant churches, even the most hierarchical. Choirs are dependent on rehearsals, voluntary cooperation and readiness to collaborate and pull together; they largely determine their own programmes, and organise festivals and competitions with other choirs.[94] In the Catholic Church the myriad sodalities function in the same

[93] Africa's new churches are hardly characterised by kingdom or dominion theology, much less reconstructionism. For these, see Gifford, *Christianity and Politics*, 252-7; Cox traces the change from pre-millennialism to a rather questionable post-millennialism in *Fire*, 287-97; see also Cox, 'The Warring Visions of the Religious Right', *Atlantic Monthly*, Nov 1985, 59-69. A failure to grasp the importance of this shift is evident in Boone, *Bible*, 53-8.

[94] See Martin on the virtues of choirs; for him, discussing the Latin American scene, they are primarily a Pentecostal phenomenon (*Tongues,* 167).

way, and need local, diocesan, regional and national coordination, often effected with only minimal reference to church professionals. The second observation is just as important. It is sometimes implied, from the Latin American scene, that membership of charismatic churches is voluntary while that of mainline churches is the result of birth; that attendance at charismatic churches denotes commitment, but at mainline churches is merely perfunctory; that charismatic churches change personal behaviour, but mainline churches have no effect on life. In Africa none of these assumptions is necessarily true. One has only to attend the Anglican or Catholic shrines on Uganda Martyrs' Day to see what Anglicanism or Catholicism means to vast multitudes. Conversely, there has been in the 1990s a change of status in the born-again churches. They are no longer necessarily countercultural. Only in Cameroon are they new enough to be still some distance from full acceptance. Elsewhere they have undergone considerable change of status in the space of less than a decade. In the late 1980s, newspapers in Uganda would not carry their advertisements; now the President's wife is likely to attend. In Zambia, as we have seen, the born-again churches form something of a new establishment. All sorts of factors can influence membership or attendance in these churches – in Ghana, for example, the superb music as much as personal commitment.

We can distinguish three areas in which churches could contribute to strengthening civil society: the political, the economic and the cultural. Where the properly political is concerned, we have focused on (in examining 'the deep politics of the churches' associational life') certain microquestions. How is power exercised? How accountable is the leadership? How transparent is the decision-making? Are constitutions observed? What subsidiarity is given to subordinate organisations? How equal are the opportunities for internal advancement?

With the mainline churches, we noted in Ghana the changing of constitutions to enable leaders to remain in office, and the flouting of constitutional regulations. In Uganda we noted the public struggle for power in Busoga and how the election of the latest Archbishop of Uganda turned on ethnic considerations. In Cameroon we saw how the PCC changed its constitution to allow the moderator to remain, and the EPC continually flouts its own constitution. We noted how a church's legal decisions cannot command much respect, since committees are often thought to be stacked beforehand, or patronage dispensed to predetermine the decision. Thus there seems little significant difference between the exercise of leadership in the churches and in national life generally; indeed, in some places it may sometimes be more autocratic and self-seeking. It is probably unrealistic to expect the churches to value legal or procedural niceties more highly than they are valued in the surrounding culture.

It is often claimed that the born-again churches function as schools of democracy, since they are groups of brothers and sisters promoting equality. Many of those we considered were personal fiefdoms, held together by the personal gifts of their leaders. We noted the tendency to authoritarianism – in Uganda one pastor would not even allow members to call him Brother, and insisted on his own views being sacrosanct and unquestioned, unlike those of his followers.[95] Some see this authoritarianism as something African, which these churches may come to modify. It is true that a traditional chief had considerable power, but it was not absolute – there were often checks, usually he had no standing army, and in places where small populations were spread thinly, it was easy for disaffected dependants simply to move elsewhere. However, in principle a chief was the representative of the ancestors, whose blessings he could bring to his people. There could be no challenge to his position, or even public criticism. A good chief had to be a strong chief, and to be able to provide help to his dependants he had to be wealthy. The people's wealth was his. In many cases he was not bound by the same rules as his subjects. Some have argued that many of the dysfunctional elements of Africa's despotisms stem from the attempts to replicate the rule of chiefs in the more complex role of leader of a modern nation state. However, Africa's new churches, far from modernising the understanding of and attitude to authority (Bayart's 'governmentalities'), or making authority more transparent and accountable, may work the other way. There is possibly a crucial dynamic within these churches that militates against democracy. Boone has well analysed the exercise of authority within fundamentalist churches. Using Foucault, she shows that a fundamentalist pastor is heir to a tradition, a participant in a discourse of which he is not the master, of which *no one* is the master. The churches we have been considering are different, appealing quite as much to the Holy Spirit as to the Bible. But authority functions in the same way, through a particular discourse. 'One stands a far better chance of challenging a [transparent] authority than a hidden one, and one stands hardly any chance at all when that hidden authority is parading in the guise of Holy Scripture' – or, in our case, the Holy Spirit.[96] Of its very nature, authority in so many of our churches cannot be transparent.

[95]   For authoritarianism in a recent Brazilian mega-church, similar to this one in Uganda, see Freston, 'Pentecostalism in Brazil', 129-32. He notes the church's strategies to increase centralisation and minimise dependence on lay demands: '1) by diversifying its income; 2) by eliminating all congregational participation in decision-making and de-emphasising strong horizontal ties among members; 3) by frequent transfers of pastors; and 4) by economising expenses through the use of many young pastors who are single and have low financial expectations because they have recently come off drugs or other disorganised lifestyles' (131).

[96]   Boone, *Bible*, 111; see also James Barr's review of Boone in *Theology Today*, Jan 1990, 422-5.

economic

Let us move from the political to the economic area. In our case studies we have argued that in all sorts of areas there is undoubtedly a close link between Africa's economic plight and the life of the churches. As economic circumstances have deteriorated, many are led to a life in the church, as one of the few opportunities available. Rev. Timothy Njoya, the outspoken Kenyan Presbyterian, has expressed this bluntly: 'Over 90% of the clergy in Kenya today have no call at all. They come to the ministry because they could not have achieved a better career.'[97] For the same reasons, the pressure to obtain and preserve the top jobs has increased, which has led to some particularly unedifying cases of clinging to power, in churches as much as in government.[98]

The fact that many capable and talented people are led to enter church leadership has a further bearing on Africa's economic development. In Chapter 1 we noted that class analysis is not particularly helpful in Africa. The bourgeoisie has tended to be linked to government, utilising government concessions, loopholes and protection, even government money. Such businessmen are not the classic wealth-creating risk-takers, but are essentially parasitic. From an economic viewpoint, the churches can appear part of this same scene. As the economic situation has collapsed, many who in the 1960s and 1970s would have gone into government jobs have moved into church or NGO employment, not creating wealth but essentially redistributing or channelling aid funds, almost as a comprador class of pastors and development officers.

Do the churches foster the middle-class virtues and skills regarded as a prerequisite for a modern economy? Cox has written at length of the way in which Korea's new Pentecostal churches inculcate economic skills. Members learn from the 'absolutely dazzling organisational genius that these churches demonstrate'. In their evangelistic campaigns and other activities, hundreds of thousands of people whose parental culture, if not their own, had been rural and traditional learned the bottom-line skills of a modern market economy. They learned to communicate a simple

---

97 *Option*, June 1995, 28; for the same phenomenon within Islam, see Jibrin Ibrahim, 'Religion and Political Turbulence in Nigeria', *JMAS* 29, 1 (1991), 121-5.

98 In 1995 the Anglican bishop of Harare in Zimbabwe refused to retire at sixty-five, because he could not see how he would live if he ceased to be bishop. He not only split the church, but ensured that the Anglican church was in no position to challenge President Robert Mugabe for personalising his office, clinging to power, or flouting the constitution. In a particularly messy lawsuit involving one of Kenya's 'retired' Anglican bishops, a lawyer argued that 'this is not about vocation. It is a question of a house, a career, and a car' (*APS Bulletin*, 8 July 1996, 6).

message: to organise promotional efforts, make lists, use telephones; to solve personality clashes in task-oriented groups; to coordinate efforts both horizontally and vertically; to set goals and reach them; and to come to meetings on time, run them efficiently, and then to implement the decisions made there. This training constitutes a 'concentrated crash course in what millions of others who fill the lower and middle echelons of modern corporations learn at business schools and sales institutes'. Their results-oriented and pragmatic spiritual life spills over to make their work life results-oriented and pragmatic too. Cox draws on the view of Peter Drucker, often regarded as the father of modern management science, that the most successful profit-making enterprises are those that do not focus primarily on making a profit, but on something he refers to as the corporate 'mission'. It is this sense of mission that Korean Pentecostals bring to everything they do, and which helps to explain Korea's economic success. Cox concludes that 'to understand the link between religion and economics in Korea... Peter Drucker is more pertinent than Max Weber.'[99] This has obviously some application in Africa. In their churches we have seen Africans learning new skills like planning and marketing, and related ones like debating and advocacy. The importance for women is particularly great.

Many of these churches tithe, and with the money they embark on projects of which they can feel a sense of pride and achievement. But sometimes the people have had no say in what their money goes into. They own a project in the sense that it was built with their money; not in the sense that it was chosen and planned and operated by them, for their benefit. The church-run bakery we met in Kampala was established with church money, but this effectively became a business of the pastor and his wife, who then employed church members (among others) in distribution. This certainly created jobs that would not have existed otherwise, but was not in any hard sense an activity owned by the church.

Let us now turn to the more cultural role of the churches. We have seen that 'inculturation' has become a key word in the Catholic lexicon. In the field of liturgy, this had already borne some fruit, particularly in a diocese like Kumasi in Ghana. Much attention is currently being focused here, even if the results to date are not especially significant. The cultural role of the new born-again churches is not that of the traditional AICs – time has moved on, and needs are different now. It must be repeated that these churches may be doing many things, even apparently conflicting things, at once. Traditional cultures can be reinforced by external links. This is exactly the process we observed in Ghana, where it was only after the visit of Derek Prince that deliverance thinking acquired public legitimacy in certain circles. We have stressed the ambiguous cultural role of deliverance churches and theology. They preserve traditional thought forms and spiritual realities, but primarily to demonise them, and thus in many ways denigrate African culture, usually to the credit of the European.

We have noted several cultural shifts brought about by Pentecostalism. The emphasis on personal decision certainly serves to develop the notion of individualism, without which it is impossible for a middle class to emerge. It is almost the same thing to say that these churches tend to break down the notion of the extended family. They provide alternative structures to oversee courtship and arrange marriage, taking these tasks away from traditional agents. We have observed how they often provide scope for youth, in a culture traditionally dominated by elders; it can be said that they re-order society for the benefit of youth.[100] The position of women too has been altered by these churches; they can assume leadership roles, determine policies as equals on committees, meet new people in institutions totally unrelated to kinship.[101] Another important cultural shift is evident in the area of competition, or accumulation of wealth. In many traditional African societies, to acquire resources noticeably beyond those of one's neighbours was profoundly threatening, often leading to accusations of witchcraft. The Faith Gospel serves to legitimise the accumulation of wealth as something willed by God. In new churches deliverance easily restores to the community those who in other conditions may have been subjected to witch-finding ordeals. Pentecostalism can even open up or revitalise whole areas of cultural expression, as we saw in Ghana in the area of gospel music.

Churches can play a role in breaking down ethnic barriers, since the intensity of conversion bestows a new identity which transcends other identities. The born-again identity creates a bond with many who previously would have been regarded as different. This is most obvious in the bigger urban churches where English or French rather than a particular local language is spoken. This can help foster democratic virtues like tolerance, respect, moderation, cooperation and compromise. But at the same time the 'born-again' label sometimes carries with it the need to distinguish others who are not born-again, and so many of these churches, under the influence of church growth thinking, demonise Islam, thus reinforcing other social divisions. It is thus hard to generalise; these churches can be doing different things at once, on different levels and among different people.

It is often assumed, as noted above, that Pentecostal churches will

---

100 R.A. van Dijk, 'Young Puritan Preachers in Post-Independence Malawi', *Africa* 62 (1992), 160-81.

101 The impact on birth control in Africa is not so evident; cf Cox, *Fire*, 137.

play the role that Methodists played in eighteenth-century England. As we have seen, one reason for caution here is that they tend to have a very different theology. But we must also make full allowance for the different contexts. The economic growth in eighteenth-century England was considerable, as the country moved to establish itself as the world's superpower. Any movement that emphasised thrift, sobriety, discipline and education was in a position to help transform its adherents, by enabling them to take full advantage of the opportunities on offer. According to the Halévy thesis, Methodism helped England to avoid violent revolution so that gradually everyone could benefit from the general amelioration of living standards; that was Methodism's contribution.[102]

And this is how Pentecostalism has functioned in the United States for most of the twentieth century. Particularly in the decades after the Second World War, there was an expanding economy, near full employment, a climate of business confidence, and low inflation to encourage savings. There was peace and stability, a judicial system increasingly enforcing equal opportunity even for Blacks, availability of good elementary schools, and expansion in higher education. This context is crucial. Churches that fostered ambition, sobriety, goals, application and education, and provided a support group for personal striving, saw their adherents advance themselves out of all recognition in the space of one or two generations. This is obviously the situation that has developed in Korea, but it is hardly Africa's current situation. Africa is undergoing a catastrophic decline. Any transformation possible through purely personal effort must be extremely limited. Africa certainly does not need violent revolution, and any institutions militating against it deserve support. But African socio-political systems just as certainly need radical restructuring, and it is not self-evident that these churches will contribute much in this direction.

Many observers of Christianity today, like Martin in Latin America, put their emphasis on the cultural.[103] He writes of the Pentecostals that their contribution depends on 'the long-term dynamics of culture. Thus whether or not you take seriously their impact on a society as a whole depends on your estimate of the power of culture.'[104] Even someone with a high estimate of the power of culture might feel that the current plight of Africa demands something structural, and something immediate.

---

[102] E. Halévy, *A History of the English People in the Nineteenth Century*, London: Fisher Unwin, 1938.

[103] Martin laments the domination of the political and economic over the cultural and religious; see 'Evangelical and Charismatic', 73-74.

[104] Martin *Tongues*, 22; see also 288.

SELECT BIBLIOGRAPHY

Abidi, Syed A.H. (ed.), *The Role of Religious Organisations in Development of Uganda*, Kampala: Foundation for African Development, 1991.

Aboagye-Mensah, Robert K., *Mission and Democracy in Africa: the Role of the Church*, Accra: Asempa, 1994.

ACIB, 'Point de vue de l'Assemblée du clergé indigène du diocèse de Bafoussam (ACIB) sur le Mémorandum des prêtres autochtones de l'Archidiocèse de Douala intitulé: Un Eclairage Nouveau', *Politique Africaine* 35 (Oct 1989), 97-104.

Africa Faith and Justice Network, *African Synod: Documents, Reflections, Perspectives*, Maryknoll: Orbis, 1996.

African Independent Churches, *Speaking for Ourselves: Members of African Independent Churches Report on their Pilot Study of the History and Theology of their Churches*, Braamfontein: ICT, 1985.

Agbeti, J. Kofi, *West African Church History: Christian Missions and Church Foundations 1482-1919*, Leiden: E.J. Brill, 1986.

Ahanotu, Austin Metumara, *Religion, State and Society in Contemporary Africa*, New York: Peter Lang, 1992.

Appiah-Kubi, Kofi and Sergio Torres (eds), *African Theology en Route*, Maryknoll: Orbis, 1979.

Apter, David E., and Carl G. Rosberg, *Political Development and the New Realism in Sub-Saharan Africa*, Charlottesville, VA: University Press of Virginia, 1994.

Assefa, Hizkias and George Wachira (eds), *Peacemaking and Democratisation in Africa*, Nairobi: Nairobi Peace Initiative, 1996.

Assimeng, Max, *Religion and Social Change in Africa*, Accra: Ghana Universities Press, 1989.

——, *Salvation, Social Crisis and the Human Condition*, Accra: Ghana Universities Press, 1995.

Atiemo, Abamfo O., *The Rise of the Charismatic Movement in the Mainline Churches in Ghana*, Accra: Asempa, 1993.

——, 'Deliverance in the Charismatic Churches in Ghana', *Trinity Journal of Church and Theology* 4,2 (1994-5), 39-49.

Auge, M., *The Anthropological Circle*, Cambridge University Press, 1982.

Auret, Diana, *Reaching for Justice: the Catholic Commission for Justice ad Peace, 1972-1992*, Gweru: Mambo Press, 1992.

Bame Bame, Michael, *Jesus Christ and the Rosicrucians*, Yaoundé: Society for Christian Growth, 1992.

Barber, Karin (ed.), *Readings in African Popular Culture*, London: James Currey, 1997.

Barkan, Joel D., 'Resurrecting Modernisation Theory and the Emergence of Civil Society in Kenya and Nigeria' in Apter and Rosberg (eds), *Political Development*, 87-116.

Bartels, F.L., *The Roots of Ghana Methodism*, Cambridge University Press, 1965.
Baur, John, *2000 Years of Christianity in Africa: an African History, 62-1992*, Nairobi: Paulines, 1994.
Bayart, Jean-François, 'Les rapports entre les églises et l'état du Cameroun de 1958 à 1971', *Revue française d'études politiques africaines*, Aug 1972, 79-104.
——, 'La fonction politique des églises au Cameroun', *Revue française de science politique*, 33 (1973), 514-36.
——, 'Civil Society in Africa' in Patrick Chabal (ed.), *Political Domination in Africa: Reflections on the Limits of Power*, CambridgeUniversity Press 1986, 109-25.
——, 'Les Eglises chrétiennes et la politique du ventre', *Politique Africaine 35* (1989), 3-26.
——, *The State in Africa: the Politics of the Belly*, London: Longman, 1993.
——, (ed.), *Religion et modernité politique en Afrique noire*, Paris: Karthala,1993
——, and Achille Mbembe, 'La Bataille de l'archidiocèse de Douala', *Politique Africaine 35* (1989), 77-84.
——, A. Mbembe and C. Toulabor, *Le politique par le bas en Afrique noire: contributions a une problématique de la démocratie*, Paris: Karthala, 1992.
Bax, M. and A. De Koster (eds), *Power and Prayer: Essays on Religion and Politics*, Amsterdam: Free University Press, 1993
Bayemi, Jean Paul, *L'Effort Camerounais ou la tentation d'une presse libre*, Paris: Harmattan, 1989.
Beckman, Björn, 'The Liberation of Civil Society: Neo-Liberal Ideology and Political Theory', *RoAPE* 58 (1993), 20-33.
Bediako, Kwame, *Christianity in Africa: The Renewal of a Non-Western Religion*, Edinburgh University Press, 1995.
Beyer, Peter, *Religion and Globalisation*, London: Sage Publications, 1994.
Boone, Kathleen C., *The Bible Tells So: the Discourse of Protestant Fundamentalism*, Albany: State University of New York, 1989
Bourdillon, M.F.C., *Religion and Society: a Text for Africa*, Gweru: Mambo, 1990.
——, 'Anthropological Approaches to the Study of African Religions', *Numen* 40 (1993), 217-39.
——, 'Christianity and Wealth in Rural Communities in Zimbabwe', *Zambezia* 11 (1983), 37-53.
——, 'On the Theology of Anthropology', *Studies in World Christianity*, 2, 1 (1996), 45-54.
Bratton, Michael, 'Beyond the State: Civil Society and Associational Life in Africa', *World Politics* 41 (1989), 407-30.
——, 'Civil Society and Political Transitions in Africa' in John W. Harbeson, Donald Rothchild and Naomi Chazan, *Civil Society and the State in Africa*, Boulder, CO: Lynne Rienner, 1994, 51–81.
——, 'Economic Crisis and Political Realignment in Zambia' in Widner, *Economic Change*, 101-28.
——, 'Micro-Democracy? The Merger of Farmer Unions in Zimbabwe', *African Studies Review* 37 (1994), 9-37.
——, and Beatrice Liatto-Katundu, 'A Focus Group Assessment of Political Attitudes in Zambia', *African Affairs* 93 (1994), 535-63.

Brouwer, Steve, Paul Gifford and Susan D.Rose, *Exporting the American Gospel: Global Christian Fundamentalism*, London: Routledge, 1996.

Brown, Rebecca, *He Came to Set the Captives Free*, Springdale, PA: Whitaker House, 1989.

——, *Prepare for War*, Springdale, PA: Whitaker House, 1990.

——, with Yoder, Daniel, *Unbroken Curses: Hidden Source of Trouble in the Christian's Life*, Springdale, PA: Whitaker House, 1995.

Bruce, Steve (ed.), *Religion and Modernisation: Sociologists and Historians Debate the Secularisation Thesis*, Oxford University Press, 1992.

——, *Religion in the Modern World: from Cathedrals to Cults*, Oxford University Press, 1996.

Bujo, Bénézet, *African Theology in its Social Context*, Maryknoll: Orbis, 1992.

——, *African Theology in its Social Context*, Nairobi: Paulines, 1992.

Burnham, Philip, *The Politics of Cultural Difference in Northern Cameroon*, Edinburgh University Press, 1996.

Callaghy, Thomas M., and John Ravenhill (eds), *Hemmed In: Responses to Africa's Economic Decline*, New York: Columbia University Press, 1993.

Carrithers, Michael, *Why Humans have Cultures: Explaining Anthropology and Social Diversity*, Oxford University Press, 1992.

Casanova, José, *Public Religions in the Modern World*, University of Chicago Press, 1995.

Chaza, Maurice, Henri Deroitte and René Luneau (eds), *Les évêques d'Afrique parlent, 1969-1992. Documents pour le synode africain*, Paris: Centurion, 1992.

Chazan, Naomi, Robert Mortimer, John Ravenhill and Donald Rothchild, *Politics and Society in Contemporary Africa*, Boulder CO: Lynne Rienner, 2nd edn 1992.

Christian Council of Ghana, *Christian Council Response to Ghana's Search for a New Democratic System*, Accra: CCG, 1990.

——, *The Church and Ghana's Search for a New Democratic System*, Accra: CCG, 1990.

——, *The Nation, the Church and Democracy*, Accra: CCG, 1992.

Church of Uganda, *Detailed Grassroot Development Programme, 1993-94*, Kampala: PDR Department, 1992.

——, *PDR Annual Report, 1993*, Kampala: PDR Department, 1994.

Clapham, Christopher, *Third World Politics: An Introduction*, London: Routledge, 1985.

——, 'The African State' in Douglas Rimmer (ed.), *Africa 30 Years On*, London: James Currey, 1991, 91-104.

——, 'International Relations in Africa after the End of the Cold War', paper delivered as part of conference on 'The End of the Cold War: Effects and Prospects for Asia and Africa', SOAS, 21-22 Oct 1994.

——, *Africa and the International System: the Politics of State Survival*, Cambridge University Press, 1996.

Coleman, Simon, ' "Faith which Conquers the World": Swedish Fundamentalism and the Globalisation of Culture', *Ethnos* 56 1 (1991), 6-18.

——, Conservative Protestantism and the World Order: the Faith Movement in the United States and Sweden', *Sociology of Religion* 54 (1993), 353-73.

Copeland, Gloria, *God's Will is Prosperity*, Fort Worth, TX: Kenneth Copeland Ministries, 1978.

Copeland, Kenneth, *The Laws of Prosperity*, Fort Worth, TX: Kenneth Copeland Ministries, 1974.

CoratAfrica, *The Socio-Economic Department of the National Catholic Secretariat, Ghana: Final Report*, Nairobi: CoratAfrica, 1993.

Cox, Harvey, 'The Warring Visions of the Religious Right', *Atlantic Monthly* Nov 1985, 59-69.

——, *Fire from Heaven: the Rise of Pentecostal Spirituality and the Reshaping of Religion in the Twenty-First Century*, London: Cassell, 1996.

Daneel, Inus, *Quest for Belonging: Introduction to a Study of African Independent Churches*, Gweru: Mambo Press, 1987.

Dartey, David, Robert K. Aboagye-Mensah and B.D. Amoa (eds), *Report of the Church Leadership Seminar on the Church, Ecumenism and Democracy*, Accra: CCG, 1993.

—— (eds), *Report of the Follow-up Workshop on the Church, Ecumenism and Democracy*, Accra: CCG, 1993.

—— (eds), *Report of the Workshop on the Role of Local Councils of Churches in the Promotion of Ecumenism and Democratic Culture in Ghana*, Accra: CCG, 1993.

de Gruchy, John W., *Christianity and Democracy*, Cambridge University Press, 1995.

de Rosny, Eric, *Healers in the Night*, Maryknoll: Orbis, 1985.

Diamond, Larry (ed.), *Political Culture and Democracy in Developing Countries*, Boulder, CO: Lynne Rienner, 1993.

Diamond, Larry, Juan J. Linz and Seymour Martin Lipset, *Democracy in Developing Countries: Africa*, Boulder, CO: Lynne Rienner, 1988.

——, *Politics in Developing Countries: Comparing Experiences with Democracy*, Boulder, CO: Lynne Rienner, 2nd edn 1995.

Dickson K.A., and P. Ellingworth (eds), *Biblical Revelation and African Beliefs*, Maryknoll: Orbis, 1969.

Dickson, Kwesi A., 'The Church and the Quest for Democracy in Ghana' in Gifford, *Christian Churches*, 261-75.

Dillon-Malone, Clive, *Zambian Humanism, Religion and Social Morality*, Ndola: Ndola Mission Press, 1969.

Doornbos, Martin, 'Church and State in Eastern Africa: Some Unresolved Questions' in Hansen and Twaddle, *Religion and Politics*, 260-70.

Dovlo, Elom, *A Review of Prof. N.K. Dzobo's Melagbe Theology Commissioned by the 50th Synod of the Evangelical Presbyterian Church of Ghana*, Accra: EP Church of Ghana, n.d.

Dozon, Jean-Pierre, *La cause des prophètes: politique et religion en Afrique contemporaine*, Paris: Seuil, 1995.

Duncan-Williams, Nicholas, *You are Destined to Succeed*, Accra: Action Faith Ministries, 1990.

——, *Taking the Promises of God in Battle*, London: Bishop House, 1995.

Eboussi Boulaga, Fabien, *Christianity without Fetishes*, Maryknoll: Orbis, 1984.

——, *Les conférences nationales en Afrique noire: une affaire à suivre*, Paris: Karthala, 1993.

EFZ, *Exposing the Unevangelised Localities/Townships and People in Lusaka Urban*, Lusaka: EFZ, 1994.

Ela, Jean-Marc, *African Cry*, Maryknoll: Orbis, 1986.

——, *My Faith as an African*, Maryknoll: Orbis, 1988.

Eni, Emmanuel, *Delivered from the Powers of Darkness*, Ibadan: Scripture Union, 1987.

Eto, Victoria, *How I Served Satan Until Jesus Christ Delivered Me: a True Account of My Twentyone Years Experience as an Agent of Darkness and of my Deliverance by the Powerful Arm of God in Christ Jesus*, Warri: Shalom Christian Mission, 1981

——, *Exposition on Water Spirits*, Warri: Shalom Christian Mission, 1988.

Fatton, Robert, *Predatory Rule: State and Civil Society in Africa*, Boulder, CO: Lynne Reinner, 1992.

Freston, Paul, 'Popular Protestants in Brazilian Politics: a Novel Turn in Sect-State Relations', *Social Compass* 41 (1994), 537-70.

——, 'Pentecostalism in Brazil: a Brief History', *Religion* 25 (1995), 119-33.

——, 'The Protestant Eruption into Modern Brazilian Politics', *Journal of Contemporary Religion* 11 (1996), 147-68.

Frostin, Per, *Liberation Theology in Tanzania and South Africa: a First World Interpretation*, Lund University Press, 1988.

Fyfe, Christopher, and Andrew Walls (eds), *Christianity in Africa in the 1990s*, Edinburgh: Centre of African Studies, 1996.

Gallagher, Mark, *Rent-Seeking and Economic Growth in Africa*, Boulder, CO: Westview Press, 1991.

Garvey, Brian, *Bembaland Church: Religious and Social Change in South Central Africa, 1891-1964*, Leiden: E.J.Brill, 1994.

Gellner, Ernest, 'Concepts and Society' in Bryan R. Wilson (ed.), *Rationality*, Oxford: Blackwell, 1974

——, *Postmodernism, Reason and Religion*, London: Routledge, 1992.

——, 'The Importance of Being Modular' in Hall, *Civil Society*, 1995, 32-55.

——, *Conditions of Liberty: Civil Society and its Rivals*, London: Hamish Hamilton, 1994.

Ghana Evangelism Committee, *National Church Survey, Update 1993: Facing the Unfinished Task of the Church in Ghana*, Accra: Ghana Evangelism Committee, 1993

Gifford, Paul, 'Prosperity: A New and Foreign Element in African Christianity', *Religion* 20 (1990), 373-88.

——, 'Christian Fundamentalism and Development in Africa', *RoAPE* 52 (1991), 9-20.

——, *Christianity and Politics in Doe's Liberia*, Cambridge University Press, 1993.

——, 'Ghana's Charismatic Churches', *JRA* 24 (1994), 241-65.

—— (ed.), *New Dimensions in African Christianity*, Nairobi: AACC, 1992, and Ibadan: Sefer, 1993.

—— (ed.), *The Christian Churches and the Democratisation of Africa*, Leiden: E.J.Brill, 1995.

Glele, Maurice Ahanhanzo, *Religion, culture et politique en Afrique noire*, Paris: Economica, 1981.

Gray, Richard, 'Popular Theologies in Africa: a Report on a Workshop on Small Christian Communities in Southern Africa', *African Affairs* 85 (1986), 49-54.

——, 'Christianity and Religious Change in Africa', *African Affairs* 77 (1978), 89-100.

——, 'Christianity and Concepts of Evil in Sub-Saharan Africa' in Gray, *Black Christians and White Missionaries*, New Haven: Yale University Press, 1991, 99-117.

Gyanfosu, Samuel, 'The Development of Christian-related Independent Religious Movements in Ghana, with special reference to the Afrikania Movement', unpubl. Ph.D. thesis, University of Leeds, 1995.

Gyimah-Boadi, E., *Ghana Under PNDC Rule*, Dakar: Codesria, 1993.

——, 'Associational Life, Civil Society, and Democratisation in Ghana' in Harbeson, Rothchild, Chazan, *Civil Society and the State*, 124-41.

Hadden, Jeffrey K., and Anson Shupe (eds), *Prophetic Religions and Politics*, New York: Paragon House, 1986.

Hagin, Kenneth E., *How God Taught me about Prosperity*, Tulsa, OK: Kenneth Hagin Ministries, 1985.

Halévy, E., *A History of the English People in the Nineteenth Century*, London: T. Fisher Unwin, 1938.

Hall, John A. (ed.), *Civil Society: Theory, History, Comparison*, Cambridge: Polity Press, 1995.

Hammond, Frank, and Ida Mae Hammond, *Pigs in the Parlor: A Practical Guide to Deliverance*, Kirkwood, MI: Impact Books, 1973.

Hansen, Holger Bernt, and Michael Twaddle (eds), *From Chaos to Order: the Politics of Constitution-making in Uganda*, London: James Currey, 1994.

——, *Religion and Politics in East Africa*, London: James Currey, 1995.

Harbeson, John W., Donald Rothchild and Naomi Chazan (eds), *Civil Society and the State in Africa*, Boulder, CO: Lynne Rienner, 1994.

Harden, Blaine, *Africa: Dispatches from a Fragile Continent*, London: Harper-Collins, 1991.

Hastings, Adrian, *African Christianity: an Essay in Interpretation*, London: Geoffrey Chapman, 1976

——, *A History of African Christianity, 1950-75*, Cambridge University Press, 1979.

——, *African Catholicism: Essays in Discovery*, London: SCM, 1989.

——, *The Church in Africa, 1450-1950*, Oxford University Press, 1994.

Haynes, Jeff, 'Human Rights and Democracy in Ghana: the Record of the Rawlings' Regime', *African Affairs* 90 (1991), 407-25.

——, *Religion in Third World Politics*, Buckingham: Open University Press, 1993.

——, 'Popular Religion and Politics in Sub-Saharan Africa', *Third World Quarterly* 16, 1 (1995), 89-108.

——, 'The Revenge of Society? Religious Responses to Political Disequilibrium in Africa', *Third World Quarterly* 16, 4 (1995), 728-37.

——, *Religion and Politics in Africa*, London: Zed Books, 1996.

Healey, Joseph, and Donald Sybertz, *Towards an African Narrative Theology*, Nairobi: Paulines, 1996.

Hebga, Meinrad, 'Le mouvement charismatique en Afrique', *Etudes*, July-Aug 1995, 67-75.

Henkel, Reinhard, *Christian Missions in Africa: a Social Geographical Study of the Impact of their Activities in Zambia*, Berlin: Dietrich Reimer, 1989.

Henriot, Peter, Edward DeBerri and Michael Schultheis, *Catholic Social Teaching: Our Best Kept Secret*, Maryknoll: Orbis, 1985.

Herbst, Jeffrey, *The Politics of Reform in Ghana 1982-91*, Berkeley, CA: University of California, 1993.

Hickey, Marilyn, *Break the Generation Curse*, Denver, CO: Marilyn Hickey Ministries, 1988.

Hinfelaar, H.F., *Bemba Speaking Women of Zambia in a Century of Religious Change 1892-1992*, Leiden: E.J.Brill, 1994.

Hobsbawm, Eric, *Age of Extremes: the Short Twentieth Century, 1914-1991*, London: Abacus, 1995.

Holland, Joe, and Peter Henriot, *Social Analysis: Linking Faith and Justice*, Maryknoll: Orbis, 1980.

Hope, Anne, and Sally Timmel, *Training for Transformation: a Handbook for Community Workers*, Gweru: Mambo Press, 1984.

Horn, J.N., *From Rags to Riches: an Analysis of the Faith Movement and its Relation to the Classical Pentecostal Movement*, Pretoria: UNISA, 1989.

Horton, R., 'African Traditional Thought and Western Science', *Africa* 37 (1967), 50-71; 155-87.

——, 'African Conversion', *Africa* 41, 2 (1971), 85-108.

Huntington, Samuel P., *The Third Wave: Democratisation in the Late Twentieth Century*, Norman, OK: University of Oklahoma Press, 1991.

——, 'The Clash of Civilisations?', *Foreign Affairs* 72, 3 (1993), 23-49.

——, *The Clash of Civilisations and the Remaking of World Order*, New York: Simon and Schuster, 1996.

Ibrahim, Jibrin, 'Religion and Political Turbulence in Nigeria', *JMAS* 29, 1 (1991), 115-36.

Ihedinma, A.U., 'Towards the Return to Traditional Religion among the Elite of Igboland, Nigeria, with Special Reference to the Godian Religion', unpubl. M.Phil. thesis, University of London, 1995.

Ipenburg, At, *'All Good Men': the Development of Lubwa Mission, Chinsali, Zambia 1905-1967*, Frankfurt: Peter Lang, 1992.

Jackson, Robert H., *Quasi-states: Sovereignty, International Relations and the Third World*, Cambridge University Press, 1990.

——, and Carl G. Rosberg, 'Why Africa's Weak States Persist: the Empirical and the Juridical in Statehood', *World Politics* 34 (1982), 1-24.

——, and Carl G. Rosberg, 'Sovereignty and Underdevelopment: Juridical Statehood in the African Crisis', *JMAS* 24 (1986), 1-31.

Jeffries, Richard, 'Urban Popular Attitudes towards the Economic Recovery Programme and the PNDC Government in Ghana', *African Affairs* 91 (1992), 207-26.

——, and Clare Thomas, 'The Ghanaian Elections of 1992', *African Affairs* 92 (1993), 331-66.

John Paul II, Pope, *The Church in Africa*, Nairobi: Paulines, 1995.

Johnson, Douglas, and Cynthia Sampson (eds), *Religion, the Missing Dimension of Statecraft*, Oxford University Press, 1994.

Johnstone, Patrick, *Operation World*, Carlisle: OM Publishing, 5th edn 1993.

Joseph, Richard A., *Radical Nationalism in Cameroon: the Social Origins of the UPC Rebellion*, Oxford University Press, 1977.

——, *Gaullist Africa: Cameroon under Ahmadu Ahidjo*, Enugu: Fourth Dimension Publishers, 1978.

——, 'Church, State and Society in Colonial Cameroon', *International Journal of African Historical Studies* 13 (1980), 5-32.

——, *Democracy and Prebendal Politics in Nigeria: The Rise and Fall of the Second Republic*, New York: Cambridge University Press, 1987.

——, 'The Christian Churches and Democracy in Contemporary Africa' in Witte, *Christianity and Democracy*, 231-47.

Kairos Document: Challenge to the Church: a Theological Comment on the Political Crisis in South Africa, Braamfontein: The Kairos Theologians, 1985.

Kaplan, Robert D., 'The Coming Anarchy', *Atlantic Monthly* Feb. 1994, 44-76.

——, *The Ends of the Earth: a Journey at the Dawn of the 21st Century*, New York: Random House, 1996

Kasambeko, Mubiru Bernard Patrick, 'The New Christian Religious Movements in Jinja Diocese,' unpubl. Dip. Theol. thesis, Makerere University, 1992

Kassimir, Ronald, 'Catholics and Political Identity in Toro' in Hansen and Twaddle, *Religion and Politics*, 120-40.

Kasumba, Simon Peter, 'The New Evangelical Church Sects in Kampala City, with Reference to Kabowa Redeemed Church of Christ and El-Shaddai Ministries, Kawempe: their Challenge to the Catholic Church', unpubl. Dip.Theol. thesis, Makerere University, 1990.

Kaunda, Kenneth, *Zambia Shall be Free: an Autobiography*, London: Heinemann, 1962.

——, *A Humanist in Africa: Letters to Colin Morris from Kenneth D. Kaunda*, London: Longmans, 1966.

Knorr, W., *A Short History of Full Gospel Mission, Cameroon*, Bamenda: Gospel Press, 1986.

Komakoma, Joseph, 'Towards a Relevant Pastoral Approach: Patoral Ministry on the Copperbelt Region of Zambia', dissertation for Licentiate, Catholic University of Louvain, 1990.

Kudadjie, J.N., and R.K. Aboagye-Mensah, *The Christian and National Politics*, Accra: Asempa, 1991.

——, *The Christian and Social Conduct*, Accra: Asempa, 1992.

Kwast, Lloyd E., *The Discipling of West Cameroon: a Study of Baptist Growth*, Grand Rapids, MI: Eerdmans, 1971

Lamb, David, *The Africans*, London: Methuen, rev. edn 1985.

Landes, David S., *The Unbound Prometheus: Technological Change and Industrial Development in Western Europe from 1750 to the Present*, Cambridge University Press, 1969.

Larbi, Emmanuel Kingsley, 'The Development of Ghanaian Pentecostalism: a Study in the Appropriation of the Christian Gospel in 20th Century Ghanaian Setting with Particular Reference to the Christ Apostolic Church, the Church of Pentecost and the International Central Gospel Church', unpubl. Ph.D. thesis, University of Edinburgh, 1995.

Leys, Colin, 'Confronting the African Tragedy', *New Left Review* 204 (1994), 35-6.

——, *The Rise and Fall of Development Theory,* London: James Currey, 1995.

Liardon, Roberts, *Breaking Controlling Powers,* Tulsa, OK: Harrison House 1987.

Lincoln, Bruce (ed.), *Religion, Rebellion, Revolution: an Interdisciplinary and Cross-Cultural Collection of Essays,* London: Macmillan, 1985.

Linden, Ian, *Church and Revolution in Rwanda,* Manchester University Press, 1977.

Longman, Timothy, 'Christianity and Democratisation in Rwanda: Assessing Church Responses to Political Crisis in the 1990s' in Gifford, *Christian Churches,* 188-204.

M'Nteba, Metena, 'Les Conférences Nationales Africaines et la figure politique de l'évêque-président', *Zaïre-Afrique,* no. 276, June-Aug 1993, 361-372.

Marshall, Ruth, 'Power in the Name of Jesus', *RoAPE,* 52 (1991), 21-37.

——, ' "Power in the Name of Jesus": Social Transformation and Pentecostalism in Western Nigeria "Revisited" ', in T. Ranger, and O. Vaughan, (eds), *Legitimacy and the State in Twentieth Century Africa,* London: Macmillan, 1993, 213-46.

Martey, Emmanuel, *African Theology: Inculturation and Liberation,* Maryknoll: Orbis, 1994.

——, 'Jesus of History, the Church and the Poor in Africa', *Trinity Journal of Church and Theology* 4, 2 (1994-5), 26-38.

Martin, David, *A General Theory of Secularisation,* Oxford: Blackwell, 1978.

——, *Tongues of Fire: the Explosion of Protestantism in Latin America,* Oxford: Blackwell, 1990.

Marty, Martin E., 'Fundamentals of Fundamentalism' in Kaplan, Lawrence (ed.), *Fundamentalism in Comparative Perspective,* Amherst, MA: University of Massachusetts Press, 1992, 15-23.

——, and R. Scott Appleby (eds), *Fundamentalisms Observed,* University of Chicago Press, 1991.

—— (eds), *Fundamentalisms and Society: Reclaiming the Sciences, the Family and Education,* University of Chicago Press, 1993.

—— (eds), *Fundamentalisms and the State: Remaking Polities, Economies and Militance,* University of Chicago Press, 1993

Maugenest, Denis, and Paul-Gérard Pougoué, *Droits de l'homme en Afrique centrale: colloque de Yaoundé, 9-11 Novembre 1994,* Yaoundé/Paris: UCAC/Karthala, 1995.

Mbembe, Achille, *Afriques indociles: Christianisme, pouvoir et état en société postcoloniale,* Paris: Karthala, 1988.

McCullum, Hugh, *The Angels have left us: the Rwanda Tragedy and the Churches,* Geneva: WCC Publications, 1995.

McGarry, Cecil (ed.), *What Happened at the African Synod?,* Nairobi: Paulines, 1995.

——, Mejia, Rodrigo, and Valerian Shirima, *A Light on our Path: a Pastoral Contribution to the Synod for Africa,* Nairobi: St Paul Publications, 1993.

McGovern, Arthur, *Liberation Theology and its Critics: Towards an Assessment*, Maryknoll: Orbis, 1989.

Médard, Jean-François, 'Identités et politiques: le cas des églises protestantes au Cameroun', paper delivered at Table Ronde, Mouvements religieux et débats démocratiques en Afrique, Pau, 8-9 Dec 1994.

Meyer, Birgit, ' "If you are a Devil, you are a Witch, and if you are a Witch, you are a Devil": the Integration of "Pagan" Ideas into the Conceptual Universe of Ewe Christians in Southeastern Ghana', *JRA* 22 (1992), 98-132.

——, 'Translating the Devil: An African Appropriation of Pietist Protestantism: the Case of the Ewe in Southeastern Ghana, 1847-1992', unpubl. Ph.D. thesis, Free University of Amsterdam, 1995.

Mihevc, John, *The Market Tells Them So: The World Bank and Economic Fundamentalism in Africa*, London: Zed Books, 1996.

Milingo, Emmanuel, *The World in Between: Christian Healing and the Struggle for Spiritual Survival*, London: Hurst, 1984.

——, *Face to Face with the Devil*, Broadford, Vic: Scripture Keys Ministries, 1991.

Moyo, J.N., 'Civil Society in Zimbabwe', *Zambezia* 20 (1993), 1-13.

Moyser, G. (ed.), *Politics and Religion in the Modern World*, London: Routledge, 1991.

Mumba, Nevers, *Integrity with Fire: a Strategy for Revival*, Tulsa, OK: Vincom, 1994

Musana, Paddy, 'The Pentecostal Movement in Uganda: its Impact with Specific Reference to Kampala City', unpubl. MA thesis, Makerere University, 1991.

New Apostolic Church, *A History of the Kingdom of God*, Dortmund: New Apostolic Church, 1991.

Ngongo, Louis, *Histoire des forces religieuses au Cameroun: de la première guerre mondiale à l'indépendance, 1916-1955*, Paris: Karthala, 1982.

Ninsin, Kwame, 'The PNDC and the Problem of Legitimacy' in Rothchild (ed.), *Ghana*, 49-67.

Nkuissi, Thomas, *Dernières Paroles d'Evêque diocésain*, Nkongsamba: l'auteur, 1993.

Nugent, Paul, *Big Men, Small Boys and Politics in Ghana: Power, Ideology and the Burden of History, 1982-94*, London: Pinter, 1995.

Nyansako-ni-Nku (ed.), *Cry Justice: the Church in a Changing Cameroon*, Buea: PCC, 1993.

—— (ed.), *Journey in Faith: the Story of the Presbyterian Church in Cameroon*, Buea: PCC, 1982.

Oger, Louis, *'Where a Scattered Flock Gathered': Ilondola, 1934-84*, Lusaka: Missionaries of Africa, 1991.

Omenyo, Cephas, 'The Charismatic Renewal Movement in Ghana', *Pneuma* 16, 2 (1994), 169-85.

——, 'The Charismatic Renewal Movement within the Mainline Churches: the Case of the Bible Study and Prayer Group of the Presbyterian Church of Ghana', unpubl. M.Phil. thesis, University of Ghana, 1994.

Oquaye, Michael, 'Decentralisation and Development: the Ghanaian Case under the Provisional National Defence Council', *Journal of Commonwealth and Comparative Politics* 33 (1995), 209-39.

Otabil, Mensa, *Beyond the Rivers of Ethiopia: a Biblical Revelation on God's Purpose for the Black Race*, Accra: Altar International, 1992.

——, *Enjoying the Blessings of Abraham*, Accra: Altar International, 1992.

——, *Four Laws of Productivity: God's Foundation for Living*, Accra: Altar International, 1992.

Pakenham, Thomas, *The Scramble for Africa*, London: Abacus, 1992.

Papini, Roberto and Vincenzo Buonomo (eds), *Ethique et développement: l'apport des communautés chrétiennes en Afrique*, Yaoundé/Rome: CLE/ Institut International Jacques Maritain, 1995.

Parratt, John, *Reinventing Christianity: African Theology Today*, Grand Rapids, MI: Eerdmans, 1995.

Peel, J.D.Y., 'Conversion and Tradition in Two African Societies: Ijebu and Buganda', *Past and Present* 77(1977), 108-41.

——, 'Poverty and Sacrifice in Nineteenth-Century Yorubaland: a Critique of Iliffe's Thesis', *Journal of African History* 31 (1990), 465-84.

——, 'An Africanist Revisits Magic and the Millennium' in Eileen Barker, James A. Beckford and Karel Dobbelaere (eds), *Secularization, Rationalism and Sectarianism: Essays in Honour of Bryan R. Wilson*, Oxford: Clarendon Press, 1993, 81-100.

——, *Religious Encounters in 19th Century Yorubaland*, (forthcoming).

Peil, Margaret, with K.A. Opoku, 'The Development and Practice of Religion in an Accra Suburb', *JRA* 24 (1994), 198-227.

Pirouet, M. Louise, *Black Evangelists: The Spread of Christianity in Uganda, 1891-1914*, London: Rex Collings, 1978.

——, 'Religion in Uganda under Amin', *JRA* 11 (1980), 13-29.

Pobee, John S., *Religion and Politics in Ghana*, Accra: Asempa, 1991.

Poewe, Karla (ed.), *Charismatic Christianity as a Global Culture*, Columbia, SC: University of South Carolina, 1994.

Pokam, Kengne, *Les Eglises chrétiennes face à la montée du nationalisme camerounais*, Paris: Harmattan, 1987.

Prince, Derek, *Blessing or Curse: You Can Choose*, Milton Keynes: Word Publishing, 1990.

Prunier, Gérard, *The Rwanda Crisis: History of a Genocide*, London: Hurst, 1995.

Ramet, Sabrina Petra, and Donald W. Treadgold (eds), *Render unto Caesar: the Religious Sphere in World Politics*, Washington, DC: American Universities Press, 1995.

Ranger, Terence O., 'Religious Movements and Politics in Sub-Saharan Africa', *African Studies Review* 29, 2 (1986), 1-69.

Reno, William, *Corruption and State Politics in Sierra Leone*, Cambridge University Press, 1995.

Rimmer, Douglas, *Staying Poor: Ghana's Political Economy, 1950-90*, Oxford: Pergamon Press, 1992.

Roberts, Andrew, 'The Lumpa Church of Alice Lenshina' in Robert L. Rotberg and Ali Mazrui (eds), *Protest and Power in Black Africa*, New York: Oxford University Press, 1970, 513-68.

Roberts, Richard H. (ed.), *Religion and the Transformations of Capitalism: Comparative Approaches*, London: Routledge, 1995.

Robertson, Roland, and Garrett, William (eds), *Religion and the Global Order*, New York: Paragon House, 1991.

Robins, C., *'Tukutendereza*: A Study of Social Change and Sectarian Withdrawal in the Balokole Revival of Uganda', unpubl. Ph.D. thesis, Columbia University, 1975.

Rothchild, Donald (ed.), *Ghana: the Political Economy of Recovery*, Boulder, CO: Lynne Rienner, 1991.

——, and N. Chazan (eds), *The Precarious Balance: State and Society in Africa*, Boulder, CO: Westview Press, 1988.

Rowlands, Michael, and Jean-Pierre Warnier, 'Sorcery, Power and the Modern State in Cameroon', *Man* 23 (1988), 118-32.

Sandbrook, Richard, *The Politics of Africa's Economic Stagnation*, Cambridge University Press, 1985.

Sanneh, Lamin, *Encountering the West: Christianity and Culture, an African Dimension*, London: Marshall Pickering, 1993.

——, *Translating the Message: the Missionary Impact on Culture*, Maryknoll: Orbis, 1990.

Schmale, Matthias, *The Role of Local Organisations in Third World Development*, Aldershot: Avebury, 1993.

Schoffeleers, Matthew, 'Black and African Theology in Southern Africa; a Controversy Re-examined', *JRA* 18 (1988), 99-124.

——, 'Theological Styles and Revolutionary Elan: an African Discussion' in van Ufford and Schoffeleers, *Religion and Development*, 185-208.

Schonecke, Wolfgang, 'What Does the Rwanda Tragedy say to AMECEA Churches?', *AMECEA Documentation Service*, 15 Sept 1994.

Shillington, Kevin, *Ghana and the Rawlings Factor*, London: Macmillan, 1992.

Shorter, Aylward, *Jesus and the Witchdoctor: an Approach to Healing and Wholeness,* London: Geoffrey Chapman, 1985.

Siewert, John A., and John A. Kenyon (eds), *Mission Handbook: USA/Canada Christian Ministries Overseas*, Monrovia, CA: Marc, 15th edn 1993.

Smith, Noel, *The Presbyterian Church of Ghana, 1835-1960*, Accra: Ghana Universities Press, 1966.

Stoll, David, *Is Latin America Turning Protestant? The Politics of Evangelical Growth*, Berkeley, CA: University of California Press, 1990.

Sundkler, B.G.M., *Zulu Zion and Some Swazi Zionists*, London: Oxford University Press, 1976.

Taylor, John V., *Christianity and Politics in Africa*, London: Penguin, 1957.

——, *The Growth of the Church in Buganda: an Attempt at Understanding*, London: SCM, 1958.

——, *The Primal Vision: Christian Presence amid African Religion*, London: SCM, 1963.

——, and Dorothea A. Lehman, *Christians of the Copperbelt: the Growth of the Church in Northern Rhodesia*, London: SCM, 1961.

Temple, Merfyn (ed.), *Black Government? A Discussion between Colin Morris and Kenneth Kaunda*, Lusaka: United Society for Christian Literature, 1960.

Ter Haar, Gerrie, *Spirit of Africa: the Healing Ministry of Archbishop Milingo of Zambia*, London: Hurst, 1992.

Thomas, Keith, *Religion and the Decline of Magic*, London: Penguin, 1973.

Thompson, E.P., *The Making of the English Working Class*, London: Gollancz, 1963.

Torres, Sergio, and Virginia Fabella (eds), *The Emergent Gospel: Theology from the Developing World*, London: Geoffrey Chapman, 1978.

Tourigny, Yves, *So Abundant a Harvest: the Catholic Church in Uganda, 1879-1979*, London: Darton, Longman and Todd, 1979.

Trevor-Roper, H.R., *The European Witch-Craze of the Sixteenth and Seventeenth Centuries*, London: Penguin 1969.

Troeltsch, Ernst, *The Social Teaching of the Christian Churches*, New York: Macmillan, 1931.

Tuma, Tom, and Phares Mutibwa (eds), *A Century of Christianity in Uganda, 1877-1977*, Nairobi: Uzima Press, 1978.

Tumi, Christian W., *Texte Intégral de la conférence de presse donnée a Yaoundé le 11 Juin 1990*, n.p.

University of Edinburgh, Centre of African Studies, *Critical Choices for the NGO Community: African Development in the 1990s*, Edinburgh: Centre of African Studies, 1990.

US Catholic Mission Association, *Annual Report on US Catholic Overseas Mission, 1992-93*, Washington, DC: Catholic Mission Association, 1993.

van Binsbergen, Wim M.J., 'Religious Innovation and Political Conflict in Zambia: the Lumpa Rising' in *Religious Change in Zambia: Exploratory Studies*, London: Kegan Paul, 1981, 266-316.

——, 'Aspects of Democracy and Democratisation in Zambia and Botswana: Exploring African Political Culture at the Grassroots', *Journal of Contemporary African Studies* 13 (1995), 3-33.

——, and Matthew Schoffeleers, *Theoretical Explorations in African Religion*, London: Kegan Paul International, 1985.

van de Walle, Nicolas, 'The Politics of Nonreform in Cameroon' in Callaghy and Ravenhill, *Hemmed In*, 357-97.

——, 'Neopatrimonialism and Democracy in Africa, with an Illustration from Cameroon' in Widner (ed.), *Economic Change*, 129-57.

van Donge, Jan Kees, 'Zambia: Kaunda and Chiluba: Enduring Patterns of Political Culture' in John A. Wiseman (ed.), *Democracy and Political Change in Sub-Saharan Africa*, London: Routledge, 1995, 193-219.

van Hoyweghen, Saskia, 'The Disintegration of the Catholic Church of Rwanda', *African Affairs* 95 (1996), 379-401.

van Slageren, Jaap, *Les Origines de l'Eglise Evangélique du Cameroun: Missions Européennes et christianisme autochtone*, Yaoundé: CLE, 1972.

van Ufford, Philip Quarles, and Matthew Schoffeleers, *Religion and Development: towards an Integrated Approach*, Amsterdam: Free University Press, 1988.

Venter, Dawid (ed.), *Towards a Democratic Future: the Church and the Current Situation*, Johannesburg: ICT, 1993.

Villa-Vicencio, Charles, *A Theology of Reconstruction: Nation Building and Human Rights*, Cambridge University Press, 1992.

Vuha, A. K., *The Package: Salvation, Healing and Deliverance*, Accra: EP Church of Ghana, 1993.

——, *Covenants and Curses: Why God does not Intervene*, Accra: EP Church of Ghana, 1994.

Wagner, C. Peter, Win Arn and Elmer Towns, *Church Growth: State of the Art*, Wheaton, IL: Tyndale, 1989.

Wagner, C. Peter, *Territorial Spirits*, Chichester: Sovereign World, 1991.

Walshe, Peter, 'Christianity and Democratisation in South Africa: the Prophetic Voice within Phlegmatic Churches' in Gifford, *Christian Churches*, 74-94.

——, 'South Africa: Prophetic Christianity and the Liberation Movement', *JMAS* 29 (1991), 27-60.

Ward, Kevin, ' "Obedient Rebels" – The Relationship between the early "Balokole" and the Church of Uganda: the Mukono Crisis of 1941', *JRA* 19 (1989), 195-227.

——, 'The Church of Uganda amidst Conflict' in Hansen and Twaddle, *Religion and Politics*, 72-105.

Warren, Max, *Revival – an Enquiry*, London: SCM, 1954.

Waruta, D.W., 'Tribalism as a Moral Problem in Contemporary Africa' in J.N.K. Mugambi and A. Nasimiyu-Wasike, *Moral and Ethical Issues in African Christianity: Exploratory Essays in Moral Theology*, Nairobi: Initiatives, 1992, 119-35.

Weber, Max, *The Protestant Ethic and the Spirit of Capitalism*, London: Routledge, 1992 (German original 1904-5, rev. edn 1920-1).

Welbourn, F.B., *East African Rebels*, London: SCM, 1961.

Westerlund, David (ed.), *Questioning the Secular State: the Worldwide Resurgence of Religion in Politics*, London: Hurst, 1996.

Widner, Jennifer A. (ed.), *Economic Change and Politcal Liberalisation in Sub-Saharan Africa*, Baltimore, MD: Johns Hopkins University Press, 1994.

Williams, Glen, and Nassali Tamale, *The Caring Community: Coping with AIDS in Urban Uganda*, London: ActionAid/Amref, 1991.

Wilson, Bryan, *Magic and the Millennium*, London: Heinemann, 1973.

——, *Religion in Sociological Perspective*, Oxford University Press, 1982.

Wilson, Monica, *Religion and the Transformation of Society: a Study in Social Change in Africa*, Cambridge University Press, 1971.

Witte, John (ed.), *Christianity and Democracy in Global Context*, Boulder, CO: Westview Press, 1993.

Woods, Dwayne, 'Civil Society in Europe and Africa: Limiting State Power through a Public Sphere', *African Studies Review* 35, 2 (1992), 77-100.

World Bank, *Accelerated Development in Sub-Saharan Africa: an Agenda for Action*, Washington, DC: World Bank, 1981.

——, *Toward Sustained Development in Sub-Saharan Africa*, Washington, DC: World Bank, 1984.

——, *Sub-Saharan Africa: From Crisis to Sustainable Growth: a Long Term Perspective Study*, Washington, DC: World Bank, 1989.

——, *The Social Dimensions of Adjustment in Africa: a Political Agenda*, Washington, DC: World Bank, 1990.

——, *A Continent in Transition: Sub-Saharan Africa in the Mid-1990s*, Washington, DC: World Bank, 1995.

Wrigley, C. C., *Kingship and State: the Buganda Dynasty*, Cambridge University Press, 1996.

Young, Tom, ' "A Project to be Realised": Global Liberalism and Contemporary Africa', *Millennium* 24 (1995), 527-46.

INDEX